Ethical Reasoning for Mental Health Professionals

To my wife, Angela Mae; my daughters, Lynette Jeanne and Caroline Ruth; and HB and the whole "hug."

Ethical Reasoning
for Mental Health
Professionals

GARY G. FORD

Stephen F. Austin State University

SAGE Publications
Thousand Oaks ▪ London ▪ New Delhi

For information:

Sage Publications, Inc.
2455 Teller Road
Thousand Oaks, California 91320
E-mail: order@sagepub.com

Sage Publications Ltd.
1 Oliver's Yard
55 City Road
London EC1Y 1SP
United Kingdom

Sage Publications India Pvt. Ltd.
B-42 Panchsheel Enclave
Post Box 4109
New Delhi 110 017 India

Printed in the United States of America on acid-free paper

Library of Congress Cataloging-in-Publication Data

Ford, Gary George.
Ethical reasoning for mental health professionals / Gary G. Ford.
     p. cm.
Includes bibliographical references and index.
ISBN 0-7619-3093-0 (cloth) — ISBN 0-7619-3094-9 (pbk.)
   1. Mental health personnel—Professional ethics. 2. Psychiatric ethics.
I. Title.
[DNLM: 1. Psychiatry—ethics. 2. Psychology—ethics. 3. Ethics,
Professional. WM 62 F699e 2006]
RC455.2.E8F67 2006
174.2—dc22

                                             2005022465

05   06   07   08   09   10   9   8   7   6   5   4   3   2   1

Acquiring Editor:	Arthur Pomponio
Editorial Assistant:	Veronica Novak
Production Editor:	Sanford Robinson
Copy Editor:	Diana Breti
Typesetter:	C&M Digitals (P) Ltd.
Cover Designer:	Janet Foulger

Contents

Preface

This book, like its predecessor Ethical Reasoning in the Mental Health Professions (Ford, 2001), is a treatise in applied ethics. While most ethics texts for professionals simply discuss the duties presented in the profession's ethical code, this book is designed to assist mental health professionals in developing the ability to reason ethically—a skill that is an extraordinarily important component of professionalism in any field, but one that is grossly underemphasized in mental health training programs. The greatest challenge to ethical professional practice is dealing with the novel situations that involve conflicts between ethical principles. Readers will learn how to resolve these conflicts in a rational manner by understanding the philosophical sources of professional ethical duties and applying that knowledge to practical problems using a revised version of my model of ethical decision making.

Two chapters have been added for this book. The first (Chapter 9) addresses computer-mediated therapy, or e-therapy, an emerging area of professional practice. The exciting prospect of providing psychological services using Internet and e-mail technology introduces some unprecedented ethical concerns, while presenting novel twists to traditional ethical considerations. The second (Chapter 10) explores issues concerning the application of psychological principles to business contexts (i.e., Industrial/Organizational [I/O] psychology). The ethical complexities of this major area of specialization certainly merit greater attention than was provided in my first book.

The primary purpose of this book is to provide mental health professionals with formal training in ethical reasoning. Four tasks that are fundamental to ethical professional practice are emphasized. The first task for mental health professionals is to become familiar with the ethical code of their profession. An overview of psychology's "Ethical Principles of Psychologists and Code of Conduct" (American Psychological Association [APA], 2002) will be presented in Chapter 2, and counseling's *Code of Ethics* (American Counseling Association [ACA], 2005) will be discussed in Chapter 3.

The second task is to develop a greater understanding of the rational basis of ethical duties. In Chapter 4, the major Western philosophical theories of ethical obligation will be presented to provide a context readers can use in their efforts to develop a rational philosophical grounding for the values that will guide their ethical conduct as professionals. As readers become increasingly sensitive to the presence of ethical issues in clinical, consulting, teaching, and research settings, they will become aware of a fundamental problem that has perpetually plagued ethical theorists in philosophy as well as professionals who seek to apply ethical principles in their work: In many situations, philosophically sound ethical values appear to conflict with one another. For example, a student asks a clinical psychology professor, whose class he had taken the previous semester, for an appointment to see her as a client in her part-time psychotherapy practice. The student is a psychology major, so the professor explains that having a psychotherapy client who is also a student in her department constitutes a dual relationship. However, the student says that she is the only person he can talk to about his problems and that he will leave school if necessary to be treated by her. This situation does involve a dual relationship, but the welfare of the individual is also an important consideration.

What is the ethically appropriate response in this situation? Unfortunately, there are not clear-cut behavioral rules that inform professionals of the ethical course of action in each novel situation they encounter. Even the ethical code of a profession provides only general guidelines for appropriate conduct, leaving considerable ambiguity regarding what professionals should do in such circumstances. To address these complex problems effectively, professionals must develop the ability to *reason* ethically, a skill that will enable them to resolve practical ethical problems by weighing the relative importance of competing ethical considerations. Learning to reason ethically is the third and most important task readers will undertake in this book.

Next, several of the most promising methods proposed by moral philosophers to resolve conflicts between ethical principles, or *ethical dilemmas*, will be described. Then, a model for ethical decision making will be presented in Chapter 5 to assist professionals in structuring their ethical deliberations in a manner that will enable them to resolve ethical conflicts rationally. At the end of each subsequent chapter, a special case scenario associated with the issues presented in the chapter will provide readers with an opportunity to practice using the model and further develop their practical reasoning skills. In addition, numerous case examples involving multiple, competing ethical considerations are distributed throughout each chapter of the book. In the early chapters, they can serve as brain teasers, but as readers develop their skills, I hope that they will revisit those cases and attempt to resolve them.

The fourth important task, which is based on mastery of the first three tasks, is to develop an increased awareness of both the obvious and subtle ethical and legal issues that arise in the daily practice of a mental health profession. The only way that professionals can be confident of behaving in an ethical manner is to develop an exquisite sensitivity to the presence of such issues in their everyday professional behavior. Both obvious and subtle ethical and legal issues pertaining to the various activities in which mental health professionals are involved (e.g., psychotherapy, assessment, consultation, supervision, teaching, research) and the organizations in which they work are discussed in greater detail in Chapters 6–12. Legal issues and applications in professional practice are presented in Chapters 13 and 14. I selected the issues to be addressed in this book based on their importance to mental health professionals and because the students in my ethics class have always found them to be intriguing. It is my hope that this book will provide readers with the tools they need to conduct themselves in an ethically effective manner throughout their professional careers.

INFORMATION FOR INSTRUCTORS

This book was written to educate readers regarding the process of ethical reasoning, whether they be practicing professionals pursuing continuing education or students training to become mental health professionals. This section will describe some features of the book that course instructors might find particularly useful and suggest ways in which these features might be incorporated into an ethics course.

The book consists of 14 chapters, so the content can be addressed at about the rate of one chapter per week over the course of an academic semester. In addition to the increased coverage devoted to I/O psychology and computer-assisted provision of mental health services in the two new chapters, I have also increased significantly the discussion of multicultural issues affecting the practice of a mental health profession. I chose to treat multiculturalism throughout the book, rather than relegating it to a single chapter, in the hope of illustrating to students its ubiquitous presence in all facets of our professional activity (and our lives). Examining their ethical and personal values and the underlying metaethical justification for those values can be a stimulating and worthwhile activity for your students. One of the many models that can be used for this purpose (i.e., Vachon & Agresti, 1992) is presented in Chapter 11. Students will certainly benefit from the opportunity to subsequently explore how others' values differ from their own, especially as a function of cultural influences, perhaps by conducting a multicultural research project.

As a starting point in preparing your class presentations and activities, you can increase your familiarity with multicultural issues by reviewing three excellent resources: APA's (2003) "Guidelines on Multicultural Education, Training, Research, Practice, and Organizational Change for Psychologists," "Guidelines for Multicultural Counseling Proficiency for Psychologists: Implications for Education and Training, Research and Clinical Practice," published by the Division of Counseling Psychology (Division 17; http:// www.div17.org/mc comp.html), and the University of Maryland's "Diversity Database" (http://www.inform .umd.edu/EdRes/Topic/Diversity/). One issue students will find interesting is the ways in which professional ethical codes and the knowledge base of the mental health disciplines reflect the values of our dominant culture. There's no question that professionals need to become more sensitive to discerning ways in which their actions reflect cultural biases and then strive to use this awareness to act in a manner consistent with their sincere respect for each individual they interact with professionally and for society as a whole.

There are considerable individual differences in the philosophical training and background of instructors of mental health ethics courses. For instructors seeking additional clarification and information concerning the philosophical theories and issues addressed in Chapter 4 (e.g., moral relativism, utilitarianism, Kant's moral philosophy) and throughout the book, I recommend the easily accessible Stanford Encyclopedia of Philosophy (http://plato.stanford.edu/ contents-unabridged.html).

Like my previous book, this book devotes considerable attention to the current versions of the ethical codes of both psychology and counseling. The ethical codes of psychology and counseling are introduced in Chapters 2 and 3, respectively. Each of these chapters is self-contained in the sense that an instructor in one of these disciplines has the option of skipping the other chapter, if necessary. However, different ethical issues of concern to all mental health professionals receive emphasis in each chapter, so there is much to be gained by having your students read both chapters. Furthermore, understanding the similarities and differences in the points of emphasis in these codes will enrich students' understanding of the range of ethical considerations relevant to mental health practice. Also, consultation between psychologists and counselors will be facilitated by understanding the similarities and differences in the ethical concerns of the two professions. Finally, many professionals who receive graduate training in psychology go on to be licensed as counselors. Likewise, master's-level counselors often enroll later in a doctoral program in clinical or counseling psychology. Familiarity with the ethical codes of both professions will make these transitions easier and avoid potential ethical difficulties resulting from confusion between the roles of psychologist and counselor.

Case Examples

Case examples that test students' ethical reasoning skills are found throughout each chapter. They provide opportunities to assist students in developing the following skills: (a) recognizing ethical complexity by identifying the different ethical considerations present in each situation, (b) determining whether each consideration identified is truly relevant in the situation presented, (c) evaluating whether the relevant ethical considerations in a situation conflict (as in a genuine dilemma), and (d) using the model of ethical decision making presented in Chapter 5 to resolve a dilemma and determine an ethically appropriate course of action.

Since case examples present scenarios involving individual professionals and their clients or students, male and female characters are alternated throughout; similarly, approximately equal numbers of cases involve counseling and psychology professionals (an attempt to avoid sexist or professionally parochial portrayals through randomization).

Following the presentation of the model in Chapter 5, a more detailed case scenario will be presented at the end of each chapter. Representing true ethical dilemmas, these scenarios, which are associated with the issues in the chapter, will provide readers with an excellent opportunity to practice using the model and further develop their practical reasoning skills. I have used these scenarios in my graduate ethics classes for ethical reasoning brainstorming sessions and as the basis for in-class "debates."

In-Class Debates

For the debate format, students sign up for a class date to participate in a debate (two students per debate), but they are not informed of their debate topic or the position they will support until the day preceding their presentation. I have found that this procedure levels the playing field for students by limiting their preparation time and forces them to focus on the conceptual issues involved, rather than engage in a lengthy literature search or extensive discussions with faculty and colleagues, which only tend to result in appeals to authority, rather than conceptually compelling argumentation. Students are instructed to use each step of the model of ethical decision making to develop a rationale for the position they are assigned to support *and* to anticipate the arguments that will be presented by the person supporting "the other side" of the issue.

The student presenting first (determined by a coin flip) has five minutes to present arguments and anticipate objections that might be raised by the other participant. The second presenter has seven or eight minutes to both present the alternative position and rebut the arguments presented by the first student. Finally, the first presenter has three minutes for a final rebuttal. Then, students in the class have the opportunity to question either presenter or to point out additional issues that were not addressed in the presentation. (Presentation grades can be based on ratings of the effectiveness of each presentation, generated by the instructor and the students in the class. I typically drop the highest and lowest student ratings to eliminate potential outliers. The instructor's rating can be weighted more strongly [e.g., three times as heavily as individual student ratings], if the instructor desires. The average of the [weighted] ratings would be used as the student's grade.)

ACKNOWLEDGMENTS

I would like to thank the many graduate students who have taken my ethics course and provided feedback on manuscript chapters. I would also like to thank Arthur Pomponio, Sage Publications acquisitions editor, for his support, patience, assistance, encouragement, and calming presence, without which I would not have been able to complete this project, and Veronica Novak, editorial assistant at Sage, for her skill and persistent kindness throughout the lengthy publication process. In addition, I would like to express my sincere appreciation to Sage production editor Sanford Robinson and copy editor Diana Breti for their many insightful contributions throughout the production process. Finally, my wife, Angela, knows very well that this book is as much a product of her editorial skill and her unwavering love and support as it is of my effort (but I felt I should tell her anyway). Thanks, Mae!

Chapter 1

Introduction

WHAT IS ETHICS?

The field of *ethics* is a philosophical discipline concerned with the morality of human behavior, with right and wrong. Some ethical theories present arguments about what is most valuable in life. This type of theory, called a *theory of value,* is considered an ethical theory because whatever is valued most highly in human life, based on its own intrinsic worth, is argued to be the greatest "good" in life. A second type of ethical theory, known as a *theory of obligation,* presents arguments that particular behaviors are morally wrong (i.e., unethical), while certain other behaviors are right and *ought* to be performed under specified circumstances. The morally prescribed behavior (i.e., the "right" thing to do) would be a person's ethical *duty,* or moral obligation, in that situation. For example, one might argue that when people see someone about to step off the curb into oncoming traffic, they ought to attempt to warn the person. Warning people whenever possible to prevent them from being harmed would be a moral duty. A theory of obligation is also a *normative ethical theory* because it presents rules of right and wrong conduct that apply to everyone. Similarly, professional ethical codes provide normative ethical expectations that apply equally to all members of a profession.

Theories of obligation also present a general philosophical justification of the meaningfulness and importance of the specific ethical duties endorsed by the theory. This component of an ethical theory is referred to as *metaethical.* Metaethical arguments explain where those specific ethical duties come from (e.g., logical thinking, cultural tradition, or a general concern for the welfare of humanity) and why those duties are sufficiently meaningful and important that everyone is obligated to obey them. Generally, theories of obligation possess both normative and metaethical components. To summarize, the normative component describes *what* behaviors represent specific ethical duties for everyone (e.g., "Stealing someone else's property is wrong"), and the metaethical component explains *why* those behaviors constitute legitimate ethical duties (e.g., "As persons [like myself], everyone is entitled to the same respect and consideration that I feel I deserve").

The relation of ethical (normative) to metaethical considerations is illustrated by the distinction between the specific duties presented in the ethical code of a mental health profession and the underlying ethical principles that provide the philosophical justification for those specific duties. When people ask why confidentiality is such an important professional ethical duty, they are addressing the rational (i.e., metaethical) justification for such a duty. A professional's metaethical response might be a brief Kantian explanation of the rational principle of respect for persons (discussed in Chapter 4).

ETHICS AND PERSONAL VALUES

All people possess *ethical beliefs,* which are guidelines that provide moral direction and organization for their conduct. Their beliefs provide them with a sense of the right thing to do in a particular situation. Underlying these beliefs are the *ethical values* they ascribe to, the general principles that constitute their sense of what is right and what is wrong, what is good and what is evil. People acquire these values from many sources: parents and family, culture, formal ethics training, religion, and their own rational analysis of ethical issues.

Cultural influences pervade individuals' personal value systems. Clearly, most *personal values,* including ethical values and cultural values, were learned as children during the process of socialization as members of a culture. For example, the enormous importance Americans place on the needs of the individual is a product of Western, individualistic culture. However, because this value is such a significant presence in their culture, Americans tend to view the importance of the individual as a *fact,* rather than recognizing it as a cultural assumption. When interacting with people from a collectivist culture, like that of India, Americans may fail to recognize the culturally based difference in perspectives on individuality or just assume that the Indian individual is wrong or backward and needs to be educated regarding the ultimate value of the individual person.

People do not normally think about why they hold the ethical values they do. The problem of providing a metaethical justification for their ethical values generally only arises when they are confronted by a person or culture that possesses particular values that are contrary to theirs. Their attempts to argue that their values are "better" or "right" require a metaethical theory that will enable them to evaluate the two sets of values against a mutually agreed upon set of rational criteria. Chapter 4 will discuss a few of the more significant ethical theories that have been advanced by philosophers over the centuries and the metaethical support the theories have provided for the existence of genuine ethical duties.

CASE EXAMPLE 1.1

A psychologist is working with a female client who is very upset about deciding whether to sign a Do Not Resuscitate (DNR) order for her terminally ill father. She is unsure whether such an action is morally consistent with the tenets of her religion. On the other hand, she cannot afford the cost of continued medical treatment. She asks her psychologist for advice. The psychologist tells her to sign the order; she has more than fulfilled her duty toward her father.

When the psychologist mentions the situation to a colleague, the colleague says that it was wrong for the psychologist to tell the client what to do because it showed a lack of respect for her personal autonomy. The psychologist felt that ignoring the client's request for help in resolving this painful dilemma would show a lack of regard for her as a person. The colleague responds that the psychologist does not understand what respect for autonomy really means.

THE ROLE OF VALUES IN THE PRACTICE OF A MENTAL HEALTH PROFESSION

Ethical values are not the only sort of personal values people hold that are important to their professional activities. Their personal likes and dislikes, along with their attitudes and beliefs about a multitude of issues in life, are also personal values that influence their perception of people and situations. For example, if a counselor prefers quiet people and considers them "nicer" than more talkative, outgoing individuals, this personal preference constitutes a value judgment. In general, people tend to be relatively unaware of the role their subjective personal, and especially cultural, values play in their daily lives. However, awareness of one's personal value system is an important component of being an ethical professional because the consulting, teaching, and research activities professionals engage in are all an expression of their values. To act on the basis of personal preferences or cultural biases, rather than be guided by objective, well-reasoned principles, would be to behave arbitrarily rather than scientifically and would involve a very significant risk of acting unethically (R. F. Kitchener, 1980).

Although long recognized in the counseling profession, *multiculturalism* (i.e., the recognition of the significance of cultural values in human behavior) has only recently begun to be appreciated by psychology (Pedersen, 2001). In the past, the importance of culture was minimized because cultural values were viewed as a threat to the scientific objectivity of psychology. Fortunately, all mental health professions are now beginning to acknowledge the pervasive influence of cultural values on the personal and professional values of mental health practitioners (e.g., APA, 2003).

Professionals' personal values also influence their view of human motivation and human behavior, thereby affecting their choice of theoretical orientation in their professional activities. In clinical work, their values influence their beliefs regarding the nature of psychopathology, the appropriate goals of treatment, and the most efficacious methods for accomplishing those goals (R. F. Kitchener, 1980, 1991). For example, humanistic psychotherapists have a very different viewpoint regarding the nature of behavior change than operant behavior therapists.[1] Moreover, therapists' values (e.g., regarding religious belief) frequently differ from those of their clients (Bergin, 1980, 1991). Clinicians must always be sensitive to the danger of imposing their values on their clients. A clinician's assumption that a client's dependency is a form of psychopathology clearly represents a cultural bias in favor of individual self-sufficiency. Obviously, mental health professionals can only address this threat to their ethical obligation to respect the dignity and autonomy of their clients effectively if they are aware of their personal values and the role their values play in psychotherapy.

Similarly, in teaching, instructors' values play a role in determining what topics they choose to include in a course and which potential explanations of a phenomenon they emphasize in class. As is the case with therapists, professors are important authority figures. Thus, the potential for their personal values to unduly influence their students' thinking is a matter to be considered seriously in deciding what to say in class. In the same vein, researchers' particular areas of interest and the projects they undertake are also a reflection of their values. In fact, every judgment mental health professionals make is, at least in part, a value judgment. Increased awareness of personal values through critical self-assessment is the best method for professionals to develop a clearer understanding of the role their values play in their professional activities and the best safeguard against arbitrarily imposing their values on the people they serve.

CASE EXAMPLE 1.2

A counselor is contacted by a couple who want her to work with their 17-year-old son. The son is sexually active, and the parents want him to stop engaging in that behavior. During an intake interview, the young man reports that he is careful about contraception and practices "safe sex." He says that he enjoys sex and experiences no guilt about his behavior. In spite of his parents' objections, he has no intention of stopping.

WHY DO PROFESSIONS DEVELOP ETHICAL STANDARDS?

The ethical standards for a profession are generally developed by the dominant professional organization. For example, the American Bar Association established the ethical code for the legal profession, the American Medical Association for the practice of medicine, the American Counseling Association (ACA) for counseling, and the American Psychological Association (APA) for the practice of psychology. Each of the mental health professions (i.e., psychology, counseling, psychiatry, and social work) has developed its own ethical code.

The creation of an ethical code can be viewed as a significant step in the development of a profession. As the profession begins to establish itself as an important contributor to society, practitioners experience an increasing need to clarify their sense of professional identity by distinguishing themselves from those practicing other professions and occupations. The establishment of an ethical code is a way of communicating to students and practitioners of the profession the basic principles, ideals, and interests of the profession. Also, as a profession becomes larger, with more practitioners operating in increasingly diverse employment contexts, the frequency of questions and problems relating to ethical matters inevitably increases. The ethical code establishes standards of professional conduct that provide some specific behavioral guidelines and serve to sensitize all members of the profession to ethical issues involved in the practice of the profession.

The publication of a professional ethical code also serves a number of other purposes, such as influencing the public's perception of a profession. The code informs the public regarding the nature of the profession and the special talents and qualifications of those practicing it. It asserts both the rights of professionals (e.g., to freedom of inquiry) and their commitment to uphold ethical standards of behavior in their dealings with consumers. For example, the public is assured that mental health professionals maintain confidentiality regarding their interactions with clients and limit their practice to areas of demonstrated competence. This assurance of the "professionalism" of psychologists, counselors, psychiatrists, and social workers is quite different from what people can reasonably expect in most business dealings. Generally, people operate at their own risk in purchasing goods or services. However, a professional ethical code informs the public that the notion of *caveat emptor* (Let the buyer beware!) does not apply when dealing with members of that profession. Thus, a code of ethics enhances the respectability and prestige of a profession in the eyes of the public by publicizing the fact that the profession will protect consumers by regulating and monitoring the conduct of its members.

This public presentation of the lofty ethical standards of the profession may also be intended to impress more than just the general population. The creation of an ethical code sends a clear message to state and federal legislators that no regulation of the profession is needed; the profession is demonstrating the ability to regulate itself and protect the interests of consumers. In presenting unique ways in which the profession can benefit society, the ethical code also represents a significant step in the process of creating a distinct niche or "turf" for the profession. The culmination of the establishment of the profession's identity comes about when state governments enact licensing laws, which specify that only members of that profession are uniquely qualified to provide certain sorts of services to the public and are permitted to use a protected professional title.

CASE EXAMPLE 1.3

A client participating in outpatient therapy with a counselor is admitted involuntarily to a psychiatric hospital following a suicide attempt. She contacts the counselor by phone from the hospital and tells him she is being treated with a major tranquilizer (i.e., an antipsychotic medication), in spite of the counselor's diagnosis of Major Depression. She reports that she is extremely sleepy and has difficulty concentrating. She tells him that she hates the way the medication makes her feel. The counselor contacts the psychiatrist responsible for the client's inpatient treatment. The psychiatrist feels that the medication he has prescribed is appropriate and tells the counselor that he is exceeding the boundaries of his professional competence in questioning the client's medication.

The counselor is concerned about his client's well-being and tells her that even though she has been committed to the hospital, she still has the right to refuse treatment that she thinks is not in her best interest. The psychiatrist is furious that a fellow professional has subverted his authority with a client in this manner.

THE HISTORY OF ETHICS IN PSYCHOLOGY

Psychology was the first mental health profession to create an ethical code. The code served as a model for those developed by the other mental health professions. The American Psychological Association (APA) first established a Committee on Scientific and Professional Ethics in 1938 to consider the possibility of developing an ethical code (Golann, 1970). The committee determined that publishing a code at that point would be premature, but it nevertheless became a standing committee of APA "to deal with charges of unethical behavior of psychologists" (APA, 1952, p. 426). In 1947, the committee determined that the time was right for psychology to develop a formal ethical code, so the Committee on Ethical Standards for Psychology was created. The committee believed that psychology's ethical code should be developed in an empirical manner, since psychology is an empirical science. They proposed that the content of the code be determined inductively by soliciting input from all APA members regarding ethical issues they had encountered in their practice of psychology. This approach was consistent with social psychology research, which indicated that a code would be followed more closely and viewed as more authoritative by people if they had a role in developing it.

In 1948, the committee contacted all APA members and asked them to submit a synopsis of a situation in which they had made an ethical judgment and to indicate what ethical issue had been involved. More than 1,000 case scenarios were provided by the APA membership. The committee sorted the submissions into six general categories: public responsibility, client relationships, teaching, research, writing and publishing, and professional relationships (Golann, 1970). Following extensive discussion within the field, the first ethical code for psychology, *Ethical Standards of Psychologists,* was published in 1953 (APA, 1953). The original *Ethical Standards* "provided a comprehensive and detailed code" covering ethical and professional issues (Golann, 1970, p. 400). In fact, the code was 171 pages in length, with a total of 106 principles under the six category sections, including many specific case examples. Critics argued that many of the principles overlapped, that matters of professional courtesy were given equal status to serious ethical issues, and that the code placed too little emphasis on nonclinical areas of psychological practice (APA Committee on Ethical Standards of Psychologists, 1958).

The committee members responsible for the original code had assumed that it would need to be revised periodically in light of future experience and developments in the field. The first major revision of the *Ethical Standards* took place in 1958 (APA, 1958). The 1958 version consisted of 18 general principles and was only four pages long. The principles were quite broad in scope, with fewer specific behavioral requirements and prohibitions. The committee believed that this approach reflected the increasing complexity of the issues facing psychologists in the wide variety of contexts in which they practiced their profession. It was thought that specific case scenarios, like those included in the 1953 code, would be of limited relevance to most psychologists and would likely be more frustrating than helpful.

During the next decade, two relatively minor revisions of the *Ethical Standards* were adopted, in 1963 and 1968 (APA, 1963, 1968). These versions consisted of 19 principles and a few moderately specific behavioral standards concerning aspects of psychological practice (e.g., advertising professional services). The 1968 version was in place for a decade, followed by two rapid-fire revisions of the code (APA, 1979, 1981a). The 1981 version consisted of 10 principles: responsibility, competence, moral and legal standards, public statements, confidentiality, welfare of the consumer, professional relationships, assessment techniques, research with human participants, and care and use of animals. (The tenth principle was added in the 1981 revision; there had been only nine in the 1979 version.) The title of the ethical code was also changed in 1981 to "Ethical Principles of Psychologists." Minor amendments to the 1981 "Ethical Principles" were adopted in 1989 (APA, 1990), reflecting APA's attempt to mollify the Federal Trade Commission, which was dissatisfied with the constraints that the "Ethical Principles" placed on psychologists' right to advertise their services to the public.[2]

In 1992, a major revision involving a substantial structural reworking of the code was published with the title "Ethical Principles of Psychologists and Code of Conduct" (APA, 1992). This version began with an introduction and preamble, followed by six general principles: competence, integrity, professional and scientific responsibility, respect for people's rights and dignity, concern for others' welfare, and social responsibility. The final section consisted of a lengthy set of specific ethical standards, grouped under eight broad headings, which provided psychologists with a set of "*enforceable* rules for conduct as psychologists" (APA, 1992, p. 1598).

"ETHICAL PRINCIPLES OF PSYCHOLOGISTS AND CODE OF CONDUCT"

The current version of psychology's ethical code, published in 2002, represents yet another substantial revision (APA, 2002). It begins with an introduction and applicability section followed by a preamble and a set of five general principles, which differ markedly from the six principles of the 1992 version. The final section again consists of specific ethical standards, now grouped under an expanded set of ten general headings. The current version of the "Ethical Principles" is presented in Appendix A. The content of the code will be detailed in Chapter 2. The "Ethical Principles," like the ethical codes of the other mental health professions, will no doubt require further revision as the ethical challenges faced by psychologists continue to evolve and the professional activities of psychologists become even more diverse.

COUNSELING: *CODE OF ETHICS*

The American Counseling Association (ACA) first published an ethical code in 1961. The code has undergone five revisions during the past 45 years. The current version of the *Code of Ethics* (ACA, 2005), the first revision in ten years, is presented in Appendix B. The format of the current version is somewhat different from the previous version (ACA, 1995) in that each of the code's eight sections (e.g., The Counseling Relationship) blends aspirational ethical principles with more specific standards of practice; previously, a separate Standards of Practice section presented minimal specific duties counselors "must" perform (ACA, 1995).

Though quite similar to psychology's "Ethical Principles" (APA, 2002) in its points of emphasis, counseling's ethical code provides much more specific guidance regarding a host of practical ethical concerns, including dual relationships, respecting diversity, group work, termination and referral, and computer technology. The content of counseling's ethical code will be discussed in detail in Chapter 3.

PSYCHIATRY: *THE PRINCIPLES OF MEDICAL ETHICS, WITH ANNOTATIONS ESPECIALLY APPLICABLE TO PSYCHIATRY*

Medical (and mental health) ethics began with the Hippocratic Oath, which was written around 400 BC (Miles, 2004). This remarkable ancient document presents the values and concerns fundamental to all of the "helping professions" today, such as beneficence (seeking to benefit and do good for others), nonmaleficence (avoiding harming anyone), integrity, justice, and professional responsibility (accountability for one's actions, including mistakes). The Oath also discusses professional ethical duties like confidentiality, the development of professional competence, respect for fellow professionals, and avoiding exploitative dual relationships (such as sexual involvement with patients). The ethical values and duties of today's mental health professionals can be traced directly to the insights of early physicians presented in the Hippocratic Oath.

Today, the ethical practice of medicine in the Hippocratic tradition is reflected clearly in the *Principles of Medical Ethics,* published by the American Medical Association (AMA).

Prior to 1973, psychiatrists had no specialized set of ethical guidelines; they followed the same ethical code that applied to all physicians. In 1973, the American Psychiatric Association published a special supplement to the AMA's *Principles of Medical Ethics*. The present version of psychiatry's ethical code, adopted in 2003, consists of *The Principles of Medical Ethics* along with extensive annotations addressing specific areas of relevance of each of its nine sections to the practice of psychiatry (American Psychiatric Association, 2003). It differs from psychology's "Ethical Principles" and counseling's *Code of Ethics* in its focus on general principles to guide the professional conduct of psychiatrists and fewer specific behavioral prohibitions. Psychiatry's code is similar in structure to earlier versions of the "Ethical Principles" (e.g., APA, 1990).

Psychiatry's ethical code addresses many of the same issues as the ethical codes of psychology and counseling. Respect for each client's human dignity is said to underlie the psychiatrist's commitment to protecting clients' confidentiality, developing and maintaining professional competence, refusing to tolerate discriminatory policies or practices, upholding standards of professionalism in dealings with other professionals, and addressing unethical behavior by other psychiatrists. One area in which psychiatry's ethical code is actually more specific (and more stringent) than the "Ethical Principles" (APA, 2002) and *Code of Ethics* (ACA, 2005) is dual relationships with clients. Section 2 states explicitly that "sexual activity with a current or former patient is unethical" (American Psychiatric Association, 2003, p. 7).

Historically, psychiatry has been the only mental health profession that must also deal with ethical issues pertaining to prescribing medication in the treatment of clients' problems. A long-standing ethical concern for psychiatrists is the conflict between their respect for the human dignity of their clients and the use of invasive treatment procedures without clients' consent, such as medicating patients involuntarily (e.g., Jellinek & Parmelee, 1977). This issue is not addressed directly in psychiatry's ethical code, except in statements that psychiatrists will always act in a manner that is consistent with mental health laws and regulations.

SOCIAL WORK: *CODE OF ETHICS OF THE NATIONAL ASSOCIATION OF SOCIAL WORKERS*

The National Association of Social Workers (NASW) adopted its first ethical code in 1960. The *Code of Ethics* was revised in 1979 and 1993; it was then substantially rewritten in 1996. The most recent revision occurred in 1999 (NASW, 1999). As stated in the preamble, "The primary mission of the social work profession is to enhance human well-being and help meet the basic human needs of all people" (p. 1). Consistent with this statement of mission, Brill (2001) identifies altruism as the fundamental motivation of the social work profession. The social work code covers the same general areas as the ethical codes of the other mental health professions; much of its content and wording is clearly derived from the models provided by psychology's "Ethical Principles" and counseling's *Code of Ethics*.

Social work's *Code of Ethics* begins with an overview followed by a preamble and statement of purpose. Next, six general ethical principles are presented, each reflecting one of the six core values of the profession. The first principle states that the "primary goal" of social workers "is to help people in need and to address social problems" (NASW, 1999, p. 5). This principle reflects the core value of *Service*. The second principle, based on the core value of *Social Justice*, concerns social workers' efforts to combat discrimination and social injustice by working to promote social change that will improve the lives "of vulnerable and oppressed individuals and groups of people" (NASW, 1999, p. 5). The third principle addresses respect for all persons, espousing the value of the *Dignity and Worth of the Person*. Social workers respect each person as a unique individual and always seek to "promote clients' socially responsible self-determination" (p. 5).

The fourth general principle concerns social workers' recognition of the central role of social relationships in people's lives. Social workers express the core value of the *Importance of Human Relationships* by relating to clients not as patients but as partners in the pursuit of life change and by seeking to improve relationships between people, families, and communities through their work. The fifth principle states that social workers are trustworthy, responsible professionals whose behavior exemplifies the value of *Integrity*. The final general ethical principle concerns the ethical value of *Competence*. Social work professionals are ethically obligated to restrict their practice to client groups (e.g., children) and issues (e.g., Attention-Deficit/Hyperactivity Disorder) with which they have established expertise through formal course work, reading, or supervised experience. Social workers develop expertise in new areas of practice and maintain their competence by pursuing continuing education opportunities.

The final section of the ethical code comprises the ethical standards of the profession, grouped under six broad headings representing a combination of "enforceable guidelines for professional conduct" and "aspirational" goals (NASW, 1999, p. 7). The first set of ethical standards concerns social workers' duties to clients. The interests of clients are always the primary consideration for social work professionals, which entails that social workers provide competent services, avoid exploiting clients in any manner, and foster autonomy by respecting the confidentiality of clients and by empowering clients to exercise their capacity for self-determination. Fulfilling their duties to clients has proven a challenging task for social workers and other mental health professionals in the face of dwindling government resources coupled with an ever-increasing demand for social services (Brill, 2001).

Social workers' responsibilities to other social workers and to colleagues of other professions are addressed in the second set of standards. The issues covered include respect for fellow professionals, consultation, handling client referrals, dealing responsibly with personal problems that might affect colleagues' professional performance, and appropriate methods for dealing with unethical conduct by colleagues. The third set of standards concerns social workers' responsibilities in the settings and organizations in which they practice. Social workers work "to prevent and eliminate discrimination" in any organization with which they are associated (NASW, 1999, p. 21). As educators and supervisors, they provide competent, professional services and do not exploit students or supervisees. In practice settings, such as hospitals and clinics, they "advocate . . . for adequate resources to meet clients' needs" (NASW, 1999, p. 20).

Social workers' duties as professionals constitute the fourth set of ethical standards. Social workers do not engage in deception or misrepresentation in their professional activities. They do not allow personal problems to adversely affect their professional practice or place their clients at risk. Ethical responsibilities to the social work profession are covered in the fifth set of standards. Social workers uphold the integrity of the profession by maintaining high standards of professional competence and behaving in accordance with the values and principles discussed earlier. When conducting research and evaluating the effectiveness of programs and interventions, social workers protect the welfare of research participants by obtaining informed consent, preserving confidentiality, and minimizing risks to participants.

The final set of ethical standards concerns social workers' duty to promote the general welfare of society "and the development of people, their communities, and their environments" (NASW, 1999, p. 26). Social work has historically experienced considerable ambivalence about the professional appropriateness of political activity and lobbying. In recent years, however, the profession has become much more active politically to advocate for the needs of its underserved, and often disenfranchised, groups in American society (Brill, 2001).

The ethical code is not intended to provide specific rules governing social workers' behavior. "The *Code* offers a set of values, principles, and standards to guide decision making and conduct when ethical issues arise" (NASW, 1999, p. 2). However, the *Code of Ethics* is supplemented by no fewer than 15 separate sets of specific standards designed to provide additional direction in particular areas (e.g., clinical social work) and issues (e.g., continuing education) of concern to the profession (e.g., NASW, 1982, 1989).

THE LIMITATIONS OF ETHICAL CODES

The ethical codes of the mental health professions are intended to guide the moral decision making of the members of a profession by informing them of both specific rules and the values and principles that are fundamental to the profession. In reality, however, the codes generally consist of a set of overly general moral platitudes, an odd combination of nitpicky specific standards regarding some matters (e.g., informed consent), and a vague treatment of other, seemingly equally important issues (e.g., sexual relationships with former therapy clients). This result should not be overly surprising, since, as Bersoff (2003a) points out, ethical codes are created by a small group of (usually politically powerful) members of a profession selected for the task. "Thus, a code of ethics is, inevitably, anachronistic, conservative, ethnocentric, and the product of political compromise" (p. 1).

A second major limitation of professional ethical codes as a guide for ethical problem solving is that they generally present ethical considerations one at a time. This approach may give students and professionals the misleading impression that ethical considerations (e.g., confidentiality, competence) are independent of one another and that behaving ethically is simply a matter of faithfully obeying the "rules" and standards presented in an ethical code, rather than learning to *think* ethically (Pedersen, 1997). Nothing could be further from the truth. Consequently, trying to follow a profession's ethical code and standards of conduct in a rote manner will not enable professionals to function ethically (Pettifor, 2001). Situations arise in the daily practice of a mental health profession that involve multiple ethical considerations. The most difficult situations are *ethical dilemmas,* in which ethical considerations actually conflict with one another (K. S. Kitchener, 1984). For example, counseling's *Code of Ethics* and psychology's "Ethical Principles" discuss the critical importance of obtaining informed consent from research participants (ACA, 2005, G.2.a; APA, 2002, 8.02). This section is followed (immediately in the *Code of Ethics*) by a discussion of the conditions under which deceiving research participants is permissible (ACA, 2005, G.2.b; APA, 2002, 8.07). Nevertheless, psychology's ethical code makes little or no mention of the potential for ethical principles to conflict. Counseling's *Code of Ethics* now acknowledges the existence of ethical dilemmas and advises counselors "to engage in a carefully considered ethical decision-making process" (ACA, 2005, Purpose). Similarly, social work's *Code of Ethics* acknowledges that it "does not specify which values, principles and standards are most important and ought to outweigh others in instances when they conflict" (NASW, 1999, p. 3).

But, how are professionals to deal with conflicts between principles when professional ethical codes have traditionally tended "to deemphasize the responsibility of individual counselors for moral thinking, moral dialogue, and moral development" (Pedersen, 1997, p. 27)? One of the primary goals of this book is to provide mental health professionals with the knowledge and skills needed to identify complex ethical situations and to resolve them in an ethical, rational manner. The next two chapters will provide a comprehensive introduction to the ethical codes of psychology and counseling, respectively. Chapters 4 and 5 will then provide the tools necessary for professionals to identify and resolve complex ethical situations.

CASE EXAMPLE 1.4

A neuropsychologist conducts an evaluation of a 75-year-old man at the request of his daughter. He has been experiencing memory problems. Although he is still quite aware and able to function fairly well, the results of the neuropsychological testing and some additional medical tests conducted by colleagues indicate that the man is in the early stages of Alzheimer's disease. His daughter meets with the neuropsychologist and pleads with her not to tell her father about the diagnosis. She says that her father has always maintained that he would commit suicide if he were diagnosed with any form of dementia, so his family would not be saddled with him as he declined physically and mentally. The neuropsychologist feels an obligation to respect the client's right to know his diagnosis, but she does not want to harm the client and his family.

ETHICS AND LAW

A final important component of professional practice, along with an understanding of moral principles, personal values, and professional ethical codes, is knowledge of the law. Some people believe that morality and law are basically the same. This belief is true in some instances. Most illegal acts are also unethical; for example, it is morally wrong for researchers to murder research participants and, of course, there are also laws forbidding such behavior. However, there have been laws that were immoral (e.g., segregation laws that legalized discrimination against African Americans in the United States). There are also some acts that would be regarded as unethical but are not illegal. For example, having a consensual sexual relationship with an adult psychotherapy client is unethical for a psychologist, but it is not necessarily illegal. Thus, morality is distinct from law, but both should serve the same basic purpose: facilitation of the satisfaction of individual needs in a manner that does not conflict with the needs of others or the stability of the society as a whole. Both laws and ethics are designed to provide standards that promote harmonious social existence.

In some situations, the law might require professionals to do something they consider unethical. For example, a state statute might require a clinician to provide his client's psychotherapy records to the court if the client becomes involved in a custody battle in the context of her divorce and the records are subpoenaed as evidence relevant to the client's fitness as a parent. Legally, the clinician is required to turn over the records to the court. However, if the client were involved in psychotherapy to deal with issues pertaining to the divorce and had explored her homosexual fantasies in the course of the therapy, the clinician might feel that his client's case for custody could be unfairly biased by having this information taken out of context. As a result, he might argue that turning over the records constitutes an unethical breach of the client's confidentiality. However, if he resists the subpoena, claiming that such disclosure is a violation of his professional ethics, he could be held in contempt of the court order. He could face substantial fines, or even imprisonment, as a result of his refusal to obey the court order.

This situation, involving a conflict between morality and law, illustrates a fundamental difference between the two that will be emphasized throughout this book. Laws are generally rigid rules applied without exception and without regard for the particular circumstances of a case. If there is no law protecting the privacy of the client's case records, then legally they must be turned over to the court when a subpoena is issued, no matter how unfair this disclosure may be to the client in that particular case. The inflexibility of the application of law in our society creates unfortunate cases in which what the law requires and what justice, or fairness, requires are two different things. (Curiously, the inflexible application of laws is intended by their creators to bring about justice by ensuring that everyone is treated the same.) Morality, on the other hand, should ideally operate more flexibly, based on an appreciation of the rightness or wrongness of a general rule of conduct (e.g., the ethical duty to obey the law) in a specific set of circumstances or context. Treating people justly does not mean treating everyone exactly the same; rather, justice requires that the interests and needs of each individual be given due consideration (Aristotle, trans. 1947).

The frequent interaction of the legal system with professional and ethical issues in the mental health professions is a compelling reason for becoming familiar with state and federal laws concerning mental health practice. For example, the confidentiality of clients' health records is legally protected by the Health Insurance Portability and Accountability Act (HIPAA), a set of federal standards addressing security and confidentiality issues in the creation, storage, and disclosure of Protected Health Information (PHI; Privacy Rule, 2003, §§ 160, 164). Failure to comply with these standards is punishable by penalties ranging from civil fines to criminal prosecution. The relevance of HIPAA standards for mental health professionals will be discussed throughout this book.

Another important legal aspect of mental health practice involves state licensing boards. All states regulate the use of certain protected titles (e.g., "psychologist"). Many states' licensing laws also specify services (e.g., personality assessment utilizing projective tests) that only members of particular professions (e.g., psychologists, psychiatrists), by virtue of their specialized training, are deemed legally competent to provide. State boards also regulate professional conduct and misconduct of those licensed to practice the profession through means such as investigating and adjudicating complaints concerning any sort of illegal or unprofessional conduct by a licensed member of the profession. The legal aspects of professional practice, including the functioning of state licensing boards and the procedures for dealing with ethical complaints against mental health professionals, will be discussed in Chapters 13 and 14.

CASE EXAMPLE 1.5

A counselor is treating a female client for an anxiety problem. The client is a lawyer trying to earn a junior partnership in a firm, so she works long hours and is under considerable stress.

She tells the counselor that she occasionally takes her frustrations out on her 10-year-old son. She gives an example of having come home from work the previous week to find that her son had not mowed the lawn as he was supposed to. The client relates that she "lost it" and began hitting the boy with the buckle end of a belt all over his body. She said that she always feels "awful" after these episodes.

The counselor informs her that her behavior qualifies as physical abuse of a child and that he is legally required to report her behavior to Child Protective Services. The client responds that the counselor had told her that everything they discussed was confidential. She says that if he violates her confidentiality by reporting her, she will sue him for malpractice.

SUMMARY

This chapter introduced the field of ethics, a philosophical discipline concerned with the morality of human behavior. The two main types of ethical theories are theories of value and theories of obligation. The former identify what is valued most highly in life (i.e., the "greatest good"), while the latter actually prescribe what one ought to do in a given situation. The ethical practice of a mental health profession requires professionals to develop a greater awareness of their ethical beliefs and values because their clinical, research, and teaching activities all reflect their personal value system. Professionals should always strive to avoid acting solely on the basis of personal biases and preferences. Rather, their judgments should be grounded in well-reasoned, objective principles. In addition to awareness of moral principles and personal values, practicing a mental health profession in an ethical manner requires knowledge of the law. Morality and law are two distinct sets of guidelines and do not always coincide, although they serve the same purpose: to provide standards of conduct that promote harmonious social existence.

Professions develop ethical standards for several reasons. Usually, the dominant professional organization establishes the ethical code of the profession. The American Psychological Association established the first ethical code for psychology in 1953. The code has undergone several revisions since then. The current version of the ethical code, "Ethical Principles of Psychologists and Code of Conduct," was adopted in 2002. Counseling created its *Code of Ethics and Standards of Practice* in 1961. The latest revision, published in 2005, is entitled *Code of Ethics;* the Standards of Practice section has been eliminated. Psychiatry established its own ethical code, distinct from that of the other medical professions, in 1973. The code, last revised in 2003, consists of the *Principles of Medical Ethics* and extensive annotations specific to the field of psychiatry. Finally, social work adopted the *Code of Ethics of the National Association of Social Workers* in 1960. The most recent revision was published in 1999.

NOTES

1. The differences between the humanistic and behavioral viewpoints regarding the nature of human behavior and their implications for behavior change were illustrated very clearly in Carl Rogers's and B. F. Skinner's classic debate regarding control of human behavior (Rogers & Skinner, 1956).

2. The specific issues addressed by the Federal Trade Commission and their implications for the "Ethical Principles" will be discussed in Chapter 2.

Chapter 2

"Ethical Principles of Psychologists and Code of Conduct"

The most recent revision of psychology's "Ethical Principles" (APA, 2002) consists of four sections: introduction and applicability, preamble, five general principles, and ethical standards. The preamble and general principles are described as "aspirational goals" of psychologists (APA, 2002). The ethical standards, on the other hand, are a set of enforceable rules of varying specificity that govern the professional activities of psychologists. This format, first adopted in the 1992 revision, reflects a shift in emphasis in the "Ethical Principles" toward greater specificity regarding behaviors that are clearly unethical and unprofessional. Obviously, the standards do not provide an exhaustive set of rules. Rather, they are designed to address some of the most common areas of complaint about psychologists' behavior. The 2002 revision also addresses technological advances affecting the delivery of psychological services (i.e., Internet, telephone, and other methods of electronic communication) more explicitly than previous versions (Fisher & Fried, 2003).

In this chapter, the general principles will be presented along with examples of ethical issues and ethical standards relevant to each principle. Their applicability to specific areas of professional practice (e.g., psychotherapy, consultation, assessment, teaching, and research) will be discussed in greater detail in later chapters. In addition, some areas of overlap between the "Ethical Principles" and counseling's *Code of Ethics* are addressed more thoroughly in the discussion of the *Code of Ethics* in Chapter 3.

INTRODUCTION AND APPLICABILITY

The "Ethical Principles" (APA, 2002) does not apply only to members of APA. Licensed or certified psychologists are bound by the code if it has been adopted by their state board (as is the case in most states). Many graduate programs in psychology also require that students admitted to the program abide by the "Ethical Principles." In addition, the "Ethical Principles" is employed by the APA Ethics Committee and review committees of any other organization that adopts these principles, along with its own rules and standards, to judge the ethicality of a psychologist's actions in the event of a complaint. It is the duty of every psychologist to be informed of the content of the "Ethical Principles" (APA, 2002). Ignorance of the code is no excuse for professional misconduct.

The "Ethical Principles" applies to the *professional* activities of psychologists; it is not intended to govern their private lives. However, any aspect of psychologists' private lives that relates to their professional activities (e.g., personal relationships with students or clients) *is* subject to the ethical standards of the profession. Psychologists retain the same freedom as any other individual to choose the values that will guide their personal lives. For example, psychologists' personal political convictions are their private business and not a matter of professional concern, unless they make public statements *as psychologists* that suggest their political stance is the position a psychologist would take based on scientific evidence. However, psychologists are obligated to behave, even in their private lives, in such a way that they do not compromise their professional responsibilities or reduce the public's trust in psychology and psychologists. Thus, psychologists behaving in an illegal or antisocial manner in their private affairs risk ethical censure as professionals and loss of licensing privileges.

Although the idea that psychologists ought to obey the law seems incredibly obvious and is generally true, you will recall from Chapter 1 that there are instances in which psychologists might experience conflict between legal requirements and ethical considerations (APA, 2002, 1.02). Some psychologists have also pointed out that mandated reporting laws, like the blanket legal requirement that suspected child abuse be reported to the appropriate child welfare authorities, can sometimes conflict with the best interests of the child and other parties involved. Mandated reporting laws generally stipulate that if professionals (or anyone else) *suspect* abuse, they are obligated to report it to the appropriate authorities, even in the absence of any direct evidence that abuse has occurred. Failure to report abuse can result in criminal penalties against a professional (VandeCreek & Knapp, 1993). Suppose, however, that a psychologist is treating a man who has a long history of problems with assertiveness and internalization of a great deal of anger. Occasionally, when the client does express anger about some situation, he experiences difficulty controlling himself adequately; he yells and curses and has even grabbed and hit his children. He reports that he feels very badly about these incidents later and wants help to manage his anger more effectively. If the psychologist suspects that her client might have grabbed or struck one of his children in an abusive manner during one or more of these episodes, she is legally required to report her suspicions. However, suppose she believes very strongly that her client does not represent a threat to his children at present and that reporting the matter will only reduce the likelihood that he will continue to be open and honest in therapy so that the situation can be resolved. As a result, she decides not to report the abuse.

Critics of mandatory reporting laws believe that clinicians should be given greater latitude to use their judgment in deciding when reporting of abuse is necessary and appropriate. On the other hand, those who advocate mandatory reporting with a very low threshold for reporting (i.e., *suspicion* of abuse) argue that a child's well-being should not hinge on the accuracy of a clinician's judgment of a very complex set of circumstances. They also point out that confronting abusive parents with the magnitude of their acts by reporting them to legal authorities should only enhance their motivation to resolve the issues that resulted in the abusive behavior. The issue of child abuse will be discussed in greater detail in Chapter 7.

There may also be instances in which the "Ethical Principles" prohibits psychologists from engaging in activities that are permitted by law. For example, though in some states it is now a felony for a therapist to engage in a sexual relationship with a current client (McMahon, 1997), the constraints put on psychologists' personal relationships with people they are involved with professionally are not generally reflected in legal statutes. In such cases, "psychologists must meet the higher ethical standard" of psychology's ethical code (APA, 2002, Introduction). In other instances, psychologists might encounter a situation that is not covered by law or by the "Ethical Principles." In these contexts, they are directed to consult professional colleagues, the specialty guidelines and standards published by APA and other "scientific and professional psychological organizations" to supplement the "Ethical Principles" (e.g., APA, 1981b, 1987, 1993), and "the dictates of their own conscience" (APA, 2002, Introduction). This instruction reinforces the view that functioning as an ethical professional requires psychologists to develop a clear understanding of their own ethical values and the philosophical basis of those values.

Any concerns regarding unethical or unprofessional behavior on the part of a psychologist can be investigated and punished by APA and the state board that has licensed the psychologist. Psychologists are ethically obligated to cooperate with ethics committees investigating a complaint (APA, 2002, 1.06). The functions of ethics committees and state boards of psychology, as well as the procedures followed in investigating alleged ethical violations, will be discussed in Chapter 14.

CASE EXAMPLE 2.1

A psychology faculty member frequently tells her classes that the U.S. government has been guilty of immoral acts against its citizens and should be overthrown, by force if necessary. A student makes a complaint to the APA Ethics Committee stating that the faculty member is behaving inappropriately in presenting these subversive ideas in class instead of teaching her students about psychology. The psychologist responds to the complaint by saying that her right to express her political opinions is protected by the First Amendment and that APA is infringing upon her academic freedom.

PREAMBLE

The primary focus of the preamble is an assertive statement concerning the roles psychologists perform and the contributions they make to society. For example, one of the services psychology is said to provide is "to help the public in developing informed judgments and choices concerning human behavior" (APA, 2002, Preamble). Critics of APA have argued that this concern with "educating" the public has been misapplied in some situations as a justification for APA's many political (e.g., abortion rights) pronouncements. (The distinction between ethical and political positions will be discussed in Chapter 13.) Even the statement regarding psychologists' respect for human and civil rights is linked to their insistence upon "freedom of inquiry and expression" in their various professional activities (APA, 2002, Preamble). Presented in somewhat parentalistic terms, the goal of the "Ethical Principles" is "the welfare and protection of the individuals and groups with whom psychologists work" (APA, 2002, Preamble). Essentially, the preamble serves to enhance the public image of psychology by stating what psychology has to offer the general public and assuring the public that the profession is committed to doing only good for people.

In closing, the preamble reiterates the point that behaving ethically as a psychologist "requires a personal commitment and lifelong effort to act ethically" (APA, 2002, Preamble). To apply the spirit of the general principles and ethical standards appropriately and resolve conflicts between ethical principles or issues not addressed in the "Ethical Principles," psychologists must strive to develop ethical competence. Psychologists must be committed personally to becoming capable of *thinking* ethically in order to *act* ethically in difficult, complex contexts.

GENERAL PRINCIPLES

Principle A: Beneficence and Nonmaleficence

Principle A incorporates two fundamental ethical duties first expressed in the Hippocratic Oath: *beneficence,* which means doing good for others, and *nonmaleficence,* which means doing no harm to others. Psychologists strive to do only good for those they serve by always working to "safeguard the welfare and rights" of any consumer of psychological services or other person affected by their actions (APA, 2002, Principle A). This statement suggests that concern for the welfare of consumers is always the primary consideration for psychologists; in fact, it is an important issue, but one that must sometimes be weighed or balanced against one or more competing considerations. Indeed, the "Ethical Principles" acknowledges that sometimes "conflicts occur among psychologists' obligations or concerns" (APA, 2002, Principle A).

Duty to Warn. One type of conflict between ethical principles that requires psychologists to weigh very carefully the welfare of each individual affected is a "duty to warn" scenario. This classic ethical-legal dilemma in clinical practice occurs when, in the context of a "special relationship" like a psychotherapeutic relationship, a client threatens to harm a specific person. The most notable legal case to address this type of ethical dilemma is *Tarasoff v. Board of Regents of the University of California* (1974/1976). The parents of Tatiana (Tanya) Tarasoff sued the University of California after their daughter was stabbed to death by Prosenjit Poddar, a graduate student from India (VandeCreek & Knapp, 1993).

The events that led to the death of Tanya Tarasoff were essentially as follows: Tanya had befriended Poddar when they met at a campus activity, and he became infatuated with her. When Tanya made it clear that she did not feel the same way about him, he became extremely upset. Poddar initiated outpatient psychotherapy with Dr. Lawrence Moore, a psychologist at a facility affiliated with the university, to deal with his anger and hurt. In the course of his treatment, Poddar confided to Dr. Moore that he intended to kill Tanya Tarasoff when she returned from her summer vacation in Brazil. After consulting with colleagues, who agreed with Dr. Moore that Poddar was psychotic and required involuntary commitment to an inpatient facility, Dr. Moore asked the campus police to take Poddar into custody and initiate commitment procedures. The campus police interviewed Poddar but found him rational and did not commit him when he promised to stay away from Tanya (VandeCreek & Knapp, 1993). Tanya was not contacted by the police nor by any of the mental health professionals who had been involved in Poddar's treatment. (He terminated treatment after the police interview.) In fact, "Dr. Harvey Powelson, the director of the department of psychiatry, . . . requested that the police chief return Moore's letters, ordered Moore to destroy his therapy notes, and requested that no further attempts be made to commit Poddar" (VandeCreek & Knapp, 1993, pp. 3–4). Shortly thereafter, Poddar killed Tanya at her home after she refused to speak with him.[1]

In such a case, an ethical respect for persons would result in the psychologist experiencing a conflict between the obligation to protect the confidentiality of a client and not reduce the client's willingness to continue psychotherapy to deal with dangerous impulses versus the obligation to ensure the physical well-being of the potential victim. Note that in this type of situation, there are no options that straightforwardly benefit each of the parties involved by producing only positive results. Rather, the object in this context is to find an ethically appropriate option that *minimizes* the harm done to the parties affected. In the Tarasoff case, the California Supreme Court ruled in 1976 that mental health professionals involved in a psychotherapeutic relationship can, under certain circumstances, incur an obligation to "protect others from harm, or to warn them of potential harm," which involves violating the confidentiality of the client (VandeCreek & Knapp, 1993, p. 5). The case was a landmark decision because it extended the duty to warn to outpatient treatment settings. Previous rulings had only concerned the obligation of a psychiatric facility to warn potential victims when an inpatient who had threatened them directly was being released. The circumstances under which mental health professionals are obligated to violate a client's confidentiality, and the implications of such decisions for psychotherapy, will be discussed in Chapter 6.

CASE EXAMPLE 2.2

A young adult being treated for depression by a clinical psychologist reveals during a session that she has thought about killing herself. When the psychologist asks her whether she has decided how she would commit suicide, she says that she would take an overdose of her sleeping medication. She then says that she really has no intention of harming herself. The psychologist, who once had a client commit suicide, calls the client's parents and tells them that their daughter is at risk for suicide and needs to be watched. When the client finds out what he did, she is very upset that he violated her confidentiality. He tells her that her life is more important than any rule about privacy.

Competence. A second issue central to the principle of doing good for others and avoiding harm is the ethical duty of competence. Psychologists only provide services in which they have developed expertise through training and experience. Competence involves psychologists' recognition of their professional limitations and weaknesses as well as their strengths and skills. This ethical issue is extremely important because professionals' blindness to areas of weakness as well as unrealistic appraisal of their strengths constitutes a major risk for harming those they serve. Although psychologists may not always be able to benefit others, they must take every measure to make certain that they do not hurt anyone. Failure to recognize one's limitations is a major source of ethical complaints and malpractice suits (APA Ethics Committee, 2004). Assuring the public that psychological services are provided by competent professionals is the ethical basis for such procedures as quality assurance reviews and peer review programs.

Sometimes the professional performance of otherwise competent mental health professionals can be impaired by personal problems (e.g., marital conflict, substance abuse) that interfere with their ability to perform their duties (APA, 2002, 2.06). The principle of nonmaleficence requires that professionals curtail the services they offer when they are impaired. For example, marital therapists going through a divorce in their own life may have difficulty viewing the marital difficulties of their clients objectively. Their anger about their personal situation could result in a negative, hostile countertransference toward some of the clients they treat. In such a circumstance, the duty of competence requires that therapists stop working with couples until their personal problems have been resolved. An even more extreme potential negative effect of impairment was revealed in the finding that male professionals' emotional distress and substance abuse are associated with increased risk of sexual boundary violations with clients and students (Thoreson, Shaughnessy, Heppner, & Cook, 1993).

CASE EXAMPLE 2.3

The caseload of a clinical psychologist working in private practice includes several couples engaged in marital therapy. The clinician questions her ability to work effectively with these couples because she and her husband have recently separated following several months of bitter conflict. After discussing the matter with several colleagues, she informs her clients of her decision to no longer see them and offers to refer them to highly competent marital therapists. However, one couple insists that she continue to work with them. Their marriage is in crisis and they feel that all therapeutic progress will be lost if they have to "start all over" with a new therapist. They inform her that they appreciate her candor and her concern for their well-being, but they regard her as a "terrific" therapist and need to continue therapy with her. The psychologist agrees to continue working with the couple.

A related threat to professional competence is the phenomenon of "burnout" (Skorupa & Agresti, 1993). Professionals experiencing burnout feel overwhelmed by the demands of their work and ineffective in their professional efforts. They typically feel underappreciated by their students or clients and disappointed in their lack of achievement. Burnout certainly impairs professionals' competence because they are not able to muster any enthusiasm for their work or to empathize with the people they interact with professionally. As a result, they may withdraw from the clients or students they serve and develop a cynical attitude toward them (Mills & Huebner, 1998). Professionals experiencing burnout or some other form of personal impairment have an obligation to seek assistance with their problems and to make certain that the people they serve are not impacted adversely. Therapist impairment will be addressed further in Chapter 6.

CASE EXAMPLE 2.4

A female clinical psychologist and a male social worker are co-leaders of a therapy group for inpatient substance abusers. They had an excellent professional rapport, which led to a social relationship in which they dated and seriously considered marriage. The psychologist broke off the relationship, but they decided to continue their professional collaboration in the group. However, she feels that the social worker has started to undercut her authority in the group by frequently disagreeing with her comments to group members. She spoke to him about it, and he accused her of trying to cover up her professional incompetence by silencing him. He insisted that his comments are always made in the best interests of group members.

Principle B: Fidelity and Responsibility

Developing Competence. The principle of fidelity and responsibility refers to the trustworthiness of psychologists in fulfilling their professional obligations and upholding high standards of professional conduct and service delivery. This principle follows quite directly from the concepts of beneficence and nonmaleficence presented in Principle A. Once again, the issue of professional competence is central. Like the disciplines of counseling and social work, psychology has developed a host of specialty guidelines and standards designed to provide additional information to assist professionals to develop and maintain high levels of professional competence in delivering services within their specialty area. "Guidelines" are recommended procedures and are not intended to be binding in the same sense that published "standards" or "ethical principles" are. Published guidelines related to specific areas of professional practice include the following: "General Guidelines for Providers of Psychological Services" (APA, 1987); "Specialty Guidelines for the Delivery of Services by Clinical Psychologists, Counseling Psychologists, Industrial/Organizational Psychologists, and School Psychologists" (APA, 1981b); "Guidelines for Providers of Psychological Services to Ethnic, Linguistic, and Culturally Diverse Populations" (APA, 1993); "Guidelines on Multicultural Education, Training, Research, Practice, and Organizational Change for Psychologists" (APA, 2003); *Standards for Educational and Psychological Testing* (American Educational Research Association, American Psychological Association, & National Council on Measurement in Education, 1999); *Ethical Principles in the Conduct of Research with Human Participants* (APA Committee for the Protection of Human Participants in Research, 1982); and *Guidelines for Ethical Conduct in the Care and Use of Animals* (APA Committee on Animal Research and Ethics, 1993). The *Publication Manual of the American Psychological Association* (APA, 2001) also includes information regarding ethical issues in conducting and reporting research.

The proliferation of specialty guidelines reflects the dramatic increase in the range of activities in which psychologists are involved. With so many specialties and subspecialties in psychology, it has become extremely difficult to produce general ethical guidelines that address the very different sorts of complex issues that arise in the dissimilar contexts in which psychologists practice their profession. Moreover, psychology has become such a technical and complex field that it is difficult to keep abreast of developments in one specialty area, let alone the entire discipline. Thus, specialty guidelines provide ethical guidance and information regarding standards of responsible, competent practice in a particular specialty area. Professional responsibility requires psychologists to stick closely to their area of training and expertise in delivering professional services as practitioners, teachers, or researchers.

The emphasis placed on psychologists' professional responsibility to develop a high level of competence in their specialty area raises the question of what constitutes sufficient training or experience to claim "competence" in an area of psychology. Is the granting of a legal license to provide a service sufficient? Is it necessary that a psychologist receive training in an APA-approved program? With regard to claims of competence in a specialized therapeutic technique, is a psychologist competent to provide a specialized service (e.g., hypnosis) after reading one or two books on the subject and attending a weekend workshop? Or is it necessary to complete an accredited certification program in the technique, including supervised experience in a clinical setting, to establish competence? A clinician may have had only limited academic exposure to a particular therapeutic orientation and yet still consider it appropriate to utilize techniques such as Rational-Emotive Therapy or Person-Centered

Therapy. Similarly, clinicians of many different theoretical orientations might have very little understanding of current theory and research concerning psychological defense and yet feel comfortable interpreting their clients' behavior as defensive (Bridwell & Ford, 1996). Still another related concern is how a clinician could be competent to treat children, adolescents, and adults (three very different areas of specialization). If you check the Yellow Pages listings in any major city, you will find that many practitioners advertise such varied expertise.

CASE EXAMPLE 2.5

A counseling psychologist is offered a contract by the superintendent of a small school district to provide neuropsychological evaluations. She explains to the superintendent that she does not have specialized training in neuropsychology beyond the Intellectual Assessment course she completed in graduate school. The superintendent thanks her for her honesty but says he has complete confidence in her ability to master the tests by reading the test manuals. He also offers to pay for the psychologist to attend workshops in neuropsychological assessment in the future, if she will agree to complete an urgently needed assessment within the next two weeks. The psychologist agrees to clear her calendar for the next two weeks to review the tests to develop competence in neuropsychology and conduct the assessment as a favor to the superintendent.

Prescription Privileges. The current debate in psychology over whether clinical psychologists should be able to prescribe psychotropic medications for their clients has focused considerable attention on the extent of academic and experiential training necessary to meet the high standard of professional competence required by the principle of fidelity and responsibility. Proponents of this initiative have argued that allowing psychologists to obtain prescription privileges would provide greater continuity of care for clients and enable clients to obtain psychotherapeutic *and* psychopharmacological treatment more economically. APA established an ad hoc task force on psychopharmacology in 1990 to make recommendations regarding appropriate training requirements for prescribing psychologists (Smyer et al., 1993). In addition, the Department of Defense initiated a demonstration pilot program in which military psychologists were trained to prescribe psychotropic medications; external evaluations of the program's effectiveness were positive (Newman, Phelps, Sammons, Dunivin, & Cullen, 2000). Proposed models for the undergraduate and graduate training of prescribing psychologists would require considerably more background in the natural sciences, neuroscience, and pharmacology (e.g., Chafetz & Buelow, 1994; Sechrest & Coan, 2002). In 2002, New Mexico granted prescription privileges to licensed, doctoral-level psychologists who have completed at least 450 hours of additional coursework "in neuroscience, pharmacology, psychopharmacology, physiology, laboratory assessment and clinical pharmacology," as well as a minimum of 400 hours of supervised (by a psychiatrist or other physician) experience treating a minimum of 100 patients, and have passed a national examination (Goode, 2002). In 2004, Louisiana became the second state to grant prescription privileges to specially trained psychologists.

Critics of this initiative have argued that to be truly competent to dispense psychotropic medications, prescribing psychologists would need to meet all of the requirements that physicians do because only by attaining the same level of mastery of biology and chemistry could psychologists achieve a thorough understanding of drug interaction effects. Acquisition of this mastery would not only require changes in graduate clinical psychology curricula but also in the undergraduate science and mathematics preparation required of applicants to clinical psychology programs (Sechrest & Coan, 2002). Critics have also argued that any graduate training curriculum adequate to produce psychologists competent to prescribe psychotropic drugs would, for reasons of length and expense, negatively impact students' exposure to the science of psychology and to training in psychotherapy (e.g., Hayes & Chang, 2002; McFall, 2002; Sechrest & Coan, 2002). In 1995, the American Association of Applied and Preventive Psychology passed a resolution opposing prescription privileges for psychologists; that group has since been joined by several other clinical science and university-based psychology organizations ("AAAPP Declares Its Own 'War on Drugs,'" 1995). They argue that prescription privileges would be detrimental to the profession of psychology because clinical psychology would become more like psychiatry, and consumers would suffer as a result of psychologists becoming less proficient in both the ability to conduct and understand scientific research in clinical psychology and the practice of psychotherapy (Hayes & Chang, 2002; McFall, 2002). These negative effects would be brought about in order to provide a service that is already provided by medical practitioners.[2]

Another disadvantage to prescription privileges is that many people experiencing emotional problems are reluctant to take psychotropic medications. They do not want their behavior and mood to be influenced by the ingestion of chemicals; rather, they want to gain greater control over their behavior and their happiness by learning to understand themselves better and enhance their ability to cope with stress (Barlow, Gorman, Shear, & Woods, 2000). If clinical psychologists begin prescribing medications, clients will be harmed because psychological treatment will gradually cease to provide an alternative to the pharmacological model of treatment that has traditionally been associated with psychiatry (Hayes & Chang, 2002). In addition, if clinical psychologists gain prescription privileges, isn't it likely that other nonmedical mental health disciplines, like counseling and social work, will pursue the same economically advantageous course? In the end, the only treatment method available to most clients, particularly under their health insurance, will be to take medication (Hayes & Chang, 2002). This debate will undoubtedly continue for many years to come (Heiby, 2002), although the initiative will likely gain momentum because graduate students and psychologists beginning their careers are much more interested than older psychologists in obtaining prescription privileges (Ax, Forbes, & Thompson, 1997; deMayo, 2002).

CASE EXAMPLE 2.6

APA is currently involved in lobbying for licensed clinical psychologists to have the legal privilege to write prescriptions for certain medications used in the treatment of mental disorders (e.g., antidepressants), The American Medical Association opposes this initiative, arguing that psychologists are not trained as physicians and, therefore, cannot possibly be competent to dispense medications. APA has responded that doctoral programs in clinical psychology could be redesigned to provide training that would make psychologists competent to provide such services. Those already licensed who desire to provide such services would participate in a comprehensive continuing education program leading to certification to prescribe. Proponents of the initiative also argue that it would provide better continuity of care for clients.

Consultation With Other Professionals. An issue related to the principle of professional fidelity and scientific responsibility is psychologists' sensitivity to the importance of consultation with other professionals and referral to other professionals (e.g., a psychiatrist) for treatment or consultation whenever such services are in the best interest of the consumer. Appropriate referral to other professionals is the hallmark of psychologists' respect for the expertise of those professionals (APA, 2002, 3.09). Another of the criticisms of the initiative to allow psychologists to prescribe psychotropic medications is that such an enterprise shows a lack of respect for the unique expertise of medical practitioners.

Maintaining Competence. The duties of professional fidelity and responsibility extend well beyond the development of expertise in an area of specialization. Once a professional is qualified to practice a psychological specialty, what sorts of effort are adequate for maintaining that level of scientific and professional competence (APA, 2002, 2.03)? Psychologists are ethically obligated to base their judgments on "established scientific and professional knowledge of the discipline" (APA, 2002, 2.04). This requirement cannot be fulfilled unless they are familiar with the current professional literature. More than 30 years ago, Dubin (1972) estimated that the half-life of a doctoral degree in psychology (i.e., the length of time before half of the information learned in training is outdated) was 10–12 years. It is certainly shorter now. Psychologists' continuing education should begin with a self-assessment of the skills and limitations relevant to their professional activities and aspirations. At the conclusion of this assessment, they will be in an excellent position to choose continuing education opportunities that directly benefit them and those they interact with professionally. In addition to ongoing didactic training, participating in peer supervision with fellow professionals can provide a very useful opportunity to benefit from other perspectives on difficult professional issues and receive informal instruction in the use of new techniques and technologies. Peer supervision also provides a support network for professionals, which is particularly valuable for psychologists in independent practice who might otherwise have few opportunities to interact with colleagues.

The issue of maintaining competence is not unique to the mental health professions. Medicine, for example, experiences dramatic advances in theory and technique quite frequently. Professions have addressed this issue by requiring continuing education for annual renewal of a professional license. Most state boards of psychology now have mandatory continuing education requirements. However, no profession has yet taken the step of requiring practicing professionals to be re-examined (i.e., to pass the current state licensing examination) for license renewal.

Changing Specialty Area. Another matter relating to professional competence that was quite controversial for many years is the retraining requirements for psychologists who want to change their specialty to that of a provider of clinical services. For example, suppose someone who was trained in graduate school as a social psychologist obtained a license as a doctoral-level psychologist and now wishes to provide psychotherapy services. What sorts of additional training experiences will be necessary for this individual to be deemed competent to engage in clinical work? APA published the "Policy on Training for Psychologists Wishing to Change Their Specialty" in 1976. This policy states that "psychologists taking such training must meet all requirements of doctoral training in the new psychological specialty" (Conger, 1976, p. 424). Some universities offer one- or two-year respecialization programs for this purpose.

The ethical principle of fidelity and responsibility is also relevant to the issue of competence and professional status of master's-level psychologists, particularly those in clinical practice. Since 1969, the number of master's degrees awarded in psychology, as a percentage of total graduate degrees earned in the discipline, has increased from 67.9% to 80.6% in 2001 (National Science Foundation, 2004). Clearly, master's-level practitioners play a very significant role in the delivery of psychological services in our society. While the profession of psychology has long acknowledged that the social need for psychologists cannot be met by the number of doctoral-level psychologists being produced (APA Committee on Subdoctoral Education, Education and Training Board, 1955), APA has nevertheless always regarded the doctoral degree as the basic professional credential in the field (Robiner, Arbisi, & Edwall, 1994).

Relatively little research has addressed the relationship between degree level and professional competence. Stevens, Yock, and Perlman (1979) found that master's-level clinicians function quite competently in the community mental health center system. Similarly, Hargrove (1991) cited evidence that master's-level practitioners can capably address the mental health needs of rural populations in the absence of adequate numbers of doctoral-level psychologists. In fact, Hargrove argues that master's-level psychologists need to be granted the autonomy under licensure laws to provide treatment without the direct supervision of a doctoral-level psychologist. In a number of states, master's-level practitioners are being granted greater autonomy. Nevertheless, in some states, a master's-level psychologist with 20 years of clinical experience could be supervised by a Ph.D. psychologist who has been practicing for only a year.

Multiple Relationships. The most important, and controversial, issue pertaining to professional fidelity and responsibility in mental health is multiple relationships (APA, 2002, 3.05). Once a psychologist has developed a professional relationship with a client, student, or research participant, is it appropriate to engage in any other sort of relationship with that person or with someone closely associated with that person (e.g., her spouse)? For example, is it appropriate for a clinical psychologist to have as a client a student currently enrolled at the institution where the psychologist teaches? Does it make a difference whether or not the client is a psychology major? Is it in any way inappropriate to teach classes taken by a *former* psychotherapy client? Is it ethically appropriate to employ a student to do yard work or babysit, since such an arrangement does constitute a dual relationship (i.e., as teacher and employer)? The concern is that factors in the first relationship (e.g., teacher-student) might affect one or both persons' conduct in the second (e.g., employer-worker). For example, students might feel pressure to accept a lower rate of pay from a professor for babysitting because refusing the job might affect their grade adversely. It is also possible that other students might view them as the "teacher's pet" because of their extracurricular relationship with the professor and believe that their high grades are a function of preferential treatment. Psychologists should always be sensitive to the implications of such relationships, particularly to the possibility that a conflict of interest may exist or that a student, client, or research participant could be harmed or exploited (APA, 2002, 3.06). Professionals must ask themselves whether a potential multiple relationship is being contemplated to meet *their* needs or to further the interests of the other party (Smith, 2003a). Obviously, a professional should never enter into a multiple relationship to fulfill their own personal or professional needs.

CASE EXAMPLE 2.7

A clinical psychologist working in an inpatient facility is conducting research on risk factors for suicide. He recruits participants from all of the psychiatric wards in the hospital but finds that most of the clients who agree to participate are from his ward, and even more specifically, are clients working with his treatment team.

However, not all multiple relationships create an ethical problem. "Multiple relationships that would not reasonably be expected to cause impairment or risk exploitation or harm are not unethical" (APA, 2002, 3.05[a]). Showing support for a client by attending a wedding or funeral, exchanging small gifts for the holidays, or being active members of the same church are examples of multiple relationships that would typically not constitute a problem. Nevertheless, mental health professionals should also be sensitive to potential implications arising from these seemingly innocuous multiple relationships and exercise careful judgment when such relationships are ongoing. They should also note the nature of their nonprofessional encounters with clients in their records (Fisher, 2003).

CASE EXAMPLE 2.8

A school psychologist begins treating an adolescent client. The client and his family attend the same church as the psychologist. It is the only church of their denomination in a small town. She notices that the client goes out of his way to engage her in conversation and sit with her at church functions. She is increasingly uncomfortable about the possibility that he might feel they are developing a nonprofessional personal relationship through these encounters. She records these concerns in the client's therapy record but is unsure about what to do. She doesn't want to stop attending church or risk making her client uncomfortable about attending church himself by speaking to him about her concerns.

Ethical guidelines regarding sexual relationships with students and clients are much more explicit (APA, 2002, 3.08). Psychologists should never engage in a sexual relationship if they "have or are likely to have evaluative authority" over a student, which covers much more territory than having the student in a class (APA, 2002, 7.07). With regard to therapy clients, sexual relationships with current clients are strictly forbidden (APA, 2002, 10.05). Psychologists should also never accept a former sexual partner as a client (APA, 2002, 10.07).

Historically, the major area of controversy has been the issue of sexual relationships with *former* therapy clients. The "Ethical Principles" states that at least two years must have passed since the appropriate termination of the therapy before such a relationship could possibly be ethically acceptable and that even then, such relationships are to be avoided "except in the most unusual circumstances" (APA, 2002, 10.08). These relationships are not regarded as inappropriate solely because of former therapists' potential power to exploit and manipulate the feelings of a former client, but also because they deprive clients of an important potential source of help, should they require mental health treatment in the future (Fisher, 2003).

Some states (e.g., Florida) have statutes or state board rules forbidding such relationships for much longer periods, or even forever. One might well question whether such a relationship could ever be ethically appropriate; so, why aren't sexual relationships with former clients completely forbidden? As Bersoff (2003a) points out, professional ethical codes are inevitably, in part, "the product of political compromise" (p. 1). Psychologists currently involved in relationships and marriages with former clients would have a strong vested interest in believing that *their* relationship had not been harmful to their former clients and would argue that such relationships are not always ethically inappropriate. The issue of multiple relationships with current and former therapy clients will be discussed in Chapter 6; multiple relationships with students and supervisees will be addressed in Chapter 11.

CASE EXAMPLE 2.9

A clinical psychologist encounters a former client three years after the successful completion of her psychotherapy. Over time, they develop a romantic relationship. After considerable thought about the ethical implications of this relationship and consultation with a marital therapist, they decide to marry. After several happy years, the former client becomes increasingly uncomfortable with her husband's "dominance" and his tendency to attribute conflicts in the relationship to her "neurosis." She feels trapped in this situation because she believes that any marital therapist they might consult would automatically side with her husband, who is a professional colleague.

Contribution to Society. The principle of fidelity and responsibility also states that psychologists "are aware of their professional and scientific responsibilities to society and to the specific communities in which they work" (APA, 2002, Principle B). Historically, APA has been very active in trying to influence legislative bodies regarding issues such as abortion and health care reform. Critics of APA's political stances argue that the organization is involving itself inappropriately in political issues under the guise of providing an objective, scientific viewpoint and opposing discrimination (APA, 2002, Principles D & E). The health care lobbying efforts of APA have also been criticized as serving the financial interests of psychologists, rather than reflecting a genuine concern for the social issue of prioritizing the expenditure of limited health care resources in the most reasonable manner. In other words, critics are suggesting that a conflict of interest exists for APA that has impaired the objectivity of its public stance.

Unfortunately, the potential for conflict of interest also exists in the multiple roles that APA has taken on to advance the profession of psychology. APA supports the interests and rights of its members (e.g., through health care lobbying); promotes the profession of psychology (e.g., by informing the public of the high standards of competence and professionalism required of psychologists); provides objective, scientific information for the benefit of the general public (e.g., through press releases and journal publication of research findings); and protects the public against mistreatment by psychologists (e.g., by investigating ethics complaints). How effectively can any organization juggle these potentially competing roles? Isn't there an intrinsic potential for bias in APA's assessment of the legitimacy of complaints against its members (e.g., mindfulness of the impact of negative publicity) or in APA's evaluation of which research findings merit publication in the journals it publishes (e.g., declining to publish "politically incorrect" yet scientifically sound research)?

The concluding sentence of the principle of fidelity and responsibility states that psychologists "strive to contribute a portion of their professional time for little or no compensation or advantage" (APA, 2002, Principle B). Professionals might fulfill this obligation by offering a sliding scale that will enable people with fewer financial resources to obtain psychological services or by donating their professional services to charitable work (e.g., volunteering to assist at a shelter for victims of domestic abuse). However, at present, there is no requirement that psychologists engage in charitable activity.

CASE EXAMPLE 2.10

Two psychologists, one a college professor and one a clinician in private practice, are discussing their work. The professor mentions that she volunteers one afternoon a week at the local shelter for victims of domestic abuse, playing with the children staying there and helping them with their homework. She says that she thinks psychologists, like everyone else, have a duty to "give something back." The clinician says that he feels the same way, so he uses a sliding scale in his practice that allows clients with lower incomes to pay as little as $40 per session, instead of his full fee of $90.

Principle C: Integrity

This principle stresses that psychologists are honest and forthright in all professional activities. The integrity of mental health professionals requires that they keep the professional commitments they make to clients, students, employers, and research participants and behave in a professional, responsible manner toward all consumers of psychological services. As a consequence, psychologists can never justify inappropriate behavior by stating that they were following their employer's instructions. Psychologists always have a professional obligation to look out for the interests of the consumer, even if no one else will. This issue is particularly pertinent to professionals working in business settings, like industrial/organizational (I/O) psychologists. Although ethical duties like confidentiality are everyday considerations for psychologists and mental health agencies, they do not commonly arise in business and manufacturing. Therefore, I/O psychologists are particularly likely to encounter situations requiring them to educate their organizational employers regarding the ethical principles of the profession and their commitment to these principles (APA, 2002, 1.03). Issues arising from practicing psychology in different organizational settings will be discussed in Chapter 10.

CASE EXAMPLE 2.11

An I/O psychologist is hired by a bank to screen applicants for teller positions. He discovers that the bank routinely shares information with other banks about applicants who fail the personality test assessing honesty; however, the bank does not inform applicants of this policy. In fact, no informed consent procedure is conducted as part of the pre-employment screening. He informs the bank president of his professional ethical duty to obtain informed consent for the screening procedure, but the president says that they prefer to keep these matters secret to avoid encouraging applicants to be overly guarded in their responses during the screening process. The psychologist tells her that he cannot in good conscience abide by the bank's policy. The bank president accuses him of applying "the rules of psychiatric treatment" to business, where they really don't apply.

Public Statements. The principle of integrity also relates to the issue of making public statements as a professional (APA, 2002, 5.0). Psychologists are responsible for the accuracy of any public statements they make, including published materials, media statements, classroom lectures, and advertisements of their services (APA, 2002, 5.01[a]). Psychologists are not only responsible for their own public statements; they are also obligated to prevent a publisher, workshop sponsor, newspaper, or other source from misrepresenting their credentials or services (APA, 2002, 5.02[a]). In other words, psychologists have an obligation to educate, if necessary, those they work with in order to avoid such misrepresentation.

CASE EXAMPLE 2.12

A psychologist published a statistics textbook. On the book jacket for the text, the publisher described her as an outstanding "mathematician and statistician." She was concerned about the validity of the description because her Ph.D. was in psychometrics; she did not have a graduate degree in mathematics. When she contacted the publisher, the marketing director informed her that they considered her undergraduate degree in mathematics adequate grounds for characterizing her as a mathematician. After thinking about it, the psychologist agreed that the description was technically accurate.

Psychologists are permitted to advertise their services on television and radio as well as in the newspaper and telephone directory. In advertising psychological services, psychologists must avoid any statement that could potentially confuse the public or be subject to misinterpretation. Therefore, they should list their degree (e.g., Ph.D.), rather than referring to themselves as "Doctor" or "Dr.," which could be misinterpreted as a medical credential. They can only list degrees they have earned (e.g., cannot list themselves as a Ph.D. candidate). Also, it would be misleading to list Ph.D. after their name if they had obtained a Ph.D. in history prior to earning an M.A. in psychology. Essentially, psychologists may include in their advertisements any information that is not deceptive or misleading and that is of potential interest to consumers.[3]

Advertising a free consultation is considered an inappropriate "bait and switch" tactic because the client is encouraged to initiate a relationship with the therapist for free, but then is required to pay after having invested considerable emotional energy in the initial free session. Similarly, if psychologists do not necessarily provide services themselves for those responding to advertisements of their psychological practice, the credentials of those who will be providing the services should be listed in the advertisement. When clients call for appointments, they should be told the professional credentials of the person they will see. Psychologists should also be very careful about listing professional affiliations to avoid the suggestion of an organization's sponsorship or endorsement. For example, clinical psychologists in private practice who are also university professors should not list the university affiliation on their practice stationery.

CASE EXAMPLE 2.13

A psychologist distributes a leaflet advertising his private practice. The leaflet has a picture of his license issued by "The University of the State of New York" and lists a variety of specialties (e.g., Adult, Adolescent, Child, Individual, Group) as if they are listed on the license.

Deception in Research. An ethical conflict regarding the issue of integrity occurs very commonly in psychologists' research activities when they use deception to keep research participants from discovering the hypothesis being tested and then debrief participants following their participation to disclose the true nature of the study (APA, 2002, 8.07). The fundamental ethical conflict is between concern for the welfare of participants (i.e., the duty to obtain fully informed consent) and the potential benefit to society of research requiring deception. Furthermore, researchers' regard for the welfare of research participants would suggest that whenever deception is used in research, debriefing should be done immediately after individuals have participated in the study. However, if the study is to be conducted over a period of several weeks with different groups of participants from the same population (e.g., undergraduate students), researchers may decide to delay debriefing participants until all data have been collected. Postponing debriefing, though inconsistent with the welfare of the client (whose right to informed consent has already been violated), is nevertheless permitted under some circumstances. The use of deception must be explained "to participants as early as is feasible, preferably at the conclusion of their participation, but no later than at the conclusion of the data collection" (APA, 2002, 8.07[c]). Ethical considerations in the use of deception in research will be discussed further in Chapter 12.

CASE EXAMPLE 2.14

During the fall semester, a psychology researcher conducts a study involving deceptive feedback about the results of a "personality test." One group of student participants receives positive feedback; the other receives negative feedback. The dependent variable is how much time they spend reading their "results" on a computer screen. The psychologist plans to conduct a second, related study during the spring semester, and she fears that next semester's participants could learn about the deception from fellow students if she debriefs fall participants now. Consequently, she decides to hold off debriefing the participants until all the spring semester data have been collected.

Principle D: Justice

The fundamental ethical principle of justice was defined by Aristotle (trans. 1947) as a matter of giving each individual his or her "due." In a similar vein, John Rawls (1971) viewed justice as "fairness" toward people (p. 12). The treatment of justice in the ethical codes of the mental health professions has evolved over the years from a focus on treating everyone equally to the recognition that professionals have a special responsibility to protect the rights of disadvantaged or especially vulnerable members of society (Pettifor, 2001). Mental health professionals endeavor to treat people justly by respecting the rights of each individual and giving the needs of everyone affected by a situation the consideration they deserve. This principle is intimately related to Principle E: Respect for People's Rights and Dignity; both ethical duties arise from psychologists' profound respect for the inherent value and importance of each individual human being.

Regard for justice charges psychologists to provide everyone equal access to the scientific knowledge and therapeutic benefits that psychology has to offer (Fisher, 2003). In small towns and rural settings, specialized mental health services (e.g., child-clinical specialists, geriatric psychologists) are often unavailable. The "Ethical Principles" stipulates that in these circumstances, "psychologists with closely related prior training or experience may provide such services in order to ensure that services are not denied" (APA, 2002, 2.01[d]). In other words, the ethical duty of competence is interpreted a bit more liberally in such situations to ensure that these consumers have access to the greatest range of psychological services possible. However, practitioners citing Ethical Standard 2.01[d] as a justification for expanding the services they provide incur an ethical duty to "make a reasonable effort to obtain the competence required" to provide effective services (APA, 2002, 2.01[d]). For example, clinical psychologists trained only in adult assessment and psychotherapy who take on the role of providing mental health services to children who would otherwise go unserved would be required to seek additional training, experience, or consultation to develop competence in assessing and treating children.

CASE EXAMPLE 2.15

A counseling psychologist is asked to provide assessment services for the local elementary school. The school psychologist who had been at the school moved to a larger city, and there is no one else in town available to conduct the special education evaluations that are desperately needed to provide children with proper educational placement. The counseling psychologist has spent his entire career working with adult clients.

Multiculturalism. The principle of justice, along with Principle E: Respect for People's Rights and Dignity, is also a fundamental motivation for psychologists to be sensitive to cultural, individual, and gender differences that might influence the value and effectiveness of their professional activities with various individuals and groups. As Pedersen (2001) points out, a multicultural perspective is a fundamental aspect of any adequate conception of justice because it enables us to avoid the natural tendency to define justice purely in terms of the value biases of the dominant culture. Cultural values and beliefs are viewed from the perspective of multiculturalism as a source of traditionally valued personal convictions that have been internalized by individuals as moral and spiritual guides for their behavior; they are regarded as an important source of strength in each individual's character that ought to be respected (Bryan, 2001). Psychologists cannot possibly provide competent services without first understanding both their own cultural values and assumptions and those of their clients (APA, 1993, 2003). In other words, they need to recognize the invalidity of the assumption that they and their clients necessarily share the same worldview (Pedersen, 2001).

Which groups of people do we need to be mindful of when discussing sensitivity to multicultural values (Pedersen, 2001)? Are we referring to ethnic and racial minorities, women, people of different sexual orientations, or individuals with physical disabilities? "Culture" is certainly not synonymous with ethnicity; it also incorporates issues of social class, subculture, gender, and religion, just to name a few (Bryan, 2001). Mental health professionals must recognize and respect the fact that *every* person operates from his or her own unique cultural, attitudinal, and behavioral perspective. Although human beings share many, many important similarities, each person is also different (Pedersen, 2001).

In 1993, APA published "Guidelines for Providers of Psychological Services to Ethnic, Linguistic, and Culturally Diverse Populations." Sensitivity to multiculturalism was presented as another *aspirational* goal of psychology (APA, 1993); psychologists were encouraged, but not required (by these guidelines or by the "Ethical Principles"), to obtain specialized training that would enable them to provide competent psychological services to ethnic minority populations (Cottone & Tarvydas, 2003). These guidelines served to remind professionals of an important component of competence discussed earlier: I they must recognize "the limits of their competencies and expertise" (APA, 1993, p. 46). The demand that ethnic, linguistic, and culturally diverse populations be served competently is obviously fundamental to the ethical principle of justice (APA, 2002, Principle D). However, it is equally important to ensure that multicultural populations, which represent more than one third of the U.S. population, actually *receive* services (Hall, 1997). Unfortunately, at present, psychologists who are not competent to provide such services can avoid engaging in unethical behavior by simply choosing not to provide services for ethnic minority clients. How is the principle of justice served by the potential failure to provide all persons with "equal quality" of all "the processes, procedures, and services being conducted by psychologists" (APA, 2002, Principle D)?

In 2003, APA published additional "Guidelines on Multicultural Education, Training, Research, Practice, and Organizational Change for Psychologists." These guidelines present "paradigms that broaden the purview of psychology as a profession" (p. 377). In addition to calling on all psychologists to achieve greater multicultural competence through increased self-awareness of cultural influences and increased knowledge of other cultures, the guidelines provide an extensive bibliography of empirical and conceptual sources that can assist professionals in achieving this goal and implementing multicultural sensitivity effectively in their specialized practice area. Although these guidelines are definitely a step in the right direction, psychology could certainly do more to encourage *all* psychologists to achieve at least a minimal level of what Sue and colleagues (1998) call "cultural skill" as part of their academic and professional training. Psychology could also strengthen its efforts to recruit ethnically diverse students and faculty members. A continuation of psychology's historical failure to address adequately the needs of multicultural clients would constitute cultural malpractice (Hall, 1997).

CASE EXAMPLE 2.16

A therapist is treating two female clients for depression. The first is an immigrant of Asian heritage and the second is a fifth-generation American of Irish descent, born and raised in New York. Both are rather passive in their marital relationships, deferring consistently to their husbands. The therapist recognizes the possible cultural basis of the Asian American client's behavior and is careful not to impose his values by identifying her passivity as a symptom or problem. He does, however, believe that the passivity of the Irish American client is a potential source of feelings of powerlessness and diminished self-esteem. He suggests that she might feel better if she asserted herself more in her marriage.

Respect for Client Values. In addition to issues of competence in providing services or instruction to individuals of different backgrounds and lifestyles, the principle of justice also requires psychologists to respect the personal, cultural, and religious *values* of students, clients, and research participants. Psychologists strive to prevent their personal biases or prejudices, or those of the organizations that employ them, from affecting their professional activities because bias and prejudice result in injustice and discrimination (APA, 2002, 3.01). Bergin (1991) has argued for many years that the religious values of psychotherapists and their clients frequently differ, with psychotherapists generally being less religious than their clients. When a therapist's values are permitted to influence the client either overtly or covertly, a serious lack of respect for the dignity and autonomy of the client is shown.[4]

This issue is complicated by the fact that religious values sometimes involve beliefs that most people would regard as discriminatory. For example, APA has historically included an exemption in the diversity requirements of its guidelines for accreditation of graduate programs in psychology so institutions with religious affiliations could continue "to use preferential treatment in admissions and employment for people who adhere to an institution's faith" (McMurtrie, 2001, p. A29). In recent years, APA's leadership became concerned that some of these institutions were discriminating against homosexuals on religious grounds. APA threatened to alter its accreditation guidelines, resulting in a storm of accusations that the organization was unfairly trying to impose its secular value system and liberal political agenda on these religious institutions by pressuring them to abandon their faith-based beliefs. APA subsequently withdrew the proposal, leaving the exemption for religious institutions intact (McMurtrie, 2001). The ethical issue of values and psychotherapy will be discussed in greater detail in Chapter 6.

CASE EXAMPLE 2.17

A client in individual therapy is involved in a very unhappy, unsatisfying marriage. He reveals that he has had a long-term extramarital affair as a means of obtaining the affection he needs because he does not want to end the marriage and break up his family. His therapist tells him that the cause of his depression must be the guilt he feels about his blatantly immoral infidelity. She informs him that she will not be able to continue treating him unless he agrees to help himself by putting a stop to the extramarital relationship that is destroying his self-esteem.

Principle E: Respect for People's Rights and Dignity

Principle E begins with a statement regarding psychologists' respect for the dignity and worth of all people as well as the rights of people to self-determination, autonomy, and privacy. The concept of personal *autonomy* involves the recognition that human beings are capable of governing themselves—that is, of initiating and controlling their own actions. Mental health professionals respect the right of individuals, as autonomous agents, to make their own decisions and behavioral choices regarding how they wish to conduct their lives; furthermore, they believe that this right to autonomous self-determination should not be denied or interfered with by others through coercion or the exercise of undue influence (even if well-intended) over people. The metaethical justification underlying professionals' regard for autonomy is that people are rational beings possessing the capacity to deliberate and choose their own behavioral paths based on good reason. Of course, human beings are *not* always reasonable; nevertheless, respect for individual autonomy entails that we acknowledge their right to act on even their idiosyncratic and irrational personal preferences, so long as their behavior does not infringe upon the legal rights of others. As autonomous, self-governing individuals, people are also regarded as responsible (morally and legally) for their actions, so long as their behavior is not being caused by some force beyond their conscious control (e.g., criminal behavior resulting from insanity).

CASE EXAMPLE 2.18

A client consults a qualified sex therapist for treatment of a sexual dysfunction. In the course of the intake interview, she reveals that she is HIV-positive and has been counseled regarding "safe" sexual practices.

Confidentiality. Respect for a client's personhood is the metaethical foundation for the ethical duty of confidentiality (APA, 2002, 4.0). Privacy is a constitutional right, protected in the Fourth Amendment, and can be violated only under certain specified conditions (e.g., when one is suspected of illegal acts, resulting in the issuance of a search warrant). Confidentiality, on the other hand, is a standard of professional conduct that implies an explicit contract not to reveal anything about a client except under certain agreed-upon circumstances (Koocher & Keith-Spiegel, 1998). The confidentiality of clients' health information is also guaranteed by federal and state law. Consequently, confidentiality is a prime example of the sort of issue discussed in Chapter 1 that involves both ethical and legal considerations. In 1996, Congress passed the Health Insurance Portability and Accountability Act (HIPAA, 1997), which provides the most stringent confidentiality standards ever enacted by the federal government. The HIPAA Privacy Rule addresses security and confidentiality issues in the creation, storage, and disclosure of Protected Health Information (PHI; Privacy Rule, 2003, §§ 160, 164). PHI includes records pertaining to past or present mental health or physical treatment, future treatment plans, and health care payment records (HIPAA, 1997). The HIPAA privacy rule stipulates the steps health care providers must take to preserve the confidentiality of PHI and that providers must obtain clients' consent prior to disclosing PHI to anyone (e.g., a client's health care insurer) for any treatment, payment, or other health care purpose (Bersoff, 2003b). HIPAA regulations apply only to "covered entities," which include health plans, health care clearinghouses, and "health care providers who transmit health information electronically" (Privacy Rule, 2003, § 164.105). However, even mental health professionals who do not qualify as "covered entities" would be wise to comply with HIPAA regulations voluntarily because the legislation is designed to better protect the privacy of clients' health records and support their right to informed consent regarding the disclosure of their confidential health records.

Ethical issues related to confidentiality include the following: (a) the circumstances under which confidentiality may be violated (i.e., the limits of confidentiality); (b) the confidentiality of clients under the age of 18; (c) which staff members at a university, clinic, or hospital should have access to confidential information; and (d) the proper procedures for maintaining and disposing of confidential records. Confidentiality issues pertaining to therapy (Chapters 6, 7, and 9), assessment (Chapters 8 and 10), and research (Chapter 12) will be discussed in greater detail later.

CASE EXAMPLE 2.19

A client with a history of Schizophrenia, Paranoid Type is being treated by a clinical psychologist at a community mental health center. The client is concerned about the possibility of losing his job because his behavior is, at times, experienced by others as "strange." He tells the psychologist that his employer knows that he is receiving treatment at the center and discusses his sense that he is being singled out for criticism at work. The next day, the client's employer calls the psychologist out of concern to let her know that her client's symptoms seem to be worsening. The employer informs her of the client's behavior at work, and the psychologist encourages the employer to call again if there is any change in the client's behavior.

An interesting related issue is whether clients should have access to their own mental health records. Legally, the records are not the property of clients; records belong to the professional or institution that creates them. In the past, if there was not a state statute pertaining to client access to institutional (hospital, clinic) mental health records, individual institutions set their own policies covering their records. However, HIPAA privacy regulations stipulate that an individual is entitled "to inspect and obtain a copy of protected health information about the individual" (Privacy Rule, 2003, § 164.524[a]). Respect for clients' rights to self-determination and to know the facts about their treatment and condition has always been an important ethical argument in support of providing clients access to mental health records. Also, one might well question how clients can provide truly informed consent (as required by Ethical Standard 4.05[a]) to release their record to a third party without knowing what it contains.

The limitations historically placed on client access have centered on two major areas of clinical and ethical concern. The first is that the client's emotional state could be harmed by information in the record. Clinicians often perceive a conflict to exist between their ethical duty to respect the autonomy of the client and the ethical principle of nonmaleficence (i.e., avoiding harm). The result has traditionally been a policy of *parentalism,* literally behaving like a parent toward clients. Acting parentally involves making judgments of what is in the best interest of clients based on the assumption that clients' judgment might be impaired by their fragile emotional state. The current regulations permit a licensed health care provider to deny client access only if the provider believes "the access requested is reasonably likely to endanger the life or physical safety of the individual or another person," although such a denial of access is subject to review (Privacy Rule, 2003, § 164.524). The second major consideration is that the record could contain information provided by, or pertaining to, some third party. Respect for a client's autonomy may conflict here with the duty to protect the confidentiality of a third party. HIPAA regulations recognize the protection of third party confidentiality as a legitimate reason for denying clients access to that portion of their record (Privacy Rule, 2003, § 164.524).

Past research supports the appropriateness of the HIPAA requirement to provide clients access to their health records, indicating primarily positive effects of client access with clinical supervision (e.g., Houghkirk, 1977; Parrott, Strathdee, & Brown, 1988; Roth, Wolford, & Meisel, 1980; Stein, Furedy, Simonton, & Neuffer, 1979). The issues associated with mental health record keeping and clients' access to their records will be addressed in Chapter 6.

Reduced Capacity. Finally, the fundamental ethical duty to respect the dignity and autonomy of each person places mental health professionals in a very difficult position when individuals' capacity for governing themselves and controlling their behavior is arguably limited by a psychiatric condition (e.g., schizophrenia, depression, dissociative disorder, or addiction) or they are deemed a danger to themselves or others (e.g., clients threatening suicidal or assaultive behavior). In these contexts, respect for individuals' autonomy and right to self-determination may conflict with the ethical duties of beneficence (i.e., the desire to do only good for others) and nonmaleficence (i.e., avoiding harm by protecting the client's well-being). The argument that psychiatric symptomatology has attenuated individuals' autonomy is frequently used as a justification for professionals to ignore the rights of those individuals and engage in parentalistic treatment, such as when depressed individuals expressing suicidal ideation are deprived of their civil liberties and hospitalized involuntarily or have their right to confidentiality violated when professionals inform legal authorities, hospital personnel, or members of the clients' family of their suicidal potential. These actions, though disrespectful of the clients' wishes and autonomy, are motivated, curiously, by professionals' deep respect for the personhood of each individual. The most fundamental duty associated with respect for persons is argued to be the protection and preservation of human life. Legal duties (i.e., the "duty to warn," discussed above) also play a role in professionals' ethical deliberations in these situations. This type of ethical dilemma becomes even more complex in cases of "rational" suicide, in which apparently competent people make the decision that they would prefer to end their life (Battin, 1999). The ethical complexities associated with suicide prevention will be discussed in Chapter 13.

CASE EXAMPLE 2.20

A psychologist is treating a client whose husband died seven years earlier. They had been happily married for 25 years and the woman has never gotten over his death. She is perfectly rational but says that life has nothing to offer her anymore. She had found happiness for many years with her husband and looks forward only to being reunited with him in heaven. She asks whether the psychologist thinks it would be wrong for her to end her life in order to put an end to her misery. She believes that God would forgive her.

SUMMARY

This chapter presented a detailed overview of the American Psychological Association's "Ethical Principles of Psychologists and Code of Conduct." The philosophical underpinnings of psychology's ethical code were highlighted in the discussion of the preamble and introduction to the code. Each of the six general principles was described in detail. Particular issues and ethical standards pertaining to each general principle illustrated the practical applications of the principles in teaching, research, and clinical activities.

NOTES

1. Prosenjit Poddar was convicted of second-degree murder, but the conviction was overturned on appeal because of errors in the instructions given to the jury by the trial judge. After Poddar was released, he returned to India (VandeCreek & Knapp, 1993).

2. As McFall (2002) points out, psychologists wishing to better serve clients by prescribing medications have always had avenues available to them for acquiring prescribing privileges "by earning an appropriate qualifying degree—such as an M.D., D.O., or nurse-practitioner degree—and by applying for a corresponding license to practice" (p. 667).

3. The authority of APA to restrict several other aspects of members' advertisements was removed in 1992 under a consent agreement signed with the Federal Trade Commission. Under the terms of the agreement, APA can no longer place restrictions on members' nondeceptive advertising that presents their services as comparatively more desirable, implies unique or one-of-a-kind abilities, presents testimonials regarding the quality of services, or includes statements "likely to appeal to people's emotions, fears, or anxieties" about the consequences of not obtaining services (DeAngelis, 1993, p. 7). Furthermore, APA cannot prevent psychologists from paying referral services as a means of obtaining clients.

4. Clients' self-evaluation of their improvement was shown in one study to be related significantly to their acquisition of the therapist's values (Beutler, Pollack, & Jobe, 1978).

Chapter 3

Counseling's
Code of Ethics

The American Counseling Association's *Code of Ethics* (ACA, 2005) is structured quite differently from psychology's "Ethical Principles," consistent with the notable differences in the two professions. Although counseling is a discipline grounded in behavioral science, it is more of an applied profession than psychology, meaning that it *applies* theory and research concerning mental health, human development, and personality functioning in the provision of services to individuals and groups. Like clinical and counseling psychologists, mental health counselors treat psychopathology, but their primary focus is on the personal growth and development of each individual, so they also deal extensively with wellness issues (i.e., the maintenance of physical and emotional well-being) and strategies for assisting people in the process of personal growth and career development. The mission of counseling, which introduces the *Code of Ethics,* "is to enhance the quality of life in society" (ACA, 2005, Mission).

Counselors provide mental health services in hospitals, mental health agencies, substance abuse treatment settings, correctional facilities, schools and universities (e.g., college counseling centers), and business organizations (e.g., employee assistance programs [EAPs]), as well as in private practice. School counselors combine their mental health expertise with certification as teachers (which school psychologists generally do not possess), working in school settings to assist parents, teachers, and administrators in promoting the educational achievement and personal development of children and adolescents. Rehabilitation counselors provide services in a variety of treatment settings to people dealing with challenges posed by physical and cognitive disabilities, as well as advocating on their behalf with governmental and social agencies. Career counselors work in rehabilitation and educational contexts to assist clients in the consideration of career options based on aptitude and interest assessments, as well as in businesses (e.g., in human resources departments), where they are involved in applicant selection and employee counseling. All of these activities serve the primary goal of enhancing the lives of those with whom counselors interact professionally. Finally, many counselors are involved in the training and supervision of future counselors in undergraduate and graduate programs.

PREAMBLE AND PURPOSE

The counseling profession has the goal of enhancing "human development throughout the life span" (ACA, 2005, Preamble). This goal is pursued by recognizing and appreciating diversity, both within and across cultures. Respect for diversity is grounded in the regard for the "worth, dignity, potential, and uniqueness of people within their social and cultural contexts" (ACA, 2005, Preamble). The major purposes of the *Code of Ethics* are to inform counselors and those they serve of the ethical principles and responsibilities of counselors, provide ethical guidance for counselors in determining appropriate courses of professional action, and create a framework for resolving ethical complaints against counselors (ACA, 2005).

The 2005 revision also acknowledges directly the fact that counselors sometimes encounter ethical dilemmas that can only be resolved effectively through "a carefully considered ethical decision-making process" that includes an "evaluation of the context" in which the ethical decision is being made (ACA, 2005, Purpose). Counselors are also advised that they need to develop the ability to employ "a credible model of decision-making that can bear public scrutiny" (ACA, 2005, Purpose). A context-sensitive model developed specifically for this purpose will be presented in Chapter 5.

CASE EXAMPLE 3.1

A counselor operating a large practice asks clients suffering from depression to complete the Beck Depression Inventory (BDI-II) twice each month when they come in for a session so she can monitor their progress. An elderly male client, fearing that his test results could be obtained by "hackers" accessing his computerized records via the Internet, always understates his depressive symptoms on the test.

ACA *CODE OF ETHICS* SECTIONS

The current version of the *Code of Ethics* (ACA, 2005) consists of eight sections, representing different areas and aspects of professional practice (e.g., The Counseling Relationship). Each section begins with an aspirational Introduction, followed by a combination of general ethical principles and more specific behavioral standards relevant to the subject of the section. Counseling's ethical code emphasizes the provision of services to clients and the development of professional counselors through counselor training.

Section A: The Counseling Relationship

The profession's applied, service emphasis is reflected in its choice to have the first section of the ethical code detail aspects of counselor-client relationships. Counselors strive to promote the positive growth and development of clients (ACA, 2005, A. Introduction). This mission contrasts with the emphasis on treating mental illness that dominates the mental health scene today. Counselors are less focused on diagnosis and "cure" than they are on helping clients to develop the ability to cope more effectively with the challenges of modern life. Nevertheless, mental health counselors are prepared to work effectively with severely disturbed clients (Cottone & Tarvydas, 2003).

Career Counseling. The subsection concerning career counseling taps another traditional component of counseling practice (ACA, 2005, A.1.e). Prior to becoming involved in the treatment of individuals suffering from psychopathology, counselors historically focused on vocational, rehabilitation, and adjustment issues. Career counselors provide information, testing, and support to individuals seeking to choose a vocational path. They also work in personnel (or human resources) settings in business and industry to identify the best candidates for available positions, matching applicants' skills with the requirements of the position. (Ethical issues pertaining specifically to personnel work will be discussed in Chapter 10.) Furthermore, they assist employees in adapting more effectively to workplace conditions and challenges and are often associated today with EAPs, where they address personal problems that impair employees' occupational performance. Issues pertaining to counselors providing mental health services in organizational settings are discussed in Chapter 7.

CASE EXAMPLE 3.2

A counselor working in the career services office of a university has a client who requests information about the job opportunities and training requirements for a career as a mortician. The client explains her interest by saying that she does not really get along with people well and has always been fascinated by dead things.

Multiculturalism. The counseling profession has long recognized the ethical obligation to respect diversity and individual differences (ACA, 2005, A. Introduction) and has developed a substantial body of literature regarding competent multicultural practice (Pettifor, 2001). The theme of multiculturalism is also addressed repeatedly in the *Code of Ethics.* The most basic multicultural duty that mental health professionals incur is not to engage in or condone discriminatory practices (ACA, 2005, C.5). A fundamental tenet of all mental health disciplines is that each individual is unique and deserving of the same respect we would want to receive ourselves. Individuals are influenced by cultural factors, their present environment, and myriad experiential and biological developmental events. Mental health professionals' fundamental respect for the autonomy and uniqueness of each individual requires that they strive to understand the cultural and personal perspectives of the people they serve.

Paradoxically, the respect for the value and autonomy of each individual that underlies the professional's regard for each person's cultural values has itself been criticized as a cultural bias. American culture prizes individualism very highly, but many other cultures view human behavior in a more collectivistic context (Pedersen, 1997). In collectivist cultures, individuals' duties to their family, community, and society vastly outweigh their own personal needs, which tend to be viewed as selfish, immoral concerns. So, if counselors were to encourage clients operating from a collectivistic cultural perspective to focus more on their own needs (e.g., by taking more time for themselves during the day), this concern for their welfare and feelings as individuals might actually constitute a disrespectful lack of regard for their cultural values. Most mental health professionals are representatives of mainstream, white, American culture. In spite of their good intentions to respect diversity, it is extremely difficult to even recognize, let alone control, the many ways in which their cultural biases and assumptions influence their interactions with clients. In fact, mental health professionals, like most people, do not tend to have a high degree of cultural self-awareness (Pedersen, 1997).

Mental health professions need to move beyond the politically correct lip service they pay to multiculturalism and acknowledge the complex, and in many cases unavoidable, problems created by the value differences that inevitably exist between professionals and the people they serve. The best strategy for professionals of *all* cultures is to become more conversant with the cultural contexts in which their clients are immersed (which requires significant changes in professional training programs) and to be more sensitive to the many ways in which therapists tend to impose both personal and cultural values on the people they interact with professionally. The role of values in counseling and psychotherapy will be discussed further in Chapter 6.

CASE EXAMPLE 3.3

A white counselor in a small Southern town is acquainted with a fellow counselor who is Mexican American. The Mexican American counselor is a private practitioner with an excellent reputation and very impressive clinical skills. Nevertheless, the white counselor generally refers clients to other counselors who, though competent, are arguably not as skilled as the Mexican American counselor; she knows from experience that white townspeople have enormous difficulty relating to a therapist of a different ethnicity. Each of the five people she has referred to the Mexican American clinician either declined to pursue treatment or requested another referral. The counselor does not want to decrease the probability that people will pursue the counseling they need.

Informed Consent. Section A of the *Code of Ethics* also addresses the important issue of informed consent in counseling (ACA, 2005, A.2). Counselors have an ethical duty to provide clients with information regarding fees, the frequency and duration of sessions, any risks associated with the process, the confidential nature of the counseling relationship, and the limits of confidentiality. In addition, the counselor and client should discuss and agree on the goals of the counseling and the methods that will be used to attain those goals. All of this information must be communicated in "both developmentally and culturally appropriate" ways—that is, in a manner that is easily understandable to the client (ACA, 2005, A.2.c). The duty of informed consent is grounded in the counselor's respect for the autonomy and welfare of clients. Clients can only make a meaningful choice regarding participation in counseling if they understand the issues that are important to consider in making that choice. The issue of informed consent in counseling and psychotherapy will be discussed further in Chapter 6.

CASE EXAMPLE 3.4

A counselor is contacted by an individual who tells him that she has been in counseling "for years" suffering from Obsessive-Compulsive Disorder. When they meet, he asks his client if she has any questions about the counseling process, and she says "No." He dispenses with most of his usual informed consent procedure because he does not want to appear patronizing.

The *Code of Ethics* also addresses the principle of nonmaleficence (ACA, 2005, A.4). Counselors avoid harming clients by not allowing their personal problems and needs to spill over into the counseling relationship and by being mindful of the dangers of multiple relationships (ACA, 2005, A.5.c). Sexual relationships with current clients are strictly forbidden and the *Code of Ethics* advises against such relationships with former clients (ACA, 2005, A.5.a).

The *Code of Ethics* addresses a number of the complications introduced into the counseling relationship by treatment contexts involving multiple clients (i.e., marital, group, and family therapy). Counselors are obligated to clarify their relationship with each of the parties involved during the process of obtaining informed consent and to consider carefully whether a group setting is appropriate for each client's needs (ACA, 2005, A.7, A.8). They also have an obligation to "take reasonable precautions to protect clients from physical, emotional, or psychological trauma" at the hands of other group members (ACA, 2005, A.8.b). Confidentiality issues unique to multiple client contexts, discussed in Section B of the *Code of Ethics,* also need to be addressed before treatment begins.

CASE EXAMPLE 3.5

A client diagnosed with Avoidant Personality Disorder is encouraged by his counselor to participate in a group she conducts, in addition to his individual counseling. The counselor tells him that the group experience will enable him to work on his interpersonal skills. When he attends his first group session, he learns that it is a psychodrama group, and he is asked to "act out" his interpersonal anxiety in front of the group. He excuses himself and flees the building.

Caring for Terminally Ill Clients. Providing end-of-life care for terminally ill clients is a specialized area of competence (ACA, 2005, A.9.b). Counselors who do not possess the technical or personal competencies required for this type of counseling should refer such clients to an appropriate professional. One of the unique issues associated with end-of-life care is the possibility that clients will elect to end their lives rather than allow their terminal condition to run its full, potentially very painful, course. The *Code of Ethics* emphasizes counselors' obligation to respect their clients' capacity for self-determination by presenting the possibility that counselors may elect to maintain clients' confidentiality in such a circumstance, rather than assuming that their suicidal ideation calls for active preventative intervention (ACA, 2005, A.9.c). Ethical considerations in suicide prevention and the possibility of "rational suicide" will be addressed in Chapter 13.

Termination and Referral. Two other important issues pertaining to the counseling relationship that are addressed in Section A are referral and termination. In some cases, counselors decide that it is in the best interest of a client to work with a different professional. Sometimes issues in the therapeutic relationship (e.g., transference, countertransference) or the appearance of treatment issues outside the counselor's range of competence (e.g., serious substance abuse) might necessitate referring a client to another professional. Generally, such a decision is preceded by a consultation with the colleague to whom the referral would be made, as well as careful deliberation regarding the potential effect of the referral on the client. Counselors making referrals are responsible for ensuring that their clients understand the reasons for the referral and do not feel abandoned (ACA, 2005, A.11.a).

The overriding issue in referral is the welfare of the client (ACA, 2005, A.11.b). Counselors should not be motivated by the desire to protect their professional "turf" by proving that their competence extends as far as that of any other professional. Likewise, counselors should not fail to make an appropriate referral because they want to avoid acknowledging an area of professional weakness. Competence involves professionals' understanding of both their strengths *and* limitations.

CASE EXAMPLE 3.6

A client suffering from depression contacts a counselor about pursuing therapy. When they meet, the client discusses her history, which involves periodic episodes of depression. The counselor asks if she is taking any medication, and the client indicates that she is not. The counselor wonders whether antidepressant medication would be helpful to the client but assumes that she does not wish to be medicated because she chose to pursue treatment with a counselor rather than a psychiatrist.

Termination of the therapeutic relationship is appropriate when the counselor believes that the client is no longer benefiting from treatment or has achieved the agreed-upon treatment goals. Even when a counselor recognizes that a client is no longer making progress, it can be difficult to terminate the relationship due to the financial benefit to the counselor of prolonging the counseling. Clients sometimes remain in therapy for years, though it is evident that most therapeutic gains are made within the first 6–12 months of treatment (Howard, Kopta, Krause, & Orlinsky, 1986). When economic self-interest becomes an issue for therapists, a conflict of interest can be said to exist because the best interest of the client should be the only relevant consideration in the matter of termination.

Counselors should raise the issue of termination during a session to learn how clients perceive the situation. Ideally, clients will agree that termination is appropriate. If not, counselors should state their reasons for raising the issue, supplementing their points with illustrations from the process of the counseling sessions. If the client raises cogent objections to termination (e.g., an additional, reasonable therapeutic goal to pursue), counselors can certainly postpone any action, though they should reflect carefully on whether their client's desire to continue the relationship is motivated by dependency (ACA, 2005, A.11.c).

CASE EXAMPLE 3.7

A counselor has been working with a client for 10 months on grief and adjustment issues following the death of his wife. The counselor recently began to notice clear indications that the client has developed an erotic transference toward her. She interprets this transference as a sign of his increasing dependence on her and decides to terminate counseling to avoid fostering a dependency relationship.

Use of Computer Technology. The final issue addressed in Section A is the use of technology (e.g., computer, telephone) in the practice of counseling (ACA, 2005, A.12). Computer-mediated therapy, or "e-therapy," has become increasingly popular over the past decade. E-therapists interact with clients via methods such as e-mail or Internet chat rooms, either as their exclusive mode of therapy or as an adjunct to traditional face-to-face meetings. Of course, intellectual, personality, and occupational assessments are also commonly conducted using computers, but new ethical considerations arise when these assessments are completed online from clients' home computers, rather than on computer equipment in a counselor's office.

A major ethical issue related to e-therapy is counselors' determination of whether technology-assisted services are appropriate for particular clients. For example, is sufficient support available from an e-therapist for a client who might become acutely suicidal? Counselors and clients must also possess considerable technological competence to be able to manage an e-therapy relationship effectively. There are also many added threats to clients' confidentiality when personal information is transmitted via the Internet. Ethical issues related specifically to the use of developing technologies in professional practice will be addressed in Chapter 9.

Section B: Confidentiality, Privileged Communication, and Privacy

Like psychology, counseling devotes a separate section of its ethical code to the issue of confidentiality (APA, 2002, 4.0). Without the assurance of confidentiality, therapy and counseling could not succeed because clients would not be willing to share their innermost thoughts and feelings with the clinician. As discussed in Chapter 2, the ethical duty to protect a client's confidentiality is based on mental health professionals' respect for the client as a person. Clinicians respect a client's right to privacy just as they would want to have their own privacy respected. Failure to preserve a client's confidentiality is one of the most serious ethical violations a mental health professional can commit because it threatens to diminish public confidence in the professionalism of clinicians and violates the trust clients place in mental health professionals. A mental health facility or practice can be ruined by even a single substantiated case of a clinician revealing information about a client inappropriately.

CASE EXAMPLE 3.8

A counselor is treating a woman who reports that she had recently been kidnapped and sexually assaulted. She reported the crime to the police. However, due to her history of emotional instability (a diagnosis of Borderline Personality Disorder) and her limited ability to provide details regarding the location of the attack and her attacker (because she was tied up and blindfolded throughout the incident), the police did not take the complaint very seriously. Another of the counselor's clients, a male diagnosed as Antisocial Personality Disorder, after posing a string of questions regarding confidentiality, describes having kidnapped and raped a woman, and the counselor realizes it was his other client that had been the victim of the attack.

Duty to Warn. A potential limitation on confidentiality discussed in this section of the code concerns "Contagious, Life-Threatening Diseases" (ACA, 2005, B.2.b). Over the past 20 years, there has been considerable controversy regarding whether mental health professionals have a duty to warn the spouse or lover of HIV-positive clients if they indicate that they plan to engage in sexual relations without informing their partner of their condition. Although this issue is not addressed explicitly in psychology's "Ethical Principles," counseling's *Code of Ethics* states that counselors are "justified in disclosing information to identifiable third parties" after assessing "the intent of clients to inform the third parties about their disease or to engage in any behaviors that may be harmful to an identifiable third party" (ACA, 2005, B.2.b).

The justification for violating a client's confidentiality under these circumstances is the counselor's "duty to warn" the third party, whose life could be threatened directly by the client's behavior, similar to the Tarasoff case discussed in Chapter 2. However, it is important to attend carefully to several points that could complicate counselors' decisions about whether to act on the basis of Section B.2.b. First, some states have specific regulations or statutes regarding the confidentiality of an individual's HIV status; in those states, counselors might be engaging in an illegal act if they disclose the information. Second, the section states that a counselor "is *justified*" in disclosing the information under the appropriate circumstances. This wording suggests that disclosure is permitted but not required. An interesting ruling by the Texas Supreme Court rejected the general notion of a "duty to warn," stating that disclosures to medical or law enforcement personnel were *permitted* but not *mandated* (*Thapar v. Zezulka,* 1999). Third, it would be extremely difficult to know for certain "the intent of clients to inform the third parties about their disease" (ACA, 2005, B.2.b). For example, when counselors inform clients that they intend to disclose the information to the third party, which would be the ethically appropriate procedure (in accordance with Section B.2.d), the clients are very likely to respond that they will inform the person themselves. They are stating an intention, but are they being honest and will this sudden change of heart really be acted upon? If counselors in this situation decide to violate a client's confidentiality, their action is certainly open to question based on the client's stated intention to inform the third party.

CASE EXAMPLE 3.9

A counselor is conducting marital therapy with a couple. The husband contacts the counselor privately and reveals that he has had two homosexual affairs during the past six months. He does not want to tell his wife about the affairs, which he attributes to his wife's lack of interest in sexual relations. He reports that he simply needed a sexual outlet. He says he decided to tell the counselor because he thinks she should know everything about the problems in the marriage. The counselor discovers that both affairs involved incidents of unprotected oral and anal sex. He has not had an HIV test, and he has never been diagnosed with a sexually transmitted disease. The counselor wonders whether she should tell the client's wife about the affairs because he could quite possibly be putting his wife at risk when they are intimate.

Multiple Client Treatment Settings. A number of additional confidentiality considerations arise in multiple client treatment settings such as marital, family, and group therapy (ACA, 2005, B.4). There are two major areas of concern that should be addressed: (a) whether information conveyed individually to the counselor outside the treatment setting will be regarded as confidential; and (b) whether group members are expected to maintain confidentiality concerning what other clients disclose during the sessions, as the counselor does. A good approach for counselors to use regarding individual interactions with such clients is to inform them before beginning treatment that individual disclosures outside of the treatment sessions can potentially complicate and subvert the treatment process. Counselors can also inform clients that when individuals do disclose information to them outside of the sessions, they will reserve the right to report the information at the next meeting, if they deem it appropriate and important for the other client(s) to know the information. This approach will allow counselors to judge on a case-by-case basis whether they want to report the information.

Counselors should never guarantee that other group clients will maintain confidentiality regarding disclosures made during the sessions. Clients are not trained to preserve confidentiality, nor do they have an ethical obligation to preserve the confidentiality of other clients. It is possible, however, for a client whose confidentiality was violated by another group member to pursue legal recourse against that group member (Roback, Moore, Bloch, & Shelton, 1996). Confidentiality matters in counseling will be discussed further in Chapter 6.

CASE EXAMPLE 3.10

A group therapy client reveals that she is not really in love with her husband anymore and that her primary attachment is to her children. She expresses concern about what will happen to her marriage when the children grow up and leave home. A member of the group meets her husband at a business seminar and comments that some "rekindling" might be needed if he expects to hold on to his marriage. The husband questions his wife about this odd comment, and she tells him what she had discussed in the group. Her husband, feeling hurt and humiliated, files for divorce. The woman sues her group therapist because of the damage that was done to her life as a result of her participation in the group.

Clients of Limited Capacity. The confidentiality of children or incompetent clients is limited under most circumstances (ACA, 2005, B.5). Parents generally have the right to know what is happening in their child's treatment because it is the parent who provides legal consent for the child to be treated. It is important that children realize their privacy is limited drastically. Child clients can then make an informed decision regarding what they wish to disclose to their counselor (and, possibly thereby, to their parents). Interestingly, many parents are far more interested in getting help for their child, or improving their child's behavior, than knowing what their child is saying to the therapist. Of course, counselors are obligated under any circumstances to inform parents of any behavior that would put their child at risk of being harmed.

Many states do permit children and adolescents to self-consent to treatment under certain specified circumstances, thereby eliminating their parents' right to know the details of the treatment. These special circumstances generally include treatment for physical or sexual abuse, substance abuse, or suicide risk. The purpose of these statutes is to encourage children to pursue treatment for these serious problems without being inhibited by fear of parental retribution. Issues pertaining to confidentiality in the treatment of children and adolescents will be discussed in greater detail in Chapter 7.

CASE EXAMPLE 3.11

A man contacts a counselor, requesting that she work with his eight year old son, who is having severe difficulty following rules at home and at school. During the intake interview, the counselor informs the father of the legal limits on the confidentiality of children and of the fact that his son may not be very willing to open up under these conditions. The father says, "I'll tell him that you won't tell us about anything that he tells you. We just want you to fix him!"

Recording Therapy Sessions. An issue pertaining to both confidentiality and the ethical duty of informed consent is the requirement that counselors obtain clients' permission prior to video- or audiotaping sessions (ACA, 2005, B.6.b; APA, 2002, 4.03). Counseling and psychotherapy sessions are routinely audiotaped in many treatment and training settings, but counselors must obtain a client's permission prior to turning on any recording device. This procedure is generally addressed prior to the first session in a statement that covers all subsequent meetings. The permission form should also explain what use will be made of the recording (e.g., supervision), how long the recordings will be retained, and how they will be disposed of or erased.

Occasionally, a client will object to being recorded. In many treatment settings, the counselor's concern for the client's comfort and willingness to participate would take precedence and no recording would be done. In training clinics, however, electronic recording or observation of sessions is necessary for adequate supervision of trainees. In such a circumstance, counselors need to explain to clients that recording is a necessary condition for being treated in a training facility. Clients should be informed of the procedures in place to safeguard their confidentiality (e.g., storing recordings in a securely locked cabinet). If a client is still uncomfortable with the idea of being taped, an appropriate referral should be arranged to enable the client to obtain treatment in a more suitable setting.

CASE EXAMPLE 3.12

Prior to his initial session with a new client, a counseling practicum student informs the client that he will need to audiotape the sessions so he can review them during his weekly meetings with his supervisor. The client says she will consent to being taped if the tapes are turned over to her when they are no longer needed for the therapist's supervision. She thinks she would benefit from listening to the sessions again to reinforce what she learns in counseling.

Consultation With Other Professionals. A final issue pertaining to confidentiality is consultation with other agencies and professionals (ACA, 2005, B.8). Counselors consult on a case only when it is in the client's interest (ACA, 2005, D.2). Consultation is very common among members of a treatment team in a psychiatric facility, between school counselors and teachers, or between rehabilitation counselors and medical personnel involved in the rehabilitation of a client with a physical disability. When consultation is appropriate, counselors generally inform clients in advance of the need for consultation and sharing of information among different treatment providers. Clinicians limit their sharing of confidential material to information that is directly germane to the consultation. When consulting about a case with professionals not directly involved in a client's treatment, counselors endeavor to avoid revealing the client's identity or any identifying information. Finally, consistent with HIPAA regulations, counselors always obtain the written consent of clients before transferring any records or reports to other mental health professionals as part of a consultation or referral.

When mental health professionals conduct a consultation with a client (e.g., for assessment purposes), they should never assume that the referring agency or clinician has informed the client regarding the purpose, procedure, and anticipated outcome of the consultation. Consultants should always discuss these issues with the client at the outset of the consultation and present the results to the client prior to obtaining the client's informed consent to provide a report of the consultation to the referring agency or clinician (ACA, 2005, D.2.d).

CASE EXAMPLE 3.13

A counselor finds it helpful to "decompress" at night by talking to her husband about some of her clients. He understands the importance of never sharing these conversations with anyone else, and he often gives her a different perspective on her interactions with clients.

Section C: Professional Responsibility

Section C begins with a statement regarding the obligation of counselors to learn and abide by the *Code of Ethics* (ACA, 2005, C.1). Next, the issue of professional competence, discussed extensively in Chapter 2, is presented. The limits of competence, the training required to claim competence, and the importance of continuing education for maintaining competence are addressed. The development of multicultural competence through increased self-awareness of cultural values and biases, sensitivity to other cultural perspectives, and skills relevant to choosing appropriate interventions for each client is stressed (ACA, 2005, C.2.a). Multicultural competence is no longer viewed by the counseling profession as an "extra," or elective, aspect of training but as an essential "primary prevention strategy" for mental health professionals (Pedersen, 2001, p. 24).

Self-evaluation. An interesting additional point included in the *Code of Ethics* is that counselors are ethically required to monitor and evaluate their professional effectiveness on an ongoing basis as a means of self-improvement (ACA, 2005, C.2.d). Clearly, claims of professional competence in any field cannot reasonably be made in the absence of evaluations of the effectiveness of one's professional performance. Although methods of conducting this evaluation are not specified, private practitioners are strongly encouraged to make arrangements with peers to obtain supervision for their cases. Many counselors welcome the end of supervision requirements after they qualify for licensure, not appreciating the importance of supervision to their ongoing professional development. Although supervision can be personally threatening at times because of anxiety about the possibility of a negative evaluation, it is the ethical duty of licensed professional counselors to continue to strive to improve their effectiveness in serving the needs of their clients.

Public Statements. Another aspect of professional responsibility is the public statements (e.g., advertisement of services) made by counselors (ACA, 2005, C.3). The *Code of Ethics* gives counselors a great deal of latitude to determine what is appropriate to include in advertisements of their professional services, provided that the information is accurate. In doing so, ACA avoids potential complaints from the Federal Trade Commission like those experienced by APA.

Section D: Relationships With Other Professionals

Mental health professionals also have responsibilities to their fellow professionals (ACA, 2005, D.1). The *Code of Ethics* points out the importance of respecting the different models and approaches used by different groups of mental health professionals in working with clients. For example, counselors who question the value of the pharmacological treatments for depression that their clients are receiving from psychiatrists should be careful not to voice these misgivings during sessions. Hearing such a criticism from their counselor could be harmful to the clients, who might begin to distrust their psychiatrist or even decide to discontinue the medication. Instead, the counselor should consult with the psychiatrists about the clients' medication regimens. Two treatment providers working with the same client should always maintain an active collaboration through periodic consultation (with the client's consent) to make certain that they are not working at cross-purposes.

Counseling professionals are also respectful of different theoretical models and treatment approaches used by others in their own field (ACA, 2005, D.1.a). For example, counselors using a psychodynamic approach do not denigrate the behavioral or person-centered models employed by fellow counselors. In the rare instances in which such attacks occur, they are generally the result of personal conflicts or jealousies. Unfortunately, they confuse clients and students, who tend to assume that an authoritative professional would not make such a statement unless it were grounded in fact. Unprofessional squabbling of this sort also diminishes the public's perception of the counseling field.

CASE EXAMPLE 3.14

A counselor working in a university counseling center has had several clients who previously received treatment from the health clinic on campus, which also provides mental health services. Three of these clients said that they were treated by a particular psychologist at the health clinic. Each of them complained about her limited understanding of their problems and ineffectiveness as a therapist, which had resulted in their seeking treatment at the counseling center. The counselor is concerned about the clinical skills of the psychologist, but he knows he has an ethical duty to respect the expertise of other professionals.

This section also deals with ethical issues that arise when counselors are employees of an organization (ACA, 2005, D.1). Mental health professionals are unlike most other employees in that they not only have obligations and duties as employees of the organization, but they are also obligated to abide by the ethical code and guidelines of their profession. These two sets of obligations can conflict at times. For example, counselors working in EAPs might encounter clients who disclose that they were told they would be fired if they did not complete treatment successfully. Counselors would have a professional obligation to discuss with their supervisors the negative implications of coercing an employee to undergo treatment and to assert the viewpoint of their profession that participation in counseling should be voluntary (ACA, 2005, D.1.h).

The *Code of Ethics* also addresses the obligations of counselors who are employers, rather than employees (ACA, 2005, D.1). Counselors must use nondiscriminatory practices in hiring and be careful to employ people who are competent and trained sufficiently to fulfill their assigned roles successfully (ACA, 2005, D.1.f). An employer's competence in personnel selection, training, and communication of goals and expectations benefits employees by creating a less stressful work environment. Finally, counselors should not exploit or harass employees; rather, they should model the professionalism they expect of their employees (ACA, 2005, C.6.d, D.1.i).

CASE EXAMPLE 3.15

A counselor's private practice expands to the point that she decides to hire a receptionist for her office to handle phone calls, billing, and filing. She mentions her plan to a friend, who immediately expresses interest in the job. The counselor hires her friend. She soon begins hearing complaints from clients about the receptionist's rude and inappropriately intrusive questions about their "problems." The counselor is concerned but does not want to strain her relationship with her employee/friend, so she asks clients to please try to ignore the receptionist's behavior. The situation calms down, and she no longer receives complaints from her clients.

No mental health professional knows how best to help every client or how to deal with every situation that arises. It is frequently helpful for counselors to consult more experienced colleagues when they are unsure about some aspect of their clinical, teaching, or research activity. Counselors can choose to consult other professionals whenever they deem it to be in the best interest of the people they serve, provided they are mindful to keep identifying information concerning their clients to an absolute minimum (ACA, 2005, D.2).

Section E: Evaluation, Assessment, and Interpretation

Psychological or educational assessment is undertaken only when it is in the best interest of the client. Testing is not done routinely or in the absence of client need. For example, clients should not be asked to complete a depression scale as part of their treatment because a clinician is trying to develop a new screening instrument. The validation or norming of a test should only involve clients who consent voluntarily to complete it as research participants.

Counselors must use only well-validated tests, and only for the purposes for which the tests were designed and validated (ACA, 2005, E.2.b). The Association for Assessment in Counseling published *Multicultural Assessment Standards* to ensure that counselors exercise due regard for multicultural factors in their selection, administration, scoring, and interpretation of tests (Prediger, 1994). Furthermore, counselors should only use tests that they are competent to administer, score, and interpret. The use of computerized test administration, scoring, and interpretation software does not diminish the clinician's responsibility for the accuracy of the test scores or the validity of the interpretations included in the assessment report (ACA, 2005, E.2.a). Counselors also need to be extremely sensitive to the fact that some clients, particularly older people, are inexperienced and, as a result, uncomfortable with computers (ACA, 2005, A.12.b). Alternative procedures that do not involve a computer should be available for clients who express discomfort with using a computer or have difficulty mastering the computer task.

The nature and purpose of testing should be explained beforehand to clients to obtain their informed consent (ACA, 2005, E.3). Feedback concerning the results of the assessment should also be provided to clients so they can make an informed decision regarding whom they want to receive the results (ACA, 2005, E.1.b). Ethical issues related to assessment are discussed in detail in Chapter 8.

CASE EXAMPLE 3.16

A school counselor has a private practice in which he provides learning disability assessments. Clients are informed at the beginning of the assessment process of the fees associated with the testing. A separate fee is assessed if the client desires to arrange an appointment to receive feedback regarding the results of the assessment following its completion.

Section F: Supervision, Training, and Teaching

Counselors involved in educational programs should be skilled both as teachers and practitioners (ACA, 2005, F.6.a). The *Code of Ethics* places considerable emphasis on the supervisory duties of faculty. Because supervisory relationships tend to be less formal and involve more self-disclosure than faculty-student interaction in the context of a typical class, supervisors must be particularly careful to avoid forming multiple relationships with supervisees and maintain the professional boundaries that preclude inappropriate sexual relationships (ACA, 2005, F.3). Supervision of counseling practica is recognized as a separate area of professional competence that faculty must develop (ACA, 2005, F.2.a). Supervisors are also responsible for ensuring that the services delivered by trainees are of professional quality (ACA, 2005, F.1.a).

CASE EXAMPLE 3.17

A young assistant professor of community counseling, newly hired out of graduate school, is assigned to provide practicum supervision for graduate students in an M.A. program. Although she is a licensed counselor, the department decides that she should also receive supervision from a senior faculty member for her supervisory work with the practicum students.

Emotional Fitness of Trainees. A difficult issue for all graduate training programs in mental health disciplines is how best to address concerns regarding a student's personal fitness for a career as a mental health professional. Some students are clearly too shy to engage clients effectively in counseling; in other cases, students might suffer from psychopathology that impairs their ability to relate well with clients and maintain appropriate professional boundaries. Training programs have an ethical duty to both their students and the clients their students serve to confront these issues and attempt to remedy them (ACA, 2005, F.9.b). After all, mental health professionals express a strong belief in the value of therapeutic counseling to stimulate behavior change and personal growth. It would be hypocritical not to encourage students experiencing these sorts of personal issues to pursue growth experiences in order to achieve their career goal of becoming mental health professionals. It would also be unethical to permit a student to work with clients if the training faculty did not believe the student could provide effective treatment.

CASE EXAMPLE 3.18

A community counseling graduate student suffering from Bipolar Disorder stopped taking her medication during a very hectic part of the semester. Two weeks later, she had to be hospitalized for stabilization. When she returned to school, she was encouraged to switch to a non-clinical program of study (e.g., vocational counseling) and was told that she would not be permitted to take a practicum class because the counseling faculty had an obligation to protect the welfare of clients treated in the training clinic.

Nevertheless, confronting students with concerns about their capabilities is generally extremely uncomfortable for everyone involved. Another complicating factor is the Americans With Disabilities Act (ADA), passed by the United States Congress in 1990. ADA prohibits discrimination against individuals with disabilities—both physical disabilities and mental or psychological disorders. Some universities, citing ADA, question whether students who have met the academic prerequisites can legally be refused admission to a practicum course on the grounds that they are emotionally unfit.

As a result, programs sometimes allow such students to continue, arguing that everyone should be given a chance to show what they are capable of. There are several problems with this approach. First, practicum supervisors are not fulfilling their professional ethical obligation to ensure that clients treated by practicum students receive professional quality treatment. Second, by failing to address students' issues proactively, supervisors are not encouraging students to pursue the opportunities for personal growth that might be essential to the attainment of their professional goals. Third, supervisors are putting clients at risk of possibly being harmed by their counseling experience. Finally, if the practicum is uneventful, they are passing on the problem to future supervisors or the state licensing board, rather than dealing with the issues in real time and attempting to remediate them.

To manage this type of situation in an ethical, professional manner, graduate training programs must establish criteria for admission to practicum that include the graduate training committee's assessment that a student currently possesses the emotional fitness to work effectively with clients. In cases where these criteria are not met, the committee should counsel students regarding the steps they should take to attain the requisite levels of academic and personal readiness. These policies must be applied in a nondiscriminatory manner to all students in the program. ADA is not incompatible with such a policy; it simply requires that employers and universities provide people who have mental or physical impairments with "reasonable accommodations" that would permit them to engage in productive work. However, there are no reasonable accommodations that would make it possible for an emotionally unfit student (or employee) to work effectively with clients. If a university policy were inconsistent with the graduate training program policy, the counselors on the graduate training committee would need to make it clear to the university that their primary obligation is to the ethical code of their profession and the welfare of clients. Students in training are also obligated to place the welfare of clients first because students must also abide by the *Code of Ethics* (ACA, 2005, F.8.a). Of course, students receiving a negative evaluation of their ability to progress in the graduate program must be given the right to appeal the ruling (ACA, 2005, F.9.b).

When it is necessary to deny a student admission to a practicum course, remediation of the student's emotional problems should certainly be the focus of the process. Counseling or assessment should be recommended, when appropriate (ACA, 2005, F.9.c). The clinician providing such services should, with the client's permission, contribute to subsequent reviews of the student's situation. Ethical issues pertaining to teaching and supervision will be addressed in greater detail in Chapter 11.

Section G: Research and Publication

Deception in Research. Counselors are permitted to deceive research participants about the true nature of a study when "alternative procedures are not feasible and the prospective value of the research justifies the deception" (ACA, 2005, G.2.b). The *Code of Ethics* distinguishes between research methodology involving "concealment" and "deception." A large proportion of personality and social psychology studies involve concealing the true purpose of the study by not fully informing participants regarding the purpose and procedures of the study (e.g., what the questionnaires are specifically designed to measure); a smaller proportion involve deception. This distinction is important because even though concealment does not involve actively deceiving participants, it nevertheless represents a failure to carry out fully the researcher's duty to obtain the informed consent of participants prior to conducting the study. The issue of deception in research will be addressed in greater detail in Chapter 12.

Reporting Research Results. In reporting the results of research studies in professional presentations and publications, counselors are obligated to present their results accurately and not withhold results inconsistent with hypotheses or desired outcomes (ACA, 2005, G.4). For example, in conducting an outcome evaluation of a day treatment program for psychiatric clients, researchers found that clients participating in the program socialized more, were more compliant with their medication regimen, and experienced fewer symptoms than a matched group of clients that did not participate in the program. The researchers were surprised to find that day treatment program participants also consumed significantly more alcohol than the matched control group participants, perhaps because they socialized with the other clients in the evening as well.

The researchers might worry that presenting the last finding would create a negative impression of the day treatment program in people's minds. Instead of focusing on the benefits of the program for clients, people might conclude that the program causes clients to be influenced by the substance abuse behavior of a few participants. Nevertheless, it would be unethical to suppress such a result (ACA, 2005, G.4.b). The researchers can certainly offer their interpretation of the meaning of the finding, but it must be reported. The recipients of the research report will draw their own conclusions regarding the result, which might include that the variation in alcohol consumption was a preexisting difference between the two groups. Suppressing research results is always unethical, even when the motivation is benevolent.

CASE EXAMPLE 3.19

A counseling professor wants to conduct a study concerning the relation of personal religious values to political party affiliation in American students. She creates a questionnaire to assess religious values and conducts a pilot study to determine the reliability and validity of the measure. She finds that the measure is reliable and that the data obtained in the pilot study reveal a strong relation between party affiliation and religiosity. She then conducts the main study, but the results fall short of providing statistically significant support for her research hypothesis. However, she discovers that when she adds the cases from the pilot study to her data set, the results achieve statistical significance. In the manuscript she is preparing to submit for publication, she decides to treat the pilot data as if they were part of her main study because the measures used in the main study were not altered at all from those used in the pilot study.

Replication Studies. One limitation of scientific research in recent decades has been the decline in the frequency of replication studies, which are studies designed to reproduce the conditions of a previous study to see whether similar results are obtained with a different group of research participants. The replication of significant research findings reduces the likelihood that a statistically significant result obtained by chance will be mistakenly viewed as a genuine phenomenon; unfortunately, such studies are unlikely to be publishable because of the perception that they do not contribute new information to the field. More frequently, researchers will conduct a study similar to one that was published, with the addition of a new variable or measure to carry the line of research a step further. When planning such a study, the researchers will typically contact the authors of the original study to obtain information regarding their methodology, measures and scoring procedures, and the like. Researchers conducting meta-analyses might also request information, including raw data, from other researchers in order to select studies for inclusion in their sample and to conduct their analyses. Researchers are ethically obligated to comply with such requests (ACA, 2005, G.4.e).

Plagiarism. A final research-related issue is *plagiarism,* or presenting the work of another as one's own. The possibility of plagiarism can be avoided in research presentations, articles, and books by citing the sources of previous research findings and ideas. Through this procedure, authors give credit to the original source of the information being presented, making a clear distinction between their original data and ideas and those borrowed from other sources (ACA, 2005, G.5.a, G.5.b). Material taken word-for-word from another source is enclosed in quotation marks, followed by the citation of the original source (APA, 2001).

CASE EXAMPLE 3.20

A counseling psychologist is preparing a manuscript about multiculturalism for publication in a counseling journal. He has previously published a number of articles concerning multicultural issues and realizes that some of the ideas in his current manuscript were presented in those articles. However, he decides that he doesn't need to cite his earlier articles because, after all, they are *his* ideas.

Section H: Resolving Ethical Issues

Counselors, like other mental health professionals, are responsible for studying the ethical code of their profession (ACA, 2005, H.1.a). If questions arise regarding the ethical propriety of counselors' professional activity, ignorance of their ethical duty will never constitute an excusing condition. The appropriate method for dealing with suspected ethical violations and the process used by state boards and ethics committees to investigate and resolve formal ethics complaints will be addressed in Chapter 14.

THE EXISTENCE OF ETHICAL CONFLICT

The ethical codes of the mental health professions discuss ethical duties one at a time, as if each ethical consideration (e.g., confidentiality, competence) were independent of the others. As noted repeatedly in the last two chapters, they are not. Although the *Code of Ethics* acknowledges the reality of ethical dilemmas in professional practice (ACA, 2005, Purpose), none of the ethical codes of the mental health professions address effectively and specifically the issue of how to resolve conflicts between ethical principles. Unfortunately, as K. S. Kitchener

(1984) has pointed out, "acting ethically involves professionals in difficult decision-making for which they are poorly prepared" (p. 43).

One of the primary goals of this book is to prepare mental health professionals to identify complex ethical situations and resolve them in an ethical, rational manner. To this end, the major philosophical approaches to ethical reasoning will be described in Chapter 4. This chapter is intended to provide an understanding of the fundamental philosophical principles underlying the ethical codes of the mental health professions, as well as the viewpoints of moral philosophers regarding the best methods of resolving ethical dilemmas. Chapter 5 will then introduce a new model of ethical decision making based on the most promising of these philosophical methods. This model will provide a framework mental health professionals can use to resolve complex ethical situations that arise in any aspect of their professional activity.

SUMMARY

This chapter presented ACA's *Code of Ethics* (ACA, 2005), which governs the professional behavior of counselors. The code consists of a preamble, purpose, and eight general sections addressing different aspects of professional practice (e.g., the counseling relationship; evaluation, assessment, and interpretation; supervision, training, and teaching). The tone of the *Code of Ethics* communicates counselors' respect for each individual and their desire to help individuals grow and cope more effectively with the challenges of life. Although the code overlaps considerably with psychology's "Ethical Principles," ACA's ethical code differs in several ways. For example, ACA's code devotes greater attention to multiple client treatment contexts (i.e., group, marital, and family counseling), ethical issues pertaining to the administration of graduate training programs, and the ethical obligations of practicum and internship supervisors. The chapter concluded with a brief discussion of the potential for ethical principles to conflict in some instances, an important problem in trying to practice as an ethical professional.

Chapter 4

Models of Ethical Reasoning and Their Effectiveness in Resolving Ethical Conflict

Consider the following situation: A psychologist decides that the best way to help her client overcome his fear of intimacy is to become involved in a sexual relationship with him. He trusts her implicitly, and she feels very strongly that the experience will be positive for him.

THE PHILOSOPHICAL BASIS OF ETHICAL JUDGMENTS

Is this type of intimate relationship ethically appropriate for a psychologist to pursue? Hopefully, mental health students and professionals would respond universally with a resounding "No!" However, to establish rules of conduct that all mental health professionals are obligated to obey, the committee that creates the ethical code of a profession must go beyond simply stating which behaviors are required and prohibited. Why is it wrong for the psychologist to engage in a sexual relationship with her client if she believes that such a relationship will be of benefit to him? The fact that there are rules prohibiting such behavior is not an adequate explanation of *why* the behavior is inappropriate. The validity of the rule must be demonstrated rationally in order to assert that the psychologist in question is *obligated* (i.e., has an ethical *duty*) to obey that rule. These explanations, though not generally stated in the ethical code, constitute the *metaethical* grounding of the ethical principles of the profession.

This chapter will critically examine two major ethical theories of Western philosophy (i.e., utilitarianism and Kant's ethical formalism) that are generally cited as providing the metaethical foundation for the ethical codes of the mental health professions and assess the adequacy of the philosophical grounding they provide for the types of ethical decision making faced by mental health professionals.

Consider another scenario: A client expresses suicidal ideation during a counseling session. She has a plan and the means to carry it out, and the counselor believes she is in imminent danger. Nevertheless, she refuses to seek help from family or friends or to admit herself to a hospital. In such a situation, the counselor has, as always, a duty to preserve the client's confidentiality. However, the counselor is also obligated to preserve the client's life, presumably by having her admitted to a hospital, where she will not be able to harm herself.

In this example, two *prima facie* (i.e., apparently valid and relevant) ethical duties appear to conflict. The potential for ethical conflict suggests that diligently following rules of ethical conduct, even when the validity of those rules is supported by a rational metaethical foundation, is not always adequate. Professionals must also be capable of resolving conflicts between ethical principles (referred to as *ethical dilemmas*) in a rational manner. Therefore, utilitarianism and Kant's ethical formalism will also be evaluated in terms of their effectiveness in enabling mental health professionals to resolve apparent ethical conflicts. Finally, two additional models that were developed to address the possibility of conflict between ethical principles (i.e., ethical relativism and ethical contextualism) will be presented.[1]

CASE EXAMPLE 4.1

A clinical psychologist is employed in a psychiatric hospital. He tells his colleague, a psychiatrist, that he is married to a woman who had been his psychotherapy client years before. The psychiatrist complains to the hospital director that the psychologist should be fired because psychiatry's ethical code prohibits sexual relationships with former clients. The director points out that the psychologist is not obligated to abide by the ethical code of the psychiatric profession. The psychiatrist argues that because he works in a psychiatric facility, the psychologist is bound by psychiatry's ethical principles.

UTILITARIANISM

Utilitarianism is one of the two major theories of ethical obligation in modern Western thought. For the utilitarian, the ethical rightness or wrongness of an action depends on the goodness or badness of its consequences; because of its focus on the outcomes or ends achieved by an action, it is categorized as a *consequentialist* or *teleological* theory of obligation (from the Greek word *telos,* meaning "ultimate end"). In most utilitarian conceptions, the notion of "the good" that people are obligated to bring about (i.e., pleasure or happiness[2]) is borrowed from ethical hedonism. So, our consideration of utilitarianism will begin with a discussion of ethical hedonism.

Ethical Hedonism

Ethical hedonism is a *theory of value.* As such, it is not a proposal about what is morally right; it is simply a statement regarding what is valued most highly in human life. Hedonism comes from the Greek word *hedone,* which means "pleasure." The Greek philosopher Epicurus (approx. 342–270 B.C.), an early adherent of the hedonistic perspective, asserted that the greatest good is that which is *intrinsically* desirable (i.e., desired for itself, not as a means to some further end) and that the only thing that is truly intrinsically desirable in life is pleasure (Russell, 1945). By pleasure, Epicurus meant that which is enjoyable. Thus, the goal of hedonism is to always enjoy oneself. "Pleasure is the beginning and end of the blessed life" (quoted in Russell, 1945, p. 243). Many things, such as money, are desirable *instrumentally* (i.e., for the desirable consequences they produce), but only pleasure is desired as an end in itself. Pain, on the other hand, is the only thing that is intrinsically undesirable.

In his original formulation of the hedonistic position, Epicurus did not propose an unbridled pursuit of sensual (i.e., "dynamic") pleasures. Rather, he advocated a simple life of philosophical reflection (i.e., "static" pleasure) as the most pleasurable, or good, life (Russell, 1945). Though strong bodily passions are perhaps pleasurable for a brief period, they tend to be followed by discomfort when the intense pleasure ends. In the example at the beginning of the chapter, the psychologist and her client might experience considerable pleasure from their sexual passion, but sexual activity can result in great discomfort later if their sexual desires are not satisfied completely or if one or both of the people experience regret about the relationship. Epicurus believed that mental activity that enabled people to achieve a clearer understanding of themselves and the world produced a less intense, but sustainable, sense of pleasure (i.e., tranquility), thereby avoiding the discomfort that tended to follow intense physical pleasure.

A long line of distinguished thinkers (e.g., Thomas Hobbes, Jeremy Bentham, James Mill, John Stuart Mill, and Henry Sidgwick) have advanced and refined the hedonistic theory of value since the time of Epicurus. Today, the general hedonistic viewpoint is that people are experiencing genuine pleasure if, and only if, at the time they are engaging in an activity the experience or activity is enjoyed *for itself;* that is, they would not wish to change the activity.

Psychological Hedonism. The hedonistic perspective has been adopted by a number of psychological theorists (e.g., Freud, 1923/1961; Thorndike, 1911, 1940) attempting to explain human motivation. These motivational theories are referred to as *psychological hedonism.* In such a model, the goal of life is the pursuit of pleasure; therefore, the motivation underlying a person's preference for one state of affairs over another is that the preferred one is expected to provide more pleasure. For example, E. L. Thorndike presented the "law of effect" in his behavioral theory, which postulates that if a behavior is followed by a "satisfying state of affairs," the association of the behavior with the situation will be strengthened, whereas if a behavior is followed by an "annoying state of affairs," the association will be weakened (Thorndike, 1911, p. 245). Similarly, Freud (1923/1961) viewed the "pleasure principle" as one of the fundamental unconscious motivations of human behavior: Human beings seek pleasure through the spontaneous satisfaction of their instinctual drives, thereby avoiding a painful buildup of instinctual tension.

Psychological Egoism. Psychological hedonism, as a theory of motivation, raises an interesting question regarding the role that self-interest plays in human behavior. If the motivation underlying all behavior is the pursuit of pleasure, does it follow that people always behave selfishly? Though all hedonists do not necessarily adopt this view, which is referred to as *psychological egoism*, a hedonist would certainly argue that human beings always act in accordance with their self-interest. Even if people behave in an altruistic manner (i.e., engage in a behavior that involves some degree of self-sacrifice out of concern for another), their behavior must be consistent with their self-interest in order to be pleasurable (e.g., they might find it very pleasurable to be regarded as charitable).

But is this behavior selfish? Clearly, it is not. Two obviously different senses of self-interest must be distinguished in ethical hedonism. What might reasonably be called selfish behavior involves a disregard for the interests of others; selfish people think only of themselves when determining their course of action. On the other hand, when people brush their teeth, the behavior shows a clear regard for the individuals' own interests, but does not necessarily involve a disregard for the interests of others. Although an ethical hedonist might justifiably argue that people never act against their own interests, even in altruistic behavior, it does not follow that all behavior is selfish, as psychological egoism would maintain (Butler, 1726/1950).

CASE EXAMPLE 4.2

A counselor attempts to encourage a depressed client to take advantage of opportunities to become involved with people by pointing out that his loneliness has made him miserable. She tells him that although there is no guarantee that people will respond positively to him, at least taking the risk of reaching out to others has the potential to bring him happiness. "And after all," she says, "isn't that what we're all looking for in life: happiness?"

Critical Evaluation of Ethical Hedonism. The first problem with the hedonistic position is that hedonists attempt to argue from facts to value. Even if pleasure is intrinsically desirable, that does not make pleasure "good" in an ethical sense. In addition, the argument that pleasure is the only thing that is intrinsically desirable can also be disputed. One could argue that to obtain pleasure, a person must want something other than pleasure for its own sake. For example, for the attainment of knowledge to be pleasurable, the person must have had an intrinsic desire to attain knowledge. Joseph Butler (1692–1752) argued that the ethical hedonist fails to recognize that there must be "particular passions" that enable people to obtain pleasure (1726/1950, p. 14).

Ethical hedonism also does not account for the obvious fact that people are motivated by factors that do not depend on the belief that the future event will be pleasant for them personally (e.g., being thought well of after their death). People will even risk personal loss rather than violate their moral principles. Of course, the hedonist will argue that under such circumstances, behaving in accordance with their values must be pleasurable. However, what is intrinsically desirable in this case is behaving in a manner consistent with their personal morality. The behavior is not simply a means to some other end (i.e., the attainment of pleasure).

Utilitarian Theory

Jeremy Bentham (1748–1832) formulated the *principle of utility,* which underlies all utilitarian ideas and transforms ethical hedonism into a theory of ethical obligation. It states that an action is ethical if it brings about the greatest positive balance of pleasure over pain because pleasure is good, and people are obligated to bring the good into existence (Bentham, 1789/1948). If all available options will produce some degree of suffering, the ethically appropriate alternative involves the least negative balance of pain. Utilitarianism boils down to this one principle, which serves as the standard for judging the morality of any proposed action. It is certainly appealing to believe that one reasonably quantifiable consideration can resolve all moral questions and dilemmas.

Act Utilitarianism and Rule Utilitarianism. There have been several different formulations of the utilitarian perspective. One distinction utilitarians have made is whether the principle of utility should be applied to particular acts or to general classes of acts (i.e., rules). In *act utilitarianism,* the pleasure criterion is applied to each particular action; therefore, a person judges the ethical status of each action by its consequences. On the other hand, in *rule utilitarianism,* the ethical status of general rules of conduct is evaluated by judging the likely consequences if everyone were obligated to behave in a similar manner (Smart & Williams, 1973). A rule will be adopted as an ethical duty (e.g., people should keep their promises) if the general consequences of behaving in accordance with this rule produce greater pleasure than those achieved by adopting an alternative rule. Act utilitarianism is generally regarded as being more flexible than rule utilitarianism because the act utilitarian is sensitive to potential changes in the ethical status of an act performed in different circumstances.

Egoistic and Universalistic Utilitarianism. Another issue for utilitarians is whose pleasure is to be taken into account when applying the principle of utility—the individual's or the community's. For the proponent of *egoistic utilitarianism,* an action's goodness depends on its consequences for the particular person engaging in the action. Conversely, an advocate of *universalistic utilitarianism* would assert that the ethical status of an action is a function of its consequences for everyone (usually within some specified community) affected by the action. Everyone ought to act so as to support the general happiness of the community to the highest degree, with people regarding their personal happiness as being of equal importance to the happiness of every other member of the community (Smart & Williams, 1973). Bentham (1789/1948) asserted that the interest of the community does not conflict with the interest of individuals. "The interest of the community then is, what?—the sum of the interests of the several members who compose it" (p. 126).

The Oregon Health Plan. An example of the application of universalistic utilitarian principles is the Oregon Health Plan, a health care reform initiative implemented by the state of Oregon in 1994. In response to escalating health care costs, the Oregon state legislature created a Health Services Commission to develop a plan to ration health care to those receiving health insurance from the state (e.g., Medicaid recipients). The plan expanded Medicaid enrollment by 50% to include working people with incomes below the federal poverty line while controlling the cost of medical coverage (Cutler, McFarland, & Winthrop, 1998). The commission developed a prioritized list of medical and mental health problems after considering the benefits of treatment to the individual and society versus the cost to society of providing or withholding treatment, the chronicity of the condition, the risk of death associated with the condition and the probability that treatment would extend life, and the effectiveness of treatment in restoring "the individual to a level of function at or close to the premorbid level" (Pollack, McFarland, George, & Angell, 1994, p. 526). The state legislature determined that sufficient funds existed to cover the top 616 diagnostic categories, which included the majority of mental health conditions. Among the mental health conditions excluded from coverage in the Oregon Health Plan were Conversion Disorder (in adults), Hypochondriasis, and a number of personality disorders, including Antisocial, Paranoid, Dependent, Avoidant, Schizoid, Obsessive-Compulsive, Histrionic, and Narcissistic (Pollack et al., 1994).

Those who prioritized the disorders recognized that conditions excluded from coverage are serious and painful for those suffering from them. However, the commission's concern was to use the limited health care dollars available to the state to provide health care coverage for as many people as possible and to benefit the most people to the greatest possible extent. These considerations outweighed the suffering of the people whose diagnoses were not covered. Such utilitarian considerations are compelling to many people, particularly taxpayers, who are aware that there is a limit to the financial resources a state can invest in health care. In practice, the prioritized list has not been used extensively to deny people needed mental health services. Instead, cost containment has been achieved by forcing Medicaid recipients into managed care programs that may provide less extensive treatment (Bodenheimer, 1997). Nevertheless, if medical costs continue to increase, the prioritized list remains a legally acceptable means of rationing health care in Oregon.

Critical Evaluation of Utilitarianism. Utilitarians, like ethical hedonists, have been criticized for arguing from facts to values. An even greater problem for universalistic utilitarians, like Bentham (1789/1948) and Mill (1863/1910), is demonstrating that it would follow from the goodness of individuals' own pleasure that they are obligated to promote "the general happiness" of their community. Why could a person not say, "Yes, the general happiness is good, but I am interested only in my own happiness"? Indeed, it appears that most people actually are far more invested in their own personal interests and do not exhibit the general attitude of "benevolence" that utilitarians assume characterizes human beings (Smart & Williams, 1973). The tendency of people's individual interests to conflict is precisely why issues concerning ethical behavior draw so much attention in the first place (Russell, 1945).

Another thorny issue for universalistic utilitarians is the question of how the good (i.e., pleasure) ought to be distributed across the community. For example, what if a particular action would produce a great deal of pleasure for a small group of people, whereas another course of action would benefit more people but produce a smaller total quantity of pleasure? An extreme example of this phenomenon is that a rule utilitarian could present an argument defending the ethicality of slavery on the basis that it is economically advantageous to the society *as a whole* (i.e., that it produces greater total happiness). However, an ethical theory that is compatible with slavery is preposterous because of its utter incompatibility with theories of justice.[3]

Utilitarianism's focus on the consequences of acts raises other issues. For example, critics of utilitarianism question the meaningfulness of ever holding individuals directly responsible for states of affairs in the world, particularly remote consequences of their acts. For example, are psychotherapists responsible for unforeseen consequences arising from their treatment decisions? Suppose a therapist decides to discharge a client prematurely from a treatment program because of countertransferential issues. While attempting to hitchhike home, the client meets someone, begins an extremely positive relationship, and goes on to live happily ever after. Can the psychotherapist be meaningfully said to have acted in an ethically appropriate manner because the long-term effect of the discharge decision was an increase in the happiness of the client? Remember that, for the utilitarian, the individual's intention in performing the act should not matter, for it is consequences that are ultimately valued (Smart & Williams, 1973).

A final problem confronting utilitarians is how people can be expected to calculate the potential consequences of their response options in situations involving conscious moral decision making. When an action produces a mixed effect of pleasure and pain, as is often the case, how are they to compare the pleasure accruing to one person with the pain accruing to another? Furthermore, are they supposed to consider only the immediate consequences of the act or the potential long-term effects—what J. J. C. Smart calls "the 'ripples on the pond' postulate" (Smart & Williams, 1973, p. 33)? What if the short-term effects are positive (e.g., increasing hospitalized clients' sense of personal autonomy by agreeing to discharge them to live independently), but the long-term effects could be quite negative (e.g., potential non-compliance with their medication regimen possibly resulting in their becoming suicidal or dangerous to others)? How much reflection is necessary prior to acting to ensure adequate consideration of the likely short-term and long-term consequences? What appeared at first to be a very practical, quantifiable, and commonsense approach to making ethical judgments actually turns out to be a very complicated model to apply successfully.

Utilitarianism and Ethical Conflict. Both rule and act utilitarians would argue that genuine ethical dilemmas do not exist because, in all circumstances, the only truly relevant ethical consideration is that of maximizing utility (i.e., the balance of pleasure over pain). If applying two different rules (rule utilitarian) or engaging in two different acts (act utilitarian) will produce equal amounts of pleasure, the decision of which rule to apply or which action to perform is of no moral significance because either will produce equally "good" consequences.

Actually, the possibility of conflict between competing ethical considerations does appear to exist within both the rule and act utilitarian perspectives. Because rule utilitarians recognize the existence of more than one ethically appropriate rule of conduct, it is always possible for conflicts to arise regarding which rule takes precedence in a given situation. For act utilitarians, ethical conflict is possible because maximizing utility is really not the *only* relevant ethical consideration. As discussed earlier, considerations of justice have led utilitarians to address how the good (i.e., pleasure) ought to be distributed. Though a utilitarian could argue successfully that the goal of maximizing the sum total of pleasure in a community is accomplished effectively in a capitalist economy like that of the United States, few would agree that the distribution of resources is a *just* one, with medical and mental health treatment frequently unaffordable for the poor while other segments of the population enjoy enormous wealth. Utilitarians interested in avoiding this problem have argued that the attitude of human beings toward others is (or should be) one of "generalized benevolence, that is, the disposition to seek happiness, or at any rate, in some sense or other, good consequences, for all mankind" (Smart & Williams, 1973, p. 7). They would conclude, then, that such injustices are inconsistent with the utilitarian model in spite of the fact that they appear to maximize utility.

Clearly, adding the principle of benevolence makes ethical conflict quite possible for act utilitarians because now there are *multiple* relevant ethical considerations (i.e., maximizing utility *and* acting in a benevolent manner), which might suggest different courses of action (Wallace, 1988). Thus, utilitarians cannot avoid the need to devise a reasonable method for resolving conflicts between principles, though they offer no such method because they continue to insist that ethical conflict is impossible.

CASE EXAMPLE 4.3

A licensed clinical psychologist specializes in neuropsychological assessment at the hospital where she has worked for many years. Needing money to pay for her child's college education, she decides to start an e-therapy Internet practice from her home on nights and weekends to increase her income. Since she has been exclusively practicing neuropsychological testing, she decides to attend a workshop to brush up on the therapy skills she learned as a graduate student before she initiates her part-time practice. She reasons that there are not enough therapists available to serve all the people who need help, so this move will benefit her and the clients who access her services.

Relevance of Utilitarianism to the Mental Health Professions. The utilitarian notion that people ought to promote the happiness of others is presented in the ethical codes of the mental health professions in the duty of beneficence, which underlies the concern that mental health professionals show for the welfare of clients, students, research participants, and others affected by their actions (Cohen & Cohen, 1999). Professionals have an ethical duty to strive to bring about good, positive consequences for the people they serve. In a situation that cannot result in pleasurable consequences for the people involved, mental health professionals have an ethical duty (i.e., nonmaleficence) to minimize the harm or pain suffered by those involved. Clearly, the metaethical basis of these duties is utilitarian reasoning.

The justification provided in professional ethical codes for the use of deception in research is also primarily utilitarian in nature. Researchers are permitted to deceive participants, thereby violating the duty to obtain informed consent, if "they have determined that the use of deceptive techniques is justified by the study's significant prospective scientific, educational, or applied value" (APA, 2002, 8.07[a]). Under certain circumstances, then, researchers' obligation to individual participants may be outweighed, at least to a limited extent, by their interest in promoting the welfare of society in general.

While the ethical codes of the mental health professions clearly reflect utilitarian ideals, the codes also attach great importance to respecting "the rights of individuals to privacy, confidentiality, and self-determination" (APA, 2002, Principle E). The value that mental health professionals place on the autonomy and dignity of the individual has its ethical roots in the other major theory of ethical obligation, Kant's formalist ethical theory.

CASE EXAMPLE 4.4

A counselor working in a community mental health center receives a telephone call from the mother of a client. The client, who suffers from Schizophrenia, Undifferentiated Type has stopped taking her medication, and her family is very upset. The counselor explains that her daughter stops taking her medication because of the extremely unpleasant side effects it produces (e.g., tremors, muscle rigidity, constipation). Her mother says she understands her daughter's discomfort with the medication, but having her on the medication makes life much easier for everyone else in the family and the neighborhood. She tells the counselor that he has an obligation to convince her daughter to go back on her medication.

KANT'S FORMALIST ETHICAL THEORY

Immanuel Kant (1724–1804), as a *rationalist* philosopher, believed that truth or knowledge could be discovered only through the principles of logic and reason. Consistent with this view, Kant asserted that moral truth is determined by assessing whether the principle guiding an action is consistent with the laws of reason. Kant's ethical theory is an example of ethical *formalism,* in that the morality of an act is determined formally, by virtue of the rational validity of the *maxim* (i.e., description of the principle embodied in an act) involved, rather than by any reference to circumstances or practical consequences of the act.[4] Since all people are rational beings, they are all capable of recognizing the universal validity of rational moral principles (Kant, 1788/1956).

Kant believed that the principles of morality revealed by reason are known to be *necessarily* true (i.e., could not possibly be false). Also, these principles are known to be true independent of experience (i.e., a priori). Just as everyone knows that $2 + 2 = 4$ without having to constantly check the fact by putting two things together with two more, everyone knows that it is wrong to steal. That, according to Kant, is why a moral maxim is always expressed in the form of a universal command, such as "Thou shalt not steal" (Kant, 1797/1964b). Kant asserted that it is obvious to anyone that stealing is wrong, though humans do not always act in accordance with moral (i.e., rational) principles. People "are unholy enough to be influenced by pleasure to transgress the moral law, although they recognize its authority" (Kant, 1797/1964b, p. 36).

Clearly, Kant makes no reference to the consequences of an act in assessing its ethical status, although he certainly believed that operating on the basis of reason benefited both the individual and others. Also, Kant was not arguing that a person's motivation in behaving morally need always be the rationality of the act. People may act in accordance with the law of reason but be motivated by a sense of justice, personal affection, or the like.

Kant's "Categorical Imperative." But how does a person know whether the maxim expressed in a particular act is reasonable (i.e., ethical)? Kant presented his "tests" of the rationality of a maxim in *Groundwork of the Metaphysic of Morals* (1785/1964a). These tests are referred to collectively as the *categorical imperative*. The first test of the categorical imperative is whether the maxim can be expressed meaningfully as an a priori universal law of reason. That is, does the maxim make logical sense when expressed as a universal moral law?

For example, suppose a therapist promises a hospitalized client diagnosed as suffering from Schizophrenia, Paranoid Type that no confidential information will be revealed to other members of the treatment team. The therapist believes that refusing to make this promise would cause the client to become agitated and refuse to participate actively in the therapy. Therefore, the therapist makes the promise, and plans to take every measure possible to preserve the client's confidentiality, but has no intention of actually keeping the literal promise. The therapist's ethical justification is that lying is in the client's best interest in this situation. The nature of the therapist's proposed act is expressed in this maxim: "It is permissible to make a promise one has no intention to keep." Is this type of act, which Kant called a "false promise" (Kant, 1785/1964a, p. 70), ethically appropriate? Kant argued that it is not appropriate because, if the maxim were universalized, it would entail that everyone make promises with no intention of keeping them. Such behavior would make the notion of a promise meaningless. By definition, a promise entails that the person sincerely intend to keep the vow made to another. Therefore, such a maxim is obviously unreasonable and immoral.

On the other hand, suppose a counseling professor is rushing across campus for an important meeting with the dean regarding the status of her application for tenure. Along the way, she is stopped by two students who had participated in her research study the previous day and want to discuss some serious misgivings they have about the study. The students are obviously quite upset. The professor wants to stop and discuss the matter because the students are apparently in great distress, but she decides not to in order to avoid being late for the important meeting with the dean. She offers to meet with the students the next morning to address their concerns. Kant would assert that the maxim expressed in this act would be something like, "I am not obligated to assist another who is in distress." Interestingly, when we express this maxim as a universal moral law, it involves no logical contradiction or inconsistency. One can indeed imagine a world where no one provides assistance to another in distress.

However, the fact that a maxim can be universalized without contradiction is not sufficient to declare it ethically appropriate. Kant (1785/1964a) asserted that for a maxim to be demonstrably moral, a rational being would also have to be able to *will* that the maxim become universal law. This requirement constitutes the second component of the categorical imperative. In the example, the professor, as a rational being, could not will that the maxim "One is not obligated to assist another who is in distress" become universal moral law because the maxim would entail that no one would be obligated to assist *her* in a time of personal distress. Rational beings would not endorse maxims that directly oppose their own interests. Thus, this maxim fails the second test of the categorical imperative.

For Kant, the morality of actions is discovered in this negative way. The tests of the categorical imperative enable people to discover those acts they should *not* engage in. Acts that are not eliminated by this process are ethically appropriate. According to Kant, when people act immorally, they do so in spite of the fact that they know the act is wrong and that the moral law they are violating is valid universally. In general, they decide hypocritically that their situation constitutes an exception to the general principle involved. However, Kant allowed for no exceptions to moral duty as it is revealed by reason.

Kant's "Kingdom of Ends." The tests of the reasonableness of maxims associated with the categorical imperative do not represent a complete explanation of the origin of people's duties toward themselves and others. Kant (1785/1964a) explained that when people act in accordance with reason, they act autonomously and freely, that is, in a manner consistent with their nature as rational beings. Such acts are self-caused because the only laws reflected in them are the laws of reason, which are the foundation of human being. Therefore, when people act reasonably, they also act in accordance with the nature of every other human being. They never impose their will on another human being when acting in a reasonable, ethical manner because what one rational being would will is the same thing any other rational being would will. Kant described this harmonious blending of autonomous human rational wills as a "kingdom of ends."

Kant (1785/1964a) argued that there is a fundamental difference between a *thing* and a *person.* The difference is that only rational beings are regarded as persons. People's regard for themselves is based upon their recognition that they possess reason, and thereby knowledge, which differentiates them from nonrational objects or beings (e.g., nonhuman animals). "Things" have "only a relative value as means" (Kant, 1785/1964a, p. 96). In other words, everything in nature exists as a means to some end, with the exception of human beings. Rational beings "are called *persons* because their nature already marks them out as ends in themselves—that is, as something which ought not to be used merely as a means" (Kant, 1785/1964a, p. 96). Thus, for Kant, all persons possess intrinsic value and are worthy of respect as ends in themselves. Therefore, it follows logically that people should "act in such a way that [they] always treat humanity, whether in [their] own person or in the person of any other, never simply as a means, but always at the same time as an end" (Kant, 1785/1964a, p. 96).

This doctrine of the *kingdom of ends* is simply another implication of the rational basis for morality provided by the categorical imperative. If people act only under maxims that can reasonably be willed to be universal moral law, they will act toward others only in ways that those others, as rational beings, would endorse as ethically appropriate. In doing so, people always show respect for others as ends in themselves (i.e., as autonomous human beings). By the same token, they can reasonably expect that they will be treated by others only in ways that they would want to be treated (i.e., in a just and respectful manner).

"Perfect" and "Imperfect" Ethical Duties. Morality, for Kant, involves not only individuals' duties to others, but their duties to themselves as well. Kant drew a distinction between people's "perfect" and "imperfect" duties to themselves and others (Kant, 1797/1964b). Maxims representing *perfect duties* specify actions that are clearly immoral. For example, the prohibition against stealing constitutes a perfect duty toward others. Stealing from clients by not pointing out their mistake in overpaying for a session is unethical because it shows a lack of regard for their humanity (i.e., personhood). Individuals' perfect duties toward themselves prohibit any action that would compromise their value as persons. For example, smoking cigarettes is contrary to people's duty to treasure and preserve their own lives.

Imperfect duties, on the other hand, do not identify specific actions. Rather, they represent ethically appropriate, rational ends that ought to motivate people's behavior toward themselves and others. Imperfect duties toward others involve promoting the welfare and happiness of others. For example, mental health professionals have an imperfect duty of beneficence to promote the welfare of their clients, students, research participants, or anyone else to whom they provide services. Imperfect duties state the goal or end to be sought but do not specify the acts that are appropriate to bring about those ends (i.e., the duty does not include specific information regarding *how* mental health professionals would achieve the end of promoting the welfare and happiness of those they encounter in their professional activities). People's imperfect duties toward themselves involve striving to perfect their human talents through "the cultivation of their capacities (or natural endowments)" (Kant, 1797/1964b, p. 44).

A Kantian's View of the Oregon Health Plan. The Oregon Health Plan had a fundamentally utilitarian rationale: The limited pool of health care funding provided by taxpayers should be used to provide health care coverage for as many people as possible by covering only those conditions that would benefit the most people to the greatest possible extent. In discussing criticisms of the plan when the proposal was being debated, Pollack and his colleagues (1994) reported that "some have suggested (only half in jest) that legislators should try the experiment on themselves (or perhaps all state employees) before changing Medicaid" (p. 535). This criticism makes the Kantian point that people are obligated to treat other persons only in a manner that they would will to be treated themselves. According to Kant, picking and choosing which people will be helped could never be willed by rational beings to be universal moral law because people would never wish to cut themselves off from receiving help if they were to suffer from a low-priority disorder in the future.

Kant's respect for persons is certainly a noble sentiment, but in reading the Kantian critique of the Oregon Health Plan, the question likely arose in many readers' minds that if we are ethically obligated to provide adequate health care for each person in need, where is the money supposed to come from? Kant's ethical formalism does not take such practical considerations into account. For each person in need of medical treatment, the money must be found somewhere. After all, rational beings could never will that medical treatment be denied if they themselves were in need.

Critical Evaluation of Kant's Formalist Ethical Theory. Kant's attempt to co-opt rationality as synonymous with *his* perspective on ethical reasoning seems more than a bit arbitrary. Consider, for example, the issue of using deception in research. In many cases, studies involving deception can yield information of direct benefit to human beings. Thus, utilitarians can provide sound reasons in support of the practice of deceiving research participants in some specific circumstances. Nevertheless, for Kant, telling a lie is *wrong* under any circumstances. He bases his arguments on different, though not necessarily better, reasons.

In fact, most people would argue that although the maxim that lying is immoral would apply under most circumstances, there are some exceptions, for in real life, conflicts between principles do occur. For example, suppose a would-be murderer approaches a counselor and asks whether a colleague (who just happens to be the person's former therapist and intended victim) is in the office today. The counselor realizes that disclosing the fact that the colleague is indeed working in the office would result in this individual going in and committing murder. The counselor's practical reasoning power is not tested seriously in coming up with the decision not to disclose the truth, on the basis that the principle of preserving life is more important in this situation than the principle of honesty. This scenario may seem simplistic or extreme, yet Kant uses a similar example in his essay "On a Supposed Right to Tell Lies From Benevolent Motives" (1797/1909). However, Kant's analysis concludes that it would be wrong to lie to the would-be murderer to save the life of the potential victim because the counselor would be violating the universal ethical principle of honesty.[5] "Truth in utterances that cannot be avoided is the formal duty of a man to everyone, however great the disadvantage that may arise from it to him or any other" (Kant, 1797/1909, p. 362). For Kant, the consequences of an act within a specific set of circumstances are irrelevant to the determination of the ethical status of the general ethical principle involved. To lie is wrong, according to Kant. Period.

This example reveals the extreme rigidity and insensitivity to contextual factors of Kant's ethical theory. Most reasonable people agree that there are situations in which telling a lie to spare someone's feelings (e.g., when asked, "How do you like my haircut?") is not only ethically permissible but, all things considered, is the *right* thing to do. However, such behavior could not be justified under Kant's model.

Like the principle of utility, the categorical imperative has a deceptive appearance of simplicity as a means of testing the reasonableness of maxims. Consider the effect of modifying particular features of a maxim on the moral evaluation of that maxim. For example, Kant would argue that it is unethical for therapists to initiate treatment with a client when they know there is no room in their current schedule to see the person regularly. However, what would be the ethical status of the maxim if therapists initiated a therapeutic relationship with a client knowing they could not see the client again the *next day?* Could a person not introduce complex situational factors that would make the application of the categorical imperative confusing, if not impossible? Like utilitarianism, Kant's moral theory proves extremely complex to apply effectively in concrete ethical decision making.

CASE EXAMPLE 4.5

A counseling professor states in the syllabus for her theories of personality class that she does not give make-up exams. Each student's lowest score on the four exams given during the semester will be dropped (i.e., not included in the calculation of the student's course grade), so if an exam is missed, the score for that exam will be dropped. A student in her class does poorly on the first exam but earns an A on each of the next two. His father dies suddenly the day before the fourth exam. He notifies the professor and asks if he can make up the exam when he returns to school after the funeral. The professor says that he need not worry about the exam; it will simply be the one dropped. The student points out that he intended to drop the first exam grade and was counting on earning an A for the course on the fourth exam. The professor says that she understands the student's predicament, but it would not be fair if she changed the class rules for one student.

Kant's Ethical Formalism and Ethical Conflict. Kant's formalist model proposes that there is a rational solution for every ethical question and that the acceptability of any ethical maxim can be established beyond any doubt purely by rational deduction (Kant, 1788/1956). Thus, like utilitarianism, the Kantian approach denies the existence of genuine ethical conflict (Wallace, 1988). For Kant, two maxims cannot both represent reasonable courses of action and yet conflict with one another. Kant (1797/1964b) also asserted that no conflict can occur between "perfect" and "imperfect" duties because perfect duties always take precedence. Apparent ethical conflicts are the result of inadequate analysis and reasoning. Wallace (1988) describes this type of moral theory as requiring a "passive" attitude toward rules; people are simply to accept the dictates of a priori universal reason (Kant, 1788/1956). There are no situations in which it would be necessary to reason further about the relevance of a rule to a particular context because genuine moral rules apply universally (i.e., in *every* situation).

However, Kant's analysis simply does not correspond to how people resolve actual moral problems. People apply rules in an active manner, judging the relevance of each competing consideration (e.g., honesty) to a given situation and actively attempting to work through conflicts between principles. People do not ignore the existence of ethical conflict nor do they throw up their hands and give up when they encounter it. Rather, they try to reason things out, as the *Code of Ethics* advises. Kant, in his insistence that reason always reveals people's moral duty, evidently did not consider the possibility that reason might inform them of a conflict between two ethical principles (e.g., honesty and respect for life). Kant's unwillingness to recognize the reality of conflicting ethical duties (i.e., moral dilemmas) presents a major problem when people attempt to apply Kantian principles to complex, real-life moral issues.

In the mental health professions, the Kantian position that there is never a genuine conflict between ethical principles has been seemingly supported by arguments that certain ethical considerations are *always* more fundamental than others. For example, there are mental health professionals who have asserted that the ethical principle of nonmaleficence (i.e., "Do no harm") is the most fundamental ethical consideration in psychological assessment (e.g., Brown, 1982) and psychotherapy (e.g., Rosenbaum, 1982). Endorsement of such a scheme would significantly reduce the problems inherent in trying to determine which consideration is most important in a given situation. However, to apply such a guideline as a universal principle again ignores the real possibility of ethical conflict. For example, when hospitalized clients behave in a violent manner toward other clients and the treatment staff, whom is the clinician obligated not to harm? When violent clients are restrained physically, they are harmed, if not physically, then at least in the sense of having their civil liberties curtailed. However, failure to restrain these clients would likely result in harm to another client or a staff member. The clinician cannot avoid harming someone, so obviously avoidance of harm cannot be the sole consideration in such a case. Additional considerations (e.g., the desire to benefit the other clients by reducing the level of stress in their environment) are also relevant. If clinicians seek instead to minimize harm relative to benefit (a very reasonable approach), they have returned to a utilitarian perspective.

CASE EXAMPLE 4.6

A clinical psychologist is the treatment coordinator for a voluntary inpatient on a ward providing assessment and rehabilitation for clients suffering from a variety of organic brain disorders. His client is a 33-year-old, married, white female suffering from encephalitis, productive aphasia, and AIDS. She is considered demented but does not communicate verbally with staff, so it is difficult to determine this for certain. She is clearly alert, obeys commands, and is generally pleasant and cooperative.

The problem is that she is incontinent of urine and stool and at times has attempted to engage in sexual activity with other patients. Staff members are concerned that her bodily fluids pose a potential hazard for the other clients, many of whom are themselves demented and might be liable to handle or ingest the patient's bodily fluids or fecal material. The psychologist decides that she must be locked in her room to protect the other clients, although this action will restrict her physical freedom and access to ward activities (e.g., television) tremendously.

Relevance of Kant's Formalist Ethical Theory to the Mental Health Professions. Kant's emphasis on the respect that should be shown for the autonomy of persons in the kingdom of ends discussion is strongly represented in the ethical codes of the mental health professions. Avoiding exploitative relationships, maintaining confidentiality, providing competent services, avoiding and correcting discriminatory practices, and respecting the rights of research participants all reflect the Kantian emphasis on the intrinsic value and importance of the individual. Kant's respect for persons is very similar to Rogers's (1961) attitude of unconditional positive regard for clients; both reflect a complete acceptance of and respect for the freedom, autonomy, and personhood of each individual.

However, in both APA's "Ethical Principles" and ACA's *Code of Ethics,* a degree of tension exists between the ultimate importance of the individual's rights and the desire to promote the practical scientific goals of the profession (e.g., through research). Although informed consent is an important value in psychology and counseling, this ethical duty can be compromised through the use of deception in research. The primarily utilitarian justification for deception appears incompatible with the Kantian emphasis on respecting "the worth, dignity, potential, and uniqueness of people" (ACA, 2005, Preamble).

THE NEED FOR ETHICAL PROBLEM-SOLVING SKILLS TO ADDRESS CONFLICTS BETWEEN ETHICAL PRINCIPLES

The discussion of utilitarianism and Kant's formalism has revealed that while each provides a valuable approach to the metaethical justification of ethical principles in the mental health professions, neither is clearly superior or completely adequate as a metaethical basis for professional ethical judgments. Also, neither model addresses effectively the very real potential for ethical principles to conflict with one another in some circumstances. Furthermore, the mix of utilitarian and Kantian metaethical justifications in the ethical codes of the mental health professions increases significantly the potential for ethical conflict. It is, therefore, extremely important that professionals be capable of recognizing conflicts between ethical principles and resolving those conflicts in a reasonable manner.

Professional ethical competence is not simply a matter of following the "rules" stated in a professional ethical code. Ethically competent practice also requires that professionals attend carefully to *all* of the ethical considerations involved in each situation they encounter. If professionals are not *thinking* ethically, there is a possibility that they might overlook subtle but important ethical considerations.[6] Furthermore, in situations in which ethical considerations appear to conflict, ethical competence requires that professionals be capable of resolving such conflicts through the use of their practical (i.e., ethical) reasoning ability (ACA, 2005, Purpose). Practical reasoning involves adapting general ethical principles to the ever-changing contexts of life in a rationally defensible manner (Wallace, 1988).

In the example of the Oregon Health Plan (Pollack et al., 1994), what makes the plan so controversial is that the situation involves not only a prima facie duty to ameliorate the suffering of each person, but also a duty to make certain that the limited available health care resources are distributed in a just and reasonable manner, and a third duty to avoid creating an onerous tax burden for the residents of the state by controlling health care expenditures.[7] It is extremely difficult, and some might argue impossible, to formulate a plan that gives due consideration to each of these important, conflicting ethical duties. Ethical dilemmas like this one represent the ultimate test of the viability of an ethical theory.

CASE EXAMPLE 4.7

A counselor receives a call from his neighbor asking him to provide counseling for her eight-year-old daughter. The girl returned recently from summer camp and has exhibited some disturbing behavior changes. Her mother says that she has become sullen and aggressive, is wetting her bed, and refuses to talk about her experiences at camp. Her parents told her that they wanted her to talk with someone. Her mother said she is calling the counselor because her daughter refuses to talk to anyone except him. The counselor knows that the situation involves potentially problematic multiple relationships, but he also feels it is very important that the girl talk with a professional.

The remainder of this chapter will be devoted to two additional approaches to ethical reasoning that, unlike utilitarianism and Kant's ethical formalism, acknowledge the existence of ethical conflict. In fact, these models, ethical relativism and ethical contextualism, are both based on the metaethical assumption that conflict between ethical principles is an extremely important and relatively common phenomenon. However, they present very different perspectives on the nature of ethical conflict and how situations involving conflicts between ethical principles are best handled.

ETHICAL RELATIVISM

Although the term *ethical relativism* has been used in many different ways by different people to refer to a variety of different ideas, ethical relativists all recognize that conflicts between ethical duties do occur and result in disagreements between individuals or groups of people (e.g., cultures) concerning the ethically appropriate course of action in a situation. They also believe that some disagreements about ethical matters reflect fundamental conflicts regarding the ethical values considered important by the people or societies involved. In a fundamental conflict, two parties do not simply disagree regarding matters of fact, as would be the case if two people disagreed about whether telling someone a bad haircut looks good meets the definition of a lie.[8] Rather, in a fundamental ethical conflict, the two parties agree on the facts of the matter (e.g., both acknowledge that it's a lie) but disagree regarding the morality of telling a lie to make another person feel good.

A second assumption that is characteristic of most forms of ethical relativism is that these fundamental disagreements cannot, at least in some cases, be resolved rationally. In other words, there is not always one demonstrably "correct" moral evaluation of an act, so two conflicting moral viewpoints may be argued to be equally correct. When this assumption is added, the position is referred to as *metaethical relativism.* The metaethical relativist would assert that either no effective method exists for resolving such moral dilemmas (a position referred to as *methodological metaethical relativism*), or if a method does exist, it is not effective in every case (*nonmethodological metaethical relativism;* Brandt, 1959). Relativism is a reaction against *moral objectivist* positions, like those of Kant and the utilitarians, that assert that there is always an objectively true or correct solution in every situation to the problem of determining the ethically appropriate course of action. Rather, they argue that moral truth is relative and varies with the perspective of the individual or cultural context within which the act is evaluated. In other words, the rightness or wrongness of an action might vary as a function of the specific details of the situation in which the act occurs or the perspective assumed by the individual performing the act. Therefore, the focus of ethical relativism has generally been on the need for tolerance in respecting the ethical values of other people or cultures, even when those values are inconsistent with one's own. One's own ethical values are, after all, not objectively (i.e., universally) valid.

With regard to the vignette at the beginning of the chapter, a metaethical relativist might argue that the ethical appropriateness of the psychologist's actions might be viewed differently by people operating from different personal or cultural perspectives. The key point is that the relative validity of the different value perspectives supporting such a practice and those condemning it might not be able to be determined objectively (i.e., rationally). Nevertheless, it does not necessarily follow from this point that moral judgments are arbitrary and have no authority (i.e., *ethical skepticism*). Instead, many ethical relativists argue that the normative authority of ethical judgments is limited to a particular society or culture of like-thinking people (i.e., *cultural relativism*), or even to each individual (i.e., *personal relativism*). Because relativists argue that the cultural or personal context, milieu, or situation in which people behave is an important contributor to their ethical perspective, people living outside that context (e.g., in a different culture or society) cannot genuinely understand the cultural context that gave rise to that value system and, therefore, cannot reasonably pass judgment on the ethicality of the actions of people operating within that context.

Cultural relativism and *personal relativism* have each received considerable support in the social sciences. Cultural relativism is the view that fundamental disagreements regarding standards of ethical justification often occur between members of different cultural groups. Cultural relativism is based on the assumptions that people acquire most of their personal values from their culture and that values and normative behavioral expectations vary from one culture to another. Some formulations of cultural relativism add the component that members of a particular culture are ethically obligated to abide by the moral standards of their culture, in which case the view is a form of *normative cultural relativism.* Normative cultural relativists differ on the question of whether people should always obey the values of their own culture or whether they should conform their behavior to the values of the culture they are currently in (e.g., when in Rome, do as the Romans do).

The perspective of *personal relativism* involves a position like the following: If people genuinely believe that it is right to do A in circumstance C, then it *is* right for them to do A in C. For example, personal relativists would consider the actions of the psychologist in the vignette at the beginning of the chapter appropriate if she genuinely believes that initiating a sexual relationship with her client will benefit him. According to personal relativism, if people believe that their action is appropriate, there is no *objective* basis from which their ethical judgment can be criticized legitimately by others. This idea is consistent with the view that people's affective *sincerity* (rather than any question of the objective "rightness" or "wrongness" of their actions) is what makes their behavior ethical. Virtually everyone technically qualifies as an ethical relativist whenever we show tolerance for ethical perspectives that disagree with our own by, for instance, evaluating people's behavior in the context of their individual or cultural perspective, rather than in relation to some objective (e.g., Kantian) moral standard.

Critical Evaluation of Ethical Relativism. Curiously, ethical relativism is far more often attributed as a criticism of those we disagree with on moral questions than professed as our own ethical viewpoint. Relativism acknowledges the existence of ethical conflict but regards these conflicts as irresolvable in at least some cases. This relativist viewpoint leaves us without a method for determining objectively whether either position is correct or incorrect in an ethical dispute. Ethical relativism can easily lead to *ethical skepticism,* the view that no ethical belief can be proven to be universally valid; therefore, all that remains are ethical attitudes or opinions.

Cultural relativism involves the additional problem of deciding which culture determines the appropriateness of people's actions (e.g., American society, their ethnic subculture, their local community). In the case of incarcerated prisoners, is their behavior to be evaluated by reference to the normative expectations within the prison? Clearly not, if the goal is to rehabilitate the prisoners to become productive members of the larger society. Another problem with cultural relativism is that we do not generally believe that the ethical status of an action is solely a function of its social acceptability. Thus, cultural relativism, in equating morals with *mores* (i.e., the habits or manners of a particular culture or group), is really a rejection of the possibility of any objective ethical standard for judging actions.

Finally, formulations of personal relativism do not generally assert any conditions under which an action is morally inappropriate. The viewpoint that a person always acts morally if she acts in accordance with her true feelings does not necessarily entail that she acts immorally if she fails to act on the basis of her feelings. Any meaningful ethical perspective must, at a minimum, specify conditions under which actions are regarded as ethically appropriate *and* inappropriate.

CASE EXAMPLE 4.8

A counselor in a small town is aware of an individual who has terrorized many of the towns-people for several years. She has harassed and committed a number of crimes against people and their property, but there has never been sufficient evidence to indict her for a crime.

Recently, a 12-year-old girl was kidnapped and murdered. Although evidence points strongly to the same woman, she has not been arrested.

In an apparent attempt to protect herself in case she is arrested, the woman comes to the community mental health center complaining of a long history of "hearing voices." The counselor performs an evaluation that indicates the woman is malingering, although she does qualify for a diagnosis of Antisocial Personality Disorder. However, to protect the community from this "evil" person, the counselor prepares a report documenting that the client is mentally ill (as she pretends to be) and extremely dangerous to others. Furthermore, the counselor contacts legal authorities and reports that his evaluation indicates that the woman should be committed to a state psychiatric facility.

Ethical Relativism and Ethical Conflict. An important insight of ethical relativism is that ethical conflict does occur. The recognition that contextual factors (e.g., cultural differences, situational variables) affect the reasonable interpretation of ethical judgments represents an important advantage over objectivist positions. However, ethical relativism is based on the assumptions that the ethical values of different individuals often conflict in fundamental ways and that there is no method available to resolve all such disagreements (Brandt, 1959). Consequently, there is *no* effective rational means of resolving conflicts between ethical principles. As discussed previously, the inability of ethical relativists to resolve conflicts in a rational manner can undermine the rational validity of the ethical values themselves, resulting in *ethical skepticism.*

So, although ethical relativism acknowledges the existence of ethical conflict, it provides no tools mental health professionals can use to resolve these conflicts reasonably. Instead, ethical relativism advocates tolerance of different ethical perspectives.

Relevance of Ethical Relativism to the Mental Health Professions. The tolerance for divergent multicultural ethical perspectives and for individual viewpoints that are inconsistent with our own personal and cultural ethical values is certainly in keeping with mental health professionals' respect for the dignity and autonomy of each person (ACA, 2005, A. Introduction, A.4.b; APA, 2002, Principle E). Carl Rogers's (1961) extremely influential concept of unconditional positive regard for clients hinges on clinicians' capacity to genuinely accept and empathize with each client's unique subjective perspective. Therefore, effectiveness as a clinician in remaining nonjudgmental and accepting clients unconditionally would seem to entail adopting a relativist perspective.

However, R. F. Kitchener (1991) has argued that ethical relativism is an untenable position for any mental health professional to espouse. While we respect clients' subjective ethical viewpoints, if there are to be any standards of professional ethical behavior, mental health professionals must be able to provide a rational metaethical justification for the ethicality and unethicality of particular actions. Failure to do so would lead to *ethical nihilism* (i.e., the position that since ethical distinctions possess no meaning or validity, arguing about ethical matters is utterly pointless). If a rational justification for a profession's ethical requirements cannot be produced, then professionals cannot reasonably be compelled to obey such requirements. Therefore, although the rational justification of ethical propositions is not an easy task, especially when there are conflicting moral considerations in a situation, a mental health profession cannot abandon the task of developing such a metaethical groundwork without abandoning all hope of establishing and enforcing standards of acceptable professional behavior.

If behaving in a manner that one sincerely believes to be appropriate constitutes ethical practice, as personal relativism would claim, then any sort of unprofessional behavior (like that of the psychologist in the opening vignette) could be argued to be permissible. Professionals cannot be permitted to "just wing it" in deciding ethically appropriate methods of treatment, teaching, and conducting research without significantly diminishing public confidence in the standard of behavior within the profession.

In addition, although the importance of understanding and respecting clients' cultural values has been stressed throughout this book, there is clearly a tension between cultural relativism and a number of the fundamental principles underlying the ethical codes of the mental health professions. Multiculturalism and respect for the individual are both based on respect for people's autonomy and dignity. However, in clinical practice, there is often a degree of conflict between the interests of the culture and the individual. For clients experiencing ambivalence about their homosexual impulses in a cultural context that is strongly heterosexual, it is questionable whether the role of the therapist is to make those individuals a better "fit" in the culture by encouraging them to behave in a manner consistent with the values of the dominant culture or to explore their feelings and determine their own course in life in an autonomous manner. Normative cultural relativism would encourage therapists, teachers, and researchers to impose their values (i.e., the values of the dominant culture) on clients, students, and research participants. Furthermore, if therapists, researchers, and teachers were ethically obligated to adopt the values of the dominant culture, how could they deal effectively and respectfully with the multicultural issues posed by clients, research participants, and students who identify with other cultures or subcultures?

In summation, ethical relativism does not appear to provide a sound metaethical framework to justify the specific ethical duties articulated in the ethical codes of the mental health professions. Relativism is also of little help in resolving the conflicts between ethical duties (i.e., ethical dilemmas) that arise frequently in professional practice.

CASE EXAMPLE 4.9

A client in a substance abuse treatment facility tells a psychologist about the activities (e.g., drug-dealing, assault) he was involved in prior to entering court-ordered treatment. When the psychologist asks him how he feels about having committed those crimes, he tells her, "That was no crime. Everyone did that. You just don't understand how it works on the street."

ETHICAL CONTEXTUALISM

As a contextualist, James Wallace (1988) acknowledged that conflicts do occur between competing ethical principles and that no principle is valid in every conceivable context (i.e., there are no universally valid ethical principles). According to Wallace, the existence of ethical conflict should not be surprising; rather, it is curious that ethicists have frequently assumed that a deductive system of ethical rules (e.g., Kant's formalist theory), derived independently of experience, could address effectively what people ought to do in the ever-changing contexts of actual human life. "How could a set of principles anticipate the continual and extensive changes in the human condition" (Wallace, 1988, p. 17)? Wallace credited John Dewey with having recognized the importance of changing contexts to ethical decision making and to people's evolving understanding of ethical issues. Dewey (1930) had said, "In quality, the good is never twice alike. It never copies itself. It is new every morning, fresh every evening. It is unique in its every presentation" (p. 197).

How are people capable of adapting their ethical understanding to new and continually changing circumstances? According to Wallace, the moral education people receive as children in the process of socialization involves more than the learning of rules. People gradually acquire an increasingly sophisticated understanding of how particular rules apply or do not apply to solving practical moral problems in different sorts of contexts. In other words, people learn that morality and justice sometimes require that rules be adapted to fit unusual circumstances. "The marvelous plasticity of response of which human beings are capable involves the ability to adapt old routines to new circumstances. Intelligence and understanding are exhibited in such adaptation" (Wallace, 1988, p. 58). This process of adapting the application of rules when deciding what the ethical course of action is in a particular set of circumstances is what ethicists call *practical reasoning* (Cohen & Cohen, 1999).

As adults, people are not generally even conscious of the need to adapt their moral reasoning to variations in context. Wallace (1988) explained that the moral education people experience as they grow up provides them with a considerable stockpile of contextually sensitive ethical guidelines, which represent the accumulated practical wisdom of their community and culture. Adults are able to employ this storehouse of practical wisdom with considerable ease to make judgments regarding the relevance of apparently competing ethical rules or to determine which ethical considerations are most important in a situation. In fact, people become aware of the need for practical reasoning only in those difficult cases (i.e., ethical dilemmas) in which it initially appears that whatever option they choose involves ignoring another, equally important ethical consideration. Individuals' practical reasoning capability is employed in such cases to devise creative solutions that best serve each of the relevant considerations. Therefore, rather than denying the existence of potential conflict between ethical principles and feeling threatened by such a possibility, the ethical contextualist recognizes that human experience has always involved such dilemmas and that the practical reasoning capability of people has generally proven adequate to address these situations reasonably and effectively.

Wallace (1988) believed that even though the ethical principles people have been taught are extremely important, rules alone are not sufficient to guarantee ethical conduct in the changing circumstances of life, in which two ethical duties might conflict. To say that "rules are rules" and that circumstances have no bearing on the ethical status of an act is a naive view that does not reflect how reasonable people actually make ethical judgments. "To be critical, in an important sense of this term, is to be good at seeing how what one already knows can be changed so that it can be brought to bear upon unprecedented situations" (Wallace, 1988, p. 58).

Wallace argued that there are two fundamental types of ethical problems: issues of relevance and genuine ethical conflicts. First, in cases involving an apparent conflict between principles, rather than applying one or the other rule in a passive, irrational manner, reasoning people assess whether each consideration is truly *relevant* to the context. For example, suppose a student in a statistics class tells his instructor in casual conversation a rumor regarding the behavior of another instructor in the department. The instructor repeats the story to the other faculty member (out of concern for the colleague's welfare). The colleague realizes which student must have reported the rumor and confronts the student about it. The student then accuses the statistics instructor of having violated his confidentiality. Although this situation might initially appear to have involved competing ethical considerations, the statistics instructor's knowledge of the "Ethical Principles" enables him to recognize that the purpose of the ethical duty regarding confidentiality is not relevant to this circumstance because neither his relationship with the student nor the nature of the information communicated meets the conditions necessary to establish a duty to maintain confidentiality.

The second type of problem involves situations in which two or more relevant ethical principles do genuinely *conflict*. An example of an ethical dilemma would be if a clinician were treating another mental health professional in therapy and she revealed to the clinician, in the context of the therapy, that she was having a sexual relationship with a current client. In this case, the confidentiality of the client is a relevant ethical consideration, as is the clinician's obligation to protect the welfare of the professional's client and to address unethical behavior on the part of another professional. The clinician would be faced with a conflict among relevant ethical duties that, at first glance, appears irresolvable (K. S. Kitchener, 1984).

Resolving situations that appear to involve multiple ethical considerations (issues of relevance) or that genuinely represent conflicts between ethical principles (ethical dilemmas) requires understanding *why* people hold the values they do. In other words, why are the ethical principles involved in the situation important to people? Wallace (1988) asserted that the reason people hold certain values dear is that those values promote human life and human activity in some important way. The key to resolving an apparent conflict between values is to understand the *point* or function of each value and determine how important that consideration is to the situation at hand, so the competing considerations can be prioritized reasonably. These metaethical reflections require a clear understanding of the sources of ethical values, which is the reason so much attention was devoted to the analysis of ethical theories earlier in this chapter.

The following example illustrates the application of Wallace's ethical contextualism: A psychology department operates a clinic for the purpose of providing practicum training for clinical graduate students. The clinic provides assessment and psychotherapy services to university students and the local community. The clinic is open only during weekday afternoons. Due to the limited availability of space in the psychology department, several clinical and nonclinical faculty ask whether the clinic space could be used to conduct research during the mornings and on weekends, citing student need for research space to complete thesis projects and the potential scientific value of both student and faculty research. Some members of the clinical faculty argue that the request should be rejected because the confidentiality of clients could be compromised, noting that client records are kept in the clinic and that clients leave telephone messages on an answering machine in the clinic during nonclinic hours.

Clearly, there are multiple, apparently conflicting ethical considerations cited by the two parties in this case. Practical reasoning, according to Wallace, first involves an assessment of the relevance of each of the considerations to the situation. As Aristotle (trans. 1947) pointed out, practical wisdom involves giving each competing consideration the weight it deserves. Obviously, an irrelevant consideration does not deserve the same weight as a relevant one. The obligation to provide sufficient space and resources for students to complete their thesis work is certainly relevant to a fundamental purpose of an academic department. The potential scientific value of faculty research projects is difficult to determine, but conducting research is part of an academic psychologist's job description, and the department is certainly obliged to facilitate faculty members' ability to do their jobs.

The issue of ensuring client confidentiality is obviously important to any clinic offering psychological services, but it is unclear how nonclinic personnel's use of the clinic when it is closed would compromise the confidentiality of clients. If client records were not locked away in filing cabinets or were easily accessible without passwords on a computer, an ethical concern would certainly be justified. However, in such an instance, the confidentiality of clients would already be at risk because custodial personnel or anyone else with a key to the clinic door would have access to the material. On the other hand, if practicum students and supervisors are diligent in their duties of putting away notes, files, computer disks, and other confidential material in locked cabinets at the close of clinic hours; making sure that computer records cannot be accessed without well-protected passwords; and keeping the telephone answering machine in a secure, private area, a breach of confidentiality should not be a potential risk.

Thus, it could be argued that the ethical consideration of protecting the confidentiality of clinic clients is being applied inappropriately to the question of how the clinic space can be used when the clinic is closed. Clinical faculty members' sensitivity to the issue of confidentiality is admirable, but the issue is not demonstrably of strong relevance to the context under consideration. If the clinical faculty were to respond that confidentiality is always the primary ethical consideration in *any* context involving the clinic, their position would be revealed to be grounded on the assumptions that there are inviolable ethical rules and that sensitivity to contextual factors is not an important part of practical reasoning. These positions were found to be untenable in the consideration of Kant's formalist theory earlier in this chapter. Thus, there does not appear to be a reasonable ethical objection in this case to using the clinic space for research purposes during nonclinic hours, provided that adequate safeguards are in place to ensure client confidentiality.

A genuine ethical dilemma, on the other hand, involves multiple, competing ethical considerations that are each relevant to the context. The following example is an ethical dilemma based on the issue of providing clients access to their mental health records: A 23-year-old client who had been hospitalized for an episode of depression requests permission to review her treatment record prior to being discharged. Her therapist is concerned because the section of the record concerning the history of the client's problems states that her first episode of depression, resulting in a suicide attempt, occurred when she was 16, shortly after her parents died. Her aunt had told the admitting psychiatrist at that time that the client's father had killed her mother and had then killed himself. The aunt provided a copy of a newspaper account of the events, which was included in the client's record. The therapist is aware that his client was told that her parents had died in an automobile accident; she apparently does not know the true story of their deaths.

Respect for the client's autonomy suggests that she has a right to review her treatment record, including the truth about her family and her own past. On the other hand, the therapist's concern for the welfare of his client is that she could be traumatized by this information and possibly take her own life. Both of these competing ethical considerations are clearly relevant. Wallace (1988) argued that such a dilemma is best addressed by trying to interpret the meaning and *purpose* of the principles involved "in ways that are faithful to the rules themselves and to the activities the rules are designed to facilitate" (Wallace, 1988, p. 10).

The principle of respect for people's rights and dignity, which entails respecting the autonomy of clients to make decisions about their own life, is grounded in people's respect for other persons. People do not believe that it is appropriate for someone else to make important decisions about their lives without their knowledge and consent. People also believe that it is inappropriate to lie to another person because such behavior displays a lack of respect for the individual's personhood. Furthermore, respect for autonomy reflects people's belief in the potential of human beings for growth and self-understanding. One cannot, then, be truly autonomous without knowledge of relevant aspects of one's past, knowledge that had been denied to this young woman through the deception perpetrated by parentalistic relatives. At the time, she was a minor, but apparently no one has informed her of the truth as an adult either. To deny her access to the information contained in her record about her family is to collude in this ongoing pattern of disregarding her autonomy.

Concern for her welfare was undoubtedly a major consideration in her family's ongoing decision not to tell her the truth regarding her parents' deaths, for her difficulties with depression have persisted episodically into adulthood. The principle of nonmaleficence is grounded in mental health professionals' respect and regard for persons, as is the competing principle of respect for a person's autonomy. Not only do clinicians have an obligation to never harm another person intentionally, they also have a duty to try to protect others from harm whenever possible.

The fundamental issue here is whether therapists are justified in protecting their clients from harm by acting parentalistically and denying them access to potentially upsetting information. Denying them access to the information might serve the purpose of protecting them from harm, but only at the expense of ignoring the obligation to respect their autonomy (and their right under the HIPAA Privacy Rule to obtain a copy of their health records). The therapist realizes that, arguably, a client is in fact "harmed" whenever others interfere with her autonomous functioning. It is rather difficult to justify harming an individual (by denying her autonomy) in order to protect her from harm. Infantilizing someone, as has been done in this woman's case, communicates a profound disrespect for her personhood. Alternatively, providing her with supervised access to the record so that she can learn the truth about her past and work through the implications of these revelations with her therapist would demonstrate respect for her personal autonomy and also address his concern about her psychological welfare and suicidal potential. This strategy would also eliminate the possibility that she might learn the truth about her parents sometime after her discharge, when she might not have any support available to help her deal with the painful discovery.

This resolution might have occurred to many readers spontaneously as they thought about the case. However, other people might have had different responses to the scenario. The important point is that the process of practical reasoning described above resulted in a solution that is supported by good reasons and is consistent with the purposes of the ethical considerations relevant to the situation, rather than an arbitrarily determined course of action that could be viewed as reflecting the personal ethical biases of the professional involved.

For the ethical contextualist, intelligent moral behavior is always based on an understanding of how ethical principles have been applied in the past and the ends that have been served by those applications (Wallace, 1988). The ethical contextualist demonstrates an understanding of the "ways of life" that represent the accumulated practical wisdom of a society (and in this case, of the mental health professions). The contextualist recognizes that practical reasoning requires that people adapt these ways to novel situations. Ethical problem solving is, therefore, a creative enterprise. Resolving an ethical dilemma seldom involves simply choosing one principle over another; rather, it requires devising a solution that is consistent with the purpose of all principles involved (Wallace, 1988).

Critical Evaluation of Ethical Contextualism. Although Wallace's (1988) contextualist theory appears to provide a very promising means of resolving ethical conflict through the use of practical reason, successful application of contextualism seems to require considerable metaethical sophistication on the part of a mental health professional. It is necessary that professionals be familiar not only with the values and ethical principles that are to guide their conduct but the metaethical justifications for those principles as well. Otherwise, they will not be in a position to understand the function of the ethical considerations involved in a situation, which is necessary in order to recognize the points of connection between the considerations and to prioritize the principles in a reasonable way.

The fact that behaving ethically is a difficult challenge is not an indictment of ethical contextualism. It is simply a reality with which the ethical professional must struggle. Exercising practical reasoning in order to behave ethically is not an easy task; however, as Wallace (1988) has pointed out, it is not impossible either.

The attention devoted to the ethical principles of mental health professionals in Chapters 2 and 3 and to models of ethical reasoning and sources of metaethical justification in this chapter represents the initial step in developing competence in practical reasoning. This process will continue in the next chapter. A model of ethical decision making based on Wallace's ethical contextualism will be presented. This model was created to provide guidance and structure for the ethical deliberations of mental health professionals that will enable them to resolve ethically complex situations in a rationally defensible manner.

CASE EXAMPLE 4.10

A 68-year-old white male, whose wife died three years ago, has been diagnosed as having Alzheimer's disease. There is no cure. The diagnosis was confirmed by several independent evaluations. He has been informed that he will gradually become demented. At present, he is not demented, though he has developed severe memory difficulties. He has no desire to experience a decline into dementia and wants to spare his family the torment of watching him decline to a vegetative state. During a behavioral medicine consultation, he tells his psychologist that he plans to terminate his life painlessly now by taking an overdose of sleeping pills, so his family can remember him as a healthy, vibrant person. He is apparently rational and tells her he has reflected on this decision for the past three months and is convinced that taking his own life is the best way to go.

SUMMARY

This chapter presented four ethical theories and evaluated their ability to provide mental health professionals with the philosophical grounding needed to make sound ethical judgments and resolve the ethical conflicts that inevitably arise in their work. The first two theories, utilitarianism and Kant's formalist theory, are the two major theories of obligation in Western philosophy and form the metaethical basis of the ethical codes. The latter two theories, ethical relativism and Wallace's ethical contextualist theory, were designed specifically to address ethical conflict.

Utilitarianism is a theory of obligation based upon the theory of value known as ethical hedonism, which asserts that pleasure is the only thing valued intrinsically (i.e., as an end in itself) by human beings. A person's ethical duty is stated in the principle of utility: An act is ethically appropriate if it maximizes the positive balance of pleasure over pain. Utilitarianism is reflected in the "Ethical Principles" (APA, 2002) in the principles of beneficence and nonmaleficence. Conversely, in Kant's formalist theory, a person's ethical duty is revealed by reason. Using the categorical imperative, a maxim can be tested to determine whether it constitutes a universal moral law consistent with the laws of reason. In his discussion of the kingdom of ends, Kant argued that when people act in accordance with reason, they always treat others in a manner consistent with the way rational beings would want to be treated. By acting in this ethical manner, people never impose their will on others because their rational will is the same as everyone else's. All humanity should be treated as an end in itself, never as a means to a person's own irrational, self-centered end. Kant's theory is the basis of many of the ethical concerns of psychology and counseling, including respect for personal autonomy and concern for the welfare of those affected by a professional's activities. Although ethical conflict is indeed possible within the frameworks of these theories, both utilitarianism and Kant's formalist theory deny the existence of ethical dilemmas.

Ethical relativism takes the position that different individuals (personal relativism) or cultures (cultural relativism) may have different conceptions of what is most valuable in life and of what action is ethically appropriate in a given context. While ethical relativists acknowledge the occurrence of fundamental conflicts, they assert that no method exists to determine objectively whether a position is right or wrong, so ethical conflicts are ultimately irresolvable.

Like relativism, Wallace's ethical contextualism also emphasizes the importance of adapting ethical guidelines to situational factors. However, Wallace argued that ethical conflict *can* be resolved rationally; people accomplish this by drawing on the store of practical wisdom communicated to them by their culture and community. When confronted with a genuine ethical dilemma, effective practical reasoning involves engaging in metaethical deliberations regarding the functions of the relevant ethical considerations (i.e., reflecting on why that ethical value is regarded as *valuable* in human life) in order to devise a solution consistent with the purpose of each ethical principle involved in the situation. One shortcoming of Wallace's theory is that he underestimates the difficulty of attaining the level of metaethical sophistication a professional would need in order to deal effectively with competing ethical considerations. The challenge of reasoning and behaving ethically is difficult, but not impossible. A model to assist professionals in ethical decision making will be presented in the next chapter.

NOTES

1. There are a number of other ethical theories that have gained adherents among mental health professionals (e.g., feminist, narrative, and Eastern ethical models). The present discussion has been limited to the few ethical models selected in the interest of simplicity, clarity, and parsimony. I certainly am not suggesting that the chapter represents an exhaustive treatment of potential sources of metaethical justification for mental health professionals.

2. Some formulations of utilitarianism, such as that of G. E. Moore (1962), assert that certain mental experiences (e.g., the acquisition of knowledge) possess intrinsic value independent of the pleasure that may be associated with them. This viewpoint has been referred to as *ideal utilitarianism* (Smart & Williams, 1973).

3. Utilitarians who believe that minimizing suffering is a more pressing concern than maximizing happiness, referred to as *negative utilitarians* (Smart, 1958), are not subject to this criticism. However, this viewpoint has never been very popular among utilitarians.

4. Kant's theory is also referred to as *deontological* (from the Greek *deon,* meaning "that which is obligatory") because ethical duties are justified independent of any theory of value. Conversely, utilitarianism is a teleological, or consequentialist, theory of moral obligation.

5. Joseph Fletcher (1966) makes the interesting point that from a legal standpoint, acting in accordance with the ethical principle of honesty in such a circumstance, as Kant suggests one ought, could cause one to become an accessory before the fact to murder.

6. Even in everyday life, subtle ethical issues are often present. For example, when I moved to Texas to take a university position, there was a restaurant in town that featured a W.O.P. burger (i.e., a hamburger topped with tomato sauce and mozzarella cheese) on its menu. "W.O.P." is a derogatory term used in the United States to refer to Italians. Immigrant laborers in the early 1900s, many of whom were Italian, often did not have the work permits required by the government to engage in various occupations. Thus, Italians were referred to as people "without permit" (i.e., as W.O.P.s). Is there an ethical issue involved in ordering the W.O.P. burger? Also, is there an ethical issue involved in eating at the restaurant?

7. One could certainly argue that there are additional duties represented in this situation. In the interest of clarity and length, the present discussion is limited to the three duties stated.

8. One person might consider it a lie, while another might argue that aesthetic judgments are so subjective that there is no objective truth concerning the appearance of the person's haircut—therefore, whatever one says cannot technically be regarded as a lie.

Chapter 5

A Model of the Ethical Decision-Making Process

Unfortunately, the development of professional ethical codes has created the impression that professionals do not need to develop their own moral reasoning ability; rather, they just need to learn and follow a set of prescribed ethical rules (Pedersen, 1997). This approach to ethical professional behavior has two major shortcomings. First, professional codes are necessarily vague. They offer general principles to guide professional conduct, along with some specific legalistic standards and prohibitions, but ethical codes cannot provide direction regarding all the circumstances that arise in the practice of a mental health profession (Pettifor, 2001). Second, mental health professionals occasionally encounter situations in which two or more ethical principles appear to conflict (e.g., the principles of confidentiality and concern for the welfare of others). The ethical codes of the American mental health professions do not provide a specific method for resolving such ethical dilemmas. As a result, professionals have little guidance, other than their personal ethical values, in deciding what to do. They are often uncomfortable with the course of action they select because it is inconsistent with one of the ethical principles involved in the situation (Smith, McGuire, Abbott, & Blau, 1991). Professionals need a rational method for determining an ethically acceptable course of action in such complex circumstances (ACA, 2005, Purpose). This chapter will introduce a new model that professionals can use to organize their thoughts regarding ethical considerations and accurately identify and resolve ethical dilemmas.

THE PURPOSE OF THE MODEL

The purpose of the model is twofold. First, it will enable professionals to differentiate contexts involving multiple, or competing, ethical considerations from those that are less ethically complex. Being mindful of the *potential* for ethical complications in a situation will enable professionals to avoid conflicts in many cases. Ethical dilemmas often have a way of "sneaking up" on people when they fail to recognize or appreciate the complex implications of seemingly minor decisions and commitments (MacKay & O'Neill, 1992). For example, suppose a counseling client asks you about your religious beliefs. What ethical consideration(s) should be taken into account in choosing a response to this query?

Second, the model provides a template of steps professionals can take to resolve complex ethical issues in a rational manner. The model does *not* provide answers to ethical problems, only a framework that will enable professionals to arrive at their own well-informed, rationally based decisions regarding what to do in a particular set of circumstances. The model is designed to apply to ethical issues that might arise in any area of the practice of a mental health profession (e.g., teaching, research, consultation).

THE MODEL

A number of others interested in ethics training in the mental health professions have recognized the value of providing students and practitioners with a template outlining the appropriate steps to take in addressing complex ethical questions and in resolving ethical conflicts (e.g., K. S. Kitchener, 1984, 2000; Koocher & Keith-Spiegel, 1998; Treppa, 1998; Tymchuk, 1981, 1986). The model presented here borrows extensively from their work but adds the important insights of Wallace's (1988) ethical contextualist theory, presented in Chapter 4.

The fundamental principle underlying this model is that the ethical complexity of a situation must be assessed initially, then continually reassessed in the light of new information and the progress of professionals' practical reasoning. Additional ethical considerations are often identified in the course of these deliberations. Whenever professionals are satisfied that they have addressed the ethical complexity of the situation adequately and a viable option for ethically appropriate action (or non-action) is available, they can make a decision and conclude their deliberations. An outline of the model is presented in Table 5.1.

In order to resolve apparent ethical conflicts in a rational manner, professionals need to apply their understanding of the metaethical sources of the ethical principles of their profession, discussed in Chapter 4, because allegiance to a professional ethical principle (e.g., confidentiality) should be superseded only by another *ethical* consideration that a professional determines to be a more powerful and fundamental obligation in a particular circumstance. "When we do override a moral principle, it should only be done for good moral reasons" (K. S. Kitchener, 1984, p. 53).

Professionals who fail to strive to resolve ethical conflicts in a reasonable manner display an unprofessional attitude of indifference toward their profession and the people they serve (e.g., students, clients, research participants). As the preamble of psychology's ethical code states, the effectiveness of ethical standards "requires a personal commitment to a lifelong effort to act ethically" (APA, 2002).

Step 1: Initial Appraisal of Ethical and Legal Considerations Involved

This initial step of appraising the presence of potential ethical and legal considerations applies to every sort of occupational situation encountered by mental health professionals (e.g., research, teaching, psychotherapy, consultation). Keep in mind that the task of evaluating the potential presence of ethical considerations is not completed when professionals have identified one principle that appears to be important to the situation. When focusing their attention narrowly on one principle, professionals will frequently overlook, and perhaps violate, other relevant principles. Professionals must also always remember their obligation to obey the law, although sometimes legal and ethical duties can conflict (APA, 2002, 1.02).

Table 5.1   A Model of the Ethical Decision-Making Process

1. Initial Appraisal of Ethical and Legal Considerations Involved

    a. If no conflict ──────────────────────────────▶ Make a Decision

    b. If a conflict apparently exists

    ↓

2. Gather Information (facts specific to the case, pertinent ethical and legal guidelines, consultation with colleagues and experts)

    ↓

3. Secondary Appraisal of Ethical and Legal Considerations Involved

    a. If conflict has been resolved ────────────────▶ Make a Decision

    b. If a conflict still apparently exists

    ↓

4. Metaethical Deliberations Regarding the Relevance of Ethical Considerations

    a. If relevance deliberations resolve conflict ──────────▶ Make a Decision

    b. If an ethical dilemma exists

    ↓

5. Metaethical Deliberations Regarding the Resolution of the Ethical Dilemma

    ↓

6. Tertiary Appraisal of Ethical Considerations—Generate Options and Estimate Consequences

    ↓

7. Make a Decision

    ↓

8. Document Rationale and Decision-Making Process (should be done throughout the process)

Effective identification of ethical complexity at this initial stage requires that professionals be appropriately sensitive to the presence of ethical considerations. Ethical sensitivity certainly requires knowledge of the ethical code. In many cases, it also involves an intuitive sense, or "gut feeling" that something about the situation is disturbing or unusual (Smith, 2003b). In the earlier example of a counseling client asking about your religious beliefs, it would be important to be sensitive to the possibility that your client might view you as an authority on this as well as other matters. The potential for the client to be unduly influenced by your personal values, presented in a professional setting, is an important ethical consideration.[1]

Also, professionals should not assume that their client is the only person whose needs have to be considered (Koocher & Keith-Spiegel, 1998). In many cases, the needs of others (e.g., the family of a potentially suicidal client) provide additional ethical considerations. Although the situation may involve a professional relationship with one principal figure (e.g., a psychotherapy client, student), frequently there is more than one person who stands to be affected by the situation (e.g., the client's family, the other students in the class).

If no competing considerations are apparent in a situation, professionals should terminate their deliberations and act in accordance with the ethical principle(s) and legalities involved. It is important for professionals to regard the ethical code of their profession as prima facie valid; that is, the ethical code is a valid guide for professional conduct unless some competing principle or special circumstance is even more compelling (Beauchamp & Childress, 1979). On the other hand, if the situation does involve apparently competing ethical considerations, the deliberations must continue.

Step 2: Gather Information

When there are apparently conflicting ethical considerations, the first task is to gather as much information as possible regarding the specific facts of the situation and the nature of the conflict. What is the potential impact of the situation on the client's life? What other parties are potentially affected and in what way? Remember that the details of a situation are enormously important to the fine distinctions that can affect professionals' ethical judgments (K. S. Kitchener, 1984), as was seen in Chapter 4. Professionals' ethical decision making is generally only as good as their information.

Professionals must always exercise care to gather information in an ethical manner, without violating clients' confidentiality (e.g., by seeking information from family members without a client's consent) or causing them undue anxiety by turning a fact-seeking interview into an interrogation. In addition, professionals must recognize that their personal values can certainly bias their perception of a situation and cause them to favor a particular course of action or give undue weight to one of the competing ethical considerations. Mental health professionals must be consciously aware of their value biases so they can avoid being unduly influenced by them during the ethical decision-making process.[2]

Information can be obtained from the client(s) involved, colleagues and ethical consultants (e.g., institutional or organizational ethics committees), ethical and practice guidelines, and other professional literature. Professionals should carefully review their professional ethical code, paying particular attention to principles and standards relevant to the competing ethical considerations they are confronting. Supplementary guidelines like those published by APA and its divisions (e.g., APA, 1981b, 1987, 1993) should be consulted if they are relevant to the context in which the conflict has arisen (e.g., research with human participants). Also, information regarding legal statutes might indicate that one of the considerations involved constitutes a legal duty in the situation.[3]

An extremely important source of information for these deliberations is the opinion of experienced, respected colleagues who have dealt with similar types of situations or the ethics committee of the professional's state or national organization (e.g., ACA Ethics Committee, 1997a). As Wallace (1988) pointed out, the practical wisdom of a community (or a profession) is based upon the values of its members and their cumulative experience in applying those values successfully to the ever-changing contexts of community (or professional) life. Effective practical reasoning is always grounded in an understanding of the ways in which similar dilemmas have been resolved in the past. The challenge is to adapt those ways to the present novel context (Wallace, 1988).

Step 3: Secondary Appraisal of Ethical and Legal Considerations Involved

If information obtained from any of the sources clearly indicates that one of the apparently conflicting duties takes priority in a situation like the present one, or if a legal duty is discovered that overrides all other considerations, the ethical conflict has been resolved and a decision can be made. If, on the other hand, the additional information has not resolved the conflict, or has even increased the ethical complexity of the situation (e.g., has introduced additional conflicting considerations or identified additional parties potentially affected), professionals must reappraise the situation in light of the new information and, if necessary, modify the list of fundamental ethical considerations that appear prima facie relevant to the situation. If any aspect of the situation or the considerations is unclear, they should, by all means, go back to Step 2 and gather more information. Always remember that the best ethical judgments are the ones based on the most comprehensive information because situational factors matter a great deal.

Step 4: Metaethical Deliberations Regarding the Relevance of Ethical Considerations

In situations involving an apparent conflict between ethical duties, professionals must next have a method for rationally determining whether each consideration is genuinely *relevant* to the situation. Although all ethical principles are important, they do not all apply to every situation. For example, confidentiality is a vitally important ethical principle, but is it relevant to a situation in which a mental health professional observes a neighbor's spousal abuse? As discussed in Chapter 4, deliberations regarding relevance involve understanding *why* each of the considerations is regarded as being of ethical importance in order to determine whether it applies in the present circumstances. Professionals need to understand the *point* of each ethical consideration; they must reflect on a metaethical level to determine why each principle, or value, is taken seriously as an ethical consideration—how the principle contributes to human life (Wallace, 1988). To deliberate effectively, professionals must be able to trace the metaethical origin of any rule of professional conduct. The background in ethical theories provided in Chapter 4 will assist in this task. In the example of the abusive neighbor, the professional's deliberations would indicate that confidentiality is an important ethical consideration in professional relationships requiring complete candor on the part of clients; however, no such relationship exists with the neighbor, so the ethical consideration is not relevant to the situation.

If the apparent ethical conflict has been addressed on the basis of the deliberations regarding relevance, leaving no further conflict, the professional is in a position to resolve the situation in an ethically appropriate manner. If conflicting, relevant ethical considerations still exist, further deliberations will be necessary to resolve the situation, which is now understood to constitute a genuine ethical dilemma.

Step 5: Metaethical Deliberations Regarding the Resolution of the Ethical Dilemma

For each ethical consideration deemed relevant to the situation, professionals must address the metaethical deliberations from Step 4 from a new perspective. Why has such a premium been placed on this value in the past? How does it contribute to the ways of life of a community or a profession? What are the implications and relative importance of this ethical consideration in the present situation? These metaethical deliberations will generally clarify and simplify a complex ethical problem because the multiplicity of ethical considerations stated in a professional code funnels down into a much smaller set of metaethical sources of value, as illustrated in Figure 5.1. Different ethical principles (e.g., concern for client welfare, confidentiality, and respect for autonomy) that appear to conflict in a given situation (e.g., a depressed individual's desire to commit suicide) are often found to reflect the same fundamental value (i.e., respect for persons is the basis for protecting clients from harm, believing that people are entitled to their privacy, and permitting clients to choose how they wish to conduct their lives). In such a case, resolving the ethical problem is then a matter of devising a solution that best serves the fundamental value (i.e., respect for persons) that is now recognized as the source of the professional's ethical duty in the situation. The metaethical foundation of respect for clients' personhood is the duty to preserve life. After all, you can't legitimately claim to respect the personhood of people you permit to be harmed unreasonably. Thus, depending on the specific circumstances of the situation, protecting the life of someone threatening suicide as a result of a depressive episode could reasonably be asserted to constitute a professional's fundamental ethical duty.

Step 6: Tertiary Appraisal of Ethical Considerations— Generate Options and Estimate Consequences

After applying their practical reasoning skills to resolve the ethical dilemma, professionals must again reappraise the situation to evaluate the progress of their deliberations. If they perceive some ambiguity in the situation that is due to inadequate information, they can always seek additional information. Once the new information is gathered and the relative importance of each of the competing ethical considerations has been determined, they should begin the process of generating behavioral options.

In generating options, professionals return to the pragmatic level of applying the ethical code to the concrete situation. The best option will be one that is consistent with the purpose of the most fundamental ethical value relevant to the situation but does not do violence to any other relevant considerations. Though options reflecting each of the conflicting considerations should be considered, it is extremely important to remember that the solution that best serves each of the competing considerations will generally be a creative solution rather than one based on the single considerations that usually guide people's thinking. Brainstorming, alone or with colleagues, to generate options that reflect the outcome and spirit of the recently concluded metaethical deliberations can introduce new ideas for action. Professionals should always also consider the possibility that the most ethically appropriate course is to not take any action. In some circumstances (e.g., a vague threat against another reported to have been made by a research participant), this option may be most consistent with the principle of nonmaleficence.

Figure 5.1   An illustration of the "funneling" phenomenon that occurs during the ethical
decision-making process as multiple, competing ethical principles in a situation
funnel down to a smaller set of metaethical sources of value.

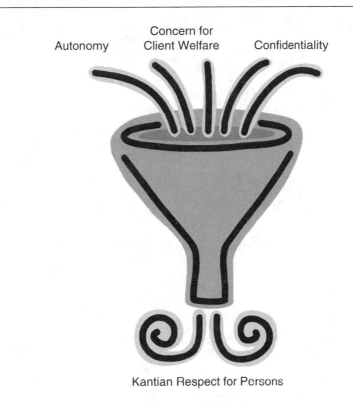

Kantian Respect for Persons

Once professionals have generated a menu of potential options for action, they should
estimate the likely consequences of each option for each person involved, utilizing any evidence available to support such estimates. Though such an estimation can never be done with
absolute precision (as was discussed earlier with regard to utilitarianism), the probability of
particular outcomes is nevertheless an important consideration. Furthermore, given the very
careful deliberations involved up to this point in the process, they will likely have a fairly
clear sense of the probable consequences of a given option. Nevertheless, situations sometimes arise in which none of the options appear ideal. In such circumstances, the principle of
nonmaleficence becomes particularly important. For example, if there is no option available
that will enable a professional to help everyone involved in the situation, is there at least an
option that will help the person who most needs help and still avoid hurting anyone else? The
utilitarian precept of minimizing the negative consequences of one's actions is emphasized
appropriately in the principle of nonmaleficence in the ethical codes of psychology and counseling. Although we are not always able to benefit those we interact with professionally, we
certainly want to actively avoid potentially harming anyone.

At the very least, the exercise of estimating the consequences of the proposed solutions will decrease the probability that professionals will act impulsively without duly considering the implications of their decision for each person affected. So, while this process may not reveal which option is absolutely the right one, it will make it very unlikely that an option will be pursued that is ethically inappropriate or insensitive.

Step 7: Make a Decision

When faced with a difficult ethical issue, it is always desirable to take as much time as possible to deliberate. Poor judgments are much more likely to occur when professionals are under intense time pressure. If time and circumstances permit, professionals might hedge their decision a bit more by proposing the solution to a supervisor or experienced colleague before implementing it. Still, in the end, they will generally need to act. Although they will not know absolutely for certain that the course of action selected is correct, their degree of comfort in acting will be significantly greater if they have attended carefully to their ethical deliberations and developed a sound, well-informed, rational justification for the action taken.

Step 8: Document Rationale and Decision-Making Process

Whenever professionals take an action involving ethical considerations, the action taken and the rationale for the decision should be documented. In situations involving an apparent or actual conflict between ethical considerations, professionals should keep careful records throughout the process of their deliberations, both to organize their thoughts on the matter and to provide a permanent record of the steps taken in their attempts to resolve the problem. When dealing with a particularly difficult dilemma, it is likely that some people will not agree with their final decision. It is important that they be able to demonstrate the care they took in reaching a decision and that they were aware of the relevant considerations, gathered information, consulted with colleagues, and so on, so that any reviewer will recognize that they acted in good faith (i.e., based on careful, rational deliberations). It is generally recognized that different individuals possessing varying degrees of experience may differ in their ethical opinions (Haas, Malouf, & Mayerson, 1986). Malpractice is not attributed to professionals based simply on a difference of opinion regarding an ethical matter; malpractice involves a judgment that the professional acted capriciously, with apparent disregard for important ethical considerations. Careful ethical deliberation, reflected accurately in official record keeping, demonstrates professionalism.

A CASE EXAMPLE APPLYING THE MODEL OF ETHICAL DECISION MAKING

Consider the following case, which will illustrate how the decision-making model can be used to resolve ethically complex situations:

A psychologist is employed on an inpatient substance abuse rehabilitation ward. One of her psychotherapy clients has been told that the medical tests conducted at the time of his admission revealed that he tested positive for the human immunodeficiency virus (HIV). He also has diagnoses of Cocaine Dependence and Antisocial Personality Disorder. He is scheduled to take a weekend pass in 10 days to see his wife and family and to attend to some personal business.

The psychologist has already discussed with her client the importance of telling his wife of his condition and of the need for them to practice "safe sex." He had indicated in response to this information that he would prefer not to tell his wife because she might refuse to have sex with him and would be likely to leave him in the future. He asked if it would be acceptable to not tell his wife about his medical condition if he agreed to use a condom, even though he does not like to use one.

When the psychologist told him that the pass would not be granted under those conditions, he responded, "Okay. Sure, I'll tell her." Her experience with this client leads her to doubt very strongly that he will fulfill his promise to inform his wife of his medical condition when he leaves on his pass.

Step 1: Initial Appraisal of Ethical and Legal Considerations Involved. What ethical considerations are involved in this example? First, there is the therapist's regard as a mental health professional for her client's autonomy. Respecting a client's autonomy involves allowing him to manage his own affairs in life, such as determining his own course of behavior on his weekend pass (ACA, 2005, A.1.a; APA, 2002, Principle E). A second consideration is the therapist's concern for the welfare of each individual potentially affected by her actions (APA, 2002, Principle A). There is more than one person potentially affected by this situation: her client, who wants to see his wife and family and attend to personal business; his spouse, who risks contracting the virus if they engage in unprotected sex; and his children, who are likely anxious to see their father as soon as possible, may be affected by whether the personal business is attended to, and certainly would be harmed if their mother contracted HIV. If protecting the welfare of the client's spouse might involve informing her of her husband's medical status, the confidentiality of information pertaining to his treatment is an extremely important consideration (ACA, 2005, B.1, B.2; APA, 2002, Principle E, 4.01, 4.02, 4.05[b]). The possibility that a state legal statute might mandate that a client's HIV status be kept confidential under any circumstances must be investigated because professionals also have an ethical obligation to abide by the law. There are undoubtedly additional considerations, but, for the purposes of a case example, these are sufficient to establish the existence of a potential conflict between ethical principles.

Step 2: Gather Information. With regard to the therapist's concern about preserving her client's autonomy, she would meet with him again to discuss his perception of the issues involved in revealing his HIV status to his spouse and the probable consequences of such a disclosure. She would also want to assess his understanding of, and feelings about, the potential consequences of nondisclosure, under both the conditions of having protected and unprotected sexual relations with his wife.

Concern for the welfare of her client would involve inquiring about the nature of the personal business that he proposes to attend to while on pass. How pressing and important is it? She would also want to consider and discuss with him the potential emotional, social, and legal consequences for him if he were to cause his wife to become infected.

Her concern for the welfare of her client's spouse would focus on the potential danger posed to the wife's health should her client fail to disclose his condition to his wife and engage in unprotected sex. It would be extremely important for the therapist to acquaint herself with the latest medical information regarding the probability that the virus could be transmitted from male to female through unprotected sexual contact.[4] It would be wise to educate her client regarding the danger of transmitting the virus and factors that would increase his spouse's risk of infection, such as the presence of lesions in the female genitalia from previously acquired sexually transmitted diseases (Quinn et al., 1988). She would also want to know whether her client's spouse is aware that he used cocaine intravenously with his substance abusing associates. If so, she might realize that she is engaging in high-risk sexual activity by having unprotected sexual relations with her husband.

Client confidentiality is another extremely important consideration. Confidentiality is fundamental to the entire psychotherapeutic enterprise; clients feel safe to reveal their innermost thoughts, feelings, and secrets because they are guaranteed that whatever they reveal will be held in absolute confidence by their therapist. This duty is particularly critical in the treatment of HIV clients, who tend to be hesitant to seek treatment because they fear being stigmatized by society (Chenneville, 2000). If the client is uneasy about discussing the matter with his spouse, the therapist might ask whether he would prefer that she inform his spouse or that the three of them meet to deal with the matter therapeutically. If he declines these options, it is clear that any disclosure made by the therapist would violate his confidentiality.

As a professional, the therapist would next consult the "Ethical Principles" (APA, 2002) to review Ethical Standard 4 (Privacy and Confidentiality), paying particular attention to Standard 4.02 (Discussing the Limits of Confidentiality) and Standard 4.05 (Disclosures), which describe the circumstances under which confidentiality may be violated.[5] She would note that Standard 4.05[b] includes the statement that "disclosure is limited to the minimum that is necessary to achieve the purpose" (APA, 2002). She would also need to review the policies of the institution in which she is working and federal and state laws regarding confidentiality of medical and mental health information, in addition to checking for state laws specifically addressing the confidentiality of an individual's HIV status. Some states directly prohibit medical professionals from revealing the HIV status of a client to anyone, including identifiable potential victims (VandeCreek & Knapp, 1993). The institution's legal counsel and ethics committee would be able to provide information regarding relevant laws and institutional policies.

The therapist would also need to reflect upon the role her personal values might play in her ethical deliberations. For example, her personal distaste for a man who would place his wife at risk for contracting a deadly disease could cause her to give greater weight to her concern for the welfare of her client's spouse than to her regard for his welfare and confidentiality. The therapist's conscious awareness of her subjective value biases can help her to evaluate her judgments even more critically and thereby minimize the role of her personal feelings in this rational, objective decision-making process.

It would also be prudent for the therapist to consult with colleagues to get their opinions of the situation and to see whether similar issues have arisen in the past. The methods that have been used to deal with previous complex situations involving confidentiality issues might be helpful to her, as would inquiring about colleagues' level of satisfaction with those solutions.

Suppose the therapist obtained the following information regarding this case:

Her client informed her that he is reluctant to tell his wife about his HIV status because he fears that his medical condition, coupled with the fact that he is hospitalized for a substance abuse problem, will cause her to leave him and take the children. He knows that his wife will be expecting him to have sexual relations with her when he goes home on his pass and that, if he brings home condoms, "she will know something is up" because he never uses them. He believes that his spouse would probably assume that he had acquired a sexually transmitted disease as a result of an affair he was having at the hospital (in which case she would also be likely to leave him). Although he reports that his wife is aware of his intravenous use of cocaine, she associates HIV infection with heroin use and has never said anything about his potential exposure to the virus.

The therapist finds that the marriage has been a troubled one, mostly because of her client's substance abuse. He feels very strongly that his wife and family are "the best thing in [his] life," and he does not want to do anything to jeopardize the relationship further. At present, lying about the situation appears to him to be his only viable option.

The client understands the seriousness of the issue of possible infection, but he believes it is very unlikely that a woman would be infected by one episode of intercourse. He reported that his wife has never contracted a sexually transmitted disease, so there would be no additional risk factors increasing the probability of her contracting the virus from him. She is using an oral contraceptive, so he is not concerned about her becoming pregnant. He believes that it will be easier to tell her of his condition when he is back at work and living a drug-free life. When the therapist asks the client how his wife will feel then about having been exposed to the virus on this pass, he thinks a moment and replies, "I'll tell her I only just found out about it a few days ago."

The client does not believe that canceling the pass is a viable option because he has been told that he must appear in person to sign important legal papers to ensure that his family continues to receive financial support during his rehabilitation.

When the therapist raises the issue of perhaps having his spouse come to the hospital so that they can tell her about his HIV status together, or doing so by telephone, he insists that now is not the time. He inquires about the confidentiality of the information. The therapist replies that although confidential information cannot generally be disclosed without the client's consent, exceptions can be made to "protect the client/patient, psychologist, or others from harm" (APA, 2002, 4.05). He is very disturbed by her statement and says that he would sue her and the hospital if any such disclosure were made.

Though the therapist has difficulty obtaining precise medical information regarding the probability of his spouse acquiring the virus through unprotected sex, the reports she accesses indicate approximately a 1 in 10 infection risk for a single episode of intercourse (Downs & De Vincenzi, 1996). Also, repeated exposure to the virus, even if an individual is already infected, may cause further damage to the individual's immune system (Aronow, 1993).

The therapist is told by the hospital's legal counsel that there is no institutional policy to cover such a situation and no federal or state statute, beyond those protecting client confidentiality in general, that specifically prohibits revealing a client's HIV status. Her colleagues all agree that this case involves an extremely difficult ethical judgment. One colleague points out that the therapist does not know for certain that the client's spouse is not already infected; in fact, he may have acquired the virus from her. (The therapist and the rest of the staff had assumed that he acquired the virus through intravenous drug use involving shared needles.) Another colleague points out that the client has only been hospitalized for two months. Since he was living with his wife prior to entering the hospital, she may well have already contracted the virus from him. (The client subsequently tells the therapist that he and his wife had been having sex only occasionally, approximately twice each month during the six months prior to his entering the rehabilitation program.) The general feeling expressed by the therapist's colleagues is that this is a very complicated issue, and she should continue her attempts to get her client to agree to disclose his HIV status to his spouse. Her colleagues would support a decision to deny the client a weekend pass if he refuses to tell his wife about his medical condition, but they are less certain about whether the circumstances would justify violating the fundamental therapeutic principle of confidentiality if the therapist decided to inform his wife herself without her client's consent.

Step 3: Secondary Appraisal of Ethical and Legal Considerations Involved. Based on all of the information obtained in Step 2, the therapist would still have good reason to believe that respect for her client's autonomy is an important ethical consideration. Whether or not to tell his spouse about his condition is a very important and personal decision. To deny him a pass or to reveal his HIV status to his wife herself would be extremely parentalistic and clearly inconsistent with Principle E (Respect for People's Rights and Dignity) of the "Ethical Principles" (APA, 2002).

She also agrees with her colleagues that protecting her client's confidentiality is a very important consideration. Violating his confidentiality could have a very negative impact on his family life and personal welfare. It could also interfere significantly with his recovery from substance abuse. If he lost his family, the additional stress resulting from the loss of social support and sense of meaning in his life would certainly increase the risk that he would resume his drug use and perhaps develop a permanent distrust of mental health professionals.

Nevertheless, the therapist is still quite uncomfortable about the threat to his spouse's welfare that will continue to exist if she is not told about his HIV status. In addition, the prospect of potentially having two parents who are HIV-positive would pose a serious threat to the welfare of the client's children.

Step 4: Metaethical Deliberations Regarding the Relevance of Ethical Considerations. First, is respect for the autonomy of the client a relevant ethical consideration in this case? Respect for the autonomy of clients is fundamental to the regard mental health professionals have for them as *persons.* Denying a client's right to self-determination is contradictory to the Kantian emphasis of the "Ethical Principles."

Concern for the client's welfare is also a relevant consideration because it, too, is grounded in the professional's respect for clients as persons. Mental health professionals have an obligation to avoid harming a client, or any other person, whenever possible. In this case, it is certainly possible that the client could be harmed if the therapist were to disclose his HIV status to his spouse without his consent.

Concern for the welfare of the client's spouse and children is also definitely a relevant ethical consideration because her physical well-being is threatened very directly by the combination of her husband's unwillingness to inform her of his HIV status and his refusal to practice safe sex or abstain from sexual contact with her.

Finally, the confidentiality of information pertaining to the client's treatment is also a relevant ethical consideration. Like respect for the client's autonomy, this duty is also based on the professional's regard for her client's personhood and subsequent right to privacy. Although disclosure of confidential material without a client's consent is permitted under certain specified circumstances (APA, 2002, 4.05), it is still unclear whether this case constitutes a legitimate exception to a therapist's obligation to maintain confidentiality.

Because there are multiple relevant, competing considerations in this case, the matter cannot be resolved at this point. A genuine ethical dilemma exists. Further deliberation is required.

Step 5: Metaethical Deliberations Regarding the Resolution of the Ethical Dilemma. In Step 4, each of the competing considerations in this case were deemed to be relevant, so the therapist must now review them again to determine their relative importance to this case. This task requires that she understand, on a metaethical level, why each of the considerations is regarded as important by people in general, that is, how each consideration improves the quality of human life.

For example, why is the confidentiality of clients regarded as such a fundamental value by mental health professionals? Confidentiality is valued because of clinicians' regard for clients' personhood, which is generally thought to entail the right to privacy. Also, physicians and mental health professionals have long recognized the importance of confidentiality to successful diagnosis and treatment of human suffering. Clients are only willing to reveal their innermost thoughts and feelings when they are secure in the belief that their therapist will never reveal the information to others inappropriately. Therefore, disclosure without the client's consent, although permissible in some circumstances, threatens one of the fundamental precepts that enables psychotherapy to work.

Respect for clients' autonomy (which is also based on the fundamental ethical value of respect for personhood) entails allowing clients to make their own choices in life. For the most part, it is not considered ethically appropriate to interfere with another person's right to choose, even when the choices made are irrational. Many people are hesitant to become involved in psychiatric treatment or psychotherapy because they fear that when they reveal their problems, "They'll lock me up!" Respecting and preserving the autonomy of clients is the only means of counteracting this impression.

The importance placed on respect for a client's personhood also extends naturally to the principle of nonmaleficence, that is, that no harm should come to the client as a consequence of what he or she discusses in a therapy session. Viewed from this perspective, it becomes evident that the principle underlying the therapist's duties to protect her client's confidentiality and to preserve his autonomy is the same regard for personhood that underlies the duty of nonmaleficence: the obligation to avoid harming her client *and,* in this case, his spouse.

When viewed from a metaethical perspective, the three distinct ethical principles of confidentiality, respect for autonomy, and concern for the welfare of others funnel down to one fundamental ethical value: respect for personhood. Although these metaethical deliberations have simplified matters considerably by reducing the multiple ethical considerations to one fundamental ethical value, there is still a conflict between the therapist's regard for the personhood of her client and that of his spouse, who is at risk of serious harm. The fact that this situation has such significant potential consequences for his spouse entails that the therapist's obligation to protect her from harm is certainly every bit as important as her duty to protect her client.

Given these considerations, the source of the ethical dilemma in this case is that disclosing or not disclosing her client's medical condition to his spouse is likely to harm one or both of the people involved. She can protect her client from the negative impact of disclosure, while respecting his autonomy and preserving his confidentiality, but only by putting the physical well-being of his spouse at considerable risk. To sacrifice her well-being to the "higher" duty of preserving the client's confidentiality would be to show a lack of regard for his spouse as an autonomous person. She would be treated as a "thing," a means to the end of protecting the client's confidentiality.

Metaethical reflection reveals that the duty to protect a person's life is clearly more fundamental than the duty to preserve confidentiality, since protecting a person's life is a prerequisite if one is to have any additional duties to value the individual's personhood in other, more specific ways. All available evidence indicates that the threat to the spouse's life is sufficient to override the duty to preserve the client's confidentiality and the therapist's concern about more ambiguous threats to her client's welfare. Her duty to protect the life of her client's spouse represents her most fundamental duty in this situation.

Step 6: Tertiary Appraisal of Ethical Considerations—Generate Options and Estimate Consequences. Two options available to the therapist that have already been mentioned are respecting her client's confidentiality by taking no action or informing his spouse of his HIV status if he declines to do so. Taking no action would demonstrate appropriate respect for her client's personal autonomy and confidentiality but is unacceptable because it totally ignores the consideration of concern for the welfare of his spouse, which was demonstrated in the previous step to be the most fundamental ethical duty in this situation. Although the immediate impact of taking the pass without informing his wife would not likely be negative for the client, he certainly could face problems in the future should his wife test positive for HIV or develop symptoms of AIDS. The client's stated willingness to keep his condition secret from his spouse in spite of the risk of infecting her with the virus would cause the therapist to question very seriously the truth of any subsequent statement on his part that he would inform his wife prior to engaging in any sexual activity. Unfortunately, among the diagnostic criteria for Antisocial Personality Disorder in the *DSM-IV-TR* is "deceitfulness, as indicated by repeated lying, . . . or conning others for personal profit or pleasure" (American Psychiatric Association, 2000, p. 706). The risk to his spouse that would result from trusting him to tell her of his condition while on a pass would make such an option extremely problematic.

On the other hand, informing the client's wife of his medical condition without his consent gives priority to the concern for her welfare but completely discounts the importance of the client's confidentiality and autonomy. Nevertheless, based on the deliberations in Step 5, this option would appear to be ethically defensible. In providing the information, the therapist could also discuss her client's fears about how his spouse would react to the news and provide her with accurate information regarding the implications of his condition for their relationship, possibly reducing the probability of her abandoning the client and the relationship precipitously. However, the therapist will have violated her client's confidentiality and refused to permit him to determine his own course of action in dealing with this highly personal trauma for himself and his family. His wife may still end the relationship. Furthermore, the client may well refuse to continue treatment for his substance abuse disorder with the therapist or any other mental health professional, feeling that therapists cannot be trusted.

Another option is that the therapist could, in consultation with the director of the unit, decide not to allow her client to leave the hospital on a pass. If he does not leave the hospital, he cannot harm his spouse. His confidentiality would not be violated, though such an action would not be consistent with the principle of respect for the client's autonomy. As stated earlier in this chapter, buying additional time to deliberate about complex ethical situations whenever possible is a sound practice. However, this option would not necessarily solve the problem. She would need to be prepared to address his likely response of requesting immediate discharge from the hospital. He would not qualify for involuntary commitment, so she would face the same decision all over again, except that now her client's substance abuse treatment would likely be at an end.

Alternatively, she could minimize the disclosure of confidential information and protect the client's spouse from harm by notifying local public health authorities of her client's HIV status (Chenneville, 2000). She could then delay his pass until health authorities have had a chance to interview her client and warn his spouse (without mentioning her client by name) that she might have been exposed to HIV. However, she would be dependent on the efficiency of public health authorities in contacting the spouse before her client takes his pass. If the spouse realizes that her husband would have been the only possible threat of exposure for her, the potential risk to her client arising from her reaction to the news remains an important issue. On the other hand, if the client's wife believes she could have been exposed to HIV in another sexual encounter, she might be afraid that if she suddenly insisted on his using a condom when he came home on a pass, he would discover her infidelity.

As was stated earlier, the process of generating options to resolve an ethical dilemma should be viewed as a creative activity, one in which a professional attempts to devise a solution that is consistent with the fundamental ethical duty in the situation (i.e., protecting the life of her client's spouse), but that also reflects, to the greatest extent possible, the other ethical considerations present (i.e., her client's confidentiality, his autonomy, and her concern for his welfare), without totally disregarding any of the relevant considerations.[6] Remember that, as discussed in Chapter 4, practical wisdom is a matter of giving each consideration its due (Wallace, 1988). None of the previous options incorporate each of the conflicting considerations involved in this case.

Is there a way that the therapist can avoid putting her client's spouse at risk without violating his confidentiality or showing a lack of regard for her client's autonomy? If the therapist decided to use the 10 days prior to the scheduled pass to discuss the situation further with her client in the context of psychotherapy, she would show respect for his autonomy by helping him to make an informed, reasonable decision. She would not be compromising his confidentiality. She could express her concern about his welfare by addressing his fears and anxieties relating to both his HIV status and his spouse's possible reaction to learning of his condition. She would also have the opportunity to discuss her ethical concern about ensuring the physical well-being of his spouse. The therapist's emphasis in these sessions would be on her responsibility to protect the well-being of his spouse, just as she has always sought to preserve his. The value and importance he places on his relationship with his spouse suggests that he certainly does not wish to harm her. To harm her would be self-defeating because it would preclude her being able to provide the support he says that he so desperately needs from her. Second, it would be essential that he attempt to look at this situation from his spouse's point of view, as the therapist has done. Were he in his spouse's place and she the one with the virus, would he not want to be told? The client needs to understand that the respect and concern that he expects from the therapist are also considerations his wife is equally deserving of. Furthermore, since it is possible that his wife may have already contracted the virus, it is essential to her health that she be informed, so she can be tested and receive information regarding treatment of her condition, just as he has been receiving at the hospital.

The outcome of these discussions might be that he would decide to inform his wife of his condition, which would address the risk to his spouse without impinging on his confidentiality or autonomy. However, the therapist should point out that dealing with such a traumatic, intense issue will be extremely stressful for both of them and should be done in a therapeutic manner. Telling her while on a pass would likely produce an emotional confrontation between the two of them that could increase the probability that his spouse would react in an extreme manner, perhaps by leaving him. If this were to occur while he was on a pass, it would dramatically increase his susceptibility to resorting to drug use to deal with the stress he would experience.

With these considerations in mind, the therapist could suggest that the client arrange for his wife to come to the hospital to meet with both of them, so the matter could be addressed therapeutically. If she were unable to come to the hospital, the issue could be addressed in a three-way conference call, or the pass could be postponed until his wife was able to visit the hospital. His decision to inform his spouse regarding his medical condition together with the therapist would address the issues of preserving his autonomy and confidentiality. Also, the therapist would be assured that she has protected the spouse's well-being and would have an opportunity to talk with the spouse about the client's welfare (e.g., his need for his wife's support with his medical difficulties and his substance abuse disorder).

Step 7: Make a Decision. Based on the deliberations described above, the therapist must decide on a course of action that she will actually follow. As a result of having worked her way through each step of this decision-making process, she will have acquired adequate information to make an informed decision.

The fundamental ethical consideration in this situation was demonstrated to be the therapist's concern for the physical safety of her client's spouse. However, she also wanted to preserve her client's sense of personal autonomy, his confidentiality, and his welfare and well-being. Consistent with these concerns, she might decide to suggest to her client that the two of them inform his wife of his HIV status together prior to his taking a pass, so the information can be disclosed and discussed in a therapeutic manner, with the therapist available as an informational resource and source of emotional support for both him and his spouse.

The least desirable outcome would be if her client refused to inform his spouse or insisted that he would handle the matter himself while on pass. As stated earlier, such an option would be ethically unacceptable because the therapist would have no way of verifying that the client had informed his wife and that his wife was not in direct physical danger. The therapist would have to explain to her client the reasons why such a plan would be ethically unacceptable to her. He would need to understand that, while he had several options available regarding how the two of them could inform his wife of his HIV status, as a mental health professional she feels ethically obligated to protect the wife's well-being by making certain that the wife is informed. If he is not ready to tell his wife, the pass would need to be denied. If he insisted on immediate discharge, the therapist would tell him that his wife would need to be informed of his HIV status prior to his discharge. The client would then be free to reevaluate his options.

Step 8: Document Rationale and Decision-Making Process. Throughout the ethical decision-making process, the therapist should document carefully the steps she has taken to address the situation. This documentation demonstrates her awareness of the issues involved; the information that she used to make a decision, including her contact with the legal representative of the hospital and her consultations with colleagues; the content of her sessions with her client regarding the matter; and the reasoning behind her final decision (and for rejecting other options she considered). The dates and names of the people with whom she had contact would be an important part of the documentation of her decision-making process.

Documenting the case carefully as it unfolds, though time consuming, is considerably easier than attempting to reconstruct the sequence of events from memory six months later, should the decision be reviewed. Furthermore, documentation completed at the time of an event will generally be regarded as a more accurate reflection of what occurred and will provide additional evidence of the conscientiousness, sensitivity, and professional competence the therapist displayed in addressing this difficult situation.

SUMMARY

Two major shortcomings of professional ethical codes are (a) that the codes cannot provide specific guidance regarding the ethically appropriate course of action in every circumstance a professional might confront and (b) that the codes do not provide a method for resolving situations in which two or more codified ethical principles seem to conflict. The model of ethical decision making presented in this chapter provides mental health professionals with a framework for reasoning more effectively when attempting to resolve complex ethical problems. In addition, employing this model will increase professionals' sensitivity to the presence of multiple ethical considerations in situations that arise in the course of their professional activity. Thus, the model will not only help professionals to resolve ethical conflicts, but it will also enable them to foresee and avoid potential conflicts that might otherwise catch them off guard.

The fundamental premise underlying this model is that the ethical complexity of a situation must be assessed initially, then continually reassessed in light of new information obtained and the progress of decision-making deliberations. Each time the ethical considerations involved in the situation are assessed, professionals must determine whether a conflict exists. If no conflict exists, they should make a decision regarding a course of action. If a conflict exists, they must go through additional steps involving gathering information and conducting metaethical deliberations. This process will enable professionals to generate viable options, estimate the likely consequences of each option, and arrive at a decision, which they will have documented as being the most rational alternative available in the case. The model for ethical decision making was demonstrated in the example of an inpatient substance abuse client with HIV who requests a weekend pass to visit his family and attend to personal business.

NOTES

1. Obviously, the ethical implications of this or any other scenario will vary in different contexts. If the question were asked during an initial counseling interview, the client might be viewed as requesting information relevant to his or her decision to proceed with counseling with you. The issue of the potential influence of therapist values on clients will be discussed in Chapter 6.

2. Therapists can work to increase their awareness of their personal and professional values through self-study programs like the one developed by Vachon and Agresti (1992), which is discussed in Chapter 11.

3. The existence of a legal statute addressing the situation may or may not eliminate the *ethical* conflict. In some instances, a law may be incompatible with a professional's ethical duty. This type of situation will be addressed in Chapter 13.

4. Unprotected sexual behavior is the primary source of concern because available evidence indicates that living with an infected person does not place one at significant risk (e.g., VandeCreek & Knapp, 1993).

5. This type of situation is addressed more specifically for counselors in the *Code of Ethics*. However, the ethical issue is not resolved because counselors are told that they "may be justified in disclosing information to identifiable third parties" concerning diseases "known to be both communicable and life-threatening" (ACA, 2005, B.2.b).

6. In some cases, it is neither possible, nor ethically necessary, to discover a solution that reflects all of the competing considerations because one duty clearly takes precedence. For example, a Tarasoff-type "duty to warn" scenario, in which a client clearly expresses the intention to kill an identifiable person, creates a situation in which the threat to human life obviously takes priority over a client's confidentiality.

Chapter 6

Ethical Issues in Psychotherapy and Counseling

This chapter will address several major ethical considerations that are fundamental to the process of psychotherapy and counseling. The encounter between the values, cultures, goals, and personal issues of the therapist and client, which is an inevitable part of any therapeutic relationship, invariably introduces a host of difficult ethical issues that test therapists' ethical reasoning skills (Cohen & Cohen, 1999).

INFORMED CONSENT

Informed consent is a critical issue in every area of professional practice (e.g., research, teaching, assessment, consultation). When clients first decide to participate in psychotherapy or counseling, they generally have a very limited understanding of what is involved. Their ideas about therapy might be based on depictions on television or in movies. At the outset of treatment, mental health professionals are obligated to provide information that will enable clients to make an informed choice regarding whether to pursue therapy. However, therapists vary considerably in how specifically they discuss the relevant issues. The fundamental areas that must be addressed in obtaining informed consent for mental health treatment are the nature and duration of the treatment (i.e., the treatment plan), potential risks and benefits associated with the treatment, confidentiality (including an explicit discussion of the limits of confidentiality), alternative treatment options (including their potential risks and benefits), and the probable effects of not pursuing treatment. Therapists are generally clearer about the issue of fees, though even in this area some details may not be addressed adequately.

The fundamental point regarding informed consent is that therapists do not ever want clients to be surprised during the course of treatment by some aspect of the therapeutic arrangement that had not been explained adequately in advance. HIPAA regulations stipulate that therapists provide a Notice of Privacy Practices to clients prior to initiating treatment, covering the therapist's policies concerning *the use and disclosure* of clients' Protected Health Information (PHI) and informing clients of the procedures used to preserve the confidentiality of this information (Privacy Rule, 2003, § 164.520). Concepts should be described in language the client understands, using vocabulary consistent with the client's level of verbal ability (ACA, 2005, A.2.c; APA, 2002, 3.10[a]; Hochhauser, 1999). Oral explanations, perhaps combined with pictorial representations of key concepts, followed by clients' oral demonstration of their understanding of those concepts, can increase clinicians' confidence that they have succeeded in obtaining truly informed client consent (Murphy, O'Keefe, & Kaufman, 1999). Taking the time needed to complete the informed consent process effectively will greatly reduce the possibility of a misunderstanding (and an ethics complaint) later.

Therapists should emphasize the voluntary nature of participation in therapy and encourage clients to act as consumers (which they are) in deciding whether to pursue therapy and in selecting a therapist (ACA, 2005, A.2.a). Most people are very careful when selecting the clothing or appliances they buy; they should certainly be just as discriminating when deciding how they want to deal with their life problems and with whom they feel comfortable discussing their innermost feelings. Therapists should emphasize that clients' task during their first meeting with a therapist is to gather as much information as possible and make sure that they are comfortable with the therapist and treatment plan before beginning therapy. A therapist can help clients to feel empowered to focus on these "consumer" considerations by asking them to think about issues such as whether they might prefer a therapist of the other gender.

CASE EXAMPLE 6.1

A counselor is contacted by an individual who says that she is interested in participating in counseling and wants to interview him to see whether she would like to pursue her journey of self-discovery with his assistance. She asks about the cost of a consultation of this type, and he tells her that his usual consultation fee will apply. She agrees and appears genuinely interested in working with him. Finally, she asks him what counseling approach he uses. He tells her that he is eclectic but generally operates from a cognitive-behavioral perspective. She responds that she is interested specifically in a person-centered approach and asks whether he would be comfortable working with her in that fashion. He tells her to come in for a consultation so they can "talk about it."

Financial Arrangements

Potential clients should be informed about therapy fees and any other financial policies (e.g., filing health insurance claims, sliding-scale fee based on family income) when they initially contact the therapist to schedule an appointment (ACA, 2005, A.10; APA, 2002, 6.04). When working in a managed care organization, therapists should inform clients of the policies affecting both fees and permitted duration of treatment. It is highly desirable for therapists to provide clients with a written copy of their fee policies at the first appointment.

Consider the following example: A counselor interested in encouraging potential clients to see whether counseling would benefit them advertises that anyone can contact him to arrange a free counseling screening appointment. The potential ethical problem with such an arrangement is that clients are encouraged to come in and discuss personal issues with the counselor at no cost, but after going through this difficult process of self-disclosure, they must pay to continue the relationship and obtain any benefit from the process. This situation could be viewed as "setting up" clients by getting them to invest emotional energy in creating a relationship at no cost, then changing the financial terms of the relationship after the client has been "hooked." This procedure is commonly known as a "bait-and-switch" among confidence tricksters.

Implications of Third-Party Payments

After obtaining clients' informed consent, the therapist should investigate their outpatient mental health coverage if they indicate they plan to use insurance coverage to pay for therapy sessions. Clients need to be fully informed about their responsibility for deductibles and copayments. In addition, if there is an annual limit for the number of therapy sessions covered by insurance, clients need to know in advance so they do not become immersed in the process of long-term therapy only to find that their insurance coverage has lapsed after 20 sessions. Furthermore, consistent with the HIPAA Privacy Rule, clients must be informed that the therapist will need to provide a diagnostic code to the insurer. Some clients are very uncomfortable with this process, fearing that their confidentiality may be threatened by the presence of a psychiatric diagnosis in their computerized insurance records. By informing them of the process, therapists allow clients to make an informed choice regarding this issue. Bear in mind that although therapists can guarantee the confidentiality of their own records, they cannot *guarantee* that information provided to an insurance company will be protected adequately. Concerned clients should be encouraged to contact the insurance company directly to learn more about the security system it uses to comply with HIPAA confidentiality regulations.

It is also important to inform clients who are interested in marital counseling or treatment for bereavement that health insurers do not necessarily provide reimbursement for treatment of life stressors.[1] Health insurers generally cover illnesses, which means that the client must be suffering from a diagnosable disorder to qualify for reimbursement. Clients can then decide whether to pursue treatment, even if insurance coverage will not be available.

Treatment Planning and Goal Setting

Clients should always be involved in treatment planning and the selection of treatment goals as part of the informed consent process. Therapists should discuss their perception of clients' needs and make appropriate suggestions regarding a treatment plan. To advance the dialogue, clients should be encouraged to provide their ideas, concerns, and questions. The outcome of these discussions should be a clear plan of action understood and agreed to by client and therapist. Having clients play an active role in treatment planning and goal setting also makes excellent clinical sense. This process will encourage clients to identify and articulate clearly their reasons for pursuing therapy as well as their hoped-for therapeutic outcomes. Also, clients are likely to be more invested in and motivated to achieve goals that they played a role in formulating. Because client motivation has been demonstrated to be a crucial determinant of therapeutic progress, including clients in treatment planning enhances the prospects for therapeutic success (Clarkin & Levy, 2004).

A therapist should be careful not to guarantee positive therapeutic results or that a problem can be solved within a specified number of sessions or time period. Offering a guarantee runs the risk of deceiving clients because there are too many variables affecting therapy outcome (e.g., client motivation) to be certain that even a well-validated treatment method will generate the desired results (Clarkin & Levy, 2004).

CASE EXAMPLE 6.2

A man seeks treatment from a sex therapist. He informs the psychologist that he is homosexual and is seeking therapy to become heterosexual in order to reduce his feelings of social alienation and discomfort. He tells her he wants to "fit in better" in society, but he has not been able to suppress his homosexual impulses effectively on his own.

Selection of Treatment Method

Therapists should discuss the methods they intend to use to achieve the agreed upon treatment goals and any potential risks associated with those methods (ACA, 2005, A.2.b; APA, 2002, 10.01). Some therapists employ a single approach with all their clients (e.g., psychoanalytic, person-centered), while others take a more eclectic approach based on their perception of the client's characteristics and the treatment issues and goals. Alternative treatments, even if they do not fall within the therapist's range of competence and would require referral, should be presented as options for the client (APA, 2002, 10.01[b]). Finally, therapists must inform clients if they intend to use a treatment of an experimental nature (e.g., e-mail therapy) or one "for which generally recognized techniques and procedures have not been established" (APA, 2002, 10.01[b]).

Treatment Risks

Although psychotherapy and counseling benefit many people, some clients are unquestionably harmed by mental health treatment (e.g., Gist & Lubin, 1999; Lambert & Ogles, 2004). For example, research has suggested that talking about traumatic memories over and over again in psychotherapy can worsen clients' symptoms of Posttraumatic Stress Disorder (PTSD); in some cases, extensive, repetitive discussion of the trauma might actually produce PTSD (Ginzburg, Solomon, & Bleich, 2002). Similarly, an avoidant client might find the communication and intimacy demands of therapy unbearable. Clinicians need to be familiar with potential risks associated with the treatment procedures they are recommending and discuss these risks with clients as part of the process of obtaining informed consent.

Psychotherapy, even when effective, tends to be a difficult emotional experience for clients, one they would likely only want to undergo in order to achieve substantial benefit. Sometimes, avoiding upsetting topics seems to work for people (e.g., Bonanno, Znoj, Siddique, & Horowitz, 1999). Therefore, clients must also be informed of the option of not pursuing treatment and the probable consequences of doing so. Eysenck (1952) was among the first to address the significant rate of *spontaneous remission* (i.e., recovery without treatment) for some mental disorders. Clinicians need to provide clients with any information available in the empirical literature regarding spontaneous remission rates for the problems they propose to treat.

CASE EXAMPLE 6.3

A clinical psychologist is the treatment coordinator for a newly admitted, female inpatient client. The treatment team meets and forms a consensus that the client qualifies for a diagnosis of Bipolar Disorder. The psychiatrist says that the client should be started on lithium. The social worker on the team says, "She's very attractive. The lithium will make her gain a lot of weight. It will ruin her nice figure." The psychiatrist says to the psychologist, "Whatever you do, don't mention that to her as a risk. After all, what's a little weight gain compared to her mental health? Besides, she can exercise." The psychologist agrees that lithium is essential to her treatment, so he decides not to say anything about potential weight gain.

Recording or Observation of Sessions

Therapists and therapists in training frequently find it useful to audiotape or videotape therapy sessions. Training clinics may also be set up to allow supervisors and trainees to observe therapy sessions remotely or from behind a two-way mirror. However, therapists are required to obtain the informed consent of clients, preferably in writing, prior to recording or observing sessions (ACA, 2005, B.6.b, B.6.c; APA, 2002, 4.03). Clients should be informed of the purpose of the recording or observation, as well as the protective measures that have been taken to safeguard clients' confidentiality (e.g., procedures for storage and erasure of recordings).

Client Access to Records and Diagnostic Information

The HIPAA Privacy Rule stipulates that clients (or their personal representative) have "a right to inspect and obtain a copy of protected health information" (Privacy Rule, 2003, § 164.524[a]). Simply put, therapists respect the autonomy of their clients, and providing clients with information regarding their condition and treatment is a behavioral indication of this respect (ACA, 2005, B.6.d). However, there is an additional reason for providing clients with access to their treatment records, which involves the issue of informed consent. Clients often sign consent forms to release their records to other professionals (e.g., physicians, health insurance, or managed care utilization reviewers); clients can only provide truly informed consent for their records to be shared with others if the clients know what information is being released (ACA, 2005, B.6.f; APA, 2002, 4.05[a]). Clients also have the right to request that a provider amend information in their record that is inaccurate (Privacy Rule, 2003, § 164.526[a]).

Historically, as discussed in Chapter 2, clients were generally not permitted to read their treatment records because of therapists' parentalistic concern that clients could be harmed emotionally by information in the record. HIPAA regulations allow professionals to deny clients access to their health records only if, in the professional's judgment, "the access requested is reasonably likely to endanger the life or physical safety of the individual or another person" (Privacy Rule, 2003, § 164.524[a][3i]). For example, a therapist might feel that a suicidal client would be harmed by receiving feedback about a recently concluded personality assessment (Cohen & Cohen, 1999). Such a judgment is subject to review, at the client's request, by an independent licensed health care professional (Privacy Rule, 2003, § 164.524[a][4]). For the most part, denying clients access to information about their treatment will only damage their trust and confidence in the therapist. Suicidal clients might want assessment feedback to find out whether the testing picked up on their intense despair. They could, in fact, be reassured by the results that their therapist does indeed understand them.

Information provided by third parties that is included in a client's record presents a difficult ethical problem. If these informants were promised confidentiality when they provided the information, therapists are ethically and legally obligated to withhold the information from their client. HIPAA regulations state that a professional's refusal to permit a client access to this portion of the record is legally permissible and not subject to external review (Privacy Rule, 2003, § 164.524.2[v]). However, an appropriate informed consent policy for these third parties (e.g., family members) would notify them in advance of the potential limitations (e.g., a court order) on the confidentiality of the information and the possibility that clients could obtain access to their records (McShane & Rowe, 1994).

Finally, clients' right to review their records also has implications for what therapists write in the record. Clients are entitled to review progress (session) notes in their health record. However, mental health professionals are *not* required to provide the informal notes they jot down during sessions; those notes are not considered part of the client's record (Privacy Rule, 2003, § 164.524[i]) as long as they are stored separately from the client's health records (Fisher, 2003). Therapists should always keep in mind that the information they record in a client's record could be read someday by the client or subpoenaed for a court proceeding. Therapists should avoid making evaluative or judgmental comments in the record and should think carefully about the implications of including information that is not directly germane to the client's treatment but could prove harmful to the client in another context (e.g., in court). Client records should be regarded as legal documents (Glancy, Regehr, & Bryant, 1998).

CASE EXAMPLE 6.4

An acutely manic client in a psychiatric hospital angrily demands to read his treatment record. He says that he is sure the record calls him "mentally ill," when the truth is that he used to be mentally ill but is not anymore. His counselor questions the value of providing her client access to his record in his present condition.

Clients of Diminished Capacity

Competence to provide consent is generally assumed unless there is clear reason to question an individual's capacity to consent (Arthur & Swanson, 1993). Some clients are deemed legally incompetent to manage their own affairs as a function of their psychiatric condition (e.g., some cases of people suffering from one of the schizophrenias or a dementia). These clients cannot legally consent to treatment. In such cases, legal consent for treatment must be obtained from a legally designated guardian or, in HIPAA terminology, "personal representative" (Privacy Rule, 2003, § 164.502[g][1]). The personal representative also must consent to any disclosure of information from the client's record.

Clients who have been deemed legally incompetent are still persons worthy of respect. They still have their own preferences and aversions, and their opinions should be respected, provided they are not endangering themselves or others. Therefore, if incompetent clients do not agree (i.e., provide their assent) to pursue treatment, their wishes should be respected, as long as the lack of treatment will not cause them or others substantial harm.

Similarly, legally competent individuals may not always be capable of fully rational decision making. The capacity to make decisions regarding one's treatment is not an all-or-none matter; it is better conceptualized as a continuum (Fellows, 1998). The capacity for rational choice must be assessed based on the client's ability to arrive at a decision through some understanding of the choices involved in a situation and the risks and benefits associated with those choices. For example, even demented clients should be encouraged to choose the foods they prefer and the activities they wish to pursue. As decisions involve greater potential risk, the requirements regarding demonstrated rational capacity should be greater. If clients wish to overrule the judgment of their treatment providers and legally authorized guardians, they will need to be capable of providing reasons why the course of treatment is not in their best interest.

CASE EXAMPLE 6.5

A recently hospitalized client suffering from Schizophrenia, Disorganized Type is experiencing severe psychotic symptoms. She becomes very agitated when approached by staff members or other clients on the unit. Her counselor decides to assign her to a private room to reduce the level of environmental stimulation and to have a staff member stay with her on one-to-one observation at all times. In her present state, the counselor decides there is no point in his explaining the treatment plan to her, so he simply implements it.

Group, Marital, and Family Therapy

In group, marital, and family therapy contexts, the informed consent of each person participating in the therapy should be obtained. Therapists must explain to each participant the nature of the therapy, their theoretical orientation, and the methods they will use. For example, in feminist family therapy, the therapist would be ethically obligated to explain to both the husband and wife the political and social assumptions that are an inherent part of the treatment prior to initiating therapy (Bryan, 2001). Full informed consent is a key element of mental health professionals' respect for the cultural values and beliefs of their clients because it enables clients to determine whether the therapist's orientation is consistent with their values and goals.

Additional guidance regarding consent issues in group, marital, and family therapy is provided in the *Code of Ethics* of the American Association for Marriage and Family Therapy (AAMFT, 1991). For instance, when a child is participating in family therapy, parental consent is legally required, and the informed assent, or agreement, of the child should be obtained as well (ACA, 2005, A.2.d; APA, 2002, 10.02[a], 10.03).[2] Also, in group therapy, release of information pertaining to the group process would require the consent of all participants in the group. The AAMFT guidelines are consistent with the APA and ACA ethical codes, though psychology and counseling do not provide as much explicit direction in these matters.

In describing the termination procedure for group therapy participants, the therapist should inform clients that they are free to withdraw from the group if they find the process is not addressing their needs and that the therapist will assist them in selecting an alternative treatment setting. Clients considering joining an existing group should be able to sit in on a group session before deciding whether to join the group as a participant.

Participants in group or family therapy should also be informed of the roles and responsibilities of the therapist and clients in the therapy (ACA, 2005, A.7; APA, 2002, 10.03). For example, when therapists function as group facilitators, they should explain that their comments will focus on keeping the group on a track consistent with its stated purpose, protecting individual clients from unwarranted attacks or unwanted intrusions into their privacy and the like (ACA, 2005, A.8.b). As with all other aspects of informed consent, this procedure will avoid unpleasant surprises for group members and will help them to understand the therapist's behavior and comments during group meetings.

CASE EXAMPLE 6.6

A counseling psychologist conducting group therapy screens each client before the client joins the group. She explains the purpose of the group as an opportunity to discuss problems and issues with other clients and to help each other deal with life problems. Although she knows that the group can be quite confrontational at times, she does not mention this point during the screening interview because the group rarely confronts new members and she does not want to scare clients about speaking up in the group.

CONFIDENTIALITY

The ethical duty to preserve clients' confidentiality is grounded in therapists' respect for clients' intrinsic value as persons and is supported by federal and state law. Clients must be confident that their therapist will keep information confidential if they are to feel comfortable revealing intimate information about their lives to the therapist. Unwarranted violations of confidentiality represent the single greatest threat to the practice of mental health treatment. As a result, HIPAA regulations require "covered entities" to designate a "privacy officer" responsible for ensuring that the confidentiality of clients' PHI is protected (Fisher, 2003).

Therapy should always be conducted in a private setting designed to minimize the chances that a therapeutic exchange will be overheard. A client's mere participation in therapy or counseling is confidential information, as is the nature and content of the client-therapist interaction. Unfortunately, no office setting is 100% secure. Also, therapists should be extremely careful about discussing confidential matters with clients on the telephone. They should inform clients of the security risk involved in telephone conversations, particularly when wireless phones are used (Masi & Freedman, 2001).

Whenever clinicians contemplate disclosing confidential information about a client, it is a good practice to ask themselves three questions (Smith, 2003a). First, has the client consented in writing to this release of information (Privacy Rule, 2003, § 164.508)? Second, on what ethical or legal basis am I making this disclosure? Third, have I limited the information disclosed to the minimum necessary to achieve the purpose of the disclosure (ACA, 2005, B.2.d; APA, 2002, 4.04)? When PHI is disclosed for any purpose other than treatment, payment, or health care operation, clients have a right to request an accounting of the disclosures, including the purpose of each disclosure and the information communicated (Privacy Rule, 2003, § 164.528). Informed consent concerning the release of PHI would require that the client know specifically what confidential information is being released and to whom (Privacy Rule,

2003, § 164.506[b]). In reference to the issue of the capacity to consent discussed earlier, a client must be competent to provide consent in order for the release to be ethically appropriate.

CASE EXAMPLE 6.7

A psychologist is employed in a college counseling center. He has been working with a 22-year-old student for six months. She told him that her mother had referred her to the counseling center. His client's mother calls and asks him to give a message to her daughter when she comes in for her appointment that day.

A therapist should never discuss a client with anyone not directly involved in the client's treatment. When working in a hospital or clinic, the content of therapy sessions should not be revealed to anyone who does not have a direct need to know. For example, if an inpatient client has expressed suicidal intentions during a session, it would be appropriate to discuss the matter with the supervisor of the nursing staff on the unit, in addition to noting the problem in the client's chart. However, therapists should not be gossips, talking about clients routinely with other staff. Also, it is unethical for therapists to tell their spouse about their clients, even if they are completely certain their spouse would never reveal the information to anyone else.

Therapists sometimes present case material in public lectures, classes they teach, or publications. They have an ethical duty to make certain that the clients being discussed cannot be identified from the information provided. This goal is generally accomplished by disguising any identifying information (ACA, 2005, B.7.d; APA, 2002, 4.07). Therapists should exercise particular care when discussing case material gathered in their clinical work in a small town because demographic data (e.g., age, gender, marital status) might be sufficient for some people to identify a client. The therapist should disguise data pertaining to clients so thoroughly that even their family and closest friends are not able to identify them. In the rare instances in which it is appropriate to provide a client's true identity, the client must first review the material to be presented and consent to being identified (ACA, 2005, B.7.e).

Privilege

Confidentiality is a therapist's professional duty, grounded in individuals' legal right to privacy. *Privilege* is a legal right of clients to prevent a professional from revealing confidential information as a witness in a legal proceeding (e.g., civil court case). Privilege resides with the client, and the therapist has an obligation to protect this right, meaning that privileged communications can only be revealed when clients consent to "waive" their right to privilege. Before releasing confidential information, therapists should always try to obtain the client's consent in writing (Anderson, 1996). When clients do waive privilege, professionals are generally compelled to reveal the information, even if they do not think it is in the client's best interest. In legal proceedings involving a client, professionals should resist a subpoena by claiming privilege on behalf of their client if their client does not want them to testify.

The existence and scope of legal privilege in communications between mental health professionals and their clients varies from state to state. Some states do not recognize privilege in psychotherapy relationships at all, some acknowledge privilege in civil cases only, and some recognize privilege between therapists and clients in both civil and criminal matters (excluding homicide). Interestingly, the United States Supreme Court has recognized psychotherapist-client privilege in civil proceedings in federal courts (*Jaffee v. Redmond,* 1996). Although the case involved a social worker, the ruling referred to "psychotherapists." Therefore, the holding is likely to apply to psychologists and counselors as well (Remley, Herlihy, & Herlihy, 1997).

Moreover, legal privilege generally does not apply to marital, family, or group therapy because, from a legal standpoint, information revealed in a context in which more than two people are present is not considered confidential (Anderson, 1996). Clients should be informed of the possibility that legal privilege might not exist in a multiple-client therapy context.

Limits of Confidentiality

Although confidentiality is an extremely important ethical duty in psychotherapy and counseling, there are contexts in which legal statutes require or permit disclosure of confidential information by therapists, independent of the consent of their clients. These legal duties, which vary from state to state, constitute limitations on clients' confidentiality. These limitations must be discussed with clients as part of the process of obtaining informed consent for treatment so that clients will understand any potentially negative consequences of revealing personal information to their therapist (ACA, 2005, B.1.d; APA, 2002, 4.02). This duty is consistent with therapists' respect for their clients' autonomy and right to self-determination.

Therapists may, for example, disclose confidential information to protect their clients or others from harm. If a client reveals an intention to kill someone, a plan to commit suicide, or reports episodes of injuring his children while punishing them physically, the therapist may be ethically (and, generally, legally) obligated to violate the client's confidentiality and inform the proper authorities. The duty to warn was discussed in Chapter 2 in relation to the Tarasoff case. When therapists are legally permitted or required to disclose confidential information, they should normally discuss the situation with the client prior to making the disclosure so the client will understand the justification for their action.

CASE EXAMPLE 6.8

A counselor reassures a client at their initial meeting about the confidentiality of their interactions, but fails to inform him about the limits of confidentiality. During the course of the counseling, the client becomes increasingly depressed and suicidal. He calls his counselor to tell her he is going to kill himself and that she should not feel responsible. She asks him to come in for a session; he refuses. She tells him she will need to call the police if he does not agree to let her intervene. He tells her she cannot do that because it would be a violation of his confidentiality. She does notify the authorities, and they intervene before he makes any attempt to harm himself. He then files an ethics complaint against her for violating his confidentiality.

Confidentiality Issues in Marital and Family Therapy

In marital and family therapy, therapists must inform clients that information discussed in the therapy sessions could be discoverable in divorce or child custody proceedings (Margolin, 1998). Therapists must also consider how they will handle individual interactions with clients that occur outside of the therapy sessions. For example, suppose a woman participating in marital therapy calls the therapist between sessions and reveals that her lack of effort in marital therapy is due to the fact that she has formed a new romantic attachment, about which her spouse knows nothing. She asks the therapist to keep this information confidential, since he is her therapist. The therapist believes that this information is extremely important for the husband to know but feels constrained from telling him by his duty to preserve his other client's confidentiality.[3]

Marital or family therapists might deal with the matter of confidentiality proactively by suggesting to the participants during their first meeting that it is undesirable for them to hide anything from each other because honesty and open communication is vital to improving their relationship. Therefore, any conversations one of them has with the therapist must be brought up at the beginning of the following session (ACA, 2005, B.4.b; APA, 2002, 4.02[a], 4.02[b], 10.02). This proactive approach prevents any negative surprises for therapists, like the marital therapy client's unanticipated disclosure, which, without previous discussion of confidentiality limits, the therapist would be obligated not to reveal to the husband (ACA, 2005, B.4.b).

CASE EXAMPLE 6.9

During a marital counseling session, the participants are discussing a series of violent confrontations in the marriage in which the husband "went off" on his wife in a jealous rage, with no apparent provocation. The couple is separated currently, and the wife has indicated that she is ready to file for divorce. The counselor strongly suspects that the husband's violent outbursts are the result of cocaine abuse. He wonders whether he should bring this matter up in a session or speak to the husband privately. He fears that raising the possibility of the husband being a substance abuser might lead the wife to file for divorce immediately.

Confidentiality Issues in Group Therapy

Therapy modalities involving multiple, unrelated clients raise additional issues concerning confidentiality. Although the therapist's duty not to disclose confidential information to persons not involved in the treatment does not change, a question arises regarding the duties of clients to one another. For example, if a client in group therapy discusses a personal issue during a session, are other members of the group free to reveal the information to family and acquaintances after the session has ended? Are members of the group permitted to discuss what went on during the session in smaller groups if they go out for coffee following the session?

These issues, like all complex ethical matters, are best dealt with proactively, before they arise, by explicitly discussing the limits of confidentiality with all group members (ACA, 2005, B.4.a; APA, 2002, 4.02[a], 4.02[b], 10.03). For example, the therapist might recommend that all members of a therapy group agree not to discuss the content of the sessions with anyone outside the group. Group members can also be encouraged not to reveal each other's secrets by informing them that they could be expelled from the group for violating agreed-upon confidentiality rules or could potentially be sued by another group member (Roback et al., 1996). However, the therapist cannot guarantee to clients that group members will actually maintain confidentiality, so clients must be warned that information they reveal in the group could be disclosed by other group members to people outside the group.

The confidentiality of group members should also be protected by maintaining individual treatment records for each client. Therapists should avoid identifying or discussing any other group members in a client's record because the other members would not be involved in consenting to the release of the client's record. As indicated earlier, interactions in group therapy settings are not generally considered privileged communications, since other people were present and heard the interaction. Thus, therapists could be compelled to testify about the content of group therapy sessions.

When group therapy clients are concurrently involved in individual therapy with the same therapist, the ground rules regarding the confidentiality of interactions in the two contexts should be clarified in advance. Clients should be assured that the therapist will never reveal anything discussed in individual therapy sessions to other members of the group, but clients are free to do so, if they wish. Of course, the possibility always exists that the therapist could mistakenly reveal something about the client in group therapy, thinking the client had discussed it previously in that setting. When group members are participating in individual therapy with another therapist, both therapists are obligated to maintain confidentiality unless the clients provide written consent for the two therapists to consult with each other regarding their treatment.

Confidentiality Issues in the Maintenance and Disposal of Records

Therapists are required to maintain confidential records concerning their clients' treatment (ACA, 2005, A.1.b; APA, 2002, 6.01–6.03). Keeping careful records promotes the efficiency of treatment by facilitating review of treatment progress and jogging therapists' memory of the content of previous meetings prior to the next session. Records are also an important means of communicating information about clients to other professionals from whom they might seek treatment.

CASE EXAMPLE 6.10

A 26-year-old client is brought to a psychiatric hospital by his parents. His mother meets with the psychologist on the unit, while his father helps him to get settled. The mother tells the psychologist that her son suffers from schizophrenia and that he has become totally unmanageable at home. He has assaulted her husband and threatened her. She says that he cannot return to their home because they are worried about having him in the house with their 14-year-old daughter. The mother asks the psychologist to keep all this information confidential. The psychologist agrees and says that they will work on a plan to discharge her son to a community care facility when he is ready.

Two weeks later, the client is doing much better, and the psychologist meets with him to discuss a discharge placement. Using his medical record, she reviews his progress and medication regimen with him. Then, the psychologist leaves the room to get a list of community care facilities. When she returns, the client is very agitated and says he does not want to talk anymore. Thirty minutes later, the psychologist receives a call from the client's mother. She says he called home and cursed her for saying he would rape his sister. His mother accuses the psychologist of violating her confidentiality. The psychologist tells her that she revealed nothing of their conversation. She wonders how the client found out about his mother's disclosure.

HIPAA regulations require a health record to be maintained for six years "from the date of its creation or the date when it last was in effect, whichever is later" (Privacy Rule, 2003, § 164.530[j][2]). If a state statute in the professional's jurisdiction mandates a longer retention period, the professional must abide by the state law. In the absence of other regulations, APA recommends that complete records be kept for seven years, which exceeds the current requirement of any state (APA Committee on Professional Practice and Standards, 1993). In addition, many states require that medical records for minor clients be maintained for the specified time period *after* the clients reach the age of majority (e.g., 18) specified by that state. Therapy notes, which are generally *not* a part of a client's record, can be destroyed at any time.

Two additional records maintenance issues that clinicians must address are what to do about outdated information in clients' records and how to dispose of records without compromising clients' confidentiality. Clinicians are obligated to protect their clients' welfare by keeping records that could potentially benefit their future treatment. Conversely, client welfare considerations require that clinicians protect their clients against the risk of being harmed by outdated or unneeded data in their records (APA Committee on Professional Practice and Standards, 1993). Outdated material most often pertains to assessment data that are no longer relevant to a client's present functioning. However, clinicians should reflect carefully before removing any information from a client's record. With regard to the disposal of records, when the legally appropriate time period has passed, clinicians are responsible for disposing of records in a manner that preserves the confidentiality of clients. Shredding paper records prior to disposing of them is common practice.

Today, many client records are kept in the form of computer files. In fact, enforcing the highest standards of confidentiality in the electronic transfer of records was the major purpose of HIPAA (1997). The use of computerized records does not diminish professionals' responsibility regarding the preservation of client confidentiality (ACA, 2005, B.6.a; APA, 2002, 6.02[a]). When working in a clinic, hospital, or other organizational setting, clinicians have a duty to make certain that the organization has developed an effective security policy to protect computerized records. Coding records, rather than putting clients' names in the computer file, and setting passwords for access to confidential records are useful means of protecting clients' confidentiality (APA, 2002, 6.02[b]).

Finally, though it is not a pleasant thought, all professionals, especially private practitioners, should make arrangements for some responsible party to take charge of their client records in the event of their death or severe incapacitation (ACA, 2005, C.2.h; APA, 2002, 6.02[c]). Failure to do so could compromise clients' confidentiality or harm them by preventing access to those records by professionals who treat them in the future.

MULTIPLE RELATIONSHIPS

A multiple relationship exists whenever clinicians engage in a social or professional relationship with clients, or someone closely associated with or related to the client, prior to initiating therapy, during the course of therapy, or subsequent to the termination of the therapy relationship (ACA, 2005, A.5; APA, 2002, 3.05[a]). Therapists who provide treatment for a neighbor, hire a current client to repair their roof,[4] provide both individual and group therapy for a client, or have their tax return prepared by a former client are engaging in a multiple relationship. Such relationships, particularly sexual relationships, are a major source of ethics complaints and malpractice suits against therapists (APA Ethics Committee, 2004; Strom-Gottfried, 1999). Similarly, therapists who are also college or university faculty members should not provide treatment for their students, the families of their students, the intimates (e.g., friends, romantic partners) of their students, people likely to become their students (e.g., non-psychology majors at the same institution), or fellow college or university employees.

Multiple relationships, no matter what their nature (e.g., sexual or social), are potentially ethically problematic because they can affect a therapist's professional judgment and thereby the welfare of the client. Conflicts of interest occur in multiple relationships when the therapist's sole interest is no longer the welfare of the client in the therapeutic relationship (Pope, 1991). For example, if a psychologist were treating a neighbor, she might be uncomfortable allowing him to explore his dissatisfaction with his wife during the session due to her friendship with the woman.

The complications introduced by a multiple relationship are also one of the reasons mental health professionals are encouraged to avoid bartering arrangements (ACA, 2005, A.10.d; APA, 2002, 6.05). For instance, if a client agrees to repair a therapist's roof in exchange for receiving therapy, until the client has completed the roof repairs the therapist might be reluctant to report to the appropriate authorities that the client seems to be abusing her children. Multiple relationships can also compromise clients' independence of judgment and action. In the example just discussed, even if the client in the bartering arrangement were dissatisfied with the progress she was making in therapy, she might feel that she could not change therapists because she had already started the roofing job on her current therapist's residence.

Of course, there are also significant disadvantages associated with a cash exchange system, even though it is the preferred method of payment according to the ethical codes. Therapists might be reluctant to take a clinically indicated action that could result in the termination of a client who has been a good source of income. Furthermore, the choice to selectively restrict bartering arrangements for mental health services can be viewed as another instance of mental health professions imposing the values of the dominant American culture on clients operating from different cultural contexts (Pedersen, 1997). Discouraging the practice of bartering has the greatest impact on rural and less affluent groups, as well as others living in cultural contexts in which money is not the only medium of exchange. Unfortunately, these groups are already traditionally underserved by the mental health professions. "The emphasis should be more on fair and equitable exchange rather than the particular . . . medium of exchange" (Pedersen, 1997, p. 27).

Therapists sometimes provide individual therapy to clients they are seeing concurrently in marital or group therapy. Although these are both professional relationships (and, in that sense, do not technically involve multiple roles), seeing a client in two settings does introduce ethical complications. A group therapy client might feel compelled to accept the therapist's offer of individual therapy, rather than provide truly voluntary informed consent. Moreover, clients will tend to develop a stronger, more intense transference to a therapist they see in two settings (Glass, 1998). Therapists might also relate differently to a group therapy client that they see concurrently for individual therapy because they know the client more intimately. This dynamic can negatively impact the group process. In addition, the therapist might unwittingly violate a client's confidentiality by mistakenly mentioning an issue that had been raised in individual therapy. For all of these reasons, and a number of others, it is generally ethically undesirable to form multiple therapeutic relationships with a client. If a group therapy client could benefit from individual therapy, an appropriate referral should be made. In any case, recruiting group therapy clients for individual therapy, or vice versa, *appears* to involve a conflict of interest: specifically, therapists' desire to expand their income by filling additional client hours (Glass, 1998).

Multiple relationships cannot always be avoided, particularly by clinicians practicing in a small town (Catalano, 1997). Some relationships develop purely out of coincidence, as when the checkout clerk at the grocery store happens to be a client (Pearson & Piazza, 1997). The "Ethical Principles" recognizes this pragmatic reality but emphasizes nevertheless that such relationships are to be avoided or handled in a professional, therapeutic manner because of their potential for harming clients.

Consider the following example: A psychologist in private practice in a small town advertises a receptionist position in the local newspaper. A former client, who had completed treatment two years earlier, calls her about applying for the job. The psychologist knows that her former client is an extremely capable person. She also believes that the woman's experience as a client would make her particularly sensitive to the feelings and needs of clients she would encounter in the office. She invites the woman for an interview and, following a frank discussion of the potential difficulties of working as employer-employee after having been in a therapist-client relationship, decides to hire her for the position because the benefits seem to outweigh the potential risks.

There are many reasons why a former client would want to work for her therapist, but it is clear that the relationship would be quite different from a normal employer-employee situation. There would be considerable potential for the former therapy relationship to affect the employment relationship. The former client might want to talk about current issues in her life with her employer. She might even feel that now there would be nothing wrong with having a social relationship with the psychologist because employees and employers are often friends. Furthermore, the psychologist might take advantage of the new relationship to pay her former client less than she would pay another receptionist of equal ability, knowing that her former client will not insist on being paid more. The bottom line is that therapists should avoid multiple relationships because of the possible harm that can result to clients. Even in a small town, the psychologist can find another receptionist.

CASE EXAMPLE 6.11

A counselor's wife is picking up her daughter from school one afternoon when she happens to meet another parent who is waiting for his own daughter. At the end of a nice conversation, the counselor's wife feels that the two families might have a lot in common, so she takes the opportunity to invite them to dinner the next evening. When the counselor comes home, his wife tells him about her encounter and their dinner engagement the next night. The counselor slowly realizes that the wife in the couple coming to his house for dinner is one of his clients

Sexual Relationships With Clients

Erotic contact between a therapist and client includes any behavior that is primarily intended to arouse or satisfy sexual desires (Holroyd & Brodsky, 1977). It is obvious to any mental health professional that engaging in such behavior with a client is unprofessional and unethical (ACA, 2005, A.5.a; APA, 2002, 3.08, 10.05). A number of studies have suggested that sexual involvement between a therapist and client is extremely likely to harm the client (e.g., Luepker, 1999; Pope & Bouhoutsos, 1986; Somer & Saadon, 1999). Some researchers have labeled the harmful effects on clients "therapist-patient sex syndrome," consisting of a set of symptoms overlapping components of both Posttraumatic Stress Disorder and Borderline Personality Disorder (Pope, 1989).[5] There is also evidence that people who were sexually abused as children might be somewhat more likely to become involved in sexual relationships with their therapist in their search for a trustworthy protector, resulting in another experience of victimization (Luepker, 1999; Pope & Bouhoutsos, 1986). Unfortunately, indications are that sexual intimacies between therapists and clients, though rare, still occur (Thoreson, Shaughnessy, & Frazier, 1995; Thoreson et al., 1993; Williams, 1992). Male therapists are much more likely to report having had sexual contact with clients than female therapists (Thoreson et al., 1995). The typical offender is a reputable male therapist working alone in a private practice (Somer & Saadon, 1999).

The only way to reduce unethical sexual behavior between therapists and clients is to provide therapists with better training in preventing such incidents from developing (Hoffman, 1995; Plaut, 1997). The context of individual psychotherapy or counseling is extremely intimate and commonly arouses romantic feelings, both on the part of the client (transference) and the therapist (countertransference). Therapists need to acknowledge such feelings when they occur. Feelings are not the problem; inappropriate behavior is. When strong countertransferential feelings exist, therapists should consult a supervisor or colleague for assistance in resolving them. The fact that sexual boundary violations are more likely to occur in private practice, where therapists are working alone, means that private practitioners should take the initiative to seek out collegial supervisory relationships in order to have a forum to discuss issues of this sort.

CASE EXAMPLE 6.12

A recently divorced clinical psychologist in private practice is treating a 25-year-old man for depression. He is very active sexually, and the psychologist finds herself encouraging him to talk more and more in their sessions about his sexual trysts. She rationalizes the discussion of his sexual behavior as an opportunity to address his self-esteem issues. She is also very stimulated by his detailed descriptions of sexual encounters. He is aware of her divorce and offers to cook her dinner some night because she must miss having home-cooked meals and someone to talk to.

Like most ethical problems, the violation of sexual boundaries occurs gradually, so timely action on the part of a therapist who acknowledges a boundary issue with a client can prevent a sexual relationship from developing. Therapists are much more likely to violate professional boundaries when they are experiencing personal problems, particularly in their own intimate relationships. The resolution of boundary problems might involve therapists seeking therapy for themselves. In some instances, referring the client to another therapist might be in the client's best interests, but this decision should be made professionally, based on what is best for the client's welfare, after due consideration of all of the issues. Clients should be informed of the reasons for the termination and the ethical rationale for taking that course of action.

In some cases, a client's romantic transference can be the starting point for an inappropriate sexual relationship between therapist and client (Somer & Saadon, 1999). Therapists must handle a situation like this very carefully. First, therapists should be careful about non-erotic physical contact with clients, as these gestures can be misinterpreted as a desire on the therapist's part for greater physical intimacy. Second, therapists should be sensitive to the possibility that clients can, and often do, form a romantic attachment to their therapist. Third, when clients express romantic feelings toward therapists, therapists should express that they feel flattered but should firmly explain that such a relationship could never occur for professional and ethical reasons, based on the potential harm that could result for the client. It is also useful to explain to clients that it is natural for them to experience such feelings in therapy; after all, it is a very intimate situation. Therapists can point out that clients are not responding to them as individuals so much as to their professionalism and the concern they show as therapists. Clients should not expect the communications they have in relationships outside of therapy to involve the same level of selfless concern that therapists express toward their clients. Therapists might point out that they themselves behave quite differently when they are not conducting therapy, focusing on *their* interests rather than solely on the concerns of others.

The professionals who interact with victims of therapist sexual exploitation have an ethical obligation to report the colleague's ethical violation to an appropriate authority, such as a state licensing board or institutional authorities (ACA, 2005, H.2.c; APA, 2002, 1.05), provided the reporting would not violate a client's confidentiality, and to encourage the victims to pursue ethical and/or legal action against the unethical therapist. Therapists must resist the desire to protect their colleagues by covering up unethical behavior (Quadrio, 1994). Incredibly, in one study, 18% of the victims of therapist sexual misconduct were subsequently revictimized by another professional (Luepker, 1999). It is *never* permissible to exploit a client. Also, no matter what the client might do to encourage such a relationship, the therapist will virtually always be held responsible when ethics complaints or malpractice suits are filed; there are no excuses. More than 15 states have created statutes that make a therapist's sexual exploitation of a client a form of criminal sexual misconduct (McMahon, 1997).

Relationships With Former Clients

There is some confusion among mental health professionals regarding when an individual's status changes from that of "client" to "former client" and how this change affects the appropriateness of multiple relationships (Mattison, Jayaratne, & Croxton, 2002). Clearly, multiple relationships with former clients should also be avoided because of the inequality inherent in such relationships due to the individuals' former roles as therapist and client. Such relationships have the potential to harm former clients and to become exploitative. In addition, such a relationship can be harmful by precluding the possibility of resuming the therapeutic relationship at some future date if the client desires additional treatment. Sexual relationships with former clients are much more common than with clients currently in treatment. In one survey, 7% of male counselors acknowledged sexual contact with former clients (Thoreson et al., 1993). These relationships are forbidden under any circumstances for a minimum of two years for psychologists and five years for counselors following the termination of the therapeutic relationship (ACA, 2005, A.5.b; APA, 2002, 10.08). The APA Ethics Code Task Force that prepared the current revision of the "Ethical Principles" reportedly recommended that sexual relationships with former clients be prohibited absolutely, no matter how much time had elapsed since the therapeutic relationship ended (Martin, 1999). However, ultimately this recommendation was not adopted (APA, 2002, 10.08). While it seems curious that the ethical codes of psychology and counseling do not forbid these relationships without exception (Gabbard, 1994), suppose a client who participated in two sessions of group therapy with a therapist meets him years later after she has completed her own clinical training. Would a relationship between the two of them necessarily be inappropriate because she had once been his client? Even in such unusual circumstances, the burden of proof would always be on the therapist to demonstrate that the relationship was in no way harmful to the former client, exploitative, or indicative of unprofessional conduct during the prior therapy. Therapists are well-served to never entertain the possibility of becoming involved sexually with a former client, no matter what the circumstances.

Multiple Relationships Among Group Therapy Clients

Group therapy clients sometimes form multiple relationships by developing friendships, or even romantic attachments, with other group members. The issues involved in client-client multiple relationships should be discussed at the beginning of the group. Therapists should point out that outside relationships between group members can complicate the group process as much as a therapist-client multiple relationship. Two group members might develop a tendency to "gang up" on another group member they feel is critical of one of them. They might defend each other against being confronted by group members or the therapist, rather than focusing on making sure they each work on their personal issues in the group. These dyadic relationships, which can play out in many different ways in the group, tend to be extremely harmful to the group process. Therefore, group members might be encouraged to agree not to form outside relationships for the duration of the therapy group.

CASE EXAMPLE 6.13

Following a group therapy session, the psychologist is invited to go out for coffee with the members of the group. He decides to go, feeling that it will enhance his rapport with the group members. When they meet at a local diner, he realizes that three of the group members are not there. He asks about them, and someone says that they had left before the idea was suggested. The therapist immediately begins to feel uncomfortable, fearing that the other three group members will think they were excluded. He wishes he had not accepted the invitation.

CONFLICT OF INTEREST

Mental health professionals try to improve the welfare of their clients while also respecting their autonomy as persons. A *conflict of interest* exists when additional motivations affect the objectivity of therapists' professional judgment. Multiple relationships are the most common source of conflicts of interest. For example, if a counselor who is a college faculty member accepts a referral from the president of the college to treat a member of her family, the therapist might be concerned with how the outcome of the therapy will affect his chances for promotion to full professor, in addition to his concern about the welfare of his client. His judgments in conducting the therapy might be less objective than usual because of his concern about impressing the president with the quality and brevity of the therapy.

Clients frequently choose to bestow gifts on their therapist around the holidays. Permitting clients to express their appreciation by giving their therapist a small gift (e.g., a book) is certainly appropriate. To refuse the gift on the grounds that theirs is a "fee for service" relationship would embarrass and demean the client and misrepresent the nature and depth of the therapeutic relationship. However, if the gift becomes something more substantial (e.g., a set of golf clubs), therapists might feel indebted to the client in a way that could affect their decision making regarding issues that arise in therapy. Large gifts should be refused politely and therapists should explain their professional duty to avoid a potential conflict of interest.

COMPETENCE

In Chapter 2, the ethical duty of competence was said to involve professionals' understanding of their strengths and limitations, both of which are extremely important to the practice of psychotherapy. Therapists' strengths (i.e., areas of professional competence) enable them to help a client with problems that fall within their area(s) of expertise, while their awareness of their limitations prevents them from potentially harming clients by attempting to work with populations or problems outside the range of their professional training and experience. Competent professionals act in accordance with the fundamental ethical principles of beneficence and nonmaleficence.

The minimum standards for competence as a psychotherapist or counselor are established by national professional organizations and state licensing boards. They involve a process of academic training and supervised experience resulting in professional licensure. However, mental health professionals' licenses do not specify what types of clients (e.g., adults, children, adolescents, families, couples) they are qualified to serve, the types of problems they are competent to treat (e.g., adjustment disorders, personality disorders, mood disorders), or the specific interventions (e.g., behavioral, psychodynamic) they are competent to use. Therapists are ethically obligated to restrict their practice to the client populations and intervention techniques with which they are qualified to practice based on their academic background and supervised clinical experience (ACA, 2005, C.2.a; APA, 2002, 2.01). In other words, the matter of determining one's competence is left largely to the ethical and professional integrity of the individual professional.

Competence With Multicultural Client Populations

Behavior is learned and enacted within cultural contexts. Even the ethical codes of the North American mental health organizations were developed within the context of the dominant, white, North American culture (Pettifor, 2001). Therefore, mental health professionals must exert considerable effort in recognizing and endeavoring to transcend their cultural assumptions if they wish to develop the ability to understand the cultural context of their clients' behavior in order to assist them with appropriate, effective interventions (Pedersen, 2003). Why is the development of multicultural competence important? The fundamental ethical duty of beneficence obligates mental health professionals to strive to help those in need. Clearly, the mental health needs of ethnic minority groups are not being met effectively at present. These groups have much higher dropout rates from mental health treatment and are less likely to use mental health services than white clients with comparable psychiatric problems (Lefley, 2002). Poor, ethnic minority clients typically do not feel understood by white, middle-class therapists representing the values of the majority American culture.

The issues and challenges involved in treating diverse populations vary considerably, depending on the client group involved. Working with children and adults, Hispanics and African Americans, or male and female clients clearly involves different cultural competencies (Hall, 1997). Therapists first need to develop an awareness of their own culturally based beliefs and biases (APA, 2003). In other words, therapists should avoid assuming that everyone views the world the way they do (Pedersen, 2001). This increased cultural self-awareness is a prerequisite to developing sensitivity to the cultural differences they will encounter in relationships with clients from diverse cultural backgrounds (ACA, 2005, A. Introduction; APA, 2002, 2.01[b]). Multiculturally competent therapists recognize and value diversity. They respect individual differences based on age, gender, education, socioeconomic status, group identifications, nationality, ethnicity, religion, and disability. While most people understand that it is wrong to view women within a cultural context as inferior, they do not necessarily realize it is equally wrong to view everyone in terms of white, male, American cultural values. Therapists must develop multicultural *skills* through their training, supervised experience, and later through continuing education and consultation with colleagues to understand how the cultural context of each client they treat affects the conceptualization of the client's issues, the formation of a helping relationship with that particular client, and the selection of the most appropriate intervention techniques for assisting that client (Pedersen, 2001). One very effective method of developing multicultural competence is through cross-cultural training, which provides professionals with an opportunity to immerse themselves in another culture and to experience what it feels like to be a minority group member (Lefley, 2002).

When gender, race, ethnicity, age, religion, sexual orientation, disability, language, socioeconomic status, or other diversity issues cause therapists to question their ability to competently serve a client's needs, they should seek consultation and, if appropriate, refer the client to a more competent colleague (ACA, 2005, A.11.b; APA, 2002, 2.01[b]). For instance, if a therapist's supervised experience has been limited primarily to the treatment of white college student and adult populations, it is inappropriate for him to offer services for ethnically diverse groups until he obtains diversity training.[6]

CASE EXAMPLE 6.14

An African American man, raised in a rural Southern community, consults a counselor about his children's behavioral problems. When she asks about his methods of disciplining the children, he tells her he does what his parents and grandparents had done. If a child disobeys an important moral or safety rule, he sends the child out to cut him "a switch" and uses it to give the child "a good whipping." He tells her that if you spare the rod, you spoil the child. The counselor tells him that hitting children with a stick is a form of child abuse and that he will need to learn new methods of discipline, emphasizing rewarding children for good behavior rather than punishing misbehavior.

Competence With Treatment Models and Interventions for Client Problems

There is considerable variation among therapists regarding the types of interventions they are competent to provide. When therapists have not established the competencies required to treat the problem a client presents (e.g., parent-child conflict requiring family therapy), they are ethically obligated to refer the client to a colleague competent in that mode of therapy. Lazarus (1995) raises an interesting issue pertaining to competence in his distinction between technical and theoretical eclecticism. Technical eclecticism involves the selection of specific intervention techniques (e.g., systematic desensitization) that are documented to be among the most efficient methods for helping clients resolve specific problems (e.g., phobias). Theoretical eclecticism involves using different theoretical models, or conceptualizations of human behavior, in working with different clients. For example, a therapist who conceptualizes a male client's anxiety problem as a manifestation of an Oedipal fixation and another client's anxiety as an existential difficulty with confronting the reality of death is practicing theoretical eclecticism.

Lazarus (1995) argues that technical eclecticism, assuming that it is based on adequate training and experience, is a particularly effective method of helping clients. Technically eclectic therapists will be able to adapt their interventions to provide each client with the methods that have been demonstrated to be the most effective means of solving the client's problems. Theoretical eclecticism, on the other hand, is criticized by Lazarus as leading to confused, incompetent therapy practice. To practice competently, therapists need to develop a stable, consistent model for conceptualizing human behavior that can guide their work with clients and the selection of techniques to address specific problems.[7]

Finally, there has been a movement in recent years in clinical psychology to encourage practitioners to limit their interventions to "empirically supported treatments" (e.g., Kendall, 1998; Sanderson, 2003). This focus on empirically based quality control of psychotherapy practice has been driven, in part, by the pragmatic demand of managed care reimbursement systems for clearer justification of the procedures used by health care providers (Sanderson, 2003). This pursuit of greater accountability for the effectiveness of psychotherapeutic interventions is a laudable initiative, consistent with the principles of beneficence and nonmaleficence. However, critics of this initiative have argued that although emphasizing empirically supported intervention techniques sounds good in theory, in practice it is a wrongheaded approach. They point out that relationship variables account for a greater percentage of the variance in the prediction of successful therapy outcome than specific treatment techniques (e.g., Norcross, 2001). In addition, a recent meta-analytic study pointed out that two thirds or more of psychotherapy clients studied suffered from more than one diagnosable problem (i.e., comorbidity), which calls into question the practical value of studies establishing the efficacy of interventions for treating single disorders (Westen & Morrison, 2001).

CASE EXAMPLE 6.15

A psychologist in a small town is treating a woman for depression. It becomes apparent to him that a major issue in the client's depression is her lack of interest in her sexual relationship with her husband. For several years, she has not been able to become aroused sexually, and it has caused her to feel that she is letting her husband down. She consulted her gynecologist, who told her that the problem is psychological and recommended therapy for her sexual dysfunction. The psychologist wants to refer her to a competent sex therapist, but there are no therapists with this specialization within driving distance.

Developing New Areas of Competence

Over time, therapists will frequently expand the range of populations they serve and the services they provide by obtaining additional education, training (e.g., continuing education workshops), and supervised experience in new therapy methods and techniques (ACA, 2005, C.2.b; APA, 2002, 2.01[c]). For example, therapists who provide individual therapy for adults might decide they would like to be able to offer marital therapy or conduct group therapy. Developing a new area of competence is not unlike training in a new area of specialization (Conger, 1976). Therapists should not offer new treatment services without first obtaining adequate training, including supervised experience. "On the job" training without adequate supervision in a new area of expertise is never ethically acceptable because it would involve a risk of providing less than competent services to a client.

Maintaining Competence

Mental health professionals are also required to *maintain* an appropriate level of professional competence (ACA, 2005, C.2.f; APA, 2002, 2.03). Therapists are expected to keep abreast of current information by reading the professional literature relevant to their practice and participating in continuing education activities. Nearly all state boards of psychology and counseling require licensees to complete continuing education requirements for annual renewal of their license. One of the indirect benefits of requiring continuing education is that independent practitioners have the opportunity to interact and network with fellow professionals at the workshops they attend. Periodic peer supervision with fellow professionals also provides an excellent method for staying current by sharing ideas with colleagues, getting fresh perspectives on difficult cases, and learning about applications and techniques used by other practitioners. In addition, meeting with colleagues provides a needed source of social support in the very stressful lives of mental health professionals.

Counseling's *Code of Ethics* presents an additional requirement that seems essential to maintaining competence: Counselors must monitor and assess the effectiveness of their professional activity as a stimulus for self-improvement (ACA, 2005, C.2.d). All therapists could certainly benefit from careful self-evaluation of the effectiveness of their interventions with clients, based on outcome data and client evaluations. The information garnered from this assessment process could then guide professionals' selection of continuing education opportunities that would most benefit their competence.

Therapist Impairment and Burnout

Everyone goes through difficult periods in life. Therapists are no different. They develop substance abuse problems, experience difficult and painful divorces, or become extremely upset and distracted by the illness or death of a loved one. Therapist impairment occurs when therapists' personal problems spill over into their professional activity and reduce their therapeutic effectiveness. The potential for interpersonal difficulties in therapists' lives to result in inappropriate multiple relationships with clients, discussed earlier in this chapter, is an outstanding example of the potential for harm arising from therapist impairment. Therapists experiencing emotional difficulties sometimes bring their problems into the therapeutic session, rationalizing that they are making the therapist-client relationship more equitable and genuine by acknowledging to clients that they too have anxieties and fears (Slater, 2003). Unfortunately, these unsolicited revelations are far more likely to confuse and upset clients.

Therapists have an ethical obligation to recognize when they are experiencing emotional or physical problems that impact their effectiveness. They should not offer services under these conditions and should seek help with their problems (ACA, 2005, C.2.g; APA, 2002, Principle A, 2.06). When appropriate, impaired therapists explain their personal situation to clients and arrange appropriate referrals, although impaired therapists have the same obligation as every other clinician not to abandon clients (ACA, 2005, A.11.a, A.11.b; APA, 2002, 2.06[b], 10.10[c]).

A potential factor in professionals' reluctance to acknowledge and seek assistance with their own mental health problems is the fear that such an admission will have a disastrous impact on their career and professional reputation. These fears are not always unfounded (Center et al., 2003). Licensing boards and professional associations have an ethical and legal obligation to monitor the professional fitness of their licensees. Although it is imperative that professionals, like clients, be treated justly and not become victims of discrimination, fear of professional repercussions is no excuse for professionals failing to respect the interests of their clients by seeking treatment for any condition that is adversely affecting their ability to provide competent mental health services.

Therapist burnout is a form of personal impairment that has received considerable attention in recent years. "Burnout may manifest itself in a loss of empathy, respect, and positive feelings for their clients" (Skorupa & Agresti, 1993, p. 281). Therapists experiencing burnout generally perceive the demands of their work as being too much for them to handle, resulting in symptoms of emotional exhaustion, depersonalization, and feelings of reduced personal accomplishment (Skorupa & Agresti, 1993). This loss of concern for clients may be evidenced by the development of a cynical attitude toward them. As a result, therapists may become uncommunicative or irritable and uncooperative toward their clients and colleagues (Mills & Huebner, 1998). Therapists might feel that their clients do not appreciate their efforts, or they might be disappointed and frustrated by their clients' lack of progress and feel that they have failed their clients.

Burnout can result from overwork, such as carrying too large a caseload. Therapists often feel that they are spread too thin: They have so many clients that they cannot devote sufficient attention to any of them. Correlational findings suggest that practitioners with smaller caseloads are less vulnerable to burnout (Skorupa & Agresti, 1993). Also, therapists working in hospital settings are at greater risk for burnout than those in private practice; this finding could be a function of the perceived meaningfulness of conducting therapy in the two types of settings (Vredenburgh, Carlozzi, & Stein, 1999). Several studies have suggested that burnout may also relate to the degree of stress associated with a clinician's area of specialization (e.g., the stress of working with terminally ill children or trauma victims), although this correlational finding might also indicate that burnout causes therapists to report higher levels of stress (Miller, 1998; Mills & Huebner, 1998). Finally, age is related inversely to burnout among therapists (Vredenburgh et al., 1999), which is consistent with the idea that younger therapists may experience greater stress as they struggle to develop competency, manage boundary issues, and achieve some degree of professional security.

Burnout impairs one's professional competence (Skorupa & Agresti, 1993). Not surprisingly, clients rate the outcome of their therapy more negatively when their therapist displays symptoms of burnout (McCarthy & Frieze, 1999). As with other forms of impairment, it is extremely unprofessional and dangerous to the welfare of clients and the public trust in the mental health professions for a therapist experiencing burnout to fail to address the situation and continue to treat clients.

Burnout risks can be addressed by training and continuing education, providing adequate supervision and social support for therapists dealing with difficult populations, instilling a strong sense of purpose or mission in therapists, and encouraging treatment providers to recognize that they, too, need to access help when professional or personal stressors begin to build (Acker, 1999; Miller, 1998). Informal interaction with professional peers can provide an excellent outlet for discharging accumulating tension and accessing both emotional and professional support.

CASE EXAMPLE 6.16

A counselor working in a state psychiatric hospital finds that the ever-increasing volume of paperwork keeps her from devoting as much time to her clients as she would like, although she doesn't feel that most of her clients are really interested in treatment. They just come into the hospital for "three hots and a cot" when they run out of money. She complains to her colleagues about revolving door admissions and needless paperwork. Some mornings, she just can't face going to work. She calls in sick and takes what she and her colleagues refer to as a "mental health day." She dreams of the day when she will be able to establish a private practice and work with motivated clients who can really accomplish something with their lives, rather than a bunch of burned out, substance abusing inpatient clients.

RESPECT FOR CLIENTS' AUTONOMY

Although autonomy could be argued to be an American cultural value, mental health professionals simply respect a client's self-directed decisions and view of life. Conducting therapy in a manner that is completely consistent with these principles can prove quite difficult, though. First, many clients who need treatment do not enter therapy voluntarily. They are coerced (e.g., by threats of hospitalization) or persuaded to pursue therapy by family members, institutions, and therapists (Carroll, 1991). Second, clients struggling with life problems generally enter therapy needing assistance and direction. However, if therapists provide direction out of concern for clients' welfare (e.g., suggesting how clients might modify their behavior), they risk showing a lack of respect for clients' autonomy by, in essence, telling them how they should live. The principles of respect for autonomy and concern for clients' welfare can certainly conflict, most notably in cases of coercive suicide prevention and involuntary hospitalization.[8]

In all forms of therapy, therapists *influence* their clients. Influencing another person occurs in any intimate relationship and means that some aspects of the therapist's beliefs, values, or behavior "rub off" on the client. This process may be deliberate or it might occur unintentionally. Many therapists give *advice* to their clients, suggesting more adaptive ways of dealing with situations. For example, therapists might suggest methods clients can use to express their feelings assertively, rather than behaving aggressively. Another term used for this process of actively providing advice to clients is giving *direction* to clients. Therapists' use of their influence in imparting their clinical expertise is related positively to clients' perception of the effectiveness of the therapy (McCarthy & Frieze, 1999). However, whenever therapists provide direction, they need to be aware that they may be fostering passivity and dependency in their clients, which is certainly not consistent with respecting clients' autonomy (ACA, 2005, A.1.a; APA, 2002, Principle E).

CASE EXAMPLE 6.17

A single mother is participating in individual therapy with a psychologist. The therapy concerns her conflict with her 15-year-old daughter. The mother asks if she and the daughter can see the psychologist for family therapy. When the three of them meet to discuss the possibility of family sessions, the daughter says that it is difficult for her to speak plainly in front of her mother. The daughter requests individual sessions, like her mother has.

The mother appears to be very controlling and strict about her daughter's behavior, based on her religious beliefs and the traditional Italian values that adhered when the mother was a teenager. The psychologist tells the mother that the only chance she has of not losing her daughter completely is to allow her to pursue individual therapy that will enable her to better understand her mother's perspective. Privately, he wonders whether the individual therapy will promote the daughter's discontent and subvert the mother's authority, but he decides that this course of action is necessary to promote the autonomy of the daughter.

The most extreme form of potential therapist influence is *coercion*. Coercion involves forcing another to do something against the person's will by exerting pressure, either psychologically or physically. People are coerced to perform a behavior when they are put in a situation in which they have no meaningful alternative. Even though coercive interventions subvert a client's autonomy, they are sometimes employed in therapy. For example, when a therapist, acting out of concern for suicidal clients' welfare, tells them they must agree to admit themselves to a hospital for observation or the therapist will call the police to take them to the hospital, the clients are being coerced. A more subtle form of coercion might involve a therapist showing obvious displeasure with a client's behavior or verbalizations. The use of personal coercive strategies has been shown to be negatively related to clients' perception of therapy outcome and may actually harm clients (McCarthy & Frieze, 1999). Pushing shy clients to pursue relationships before they really feel ready could result in rejection and greater suffering. Also, therapists dealing with women who are in domestic abuse situations frequently urge them to muster the courage to leave. Unfortunately, many women have been murdered by their male partner because they were trying to leave.

Carl Rogers developed his person-centered approach to therapy because he believed any sort of therapist influence demonstrated a lack of regard for clients' autonomy (e.g., Raskin & Rogers, 1995). Rogers respected the autonomy of his clients by attempting to be as non-directive as possible. He believed that therapists should create an atmosphere of trust and support clients in devising their own solutions to their life problems. The Rogerian legacy has highlighted the ethically problematic nature of therapy techniques that involve deception or coercion (Cohen & Cohen, 1999). For example, some therapists employ a technique called "paradoxical intention" or "antisuggestion." A marital therapist treating a couple who argue constantly and seem unwilling to work on improving their relationship realizes that he is reinforcing their combativeness by constantly urging them to deal with conflicts calmly. He decides to offer a paradoxical intention by saying they have convinced him that their marriage has become one long battle and that the only solution is divorce. (He does not really mean this, but is hoping that his statement will cause them to rally against him for dismissing their relationship so lightly.) This type of strategy, often used by parents in old situation comedies on television, is referred to popularly as "reverse psychology." Such dishonesty with clients is certainly disrespectful of them as persons. Therapists ask clients to be completely open and honest with them; in doing so, therapists certainly incur an obligation to be genuine and honest in return.[9]

CASE EXAMPLE 6.18

A counselor encourages a client suffering from depression and social anxiety to participate in a weekly therapy group she conducts. She does not tell the client that it is an incest survivors group because she doesn't want to bias his approach to the group. She believes it is possible that her client was a victim of sexual abuse at some point in his life. After attending the group for two months, the client reports that he has been remembering how, when he was a little boy, his father would "play" with him on his bed. The group explores these memories with him, and he becomes increasingly convinced that his father had abused him. Only then does the counselor mention that she had suspected all along that he had been a victim of sexual abuse.

Respect for Client Values

Another facet of mental health professionals' respect for client autonomy and diversity is their regard for the personal values clients bring to therapy. The relationship between a therapist and a client is inherently value-laden, in that it necessarily reflects the values of each person involved. For example, the importance that therapists place on preserving their clients' autonomy represents a value position. Similarly, clients' willingness to endure the often uncomfortable process of therapy is evidence of the value they place on self-understanding and personal development. The fact that the values of all parties involved permeate the therapy relationship is not necessarily a problem; it is simply a fact.

However, this mixing of value systems (which is another aspect of multiculturalism) does raise some important ethical issues (ACA, 2005, A.4.b). Allen Bergin (1980, 1991) pointed out that at least three sets of values are present in a therapy context: those of the therapist, those of the client, and those of the community or society in which they live. The role of values in the therapy process becomes a particularly important ethical issue when these value orientations differ. There is substantial empirical evidence that therapists seem to perceive clients as having changed for the better when the client's values become more like those of the therapist (e.g., Arizmendi, Beutler, Shanfield, Crago, & Hagaman, 1985; Beutler et al., 1978; Kelly & Strupp, 1992; Richards & Davison, 1989). Although it is not unreasonable to suppose that some clients will be influenced by the values of their therapist as they work on clarifying their personal value system, value imposition is generally not an explicit goal of therapy (Beutler et al., 1978; Schwehn & Schau, 1990).

Bergin (1980) focused on the issue of religious beliefs to illustrate this point. He asserted that psychotherapists are less religious than the general population. As the therapeutic relationship develops, the approach to understanding emotional conflicts and resolving behavioral problems taken by a nonreligious therapist and a religious client may very well differ based on their personal value systems. For example, suppose a client who is a very devout religious believer is being treated for marital dissatisfaction by a psychologist who is an atheist. Bergin (1980) argued that the differences in the two individuals' values will necessarily affect the course of the therapy, even if the therapist never explicitly expresses an atheistic orientation. The psychologist might conceptualize the client's marital dissatisfaction and depression as an indication that a divorce should be considered. If the client responds that, as a Roman Catholic, divorce is out of the question, the psychologist might be inclined to view this statement as indicative of personal rigidity or a punishing superego. The fundamental difference in value orientations could not help but come into play in a variety of ways. Some might be obvious, but others could be quite subtle. As a non–Roman Catholic, the therapist would have an ethical obligation to become more familiar with the client's value system in order to better understand this religious perspective so as to work with the client more effectively (ACA, 2005, C.2.a; APA, 2002, 2.01[b]).

Bergin's (1980, 1991) concern was that clients tend to be influenced very strongly by their therapists, who are not only authority figures, but models of effective living. Therefore, when clients perceive a discrepancy between their thinking and that of their therapist, they might tend to modify their value position to bring it more in line with the "correct" perspective expressed by their therapist. He argues that therapists run the risk of subverting clients' value systems and imposing their own values on clients in their conduct of therapy. Such activity is profoundly disrespectful of clients' autonomy as individuals, which mental health professionals profess to support so strongly.

Bergin makes an excellent point. It certainly is ethically inappropriate for therapists to impose their values on clients, no matter how unintentionally (ACA, 2005, A.4.b; APA, 2002, Principle E). The issue then becomes, if value perspectives are indeed ubiquitous in therapy, how can therapists prevent or minimize the potential for their clients' value systems to be subtly influenced during therapy? Unfortunately, there is no simple answer to such a complex issue.

Bergin suggested that therapists disclose their value orientation to potential clients as part of the informed consent process prior to beginning therapy, so clients can make an informed choice of a therapist they will feel comfortable with (Bergin, 1980; Bergin, Payne, & Richards, 1996). This solution would require that therapists increase their awareness of what their values are, then determine what information they should disclose to clients concerning their personal values.[10] Clearly, clients should not be subjected to long discourses regarding the therapist's beliefs, particularly those that are not directly relevant to the client's concerns (Tillman, 1998). In addition, if clients are indeed vulnerable to being unduly influenced by the therapist's values, it might be unwise to encourage such modeling by revealing too many of the therapist's beliefs. Nevertheless, a limited discussion of the therapist's values may be appropriate when the therapist can identify areas of potential value conflict based on information provided by the client during the intake process. As discussed earlier in this chapter, therapists should talk with clients about their conceptualization of therapy and of the client's presenting problem prior to beginning therapy. This information should provide clients with a reasonable understanding of what they are likely to experience if they proceed with the therapy.

It is extremely important for therapists to ensure that the client understands that they are presenting their beliefs about certain issues because these beliefs are relevant to concerns the client raised and that they are in no way suggesting that their beliefs are correct, or "scientific," or better than the client's viewpoint (Tillman, 1998). On the contrary, they should explain that mental health professionals have great respect for individual differences and people's right to choose their own values and beliefs. They should also emphasize repeatedly that they simply want to make sure that they both understand the differences in their viewpoints, so the client can make an informed choice about whether to proceed with therapy. In taking such action, therapists are modeling genuineness and respect for the client's autonomy (Cohen & Cohen, 1999).

Value-related discussions could be initiated by therapists at other points in the therapy, as needed, to make certain that they do not impose their personal values on clients, since therapists cannot possibly know in advance which personal values might turn out to be relevant to the issues that will emerge during the course of therapy. As in all ethical matters, sensitivity to, and respect for, the client's welfare are the key components of professional, competent practice.

CASE EXAMPLE 6.19

A humanistically oriented, but not traditionally religious, psychologist is assigned an inpatient client who asks him to pray with her during a session for relief from her depression and despair.

Although Bergin (1980, 1991) argues that a therapist's religious values need to be disclosed so that the client can make an informed decision regarding whether to pursue therapy with someone whose religious beliefs are similar or dissimilar to his own, Zeiger and Lewis (1998) point out that the initial similarity of therapist and client values has not been demonstrated to be a positive predictor of therapeutic outcome. Rather, it is the moderate convergence of their values over the course of therapy that is related to therapeutic success (Kelly & Strupp, 1992). Thus, a high level of value similarity at the outset of therapy may actually impede the development of a successful therapeutic process. An important benefit of therapy is learning new ways of thinking about and responding to situations, which is more likely to occur when the perspectives of client and therapist differ.

A final difficult issue concerning the role of therapists' personal values in therapy is whether a client might present values or goals that so directly contradict the values of therapists that they would feel they cannot treat the client effectively. For example, suppose a therapist is very strongly opposed to abortion on religious grounds. What should he do if a client comes in for an intake interview and reveals that she is trying to decide whether or not to terminate an unwanted pregnancy? Therapists are never obliged as professionals to behave in a manner that violates their personal moral principles. On the other hand, a therapist should not agree to work with such a client in order to convince her not to terminate the pregnancy because intentionally attempting to alter the value perspective of a client would demonstrate an unethical lack of respect for her autonomy. If the therapist realizes he cannot view the client's situation objectively and assist her effectively due to the depth of his personal moral convictions concerning abortion, he should show appropriate respect for her autonomy by arranging a referral to another therapist. But, what if the therapist works in a rural area where referral is not a realistic option? Would this situation affect the therapist's duty to help the woman? It would certainly intensify the conflict between his concern for the welfare of the pregnant woman and his desire not to subvert her autonomy and personal values. In such a circumstance, he might benefit from using the model of ethical decision making to devise a course of action designed to serve both duties.

TERMINATION

Three reasons to end a therapy relationship through termination or referral have long been recognized as ethically appropriate (ACA, 2005, A.11; APA, 2002, 10.10). First, if clients no longer require therapy because the issues that were troubling them have been resolved, the therapy has reached a successful conclusion. Second, if clients are no longer deriving any benefit from therapy, but are perhaps willing to continue due to dependency on the therapist, termination is indicated. (If therapists believe that their client might make better progress with another therapist, the possibility of a referral should be discussed.) Third, as discussed earlier, clients are sometimes harmed by therapy (Lambert & Ogles, 2004). If the therapist believes that continuing the therapy relationship could be harmful to the client, the issue of termination or referral should definitely be addressed. New to the 2002 revision of the "Ethical Principles" is a statement that clinicians have the right to terminate the therapeutic relationship "when threatened or otherwise endangered by the client/patient" or someone associated with the client (APA, 2002, 10.10[b]).

In all other circumstances, termination or referral should not be done precipitously. When the issue of termination is raised by the therapist or client, the matter should be discussed thoroughly and the reasons for the proposed termination should be clear to both parties. Ethical therapists do not abandon clients (ACA, 2005, A.11.a; APA, 2002, 10.10[c]). In dealing with termination and referral, therapists must be careful not to let factors other than the best interest of the client influence their decision making. Therapists should evaluate carefully their motivations for considering termination in order to avoid potentially harming a client.

CASE EXAMPLE 6.20

A client's insurance runs out, and he is no longer able to pay the full fee for counseling sessions. The client is stable, but wants to continue the sessions to more fully address unresolved issues from his childhood. The counselor cannot afford to have him pay the greatly reduced fee for a regular weekly time slot due to overhead costs associated with her practice. The counselor and client agree that he can continue to attend sessions on a "standby" basis; that is, he can take the time slots of vacationing clients or clients who cancel appointments. He agrees to this arrangement in spite of having as little as 24 hours' notice on some occasions. Of course, he can decline the opportunity for an appointment if it does not fit his schedule.

PRACTICE CASE INVOLVING THE MODEL OF ETHICAL DECISION MAKING

A counselor is working with a family adjusting to the father's physical disability due to kidney disease. During the course of counseling, issues of intense sibling rivalry between the two sons emerge. In a phone conversation with the counselor, the mother reveals in confidence that she had an affair at the time her younger son was conceived and has always questioned whether her husband was the boy's biological father.

When the father learns that he will need a kidney transplant, the two sons both express a willingness to donate one of their kidneys to their father. The mother pleads with the counselor, again in a private conversation, to support her view that the firstborn son should make this sacrifice for his father. She fears that if the younger son were tested, his kidney would be deemed genetically incompatible with his father, and her infidelity (and her son's true parentage) would be discovered. She argues that such a situation would do irreparable harm to the family, her husband's health, and her younger son's emotional well-being.

SUMMARY

The ethical issues that arise inevitably in therapy are so numerous and complex that mental health professionals must be able to reason ethically if they are to manage their responsibilities competently. During the informed consent process at the outset of therapy, therapists must explain adequately all relevant issues (e.g., length and duration of treatment, limits of confidentiality) so clients do not encounter any surprises during therapy. If a client is legally incompetent to consent to treatment, a personal representative must provide consent and the client's assent should be obtained. Additional informed consent issues in group, marital, and family therapy were discussed.

Therapists' respect for the autonomy and personhood of clients is demonstrated in the importance placed on confidentiality as an essential part of the therapeutic relationship. Providing clients with access to their treatment records is also done out of respect for clients' autonomy and may actually benefit clients. In addition, clients must know what is in their record before they can consent to sharing it with another professional. Therapists should be very careful to maintain and dispose of treatment records without endangering clients' confidentiality.

Multiple relationships occur when a therapist engages in another professional or social relationship with a client before, during, or after the therapy relationship. These relationships can cause a professional's judgment to be clouded by considerations other than the client's best interests. Multiple relationships involving improper sexual behavior are a major source of ethics complaints.

Although therapists inevitably influence the thinking and behavior of their clients, the use of coercion is generally inappropriate. Therapists should be sensitive to the potential for their personal values to unduly influence clients during the course of therapy. Bergin pointed out the danger of subverting clients' autonomy by subtly imposing religious values in therapy. This controversial problem was discussed, along with proposed solutions.

Therapy should be terminated when clients resolve their problem, are no longer benefiting significantly from therapy, or are actually being harmed by therapy. Referral is appropriate if a client requires treatment but may derive greater benefit from working with a different therapist.

NOTES

1. In the *Diagnostic and Statistical Manual of Mental Disorders* (2000), life situations that may be the focus of treatment but do not involve clinically significant maladaptive reactions on the part of the client (e.g., Partner Relational Problem, Bereavement) are referred to as "V-codes." They are found in the section "Other Conditions That May Be a Focus of Clinical Attention" in the *DSM-IV-TR* (p. 736).

2. Informed consent and confidentiality issues concerning the treatment of children will be discussed in greater detail in Chapter 7.

3. In some states, if the marital therapist did maintain the woman's confidentiality by keeping his knowledge of an extramarital affair secret, he could be setting himself up for a charge of criminal conspiracy or "alienation of affection" (Cottone, Mannis, & Lewis, 1996).

4. Bartering one's professional services (e.g., a therapist agreeing to treat an individual in exchange for the client repairing the therapist's roof) was strongly discouraged by APA in the past. The previous version of the "Ethical Principles" pointed out the "inherent potential for conflicts, exploitation, and distortion of the professional relationship" in such an arrangement (APA, 1992, 1.18). Bartering should be handled with extreme care. The burden of proof that the barter relationship was "not clinically contraindicated" or "exploitative" would rest on the professional (APA, 2002, 6.05). Such arrangements are fertile ground for ethics complaints.

5. Because of the potential for sampling bias in the studies that have been conducted, it is difficult to evaluate the validity or prevalence of the "therapist-patient sex syndrome" and whether it is a causal factor or a result of the sexual relationship with a therapist (Williams, 1992). Nevertheless, there is strong agreement that clients can and have suffered considerable harm as a result of the unethical sexual behavior of therapists.

6. Unfortunately, as discussed in Chapter 2, so few psychotherapists in psychology today possess the competence needed to provide effective services to ethnically diverse clients that we run the risk of leaving these clients without adequate (not to mention equal) access to mental health services. Ultimately, the only solution to this problem is to encourage greater numbers of ethnically diverse students to study psychology and to increase the ethnic diversity of psychology faculty who can serve as models and mentors for psychology students striving to develop multicultural competence (APA, 2003; Hall, 1997).

7. Lazarus's (1995) critique of theoretical eclecticism should not be interpreted as extending to *theoretical integration,* in which clinicians integrate two or more systems of psychotherapy, not merely by combining elements of two schools of thought but by synthesizing the best elements of diverse theories in the creation of "an emergent theory that is more than the sum of its parts and that leads to new directions for practice and research" (Prochaska & Norcross, 1999, p. 464).

8. These topics are discussed in Chapter 13.

9. Paradoxical intention does have many useful applications that do not involve deceiving clients, such as encouraging clients to exaggerate a compulsive symptom in order to recognize their voluntary control of the behavior (Frankl, 1963).

10. A training model for increasing therapists' awareness of their personal and professional values is discussed in Chapter 11.

Chapter 7

Organizational Settings and Special Populations

Most mental health professionals become employees of an organization, rather than practice completely independently. Psychologists and counselors work in hospitals, universities, clinics, correctional institutions, corporations, schools, Health Maintenance Organizations (HMOs), and many other settings. In a recent APA member survey, 75% of respondents were primarily employed by an organization (APA Research Office, 2000). This chapter will examine some of the organizations employing therapists and ways of managing the ethical issues and conflicts that can arise in these professional contexts. Special ethical issues concerning the treatment of children will also be addressed.

WORKING WITHIN AN ORGANIZATION

When most people take a job with a company, institution, or government agency, they take on a straightforward set of responsibilities as an employee of the organization. However, the situation is somewhat more complex for a psychologist, counselor, or other mental health professional. These individuals already accepted a set of professional duties (e.g., ACA *Code of Ethics*, 2005) when they chose to become members of their profession; by accepting a position within an organization, they assume a second set of obligations prescribed by the employment policies and values of the organization. In the case of government-supported agencies, federal and state regulations also apply. Generally, this dual role (e.g., psychologist and HMO employee) does not create an ethical problem for the professional. However, as discussed earlier, any situation involving multiple duties or obligations has the potential for conflict.

In any organizational setting, the fundamental ethical point for mental health professionals to remember is that the ethical principles and standards of their profession take precedence over their employer's regulations and policies when the two conflict. In a situation involving an apparent conflict, professionals should use the model of ethical decision making (see Chapter 5) to devise a solution that is consistent with the employer's guidelines *and* their ethical duties as professionals. If their analysis indicates that the two cannot be reconciled, they should inform the relevant parties of their primary obligation to the ethical principles of their profession (ACA, 2005, H.2.e; APA, 2002, 1.03). For example, in some states, master's-level counselors hired by a state-operated substance abuse rehabilitation facility immediately following their graduation could be assigned to a clinical supervisor who holds only a bachelor's degree in substance abuse counseling (West, Mustaine, & Wyrick, 1999). They would need to inform the director of the facility that ACA requires that they receive supervision from a licensed professional counselor. They should not take on a holier-than-thou stance toward the supervisor or organization; rather, they should work with the organization, educating policy makers about potentially unethical institutional policies and attempting to modify and improve them. In some instances, the organization's values or policies may be so inconsistent with professionals' ethical duties that they cannot continue working there.

CASE EXAMPLE 7.1

A counselor working in the counseling center of a Roman Catholic college is treating an adult female student who reveals that she is pregnant as the result of date rape. She is extremely distraught and wants his help in obtaining information about abortion services. He is not personally uncomfortable with providing the information, but he knows that abortion is radically inconsistent with the values of the institution.

CONFLICT OF INTEREST

Conflicts of interest occur when the objectivity of a professional's judgment is affected by personal interest in a situation, usually as the result of a multiple relationship. For example, a clinician who is an employee of a psychiatric inpatient facility has an outpatient practice as well. One of her outpatient clients is severely depressed and is threatening suicide. The clinician knows of a psychiatric hospital that specializes in the cognitive-behavioral treatment of depression, but she advises the client to enter the facility where she works because he will be able to continue therapy with her. Is this recommendation in the client's best interest? Or, is it motivated, at least in part, by the clinician's desire to generate business for the facility that employs her or to retain the client for outpatient treatment following his hospitalization?

A different type of conflict of interest can develop when professionals are asked to evaluate the effectiveness of a program offered by the agency that employs them (Hammond, 1998). For example, a clinician serving as a consultant to a local Head Start facility is asked to conduct an evaluation of the Head Start program. This evaluation must be completed in order for the facility to qualify for continued federal funding. Even if the clinician has the competence in design, analysis, and report writing required for the evaluation, his vested interest in the outcome of the evaluation makes the arrangement ethically questionable (Hammond, 1998). First, the clinician undoubtedly helped to structure at least some of the facility's programs. Second, the continuation of the clinician's contract as a consultant might be affected by the outcome of the evaluation; if the facility were to lose funding or if he were judged to have conducted a poor evaluation, he would likely not be retained. This situation involves an apparent conflict of interest because the consulting clinician is not in the best position to conduct an objective, unbiased evaluation of the Head Start program. A competent evaluator who has no financial or personal stake in the outcome would be a much better choice. The clinician would be obligated to point out this conflict of interest to the Head Start director and inform the director that it would be unethical for him to conduct the evaluation himself.

When a situation does involve a conflict of interest, or has the potential to give rise to such a conflict, mental health professionals should clarify their role with all parties concerned (APA, 2002, 3.06). Specifically, they should inform the client, supervisor, student, or anyone else affected directly that a conflict exists and explain the limits they must place on their activity within the organization to avoid an unprofessional conflict of interest. Professionals should also avoid the appearance of conflicts of interest. If a situation could be perceived by other professionals or the public as a conflict of interest, the professional should avoid becoming enmeshed in the situation, even if it technically does not involve a conflict.

CASE EXAMPLE 7.2

A psychologist frequently refers clients to a psychiatrist, who happens to be her husband, for medication consultations. She does not have the same last name as her husband, and she generally does not mention that he is her spouse because she does not want clients to feel pressured to accept the referral. She refers clients to him because she thinks he is the most competent psychiatrist in the local area.

WORKING IN A PSYCHIATRIC HOSPITAL

Many therapists work with inpatients in psychiatric or medical hospitals. Inpatient therapy involves a number of special ethical issues, in addition to the ones discussed in the previous chapter. The dominant philosophy in psychiatric hospitals tends to be the *medical model,* which is the assumption that diagnosable conditions are a function of underlying, internal pathology or illnesses (Carson, Butcher, & Mineka, 2000). The dominance of biological explanations in psychiatric hospitals is not surprising, given that they are medical facilities managed by psychiatrists. One implication of this medical philosophy is that psychiatric practitioners tend to behave in a parentalistic manner toward clients, feeling that clients cannot understand (nor do they need to understand) the complex explanations associated with their conditions. Clients just need to follow appropriate medical advice. Therapists must avoid letting this organizational culture alter their perspective regarding their professional duties to clients. Respect for clients' autonomy and their right to self-determination is particularly important in such settings. Mental health professionals also have a duty to advocate for their clients if their rights are being infringed upon unreasonably.

Informed Consent and Confidentiality

Informed consent procedures for inpatient treatment are the same as those discussed in the previous chapter, including the HIPAA requirement that each client receive a Notice of Privacy Practices (Privacy Rule, 2003, § 164.520). There are also a few additional informed consent considerations relevant to inpatient settings. First, inpatient clients might not be receiving treatment voluntarily. Their family might have pressured them to enter the hospital, or they might have been involuntarily committed.[1] Therapists must make certain that their clients, including those admitted involuntarily to the hospital, understand the voluntary nature of therapy and their right to refuse to participate.

CASE EXAMPLE 7.3

A voluntary inpatient client on a dual diagnosis unit (for clients diagnosed with both a mental disorder and substance abuse disorder) requests discharge. The clinical psychologist treating her does not feel that she is ready. He talks with the client for nearly two hours, trying to convince her that she needs further treatment before she will be ready to face the world without resuming her substance abuse behavior. Finally, the client relents and agrees to stay.

Confidentiality issues are also more complex in inpatient settings. In a psychiatric hospital, the therapist will not be the only professional involved in a client's treatment. Psychiatrists, social workers, and nursing staff will also provide treatment and monitor the client's progress. As a result, information must be shared with other professionals; failure to provide the treatment team with relevant information obtained in therapy sessions will restrict the effectiveness of the client's treatment. However, therapists should only share information in team meetings or in the client's record that is directly relevant to the client's treatment. For example, the fact that the client had been arrested for shoplifting as an adolescent might not be relevant to the client's treatment for depression as an adult, whereas a report of suicidal ideation definitely needs to be brought to the treatment team's attention.

During the informed consent process, therapists must, of course, inform clients that the treatment team exists and that information regarding clients will be shared with other team members. Clients should be assured that the other members of the treatment team are also professionals who can be trusted to fulfill their obligation to protect client confidentiality (ACA, 2005, B.3.b, D.1.c; APA, 2002, 3.09, 4.06). If therapists become aware of a member of the treatment team disclosing confidential information to anyone not directly involved in the client's treatment without the client's consent, they have an ethical duty to address the breach of confidentiality with the staff member and, if necessary, with the staff member's supervisor.

In alcohol and drug abuse treatment programs, federal guidelines also govern the confidentiality of information. Therapists working in a facility of this type should become familiar with these rules, which generally place tighter restrictions on the release of treatment information. Even the names of clients pursuing treatment in such a facility cannot be revealed because, unlike admission to a medical or psychiatric hospital, entering a substance abuse treatment facility specifies the nature of clients' diagnoses (Arthur & Swanson, 1993).

Utilization Review

Psychiatric hospitals frequently receive reimbursement from insurance companies, managed care organizations, and state and federal government agencies based on clients' diagnoses. For example, a health insurance provider might reimburse a hospital for 28 days of treatment for a client diagnosed with Alcohol Dependence. If the client is discharged prior to the 28-day limit, the hospital comes out ahead financially. If a longer hospitalization is required to provide effective treatment, the hospital receives little or no additional reimbursement. Utilization review, then, is the process by which treatment facilities and health insurers monitor whether the length of clients' stay in a hospital is consistent with their diagnoses. This type of system puts considerable pressure on hospitals, and, in turn, mental health professionals, to complete treatment and discharge clients within a specified time limit. However, as always, mental health professionals' primary consideration is the best interest of their clients. Therapists must advocate assertively for their clients if further treatment is clinically indicated when their diagnosis-related length of stay has been exhausted. Therapists must be able to present documented clinical evidence to support their assertions. The hospital administrative authorities might be particularly receptive to these arguments if therapists point out the litigation risk associated with discharging a client in need of continued treatment (e.g., a potential suicide risk).

CASE EXAMPLE 7.4

A client suffering from chronic Alcohol Dependence and Borderline Personality Disorder is receiving treatment on an inpatient alcoholism unit. His counselor lists his primary diagnosis as Borderline Personality Disorder, even though personality disorders are not the focus of treatment on the unit, because this diagnosis will permit him to stay on the unit longer. The counselor believes that it is her professional duty to "work the system" whenever doing so serves the best interest of a client.

Coercion and Treatment

Some hospitals use token economies and other operant conditioning programs to improve clients' self-care skills (e.g., on wards with long-term clients suffering from the schizophrenias) and to give clients a degree of responsibility for maintenance of their environment. Clients, particularly those admitted involuntarily, must be informed that participation in such programs is voluntary.[2] In addition, mental health professionals must ensure that only privileges (e.g., special snacks, additional trips off the ward) are used as reinforcers. Basic rights of hospital clients, such as regular meals, the ability to receive mail, and the right to the least restrictive treatment setting, cannot be withheld. If hospitalized clients are asked to do work normally performed by paid employees (e.g., cleaning or painting the ward) as part of a rehabilitation program, they should be paid for the work just like regular employees. Hospitals cannot exploit clients.

CASE EXAMPLE 7.5

A substance abuse unit in a Veterans Administration Medical Center operates on the Therapeutic Community model. Inpatients on this unit are required to perform maintenance and custodial tasks as a means of holding down the cost of the program for the hospital and as a part of their treatment (i.e., taking responsibility as a member of the community for the care and maintenance of their environment). The unit's counselor also feels clients learn an important lesson regarding humility by performing these custodial tasks. In spite of his efforts, the program has not been able to obtain funding to pay patients for this activity.

MANAGED CARE PRACTICE

Most private insurance and many state-funded programs (e.g., Oregon Health Plan for Medicaid recipients) involve some form of managed care today. The goal of managed care organizations (MCOs) is to provide medical and mental health benefits for their customers in the most cost-effective manner possible (Ambrose, 1997). Among the most common MCO formats are Health Maintenance Organizations (HMOs), Preferred Provider Organizations (PPOs), and Employee Assistance Programs (EAPs). Each MCO is organized somewhat differently, with different allowable services and reimbursement schemes. Some programs only allow clients to use health care providers who are part of the managed care network, while others allow clients to use non-network providers, but at a lower rate of reimbursement. Also, many MCOs require a referral from a client's primary care physician or pre-approval through a separate review system before a client can receive behavioral or mental health treatment. What these different types of MCOs all have in common is that case management is no longer the exclusive province of treatment providers; financial managers, focusing on cost containment, are involved actively in decisions about the provision and continuation of treatment services (Butcher, 1997a).

The increased focus on accountability, intended to ensure that the nation's limited health care resources are expended for necessary, effective treatment, is a very positive aspect of managed care systems (Butcher, 1997a). However, many mental health professionals question the ethicality of MCOs, arguing that decisions regarding a client's treatment needs should be made by people who understand the client's problems and circumstances and put the client's best interest ahead of economic considerations. Mental health professionals have frequently been at odds with MCOs because they feel their professional judgments can be overruled by MCO case managers, who are constantly looking over their shoulder (Butcher, 1997a). However, professionals need to recognize that managed care is likely to exist for a long time and that viewing MCOs as enemies does not serve anyone's needs, including clients' (Ambrose, 1997).

Therapist-providers can best serve the needs of clients by learning to work within managed care systems to provide needed services in a cost-effective manner. First, therapist-providers need to become competent in brief forms of therapy. Second, prior to initiating service, they should research carefully what a client's program will allow. Finally, they should become proficient at advocating for their clients by making a concise, reasonable case to educate MCO case managers regarding the benefits to the organization and its clients of providing additional mental health services (Ambrose, 1997). For example, after spending 10 sessions working to modify a client's inappropriate, explosive interpersonal behaviors, a follow-up session or two over the next few months is vitally important to make certain that the new skills are being used effectively. An MCO that fails to recognize this need for follow up is wasting its money; the value of the 10 treatment sessions is seriously threatened by the MCO's poor conceptualization of the behavior modification process. Therapy certainly should not drag on forever, but neither should clients be denied a chance to complete their treatment.

CASE EXAMPLE 7.6

A psychologist working for an MCO is assigned a client suffering from depression. The therapist quickly determines that the client is experiencing uncertainty regarding his sexual orientation. Although the MCO strongly advocates the use of cognitive-behavioral therapy (CBT), the therapist believes that the client can only be served effectively through a psycho-dynamic exploration of significant Oedipal issues in his background. The therapist's supervisor, also a clinical psychologist, informs her that the MCO will only fund 13 sessions, so the client must receive CBT.

Providing mental health services for an MCO requires that therapist-providers sharpen their assessment skills, so they can distinguish between clients who can benefit substantially from short-term treatment and those in need of longer-term care. Therapist-providers must be competent diagnosticians and avoid the temptation to manipulate clients' diagnoses in order to provide them with the treatment they need. For example, a therapist-provider might be tempted to misdiagnose a client suffering from a complex Adjustment Disorder With Depressed Mood as a case of Major Depression because the latter diagnosis will provide a larger allotment of treatment sessions. However, the ethical end of providing adequate treatment for the client does not justify the use of unethical means (i.e., deliberate falsification of treatment records). Therapist-providers have a professional obligation to their MCO to conduct themselves with integrity (ACA, 2005, E.5.a; APA, 2002, 2.04, 9.01[a]). (Issues pertaining to diagnosis are discussed more thoroughly in Chapter 8.)

Mental health professionals working in HMOs must make certain that information they provide is not misunderstood or misapplied by other providers within the organization. For example, providing physicians with reports summarizing a client's emotional issues could contribute to the misdiagnosis of the client's physical symptoms as emotionally based (e.g., somatization). In fact, the more psychological information physicians receive, the greater the tendency might be to attribute symptoms to psychological issues (Belar, 1997). Mental health providers should consult directly with primary care physicians or provide continuing education workshops for them to reduce the likelihood that psychological assessment information will be misinterpreted.

When therapist-providers are treating both network and non-network clients, who receive different levels of reimbursement, they are obligated not to vary the care and attention provided to the two groups of clients. Therapists' agreement to accept smaller fees from network clients is no justification for treating them differently. For example, therapists would be ethically obligated to provide additional sessions needed to complete a network client's treatment, even if a higher-fee client is interested in starting therapy during the network client's current time slot.

CASE EXAMPLE 7.7

A counselor provides outpatient substance abuse rehabilitation as part of a Preferred Provider Organization (PPO). He is permitted to see PPO clients for as long as he deems necessary, but he is paid only $40 per session by the PPO, compared to the $80 fee he receives from his private clients. Most of his clients are referred to a self-help group (e.g., Alcoholics or Narcotics Anonymous [AA or NA]) after 8–10 individual sessions. Only clients requiring more intensive psychotherapy are seen for longer periods. During a review of his records to determine the average length of treatment in his practice, he finds that PPO clients are seen for an average of 8.2 sessions, while private clients are seen for an average of 15.7 sessions.

Informed Consent and Confidentiality

Therapist-providers in an MCO have informed consent obligations to both the organization employing them and to their clients. They need to make certain that their clients are aware of a clinician's duties to the MCO (e.g., to provide treatment summaries for each group of three sessions). MCOs are "covered entities" under HIPAA and are, therefore, subject to all the informed consent and confidentiality provisions of HIPAA discussed previously, including providing clients a Notice of Privacy Practices outlining the extent to which clients' PHI is shared within and beyond the organization in order to provide treatment and coordinate payment for services (Privacy Rule, 2003, § 164.520).

Prior to the initiation of therapy, providers should also inform clients about the permitted duration of treatment, the availability of alternative treatments, the option of not pursuing treatment, and the limits of client confidentiality. Confidentiality issues that might arise in providing treatment for an MCO include the sharing of diagnostic and other information within the MCO system to determine clients' need for treatment, clients' right to appeal decisions affecting access to treatment, and the types of information shared with employers (and the potential implications for clients of disclosures to their employer). Utilization reviews to monitor the need for continued treatment are part of any managed care setting.

CASE EXAMPLE 7.8

A male high school teacher is referred through an EAP because, recently, he has frequently been unprepared for his classes. His principal is concerned about him because he has been a very effective teacher in the past. The client asks his psychologist not to reveal that he had a homosexual experience with another teacher at work that has caused him to become very anxious and confused about his sexual orientation. The psychologist knows that revealing this information could cause the teacher to be fired, but she also believes it is very likely the reason he has been having so many difficulties with preparation for class.

(After considering that scenario, suppose the client had also mentioned having fantasies about some of the boys in his classes. Though he said he would never act on such ideas, the client has wondered about which boys might be receptive to sexual advances.)

Multiple Relationships and Conflict of Interest

Clients are very likely to view therapists working for an MCO as part of the system, whereas the primary concern of therapist-providers should always be the client's welfare. When health care providers work for an MCO, the potential for conflict between organizational profit and the best interest of clients always exists. Suppose a psychologist working for an MCO conducts an assessment that indicates the strong possibility of neurological impairment in a 35-year-old woman diagnosed with Major Depression. The psychologist recommends that the woman be referred for a neurological assessment. Her primary care physician makes the referral, but treatment review administrators refuse to approve the referral and request further information from the psychologist. The psychologist speaks with an administrator and reiterates the justification for the referral stated in the assessment report, emphasizing that failure to obtain the neurological assessment could be harmful to the client's health. The psychologist is notified a week later that the referral has been disapproved again. The psychologist, genuinely believing that the referral is in the client's best interest, has an ethical obligation to continue to advocate on the client's behalf in writing and to remind the MCO of its duty to provide services necessary to meet the needs of its clients. Even if the organization drops the psychologist as a service provider, the psychologist's ultimate responsibility is to the client. Mental health professionals must advocate for organizational change when clients are being treated unjustly.

A final issue concerning therapists' duties when working for an MCO is termination of treatment. When clients who are genuinely in need of continued treatment are denied additional coverage, their therapists cannot abandon them simply because an MCO case manager says that the maximum number of sessions has been reached. If advocating with the MCO on clients' behalf produces no results, therapists are obligated to either provide services on a reduced fee or pro bono basis (ACA, 2005, A. Introduction; APA, 2002, Principle B) or arrange an appropriate referral to another treatment provider (ACA, 2005, A.11; APA, 2002, 10.10).

CASE EXAMPLE 7.9

A clinical psychologist working in an MCO is only able to see clients for 15 sessions when they are diagnosed with Dysthymic Disorder. He frequently finds that his clients have only begun to address the important issues in their lives during that period. In such cases, he recommends that clients seek additional private therapy. He offers to refer them to a local practitioner or to continue working with them in his private practice at his standard private practice fee.

WORKING IN FORENSIC (CORRECTIONAL) SETTINGS

The number of convicts in the state and federal prison systems increased by 234% between 1985 and 1996. A recent study concluded that as many as 20% of inmates suffer from serious mental disorders (Butterfield, 2003). As a result, a growing number of mental health professionals provide assessment, diagnostic, and treatment services to convicts who suffer from mental disorders or mental retardation, as well as routine assessment of the general prison population (Brunswig & Parham, 2004). Crisis intervention services are also an important component of mental health services in prisons because the suicide rate among convicts is much higher than in the general population (Mobley, 1999). Forensic psychologists working in prison settings report spending the majority of their work time on administrative (30% of work time), treatment (26%), and assessment (18%) duties (Boothby & Clements, 2000).

Clients who are prison convicts are, quite literally, a captive population for mental health services. As a result, their participation in mental health treatment is never truly voluntary or completely free of coercion (Bell, 1999). This fact introduces a number of special ethical obligations for mental health professionals to protect the welfare of their clients. Correctional clinicians are also in a privileged position to contribute to the institutions they work for by using their psychological expertise to foster the development of more humane and effective prison environments (Milan, Chin, & Nguyen, 1999).

Informed Consent and Confidentiality

Mental health professionals are ethically bound to show the same respect for the rights of prisoners as for any other client. By demonstrating respect for the dignity of each convict as a person, mental health professionals may also be enhancing their therapeutic effectiveness:

Convicts are more likely to trust that the professional is truly concerned with their welfare (Bell, 1999). For example, convicts entering a correctional facility may be required to complete psychological testing, including intelligence and personality assessments. Although this testing is required, clinicians conducting the testing should nevertheless inform clients of the nature and purpose of the testing; the limits placed on the confidentiality of their interaction; clients' right to refuse testing (along with the consequences of such refusal); what, if any, feedback will be provided concerning the testing; and what use will be made of the results. Clinicians should also attempt to answer any questions posed by clients.

Similarly, when conducting therapy with a convict, therapists should make it clear that they are employees of the institution and inform the client of the nature of the therapist-client relationship in that context. Specifically, they should explain clients' right to decline to participate, prison policies regarding the length and frequency of therapy sessions, the information included in their treatment record, and who will have access to their record. Therapists working in prisons need to be aware of the combination of state and federal statutes affecting the privacy of client information so they can inform clients about the extent of confidentiality in the relationship. The confidentiality of prison records is becoming more and more limited in many jurisdictions (Arthur & Swanson, 1993). In some settings, parole boards, mental health services, and others have relatively open access to convicts' treatment records.

In group therapy contexts, clinicians need to make clients aware that other group members might reveal information to inmates outside the group. A discussion of group members' feelings about the importance of "respect" and their view of "snitching" can help clarify confidentiality issues (Mobley, 1999). Another issue that should be addressed in both group and individual therapy is the implication of therapy participation for good conduct and parole reviews, to correct any misunderstandings clients might have developed.

CASE EXAMPLE 7.10

A counselor working in a prison is told by an inmate client that another inmate has a knife and intends to stab the client's cell mate in retaliation for a previous altercation. The counselor suggests that the client tell a correctional officer, but the client tells her he fears that word would get out that he had squealed on another inmate.

Goal Setting

When working with convicts, therapists have the same concerns as with any other clients: promoting the self-determination and autonomy of clients and assisting them in resolving behavioral and emotional problems. An additional stated goal for incarcerated prisoners is rehabilitation, or developing the abilities needed to become productive members of society and avoid returning to prison (Mobley, 1999). Most clients receiving psychotherapy in prison are management problems (e.g., violent prisoners); prisoners with diagnosable mental disorders, identified upon admission and now receiving maintenance therapy; and participants in sex offender and substance abuse treatment programs. Within the limits imposed by the availability of mental health staff, convicts can also self-refer for therapy services (Mobley, 1999).

Therapists should communicate their professional purpose of helping clients deal with emotional problems, the prison environment, and reintroduction to society when their sentence is completed. Although therapy participation is not truly voluntary, as clinicians would like it to be, clients' autonomy in the situation can be maximized by involving them actively in establishing treatment goals. The goals should be consistent with the rehabilitative goals of the penal system, but they need not focus on making the client more manageable or an easier "fit" in the system. Clients are much more likely to benefit from treatment if they are motivated to achieve the stated goals (Clarkin & Levy, 2004).

CASE EXAMPLE 7.11

An inmate requesting therapy is assigned to a male counselor. In the initial interview, she says that she wants to address her long history of violence against other women. She feels strongly that she can best accomplish this goal by working with a female therapist. The counselor understands and, to some extent, agrees with the client's reasoning, yet he wonders whether the request is a manipulation that could place his female colleague at risk.

Multiple Relationships

Mental health professionals working in prisons are employees of the correctional system. As such, therapists occupy an amorphous middle ground between corrections officers and inmates and are generally viewed with suspicion by both (Mobley, 1999). Avoiding drifting too far to one side and becoming identified exclusively with one of these groups requires a very careful articulation of one's roles and responsibilities to all concerned parties.

Mental health professionals concerned with improving the prison system should be careful not to address this issue with their clients. Prison administrators will view such employees as attempting to subvert the organization's structure and may retaliate against the clients the clinicians are seen as aligning themselves with (Mobley, 1999). Well-formulated ideas regarding positive changes in a prison's operations should be presented through the appropriate chain of command. Mental health professionals should use their training to devise effective, nonthreatening ways of proposing positive change.

Therapists working with prison populations are sometimes interested in conducting research to increase society's understanding of both the causes of criminal behavior and the effects of incarceration. Prisoners are in great demand as research participants; in fact, this demand became so great that prison systems have greatly reduced researchers' access to prison populations. Therapists working in prisons should not take advantage of their position to encourage clients to participate in their research projects.

Competence

With the majority of prisoners in the state and federal prison systems being African American or Hispanic, therapists' understanding of cultural diversity and development of multicultural competence are essential for competent provision of mental health services in a prison (APA, 2003; Milan et al., 1999). As in any therapeutic context, therapists should not make assumptions about clients' cultural background based on their physical appearance; they should let clients describe their cultural background and the extent to which they identify with that culture (Milan et al., 1999). This process can help to prevent misdiagnosis and forge a better understanding of clients' life experience, leading to more effective treatment.

Prison settings also require competence in other areas. Crisis intervention is an important area of competence for dealing effectively with acts of violence and suicidal behavior (Mobley, 1999). In addition, a very large segment of the prison population is in need of substance abuse treatment (Milan et al., 1999). Providing competent substance abuse treatment requires expertise in substance abuse theory and the translation of this theory to the development of comprehensive treatment programs. Traditional rehabilitation strategies based on the disease model of addiction have proven relatively ineffective (Ford, 1996; Milan et al., 1999). Finally, competence in research methods is also needed to evaluate the effectiveness of substance abuse and other mental health programs used in prisons.

Therapists working in prisons must learn to cope with the institutional environment and the coercive reality of prison life without either withdrawing from offering needed services out of the desire to be noncoercive or becoming insensitive to the personhood of prisoners (Bell, 1999). Therapist burnout is a significant threat to competence in the prisons, as in other therapy contexts. Consequently, many therapists abandon prison work within a few years, leaving the prison system to cope with an ongoing shortage of trained forensic therapists (Mobley, 1999).

Directive interventions have generally proven to be the most effective with prisoners (Mobley, 1999). Boothby and Clements (2000) conducted a survey of correctional psychologists and found that more than half the respondents used a behavioral orientation and 40% indicated they operate from a rational-emotive (i.e., cognitive) approach. However, as discussed in the previous chapter, therapists must learn how to be directive without diminishing the autonomy of the client. Confrontation can be a very effective technique with convicts, but it is a skill that must be developed through supervised experience. Otherwise, confrontation can easily become little more than an unprofessional outlet for the therapist's own hostility.

CASE EXAMPLE 7.12

A psychologist who has worked in prisons for 15 years feels that her younger, less experienced colleagues are constantly being manipulated by the inmates. She tells them that they need to always remain aware of the type of people they are dealing with: prison inmates who would slit their own mother's throat to get something they want. Her colleagues question how effective she can be as a therapist if she has so little regard for her clients. She says that she is very effective because she confronts them every time they attempt to manipulate her. Most of her clients want another therapist because all they want to do is manipulate.

MENTAL HEALTH PROFESSIONALS IN THE MILITARY

Psychologists and other mental health professionals have been involved with the military throughout the past century. Many personnel testing methods were developed by psychologists working in the military during World War I. To this day, the armed forces remain the largest consumers of employment tests in the United States, both to screen applicants for military service and to assess job-related skills (Murphy & Davidshofer, 1994). Also, beginning in World War II, mental health professionals working in the military have become involved increasingly in the treatment of psychiatric disorders in military personnel in both peacetime and war.

An ethical tension has always existed for health care professionals working in support of the military. On the one hand, therapists working in the military are committed to supporting the goals of the armed forces and those of their individual clients. However, as mental health professionals, they also seek to support and protect the welfare of all humankind; they "respect the dignity and worth of all people" (APA, 2002, Principle E). In other words, they work to reduce human suffering (ACA, 2005, A.1.a). Some ethicists have questioned whether the ethical concerns of mental health professionals are congruent with the goals of the military, pointing out that professionals are not concerned with reducing the suffering of Americans only and that national interests do not take precedence over professionals' concern for the welfare of all people (Summers, 1992).

CASE EXAMPLE 7.13

A clinical psychologist in the U.S. Army treated soldiers during the Vietnam conflict for combat-related stress disorders. At field hospitals near combat areas, he would assess a soldier's condition initially to determine whether the soldier might regain his fitness for duty with treatment. The psychologist treated those who had the potential to function as soldiers again, with the goal of enabling them to return to combat. Throughout that period, and ever since, he has questioned whether his role as a facilitator of war and possibly the death of his clients was ethically appropriate for a psychologist.

Multiple Relationships

The dual obligations faced by mental health professionals working in the military can be particularly difficult to clarify and resolve (Hines, Ader, Chang, & Rundell, 1998). Many clinicians working for the military are actually active duty military personnel. These mental health professionals are clearly part of the military organization, usually as officers. As military officers, they have a duty to abide by their oath of military service and to obey the orders of superior officers. However, as mental health professionals, they also have obligations to their clients. Therefore, therapists in the military must constantly balance and weigh the relative importance of these two sets of duties. Suppose a psychologist working in the military was ordered by a superior officer to document that a soldier-client of hers was unfit for duty because of his depressive symptoms, though she did not consider him incapacitated. She would need to inform the officer that she has a professional duty as a psychologist to consider what is in the best interest of her client, even if it means not carrying out an order from a superior officer.

Informed Consent and Confidentiality

Therapists working in the military, like therapists working in forensic settings, must emphasize the voluntary nature of psychotherapy participation. Even when military personnel are ordered to seek psychological services, therapists should inform clients that they can refuse to participate in therapy and inform them of the likely consequences of such a refusal. Clients should also be told that the therapist will be functioning in the relationship as a mental health professional, not as a superior officer. For example, clients would never be ordered to self-disclose; what they reveal in therapy is their autonomous choice. The voluntary aspect of treatment can be augmented further by having clients play an active role in setting therapy goals.

The APA Ethics Committee published a statement on the complex issues regarding confidentiality for psychologists working in the military ("Ethics Committee Statement on Military," 1993). According to this statement, therapists must strive to preserve the confidentiality of their clients, as they would in any other setting. However, they must also abide by Department of Defense rules regarding access to information. The limited nature of confidentiality in a military setting must be explained to clients at the beginning of the therapy (ACA, 2005, B.1.d; APA, 2002, 4.02[a], 4.02[b]). Therapists should not guarantee the confidentiality of mental health records. (For this reason, therapists should also think very carefully about what they write in a client's record.) When the disclosure of confidential material is required, therapists should present the information in a manner designed to minimize the intrusion into the client's privacy (ACA, 2005, B.2.d; APA, 2002, 4.04).

Confidentiality should *not* be maintained regarding any information that could significantly affect clients' performance of their military duties. This limitation on confidentiality, resulting from a military therapist's dual role as an officer and a mental health professional, can be confusing. For example, when a senior officer requests information about a soldier-client's substance abuse history, clinicians need to weigh the importance of that information to the client's functioning as a soldier and to the welfare of her unit versus the clinicians' duty to protect her privacy. Again, clinicians must endeavor to minimize the intrusion of such disclosures into a client's privacy because revealing information about a client, even regarding diagnosis, can negatively impact the client's military career (Arthur & Swanson, 1993).

CASE EXAMPLE 7.14

A military counselor is treating the adolescent son of an Air Force pilot. The client had gotten in trouble with the military police for drinking at a party. He tells the counselor that his father is the one with a serious alcohol problem. He says that most nights his father passes out from drinking and then has a drink to get going in the morning.

The counselor tells her client that, if this is true, she has a duty as a military officer to report his father's problem to a superior officer. The client refuses to provide his consent for the counselor to violate his confidentiality, saying that his father would "kill" him if he found out about it. Then, he says that he exaggerated his father's drinking so the counselor would not make too big a deal out of his own party incident.

PSYCHOTHERAPY WITH CHILDREN

Mental health professionals encounter a number of special ethical considerations in the treatment of children. First, as minors, children generally cannot legally consent to participate in therapy. Therefore, although the child is usually recognized to be the therapist's client, the child's parent(s) or legal guardian is involved directly in the consent process. In HIPAA terms, the parent or guardian functions as the "personal representative" of the child (Privacy Rule, 2003, § 164.502[g][1]). The parents may also be involved in the treatment as clients if the decision is made to conduct family therapy or if the therapist provides parenting skills training to the parents separately from the child's sessions. Second, the legal limits of confidentiality are dramatically different for children. Third, children are even more susceptible than adult clients to being influenced by a therapist's values (Cottone & Tarvydas, 2003).

Informed Consent With Children

Informed consent for therapy with a minor must be obtained from the child's parent or legal guardian. The parents should be provided with a complete explanation of all issues pertaining to informed consent (as discussed in the previous chapter), including a thorough consideration of the potential risks (e.g., interacting with an adult they do not know well can be frightening to young children) and benefits of treatment. Alternative methods of resolving the presenting problems should be described, as well as the option of not pursuing treatment. Entities covered by HIPAA must also provide the child client's personal representative with a Notice of Privacy Practices (Privacy Rule, 2003, § 164.520).

One problem with parents providing consent for their child's treatment is that parents might tend to focus more on the potential benefits of treatment than on any risks to the child. When parents bring a child to a therapist to address a behavioral problem, they frequently just want their child "fixed" (i.e., cured). Analogue informed consent research indicates that the severity of the child's symptoms is much more salient to mothers than the balance of risks and benefits associated with treatment (Gustafson, McNamara, & Jensen, 1994).

Therapists should always discuss the purpose of the therapy (e.g., to reduce the level of conflict between the child and parents) and the methods that will be used in the sessions with the child (e.g., talking awhile, followed by playing a game the child brings to build rapport). Because children cannot legally consent to treatment, the voluntariness of the therapy should be maximized by involving them as much as their age and understanding will permit in treatment planning and goal setting. Involving children actively in treatment planning may also increase their motivation to participate in therapy, thereby reducing the likelihood of premature termination and increasing the effectiveness of treatment (Kazdin, 2004). Children who do not want to participate in therapy should not be coerced to do so by therapists (Yanagida, 1998). The limits of confidentiality, which will be discussed below, must also be described very carefully to children in a manner appropriate to their age and understanding.

In many states, there are special circumstances in which children do have a legal right to consent to treatment (e.g., if counseling is sought for physical or sexual abuse, substance abuse, pregnancy, sexually transmitted diseases, or contraception). These laws vary by state, so therapists need to be familiar with the relevant statutes in their state. In some states, adolescents can legally self-consent for psychological treatment. Also, emancipated minors are generally regarded as adults in terms of their ability to provide informed consent.

Confidentiality Considerations With Children

The major difference concerning the confidentiality of child clients is that children do not generally have the right to have information kept private from their parents. Statutes concerning the confidentiality of minors vary from state to state, so therapists working with a child client must be aware of the laws governing their practice, as well as the policies of their employing organization. In Texas, for example, therapists are not required to inform parents that their child has initiated therapy for suicide prevention; substance abuse; or physical, sexual, or emotional abuse (Texas Family Code, 2000). However, the statute does not *prevent* the therapist from notifying and involving the parents without the child's consent; the matter is simply left to the therapist's judgment of what best serves the interests of the child. In some states, the age of the child is a factor; for example, if 14-year-olds have the legal right to consent to treatment, information cannot be released to the parents without the adolescent's consent.

CASE EXAMPLE 7.15

A 16-year-old female client being treated for depression with her parents' consent tells her counselor that she underwent an abortion without the permission of her parents shortly before beginning treatment. (She resides in a state that does not require parental notification or consent prior to an abortion for a 16-year-old.) The counselor is acquainted with the parents and agrees with his client that the parents would punish her severely and kick her out of their home if they knew what she had done. On the other hand, the counselor is concerned about his ethical and legal obligations to her parents. He is also concerned that his client's therapy would be terminated prematurely if her parents discovered that he knew of the abortion.

Children, like any other clients, should be informed before confidential information is shared with anyone else, including parents, and their concerns about the sharing of information should be weighed carefully in a clinician's judgments of what to reveal to parents. Clearly, if a therapist were to reveal to the parents information their child had shared about the parents' behavior, the child-parent relationship might be negatively impacted. In general, parents should certainly be informed of anything children communicate that suggests that they could be in danger (e.g., abuse, violence, drug use, suicidal ideation).

Prior to initiating treatment, therapists should always discuss with parents the legal limitations on children's confidentiality. Some therapists point out that children may be reluctant to discuss personal issues that are affecting them after they have been informed that the information will be accessible to their parents. Parents are generally most concerned about the effectiveness of the treatment and do not want confidentiality issues to interfere with their child's full, voluntary participation. In some cases, the parents and therapist enter into a professional services agreement in which the parents allow the therapist to maintain confidentiality regarding the content of the child's therapy sessions, with agreed upon limitations, such as dangerous behavior on the part of the child (Gustafson & McNamara, 1987). The terms of the agreement are presented to the child, with the parents present, to make certain that all parties understand the confidentiality ground rules for the therapy. The agreement is then signed by the parents, child, and therapist. Parents are left with the option of changing the terms of the agreement at a later date if they become uncomfortable with the arrangement, though parents seldom, if ever, exercise this option. If they did, the child would then be informed of the changes in the conditions of the therapy to make sure the child understands that the earlier promise of confidentiality is no longer in force. Of course, the child might then ask to terminate the therapy.

CASE EXAMPLE 7.16

A 14-year-old white client reveals to his counselor that he is secretly dating a classmate of a different race. He feels very positively about the relationship, but says his parents would never allow it if they knew. The counselor is uncertain about what she should do.

Termination With a Child Client

Parents often decide that their child's therapy ought to be terminated, regardless of the advice of the therapist and the feelings of the child. A therapist working with a child is obligated to urge the parents to allow an orderly ending to occur, so the child will not experience the termination of the relationship as abandonment (Yanagida, 1998). In other situations, parents simply do not implement the treatment plan (e.g., a behavior modification program) at home, even though the critical importance of consistency in the child's environment was stressed to the parents when the treatment plan was developed. If the parents are subverting the effectiveness of the treatment by not following the therapist's advice, the therapist should point out the limited value of continuing the therapy (Yanagida, 1998). On the other hand, terminating the relationship might eliminate the child's only opportunity to interact with a concerned, caring adult figure. Therapists must attempt to determine what is in the child's best interest in this type of situation.

Mandatory Reporting of Child Abuse and Neglect

In all 50 states, mental health professionals, like other professionals, are obligated to report suspicions that a child has been or may have been abused or neglected to state or local law enforcement personnel or a legally designated child protective agency (Kalichman, 1999).[3] Any person making a good faith report is generally protected against civil or criminal liability, should the report turn out to be false. Different forms of abuse (i.e., sexual, physical, and emotional) and neglect are covered by mandatory reporting laws.

Sexual abuse involves a person using a child to achieve sexual gratification. Sexual abuse of a child can range from watching a child undress or bathe, to masturbating in the presence of a child, to acts of oral, vaginal, or anal penetration. In many states, sexual behavior between minors would also constitute statutory rape (although the difference in the ages of the two participants is often a factor), thus requiring mandatory reporting by mental health providers (Findholt & Robrecht, 2002); this issue presents a significant consideration for professionals working with adolescents.

The prevalence of child sexual abuse is difficult to determine; prevalence studies are generally thought to underestimate rates of abuse. Recent national survey data indicate that 15.3% of girls and 5.9% of boys have been victims of sexual abuse (Swenson & Hanson, 1998). Only about 10% of all cases involve a stranger as the perpetrator of the abuse.

Physical abuse is physical injury to a child that harms the child (in some states, producing visible marks is the criterion), or the genuine threat of such injury. *Mental* or *emotional abuse* is emotional injury to the child that impairs the child's development or psychological functioning. Failure to prevent the abuse of a child can also be grounds for charges of abuse. *Neglect* can involve several different scenarios: leaving a child alone, leaving a child in a situation where the child is exposed to a significant risk of physical or emotional harm, not protecting the child's interests (e.g., leaving a child with caretakers who are known to be abusive, ignoring a serious medical problem), or abandonment (i.e., leaving a child with the intent not to return). In 1999, more than 800,000 children were victims of child abuse or neglect in the United States (Rovi, Chen, & Johnson, 2004).

It is extremely important that child abuse and neglect be identified and stopped and that both abuser and victim receive treatment. Child deaths resulting from abuse have increased dramatically during the past 20 years (Kalichman, 1999). Moreover, children, adolescents, and adults who were once victims of child abuse and neglect experience an increased incidence of depression, anxiety, posttraumatic stress disorder, alcohol abuse, interpersonal problems, and indiscriminate sexual behavior, as well as higher levels of anger, aggression, and suicidality (Briere & Elliott, 1994; Brown, Cohen, Johnson, & Smailes, 1999; Luster & Small, 1997; Muller & Diamond, 1999).

CASE EXAMPLE 7.17

A clinical psychologist is providing psychotherapy for a clinical psychology graduate student who is preparing for a career as a child psychologist. During one discussion of her sexual fantasies, his client tells him about her fantasies of having sexual relations with underage males to initiate them sexually. The psychologist inquires whether she has ever engaged in sexual behavior with a child and she informs him that she has not, although she does say that she doesn't believe that adolescent boys are necessarily harmed by sexual contact with adults, "as the media claims." The psychologist inquires whether she has ever had recurrent fantasies about a particular boy, and she replies that she has not. She just has sexual fantasies about pre-adolescents periodically. The psychologist makes note of the issue in the client's record but decides that it would not be appropriate to violate her confidentiality by taking any further action on the basis of her fantasies.

The client completes therapy, completes her training program, and is licensed as a child-clinical psychologist. Two years later, she is charged with molesting two male clients, ages 11 and 12. During her trial, the psychologist-defendant discloses that she had "struggled" with her obsessional thoughts about sexual activity with boys for a long time and had addressed the issue in her previous therapy. As a result, the family of one of the boys sues the clinical psychologist for negligence stemming from his failure to report his client's "pedophiliac tendencies."

Reporting child abuse to legal authorities is frequently a difficult and sensitive issue for mental health professionals. In many instances, therapists might question whether they have sufficient evidence to make a report, whether any positive results for the protection of the child will result from the report (e.g., report of excessive hair-pulling by a parent), and whether the report could interfere with the therapeutic relationship established between a therapist and a client suspected of abuse. A therapist might be concerned that an abuser-client will terminate therapy prematurely following a report, thereby actually increasing the likelihood that the abuse will recur. Might the report result in additional abuse, before the investigation by child protective services gets underway, as a means of pressuring the child to deny any history of abuse? As a result of considerations like these, many clinicians fail to comply consistently with mandatory reporting laws (Hess & Brinson, 1999; Kalichman, 1999).

Therapists need to consider carefully the motivations behind their reluctance to comply with the legal mandate to report abuse. It is certainly uncomfortable to confront, and possibly anger, violent people. It is awkward to place oneself in the middle of a potentially explosive family situation without having any control over the events that follow. The discomfort and sense of limited power experienced by therapists should help them to identify with the child, who has no protection within the family. The child's welfare is clearly best protected (though not necessarily perfectly so) by the legal authorities. Legislators and government policy makers in every state have come to that conclusion. If therapists have reason to believe that the report of abuse will lead to greater harm to the child, they are obligated to inform legal authorities of this concern as well. In several cases, professionals have been held legally responsible for failing to report suspected child abuse (Kalichman, 1999). Clearly, the best means of protecting the interests of the child is to report.[4]

Mandatory reporting of child abuse and neglect again underscores the importance of informing clients of the limits of confidentiality, including therapists' legal obligation to report any suspicion of abuse, prior to initiating therapy (ACA, 2005, B.1.d, B.2.a; APA, 2002, 4.02, 4.05; Kalichman, 1999). Addressing this issue proactively will prevent clients from experiencing mandatory reporting as an unexpected breach of confidentiality and feeling betrayed by their therapist. When therapists suspect that abuse has occurred, they should inform their clients of their concern and remind them of the legal duty to report suspected abuse. The critical importance of protecting the welfare of children can be presented as the rationale for the law. Adult clients should be given the option of making the report themselves, which, along with their participation in therapy, should suggest to child welfare authorities that they are attempting to address their behavioral problems. The client would need to make the report in the therapist's presence to absolve the therapist of the duty to report the abuse. The therapist can offer to speak to the child welfare authorities to corroborate the client's report of participation in treatment that will address the abusive behavior and the emotional issues underlying it.

CASE EXAMPLE 7.18

A school psychologist is working with an eight-year-old boy who was sexually abused three years earlier by an older cousin. The case was investigated, and the cousin and her family no longer have any contact with the client's family. His mother met with the school psychologist several times about the boy's progress. The mother mentioned that she and her husband were under a great deal of financial stress and that her husband sometimes had trouble controlling his temper when the boy misbehaved. He "spanked him pretty hard" on those occasions.

The psychologist had perceived symptoms of abuse in the child's behavior but assumed they were the result of the sexual abuse incident. She now wonders whether the boy might be experiencing physical abuse, but she has not seen any physical evidence of abuse or injuries. The boy did not respond to the counselor's questions about physical abuse or being hurt by his father, other than saying, "No." The psychologist decided not to make a report.

SCHOOL PSYCHOLOGY AND COUNSELING

Another unusual aspect of providing mental health services to children is that they are seen in a wide variety of settings, including school (Kazdin, 2004). Mental health professionals working in schools are generally either school psychologists or school counselors. School psychologists and counselors are typically master's-level practitioners with a specialized degree that requires coursework in education in addition to counseling or psychology training. *School psychologists* provide assessment and treatment services to schoolchildren. *School counselors* provide students with academic and career guidance, in addition to mental health counseling.

Competence in School Psychology and Counseling

School psychologists are competent to administer a wide range of tests to school-age children to assess their personality and cognitive functioning. Frequently, school psychologists are called upon to conduct intellectual assessments to evaluate whether a child qualifies for a diagnosis of mental retardation or a learning disorder. School psychologists must be very familiar with federal and state statutes (e.g., ADA, 1990) and policies concerning the diagnosis of disabilities and the provision of educational services and accommodations for intellectually and physically challenged children.

Both school psychologists and counselors treat emotional and behavioral disorders affecting school behavior. An important aspect of competent practice as a school psychologist or counselor is recognizing when the issues affecting a child exceed the limits of school-based treatment. School professionals should have an established network of competent child psychiatrists and child-clinical psychologists to whom they can refer these students.

Suicide is an extremely serious and difficult issue to assess and treat effectively in children and adolescents. School psychologists and counselors must recognize the instability of adolescents' moods and the impulsivity that can characterize their behavior. Any mention of suicidal intent must be taken very seriously. Subsequent denial of suicidal thoughts does not necessarily mean that an adolescent is not at risk. Children and adolescents who are contemplating suicide need more intensive treatment than a school psychologist or counselor can provide, so, once again, competent practice requires identification and referral. Case precedents and legal guidelines for the state in which a school psychologist is practicing should be consulted carefully to determine whether it is appropriate to inform parents their child is seeking mental health services for suicidal thoughts and impulses (Fischer & Sorenson, 1996).

Currently, student violence in schools is a major concern of school districts. School psychologists and counselors need to pursue continuing education opportunities to develop competence in recognizing risk factors for violence and providing educational programs for students to prevent school violence.

CASE EXAMPLE 7.19

A school counselor working in a suburban high school is asked to develop an assessment plan for identifying students at elevated risk to commit violent acts against others. He points out to the principal that no valid method exists for accurately predicting such behavior in an adolescent population. The principal says the assessment program will serve an important political purpose, showing parents that school officials are doing something about the school violence problem. The parents of high-risk students will be notified, and these students will participate in a mandatory counseling program.

Informed Consent and Confidentiality Issues

As discussed in the previous section, parental consent is generally required to provide mental health assessment or treatment services to children and adolescents. The child's assent to participate in an evaluation or treatment program is also essential, for two reasons. First, obtaining children's assent shows a proper ethical regard for their autonomy as persons. Second, children are likely to be more positively motivated to participate in and complete a procedure if it has been explained to them and they have agreed to it.

During the informed consent process, parents and children should both receive a thorough explanation of the purpose and nature of any testing or treatment procedure. When children are going to be tested or evaluated by a school psychologist, their parents will be particularly interested to know what use will be made of the results of the procedure and what kind of feedback will be provided to them regarding their child's performance. Children who are assessed should also be provided with testing feedback in language they will understand.

Maintaining confidentiality is an extremely important duty for school-based mental health professionals. They are frequently faced with questions from teachers, other students, and concerned neighbors about the students who are being evaluated or treated. Information about a student should never be disclosed to any nonprofessional other than the student's parents or legal guardian. School staff members should only be given information about a student on a need-to-know basis. For example, a student's teachers will be provided with limited information regarding a student's functioning if they are asked to implement a behavior modification program in their classroom. However, even when school personnel do become involved in delivering psychological services to a student, school psychologists and counselors should respect the student's confidentiality by limiting the disclosure of information to what is absolutely necessary for personnel to assist the student effectively (ACA, 2005, B.2.d; APA, 2002, 4.04). Teachers and administrators are not obligated to keep their interactions with students confidential, so they might not recognize that the duties of a school psychologist are different.

Students should be informed very carefully about the limits of confidentiality. Therefore, school psychologists and counselors must be familiar with federal and state statutes, as well as school board, state, and federal education policies regarding their duties to protect students' privacy and to inform parents about matters pertaining to their child. For example, school psychologists and counselors are required to report child abuse and neglect, but requirements regarding their obligation to inform parents about such matters as students' sexual activity or treatment for a sexually transmitted disease vary from state to state (Fischer & Sorenson, 1996). School psychology and guidance counselor journals, along with state board newsletters, are excellent ways to stay abreast of legal developments that might impact school psychology practice. School psychologists and counselors should always inform students of what will be reported to their parents or anyone else.

Parents have a right to examine their minor child's primary and secondary school education records under the Family Educational Rights and Privacy Act of 1974 (FERPA; Pub. L. No. 93–380). Both FERPA and HIPAA regulations give a parent or guardian (who, under HIPAA, functions as the child's "personal representative") the right to examine the child's PHI contained in school mental health records (Privacy Rule, 2003, § 164.502[g][1]). When children reach the age of 18, parents can no longer access these records without their child's consent. A counselor's personal session notes, consistent with the record keeping discussion in Chapter 6, are not part of a child's education record, so long as they are not kept in the student's official file. As always, school professionals should regard therapy and assessment records as legal documents and consider carefully the implications of the information they include.

The situation is somewhat different for minor college students receiving mental health services through their educational institution (e.g., in a university counseling center). Mental health records of students attending postsecondary educational institutions (e.g., college, university) are not accessible by parents without the student's permission, even if the college student is under 18.

Multiple Relationships

Most school-based mental health professionals confront the issue of multiple relationships. As residents of the community they serve, school psychologists or counselors may have preexisting relationships (e.g., as neighbors or friends) with the parents of the students they counsel. Mental health professionals' children might, particularly in smaller communities, attend the schools where their parents work and know the students who are being evaluated or treated. These relationships generally cannot be avoided, but they place a heavy responsibility on school psychologists and counselors to remain as objective as possible in their judgments and recommendations. School administrators should be informed when a student requiring services has a preexisting relationship with school psychologists or counselors that would be likely to interfere with their ability to assist the student in an objective, professional manner.

CASE EXAMPLE 7.20

A principal refers a very troublesome student to a school psychologist. She is told that the student is disruptive in class and, during a two-week suspension, allegedly flattened the tires on the principal's car. The principal tells the psychologist that she believes the boy suffers from Attention-Deficit/Hyperactivity Disorder. She asks the psychologist to provide the diagnosis so he can be sent to an alternative school. The principal clearly wants the student out of her school.

Enhancing the Learning Environment

For school-based mental health professionals, one of the most uncomfortable aspects of the learning and discipline strategies in schools is the frequent use of coercion with students (e.g., corporal punishment, negative reinforcement). School psychologists and counselors have the expertise to recognize that even though coercion might reduce undesirable behaviors in the short run, it is not the most effective long-term behavior modification strategy (Sidman, 1999). School psychologists and counselors have a professional duty to educate school personnel about the effectiveness of positive reinforcement strategies (e.g., token economies) in modifying students' behavior and enhancing academic performance. Input from school psychologists and counselors will be received much more positively if these professionals are perceived by teachers and administrators as a useful resource for solving practical problems with students. They will be less effective in promoting the best interests of students if they present themselves as mental health experts whose purpose is to tell teachers what they are doing wrong.

PRACTICE CASE INVOLVING THE MODEL OF ETHICAL DECISION MAKING

During the mid-1980s, New York City had several incidents of homeless citizens freezing to death overnight while living on the streets during the winter months. In response to this problem, Mayor Edward I. Koch initiated a policy of having police escort homeless individuals to shelters on dangerously cold nights (temperature below 20 degrees Fahrenheit). However, many homeless individuals refused to go to shelters, arguing that they were dangerous places where one's property was often stolen while one slept. Repeated attempts to reassure homeless individuals that shelters were being made safer (e.g., by the hiring of security personnel) had little effect.

Mayor Koch responded by initiating another policy: A homeless individual refusing to be transported to a shelter on such occasions would be taken into protective custody by the police and transported to a city psychiatric facility, with the rationale that exposing oneself to such imminent danger indicated that one's reasoning ability was seriously impaired and that one needed to be protected. These individuals would be evaluated by a psychiatrist the following day and then released, voluntarily admitted, or involuntarily committed, as deemed medically appropriate.

For the mental health professionals who are being asked to assess these homeless individuals, is there a conflict between their duty as employees of the New York City health care system and their ethical obligations as professionals, delineated in their profession's ethical code?

SUMMARY

This chapter dealt with the special ethical challenges faced by therapists practicing within organizations or working with special populations. Mental health professionals in organizations must harmonize their duties as employees with their ethical obligations to their profession. Conflicts of interest can easily arise as professionals try to serve both their employing organization and the needs of their clients. Therapists working in psychiatric hospitals must deal with sharing confidential information within a treatment team and the pressure to discharge clients as quickly as possible. MCOs pose similar issues for professionals, who must be prepared to advocate for clients when they are denied needed services due to financial considerations.

Correctional therapists strive to minimize the coercive aspect of treatment in a prison by emphasizing clients' right to refuse treatment and having clients play an active role in setting therapy goals. Clients should be informed of the limits placed on the confidentiality of their treatment and records. Correctional therapists must avoid having their role as prison employees interfere with their professional duties to clients. Similarly, mental health professionals working in the military must strive to uphold professional standards of informed consent and confidentiality within the regimented military environment.

Psychotherapy with children is complicated by children's inability to consent to treatment. Parents not only must consent for their child to be treated, but, with few exceptions, they also have the right to know what is discussed during their child's therapy sessions. Professionals are legally required to report any suspicion that a child is a victim of neglect or physical, sexual, or emotional abuse. Nevertheless, many therapists are reluctant to comply with mandatory reporting laws. School psychologists and counselors must also report suspected abuse or neglect. They must look out for the best interests of their clients while promoting the safety and welfare of all students in their school and supporting its educational mission.

NOTES

1. Ethical issues pertaining to involuntary commitment procedures will be discussed in Chapter 13.

2. There are serious ethical questions about using such a program with involuntarily committed clients, for whom treatment already involves a degree of coercion. These clients should receive all privileges for which they are eligible in light of their psychiatric condition.

3. Mental health professionals with specialized knowledge and experience in issues pertaining to child abuse may also conduct child protection evaluations. This and other types of forensic evaluations (e.g., child custody assessments) will be discussed in Chapter 13.

4. I once attended a talk given by a child-clinical psychologist who said that he makes a case-by-case judgment regarding whether situations involving apparent child abuse can be managed effectively in family therapy or require reporting. I was shocked by his willingness to stake a child's life on the accuracy of his professional judgment (besides encouraging other professionals to consider disobeying the law). Therapists should never place themselves in the position of being above the law in their ability to make an omnipotent judgment regarding what is truly in the best interest of the child. Also, reporting suspected abuse is simply abiding by the terms of the informed consent agreement a therapist should make with the client before therapy begins. If clients observe that their therapists can be manipulated to disobey the law, what kind of model are they of good citizenship and the unbiased protection of children's welfare?

Chapter 8

Ethical Issues in Assessment and Testing

Mental health professionals working in clinical and educational settings are involved continuously in assessment. In addition to formal intake assessment and psychological testing geared toward determining a client's needs and diagnosis, clinicians assess their client's condition and progress each time they meet. Likewise, school psychologists assess the personality and intellectual functioning and academic achievement of students. This chapter will first examine the major ethical issues pertaining to clinical assessment and diagnosis and then consider the ethical concerns related specifically to psychological and educational testing.

THE VALUE AND ETHICAL IMPLICATIONS OF PSYCHIATRIC DIAGNOSES

In making a *DSM-IV-TR* (2000) diagnosis, clinicians are asserting that their client's behavior is not just unusual or different from most people's but is actually disordered, or "sick" (i.e., psychopathological). This diagnostic process involves important ethical considerations because a diagnosis represents, among other things, a culturally based value judgment concerning the behavior or beliefs of a client (ACA, 2005, E.5; APA, 2002, 9.01[a]). For example, in American culture, dependency is viewed as a personality flaw, an inability to stand on your own two feet and deal with life in an independent, assertive manner. The dependent behavioral style is pathologized in the *DSM* with the diagnosis of "Dependent Personality Disorder" (*DSM-IV-TR*, 2000), whereas in a collectivist culture, the American preoccupation with individual identity and goals would be viewed as selfish and unhealthy.

The meaning of a behavior may change when viewed in the appropriate cultural context. The APA "Guidelines for Providers of Psychological Services to Ethnic, Linguistic, and Culturally Diverse Populations" gives the example of "'healthy paranoia,' whereby ethnic minorities may develop defensive behaviors in response to discrimination" (APA, 1993, p. 46). This culturally based behavior would be regarded as diagnosable by professionals operating from the dominant, white American cultural perspective (ACA, 2005, E.5.b, E.5.c).

In addition, although the explicit goal of mental health treatment is to help clients become "healthier," the cultural values underlying many *DSM* diagnoses seem to entail that the implicit goal is to make clients a better "fit" in mainstream American culture (Pedersen, 2001). In making diagnoses, professionals should be sensitive to multicultural considerations and strive to reduce this culturally biased lack of respect for multicultural individual differences (ACA, 2005, E.5).

The Values Underlying the *DSM* Diagnostic Scheme

The *DSM-IV-TR* (2000) psychiatric classification system uses a medical model to conceptualize behavioral disorders. For example, the schizophrenias are regarded as illnesses or diseases, presumably caused by some biological malfunction in the individual's central nervous system (Sarbin, 1990). Disorders tend to be viewed from the context of the individual's biological functioning, thereby minimizing the role of personality, social, and cultural factors in producing individual differences in behavior (Peele, 1990). The medical model appears to be inconsistent, then, with the ethical importance that mental health professionals attach to recognizing and respecting individual differences and sources of diversity in people (e.g., ACA, 2005, C.5, E.5.b, E.8; APA, 2002, 3.01, 9.02[b], 9.02[c]).

Critics of the *DSM-IV-TR* point out that the biological basis of mental illness, assumed by the medical model, has been supported by the identification of specific biological mechanisms in very few of the disorders listed in the *DSM-IV-TR* (Lilienfeld & Marino, 1995; Sarbin, 1997). Even when biological factors have been identified as contributing to a syndrome (e.g., inadequate serotonin activity in Major Depression), there are many instances in which cognitive and social factors (e.g., the death of a spouse) appear to play a far more significant role in the development and persistence of the disorder (e.g., Lilienfeld & Marino, 1995; Peele, 1990; Sarbin, 1990, 1997; Szasz, 1974).

The *DSM-IV-TR* has been designed to maximize the *reliability* of psychiatric diagnosis. Reliability is the extent to which independent evaluators would classify the same set of behaviors as fitting a particular diagnosis. This consistency of diagnostic classification is a prerequisite for a *valid* diagnostic system. Validity refers to the meaningfulness of a diagnosis; that is, whether the diagnosis provides important clinical information concerning a person's functioning and the prognosis for the individual's future adjustment. However, the validity of both the medical model and the practice of psychiatric diagnosis has been questioned increasingly as the number of mental disorders in the *DSM-IV-TR* has burgeoned to over 300. Media fascination with the coining of new syndromes and people's desire to reduce their individual responsibility for their behavior have certainly contributed to this process. Nevertheless, political support in the psychiatric community appears to be a key factor in a syndrome gaining official "mental illness" status (Sharkey, 1997). As a result, American society appears to be moving closer and closer to the point where virtually everyone will qualify for some type of psychiatric diagnosis (Gergen, 1990). If everyone is "sick," the concept of mental illness ceases to make an important distinction between people. Critics have also questioned whether the proliferation of diagnostic syndromes (e.g., "Road Rage") has been motivated, in part, by mental health professionals' desire to ultimately have these disorders added to the *DSM,* thereby increasing mental health professionals' share of the health care funding pie (Sharkey, 1997). Shouldn't mental health professionals' respect for personal autonomy and capacity for self-determination lead to a greater emphasis on individuals' responsibility for their behavior, rather than attributing all forms of socially inappropriate behavior to an illness or syndrome (Sarbin, 1997; Szasz, 1974)?

CASE EXAMPLE 8.1

An I/O psychologist working in a human resources office is asked to recommend an alcoholism screening instrument for his firm to use in monitoring the safety risk presented by the company's truck drivers. He presents two screening instruments: One is exceptionally sensitive to the presence of alcohol problems but yields a high rate of false positives (i.e., incorrect identification of people who do not really have a drinking problem as alcoholics); the other test is more likely to produce false negatives (i.e., fail to identify people who are problem drinkers) but very few false positives. The CEO tells him to adopt the second test because the company would be obligated to provide treatment for anyone identified as a problem drinker by the screening procedure, and they do not want to pay for treatment for anyone who does not need it.

After thinking about the issue, the psychologist agrees because a test that misidentifies anyone as an alcoholic would violate the principle of nonmaleficence.

The Pros and Cons of Labeling Clients

Psychiatric diagnosis is intended to benefit clients by enhancing clinicians' understanding of their clients' problems and facilitating communication between mental health professionals, thereby increasing the effectiveness of treatment. However, the diagnostic process has been criticized on ethical grounds by clinicians and researchers who argue that the use of diagnoses actually does more harm than good for clients. Many of these arguments have focused on the impact of diagnostic "labels" on clients. First, critics have asserted that once an individual receives a diagnosis of a mental disorder, it is difficult for others to ever view the person as normal again (e.g., Link, Cullen, Frank, & Wozniak, 1987). A famous case of this phenomenon involved Senator Thomas Eagleton, who was the Democratic vice presidential nominee in 1972. During the campaign it was revealed that, years before, Senator Eagleton had been hospitalized in a psychiatric facility and treated successfully for depression with electroconvulsive therapy (Lydon, 1972). Even though Senator Eagleton had not suffered any additional episodes and had served effectively for several years in the United States Senate, the outcry was so great against having a "nut" just a heartbeat away from becoming president that Senator Eagleton had to withdraw from the campaign (Naughton, 1972). Apparently, popular opinion still held that no one diagnosed with a serious psychiatric condition should ever be regarded as completely cured.

A second problem with diagnosis is that it can result in individuals adopting a "sick role"; that is, individuals may devalue themselves by perceiving themselves as seriously incapacitated and cease to believe that they are capable of coping effectively or of improving their situation (Link, 1987). They might view themselves as disabled and begin to focus on obtaining relief from their responsibilities (e.g., by qualifying for disability compensation) than on resolving their problems and getting on with their lives (Link, 1987; Link et al., 1987; Szasz, 1974).

Although proponents of psychiatric diagnosis assert that diagnostic information provides clinicians with a better understanding of their clients, critics argue that diagnosis actually *decreases* many clinicians' understanding of their clients as individual human beings.

Determining a client's diagnosis has become an end in itself, rather than representing one important piece of information in the process of understanding clients' experience and assisting them with making life changes (Tucker, 1998). When individuals receive a psychiatric diagnosis, their individuality is too often subsumed by that label. According to critics, diagnostic categorizations encourage a clinician to pigeonhole people rather than focus on their unique life history, current situation, and life goals. Clinicians will assume that they know the major facts about a person once they read the diagnosis of Schizophrenia, Paranoid Type in the individual's medical record, whereas effective treatment is based on a comprehensive understanding of an *individual* as an agent responsible for behavioral choices, not a diagnostic label (Sarbin, 1997).

On the basis of arguments like these, some mental health professionals believe that diagnosis is unethical because of the exaggerated and harmful significance attached to such labels in current mental health practice. Clearly, ethical, competent diagnosis should be based on a comprehensive assessment of the individual's functioning by a highly competent clinician with a keen sensitivity to the potential impact that receiving a psychiatric label can have on a client's life (ACA, 2005, E.5; APA, 2002, 9.01[a]).

Prediction of Low Base Rate Behaviors

In many instances, the information most important for determining a psychiatric diagnosis is a person's score on a diagnostic test. The diagnosis is applied if the person's score exceeds a cut-off level that has been established as a valid indicator of the presence of the disorder. In fact, actuarial (i.e., statistical) prediction based on a client's assessment profile or test cut-off score yields greater diagnostic accuracy than the clinical judgment of even experienced clinicians (Walters, White, & Greene, 1988). However, Meehl and Rosen (1955) pointed out long ago that effective behavioral prediction cannot occur without an understanding of the *base rate,* or antecedent probability, of a behavior in the population being tested (i.e., how often the behavior or condition occurs in the population). Accurate classification is dependent on both the probability of detecting a condition using a specific criterion and the proportion of the population that is actually affected by the condition (Gottesman & Prescott, 1989). Evaluating the efficiency of a diagnostic test involves comparing its rate of success in classifying people correctly, also known as the "hit rate," with the base rate of the condition in the population being studied.

For example, the MacAndrew Alcoholism Scale (MAC) was developed during the 1960s to differentiate clients who were in need of treatment for alcoholism from other psychiatric outpatient clients (MacAndrew, 1965). It was included as a supplementary scale on the Minnesota Multiphasic Personality Inventory (MMPI). In the original validation sample for the MAC, the base rate of alcoholism was 50%: Half of the sample consisted of alcoholics in treatment and half of nonalcoholic psychiatric clients. Using a cut-off score of 24, the MAC correctly classified 81.8% of the standardization sample as alcoholic or nonalcoholic, which is much better than the 50% hit rate that would have been obtained by randomly classifying individuals in that sample as alcoholic or nonalcoholic (Gottesman & Prescott, 1989).

However, the base rate, or lifetime prevalence, of alcoholism in the United States population is 13.4% (Grant, 1997). The MAC, with a hit rate of 81.8% (which sounds very impressive), would not be an effective classification tool for a behavior with such a low base rate in the general population. Suppose, instead of administering the MAC, a psychologist decided to simply classify 100% of the general population as nonalcoholics. The hit rate (i.e., percentage of nonalcoholics correctly classified as nonalcoholics) would be 86.6% (100% − 13.4% = 86.6%), which is even better than the 81.8% hit rate of the MAC! When a test is used with a population that has a significantly different base rate for a condition than the population used to validate the test, a high frequency of misdiagnoses will occur. In the case of the MAC, incorrect classifications would have tended to be false positives (i.e., people classified as alcoholics who really were not). Using the MAC in a personnel screening context, then, would have led to the misclassification (and, presumably, the inappropriate rejection) of many job applicants as alcoholics. Clearly, this would have been an unethical use of the test.

Test developers have an ethical obligation to validate the use of cut-off scores and classification schemes for the population (e.g., male prison inmates) with which the test will be used (ACA, 2005, E.8; APA, 2002, 9.05). Likewise, professionals are ethically obligated to make themselves aware of the population base rates of the behaviors being classified and not use tests or other assessment procedures that have not compiled clear evidence of predictive efficacy for the population in question (ACA, 2005, E.6; APA, 2002, 9.02[b]). Test users must also be sensitive to potential differences in base rates and appropriate cut-off scores based on ethnicity, age, and gender (Sandoval, 1998). When test scores and other relevant variables are used *competently,* specific predictors of low base rate behaviors can, in some instances, be identified (Janus & Meehl, 1997). Unfortunately, many clinicians have little understanding of the correct use of base rate information (e.g., Walters et al., 1988; Whitecotton, Sanders, & Norris, 1998).

PSYCHOLOGICAL AND EDUCATIONAL ASSESSMENT AND TESTING

Psychological assessment is the process of gathering information about individuals that will be useful in determining their need for treatment and which treatment methods will be most effective with them. It is essentially a problem-solving task, based on the questions regarding the individual that are being addressed in the assessment (Tallent, 1987). *Testing* is often a component of this assessment process. Psychological testing is undertaken when professionals believe it can yield information needed to help the client more effectively. (Unnecessary testing constitutes an unwarranted intrusion into the client's privacy and exploits the client financially.)

Two sets of specialty guidelines pertaining to the use of psychological and educational tests have been developed. The American Educational Research Association, American Psychological Association, and National Council on Measurement in Education published a revised set of *Standards for Educational and Psychological Testing* in 1999. In addition, ACA, in cooperation with the Association for Assessment in Counseling, updated its specialty guidelines for users of standardized tests in 2003.

Informed Consent Issues in Psychological Testing

Assessments, like any other aspect of professional activity, require the informed consent of the individual(s) involved (ACA, 2005, E.3.a; APA, 2002, 3.10, 9.03). Many assessment referrals are made to clinicians by other practitioners or agencies that are providing treatment services to clients. However, it is extremely important that clinicians never assume that the referring practitioner or agency adequately explained the purpose of the assessment and the testing procedure. Clinicians should always obtain clients' informed consent themselves.

The informed consent procedure for psychological testing is similar in many ways to the process described for therapy and counseling in Chapter 6. HIPAA regulations (if applicable) require that clients be provided a Notice of Privacy Practices describing the security measures employed by the practitioner or organization to prevent inappropriate disclosure of confidential information (Privacy Rule, 2003, § 164.520). However, there can also be some significant differences in the informed consent process in assessment contexts. For example, information provided during the interview and testing process is frequently not confidential between the client and the clinician in that all information provided by the client can be included in the test report generated for the referring agency. Because many assessment clients are either participating in therapy currently or have been in therapy in the past, it is extremely important to inform clients of this special limitation during the discussion of confidentiality issues. Clients also need to know the types of tests that will be used, the purpose of the tests, and the types of responses they will be asked to provide (e.g., impressions of inkblots, answers to true-false questions, drawings), as well as the fees for the proposed assessment. The clinician should also tell clients who will provide feedback to them regarding their assessment results, whether a report will be generated, and the process that will be used to obtain their consent for the report to be sent to the referring agency or any other professional or agency they designate (ACA, 2005, E.1.b; APA, 2002, 9.10).[1] Finally, clients must be informed of their right to refuse to participate in the assessment and any consequences resulting from their refusal.

CASE EXAMPLE 8.2

A counselor is testing a client referred by a community mental health center. They want to know whether he is suffering from a mood disorder, a personality disorder, or both. The counselor finds him to be very anxious and hostile when she interviews him. She explains the purpose of the testing as an attempt to find "how best to help [him]." The client continues to be hostile and evasive throughout the testing. When the testing is complete, the counselor tells the referring agency that she has not obtained sufficient data to make the differential diagnosis they requested. When the client's therapist asks him how the testing went and explains the purpose of the procedure in greater detail, he looks greatly relieved and says that he thought the testing was being done to gather evidence to "put [him] away in a nuthouse."

Informed Consent Issues When Testing Children

When children are the focus of assessment, ethical guidelines stipulate that informed consent must be obtained from a parent or guardian acting as the "personal representative" of the child (ACA, 2005, A.2.d, E.3; APA, 2002, 3.10[b], 9.03[b]; Privacy Rule, 2003, § 164.502[g][1]). Clinicians must ensure that parents understand the purpose of the testing, which tests will be administered, and what use will be made of the test results. Children are often tested in situations where a particular diagnostic label is necessary for the child to receive services (e.g., to qualify for a special education program). The consent form signed by parents would specify the use to be made of any diagnosis resulting from the assessment and whether the parents' consent will be required after the procedure is completed for any further steps to be implemented (e.g., whether the parents will control the placement of their child in a special education program after receiving the assessment results or whether the child's diagnostic status will automatically trigger a placement decision). Clinicians also have an ethical duty to explain the nature and purpose of the testing to child clients, at a level commensurate with their understanding, and to obtain their assent (ACA, 2005, A.2.d; APA, 2002, 3.10[b]).

Client Feedback

The informed consent process continues after the assessment has been completed. The clinician conducting the assessment is responsible for providing feedback to the client regarding the results (ACA, 2005, E.1.b; APA, 2002, 9.10), unless some other arrangement has been agreed upon with the referring agency (e.g., that feedback will be provided by the client's individual therapist). When testing a child, feedback is provided to the child's parents and to the child. Depending on the age of the child, the parents might receive feedback first, then sit in while the clinician explains the results to the child. Assessment feedback is considered an aspect of informed consent because client consent is needed in order to send copies of an assessment report to the referring agency or any other professional. Clients cannot provide informed consent if they do not understand the information in the assessment report.

The written summary and supplementary information provided to the client (or, in the case of a child, the child's parents) during the feedback session should be communicated in language consistent with the client's level of verbal achievement (ACA, 2005, E.1.b). Avoiding psychological jargon will also reduce the likelihood that the client will misunderstand the results. Diagnostic information should be explained to children based on the clinician's judgment of what the child can understand and benefit from knowing. In the past, psychologists generally did not release "raw test results or raw data" to clients because clients lacked the qualifications to understand and use the data appropriately (APA, 1992, 2.02). However, consistent with the HIPAA requirement that providers release health records to clients requesting them, the "Ethical Principles" now states that "psychologists provide test data to the client/patient or other persons" upon the client's request (APA, 2002, 9.04[a]; Privacy Rule, 2003, § 164.524[a]).

CASE EXAMPLE 8.3

A counselor receives a testing referral for an adult female client to assess her apparently delusional beliefs about her neighbor. She is also suspicious about the testing process and agrees to be tested only after the counselor says that he will provide her with feedback regarding the test results and any diagnostic conclusions. Throughout the testing, the client insists that there is nothing wrong with her and is clearly very upset about the possibility that she is "crazy." The results of the assessment indicate clearly that the client qualifies for a diagnosis of Schizophreniform Disorder. The counselor feels that his client has the right to know this diagnosis, and she undoubtedly wants to know. On the other hand, he wants to protect her from being upset by the news because he fears she might decompensate further.

Confidentiality Issues in Psychological Assessment

The limitations of confidentiality in assessment situations may be quite different from those discussed for psychotherapy and counseling in Chapter 6. When clients are referred to a clinician for the sole purpose of assessment, they should be informed at the outset that all the information they provide may be used for the assessment report and communicated to the referring agency, so they will not mistakenly assume the assessment situation can be treated like an opportunity to receive therapy from a different therapist. Of course, clients should be assured that the clinician will not provide assessment information to anyone without their permission, except upon court order (APA, 2002, 9.04[b]; Privacy Rule, 2003, § 164.512[e][1]).

The same limitations on confidentiality discussed in Chapter 6, concerning risk of harm to self or others and abuse or neglect of children, apply to the assessment situation (ACA, 2005, B.1.d; APA, 2002, 4.02). For example, suppose a client had not indicated any suicidal plan in his sessions with his therapist, but while completing the Thematic Apperception Test, he tells a story on Card 3BM about a suicidal individual. He then follows up the story by talking about his own plan to kill himself. The clinician administering the test would need to determine whether to seek to have the man hospitalized to prevent him from carrying out his plan. The ethical responsibility to protect the client from harm while preserving the client's confidentiality to the greatest possible degree is no different than in therapy.[2]

After obtaining the informed consent of the client, a test report is always sent to a specific person, designated by the client or the referral source, who is professionally qualified to understand the information provided in the report. The envelope is marked "Confidential" so it will not be opened by anyone in a hospital mailroom or by clerical staff (ACA, 2005, B.6.f, E.4; APA, 2002, 4.04, 4.05). An assessment report can be faxed only if immediate receipt of the report is in the best interest of the client and the clinician has been assured by the person receiving the report that the facility's fax machine is in a secure environment.

CASE EXAMPLE 8.4

A clinical psychologist accepts a testing referral from a therapist, so she conducts several days of testing with the client. Her agreement with the client is that he will pay the fee in full before the testing is finished. Although he makes partial payments, he still owes nearly half of the fee when the assessment is completed. The psychologist informs the client that she will not send the report to his therapist until he pays the remainder of the fee.

Competence in Psychological Assessment

A substantial proportion of successful malpractice claims arise in the context of psychological assessment, in part because testing involves a permanent record that can easily be evaluated by independent experts to detect incompetent practice. A second major reason is that competent test administration, scoring, interpretation, and report writing require the development of a highly sophisticated set of clinical skills.

Many clinicians prefer doing therapy or counseling to conducting assessments, yet assessments can be a lucrative component of professional practice. As a result, many clinicians and agencies will hire practitioners beginning their professional careers to conduct assessments under the supervision of more experienced clinicians. Positive aspects of this situation are that assessment skills are a very marketable commodity for beginning clinicians and that these clinicians have the opportunity to obtain additional supervised clinical experience to enhance their assessment ability. However, people hired to conduct assessments need to be certain that they are competent to administer, score, and interpret each of the tests they use (ACA, 2005, E.2.a; APA, 2002, 9.02). Before using a new test, ethical guidelines require that clinicians have knowledge of the test's development, the makeup of the normative sample, and its reliability and validity (ACA, 2005, E.2.a; APA, 2002, 9.02[a], 9.02[b]). In addition, they must obtain experience by administering the test to a nonclinical population and then a clinical one, while under the supervision of a clinician knowledgeable about the test. Clinicians conducting assessments under supervision are responsible for demanding adequate supervision to be able to conduct the assessment correctly (ACA, 2005, F.8.a; APA, 2002, 9.07). Supervising clinicians bear primary responsibility in such a situation, but supervisees are equally responsible for making certain that they do not exceed the limits of their competence (ACA, 2005, F.1.a; APA, 2002, 2.05).

A survey of departments training doctoral students in psychology found that a substantial majority of the departments did not believe that their graduates had developed competence in methods of assessing the reliability and validity of tests (Aiken et al., 1990). Geisinger and Carlson (1998) point out that although competent assessment does not require the ability to construct tests, an understanding of psychometric concepts is needed to understand the information provided in test manuals and recognize the potential for bias and invalidity when tests are used with different populations.

CASE EXAMPLE 8.5

A counselor receives a referral for an intellectual assessment of a child. The referral source asks specifically for the child to be assessed using the Stanford-Binet rather than the WISC-IV. The counselor has not used the Stanford-Binet, but he does not want to disappoint the referral source and decides that this would be an excellent opportunity to develop competence with a new test. He agrees to conduct the assessment.

MULTICULTURAL ISSUES IN PSYCHOLOGICAL ASSESSMENT

When testing members of diverse groups, it is extremely important to ensure that the tests used and the conditions under which they are administered do not place members of any group at a relative disadvantage (ACA, 2005, E.6.c, E.8; APA, 2002, 9.02). Tests must be selected carefully, "based on a thorough review of the available information" (Prediger, 1994, p. 69). An important part of this review is attending to the makeup of the normative sample used in the construction of the test, to ensure that the test can provide useful, valid information for the groups the clinician wants to assess (ACA, 2005, E.6; APA, 2002, 9.02[b]; Geisinger, 1998).

Are some groups of test takers being placed at a disadvantage when a test is administered in English? If so, the professional should investigate whether translations of the test exist (ACA, 2005, E.8; APA, 2002, 9.02[c]). If a translation does exist, the validity of the translation (i.e., that the translation measures the same constructs as the original language version) must be confirmed (Geisinger, 1994). If a valid translation of the test is not available, perhaps a different test can be used to measure the same characteristics more effectively in linguistically diverse groups (APA, 2003).

People with disabilities comprise a group whose special testing needs must also be considered. For example, large print, Braille, or audiotaped versions of a test might make it possible for individuals with visual impairments to perform up to their true potential on a test. It is important to recognize, however, that whenever accommodations or variations are introduced, the nature of the test might be altered. The professional using the test is responsible for considering whether the change from a standard administration might affect the reliability or validity of the client's scores (Geisinger, Boodoo, & Noble, 2002).

In training professionals to use psychological and educational tests, Geisinger and Carlson (1998) emphasize the importance of helping them to develop an understanding and appreciation of "individuality" (i.e., human differences resulting from each individual's unique experiential background). To develop competence in this area, it is extremely important to obtain supervised experience in testing diverse groups of clients. A knowledge and appreciation of individual and cultural differences is also needed to competently interpret the results of assessment procedures conducted with diverse groups of clients (Velasquez & Callahan, 1992). Like therapists, assessment professionals need to be capable of interpreting clients' responses within the appropriate cultural context in order to draw valid conclusions (Prediger, 1994). Finally, consultation with professionals possessing greater expertise in issues of test administration and interpretation with diverse populations should not be presented in training as a rare event, but as a common practice of competent clinicians concerned with delivering the highest quality assessment services possible (Geisinger & Carlson, 1998).

CASE EXAMPLE 8.6

A psychologist provides testing services for a number of nursing homes. Frequently, she finds it necessary to deviate from standard administration procedures to accommodate the special needs of her elderly clients. She encourages them by reinforcing their responses, taking breaks within lengthy subtests, and repeating information to be certain they heard it correctly. She believes that her methods ensure that the results reflect clients' optimal level of functioning. She is careful to mention the deviations from standardization in her assessment reports.

ETHICS AND TEST VALIDITY

For an assessment to yield useful information, the tests used must be reliable and valid; that is, clients' performance on the test must convey important and meaningful information about them that corresponds to what the test was designed to measure. Test developers are responsible for establishing strong evidence of the reliability and validity of a test before publishing it (ACA, 2005, E.12; APA, 2002, 9.05). However, there are published tests whose reliability and validity have been criticized. For example, many critics have questioned the ethicality of the widespread use of the Rorschach in personality assessment, given the paucity of evidence regarding its reliability and validity as a predictor of personality functioning (Hunsley & Bailey, 1999).

Clinicians using a test need to be familiar with its construction and purpose, as well as its limitations (ACA, 2005, E.6.a, E.8; APA, 2002, 9.02). Clinicians must be careful not to use a test for any purpose other than the one for which it was designed because conclusions drawn from such use could very well be invalid. For example, although the Beck Depression Inventory-II can be a valid measure of depression in college students, it would be invalid to infer that a student receiving a score of 10 is twice as depressed as a student with a score of 5 (Beck, Steer, & Brown, 1996). First, the test is not designed to use a ratio scale of measurement; a score of zero does not indicate the complete absence of depression. Second, both scores fall within the range of "minimal" depression, and the test is not designed to make discriminations within that range.

Clinicians should also be aware of variables that might affect a client's functioning in an assessment context (ACA, 2005, E.7.a; APA, 2002, 9.02[c]). A good rule to follow, consistent with the ethical dictum of nonmaleficence, is that a clinician always wants to give clients the opportunity to perform as well as they can in assessment situations (ACA, 2005, E.7.d; APA, 2002, 3.04). To that end, clinicians always provide test takers with the best test-taking conditions possible; tests should be administered under private, quiet, and physically comfortable conditions. Clients should be tested when they are physically alert and able to perform up to their potential. For example, if a client has an automobile accident on the way to the testing appointment, the testing should be postponed. If the client was tested on the day of the accident and produced a high score on an anxiety measure, it would not be reasonable to conclude that the results were indicative of the client's functioning in general.

Preserving test security is another important duty of mental health professionals (ACA, 2005, E.10; APA, 2002, 9.11). The validity of many psychological tests can be compromised if potential test takers have prior access to the test materials (American Educational Research Association et al., 1999). Clinicians should be careful not to reveal too much about test stimuli and typical responses in their teaching or public presentations.[3] Also, they should not allow clients to look over test materials or discuss clients' responses with them in any detail, even after clients have completed the assessment process. They should always bear in mind that clients might need to take the same tests again to evaluate changes in their condition.

A special case affecting the issue of test security for the Rorschach is the "testing the limits" procedure that some clinicians use when clients produce a very limited Rorschach record (Exner, 1993). For example, if a client rejected (i.e., could not generate a response for) 6 of the 10 cards during the Rorschach administration, the clinician might test the limits by showing the client Card V again and saying, "You did not see anything on this card. Some people see a _____ on this card. Can you see that?" Testing the limits on the Rorschach can be problematic because the procedure contaminates future testing for clients. They will no longer be naive; they will know one or more of the "right" answers. Another reason to avoid testing the limits is that the clinician is communicating to clients that they did not perform well on the test. This information could significantly increase clients' anxiety level and affect their performance on the remaining tests in the assessment battery.

CASE EXAMPLE 8.7

A psychologist working in a psychiatric hospital receives the results of an MMPI-2 completed by his client following her admission to the hospital. The results indicate that the client likely qualifies for a schizophrenia diagnosis. When the psychologist discusses the results with the client, she disagrees vociferously and insists that he tell her how he could arrive at that conclusion based on her test responses. He proceeds to show her items she endorsed from the Paranoia and Schizophrenia scales.

USE OF COMPUTERIZED TEST ADMINISTRATION, SCORING, AND INTERPRETATION

Computer-based test administration, scoring, and interpretation have become extremely popular in clinical practice, particularly during the past 30 years. The majority of psychologists involved in assessment have used these technological aids (Pope, Butcher, & Seelen, 2000). The test most commonly associated with computer scoring and interpretive technology in mental health settings is the Minnesota Multiphasic Personality Inventory-2 (MMPI-2; Butcher et al., 2001). Computer-based test scoring is a recommended procedure because it eliminates scoring errors, thereby increasing the reliability of scoring and making valid interpretation of the test data possible (Allard, Butler, Faust, & Shea, 1995; McMinn, Ellens, & Soref, 1999). Of course, clinicians and their staff must be competent in using the relevant software in order to realize these benefits (ACA, 2005, E.7.b; APA, 2002, 9.09[c]). If mental health professionals use an independent test scoring and interpretation service, they must obtain a client's informed consent to this transmittal of test data prior to conducting the assessment (APA, 2002, 4.05[a]).

As discussed earlier, clinicians are obligated to provide clients with a testing environment that enables them to perform up to their full potential (ACA, 2005, E.7.d; APA, 2002, 9.02). Computerized test administration affords clients greater privacy for test-taking and simplifies the process of responding to test items. However, for clients who have little or no experience with computers, computerized tests can provoke extreme anxiety and discomfort. Clients with higher levels of computer anxiety have been shown to produce more negative mood ratings when questionnaires were administered on a computer rather than in a paper-and-pencil format (Tseng, Macleod, & Wright, 1997; Tseng, Tiplady, Macleod, & Wright, 1998). Clinicians are particularly likely to encounter this situation with rural, older, and lower socioeconomic status clients. Clients' experience and level of comfort with computer tasks can be assessed prior to testing. Clients expressing reservations about using the computer can practice making responses on the computer until they are comfortable doing so. If they remain uncomfortable or practice cannot be provided, an alternate testing format (e.g., responding on an answer sheet) should be used (APA, 2002, 9.02[c]). (The client's responses can be entered on the computer later, if desired.) Test publishers should provide data regarding any differences in performance that are likely to occur in computerized versus paper-and-pencil test administration so that interpretive assumptions made by clinicians are reasonable (Geisinger, 1998).[4]

Computer-based test interpretation can be a useful tool in the assessment process. Controlled studies support the superior reliability and validity of actuarial interpretation over clinicians' judgment when the two have the same client information available to them (e.g., Tsemberis, Miller, & Gartner, 1996). The large empirical database underlying quality computer-based interpretive systems enables them to provide extremely valuable hypotheses concerning personality functioning and diagnosis, reflecting not only test scores but a host of other variables (e.g., base rate information regarding various conditions in the relevant population). Documentation of the empirical sources of diagnostic conclusions is another advantage of computer-based interpretation (Sampson, Purgar, & Shy, 2003). The closer the client comes to fitting a prototype score pattern, the more accurately the actuarial model is likely to describe the client's functioning (Butcher, 1997b). Computer-based reports also often provide treatment recommendations that might not have been considered otherwise (Butcher, 1997b; Tsemberis et al., 1996).

However, a computer-based interpretation is best viewed as one of several useful sources of information for a clinician, like a consultation with an experienced colleague, rather than as the final product of the assessment process (McMinn, Ellens, et al., 1999; Tallent, 1987). In a recent survey, 86% of psychologists said it is unethical to use a computer-based test interpretation "as the primary resource for case formulation" (McMinn, Ellens, et al., 1999, p. 75). The reason for this view is that the output of "expert" computerized interpretation systems are based on algorithms that simplify the considerable variability of test scores and provide interpretations based on a limited set of decision rules. In other words, a client's data are analyzed and summarized in such a way that some of the individual variability is overlooked in order to "fit" the client's performance into one of the limited set of interpretive options programmed into the system. Because these systems cannot "adequately anticipate all possible human variation, they are inaccurate or misleading at times" (McMinn, Ellens, et al., 1999, p. 75). Clinicians, on the other hand, can obtain additional relevant information regarding a client's past and present functioning by interviewing the client, consulting past treatment records, and administering a complete battery of tests, supplemented by behavioral observations obtained throughout the process (Carson, 1990; Tallent, 1987; Whitecotton et al., 1998).

Unquestionably, computer-based test interpretation using well-validated software programs can play an important and useful role in psychological assessment when combined with the skills and judgment of a competent clinician (Carson, 1990; Downey, Sinnett, & Seeberger, 1998; Whitecotton et al., 1998). Professionals should evaluate carefully the quality of any computer-based test interpretation software they are considering using (ACA, 2005, E.2.b; APA, 2002, 9.09[b]) and not make the mistake of assuming the credibility of the program's creators and the validity of the impressive-looking results generated by the program (Sampson et al., 2003). Research studies and reviews of the interpretive system are good sources of information, as is the record of scholarship of the program's creators pertaining to the validity of the test and computer-based test interpretation (Moreland, 1987).

CASE EXAMPLE 8.8

A clinical psychologist administers an MMPI-2 to a client in a substance abuse rehabilitation center. The computer-based test interpretation indicates that the client's profile could be consistent with a diagnosis of Schizophrenia, Paranoid Type. The psychologist puts the computer-generated report in the client's record, along with the diagnosis. As a result, the client is transferred to a psychiatric facility. A counselor on the psychiatric unit reads the report and interviews the client. She believes the client is clearly not schizophrenic. She asks the client about a number of his MMPI-2 responses and finds that he answered that someone was trying to poison him because he was poisoning himself with alcohol. He reported strange and bizarre thought processes because they occurred when he was intoxicated. He said that people were trying to influence his mind because he was receiving therapy.

The counselor changes the client's diagnosis back to Alcohol Dependence and transfers him back to the substance abuse rehabilitation unit.

REPORT WRITING

In an assessment context, the final assessment report is generally the only information released to other professionals or to clients upon their request (ACA, 2005, E.4; APA, 2002, 4.04; Privacy Rule, 2003, § 164.524[a]). Test data and protocols are retained by the clinician who conducted the assessment (ACA, 2005, E.4; APA, 2002, 9.04). Not releasing test data reduces the chance that the scores will be misinterpreted or misused and minimizes the invasion of the client's privacy.

In preparing an assessment report, clinicians should, as always, be sensitive to the ethical importance of clear, understandable communication. They should assume that professionals reading their reports are not as familiar as they are with the tests used or with clinical terminology. After all, they did refer the client for testing, presumably to a clinician with more expertise in the area. Clinicians should avoid using clinical terminology (e.g., paranoia) in a report because those terms have weighty connotations for nonprofessionals and professionals alike (ACA, 2005, E.1.b). Rather, the goal of report writing is to describe the client's behavioral, cognitive, and emotional characteristics (i.e., how the client could be expected to behave, think, and feel in various situations) based on the assessment findings. Competent reports avoid value judgments concerning the client's behavior and focus on describing the person in terms of both strengths and weaknesses. Clinicians should also note any factors in the testing context that may have had a negative effect on the client's performance and might affect the accuracy of the interpretations provided in the report (ACA, 2005, E.9.a; APA, 2002, 9.06).

Providing an accurate sense of the individual's functioning is an important contribution to the client's future treatment, independent of a diagnosis. Occasionally, a clinician perceives some pressure to provide a diagnosis in an assessment case because the client will not be eligible for services (e.g., accommodations for learning difficulties) without a qualifying diagnosis (i.e., learning disability). As a professional, it is certainly unethical to provide an invalid diagnosis, regardless of the potential benefit to the client (ACA, 2005, E.5.a; APA, 2002, Principle C, 9.01[a]). Always remember the potential costs to the client associated with diagnosis, which were discussed earlier in this chapter (ACA, 2005, E.5.d).

Clinicians should focus on answering the referral question in an assessment report. They should not include information in the report that is not directly relevant to the client's treatment (e.g., suggestions in projective data regarding possible sexual orientation issues in an assessment of the client's competency to stand trial). Such information could be harmful to the client (ACA, 2005, B.2.d; APA, 2002, 3.04, 4.04[a]).

In making recommendations in an assessment report, clinicians should be clear and concise and must bear in mind that they are advocates for the client. Clinicians often confront issues regarding whether their recommendations should be based on what the client needs or what can realistically be provided. For example, if a client has no health insurance coverage and is being treated at a small clinic, is it worthwhile to recommend that the client obtain a neurological evaluation if testing indicated the possibility of neurological impairment? Clinicians might be concerned that the referring agency will be unable to act on such a recommendation but that it might feel pressured to do so if the recommendation is included in the report and becomes part of the client's record. Moreover, this situation, in turn, could reduce the likelihood that the clinicians will receive assessment referrals from the agency in the future.

In such a situation, the clinicians' duty is clear: The best interest of the client must take precedence over the other considerations involved. Clinicians' respect for other professionals entails that they should assume the referring agency also has the best interest of the client in mind.[5] At the same time, clinicians should take pragmatic considerations into account by trying to think of recommendations that utilize available services in a creative manner. For example, a child with self-esteem and social skills deficits might benefit considerably from participation in a Big Brothers/Big Sisters program rather than more costly psychotherapy.

CASE EXAMPLE 8.9

A counselor refers a client to a clinical psychologist for intellectual and personality assessment to evaluate the severity of the client's depressive symptoms and their impact on her cognitive functioning. The client calls the counselor after a feedback session with the psychologist. She is very upset and says that she needs to make an appointment with a neurologist because she is brain damaged. The counselor is very surprised by the finding. When he receives the test report from the psychologist the next day, he reads it carefully. He finds that her intellectual functioning is normal, though there is considerable variability between subtests. Personality testing indicated moderate depression. Nevertheless, there is a recommendation that she obtain a neurological evaluation for possible organicity.

After reassuring the client that there is no apparent evidence that she has suffered brain damage, the counselor calls the psychologist and asks about the reason for the recommendation. The psychologist says she always includes that recommendation in test reports to rule out the possibility that a client's psychiatric symptoms are due to central nervous system pathology.

SPECIAL CONSIDERATIONS IN COLLEGE ORIENTATION TESTING

Many counselors and psychologists are involved in the testing of first-year college or university students during the student orientation process. Students may be asked to complete career interest tests, psychological adjustment screening measures, and even measures being used in faculty members' research. Group testing of this sort does not affect testing professionals' ethical duty to obtain the informed consent of each student. The tests should be described and the purpose of students' taking them explained. Any limitations on the confidentiality of students' test scores and responses must also be enumerated. Students must be informed that they have the right to refuse to complete the tests, without penalty. They should also have the opportunity to receive feedback on their test performance because it would be unprofessional and unethical to simply use students as a vehicle to amass assessment data. Finally, if the testing process is in any way related to a research study, students' informed consent as research participants must be obtained. Ethical issues pertaining to research participation will be addressed in Chapter 12.

CASE EXAMPLE 8.10

The director of the honors program at a large university is a personality psychologist. She realizes that personality variables distinguishing high achieving students from average achievers have been studied extensively. She is interested in conducting research on the personality characteristics that differentiate the highest achieving students within a group of high achievers (i.e., honors students). She proposes to institute psychological testing as part of the freshman orientation for students admitted to the honors program and then chart the students' academic progress at the university. She will obtain the students' informed consent for testing, offering personality feedback based on the test results to those who consent to be tested.

PRACTICE CASE INVOLVING THE MODEL OF ETHICAL DECISION MAKING

A woman is hospitalized voluntarily for depression, although the admission was clearly influenced by her husband's insistence that she was "having a nervous breakdown." She was not very communicative when admitted, so most of the information obtained during the admission process was provided by her husband. At her husband's urging, she signed a consent form allowing hospital staff to continue to consult with him about all aspects of her treatment.

A counseling psychologist on the hospital staff conducts an intellectual and personality assessment to evaluate her condition. As the assessment progresses, the woman gradually becomes more comfortable and willing to discuss her situation with him. The psychologist learns that the client's depression had developed during the previous two months, largely as a result of the conflict she had been experiencing with her husband. She had found out that he had engaged in a series of extramarital affairs. The "breakdown" occurred when he filed for divorce. She reports feeling "totally overwhelmed" by the situation. Her biggest fear is that her husband will gain custody of their sons in the divorce proceedings.

The psychologist learns, in a consultation with the woman's inpatient therapist, that the husband denied having an affair. The husband said that his wife had developed this strange belief as she became increasingly depressed and that the breakup was a result of her psychiatric deterioration, rather than a cause of it.

The testing reveals that she is indeed suffering from Major Depression and also qualifies for a diagnosis of Avoidant Personality Disorder. She is painfully shy, extremely sensitive, and very easily intimidated by other people. Her husband has managed her entire life, which is why the breakup has been so devastating for her. The psychologist does not believe that the woman's report of her husband's affairs is delusional in nature, so he decides not to include the information about the affairs in his assessment report.

The husband requests a copy of a summary of the assessment report, ostensibly to ensure that his wife receives appropriate outpatient care after she leaves the hospital. When the psychologist consults his client about releasing the information to her husband, she simply says, "Okay, whatever he wants." When the psychologist asks, "But what do you want?," she simply answers, "My children."

The psychologist is concerned that some of the information in the assessment summary could reflect negatively on his client in a custody determination and is hesitant to release it to the husband. The psychologist wishes he had included more of the client's statements about her husband's possible misbehavior during the marriage in the report.

What should the psychologist do?

SUMMARY

This chapter addressed issues in diagnostic assessment and psychological and educational testing. Although psychiatric diagnosis is intended to enhance clinicians' understanding of clients' problems, critics argue that clients are simply pigeonholed by diagnostic classifications, with little attention paid to their individual life circumstances. The fascination with diagnostic testing can also lead to the misclassification of clients if clinicians fail to take into account the population base rates of the conditions they are attempting to diagnose.

Informed consent issues for testing include discussing with clients the tests to be used and the purpose of the testing, as well as providing feedback when testing is completed. Feedback enables clients to make an informed decision about sharing evaluation reports with other agencies and professionals. Clinicians should use only well-validated tests and only for the purpose for which they were developed and the populations with which they were validated. Clinicians should be sensitive to diversity issues in assessment and avoid evaluating members of diverse groups by reference to norms developed with more homogeneous samples.

Computer-based test administration and scoring are very useful technological aids that reduce response and scoring errors. However, taking a test on computer may have an adverse effect on the performance of clients unused to computers. Actuarial computer-based test interpretations are a useful component in the interpretation process, but assessment reports should not simply consist of printouts of actuarial interpretations. Reports should integrate information from all the sources available to a competent assessment professional.

NOTES

1. McMinn, Ellens, and Soref (1999) suggested that professionals might also need to inform clients prior to testing if they intend to use a computer-based test interpretation as the final test report because this practice is inconsistent with standards of professional practice.

2. Ethical issues pertaining to suicide prevention will be discussed in Chapter 13.

3. Most tests are also protected by copyright, which would make it a violation of copyright law, as well as an ethical violation, to publish or reveal the content of tests.

4. Clinicians using computer-based test interpretation software should clarify whether the program's interpretations are based on data from computerized, rather than paper-and-pencil, administration of the test.

5. As discussed in Chapter 7, these issues can also arise when a clinician is working for an MCO that rewards efforts to contain costs.

Chapter 9

The Use of Computer Technology in Professional Practice

The mental health professions, along with the rest of the world, have been revolutionized by developments in computer technology during the past 40 years. Since the early 1990s, the use of Internet technology in the delivery of psychological services has been described as "the fastest growing aspect of telehealth" (Fisher & Fried, 2003, p. 103).[1] Current estimates indicate that hundreds of Web sites offer some sort of mental health services, although recent surveys located only 136 Web counseling sites (Heinlen, Welfel, Richmond, & Rak, 2003) and "only 44 separate active sites" operated by doctoral-level psychologists (Heinlen, Welfel, Richmond, & O'Donnell, 2003, p. 121). A small minority of online providers (11% in one survey) offer psychological assessment services, consisting mainly of personality tests (Heinlen, Welfel, Richmond, & O'Donnell, 2003). In addition, many mental health organizations conduct online support groups.

Most of the Internet sites offering psychological services use either simultaneous (synchronous) or time-delayed (asynchronous) text-based methods of service delivery (Manhal-Baugus, 2001). Chat technology is an example of a synchronous method, while e-mail communication, the most common form of e-therapy, uses asynchronous communication. Synchronous televideo and audio conferencing (e.g., voice over IP) are less frequently used technologies (Heinlen, Welfel, Richmond, & O'Donnell, 2003; Manhal-Baugus, 2001).

Online group activities, like traditional face-to-face groups, involve even more complex ethical issues than e-therapy with individual clients, including therapists' reduced ability to control interactions between group members during sessions (Oravec, 2000). The remainder of this chapter will be concerned with issues pertaining to the provision of Internet-based mental health services to individual clients.

In spite of the rapid growth of Web-based psychological services, the financial viability of e-therapy for providers remains questionable. In fact, both of the survey studies of e-therapy Web sites cited previously reported that a large percentage of sites (up to 37%) were no longer operational a year later (Heinlen, Welfel, Richmond, & O'Donnell, 2003; Heinlen, Welfel, Richmond, & Rak, 2003). When submitting claims for payment or client reimbursement, e-providers are ethically obligated to inform third-party payers (e.g., health insurance providers) that services were provided using computer technology (ACA, 2005, C.6.b; APA, 2002, 6.06). However, most health insurers require face-to-face meetings for reimbursement, creating a major financial restriction for e-therapy (McCarty & Clancy, 2002).

SPECIALTY GUIDELINES FOR E-THERAPY

Computer-assisted therapy raises a number of extremely serious ethical concerns, besides those affecting therapy in general. In fact, 36% of the psychologists surveyed in one study regarded e-therapy as inherently unethical due to intractable ethical problems (McMinn, Buchanan, Ellens, & Ryan, 1999). Others believe that the ethical complexity of e-therapy at least requires "specialized suggestions for ethical practice" (Ragusea & VandeCreek, 2003, p. 95). Unfortunately, APA has chosen to regard the Internet delivery of mental health services as essentially similar to traditional face-to-face psychotherapy, but there is little question that the two methods differ substantially (Heinlen, Welfel, Richmond, & O'Donnell, 2003). On the other hand, coverage of issues unique to e-therapy was expanded significantly in the current version of the *Code of Ethics* (ACA, 2005, A.12). In addition to the ACA and APA ethical codes, diverse professional organizations have published guidelines to specifically address the ethical provision of online mental health services. ACA published a set of *Ethical Standards for Internet Online Counseling* (1999), and the APA Ethics Committee (1997) published the *APA Statement Concerning Services by Telephone, Teleconferencing, and Internet.* In addition, the National Board for Certified Counselors (NBCC, 2001) created standards in *The Practice of Internet Counseling,* and the International Society for Mental Health Online (ISMHO, 2000) published its *Suggested Principles for the Online Provision of Mental Health Services.* The guidance provided in these documents overlaps considerably, but it is clear that providing competent, ethically sensitive e-therapy is an extremely complex and challenging undertaking requiring a strong personal commitment on the part of the pioneers to preserve the highest professional standards and ethical ideals of their profession (Fisher & Fried, 2003).

CASE EXAMPLE 9.1

A couple interested in marital therapy contacts an e-therapist. They report that they have been experiencing marital conflict for the past six months and that the husband has become very depressed. They are uncertain whether they should pursue therapy online or with a face-to-face therapist. The e-therapist informs them that marital conflict (i.e., Partner Relational Problem) is generally not a diagnosis covered by health insurance plans (which is true), so they might want to consider the fact that e-therapy is generally less expensive than traditional therapy sessions.

BENEFICENCE

Computer-assisted therapy can enhance the availability of mental health services for people who find it difficult to arrange face-to-face therapy meetings. Rural populations, the elderly, and people with physical disabilities are groups who could benefit from the opportunity to access mental health services in their homes. Other client populations (e.g., bulimics) unlikely to seek traditional face-to-face therapy may also be attracted to e-therapy (Robinson & Serfaty, 2003). Unfortunately, many of these traditionally underserved populations, including lower socioeconomic status individuals, are less likely to have Internet access, so this method might do little in the short term to alter the cultural inequality of access to treatment (Bloom, 1998).

Those who do gain access will find that e-therapy is generally less expensive than traditional mental health services (Manhal-Baugus, 2001). Other potential advantages of e-therapy include easing the problem of scheduling therapy contacts, allowing clients to access services without the risk of being observed entering or leaving a psychotherapist's office, and simplifying clients' completion of assessments and between-session homework assignments (Ragusea & VandeCreek, 2003; Sampson, Kolodinsky, & Greeno, 1997). When e-therapy is conducted by e-mail, no set appointment time is involved. Clients gain the flexibility and convenience of e-mailing at their own pace; they have the opportunity to edit messages to describe their life circumstances, thoughts, and feelings as effectively as possible and to retain a complete record of their e-therapy interactions on their computer (ISMHO, 2002). Some clients might also be more comfortable self-disclosing via typewritten computer exchanges than in face-to-face conversation (Heinlen, Welfel, Richmond, & O'Donnell, 2003).

In recent years, telephone therapy has proven to be an efficient and cost-effective intervention modality (Manhal-Baugus, 2001). Likewise, interactive computer programs have been used successfully in the treatment of anxiety and mood disorders as supplements to in-person psychotherapy and as a stand-alone treatment method (Taylor & Luce, 2003). However, the few preliminary assessments of the efficacy of e-therapy, relative to traditional psychotherapy, have produced mixed results (Heinlen, Welfel, Richmond, & O'Donnell, 2003). Therefore, the exciting *potential* benefits of computer-assisted therapy are as yet unproven.

CASE EXAMPLE 9.2

A licensed therapist creates a psychoeducational Web site encouraging people to seek mental health services and explaining the various forms of e-therapy as a 21st-century alternative to traditional psychotherapy. The site has a link to the therapist's e-therapy practice Web page.

NONMALEFICENCE

In addition to concerns about its effectiveness, there are significant risks associated with clients' participation in e-therapy (ACA, 2005, A.12.b). At present, the most problematic ethical issue is the terribly inadequate risk management options of most geographically distant e-therapists (Smith & Reynolds, 2002). Even if an e-therapist did respond in a timely manner to a client's e-mail, would an e-mail response be sufficient to manage a crisis in the client's life? An e-mail message is not likely to be of substantive assistance to an acutely suicidal client (ACA, 2005, A.12.g.9). Critics argue that the problematic nature of risk management procedures associated with e-therapy makes it an unethical form of mental health service delivery at present (Smith & Reynolds, 2002).

Clinicians contemplating practicing e-therapy can take proactive steps to minimize client risk. They need to obtain accurate documentation of a client's identity and location, in part so they can arrange in advance for mental health professionals in the e-client's local area to be on-call to provide a face-to-face intervention in a crisis (Heinlen, Welfel, Richmond, & O'Donnell, 2003; NBCC, 2001; Ragusea & VandeCreek, 2003). E-therapists could even require distant potential e-therapy clients to obtain an initial screening assessment from a local practitioner, so clients will create a connection with a practitioner who can intervene in the event of a crisis; alternatively, clients might decide to participate in conventional psychotherapy with their local practitioner (Fisher & Fried, 2003). Clearly, limiting online therapy to clients in the e-therapist's local area reduces the ethical (and legal) complications associated with e-therapy, like the crisis intervention issue. The trade-off is that such a policy also reduces the potential benefits of online technology to rural clients in need of such services (Ragusea & VandeCreek, 2003).

E-therapists also need to develop proactive guidelines regarding the circumstances under which e-therapy sessions should be replaced or supplemented by face-to-face meetings with a therapist (ACA, 2005, A.12.c; Oravec, 2000). Indications of the need for face-to-face sessions might include ongoing concerns about a client's social isolation, increasing dependency on computer usage, or more traditional signs of the need for increased therapeutic vigilance (e.g., exacerbation of problems, suicidal ideation, development of psychotic symptoms).

CASE EXAMPLE 9.3

An e-therapist begins conducting synchronous "chat" therapy with a female client. After two sessions, she asks him if he is the same "Ron, the psychologist" she had met in an online dating chat room several months earlier. He immediately realizes that she is the "Betty" with whom he had chatted extensively and shared a lot of personal information.

INTEGRITY

The ethical standard concerning media presentations applies to therapeutic activities (e.g., assessment, consultation, counseling) carried out electronically (ACA, 2005, C.6.c). Therapists also incur an ethical obligation to be extremely careful about presenting their credentials and licensure status accurately on their own Web page and other Internet sites (ACA, 1999; APA, 2002, 5.01[b]). They should provide a vita that potential clients can peruse to familiarize themselves with the therapist's background and education; more extensive documentation of their credentials should be available upon request (Barak, 1999; Bloom, 1998; Heinlen, Welfel, Richmond, & O'Donnell, 2003). Sites for Web practices involving more than one professional should provide the credentials of each practitioner providing services to online clients. Although these points might seem obvious, a recent survey indicated that 36% of sampled Web sites provided no information on the professional credentials of service providers (Heinlen, Welfel, Richmond, & Rak, 2003). Psychological services Web sites should also provide contact information and links to the Web sites of the certification and licensing boards through which the professionals practice, so consumers will have easy access should they desire to file a complaint (NBCC, 2001). In another study, only 34% of the surveyed sites even indicated the state in which the practitioner was licensed (Heinlen, Welfel, Richmond, & O'Donnell, 2003).

From a client's point of view, it is difficult, if not impossible, to verify the competence of an e-therapist. Although some services (e.g., http://www.metanoia.org/imhs/directry.htm) will help clients verify e-therapists' credentials, ultimately clients cannot even be certain that the e-mail correspondence they receive was actually composed by the therapist they agreed to correspond with (Smith & Reynolds, 2002). E-therapists need to recognize their obligation to communicate effectively and extensively with their clients to minimize the ambiguity inherent in e-therapy contexts (ACA, 2005, A.12.g).

CASE EXAMPLE 9.4

A Web site advertises individual and group therapy services via the Internet provided by "a master's-level counseling student" with both individual and group counseling experience.

COMPETENCE

The provision of online mental health services requires special competencies of both therapists and clients.

Therapist Competence

In addition to the "normal" competence issues relevant to conducting therapy and assessment, e-therapy should be regarded as a wholly new area of professional competence (Barak, 1999; Bloom, 1998). When entering into a new area of practice, mental health professionals are ethically required to "undertake relevant education, training, supervised experience, consultation, or study" to develop competence (APA, 2002, 2.01[c]). The APA Ethics Committee (1997) statement and the ACA *Ethical Standards for Internet Online Counseling* (1999) and *Code of Ethics* (2005, C.2.b) all emphasize this point. Unfortunately, since e-therapy is an emerging area of professional practice, clearly established standards for competent service delivery have not yet been formulated. In such cases, professionals "nevertheless take reasonable steps to ensure the competence of their work" and protect their clients from harm (APA, 2002, 2.01[o]).

As a first step, professionals interested in practicing online incur an ethical duty to develop the technical expertise with computers necessary to conduct effective, confidential interactions with clients[2], as well as to troubleshoot their own computer systems and advise clients on theirs when problems arise, as they inevitably do (Glueckhauf, Pickett, Ketterson, Loomis, & Rozensky, 2003; Ragusea & VandeCreek, 2003). Since most clinicians do not possess this degree of technical knowledge, they are obligated to acquire additional training in computer science or the assistance of a technical support person to achieve this standard of technical competence.

Second, the burden is squarely on the e-therapist to determine, through a thoughtfully developed screening process, whether online services are appropriate for a given client and to develop a clearly articulated treatment plan for each client (ACA, 2005, A.12.b, A.12.c). (Some of the client variables relevant to this determination are discussed in the next section.) This task is considerably more difficult than it might first appear. Assessing mental status and generating an accurate diagnosis in the absence of the behavioral and sensory cues available in face-to-face assessment is a significant clinical challenge. Conducting televideo diagnostic interviews with e-clients over the Internet (meaning the therapist can actually see the client) can enhance the reliability and validity of the online assessment process. Studies have indicated that the use of computers supporting broad bandwidth connectivity, and consequently high-quality audio and video, resulted in diagnostic ratings comparable to face-to-face interviews (Yoshino et al., 2001). However, state-of-the-art equipment is required at both ends of the Internet connection to achieve these benefits. Narrow bandwidth televideo interviews were less effective, due to breaks in audio transmission and video distortions that made it impossible to use important verbal and nonverbal information, such as tone of voice, facial expression, and behavioral gestures (Yoshino et al., 2001).

Third, e-therapists should seek opportunities to learn more about fostering client relationships built primarily on written communication, as relationship issues are known to be a major determinant of therapeutic success (e.g., Norcross, 2002). Clearly, the therapeutic alliance is likely to develop very differently in text-based e-therapy communications due to the absence of verbal and nonverbal cues (Ragusea & VandeCreek, 2003), which can also create considerable potential for misinterpretation of text messages (Heinlen, Welfel, Richmond, & O'Donnell, 2003; NBCC, 2001; Smith & Reynolds, 2002). Currently, therapists do not receive much, if any, training in narrative interpretation or text-based communication; therefore, their competence in delivering such services is likely to be quite limited (Manhal-Baugus, 2001).

On the other hand, some aspects of communicating with clients via e-mail can potentially enhance e-therapists' competence. When using e-mail, professionals have more time to reflect on their clients' statements and inquiries and to construct their responses carefully and thoughtfully. When complex issues arise, they can draft an e-mail reply, review and edit the message, and even obtain feedback from a senior colleague or supervisor before sending it to their client (Robinson & Serfaty, 2003).

CASE EXAMPLE 9.5

A counselor who is a heavy smoker has had many clients ask her not to smoke during sessions. She finds it very difficult to go for 50 minutes without a cigarette; as a result, she feels she is less effective in counseling when she does not smoke. She has tried to quit smoking in the past, but with no success. She is no longer interested in quitting. When she learns about e-counseling, she thinks that practicing from her home computer would allow her to continue to smoke during sessions without imposing her habit on her clients.

Fourth, professionals contemplating the practice of e-therapy across state lines should consult the licensing and certification authorities of their own state to ensure that they are not violating board rules by treating e-clients in other states (ACA, 2005, A.12.e, A.12.f; Smith &

Reynolds, 2002). E-providers must also familiarize themselves with the mental health regulations in the client's state because the professional could be held to that standard (McCarty & Clancy, 2002).

Malpractice issues can easily arise in connection with e-therapy because most ethics complaints assert that the professional failed to provide services consistent with the profession's standard of care; of course, specific standards do not yet exist for many aspects of e-therapy (McCarty & Clancy, 2002). The lack of specific standards does not free professionals who claim competence in e-therapy from legal responsibility for any adverse consequences arising from their failure to provide services at a level consistent with the ethical code of their profession. In other words, professionals providing e-therapy services will be held to the professional standards applicable to the provision of face-to-face psychotherapy, counseling, and consultation. Complaints arising from e-therapists' limited ability to intervene in crisis situations are especially likely. Therapists' responsibility for protecting their clients from harm is not diminished, though their ability to recognize and accurately assess suicidal potential through typed exchanges may be limited (Bloom, 1998; Sampson et al., 1997). Professionals should consult their professional liability insurance provider to see if their coverage applies to the provision of online mental health services (Watson, Tenenbaum, Lidor, & Alfermann, 2001).

Remember the study cited earlier (i.e., McMinn, Buchanan, et al., 1999), in which 36% of the surveyed psychologists regarded the current practice of e-therapy to be inherently unethical? Therapists would be well advised to give considerable thought to the risks associated with conducting e-therapy; those deciding to practice e-therapy need to be extremely cautious in their preparation for, and delivery of, online therapeutic services.

CASE EXAMPLE 9.6

A counselor with 15 years in private practice has been experiencing increasing symptoms of burnout. He is having trouble maintaining professional boundaries; he even asked one of his clients to meet him for a drink, so they could continue their discussion after a session. He decides to start an e-therapy practice because he believes that computer-mediated therapy relationships will be less intense and provocative for him.

At present, e-therapists have been trained to work from models of counseling and psychotherapy developed for traditional therapy contexts. It is likely that new models for conducting text-based therapy will emerge in time, but currently, e-therapy clients are receiving services that have been validated only for face-to-face therapy interventions (Manhal-Baugus, 2001). Clearly, a great deal of research is needed regarding the additional variables affecting the therapeutic relationship in computer-assisted therapy (Sampson et al., 1997).

E-therapy competence will likely improve as future therapists receive greater exposure to e-therapy contexts during their graduate training. Even if they do not go on to provide e-therapy services, their appreciation of the role of narrative in face-to-face therapy interaction will improve through experiences with purely text-based self-presentations of clients (Oravec, 2000). Provided that competent supervision is available, mental health professionals should be encouraged to experience this "brave new world" of text-based therapy during the course of their formal and practicum training.

Client Competence: Appropriateness of E-Therapy

What of the "competence" required of clients in order to benefit from e-therapy? There are many opinions on this issue but very little data to support them (Ragusea & VandeCreek, 2003). The ISMHO (2002) guidelines present nine basic issues professionals should consider in determining the appropriateness of online therapy for a client. Clients, like therapists, would need to have private access to computer equipment adequate for the desired e-therapy modality (e.g., videoconferencing, e-mail). Unfortunately, such a requirement might dispro-portionately exclude culturally diverse populations from access to this new therapeutic oppor-tunity (Ragusea & VandeCreek, 2003). Client communication skills are also important, but rather than the oral expression essential in traditional psychotherapy, reading ability and writ-ing skills are critical for text-based forms of e-therapy. Clients with poor writing skills or low intelligence would, therefore, be poor candidates. The presence of physical conditions that affect a client's ability to see the computer screen (e.g., visual limitations) or to type might also exclude some clients. Moreover, the advisability of face-to-face treatment options is affected by the nature of the client's presenting problems, the client's involvement in any other therapeutic relationship, and the availability of traditional treatment options. Clients suffering from significant psychiatric impairment require closer supervision than an e-therapist can provide. Ultimately, e-providers need to make their own judgments based on their assess-ment of their competence and the potential risks and benefits of e-therapy for different types of clients, then include on their Web site a list of presenting problems that are *inappropriate* for e-therapy with them (NBCC, 2001). Furthermore, therapists should develop a policy and intake procedure to determine whether e-therapy is appropriate for a potential client; this pol-icy should be communicated explicitly to potential clients (ACA, 1999). As discussed earlier, the prospective client's location might also be a determinant of the appropriateness (and legal-ity) of providing e-therapy (ACA, 1999; Ragusea & VandeCreek, 2003).

Because so many minors use the Internet, mental health Web sites should post a clearly understandable policy regarding the availability of treatment services to minors (ACA, 1999). Most e-therapy sites are limited to serving adults (Heinlen, Welfel, Richmond, & O'Donnell, 2003). Written permission of a parent or legal guardian is required in order to provide e-therapy to a minor or individual incapable of providing legal consent; the identity of the individual providing consent must also be verified (ACA, 1999; NBCC, 2001). Better methods of veri-fying the age of e-clients need to be developed "to avoid ethical and legal complications from serving minors without parental permission" (Heinlen, Welfel, Richmond, & O'Donnell, 2003, p. 122). Laws regarding minors' ability to self-consent to therapy vary from state to state, which again highlights the importance of e-providers learning the mental health laws for each state in which they practice e-therapy (ACA, 1999).

CASE EXAMPLE 9.7

A clinical psychologist discovers that the client she is treating via e-mail appears to be suf-fering from Dissociative Identity Disorder. She finds the process of corresponding with his different personalities a fascinating experience. With his consent, she saves all of their corre-spondence because she expects to write extensively about his case in the future. However, he reports that his life problems are getting worse. His marriage is falling apart. He says that he heard about an inpatient facility in another city that specializes in the treatment of dissocia-tive disorders. He wonders if he would benefit from pursuing treatment there.

The psychologist tells him that inpatient programs are a last resort and encourages him to continue e-therapy with her. She offers to communicate with his wife so that she will better understand what he is going through.

INFORMED CONSENT

All information and policies relevant to a client's decision to participate in treatment must be available to the client (ACA, 1999). In addition to the issues normally associated with informed consent (e.g., disclosure of professional credentials, services provided, fee structure, limits of confidentiality) discussed in previous chapters, there are other ethical considerations unique to conducting computer-assisted therapy and assessment (ACA, 2005, A.12.g). This information can be posted on Web pages that the client must visit during the enrollment process, or it can be delivered to potential clients via e-mail. With regard to clients' ability to comprehend informed consent materials, professionals must develop methods for identifying special language needs of online clients so the reading level and primary language of the client can be taken into account (ACA, 2005, A.12.h.7; APA, 2002, 3.10[a]). Formal informed consent for online therapy and assessment (including an HIPAA Notice of Privacy Practices) is generally obtained by having a client download a consent statement (or receive it by fax transmission), sign it, and return it to the provider, although some provider Web sites have electronic signature capabilities (Heinlen, Welfel, Richmond, & O'Donnell, 2003). A statement concerning measures taken to ensure the security and privacy of information transmitted by and to clients should be posted on the provider's Web site, consistent with HIPAA regulations (Fisher & Fried, 2003). APA provides a sample on its Web site (http://helping.apa.org/privacy.html). Welfel (2003) has also suggested that providers obtain clients' informed consent for release of information before they initiate professional communication involving e-mail or Internet chat rooms.

Professionals must provide a clear description of the range of services offered online, the method(s) used to deliver those services (e.g., e-mail, teleconferencing, instant messaging), and the identities, qualifications, and licensure status of all those providing services, as well as contact information clients can use to reach the provider's state board or other licensing body or professional organization in the event that they have a question or complaint (NBCC, 2001). E-therapists should disclose the circumstances under which other members of their staff might read a client's e-mails or generate responses to them (Ragusea & VandeCreek, 2003). Some therapists seek to avoid legal liability issues by describing their online services as "psychoeducational" or "coaching." If these terms are used, they should be described explicitly, particularly as to how they differ from traditional psychotherapy or counseling (ACA, 1999; APA, 2002, 10.01[a]). Descriptions of services should also include other details of obvious interest to clients. For example, in e-mail interactions, how quickly can clients expect a reply to their e-mail? How quickly are clients expected to communicate again after receiving a response from the therapist? What steps can clients take if they do not hear from the therapist within the expected timeframe (ACA, 1999; Ragusea & VandeCreek, 2003)? What are the procedures for contacting the therapist in an emergency if the therapist is offline (ACA, 2005, A.12.g.9; NBCC, 2001)?

A description of the fee structure should address all potential charges, particularly if clients making frequent use of services will incur additional charges, or if clients making no use of services (e.g., not submitting an e-mail during a seven-day period) will nevertheless be charged. Clients need to know how to determine whether their health plan will cover e-therapy services (Fisher & Fried, 2003); the range of payment options, including acceptable forms of online payment (and the security procedures employed); as well as the process for payment by mail or telephone (ACA, 2005, A.12.a; APA, 2002, 6.04).

Consistent with the principle of nonmaleficence, professionals should inform potential clients of the risks of e-therapy discussed earlier (ACA, 2005, A.12.a). For example, providers should point out the limited availability and efficacy of online assistance in the event of a crisis or emergency (including power outages). Providers are also required to inform clients that online therapy is an experimental area of practice, the effectiveness of which has not yet been validated empirically (APA, 2002, 10.01[b]; Ragusea & VandeCreek, 2003). Clients should be reminded of the alternative mental health resources available in their community (ISMHO, 2002).

Like all therapy clients, e-clients must be informed of limitations of their confidentiality; if offering services to clients in other states, providers should be familiar with disclosure laws for each client's state of residence (APA, 2002, 4.02). Clients must also be made aware of potential threats to the confidentiality of information transmitted over the Internet that may be beyond the control of even competent and conscientious mental health professionals (ACA, 2005, A.12.g.1; APA, 2002, 4.02[c]). For example, clients using Internet service providers (ISPs) like America Online (AOL) or Microsoft Service Network (MSN) should be aware that these services monitor e-mail transmissions and are capable of accessing copies of subscribers' e-mail communications (Heinlen, Welfel, Richmond, & O'Donnell, 2003). Consistent with HIPAA guidelines, clients should be informed of the provisions the therapist has made to protect the security of the information they exchange and of additional steps clients can take to preserve their privacy. Clients should also be informed of how the therapist will store transcripts of sessions or client e-mails and who (e.g., employees) might have access to those records (ACA, 1999).

Finally, e-providers should present the potential advantages of e-therapy, consistent with the ethical duty of beneficence discussed earlier (ACA, 2005, A.12.a). However, they should be careful not to exaggerate the potential benefits; professionals must be honest and accurate in these, as in all, public statements (APA, 2002, 5.01[b]; Welfel, 2003).

CASE EXAMPLE 9.8

A counselor offering online services receives an inquiry from a man about providing counseling for his 10-year-old son, who is having increasing problems abiding by the rules set for his behavior at home and at school. Although the counselor had expected her online practice to attract only adult clients, she says that she has no problem with the arrangement, as long as the parents fax her their consent to treat their son and the boy agrees. She says that she has treated children with behavioral problems in her practice before.

CONFIDENTIALITY

Along with the usual concerns about confidentiality in psychotherapy, delivering psychological services via computer technology adds a host of new threats to the confidentiality of clients' identity and PHI. Fittingly, ACA (1999) has established standards that emphasize confidentiality issues unique to Internet counseling. Unfortunately, in many cases, "online counselors seem oblivious to the difficulties" (McCarty & Clancy, 2002, p. 158).

Confidentiality is impossible to guarantee on the Internet because few users understand the complexities of Internet security. Counselors are required to execute a waiver agreement with clients stating that clients recognize that confidentiality cannot be guaranteed for information transmitted online, in spite of the best efforts of the counselor (ACA, 1999). As discussed earlier, knowledge of cyber-technology or the availability of expert technical consultation is a vital aspect of the competence needed to adequately protect clients' privacy. Not long ago, most providers of psychological services on the Internet used unsecured Web sites (Barak, 1999); unfortunately, many still do. Mental health professionals should use only secured sites (i.e., sites providing state-of-the-art data encryption security) to transmit confidential information.

E-mail communications between providers and clients must use encrypted data transmission to prevent breaches of confidentiality if messages are stored on clients' computers, though this may require that therapist and client acquire the same encryption software (ACA, 2005, A.12.g.5, A.12.g.6; Mathy, Kerr, & Haydin, 2003). Downloading free e-mail encryption software and secure e-mail services are options for both clients and providers (Manhal-Baugus, 2001). Nevertheless, one recent survey revealed that only 27% of sampled e-therapy sites used encryption (Heinlen, Welfel, Richmond, & O'Donnell, 2003). The use of firewalls and virus detection software is also essential to prevent unauthorized access to confidential information and protect clients from transmission of viruses, worms, and the like (ACA, 1999; Fisher & Fried, 2003; Mathy et al., 2003). Perhaps not surprisingly, privacy protections used to collect fees tend to be much more sophisticated than those used to ensure that other types of client communications are kept secure (Heinlen, Welfel, Richmond, & O'Donnell, 2003). Clearly, professionals should not be so self-serving and selective in enacting state-of-the-art security measures. E-mail software and files can also be stored on removable drives, though wherever they are stored, password protection should be employed.

Although user errors could still potentially compromise the confidentiality of transmissions, with the addition of intruder detection systems (IDS), at least on the part of the therapist, the risks to privacy and confidentiality can be argued to be "approximate to the risk in a traditional office" (Ragusea & VandeCreek, 2003, p. 97). Remember that in traditional therapy settings, conversations can be "overheard" and theft of recorded information can occur. Use of telephones, particularly wireless phones, is also far from secure, so e-therapy is not the only treatment modality that involves risks to confidentiality (Masi & Freedman, 2001). Ultimately, professionals must determine the level of security risk they deem acceptable, just as they do in the operation of a traditional psychotherapy office (Ragusea & VandeCreek, 2003). (Is a locked filing cabinet sufficient to safeguard records, or is a steel office door also required?)

As with any mental health records, therapists are responsible for taking all possible precautions, including using passwords and hidden files, to prevent unauthorized access to client information. There have been numerous illustrations of the dangers of storing confidential client information on the same computer system used to store and post Web site material. One was the accidental posting of the confidential psychological treatment records of 62 children and adolescents on the University of Montana Web site for eight days in 2001 (Piller, 2001).

The use of chat rooms and instant messaging has the advantage of not leaving a permanent record of the interaction on either party's computer, unless the person chooses to save the information. On the other hand, these interactions are very difficult to secure and make identity verification an even more complex issue. Ragusea and VandeCreek (2003) suggest that the therapist and client begin their exchanges with a keyword or phrase known only to them whenever they initiate a chat room conversation. However, the possibility always exists that these conversations (and hence, the keywords) could be intercepted.

Clients should be advised to address the need for privacy in their home and to terminate a telephone or computer contact if they experience an intrusion into the privacy of a session (Ragusea & VandeCreek, 2003). E-therapists can also recommend that clients delete old therapy-related e-mails. Both clients and therapists should use some innocuous expression in the subject line of therapy e-mails that will not arouse the interest of family members accessing the client's mailbox. (However, care must be taken that the client does not accidentally delete such messages without opening them, failing to realize what they are.)

A final issue related to both privacy and avoiding inappropriate charges to clients is the need for online providers to establish a reliable, valid method for determining the identity of the client who is participating in online treatment (ACA, 2005, A.12.h.4). Providers need to make certain that the person they are communicating with and charging for services is the same individual that consented to participate in e-therapy. This issue is relatively easily resolved if an initial face-to-face screening interview is conducted and video conferencing technology is used for subsequent sessions. In other online contexts, establishing client identity is more complicated. The use of passwords is helpful both in ensuring confidentiality and establishing the identity of the person the professional is interacting with (Fisher & Fried, 2003).

CASE EXAMPLE 9.9

A counseling psychologist interacts with his e-therapy clients via e-mail. One day, he receives an e-mail from a client's daughter. The e-mail was sent from the client's computer, and the therapist remembers that the client has mentioned her daughter being a "troubled girl." The daughter informs the therapist that her mother is physically abusive toward her and her brother. She asks the therapist to help them and not to reveal to her mother that she has contacted the therapist because she fears physical reprisals from her mother.

CONDUCTING ASSESSMENTS USING THE INTERNET

The use of computers in administering and interpreting psychological tests was discussed in Chapter 8. That discussion concerned a client completing an assessment on a computer in a clinician's office. The ethical considerations are somewhat different when clients are using home computers to complete tests and receive feedback on their performance. Many mental health Web sites operated by NIMH and various professional organizations offer interactive screening and assessment for depression and other mental health problems. Internet-based testing has the obvious advantage that it can be conducted anywhere the client can access an Internet connection (Sampson et al., 2003). "Overall, the evidence suggests that computers can make assessments more efficient, more accurate, and less expensive" (Taylor & Luce, 2003, p. 18).

Obviously, the selection of tests to be administered via the Internet is crucially important. Assessment instruments (tests, checklists, etc.) are generally adapted very easily to computerized administration, but there must be adequate evidence supporting their reliability and validity when administered via computer, as opposed to a paper-and-pencil administration

(ACA, 2005, E.6.a; APA, 2002, 9.02). Clearly, taking a test on the Internet is a different assessment context than even a computerized administration in a clinician's office. One significant issue involves the possibility of a testing session being interrupted by the temporary loss of Internet connectivity (Buchanan, 2002). This situation could distort the data received by clinicians and create confusion regarding what clients should do about completing the assessment when they reconnect to the Web site. Conducting assessments and properly substantiating conclusions drawn from assessment procedures is also trickier when done over the Internet because professionals lack behavioral observations that typically provide important data in traditional assessment contexts (Fisher & Fried, 2003).

The ethical obligation to provide competent, understandable feedback following an assessment procedure also applies to Internet testing. Simply providing clients with direct Internet access to computer-generated interpretations of test results is definitely unethical, as clients are not qualified to differentiate valid and invalid interpretations (Sampson et al., 2003). Providing ethically appropriate testing feedback is complicated by the increased difficulty in assessing how well clients understand feedback presented via telephone, e-mail, or some other form of electronic communication (ACA, 2005, E.1.b; APA, 2002, 9.10). The clinician cannot see (or necessarily hear) clients' reaction to the feedback, and clients might not bother to ask questions of interest to them because of the effort involved and the time delay in receiving a response. At present, it would be ethically inadvisable to engage in Internet assessment involving potentially disturbing client feedback unless the testing is conducted by an e-therapist in the context of a previously established therapeutic relationship (Buchanan, 2002).

Finally, in addition to testing, "handheld computers or personal digital assistants (PDAs) have been used to collect real-time, naturalistic data on a variety of variables," such as mood or the cognitive and environmental contexts of behaviors, like bulimic episodes (Taylor & Luce, 2003, p. 18). Clients can use these devices to conveniently store and transmit data to their therapist, whether they are engaged in e-therapy or traditional, face-to-face therapy sessions.

CASE EXAMPLE 9.10

A large online psychology practice offers a variety of fee-based personality assessment and interpretation packages using objective personality measures that have been validated extensively in the United States. The provider is very careful to ensure that people from non-English-speaking countries do not access the tests. However, she decides that people living in Great Britain can obtain valid interpretations because they also speak English.

CONCLUSION

To date, the mental health professions seem to be focused on requiring e-therapy to achieve equivalence to face-to-face psychotherapy. Clearly, it is a very different treatment context, in both positive and negative ways. Hopefully, professionals will continue their efforts to minimize the risks associated with e-therapy (e.g., threats to client confidentiality), while focusing on developing the positive potential of this radically new method of service delivery. Web-based delivery of mental health services has the potential to combine interaction with a licensed provider and social support (through chat groups), frequent monitoring of symptoms and progress in treatment, and interactive psychoeducational information, all of which can be accessed by clients without leaving their homes (Taylor & Luce, 2003). The fact that e-therapy is not equivalent to conventional psychotherapy is not necessarily a liability. Professionals simply need to recognize it as a unique treatment modality and develop thoughtful, creative solutions to its ethical complexities in order to realize its potential for benefiting clients whose needs can be better addressed with the assistance of computer technology.

PRACTICE CASE INVOLVING THE MODEL OF ETHICAL DECISION MAKING

An e-therapist was contacted by a couple requesting that she conduct marital therapy with them via e-mail. The counselor agreed when they insisted that face-to-face marital sessions were not a viable alternative. Both husband and wife appeared highly motivated to work at improving the relationship, though they had become quite alienated from each other during recent years. One day, the therapist received an e-mail from the wife. It was written to a friend of hers but inadvertently sent to the counselor. (The first letter of her e-mail address was the same as that of the intended recipient. Apparently, the client had clicked on the wrong address from a drop-down menu.) The e-mail contained several revelations for the therapist. First, her client revealed that she and her husband had pursued marital therapy online because the husband was a very prominent entertainer who would certainly be recognized by any therapist in a face-to-face meeting. Second, the client described details of a long-term extramarital affair and made it clear that she intended to marry her lover after divorcing her husband. She told her friend that she had encouraged her husband (who knew nothing of her affair) to pursue the marital therapy to show her commitment to the relationship. She believed that she would be able to sabotage any therapeutic progress while making her husband appear responsible for the failure. Ultimately, she said, this strategy would enable her to garner a much larger divorce settlement than if she just left the relationship to be with another man.

The next day, realizing the error she had made, the client e-mailed the therapist to say that if the therapist revealed anything to her husband about the misdirected e-mail message, she would sue her for breach of confidentiality. She told the therapist that she was ethically obligated to continue the e-therapy as if she had never received the other message.

What course of action should the e-therapist take?

SUMMARY

Recent advances in computer technology have revolutionized the provision of mental health services, resulting in complex ethical issues for professionals. Several organizations, including APA and ACA, have issued guidelines or statements pertaining to e-therapy. Although APA does not really distinguish e-therapy from face-to-face therapy, e-therapy is different from traditional therapy in important ways that introduce numerous ethical complexities.

Computer-assisted therapy may potentially benefit clients by reaching traditionally underserved populations, offering services at a lower cost, facilitating client self-disclosure, and providing greater flexibility and convenience in scheduling, especially when e-mail is the primary method of communication. However, professionals must consider the risks of e-therapy, most notably the lack of adequate response options in crisis situations. E-therapists need to be proactive in minimizing such risks.

Online providers should be careful to present their credentials and services accurately on their Web sites. Competence in conducting e-therapy should be considered a separate area of expertise, developed through specialized training, study, and consultation. However, no clear standards currently exist. E-therapists need to develop the technological expertise to interact effectively with clients while preserving confidentiality and to troubleshoot computer problems. They also must identify ways to foster a relationship built primarily on text-based communication and become versed in the mental health laws of those states in which they serve clients. To benefit from e-therapy, clients also need to possess competence in certain areas (e.g., computer skills, reading and writing ability) and have presenting problems that lend themselves to online treatment.

NOTES

1. Telehealth services include telephone contact, teleconferencing (with or without video), e-mail, and Internet chat technology.

2. Since PHI is exchanged electronically in any form of e-therapy, there is no question that e-providers are "covered entities" subject to all HIPAA regulations governing the confidential creation, transmission, and storage of client information.

Chapter 10

Practice and Assessment in Organizational and Business Settings

Many psychological professionals become employees of organizations in a variety of management areas, such as human resources and organizational development, or fulfill specific roles in recruiting, hiring, and evaluating personnel for a company. Others provide services to business organizations as personnel or organizational consultants. Business organizations tend to operate very differently from the institutional mental health settings discussed in Chapter 7, where the professional concerns and responsibilities of physicians, psychologists, counselors, and allied professionals are an integral part of the agency's structure and policies. In business organizations, the ethical values of psychology (e.g., client confidentiality) tend to be far less familiar, but they are still fundamental duties for mental health professionals in such settings. This chapter will examine some of the ethical issues and conflicts encountered most frequently in industrial and business contexts and conclude with a general discussion of concerns that arise in the entrepreneurial practice of a mental health profession, regardless of specialty area.

CASE EXAMPLE 10.1

A counselor working for a manufacturing firm is assigned the task of reducing employee turnover among workers performing a simple, repetitive assembly task. He discovers that brighter employees seem more likely to quit, while employees of lower intelligence stay longer. Both high- and low-intelligence employees can easily become competent at the task. The counselor recommends assessing the intellectual functioning of applicants and hiring those with IQ scores in the low average range. Applicants scoring in higher or lower ranges are told only that their score did not qualify them for the position.

WORKING FOR A BUSINESS ORGANIZATION

As discussed in Chapter 7, professionals who take a job with a company incur a dual set of ethical responsibilities: As psychological professionals, they are obligated to abide by their professional and ethical duties set forth in the "Ethical Principles" (APA, 2002); as employees of a company, they are bound by the policies, goals, and values of that organization. This dual role requires psychologists to always be mindful of their duties as professionals no matter how deeply immersed they become in the operations and pursuit of the financial goals of the organization. Even if psychologists become CEOs of major corporations, as long as they continue to identify themselves professionally as psychologists, their primary duty is to fulfill their ethical obligations as mental health professionals (ACA, 2005, H.2.e; APA, 2002, 1.03).

COMPETENCE

Industrial/organizational (I/O) professionals complete graduate training in this area of psychological specialization, typically with a focus on either industrial (personnel) psychology or organizational behavior. The Society for Industrial and Organizational Psychology (SIOP, Division 14 of APA) has set guidelines for education and training in I/O psychology at both the master's and doctoral levels (SIOP, 1994, 1999). These guidelines require the development of competence in core areas of psychology (e.g., social psychology, personality, history of psychology); data collection and analysis (e.g., statistics, research methods, test construction); and domains specific to I/O psychology, including employee selection, performance appraisal, and organizational development. Psychologists with other areas of specialization (e.g., clinical, experimental) who wish to pursue I/O consulting opportunities would be ethically obligated to follow APA's "Policy on Training for Psychologists Wishing to Change Their Specialty" (Conger, 1976). As discussed in Chapter 2, the policy requires that professionals "meet all requirements of doctoral training in the new psychological specialty," including those for supervised experience (Conger, 1976, p. 424).

Specialty guidelines and ethical guidance are also available for I/O professionals. APA (1981b) published "Specialty Guidelines for the Delivery of Services by Clinical Psychologists, Counseling Psychologists, Industrial/Organizational Psychologists, and School Psychologists." In addition, a number of professional organizations in the business world have produced ethical codes relevant to I/O activities. A particularly useful set for I/O professionals is the Academy of Management's (AOM) *Code of Ethical Conduct* (AOM, 2003).

Although many psychological professionals practice in business settings, business people are not generally very knowledgeable about the mental health professions. They sometimes equate being a psychologist with being an expert in I/O matters, focusing more on the skills and services psychologists can offer than the details of their training and specialty area. Nevertheless, mental health professionals have an ethical duty to limit their activities to areas of practice for which their training has specifically prepared them (ACA, 2005, C.2.a; APA, 2002, 2.01[a]).

CASE EXAMPLE 10.2

A counselor who recently completed her Ph.D. is disheartened by the limited employment prospects for clinicians. She possesses excellent skills in behavior analysis and behavioral therapy techniques. After talking to some friends who work in industry, she decides that she would make more money offering stress management and communications skills workshops for businesses. She sends a resume to local industries in which she presents herself as an "Industrial Behavior Consultant" and accentuates her "graduate background" in I/O psychology. In reality, she took one graduate course in business and career counseling. She is comfortable with the resume because she is extremely competent to provide the services she is offering.

CONSULTING RELATIONSHIPS

Many I/O professionals provide services to business organizations on a consulting basis, rather than as regular employees. I/O consulting arrangements involve many of the same ethical issues as clinical consultation (e.g., informed consent, confidentiality); they are based on the principles of competence, integrity, and objectivity (AOM, 2003). However, other ethical issues, such as fee setting and multiple relationships, take on different forms in I/O consulting.

Financial Arrangements

I/O consultants negotiate contracts with businesses based on the nature of the job and the professional's assessment of the time and resources required to complete it (ACA, 2005, D.2.d; APA, 2002, 6.04[a]). When charges are to reflect actual services rendered, consultants provide realistic estimates; if they find later that the work is going to cost significantly more than they had estimated, they discuss this issue with the recipient of services as soon as possible to obtain approval of the revised budget (APA, 2002, 6.04[d]). Other than their fees, consultants do not seek personal or financial advantage for themselves through their consulting relationships, nor do they allow others to profit from the knowledge they obtain through their consulting activities (AOM, 2003).

CASE EXAMPLE 10.3

An I/O psychologist is hired as a consultant by a software firm to improve a company's procedure for evaluating employee performance, so he interviews several supervisors and employees individually to gather information about the current evaluation process. One employee mentions that she feels she has not been given sufficient credit for developing new banking software that the company expects will double its profits when the software is introduced in the near future. The psychologist wonders on the way home whether he should buy some of the company's stock to take advantage of the anticipated boost in earnings.

Conflict of Interest

Conflicts of interest occur when the objectivity of professionals' judgment is affected by personal interest in a situation, usually as the result of a multiple relationship. Although acting in a manner consistent with their self-interest is not necessarily unethical, professionals must be particularly sensitive to the possibility that their judgment has been unduly influenced by factors of self-interest. If a conflict of interest does exist, or a situation has the potential to result in such a conflict, mental health professionals should inform the client and all others affected directly by the situation about the conflict and what limits must be placed on their activity within the organization to avoid engaging in unprofessional conduct (APA, 2002, 3.06). Even if a situation merely has the potential to be perceived by other professionals or the public as involving a conflict of interest, professionals should avoid the situation, regardless of whether a conflict actually exists.

For example, suppose an I/O psychologist teaching at a university decides to seek part-time outside employment as an organizational consultant for local industries. He meets with the employee relations director of a manufacturing plant, who also turns out to be an I/O psychologist. In the course of their discussion, the director mentions that she has been thinking for some time about pursuing opportunities to teach I/O courses part-time as an adjunct professor. The professor/psychologist tells her that he thinks he can arrange an adjunct appointment for her because he needs help meeting the demand for I/O courses at the university. She replies that the prospects look very good for their relationship to be "mutually beneficial."

In this case, considerable potential for conflict of interest exists on both sides of the relationship. While the university may well need part-time faculty to teach psychology courses, the professor's colleagues might find it suspicious that he is recommending an adjunct whose company has hired him as a consultant. Similarly, if the employee relations director's supervisor hears that she has begun teaching courses in the department in which the firm's new organizational consultant is employed, he might well question whether a *quid pro quo* arrangement (i.e., something given in exchange for something else) was the true explanation of the two events. Even if the two hiring decisions were completely unrelated and serendipitous (if the university had been looking for instructional help in the department of psychology, and the employee relations director had been considering bringing in an organizational consultant) and the two individuals were both very competent and highly qualified for the positions, many observers might wonder whether the situation involved unethical behavior. When situations involving the potential for conflict of interest cannot or should not reasonably be avoided, disinterested third parties (e.g., the department chair at the university, the manager of the manufacturing plant) should be brought into the decision-making process, and the process should be documented carefully and extensively (ACA, 2005, C.3.d, C.6.d; APA, 2002, 3.06).

I/O professionals frequently have consulting arrangements with multiple companies. Working for two competing companies (e.g., two athletic shoe manufacturers) constitutes another sort of multiple relationship and also potentially involves a conflict of interest. Consultants have an ethical duty to avoid such a dual relationship unless they first obtain the consent of all parties involved (AOM, 2003; APA, 2002, 3.05[a]).

Integrity

I/O consultants often become intimately acquainted with the details of a company's operation during the course of their work. They should keep information pertaining to their business clients confidential. However, if consultants discover anything unlawful about the company's activities (e.g., accounting irregularities), they must investigate whether the nature of their relationship with the company would obligate them to report the violation to the proper authorities (ACA, 2005, H.2.e; AOM, 2003; APA, 2002, 4.05[b]).

Mental health professionals also have an obligation not to misrepresent the potential effectiveness of their services. In many instances, I/O professionals might need to educate their business associates about the proper context for evaluating the impact of personnel strategies or program innovations. While psychologists are trained to assess how well an intervention works, people in business sometimes view such matters in simpler, more clear-cut terms: A strategy either works or it doesn't. Psychologists know that in most situations, the reality lies somewhere between and that meaningful change is a lengthy, challenging process. For example, a company that has received many complaints from employees about the subjective nature of supervisors' evaluations of their performance brings in a consultant to suggest improvements to the firm's performance evaluation procedure. The plant manager informs the consultant that the immediate goal is to increase worker satisfaction with the evaluation process. The consultant displays professional integrity by pointing out that virtually *any* change in the current evaluation process is likely to be viewed positively by workers, explaining further that creating an effective, objective evaluation procedure will involve a lengthy process of acquiring input from workers and supervisors and conducting a thorough job analysis for each type of position. At the end of their meeting, the manager will be in a much better position to conceptualize the task facing the company (and to recognize the competence and professionalism of the consultant).

Similarly, personnel professionals should explain the actuarial nature of statistical methods of predicting job applicant behavior. Even tests with excellent predictive validity will not yield accurate predictions for *every* applicant. Professionals should avoid speaking in vague terms about the potential for "improvement" in some area of company performance based on their services; rather, they should provide conservative, data-based expectations, in terminology familiar to the non-psychologists to whom they report.

CASE EXAMPLE 10.4

An I/O psychologist serves as a personnel consultant for local industries. When recruiting new business for her consulting practice, she points to positive changes in employee retention rates for companies that have implemented her suggestions. She knows that business people tend to be very impressed with numbers. No one has ever asked her whether the increases in retention rates she cites represent statistically significant improvements. (They do not.)

SPECIAL CONSIDERATIONS IN INDUSTRIAL/ ORGANIZATIONAL ASSESSMENT

I/O professionals are often involved in personnel assessment, which includes testing, interviewing, and reviewing applications and work samples (Murphy & Davidshofer, 1994). Testing is used in employment contexts both for screening job applicants and making promotion decisions. Tests used by personnel professionals provide information about a person's skills and abilities, personality functioning, and life experiences that can be useful in selecting the most qualified applicant for a job and in matching the right person with the right job. SIOP (1987) has published specialty guidelines for I/O professionals involved in assessment: *Principles for the Validation and Use of Personnel Selection Procedures.*

When administering employment tests, personnel professionals should obtain the informed consent of test takers, as discussed in Chapter 8 (ACA, 2005, E.3.a; APA, 2002, 9.03[a]). The major issues addressed in the informed consent process are as follows: the nature and purpose of the test(s) to be taken; what the test scores will or might be used for, at present and in the future (e.g., employment selection, performance evaluation, promotion review); who will have access to the test scores (e.g., personnel professionals, potential supervisors, performance evaluators); what feedback will be provided after testing; and where the test data will be kept on file and for how long. Protection of the confidentiality of test data is as important in personnel settings as in any other assessment context.

Personnel professionals responsible for employment testing must be competent in the administration, scoring, and interpretation of the tests they use. Consultants who develop or recommend employment tests for organizations that do not have a staff psychologist or counselor competent in employment testing are obligated to ensure that the organization's personnel staff are sufficiently trained in the use of any tests being adopted (ACA, 2005, E.2.a; APA, 2002, 9.07). Alternatively, the consultant should advise the organization to hire a competent testing service to conduct the employment testing.

A wide range of tests are used in employment settings, which can also raise ethical issues. For example, the use of clinical tests (e.g., MMPI-2) in employment screening is certainly an invasion of applicants' privacy and should be justified by the critical importance of applicants' emotional state to their performance of the job (e.g., police officer) in question (ACA, 2005, E.2.b; APA, 2002, 4.04, 9.02). Clinical tests used in such settings must also be well-validated for use with a nonclinical population. The Rorschach, for instance, has questionable validity with normal populations, so it is generally not appropriate for personnel settings (Hunsley & Bailey, 1999). In addition, the questionable validity of integrity (i.e., honesty) tests sometimes used in personnel selection (Camara & Schneider, 1994) highlights the importance of personnel professionals possessing adequate knowledge of the validation of cut-off scores used in employment decisions for the groups being tested (ACA, 2005, E.6.a, E.8; APA, 2002, 9.02). I/O professionals are obligated to point out the questionable validity of trait measures (e.g., friendliness scales) for predicting behavior in specific situations, like an office context. They can present alternatives to testing, such as creating behavioral assessments of applicants' ability to perform behaviors critical to successful job performance, and stronger consideration of other variables (e.g., work history, performance appraisals, motivation) in predicting performance.

CASE EXAMPLE 10.5

An African American job applicant is rejected by a construction firm because her score on the MAC is above the cut-off of 24, indicating that she is likely to abuse alcohol. Researchers subsequently discover that the mean score for African Americans is higher than it was for the norm group, making this test an even worse predictor of alcohol abuse for African Americans than for the population in general. When the norms for African Americans are published, the counselor responsible for personnel testing at the firm stops using the test.

Personnel professionals may be called upon to develop employment tests. Competence to perform this task requires extensive knowledge and expertise in test development theory, psychometrics, and diversity issues (ACA, 2005, E.12; APA, 2002, 9.05). In many instances, personnel professionals may not possess the skills needed to produce a reliable, valid, and fair test. Their ethical duty would then be to inform their supervisors of the need to hire a consultant competent to develop the test. As in other areas of professional practice, knowing the limits of one's abilities is a critical component of competence (ACA, 2005, E.2.a; APA, 2002, 2.01[a]).

Decisions based on employment test results have significant economic implications for applicants, employees, and organizations, so it is not surprising that the use of tests in personnel settings has given rise to many legal challenges and to legislation concerning the appropriate use of tests in personnel decision making (Sireci & Geisinger, 1998). The two key issues are relevance and fairness. The relevance of a test for selecting the most qualified applicants for a job is a validity issue. A test is valid if its content addresses effectively the skills, abilities, or characteristics relevant to the job (i.e., content validity) and if the possession of those skills, abilities, or characteristics can be demonstrated to be essential to the successful performance of the job (i.e., predictive, or criterion, validity). A comprehensive evaluation of what the job entails, referred to as a job analysis, is an important prerequisite for the development of a test with adequate content and criterion validity (Sireci & Geisinger, 1998).

A valid test must predict job performance, not just for workers in general, but for each group being tested (e.g., males, females, African Americans, Hispanics); otherwise the test is unfair. The issue of fairness concerns whether the test favors one group of applicants over another due to factors that are not essential to job performance (Sireci & Geisinger, 1998). Personnel professionals have an ethical duty to identify situations in which they might have to "adapt" an assessment technique because of diversity issues, such as gender, ethnicity, disability, or socioeconomic status (APA, 2002, 9.02[a]). For example, if the instructions on an accounting test are in English, Hispanic applicants could be placed at a disadvantage, even though they might possess the skills needed to perform the job (ACA, 2005, E.8). If all applicants are required to take the test in English, then knowledge of English must be essential for performing the job. It might still be fairer to applicants from diverse groups to provide instructions in other languages, even if the test items are in English (Sireci & Geisinger, 1998).

Similarly, the Americans With Disabilities Act (ADA) requires that an employer provide testing accommodations for individuals with disabilities if a disability prevents them from completing a standard test administration but not from performing the job for which they are applying (ADA, 1990). Depending on the nature of the disability, accommodations might involve altering the time limit for a test, how the applicant's responses are recorded, the format of the test (e.g., changing or eliminating items that present information graphically, providing a large print or Braille version of the test), or how it is administered (e.g., oral administration). For accommodations based on diversity or disability issues to be acceptable, they must not impact the validity of the test for its purpose of selecting the most qualified applicants or employees. Personnel professionals are responsible for confirming the validity of the accommodated version of the test empirically (Geisinger et al., 2002).

CASE EXAMPLE 10.6

Because he has a visual impairment, an applicant for a police dispatcher position requests a large print version of the MMPI-2 for his employment testing. The personnel psychologist supervising the testing refuses his request because she cannot find any information concerning the effect of this altered format on the validity of MMPI-2 results.

Increasingly, computer-based test administration and interpretation software is being used in employment screening (Sampson et al., 2003). As discussed in Chapter 8, I/O professionals are obligated to possess the same level of testing competence when using computer-based testing software as when using paper-and-pencil versions of tests.

Professionals should not depend on a convenient computerized interpretation to conceal their lack of training (Sampson et al., 2003).

Adverse Impact in Employment Testing

When diverse groups of applicants produce substantially different scores on an employment test, the test is said to produce an *adverse impact* (Sireci & Geisinger, 1998). For example, if 80% of white applicants achieve passing grades on an employment screening test compared to only 60% of African American applicants, the test produces an adverse impact against African American applicants. In 1978, the Equal Employment Opportunities Commission (EEOC), U.S. Civil Service Commission, U.S. Department of Labor, and U.S. Department of Justice adopted a set of Uniform Guidelines on Employee Selection Procedures. Adverse impact was defined in these rules as any situation in which the passing rate for a protected group is less than four-fifths (80%) of the passing rate for the highest-scoring group.

The legality of a test used for employment purposes is questionable whenever the test produces an adverse impact (Sireci & Geisinger, 1998). The company using such a test is legally required to demonstrate the test's content and/or criterion validity. Therefore, professionals should be familiar with the validation procedures outlined in the *Standards for Educational and Psychological Testing* (American Educational Research Association et al., 1999). The adverse impact of a valid employment test can often be reduced by *banding* scores falling within a range determined by the test's standard error of difference—an index of statistical significance for the difference between test scores (Sireci & Geisinger, 1998). All scores within a band are treated as equal, which permits members of diverse groups with lower scores falling within the band interval to be selected when they would not have been selected based on raw test score alone. Although banding methods have been criticized, they do reduce adverse impact without ignoring the importance of selecting individuals with the best test scores (Sireci & Geisinger, 1998).

When a test is demonstrated to be valid for predicting performance in a particular job but produces adverse impact, assessment professionals incur additional duties to prevent discrimination and promote diversity within their organization (ACA, 2005, C.5; APA, 2002, 3.01). First, professionals can conduct an exhaustive search for other valid tests that can help evaluate applicants for the job in question without producing adverse impact. They also have an ethical duty to promote nondiscriminatory practices by investigating their organization's recruiting practices to determine why they are not attracting qualified applicants from diverse groups. They would then endeavor to improve the organization's methods of recruiting or training applicants. For example, using the Internet and e-mail in the recruiting process (referred to as *e-recruiting*) can help an organization access a larger, more diverse pool of applicants.[1] Unquestionably, the active recruitment of highly qualified minority, female, and disabled applicants is the best solution to increasing diversity (Sireci & Geisinger, 1998). If the ethics of a company do not involve an organizational concern about promoting diversity and eliminating discriminatory practices, I/O professionals should inform the organization of their ethical commitment to those values (ACA, 2005, H.2.e; APA, 2002, 1.03).

CASE EXAMPLE 10.7

The EEOC filed suit against a statistical software manufacturer after finding that a statistics test used to screen applicants for programming positions adversely impacted African

American applicants. The company was able to demonstrate the validity of the test for predicting competence of statistical programmers, and the suit was dismissed. The personnel counselor in the human resources department was told by the CEO that she should continue to use this highly effective test and that no changes would be made in the company's hiring procedures.

Assessment of Employee Performance

Another common duty of personnel professionals is the development of methods to assess employees' job performance. Professionals can use performance appraisal as an additional means to promote the development of nondiscriminatory organizational practices and policies (ACA, 2005, C.5; APA, 2002, 3.01). Although the judgments and ratings of supervisors or other evaluators are never completely objective, professionals have an obligation to develop appraisal methods that are as objective and behaviorally based as possible (Murphy & Davidshofer, 1994). I/O professionals can advocate for the development of a performance appraisal procedure based on a careful job analysis, with input from the employee(s) doing the job, so the process involves a comprehensive assessment of the tasks involved in the job. Also, using multiple raters will reduce the likelihood of a biased appraisal.

The performance appraisal system should include adequate feedback to employees. Personnel professionals encourage organizations to view performance appraisal as a learning experience and an opportunity for employees to improve their skills. Raters (e.g., supervisors) should be informed in advance whether their individual ratings or the average of several ratings will be disclosed to employees. Finally, the confidentiality of performance ratings, like any other assessment results, should be protected within the organization, but raters should be informed that their ratings will, in all likelihood, not remain confidential if employees pursue complaints concerning the fairness of their performance evaluation.

CASE EXAMPLE 10.8

An accounting supervisor provides performance appraisal ratings for the six accountants under her supervision. When the employees receive feedback on the ratings, one accountant asks the supervisor why he received such a low rating on "collegiality." The supervisor replies that the accountant is very shy. The accountant then informs the supervisor that she misunderstood the meaning of the term "collegiality." The supervisor says that the term had not really been explained by the I/O psychologist who conducted the training session for supervisors, and she had thought it meant friendly and outgoing. The supervisor contacts the psychologist to let him know of the issue because other supervisors might have made similar errors.

ENTREPRENEURIAL PRACTICE OF A MENTAL HEALTH PROFESSION

People practice mental health professions as their *profession,* or livelihood. Although every professional wants to earn a decent living, some are interested in doing more than just earning a salary from a clinic, university, or company. Some professionals in every specialty area (e.g., I/O, clinical/counseling, rehabilitation, forensic, psychometrics) manage to create extensive practice or consultation networks involving hundreds of thousands, or even millions, of dollars in fees each year. Obviously, the importance of acquiring wealth varies from person to person, just as it does among practitioners of any profession. While there is certainly nothing inherently unethical about entrepreneurially motivated professional businesses, the *business* of professional practice does heighten the possibility of conflicts of interest and other ethical problems.

The mental health professions are referred to as "helping" professions. Mental health professionals "strive to benefit those with whom they work and take care to do no harm" (APA, 2002, Principle A). The metaethical justification for this ethical obligation is a Kantian respect for the value of each individual person. On the other hand, the justification under-lying the pursuit of wealth is utilitarian: professionals desire to maximize the benefits accruing to them as a result of their professional activities. As discussed earlier in this book, these two metaethical models sometimes conflict. For example, if I/O psychologists' consulting fees are too expensive for a struggling business, causing them to decline to provide important expertise to the owner, could they not be argued to be harming that business, the owner, and the employees? Similarly, when the most experienced and effective therapists command the highest psychotherapy fees, aren't poorer clients who are relegated to seeking treatment from relatively inexperienced, poorly paid young therapists working in state-subsidized agencies being denied equal quality? When forensic practitioners offer expert testimony only for a defendant who can pay $250 per hour for these services, are they not discriminating against people of lower socioeconomic status who could benefit as much or more from their knowledge and skills? Mental health professionals "do not condone or engage in discrimination based on . . . socioeconomic status" (ACA, 2005, C.5). They should "recognize that fairness and justice entitle all persons to access to and benefit from the contributions of psychology and to equal quality in the processes, procedures, and services being conducted by psychologists" (APA, 2002, Principle D). Economic discrimination clearly violates the Kantian duty to respect each individual equally. Unquestionably, an ethical tension exists between the lofty Kantian statements in the professional ethics codes and the common utilitarian practice of seeking ways to maximize income from a profes-sional practice.

Although professionals must ultimately look to "the dictates of their own conscience" in their attempts to balance their economic aspirations with their professional ethical obliga-tions, the ethical codes do place some limitations on practitioners' pursuit of economic gain (APA, 2002, Introduction and Applicability). Professionals are obligated to be sensitive to the socioeconomic status of potential clients (ACA, 2005, A.10.b; APA, 2002, Principle E). For example, I/O consultants might use a sliding scale formula based on the net income of a business to set an appropriate fee for their work. Therapists might do the same based on an individual client's income. A sliding scale is also somewhat consistent with the spirit of the ethical expectation that professionals "strive to contribute a portion of their professional time for little or no compensation or personal advantage" (APA, 2002, Principle B). Providing professional services without receiving *any* compensation is referred to as *pro bono* (i.e., for the good of another) work. Although donating professional services is not required, it is certainly encouraged as a way of "giving something back," reflecting the strong sense of social responsibility that professionals should possess (ACA, 2005, A. Introduction).

CASE EXAMPLE 10.9

A counselor providing I/O consultation services gives an estimate of her fee based on her careful analysis of the time and resources required to complete the task of evaluating a company's employee recruitment program. However, after interviewing a few of the human resources staff, she discovers that the process will be much more involved than she had thought. She decides it would be unethical to submit a bill for more than her estimate and that she'll just have to absorb the extra costs.

A final issue related to the business aspect of professional practice arises when clients fail to pay the fees billed for treatment, consultation, or other professional services. When clients fail to pay the agreed-upon fee, mental health professionals are placed in a difficult position. For example, if psychotherapists engage a bill collection agency to collect the debt, they would be violating the confidentiality of their client. However, professional ethical codes permit this limitation on confidentiality because it would be unfair to professionals if clients could willfully withhold payment and prevent professionals from pursuing collection by invoking the ethical duty of confidentiality (ACA, 2005, A.10.c; APA, 2002, 4.05[b]).

Professionals must abide by two stipulations to avoid unethical violations of confidentiality in pursuing payment for services. First, at the beginning of the professional relationship, clients must be informed of this (and any other) foreseeable potential limitation on their confidentiality (ACA, 2005, A.10.c; APA, 2002, 4.02[a], 4.02[b]). For HIPAA-covered entities, this information would need to be included in the Notice of Privacy Practices provided to clients (Privacy Rule, 2003, § 164.520). In other words, they must be informed of the steps that will be taken if they fail to pay the agreed-upon fees. (They should also be given ample warning in the billing statements they receive prior to the initiation of collection procedures.) Second, professionals are obligated to limit the disclosure to the minimum information required to achieve the goal of collecting the fee (ACA, 2005, B.2.d; APA, 2002, 4.05[b]). The client's name and contact information can be provided to a reputable collection agency that understands the importance of confidentiality in collecting professional fees, but obviously no information regarding the client's diagnosis or length of treatment is required.

Even if addressed in an ethically acceptable manner, revealing confidential client information to a collection agency would be undertaken only when every other confidential recourse to obtain payment has been exhausted. Also, if the collection agency violates the confidentiality of a client, the professional will likely be held at least partly responsible. Therefore, when the debt does not constitute a significant sum, professionals might strongly consider regarding the services rendered as *pro bono* work and letting the matter drop. When the unpaid fee is a substantial amount, professionals should review their billing and payment policies to try to prevent a recurrence of the situation. They could, for example, adopt a policy requiring payment (or co-payment for clients with insurance) at the time of service.

CASE EXAMPLE 10.10

An I/O psychologist with considerable expertise in organizational behavior designs a four-hour workshop to improve supervisors' communication skills. He offers the workshop for groups of up to eight supervisors so he can closely monitor the exercises and provide individual feedback to each participant. The workshop is quite successful, and he is soon contacted by a large local industry about conducting a workshop for a group of 75 supervisors. He is hesitant initially because working with such a large group would change the nature of the workshop. However, he decides that the fee (and the possibility of additional large referrals) is too good to turn down. Besides, he reasons that even a slightly watered-down version of his workshop will still meet the goal of improving supervisors' communication skills.

PRACTICE CASE INVOLVING THE MODEL OF ETHICAL DECISION MAKING

An industrial/organizational psychologist is working as a consultant for a manufacturing business to help increase worker productivity. In her initial assessment of the situation at the manufacturing plant, she conducts informal interviews with a sample of workers to get their suggestions regarding possible strategies for increasing efficiency. While interviewing a forklift operator, the psychologist notices that his personnel file lists three forklift accidents during the past year. In one of these accidents, a worker was seriously injured. The psychologist asks the employee about the accidents and how such incidents might be avoided in the future. He acknowledges that the accidents were his fault. He says, "You're a psychologist, so I know I can confide in you." Before she can respond, he continues, "Off the record, I've been having a lot of problems at home. I've been drinking pretty heavily for the past couple of years, and sometimes I have problems driving the forklift after lunch. I'm trying to cut back, but it's awfully hard. I think I'm getting a handle on it, though. I can tell you because you're a psychologist. They'd fire me for sure if they found out. At my age, I'd never get another job this good."

At the end of the interview, he says, "I'm glad to tell someone about my drinking. I've felt so guilty about nearly killing my friend. Don't worry though; I'm gonna lick this problem."

What should the psychologist do?

SUMMARY

Mental health professionals who function within a business organization, either as an employee or a consultant, incur a dual set of ethical responsibilities. However, their fundamental duty is to act ethically as a mental health professional. To practice competently as an I/O psychologist in a business setting, formal graduate training or respecialization is required. This area of psychology has its own specialty guidelines and additional sources of ethical guidance.

Consulting relationships with business organizations involve special ethical considerations in matters such as fee setting and avoiding conflicts of interest. In addition, professionals must demonstrate integrity by maintaining client confidentiality and portraying accurately the effectiveness of their services, especially to those who know less about the complexities of evaluating new programs or assessments.

I/O professionals are often involved in screening job applicants and evaluating employee performance, both of which have a significant impact on people's lives. Professionals must always obtain informed consent and only use tests they are competent to administer. Tests used to screen job applicants must be relevant and fair. If a test produces an adverse impact, it may not be legal. When assessing employees' job performance, professionals should develop appraisal systems that are as objective and nondiscriminatory as possible.

Finally, in the entrepreneurial practice of a mental health profession, a tension exists between the Kantian respect for the value of each person and the utilitarian desire to maximize the financial benefits accruing to the professional. Professionals should seek ways to assist those with fewer resources and might consider giving back to society by providing some *pro bono* services.

NOTE

1. The informality of contacting applicants by phone or e-mail creates a challenge for maintaining proper recruitment procedures. Professionals must take steps to counteract the increased potential for inappropriate interactions with applicants in these unsupervised situations.

Chapter 11

Ethical Issues in Teaching and Supervision

A substantial proportion of counselors and psychologists take on the role of faculty or supervisor, on a full- or part-time basis, to train the next generation of professionals. Many of the ethical issues of concern to faculty members are related to those affecting professionals in other contexts; others are unique to instructional settings.

COMPETENCE

College and university faculty are expected to make professional contributions in the areas of teaching, scholarship (e.g., research), and service to their institution, profession, and community. Effective faculty must develop competence in each of these areas (ACA, 2005, C.2.a, C.2.b; APA, 2002, 2.01).

Developing Competence in Teaching

Historically, mental health professionals received relatively little graduate training in providing instruction to students. Professionals beginning their teaching career were generally well-versed in their specialty area and in their academic field in general but had little or no specific training in methods of conveying those ideas effectively to students. Of course, they had been exposed to numerous teaching styles as students themselves and many had also worked as graduate teaching assistants, which gave them an opportunity to learn about the mechanics of organizing a course, grading students' work, and preparing and delivering an occasional class lecture. However, beginning faculty members learned teaching skills on the job. Initially, they attempted to blend the styles of a few of their favorite teachers and, over time, developed their own teaching style based on feedback from colleagues, supervisors, and students.

In recent years, the importance of assisting graduate students and faculty members in developing develop teaching competence has received much more attention. Many graduate programs in the mental health professions provide courses devoted specifically to instructional theories and methods. Graduate students are also frequently given the opportunity to teach one or more courses as teaching apprentices. APA has long recognized the teaching of psychology as a distinct area of specialization and research. APA Division 2 (Society for the Teaching of Psychology) is devoted specifically to teaching issues and publishes its own journal, *Teaching of Psychology*.[1] National and regional teaching institutes and conferences provide additional resources for graduate students and faculty to augment their repertoire of instructional skills.

CASE EXAMPLE 11.1

A first-year member of the counseling faculty thinks that he might have a tendency to identify too strongly with the struggles of his students. He does not want to be perceived as an "easy" instructor, so he creates more rigorous requirements in his sections of courses than anyone else in the department. He makes a point of telling his colleagues about the high percentage of students failing his exams.

Developing Multicultural Competence in Teaching

As discussed throughout this book, the paradigm of psychology and counseling is changing to incorporate multicultural issues (APA, 2003; Pedersen, 2001). Like any paradigm shift in a discipline, multiculturalism requires faculty to take pains to develop new competencies to train the next generation of professionals effectively. Instructors must modify their presentation of theories and treatment methods to consider the cultural limitations of psychological theory and practice; that is, which theories and treatments can be applied most effectively in which cultural contexts (Pedersen, 2001)? A major benefit of developing multicultural competence as an instructor is that the presentation of concepts in class will have greater relevance to students' lives and future professional activities because it will better reflect "the complex and dynamic reality in which we all live" (Pedersen, 2001, p. 20).

One basic method of increasing multicultural awareness in students is to have them construct a genogram of their family to discover the cultural complexity of their own origins (Bryan, 2001). Interviewing classmates of different cultural backgrounds and attending church services of different faiths are additional ways to increase multicultural awareness. The class can read literature or view videos relevant to the course's subject matter with racially diverse casts and plots involving other cultures. Instructors can coordinate additional activities with their institution's Office of Multicultural Affairs.[2]

Discussing the role of sociocultural factors, such as racism and sexism, in the etiology of life problems in a personality or psychopathology course might enhance students' sensitivity to the detrimental effects of cultural biases. Instructors can also address the issue of whether certain cultural values (in American culture and other cultures) might reduce the personal autonomy of some individuals (e.g., women) and conflict with mental health professionals' fundamental value of respecting human rights (Bryan, 2001).

Finally, Vachon and Agresti's (1992) self-study program designed to increase therapists' awareness of their personal values, discussed later in this chapter, is a useful exercise for both faculty and students interested in increasing their awareness of their attitudes, beliefs, and values regarding diversity issues.

Maintaining Competence as a Teacher

Today faculty members are generally well-trained prior to beginning their instructional career; however, it is extremely important that they remain up-to-date concerning developments in teaching theory, applications, and technology, as well as in the content areas they teach (ACA, 2005, C.2.f; APA, 2002, 2.03, 7.03[b]). As discussed in Chapter 2, Dubin estimated in 1972 that half of the knowledge gained in graduate study in psychology was outdated within 10 to 12 years. The revolution in information technology that has occurred during the past 25 years has undoubtedly caused professionals' knowledge to become outdated even more quickly today. New editions of textbooks help in maintaining competence, but faculty must also read journals in their specialty areas as well as those devoted to instructional issues, attend teaching conferences and professional meetings, and pursue continuing education opportunities.

Competent faculty should incorporate updated information into their class presentations, rather than relying on old lecture notes. Students become extremely frustrated when outdated information presented in class is inconsistent with what they read in their recently published textbook. Also, faculty members should always strive to increase their awareness of diversity issues relevant to the subject matter they are presenting (ACA, 2005, F.6.b; APA, 2002, 2.01[b]). For example, when discussing the issue of diagnosis, the potential significance of culture, ethnicity, gender, age, and socioeconomic status for the validity of diagnostic assumptions should be discussed. The task of maintaining competence as a faculty member, like most ethical duties, is a very challenging, though not impossible, one.

"Jack" of All Subject Areas, Master of None?

The challenges encountered by faculty members in developing and maintaining competence vary considerably depending on the context in which they teach. At a large, doctoral degree-granting institution, faculty members might teach one or two courses each semester within their specific area of expertise. On the other hand, faculty members at a small undergraduate college might be expected to teach a wide variety of courses as part of a small department. In a single semester, a clinical psychologist might be asked to teach introductory psychology, abnormal psychology, developmental psychology, and statistics. Consequently, faculty members at "teaching institutions" must devote considerably greater energy to becoming and remaining competent in these varied teaching areas (ACA, 2005, C.2.b, C.2.f; APA, 2002, 2.01[c]). (This demand is one of the reasons why, historically, faculty members at such institutions have not been expected to engage in as much research activity as those with less diverse or lighter teaching loads.) Regardless of their situation, faculty members should remember that it is ethically inappropriate for them to teach a course outside the boundaries of their competence (ACA, 2005, C.2.a; APA, 2002, 2.01[a]).

Burnout

Like clinicians, faculty members can become discouraged and cynical about their work. Personal problems, professional setbacks, and negative feedback from students (particularly if it is felt to be undeserved) can all cause faculty members to feel like failures who are not achieving their goals in life. Their perceived lack of personal accomplishment will likely cause them to become less committed to maintaining a high level of professional performance (Vredenburgh et al., 1999). Like clinicians, faculty members suffering burnout may become withdrawn and irritable. Faculty members may evidence signs of burnout by adopting an adversarial relationship with students. They might react to student criticism of their performance by complaining that students are lazy, unmotivated, and always seeking to blame someone else for their own failures. Faculty might then set unreasonably difficult standards in their classes, ostensibly to motivate students, but perhaps with the added motivation to punish them for their criticisms. In other cases, genuine disappointment in students' lack of interest in faculty members' chosen field can reduce their investment in and enjoyment of teaching.

The "publish or perish" expectations for scholarly productivity at many academic institutions can also contribute significantly to faculty burnout. The externally imposed pressure on faculty to produce meaningful research in order to earn tenure and promotion can make research activity extremely stressful and interfere with faculty members' experiencing any intrinsic enjoyment from conducting research (Singh, Mishra, & Kim, 1998). Clearly, when people no longer enjoy their work, they are at elevated risk for burnout.

Obviously, any decline in the motivation or professionalism of faculty members impairs their competence as teachers (ACA, 2005, C.2.g; APA, 2002, 2.06, 3.04). It is faculty members' ethical obligation to identify and seek help for any emotional problems they are experiencing that could impinge on their professional performance. Remediation might involve a break from teaching, the pursuit of faculty development opportunities to enhance their skills, or, in extreme cases, recognition that teaching is not an appropriate career path for them.

CASE EXAMPLE 11.2

A psychology faculty member has developed a very unfavorable opinion of students over the years. She feels that all they care about is their grade for a course, not about how much they learn. She tells students that they are the only group of consumers who demand less for their money. She sees her task as being to challenge students to think. She asks extremely difficult exam questions that require students to go well beyond the information presented in the lectures and textbooks in order to synthesize a comprehensive answer. A substantial majority of students fail her courses, even her graduate courses.

When students complain about the exams, the chair of the department finds that even he cannot answer several of the questions. He discusses the matter with the faculty member, suggesting that perhaps she expects too much of her students. She replies that everyone else in the department expects too little.

INFORMED CONSENT

Providing a Syllabus

When students enroll in a course, the ethical duty of informed consent obligates the instructor to provide them with information regarding course goals and material to be covered, course requirements, assessment methods, and grading procedures (ACA, 2005, F.9.a; APA, 2002, 7.03[a]). The course syllabus serves as the primary informed consent document in academic courses. It should be distributed at the first meeting, or at least early enough that students can still elect to change their schedule. Once the syllabus has been distributed, instructors should make every effort to conform to the schedule and terms set forth in it. The syllabus should be viewed as an informal contract between the instructor and students. If changes in the schedule or course requirements do become necessary, they should not impact students negatively (ACA, 2005, F.9.a; APA, 2002, 3.04, 7.03[a]).

CASE EXAMPLE 11.3

After the semester has begun, a psychology instructor takes on a research project that will require a great deal of his time near the end of the term. He realizes that he will not have sufficient time to grade the term papers he had assigned in one of his classes. He notifies students at mid-semester that he is canceling the research paper that had been listed in the syllabus and that the final exam will now account for 40% of the course grade, instead of the 20% stated in the syllabus.

Providing Letters of Reference to Students and Supervisees

Faculty members and supervisors are frequently asked to provide references for students seeking admission to further academic training or applying for academic awards, financial aid, certification and licensure, or employment. A letter of reference is a public statement made by professionals; they are ethically obligated to be truthful and forthright in all such statements (ACA, 2005, C.6.b; APA, 2002, 5.01[b]). Therefore, they should not agree to provide a letter of reference unless they are very comfortable with the student's qualifications (ACA, 2005, F.5.d; APA, 2002, 7.06[b]). Unfortunately, the trend in recent years has been to provide positive letters of reference for all students requesting them, even less qualified students (Rosovsky & Hartley, 2002). Many factors have contributed to this trend, including the fact that students have legal access to their application files, enabling them to review their letters of reference.

Providing letters of reference involves informed consent issues because students are often asked to waive their legal right to review the letters, as a means of protecting the writer's confidentiality. As with other informed consent situations discussed previously, it would be difficult for students to meaningfully consent to waive this right unless they had at least a general notion of the letter's contents. If faculty members feel that they cannot write a very positive, helpful letter, they should model professional integrity for students by simply being honest with them regarding any reservations they have (and would need to include in a letter) about students' qualifications. From a student's point of view, it is much better to have professors or supervisors decline to provide a reference than to have them write a lukewarm or negative letter.

MULTIPLE RELATIONSHIPS

Mental health professionals endeavor to avoid multiple relationships in teaching, as they do in other areas of their professional activity (ACA, 2005, F.3; APA, 2002, 3.05[a]). When a multiple relationship cannot be avoided, the faculty member should be sensitive to the potential for students to be harmed by such relationships and take appropriate steps to protect students' interests (ACA, 2005, F.10.d; APA, 2002, 3.08). A common multiple relationship in teaching involves students taking courses from faculty members and being involved simultaneously in an employee-employer/supervisor relationship with them. For example, graduate students often take a class from professors they are assigned to as a teaching or research assistant for the semester. While there is nothing inherently improper about such an arrangement, it does fit the definition of a multiple relationship and, thus, requires that the faculty member be vigilant in ensuring that the relationship does not in any way exploit or harm the student or other students in the class. In the context of interacting with students as assistants, the faculty member should not provide any information regarding the class in which the assistants are students that would not be equally available to the other graduate students in the class. Also, the faculty member should be careful not to assign duties to assistants that exceed their job description. Students with a 20-hour per week assistantship might be less likely to object to being assigned 25 hours of work each week by a professor they are also taking a class from, fearing that the protest might adversely affect the professor's perception of them and, in turn, their grade in the professor's course.

A similar issue could arise if faculty members were to ask students in their class if they would like to earn some extra money by babysitting or by doing yard work for them. This type of multiple relationship is potentially problematic because students might feel, rightly or wrongly, that if they declined the offer, it would negatively impact their course grade. If the students did decline the offer and performed poorly in the class, they might attribute their low grade to the multiple relationship issue. An ethical professional is sensitive not only to avoiding treating students unequally, but also to the potential for students to *believe* they were treated unequally.

Alternatively, a multiple relationship with a student might be perceived by *others* as affecting the faculty member's evaluation of that student's performance (Blevins-Knabe, 1992). For example, graduate assistants might interact with the faculty member in a more informal manner than other students, resulting in other students perceiving the assistants as the "teacher's pets" and believing that they receive preferential treatment. The same situation could develop with an undergraduate student who works as a babysitter for faculty or assists with their research. Again, the important element to be aware of here is students' *perception* of the situation.

The issue of multiple relationships outside the college or university is more likely to arise in a smaller town, as mentioned in Chapter 6 (ACA, 2005, F.10.f; APA, 2002, 3.05[a]). Faculty members in a small college town encounter their students everywhere (e.g., working in the grocery store, the bank, their child's preschool). Their neighbors' children might well become students in their classes. While such multiple relationships are a fact of life in such contexts, it is the professional's obligation to ensure that there is no potential for students to be harmed or exploited in any way. If such potential exists, the professional must refrain from entering into the relationship. If the relationship already exists and is found to be problematic, the professional "takes reasonable steps to resolve it with due regard for the best interests of the affected person and maximal compliance with the Ethics Code" (APA, 2002, 3.05[b]).

No matter how tempting it may be for a faculty member with a part-time private practice to treat current or former students, it is not appropriate in most cases because the preexisting relationship results in a mixing of professional roles (ACA, 2005, F.10.e, F.10.f; APA, 2002, 3.05[a], 7.05[b]). Students will ask clinical faculty members to provide therapy for them because they trust and admire their instructors, but faculty should recognize that it is better for them to begin therapy with someone they can approach on a more equal footing, as opposed to someone who is already an authority figure for them from another context (Pearson & Piazza, 1997).

CASE EXAMPLE 11.4

A neighbor and close friend of a counseling faculty member tells her that he will be taking a counseling course as part of his interdisciplinary studies degree. He says he plans to enroll in her section of the course because the time at which her section meets is more convenient for his schedule than the other time the course is offered. The faculty member is aware of the multiple relationship issue, but she questions whether she has the right to prevent him from taking the course at a time that is convenient for him. The course involves objective (true-false) exams, so she does not envision a problem with the objectivity of her judgment regarding his academic performance. She decides to say nothing and allow him to enroll.

Sexual Relationships With Students and Supervisees

Historically, the appropriate limits on multiple relationships in academic settings were considerably more controversial than those in therapy contexts. While sexual relationships with clients have long been recognized as unethical, psychology's ethical principles had never stated that such relationships with consenting adult students were strictly unethical until the 1992 revision (APA, 1992, 1.19[b]). Prior to that, faculty members were prohibited only from pursuing a personal relationship with a student taking their class (APA, 1990, Principle 7[d]). One reason for the slow development of these guidelines, as well as the controversy surrounding them, is that it was not uncommon for faculty to become involved with, and even marry, currently enrolled graduate students.

Eventually, the ethical codes of the mental health professions were expanded to address more comprehensively the significant inequality of power present in teacher-student relationships (ACA, 2005, F.10.a; APA, 2002, 7.07). The "Ethical Principles" now states that psychologists should not engage in a sexual relationship with students "who are in their department, agency, or training center or over whom psychologists have or are likely to have evaluative authority" because such relationships are so likely to impair judgment or be exploitative (APA, 2002, 7.07). Most colleges and universities also have institutional policies prohibiting such relationships between a faculty member and any enrolled student.

APA and ACA do not prohibit a faculty member from having a relationship with a former student following graduation because this situation is recognized as being quite different from sexual involvement with a currently enrolled student. Also, faculty members are not generally as authoritative and emotionally significant to their students as therapists are to their clients. Consequently, sexual involvement between a faculty member and a former student is not viewed as involving a significantly greater potential for emotional harm than any other intimate relationship. However, the potential for inequality in such relationships remains an important consideration for ethical professionals (ACA, 2005, F.10.c).

Using Students as Research Participants

Faculty members are often tempted to use the students in their own classes as research participants. If instructors offer their students the opportunity to participate in their research project, they are initiating a multiple relationship. It would be improper for instructors to coerce their students in any manner to participate in their particular research study by, for example, making participation in the study a course requirement (ACA, 2005, G.2.c; APA, 2002, 8.04). Even if research participation is voluntary, instructors should also be sensitive to the fact that students in their class might be more reluctant to refuse to participate in their research than in a study conducted by another researcher (Galassi, 1991). Therefore, if the instructor has a research participation requirement, it must apply to a wider range of studies, perhaps to all projects using the student subject pool. Also, if instructors offer students any incentive (e.g., extra credit) to participate in their study, the same benefit must be available if students choose to participate instead in a different study being conducted in the department. Finally, instructors should have equitable alternative means available for students to earn the extra credit if they choose not to participate in any research study (ACA, 2005, G.2.c; APA, 2002, 8.04[b]).

CASE EXAMPLE 11.5

A counseling professor teaches a class in personality assessment each year. One semester, there are only five students in the class. The anonymous student evaluations provided by the class are extremely negative. The following semester, the professor encounters one of the students from this class in the hall. He says that because the evaluations were anonymous, he doesn't know which students provided the negative evaluations, but he asks the student why she thought he had received such poor evaluations from the students in the class.

CONFIDENTIALITY

Student records, including information regarding a student's performance in a faculty member's course (e.g., test grades), are confidential (APA, 2002, 4.04[b]). The release of student information is protected by the Family Educational Rights and Privacy Act of 1974 (FERPA, Pub. L. No. 93–380), often referred to as the "Buckley Amendment." Faculty cannot post students' grades by name or social security number because this information might enable students to be identified. Instructors wishing to post grades should obtain students' consent; the student should be identified by a code number known only to the faculty member and student.

However, other communications between a student and a faculty member are not typically regarded as confidential, unless both parties agree in advance to make it so. This fact can pose a problem for faculty in the mental health professions because students often equate a discussion with their psychology or counseling professor (even one who is not a clinician) with psychotherapy, assuming that anything they say will be confidential. Faculty should be sensitive to this perception and avoid potentially harming a student by being very careful about sharing any personal information revealed by a student (APA, 2002, 3.04).

CASE EXAMPLE 11.6

A psychology faculty member posts her students' grades using only the last four numbers of their social security numbers after obtaining their consent to do so. One of her classes has only six students. They quickly figure out that although students' names do not appear on the grade sheet, the grades are posted in alphabetical order. One of the students complains that the faculty member's procedure for posting grades violates his right to privacy.

PROFESSIONAL AND SCIENTIFIC RESPONSIBILITY

Administering an Undergraduate or Graduate Curriculum

Mental health professionals responsible for the administration of academic programs are obligated to make certain that those programs operate in a manner consistent with the ethical code of their profession and federal and state statutes. Selection criteria for admitting students into an academic program must be unbiased, valid predictors of academic performance. Policies regarding retention, academic probation, and dismissal must be explained thoroughly to students during their orientation to the program and administered fairly (ACA, 2005, F.7.a; APA, 2002, 7.02). Furthermore, students must be provided with timely evaluative feedback concerning their performance (ACA, 2005, F.9.a; APA, 2002, 7.06). If participation in psychotherapy is a degree requirement for graduate training in a clinical or counseling program, that fact must be stated explicitly in the program description provided to applicants (ACA, 2005, F.7.b; APA, 2002, 7.02). Students must be given "the option of selecting such therapy from practitioners unaffiliated with the program" (APA, 2002, 7.05[a]). Faculty who provide academic instruction or are potentially responsible for evaluating students' academic performance cannot function as therapy providers for students in the program (APA, 2002, 7.05[b]). Students cannot be required to disclose personal information "regarding sexual history, history of abuse and neglect, psychological treatment," and personal and familial relationships unless this requirement is made clear in a program's admissions materials or a judgment is made that these issues are preventing the student from performing competently in the program (APA, 2002, 7.04).

Infusing Multiculturalism. The most effective method of increasing students' sensitivity to multicultural issues is to address these issues both in courses specifically concerning multicultural topics (e.g., the importance of differences in culture, family structure, language, socioeconomic level, and political disenfranchisement in understanding behavior) and across the curriculum, at both the undergraduate and graduate levels (ACA, 2005, F.6.b, F.11.b; APA, 2003). Courses devoted specifically to multicultural issues are being offered by an increasing number of institutions (Helms et al., 2003). The ethical mandate for sensitivity to multicultural issues and the development of multicultural competence (ACA, 2005, F.11; APA, 2002, Principle E, 2.01[b]) strongly supports administrative policies requiring students to complete such a course as part of an undergraduate or graduate major in a mental health field (Helms, 2003). Departments relegating multicultural issues solely to elective, rather than required, courses run the risk of producing culturally incompetent graduates. Cultural malpractice is as unethical as any other type of incompetent professional practice (Hall, 1997).

Hiring an ethnically diverse faculty provides much-needed expertise in multicultural matters and affords students the opportunity to interact with a diverse set of faculty mentors and role models during training (ACA, 2005, F.11.a; Hall, 1997). Increasing the diversity of both faculty and students in a department is ultimately the only means of producing a new generation of professionals with greater multicultural sophistication.[3] The goal of instilling multicultural competence in students can also be advanced by emphasizing the general theme of social justice as part of the ethical mission of all mental health professions (Helms, 2003). Conceptualizing mental health services as group and community services, rather than simply as assisting individuals, will broaden students' perspective regarding the applicability of multicultural concerns.

Evaluating Student Performance

The primary means of assessing student performance is the assignment of grades for exams, papers, participation, and the like, culminating in a single course grade. Faculty have an ethical duty to evaluate students fairly, "on the basis of their actual performance on relevant and established program requirements" (APA, 2002, 7.06[b]). The fairness of the grading process is difficult to evaluate because it is idiosyncratic to each course and each faculty member teaching the course. However, faculty should be able to document their grading procedures and the criteria for evaluating student performance on each assignment (ACA, 2005, F.9.a).

During the past 30 years or so, faculty members have displayed a general tendency to give higher grades to students than their level of mastery of course material would have merited in the past (Rosovsky & Hartley, 2002). The phenomenon of "grade inflation" occurs as a result of more lenient grading, less challenging exams, and less work (e.g., reading) being required in classes. Educational researchers point to several motivations for greater leniency on the part of faculty members. One is the popularity of the perspective that students are "consumers" of education who must be provided with a positive, self-esteem-enhancing experience. Another factor has been the ubiquitous use of student evaluations of faculty performance; there is clear evidence that faculty providing higher grades receive more positive student evaluations. Because these evaluations play an important role in tenure and promotion decisions, faculty members are naturally inclined to court the favor of their students (Rosovsky & Hartley, 2002). Despite these political and social pressures, faculty members still have an ethical duty to evaluate students fairly and meaningfully. In the long run, students and those they serve professionally will be harmed significantly if students achieve grades that meet program requirements without having learned the concepts and skills the program was designed to teach.

CASE EXAMPLE 11.7

A psychology professor receives a letter from a psychotherapist stating that a young woman he had been treating for the past three years is now enrolled in one of the professor's classes. The therapist indicated that the client had given him permission to contact the professor to inform him of her history. The letter went on to describe the young woman's traumatic life history and present familial, financial, and mental health problems. It said that the woman was not looking for any special consideration, but she wanted the professor to understand why her performance would likely not reflect her true potential. The therapist encouraged the professor to contact him if he had any questions about his client or wanted any additional information.

The professor realized that it would be unfair to the other students to give the young woman any extra time for assignments or grade her work more leniently, but he decided to "give her a break" if her final grade was borderline between two letter grades. (Usually, he was a stickler in such matters, following the cut-offs stated in his syllabus very precisely.)

Presenting a Balanced Viewpoint on Controversial Issues

All mental health professionals have preferences for particular theoretical perspectives based, to a significant extent, on their personal values. When presenting information in class, it is important to remember that models in psychology, including those a faculty member has adopted, are theories, not facts. Thus, if instructors present only their perspective (e.g., a Rogerian one) regarding psychopathology, they are arbitrarily imposing their values on students (ACA, 2005, A.4.b; APA, 2002, Principle D, 3.08). Responsible faculty members present a variety of models in an unbiased fashion so students can get as much information as possible (APA, 2002, 7.03[b]). Instructors should consider it a credit to the objectivity of their class presentations if, at the end of the semester, students are unsure which model the instructor prefers. Also, instructors should always respect the viewpoints expressed by students, particularly those that disagree with their perspective (APA, 2002, Principle E).

It is also highly unprofessional to derogate or belittle other professions or areas of specialization when presenting information to students (ACA, 2005, D.1.a; APA, 2002, Principle C, 3.04). Such behavior demonstrates a lack of respect for other professionals and betrays the limited competence and lack of integrity of the instructor. Instructors should, instead, serve as role models of professional, ethical behavior (ACA, 2005, F.6.a; APA, 2002, Principle C).

Making Students Skeptical Consumers of Research Findings

The task of faculty members is to educate, not to convince students that their research or profession is infallible. Faculty members must exercise great care to avoid overstating the evidence in support of a particular theory or research finding. For example, in presenting research results, instructors should be careful to distinguish *statistical* and *practical* significance to prevent students from exaggerating the importance of research findings. Instructors should explain that statistical significance refers to the probability that observed group differences reflect genuine differences in the underlying populations (Keppel, Saufley, & Tokunaga, 1992). Statistically significant differences between groups are affected by sample size, such that with large samples, very small differences of little practical importance can sometimes achieve statistical significance. For example, in studies of gender differences in children's cognitive abilities, small differences in the average scores achieved by boys and girls constituted a statistically significant difference due to the studies' very large samples. Instructors presenting these findings should also point out that the variation in performance within each gender group (e.g., among girls) was much greater than between the two groups (Maccoby, 1990).

CASE EXAMPLE 11.0

In her classes, a counseling faculty member takes every opportunity to criticize projective assessment as "voodoo psychology." She is not a clinician and has no expertise with projective tests. When clinical faculty members ask her to discuss her criticisms with them, she tells them that a voluminous empirical literature exists that attests to the invalidity of projective techniques. She says that she talks about this issue in her classes not to present her clinical colleagues in a negative light but to make her students skeptical consumers of their psychology training.

Distance Learning

Increasingly, academic programs are making courses available through distance learning arrangements with other institutions or over the Internet. The instructional technologies used in these initiatives hold tremendous promise for making academic and professional training more accessible to students. Although distance learning arrangements may involve learning environments that are very different from a traditional classroom, they do not in any way alter the obligations of program administrators and faculty members to their students. Faculty should receive the relevant technological training prior to providing Internet instruction; at present, this does not always occur (Vodanovich & Piotrowski, 2001). Also, all students accepted for enrollment in such a course must be given the same opportunity to succeed. For example, all students must have access to study materials; if students at a distant location cannot get to the university library to read materials placed on reserve, the faculty member should consider making materials available online on "virtual reserve."

The ethical concerns about distance learning become much greater if all or most of a training curriculum is delivered in this format, as opposed to just a course or two. It is considerably easier to teach courses addressing a content area (e.g., personality) via distance learning than a skills development course (e.g., personality assessment). Educational institutions must determine that competent instruction and student mastery of a course's subject matter can be achieved through distance learning before offering the course in such a format.

TEACHING STUDENTS ABOUT VALUES AND PROFESSIONAL ETHICS

Teaching Students About Ethics in Courses Other Than Ethics

Faculty members teaching undergraduate and graduate courses in psychology and counseling deal generally with one or more of the content areas addressed in this book: therapy, assessment, and research. Each of these areas involves important ethical issues. Instructors should seize every possible opportunity to communicate ethical standards and values to their students in the context of their courses (ACA, 2005, F.6.d; APA, 2002, Preamble). For example, research methods courses present opportunities for instructors to discuss issues of informed consent, confidentiality, and debriefing, as well as to explain how Institutional Review Boards (IRBs) protect the interests of research participants. An early introduction to ethical considerations in their field will increase students' sensitivity to these issues as they prepare to enter the profession. Ethics training was never intended to be reserved for ethics courses.

Addressing the Issue of Personal Values in Training Mental Health Professionals

In Chapter 6, the important role of therapist values in conducting psychotherapy was discussed. Professionals in training (and in practice) can increase their awareness of their personal and professional values through self-study programs like the one developed by Vachon and Agresti (1992). Their three-phase model can be used by training programs to increase novice professionals' awareness of their personal and professional values and to help them manage more effectively the role of their values and client values in their professional interactions.

Phase 1 of the program involves increasing students' awareness of their personal values. It encourages students to identify and explore the personal values underlying their views of psychotherapy (or other professional roles), client diversity (e.g., ethnic, diagnostic), psychiatric diagnosis, and other issues (e.g., religious belief) that play a role in their approach to working with clients. This process enables students to reflect consciously on the personal, subjective values that guide their choices of an orientation to their work and a style of relating to clients, as well as their positions on other professional issues. Some of these value issues (e.g., choice of psychotherapy orientation [Chapter 6], attitudes regarding the diagnostic process [Chapter 8], and entrepreneurial aspects of professional practice [Chapter 10]) have been addressed in this book. In fact, each topic addressed in this book is intended to encourage readers to reflect consciously on their personal values concerning fundamental issues in professional practice.

Phase 2 of the training model helps students and professionals develop an ethical framework that integrates their increased conscious awareness of their personal values from Phase 1 with their knowledge of their ethical obligations as professionals. In other words, in Phase 2, students and professionals develop the ability to apply their increased sensitivity to the personal values and issues of self-interest that might influence their professional judgments in the ethical decision-making process. Their awareness of their personal values represents important information for them to consider in Phase 2 of the model of ethical decision making presented in Chapter 5 of this book.

Phase 3 develops methods to deal with religious values and issues involving "a client's general philosophy of life" in therapy (Vachon & Agresti, 1992). Clearly, respect for the diverse values of clients is fundamental to the therapy process and all other professional interactions. However, professionals' personal values will influence their perception of a client's perspective on life. For example, behavior analysts who view life in a baldly empirical manner and firmly believe that a scientific model is the best perspective for understanding each and every aspect of human existence can respect a client's religious beliefs but cannot relate fully to the phenomenological experience of the client. Much as they might try, they will not be able to avoid viewing the client's beliefs as an ultimately incorrect attempt to comprehend the nature of existence. Vachon and Agresti (1992) suggest that professionals whose values differ markedly from those of a client use a "levels of analysis" approach to better understand the client's view. Instead of seeing a phenomenon from only one perspective (e.g., a client's religious belief as a failure to comprehend the true contingencies influencing events in life), professionals can consider other levels of meaning associated with religious beliefs (e.g., as philosophies of life or mythic systems). The behavior analysts in the previous example might be better able to relate to the logical rigor of the philosophical and theological tenets of religious systems. The important thing is professionals' ability to find points of connection with their clients' philosophy of life, so they can relate to their clients more fully and genuinely. This effort will enable students and profes sionals to understand their clients and be respectful of their religious values or philosophy of life (Grimm, 1994; Kelly & Strupp, 1992), an important aspect of multicultural sensitivity.

CASE EXAMPLE 11.9

A counseling graduate student objects to the values training component of her counseling methods course. She argues that disclosure of her personal values to a faculty member and other students is an invasion of her privacy. She also asserts that the exercise is pointless because students do not present their true personal values. They simply talk about values they know the instructor will approve of. "They just tell him what they think he wants to hear."

ETHICAL AND LEGAL ISSUES IN SUPERVISION

When providing supervision for students completing practica or internships in such areas as counseling, clinical psychology, school psychology, and I/O psychology, faculty members incur obligations to the clients being served by the students, in addition to their obligations to the students themselves. In addition to the guidance provided in professional ethical codes (ACA, 2005, F.1–5; APA, 2002, 2.05), counseling supervisors can consult the "Standards for Counseling Supervisors" published by the Association for Counselor Education (1990).

Competence Issues in Supervision

Supervision involves a combination of theoretical and applied knowledge and skill that is not possessed by all faculty members in the mental health professions. Faculty should receive additional preparation in models and methods of supervision prior to entering into supervisory relationships (ACA, 2005, F.2.a). Some graduate training programs assist counseling and psychology students with developing supervision skills by providing the opportunity to function as peer supervisors to other trainees. Peer supervisors are themselves supervised by a fully qualified, licensed supervisor (ACA, 2005, F.6.e). In the absence of this type of training opportunity, novice supervisors should have the opportunity to observe and work with more experienced supervisors before taking on full supervisory responsibilities themselves. This process will help novice supervisors develop a clearer conception of the skill level of practicum students or interns, rather than basing their expectations for students' performance on their own abilities. An accurate assessment of the capabilities of supervisees is essential in protecting them and the clients they serve from harm (ACA, 2005, F.1.a; APA, 2002, 2.05).

Supervisors should have a clear sense of the supervision model they will use with their students and of the theoretical orientations to which they want students exposed (ACA, 2005, F.2.a). Also, supervisors must have a thorough knowledge of the ethical, professional, and legal issues that supervisees should learn during their initial opportunities to function as mental health professionals (ACA, 2005, F.6.d; APA, 2002, 2.05). Many of the issues that students are exposed to in their academic training (e.g., confidentiality, cultural diversity) need to be reinforced strongly as they enter an applied setting, so they will develop an appropriate ethical sensitivity.

Informed Consent and Confidentiality Issues in Supervision

There are two sets of informed consent issues in supervisory relationships: one set concerning supervisees, the other concerning the clients they serve. A clear, detailed syllabus is every bit as important in a practicum course as in a traditional classroom setting. Supervisors may tend to underestimate the importance of a practicum syllabus because of the unfortunate perception that a practicum "class" has a less formal structure. (Actually, supervisors' professionalism and careful attention to academic procedure are vitally important if a practicum course is to provide the optimal learning experience for supervisees.) An enormous amount of information needs to be provided to practicum students regarding the supervisor's expectations of them (e.g., if they must self-disclose personal issues that may give rise to countertransferential experiences), the evaluation methods that will be used in the course, the procedures to be used in contacting and dealing with clients, the mechanics of keeping track of practicum hours, and the nature and frequency of supervision meetings (ACA, 2005, F.4.a; APA, 2002, 7.03[a]). Practicum students, particularly those working at off-campus agencies, should be told whether they are permitted to communicate with their supervisor about client issues by e-mail. If technology is used to provide supervision (e.g., telephone, e-mail, video conferencing), clients should be informed of that fact and adequate procedures to protect both the client's and supervisee's confidentiality should be explained and implemented (Olson, Russell, & White, 2001). Supervisors must remember that computer-assisted supervision is an emerging area of clinical practice (APA, 2002, 2.01[e]). Therefore, these supervision methods should be implemented with considerable care and in slow increments as professionals await empirical evidence of their efficacy (Olson et al., 2001); they should not yet be considered an acceptable substitute for face-to-face interaction with supervisees in a supervised training experience.

CASE EXAMPLE 11.10

A psychology practicum supervisor conducts individual initial meetings with each of her supervisees on the first day of the semester to discuss their practicum duties and to assign clients to each of them. The supervisor is struck by one student who seems very depressed. He becomes tearful during the session while discussing the recent break-up of his marriage. The supervisor suggests that he postpone his practicum, but he assures her that he will be okay, though he thinks it would be wise not to assign any marital therapy cases to him.

The supervisor decides that, at present, the student lacks the emotional stability to work with clients effectively and to complete the practicum successfully. She tells him that she is canceling his registration for the course and suggests that he pursue psychotherapy to resolve his personal issues. The student complains to the department chair that the supervisor's actions were inappropriate.

The supervisor-supervisee relationship involves more one-on-one interaction than is typical between faculty and students, and those interactions tend to be conducted more informally than classroom interactions. This informality is subject to misinterpretation by supervisees as intimate interaction. As a result, there is an even greater tendency for inappropriate multiple relationships to develop (Thoreson et al., 1993; Thoreson et al., 1995). Supervisors are obligated to clearly define appropriate relationship boundaries for their supervisees and to discuss the ethical importance of those boundaries with them (ACA, 2005, F.3.a; APA, 2002, 3.05[a]). The supervision relationship also provides an excellent opportunity for supervisors to model the professionalism that supervisees should maintain in their relationships with people they serve in a professional capacity.

Clients served by supervisees must be told that professional services are being provided by a trainee under the supervision of a licensed professional. The qualifications of the trainee providing services and the supervisor must be specified (ACA, 2005, F.1.b; APA, 2002, 10.01[c]). Also, clients need to be told that all aspects of their interactions with a trainee will be shared with the trainee's supervisor. The supervisor's professional obligation to maintain the client's confidentiality should also be explained. In many training settings, sessions are observed by other practicum students and aspects of the client's treatment are discussed in group practicum meetings. Of course, the client's informed consent must be obtained for these procedures, as well as for any electronic recording of sessions (ACA, 2005, B.6.b, B.6.c, F.6.h; APA, 2002, 4.03). Clients who are uncomfortable with confidential information being shared with the supervisor or other trainees should be referred to a licensed professional who does not require supervision.

Conflicts of Interest in Supervision

The potential for conflicts of interest can also arise when supervising students. For example, suppose I/O faculty members are responsible for placing students in practicum settings. Suppose further that the faculty members are sometimes paid consultants to one of the agencies serving as a practicum site. They might be tempted to place the best students with this agency, both because they would be the best students to supervise and because the agency might be more likely to retain them as a consultant if they prove to be a reliable source of excellent practicum students. Supervisors can minimize the potential for conflicts of interest by avoiding placing students with agencies where they have a consulting relationship and by declining opportunities to work as a consultant with agencies where they place students (ACA, 2005, F.10.d; APA, 2002, 3.06). Such issues are ethically complex because the agency they serve as a consultant might provide the best quality practicum experience. Again, this is particularly likely in a smaller city. In such a case, professionals must weigh the relevant concerns and use the model of ethical decision making to rationally devise a solution that will minimize the likelihood that a conflict of interest will arise.

Legal Responsibilities of Supervisors

Supervision is a formal, structured relationship developed to ensure an adequate standard of care for clients (Anderson, 1996). Therefore, supervisors can be held liable for actions of a supervisee that are harmful to a client, though the courts generally consider whether the supervisor could have reasonably known of and prevented the danger (ACA, 2005, F.1.a, F.4.c; APA, 2002, 2.05). For example, suppose a supervisee meets his client in a local bar, and they wind up spending the night together. The next week, she files a complaint against both the supervisee and his supervisor. If the supervisor had taken the proper pains at the beginning of the practicum to make certain that her supervisees were aware of the ethical rules prohibiting sexual relationships with clients, it would be unlikely that the supervisor would be held legally accountable for the inappropriate behavior of the supervisee, unless the supervisee had discussed his attraction to the client in supervision and the supervisor had failed to take appropriate action.

Supervisors must be careful to document their supervisory activities in writing, including the decision-making process conducted for all complex treatment matters such as termination, referral, suicidal ideation, and child abuse (Anderson, 1996). At the outset of the relationship, they should discuss with supervisees the shared nature of their ethical and legal responsibility for the treatment of clients. Supervisees should perceive the supervisor as a resource who will enable them to avoid making errors in the treatment of clients through timely consultation.

PRACTICE CASE INVOLVING THE MODEL OF ETHICAL DECISION MAKING

As the result of a colleague's sudden serious illness, a clinical psychologist is asked to teach a physiological psychology course, which is definitely outside his area of expertise. The course begins in one week. The department chair recognizes that the psychologist is not competent in this area, but he is as qualified as anyone else in the department and is the only person whose schedule can accommodate the course. The course is required for graduation, and several seniors will not graduate at the end of the semester if they do not take the course now.

What should the faculty member do?

SUMMARY

This chapter addressed issues pertaining to the teaching and supervision activities of mental health professionals. Establishing and maintaining competence as an instructor requires specialized training and scholarly diligence. Strategies for developing multicultural competence in teaching and for promoting multicultural awareness among students were outlined. Faculty members should regard their course syllabus as an informed consent document and employ grading procedures that are fair and equitable to all students. Multiple relationships with students should be avoided because they can impair the objectivity of faculty members and supervisors or be perceived by students as doing so.

Faculty members should remember that the privacy of students' academic performance is protected by federal law. Also, faculty in the mental health professions should be circumspect about discussing a student's personal disclosures with colleagues because the student might assume that psychology and counseling faculty maintain confidentiality in non-therapy settings.

Ethics training should not be limited to ethics courses. Vachon and Agresti's (1992) model for instructing future therapists about the role of values in therapy was presented to highlight the importance of addressing this issue in training programs. Practicum and internship supervisors must recognize that supervision involves specialized competence, which they must attain in order to fulfill their legal and ethical responsibilities to both supervisees and practicum clients.

NOTES

1. The following journals are among those devoted to instructional issues in higher education: *Active Learning in Higher Education, College Teaching, Journal of Excellence in College Teaching, Teaching in Higher Education,* and *Teaching of Sociology.*

2. There is a wide array of Internet resources concerning multicultural issues that can be investigated by students and instructors. The University of Maryland Web site provides a very useful starting point (http://www.inform.umd.edu/EdRes/Topic/Diversity). It contains links to many other valuable resources relevant to multiculturalism. In addition, APA's "Guidelines on Multicultural Education, Training, Research,

Practice, and Organizational Change for Psychologists" (APA, 2003) cites a wide variety of empirical and conceptual sources of multicultural information. It is an excellent heuristic starting point for students exploring multicultural issues.

3. The issue of encouraging organizations to hire ethnic minority applicants has proven to be extremely controversial. However, it is difficult to see how academic institutions and the mental health professions can fulfill their avowed mandates regarding multiculturalism without increasing the ethnic diversity of their faculty and membership, respectively.

Chapter 12

Ethical Issues in Research

Most mental health professionals conduct research during their academic training; many continue to pursue research as an important part of their professional activity. Ethical considerations are as important and complex in research settings as they are in clinical practice. In both cases, there is great potential for harm, as well as benefit, to those affected by the professional's decision making. Concern about the potential for harm to human research participants focused initially on biomedical research. However, notable instances of participants being harmed emotionally by behavioral studies increased awareness of the ethical complexity of psychological research. Milgram (1963) deceived the participants in his study by making them believe they were administering shocks each time the participant they were paired with (actually, a confederate of the experimenter) made an error on a paired associates learning task. Participants became increasingly upset as they were instructed to administer stronger and stronger shocks, but most of them continued to obey the experimenter's instructions. Although they were debriefed and told they had not harmed anyone, many of the participants were extremely upset and embarrassed about how they had behaved in the study.

Milgram's study raised questions about the appropriateness of the common practice of deceiving research participants. His participants were deceived about the true purpose of the study, the confederates, and the fact that no shocks were really administered. Also, he had not warned the participants in advance about the risk of emotional harm. Ethical duties concerning protecting participants from harm, informed consent, and the confidentiality of research data, as well as ethical concerns related to data collection, analysis, and the publication of research findings, will be discussed in this chapter. Because researchers still deceive participants in some studies, the ethical considerations involved in the decision to use deception and the consequences of deceiving participants will also be addressed. Finally, ethical issues unique to research conducted on the Internet and research using animals will be presented.

CASE EXAMPLE 12.1

A social psychologist proposes the following study as part of her research concerning sexual behavior. An experimenter will approach individuals of the same sex on a city street. He will say that he has noticed the person before and that he finds the person attractive. He will then ask the person to go out on a date (Condition 1) or go somewhere private to have sex (Condition 2). After the participant responds to this offer, the experimenter will inform him that this is a research study; ask him to sign a consent form; and, if consent is granted, ask him additional questions about his dating and sexual behavior. A participant's initial reaction data would not be included in the study results if he refused to consent to participate.

ETHICS, VALUES, AND THEORY CONSTRUCTION

Behavioral research is generally conducted to test specific hypotheses arising from psychological theories. That is, researchers have ideas about the variables influencing some psychological phenomenon, and they test their beliefs about those variables under specified conditions. Researchers decide which questions about human and/or animal behavior will be the most interesting ones to address based upon their theoretical viewpoint regarding how motivation, behavior, and human nature are best explained. Mental health professionals generally adopt theoretical viewpoints that have proven useful to them for understanding themselves and the people they know. Researchers' choice of a model of human personality, for example, is generally based upon their own subjectively held values and beliefs regarding such issues as freedom of choice, biological influences, and the relative contributions of emotion and cognition to behavior, rather than an objective scientific appraisal of the issues.

This point is important because it illustrates again the ubiquitous role of subjective, personal values in every aspect of mental health professionals' activities. The fact that values are involved in a researcher's choice of phenomena to study raises the ethical question of whether there are research questions that should or should not be studied. Obviously, research that involves deliberately harming human participants would be unethical, but what about studies that are potentially socially divisive, like those looking for racial differences in intelligence? Defenders of these studies point out that scientific research should never avoid issues for social or political reasons and that uncovering social problems is a necessary first step toward remediating them. Nevertheless, researchers must consider the ethical and social implications of the phenomena they choose to study.

Researchers' personal values might affect not only what issues they study, but also how they evaluate the evidence (i.e., data) they obtain. Research is a scientific enterprise in which data are to be evaluated in an objective, dispassionate manner. However, in reality, researchers might be more open to accepting data that support their assumptions, even when these data are flawed. Researchers must always strive to be as objective as possible in their activities (ACA, 2005, G.4; APA, 2002, 2.04), which requires that they consciously acknowledge their theoretical biases and approach research as a quest to *disconfirm* their theories (Popper, 1965).

Multicultural Research Considerations

Psychological research has too often been limited to describing the behavior of white, American introductory psychology students (Guthrie, 1998). The inclusion of ethnically and racially diverse groups in research samples is of enormous importance if the mental health professions are to fulfill their self-declared mandate to increase multicultural awareness and understanding (ACA, 2005, G.1.g; APA, 2003). An increasing amount of research is being conducted internationally, incorporating samples from diverse cultures. This is certainly a positive development; however, it does raise both methodological and ethical concerns, in that human participant protections and scientific oversight vary substantially in different countries around the world (e.g., Marino & Cirillo, 2004).

Increasing the multicultural nature of psychological research is not simply a function of accessing more diverse research samples. It also requires changing the way we conceptualize the research enterprise (APA, 2003). Historically, psychological research has focused on the search for universally valid predictors of behavior. Multicultural research, or research including participants of different cultures, requires a different paradigm (Pedersen, 2001): a more holistic perspective, involving more of the "real-life" complexity of interacting networks and considerations that influence behavior on both the individual and group levels (Smith, Harre, & Van Langenhove, 1995). The focus is more on description of socially important phenomena through a narrative understanding of people's varied perspectives of events and issues. Ultimately, for research to be relevant to our multicultural society, researchers must move away from the notion of finding *the answer* regarding a behavioral phenomenon toward a clearer appreciation of the subjective perceptual, attitudinal, and behavioral priorities of different cultural groups and individuals.

If it seems to you that this research paradigm will reduce researchers' sense of clarity and certainty regarding the prediction and explanation of behavior, you're right. If research is to be relevant to our multicultural world, researchers must address the real complexity of human behavior. In doing so, they need not become sloppy thinkers, but they do need to increase their tolerance for ambiguity (Pedersen, 2001). Clearly, this new paradigm is still in its beginning stages, but researchers have an ethical obligation to increase the representation of multicultural participants in all research endeavors in order to produce findings that will be socially meaningful (ACA, 2005, G. Introduction; APA, 2002, Principles D, E).

CONDUCTING RESEARCH WITH HUMAN PARTICIPANTS

In 1977, the National Commission for the Protection of Human Subjects of Biomedical and Behavioral Research (NCPHS) was created under the National Research Act of 1974 (Pub. L. No. 93-348). The commission's primary purpose was to identify the ethical principles involved in research with human participants and to make recommendations to the Department of Health and Human Services (DHHS). The work of the commission resulted in *The Belmont Report* (1979), which focused on the ethical principles of respect for persons, beneficence, and justice. In addition, in 1982, APA's Committee for the Protection of Human Participants in Research published its own research guidelines.

Institutional Review Boards (IRBs)

Based on the principles articulated in *The Belmont Report,* DHHS published federal regulations in 1981 that formalized the role of the Institutional Review Board for the Protection of Human Subjects in Research (IRB). In an institution conducting research (e.g., hospital, university, medical school), the IRB is the official entity that reviews research proposals involving human participants to determine whether the studies are ethically acceptable. The IRB is composed of at least five members of varying backgrounds who provide expertise in the areas of research commonly conducted at the institution. At least one member of the board must have no affiliation with the institution. All members have a responsibility to ensure the following: that the risks and benefits to participants are reasonable, that consent is informed and voluntary, that research conditions are safe, that the privacy of data is protected, that the selection of participants is equitable, and that vulnerable groups such as children are protected (Porter, 1996). Mental health professionals are ethically required to cooperate with IRBs by providing accurate information in their research proposals and abiding by the research procedures for their study approved by the IRB (ACA, 2005, G.1.a; APA, 2002, 8.01). Ongoing research projects must be reapproved by the IRB each year (Protection of Human Subjects, 2001, § 46.109[e]).

PROTECTING RESEARCH PARTICIPANTS FROM HARM

The ethical duty to protect research participants from physical and psychological harm was stated in the Nuremberg Code, which was developed after the Nuremberg trial of Nazi medical researchers following World War II (Beecher, 1970). Compared to medical research, most psychological research involves relatively little risk to participants' health (and correspondingly, little potential benefit). For the most part, the potential risks concern harm to participants' emotional well-being. Nevertheless, the potential for lowered self-esteem, embarrassment at being manipulated to perform negative behaviors, emotional upset from recalling painful life events, negative reactions to being deceived, and harm from potential breaches of confidentiality can be very real risks in mental health research (Bersoff & Bersoff, 1999). Generally, the short-term manipulation of variables like anxiety in behavioral research is not very powerful. Nevertheless, researchers have no right to place participants at even short-term risk without informing them of the potential for emotional upset.

Assessing the significance of research risk always involves weighing the potential risks to participants against the potential benefits of the research to participants and others; in an acceptable study, the potential benefits should always outweigh the potential risks. For example, in a behavioral study of honesty in children in which there is little potential for direct benefit to the participants, an IRB would require that the study involve no more than minimal risk. On the other hand, an ethically acceptable treatment study of an aversive conditioning method to reduce head banging behavior in autistic children might involve a higher level of risk but would be balanced by the potential for directly benefiting the participants by reducing such a dangerous behavior.

As R. A. Thompson (1992) points out, risk-benefit assessment appears initially to be a purely utilitarian calculation of what will produce the greatest positive balance of pleasure over pain to the greatest number of people, but researchers actually have an ethical duty to always minimize risks to participants, reflecting the principle of nonmaleficence, and to only conduct research that benefits participants, consistent with the principle of beneficence (ACA, 2005, G.1.d; APA, 2002, 3.04). Respect for the personhood and autonomy of participants is the metaethical basis for the requirement that they be informed of any potential risks associated with their participation in a study.

Ideally, behavioral studies should involve no more than *minimal risk,* in which "the probability and magnitude of harm or discomfort anticipated . . . are not greater . . . than those ordinarily encountered in daily life or during the performance of routine physical or psychological examinations or tests" (Protection of Human Subjects, 2001, § 46.102[i]).

Unfortunately, this definition is quite vague, both in terms of the breadth of experiences that might be involved in "routine physical or psychological exams or tests" (e.g., having your temperature taken versus completing the Rorschach) and in terms of what qualifies as minimal risk for the reference group we are supposed to have in mind as undergoing the procedure (e.g., a normal population or a sample of depressives being studied in a particular research project?). For example, for a sample of people in the early stages of Alzheimer's disease, completing a "routine" intelligence test can be extremely painful because, as they try to answer the questions, they are repeatedly reminded of how much their intellectual abilities have declined. Thus, there is no reasonable universal determination of minimal risk. The metaethical foundation of mental health professionals' concern for protecting research participants from harm is the profound respect they have for the personhood of each unique individual. Therefore, researchers (and IRBs) have an ethical obligation to calibrate the standard that will qualify as "minimal risk" in relation to the characteristics of the specific group that will be sampled, consistent with the principle of nonmaleficence (ACA, 2005, A.4.a; APA, 2002, Principle A).

Potential risk factors in any behavioral research would not be expected to affect all participants equally. Participants experiencing anxiety or mood disorders would be at considerably greater risk than other participants in a study designed to induce anxiety. When conducting such a study, the researcher might be required by an IRB to use a screening procedure to identify high-risk individuals who should not be subjected to the manipulation. Prebriefing procedures, in which potential participants are informed of risk factors in solicitations for the study, can also help to reduce the potential for participants to be upset by stimuli, such as traumatic childhood experiences, snakes, vignettes depicting violent crimes, or sexually explicit material (Allen, D'Alessio, Emmers, & Gebhardt, 1996; Korn, Huelsman, Reed, & Aiello, 1992).

Everyone agrees that researchers have an ethical duty to inform participants of potential study risks; however, they sometimes disagree about what constitutes a risk that needs to be mentioned. For example, a researcher wants to elicit anxiety by providing false feedback on the results of a "personality" test. The items will not really be scored, but half the participants will be shown a set of negative trait terms and told that the testing software generated the personality descriptors. They will be debriefed immediately following their participation. Does this procedure involve a significant risk of harm to participants? To some participants?

CASE EXAMPLE 12.2

A student in a counseling research methods class has a large python snake as a pet. For her experiment, she proposes to have college students attempt to complete a set of 10 anagrams in five minutes under one of two conditions. She will walk around the room with her pet snake around her shoulders while Group 1 completes the anagrams and without her snake while Group 2 completes the anagrams. She is interested in knowing whether most people's concentration is affected by anxiety about snakes. After receiving assurances that the snake will not attempt to molest any of the students, the instructor gives his permission to conduct the study.

Risk is a particularly potent concern in research with children, in part because adult researchers and IRB members often experience difficulty in evaluating a research study's potential harm to children. Risks to child participants must be minimal or nonexistent in most cases for a study to receive IRB approval because children depend on someone else (i.e., their parent or guardian) to make consent decisions for them. The only exception might be therapeutic research concerning life-threatening problems, where the promise of direct benefit to the child participants reasonably outweighs the risk involved. The informed consent agreement in such a study should stipulate that all participants, including the children in control groups, will be provided access to any therapeutic benefit resulting from the study.

IRBs look very carefully at the potential risks to research participants; in fact, some have argued that IRBs have moved toward a "zero risk" criterion in their zeal to protect participants (Mueller & Furedy, 2001). However, other critics point out that most IRB members are researchers themselves, which makes them more likely to view the situation from a researcher's perspective. Although all IRB members take their duty to protect participants from risk seriously, the assessment of risk is a major reason why IRBs include a community member who has no investment in research. This individual is best able to represent the perspective of potential participants when evaluating risks associated with participation in a proposed study.

Of course, research risk to participants could be eliminated completely if IRBs refused to approve any study involving greater than minimal risk, but at what cost to the scientific, educational, and applied goals of research? For example, social psychology researchers conduct studies investigating anger and antisocial behavior, such as the phenomenon of road rage. When researchers elicit negative emotions or behavior in these studies, the risks that participants might be embarrassed about their behavior in the study or may carry the anger elicited by the study with them when they leave are very real. However, these are important phenomena for researchers to investigate because the results could assist in generating solutions to a serious social problem. Whenever a study involves any risk to participants, researchers' responsibility for demonstrating the potential value of the study becomes much greater.

Risks to Control Group Participants in Treatment Research

Although it is essential to use a control group in studies testing the effectiveness of new treatments for medical conditions or emotional problems (e.g., depression), it is not ethically appropriate to place people suffering from the disorder at increased risk by denying them treatment (ACA, 2005, G.1.f; APA, 2002, Principle A). Researchers should provide control group participants with a baseline level of treatment; ideally, this treatment will be the most popular intervention currently used for the condition. At a minimum, concern for the welfare of control group participants requires use of an attention-placebo control group so that the condition of control group participants can be monitored carefully (Bersoff & Bersoff, 1999).

INFORMED CONSENT

A researcher must obtain the informed consent of research participants prior to their participation in a study (ACA, 2005, G.2.a; APA, 2002, 8.02), unless the research is "exempt" under HIPAA and federal human subjects regulations (Privacy Rule, 2003, §§ 164.501, 164.508, 164.512[i]; Protection of Human Subjects, 2001). The following types of research may qualify as exempt from IRB review and informed consent requirements: research conducted in educational settings that involves only normal educational practices; studies using only archival data that are either publicly available or cannot be linked with a particular person (Protection of Human Subjects, 2001, § 46.101[b]); survey and interview research that does not involve any identifiable private information or any intervention or interaction with people that is not an ordinary part of daily life (Protection of Human Subjects, 2001, § 46.102[f]); and most observation studies in public settings, unless the research concerns "sensitive matters" and the participants can be identified and linked to their responses (Areen, 1992). An IRB can also waive or alter informed consent procedures in any study involving no more than "minimal risk" when the waiver or alteration is essential to conducting the study and will not abridge participants' rights or deny them any pertinent information prior to or following their participation (Protection of Human Subjects, 2001, § 46.102[i]). These exemptions have been incorporated in the 2002 revision of the "Ethical Principles" in the discussion of situations in which researchers "may dispense with informed consent" (APA, 2002, 8.05).

Obtaining consent simply means that participants agree to participate. It is the "informed" aspect of informed consent that involves most of the tricky ethical issues. Ideally, participants should be fully informed regarding the purpose of the research, every aspect of their participation, and anything else that would be likely to affect their willingness to participate. The following information should be explained in the informed consent process:

1. the voluntary nature of participation

2. the amount of time required for participation

3. the procedure(s) participants will complete

4. any risks that participants might encounter as a result of their participation

5. what use will be made of the study results

6. any inducement (e.g., money) to participate

7. any prospective benefits for participants (e.g., educational, emotional) or society

8. the protections used to ensure the confidentiality of non-anonymous data and any potential limitations on confidentiality

9. the right to withdraw from participation

10. addresses and telephone numbers of the primary researcher and the chair of the IRB in the event participants have any questions or concerns about their participation

11. the right to ask the researcher(s) any questions at any point during the study or afterwards

12. how to obtain information regarding the results of the study

13. any debriefing procedure that will occur following participation

14. participants' legal rights, including their right to sue the researcher, even though they have consented to participate

CASE EXAMPLE 12.3

A counseling researcher wishes to conduct a follow-up study concerning women's psychological adjustment following breast augmentation surgery. She receives the approval of the IRB of her university to mail surveys to women identified by their plastic surgeon as potential participants. The researcher has procedures in place to preserve participants' privacy by carefully protecting the list of names and contact information.

Voluntary Research Participation

IRBs require that participants be free to decide whether they want to participate and to choose to withdraw from participation at any time (ACA, 2005, G.2.a.9; APA, 2002, 8.02[a]). Research in institutional settings, or in any other context involving perceived differences in power between participants and researchers (e.g., research with involuntarily committed clients or prisoners), is scrutinized very carefully by IRBs (ACA, 2005, G.2.d; Draine, 1997; Grisso, 1996). The use of incentives (e.g., extra credit for students, toys for children, free treatment following participation for depressed participants) can also potentially affect the voluntariness of research participation.

Consent Forms

Researchers generally obtain the informed consent of participants by having them read and sign a consent form. Participants' signatures attest to the fact that they have read and understood the consent form and agree to participate in the study. The IRB may waive the requirement to obtain a signed consent form when research participation involves "no more than minimal risk to subjects and involves no procedures for which written consent is normally required outside of the research context" (Protection of Human Subjects, 2001, § 46.117[c]). The benefit to participants of *not* signing a consent form is that their participation can be anonymous. In some research contexts, anonymity is especially critical because participants would be placed at risk if the fact that they had *participated* in the study became known to others (e.g., in a study of the psychological impact of suffering from a sexually transmitted disease). If having signed informed consent documents as the only identifier of an individual's participation in such a study would constitute "the principal risk" of harm to study participants, signed consent should not be obtained (Protection of Human Subjects, 2001, § 46.117[c]). In such cases, participants' consent is indicated by their subsequent participation in the study.

The use of consent forms is only an effective means of obtaining informed consent if the potential participants actually do read and understand the information provided. For participants who are not fluent in English, the informed consent information must be presented "in language understandable to the subject" (Protection of Human Subjects, 2001, § 46.116). In addition, studies have indicated that consent forms tend to be written at a reading level higher than would be appropriate for the participant population (e.g., Hochhauser, 1999; Ogloff & Otto, 1991; Young, Hooker, & Freeberg, 1990). Researchers are obligated to ensure that their consent forms can be understood by potential participants. Helpful strategies include having a member of the participant population review the form and provide suggestions for making the form more readable, checking the vocabulary level of the form using a word processing program, providing visual illustrations to accompany the verbal information, and presenting information orally as well as in writing (Hochhauser, 1999; Murphy et al., 1999; Tymchuk & Ouslander, 1990).

Do participants really bother to read consent forms carefully and ask questions about matters they do not understand? Evidence suggests that shorter consent forms are understood better than longer ones, so it is probably desirable to address only the key issues listed earlier that might affect participants' willingness to take part in the study (Mann, 1994; Young et al., 1990).

Participants must be informed of any potential risks to their well-being (ACA, 2005, G.2.a.3; APA, 2002, 8.02[a]), even in research involving deception (Bersoff & Bersoff, 1999). If a study involves greater risk for particular groups of participants, the researcher must make certain that these additional risks are communicated (APA, 2002, 3.04). For example, a retrospective study about childhood memories may involve special risks for individuals who experienced traumatic events (e.g., abuse, death of a parent or sibling) as children.

In studies involving data that are not anonymous, informed consent documents should state the extent of confidentiality afforded to participants and the protections in place to ensure the confidentiality of participants' data (e.g., using numerical codes for data files so individual participants' data cannot be identified). The limits of confidentiality, which will be discussed later in the chapter, should also be presented (ACA, 2005, G.2.e; APA, 2002, 8.02[a]).

Some research projects involve agencies as well as individual participants. In such cases, researchers must also develop an informed consent agreement for the agency (ACA, 2005, G.2.i; APA, 2002, 8.01, 8.02[a]). Researchers should create a contract stipulating the records or information the agency will provide, the role agency personnel will play in the data collection process, and the types of information the researchers will provide to the agency (e.g., group or individual results). Researchers are then ethically bound to fulfill these commitments.

CASE EXAMPLE 12.4

A psychology instructor teaching a research methods course at a university requires each student to conduct a research project for the class. One of his students is especially interested in the topic of therapist bias, with particular emphasis on sexism. The student suggests that for her research project, she will have female confederates pose as clients at various clinics in town and gather data regarding sexist behavior of male and female therapists toward female clients.

Informed Consent With Participants of Reduced Capacity

The decision-making capacity of potential research participants must be assessed if their competence to provide consent is questionable. Visual and auditory functioning, mental status, and reading comprehension are all relevant factors, which can be assessed through interview and testing procedures. Some mental health research activities, such as clinical brain research, will typically involve participants "suffering from psychiatric, neurological, and other conditions that may reduce their ability to give what we call informed consent" (Cook-Deegan, 2000, p. 74). It is not reasonable or ethical to suggest that these individuals not be permitted to participate in research because, in many instances, important potential benefits *for them* (e.g., the discovery of a new, more effective treatment for their condition) might result from their participation. On the other hand, people experiencing cognitive, physical, or emotional impairment are particularly vulnerable to the "therapeutic misconception"—the tendency to confuse research participation with medical or mental health treatment (Cook-Deegan, 2000, p. 84). Researchers have a duty to explain to potential participants and those providing proxy consent the differences between participation in the research protocol and actually receiving treatment for their condition (e.g., the possibility of being assigned to the control condition).

The assessment of participants' ability to consent should be made by competent, disinterested experts who are not otherwise involved in the study. Individuals lacking adequate capacity in a function that is important to the consent process, as well as anyone who is not legally competent to consent to participate, require proxy consent from a legally authorized guardian (ACA, 2005, G.2.f; APA, 2002, 3.10[b]). In addition to proxy consent, the *assent* of these participants (i.e., their agreement to participate after being given an explanation of the nature and purpose of the research that they can comprehend) is generally required. However, an IRB may waive this requirement if participants' rights will not be adversely affected and the research cannot practically be carried out if information about the study is provided prior to participation (Protection of Human Subjects, 2001, § 46.116[d]). Because these individuals cannot legally consent to participate, a stronger justification is needed for invading their privacy by including them in a study, even though proxy consent has been obtained and participants have assented. Using participants of diminished capacity should involve some direct potential benefits to them or others suffering from similar problems (Delano & Zucker, 1994).

Another important issue in working with research participants of reduced capacity is how to make certain that their right to withdraw from participation at any time is respected. These participants may be less likely to exercise this right because of their willingness to comply with the directions of authority figures. Fisher and Rosendahl (1990) suggest that participants "can simply be instructed to say, 'I'd like to stop now,' or to signal by picking up a picture of an arrow provided by the experimenter and pointing it toward the door" (p. 50). Behavioral indications of discomfort, such as crying, yawning, wringing of hands, looking away from the task, or requesting to use the bathroom, are also indications of a participant's desire to stop.

Inducements to Research Participants

In studies evaluating the effectiveness of new treatments for physical illnesses or emotional problems, participants are frequently offered free treatment in exchange for their participation. The offer of free treatment, which implies the promise of relief from suffering, could be viewed as coercive. Therefore, researchers conducting treatment studies must include an explanation of the following issues in their informed consent statement: the nature of the treatment services and the fact that they are *experimental,* the length of treatment provided in the study, any risks and limitations associated with the treatment, the possibility that the participant could be assigned to a control group condition and not receive the experimental treatment, the availability of services to control group participants at the conclusion of the study, treatment alternatives if the participant decides not to participate or to withdraw from the study after it has begun, and compensation or monetary costs associated with participation (APA, 2002, 8.02[b]). Participants in treatment studies should be offered the opportunity to receive the new treatment for free if it proves effective.[1]

Researchers conducting non-treatment studies also frequently offer to compensate research participants in some way for their time and effort, consistent with the respect mental health professionals have for their participants' value as persons. However, inducements can interfere with the voluntariness of a participant's decision to participate (APA, 2002, 8.06). For example, offering poor families money as an inducement to participate in family research could be construed as coercive (Bersoff & Bersoff, 1999). There is no straightforward formula that researchers can use to determine what constitutes reasonable, non-coercive compensation for participants' time and effort because the degree of effort associated with participation varies tremendously across studies. Also, the coercive potential of a financial inducement depends largely on participants' economic situation and the value they place on money.

Any inducement offered to children is potentially coercive, even though the parents actually provide consent. If children are aware of a desirable inducement to participate (e.g., a toy that most children want), they might insist that their parents sign the consent form so they can obtain it. Researchers should give children the inducement after they participate, with the parents' consent, without advertising it to the child beforehand (Powell & Vacha-Haase, 1994). Paying money to pre-adolescent children for participating in research is also an ethically ill-advised procedure (Powell & Vacha-Haase, 1994). First, the money might be a coercive influence on the process of obtaining parental consent. Second, because the money is generally given to the child's parents, researchers do not know whether the child will ever receive it.

In some cases, the parental consent requirement in research with children can present an economic obstacle to children's participation if a parent has to leave work in order to provide informed consent, thus interfering with researchers' attempts to obtain a broad multicultural sample. Reimbursement for travel and lost work time has been suggested as an appropriate method of participant compensation to address this problem (Fisher et al., 2002).

CASE EXAMPLE 12.5

A counseling researcher comparing college students' scores on a short form of the MMPI-2 with scores on the complete test offers participants an inducement of receiving a free copy of a computer-based interpretive report of their MMPI-2 performance if they participate in her study. Participants will be able to pick up their report the day after they complete the tests.

Debriefing Participants

Researchers are obligated to provide participants with comprehensive information regarding the study following their participation (ACA, 2005, G.2.h; APA, 2002, 8.08[a]). Debriefing procedures are intended to correct any misconceptions and answer any questions participants might have. In addition, if participants were not fully informed regarding the purpose and procedures for the study or were actively deceived, they must be informed as soon as possible following their participation to ameliorate any negative experiences that may have resulted from their participation (Blanck, Bellack, Rosnow, Rotheram-Borus, & Schooler, 1992). Debriefing is the responsibility of the principal researcher and must be done carefully because debriefing can itself evoke anger, suspicion, and emotional upset (Oliansky, 1991).

Although debriefing should occur immediately, it is often delayed until all study data have been collected because researchers fear that debriefed participants will reveal the true details of the study to future participants (ACA, 2005, G.2.h; APA, 2002, 8.08[b]). Evidence supports this concern about participant contamination, particularly when participants are recruited from a student subject pool. Having students sign a pledge to maintain confidentiality reduced, but did not eliminate, the problem (Klein & Cheuvront, 1990). While the practice of delaying debriefing is not prohibited, it is ethically problematic because it gives priority to the concerns of researchers over their duties to participants. Furthermore, researchers question whether delayed debriefing is of any value because most participants do not attend the sessions.

Debriefing participants is also intended to serve an educational function. In some studies, participants are able to obtain feedback regarding their personal performance (Blanck et al., 1992). For example, in clinical research concerning depression, clients can receive feedback about their depression score and any change that occurred from pretest to posttest. When college students are the population studied, debriefing affords an excellent opportunity to enhance participants' understanding of the research process. If debriefing is delayed until all the data have been collected, the results and conclusions of the study can also be presented. In any case, participants should always be given the opportunity to obtain a copy of the results and conclusions of the study (APA, 2002, 8.08[a]).

Delayed debriefing and providing study results is now much easier because of Internet technology. At the time of their participation, participants can be given the researcher's Web address and the date that the results of the study will be posted there. Participants can then view a summary of the study, its results, and conclusions. If they have questions, they can contact the researcher by telephone, mail, or e-mail. Online debriefing does not require finding a way to contact participants at the end of the study. Of course, participants who do not have Internet access should be given the option of receiving debriefing materials by mail.

Finally, researchers should also regard debriefing as an educational opportunity for themselves to find out from participants how well the methodology of the study worked, what expectations participants had, and whether participants' behavior was affected by any extraneous variables (Blanck et al., 1992). For example, in studies using deception, researchers can learn whether participants were at all suspicious of the manipulation. Previous experiences in research involving deception can increase participants' suspiciousness about possible manipulations in studies they participate in subsequently (Epley & Huff, 1998; Oliansky, 1991).

CASE EXAMPLE 12.6

A social psychology professor conducts a research study to assess the willingness of college student participants to provide aid to a female participant (actually a confederate of the experimenter) who asks to borrow a dollar to buy a soda because she is feeling "shaky." Due to the deception involved in the study, he delays debriefing until all data are collected for the project. Participants are informed that the full details and results of the study will be posted during the final week of classes on the departmental bulletin board where students sign up to participate in research studies.

SPECIAL CONSIDERATIONS IN CONDUCTING RESEARCH WITH CHILDREN

Informed Consent Issues With Children

In 1983, DHHS adopted additional guidelines for research with children based on recommendations issued in a report titled *Research Involving Children* (NCPHS, 1977). These guidelines are found in "Additional DHHS Protections for Children Involved as Subjects in Research" (Protection of Human Subjects, 2001, Subpart D). Research with children must involve no more than minimal risk and adequate provision for obtaining the informed consent of the parent or guardian and the assent of the child (ACA, 2005, G.2.f; APA, 2002, 3.10[b]). Assent is "a child's affirmative agreement to participate in research" (Protection of Human Subjects, 2001, § 46.402[b]). The IRB will consider the age, maturity, and psychological status of the children involved in determining whether assent is needed (Protection of Human Subjects, 2001, § 46.408[a]). Research with children that poses more than minimal risk will receive IRB approval only if it involves the prospect of direct benefit to the child participant. Understandably, the standards for approval of research with children are more stringent because children cannot provide consent (Ondrusek, Abramovitch, Pencharz, & Koren, 1998). Children of any age should also be informed that they can stop if they no longer want to participate.

Obtaining parental informed consent protects both children and researchers against a number of potential ethical problems. First, the process reduces the pressure on researchers to make certain that children understand every implication of the consent agreement (Grisso, 1992). Second, the consent form can involve a more complete explanation of the details of the study than might be given to participants. For example, an incidental learning procedure (e.g., instructing children to attend to the different colors of cards with printed words, then testing their ability to recall the words) can be explained completely in the parental consent form, whereas it will spoil the study if participants are told about this aspect of the research in advance. Finally, in obtaining parental informed consent, researchers have the opportunity to inform parents that, as mental health professionals, researchers have an ethical and legal duty to report any suspicions of child abuse or neglect that might arise in the course of the research (Kalichman, 1999).

When appropriate, the IRB may waive or alter the parental consent requirement if four conditions apply: (a) the research poses no more than minimal risk, (b) the waiver or alteration will not jeopardize the rights and welfare of the participants, (c) the research cannot be conducted without the waiver or alteration of the consent process, and (d) if appropriate, the participant may be informed of pertinent information after the research is completed (Porter, 1996). A waiver is also permitted in situations in which parental consent is not a reasonable requirement for the protection of the child participant, such as in research with neglected or abused children (Protection of Human Subjects, 2001, § 46.408[c]). In spite of IRBs' ability to waive parental consent in some research (when such a waiver does not conflict with state or local law), IRBs are usually very reluctant to do so.[2]

Additional informed consent considerations arise in conducting research with ethnic minority children. Researchers need to be even more diligent in their efforts to explain the purpose and procedures of their study in clear, easy-to-understand language because multicultural parents and guardians, as well as children, may be less familiar "with the research process and scientific terminology" (Fisher et al., 2002, p. 1029). Translations of informed consent documents must be accurate and, whenever possible, presented in the appropriate vernacular for the participants. Whether written or oral consent procedures are used, an interpreter should be present to explain anything the participants or parents do not understand and answer their spontaneous questions (Protection of Human Subjects, 2001, § 46.117[b]). Choosing an interpreter based on convenience rather than competence is a violation of the researcher's ethical duty (ACA, 2005, D.1.f; APA, 2002, 2.05). Furthermore, in some cultures and families, grandparents, other relatives, or respected community members may be routinely sought out for advice or depended upon to make important decisions (Fisher et al., 2002). The researcher might ask families of prospective participants if there is someone else they would like to be involved in the decision regarding their child's participation.

When research is being conducted in a service delivery setting (e.g., school, social service setting, or clinic), it is extremely important that investigators make every effort possible to clarify that parents' refusal to consent to their child's participation in a research study will in no way affect the child's eligibility to receive professional services (Fisher et al., 2002).

Debriefing Child Participants

Ethical issues concerning debriefing are even more complex in research involving child participants. When children are deceived or manipulated to engage in negative behaviors, debriefing is necessary to reduce the possibility that the children will make negative self-attributions regarding their behavior in the study (Fisher & Rosendahl, 1990). However, debriefing children is not the same as debriefing adults. The terminology used must be understood by the children, and they should be asked to demonstrate their understanding of the points communicated in the debriefing. Pilot testing of the debriefing procedure prior to conducting a study is certainly indicated; if an effective debriefing procedure that eliminates all risk of lingering emotional or behavioral harm to the participants cannot be developed, the researchers cannot ethically conduct the study (Fisher & Rosendahl, 1990).

CASE EXAMPLE 12.7

A child counseling professor conducts a study with seven-year-olds concerning honesty. Children are left in a room with loose change on a table. He tells one group of children that they will be watched through a two-way mirror when he leaves the room; the researcher does not tell the other group of children anything. He anticipates that a child who does not expect to be monitored will pick up some money. He decides not to debrief the children or their parents following children's participation because he thinks that children who took money and their parents will be embarrassed and will think that he is calling the children thieves.

The Importance of Conducting Research With Child Participants

The additional safeguards required for research with children have, at times, affected researchers' willingness to conduct such research. However, excluding children from health-related research samples does an injustice to them as a group and places them at risk because it results in a lack of valid information regarding the effects of proposed behavioral and biomedical treatments on children (Levine, 1995b). The generalizability of research results can only be ensured by including children from the gender, age, cultural, and ethnic groups that the researchers intend the treatment to benefit (Laosa, 1990). The National Institutes of Health (NIH) implemented a policy requiring the inclusion of children in federally funded research samples unless there are compelling scientific or ethical reasons for excluding them (NIH, 1998).

Unfortunately, racial and ethnic minority children, as well as low-income children in general, tend to be underrepresented in research samples (Scott-Jones, 1994). This situation has begun to change in recent years as the increase in sensitivity to multiculturalism has extended to researchers. However, the inclusion of multicultural populations in child research samples introduces some new concerns. Including race or ethnicity as research variables requires that these terms be defined meaningfully and operationalized with great precision. Furthermore, the emphasis placed on these labels introduces the risk of researchers ignoring or undervaluing within-group differences in these samples (Fisher et al., 2002). For example, an American researcher would be unlikely to incorrectly assume that the behavior of all Caucasian children can be understood in terms of race. Researchers must show equal consideration to within-group differences among African American or Hispanic American participants.

In clinical research, multicultural populations are at risk of being stigmatized as deficient if "normal" or "healthy" is defined in terms of developmental norms for the cultural majority white child population; culturally relevant norms must be developed. Finally, researchers should be aware that parents and adolescents from multicultural populations might expect them to take an active role in accessing professional resources to assist them in resolving health problems revealed in the course of research participation, rather than just providing information or a diagnosis during debriefing (Fisher et al., 2002).

THE USE OF DECEPTION IN RESEARCH

The most common limitation placed on the duty to obtain informed consent in psychological research involves the use of deception. In 1985, 47% of published studies in social psychology utilized deception (Adair, Dushenko, & Lindsay, 1985). Two types of deception are employed in behavioral research. The first, which the *Code of Ethics* refers to as "concealment," occurs when researchers fail to tell participants the "whole truth" about a study (ACA, 2005, G.2.b). For example, a researcher studying the relation between depression and interpersonal behavior tells participants that they will be asked to complete a questionnaire about some of their "behaviors and attitudes." Participants are not actively deceived in the description of the study; however, they are not told that the questionnaire concerns depressive symptoms, even though this information could be important to some people's decision to participate. This limited type of deception is present in a large proportion of psychological research. The second type of deception involves actively deceiving participants regarding the true purpose and procedures of the study. Milgram's (1963) study of obedience to authority is a classic example of researchers actively lying to participants.

In such studies, the ethical duty to obtain informed consent is not being compromised by behavioral researchers due to a lack of ethical sensitivity; rather, it is done in the interest of using the best methodology possible in their research. Deception is used when (a) the researcher believes that informing participants fully regarding a study's purpose or procedures will affect participants' responses, thereby threatening the validity of the study; and (b) there is no workable nondeceptive method of addressing the research question (ACA, 2005, G.2.b; APA, 2002, 8.07[a]). For example, if participants are told in advance that the purpose of a study is to evaluate people's honesty in different situations, their behavior will likely reflect a social desirability response set (i.e., they will behave honestly to create a positive impression on the researcher). The use of deception reduces the response cues available to participants, thereby making the results more valid and straightforwardly interpretable.

As with other research risks, the ethical justification for using deception is conceptualized as a cost/benefit analysis. The potential cost to participants of being deceived is weighed against the study's potential benefit to science, or, in some instances, to the participants themselves (ACA, 2005, G.2.b; APA, 2002, 8.07[a]). There are both ethical and metaethical problems with this method of justification for deceiving research participants. On a pragmatic, ethical level, the first problem with this analysis is that all the costs affect participants, while the benefits generally accrue to the researcher or to "society." Indeed, Michaels and Oetting (1979) found that participants' views of the ethicality of hypothetical research projects and their willingness to participate varied as a function of the costs, whereas researchers focused on the potential benefits. A second ethical criticism is that the costs of deception are quite apparent, but the potential benefits of research are extremely difficult to predict and often never materialize.

Metaethically, the ethical duty of informed consent and the practice of deceiving research participants are completely incompatible (Pittenger, 2002). As discussed in Chapter 4, the metaethical basis of informed consent is mental health professionals' Kantian ethical regard for persons; respect for participants' personhood is radically inconsistent with the practice of taking advantage of them through deception. In terms of the Kantian *kingdom of ends,* when research participants are intentionally deceived, they are being treated as a *means* to enable researchers to achieve the *end* of conducting a potentially valuable research study (Kant, 1785/1964a). The metaethical justification for deception is the utilitarian concern with beneficence—the desire to conduct research that will benefit the participants involved or humankind in general. What makes deception such a thorny issue for ethicists is how the harm being done to research participants by lying to them (in violation of the ethical duty of nonmaleficence) can possibly be offset by the potential benefits that *might* accrue later based on the research findings. Deception in research involves an inherently paradoxical mixing of incompatible metaethical models (Kantianism and utilitarianism), as well as pitting two utilitarian considerations (i.e., beneficence and nonmaleficence) against one another (Pittenger, 2002). As a result, the relative importance of informed consent considerations (i.e., the costs of deception) and the potential value of research (i.e., the benefits of deception) cannot usually be directly and meaningfully compared. Nevertheless, researchers are instructed in their ethical code to weigh all these competing considerations in deciding whether it is necessary and appropriate to use deception (ACA, 2005, G.2.b; APA, 2002, 8.07).

These metaethical complexities have led some researchers to argue that intentional deception is never appropriate in psychological research because it denies participants the right to self-determination and causes professionals to violate their duty to be trustworthy (Baumrind, 1990; Ortmann & Hertwig, 1997). These researchers point out that many participants now approach research studies assuming that they will be deceived. This phenomenon suggests that the use of deception reduces the respect participants have for psychological research and researchers and impacts the quality of data obtained by researchers (Ortmann & Hertwig, 1997). Also, even after debriefing, participants may still be upset about having been deceived.

There are some issues researchers are never permitted to deceive participants about. First, participants must be informed of any potential risks or other factors that might affect their willingness to participate in the study (ACA, 2005, G.2.b; APA, 2002, 8.07[b]). Second, researchers cannot promise participants an incentive for participating without fulfilling the promise (ACA, 2005, G.2.g). Third, researchers cannot create audio or video recordings of participants without obtaining their informed consent (ACA, 2005, B.6.b; APA, 2002, 8.03).

CASE EXAMPLE 12.8

A psychology researcher proposes a study to investigate whether interpersonal influences on cognitive performance vary as a function of depression. Her participants will be told that they will complete a mood questionnaire and then a cognitive task. Two participants will be assigned to each small room being used for the study. However, the participants will not be told that the person they will be paired with is a confederate of the experimenter. The confederate in each pair will talk and act either like a very bright, confident person or like a very dumb person.

The statement in the "Ethical Principles" that "psychologists do not deceive prospective research participants about research that is reasonably expected to cause physical pain or severe emotional distress" (APA, 2002, 8.07[b]) represents an interesting change from the previous version of the code, which prohibited psychologists from deceiving "participants about significant aspects that would affect their willingness to participate" (APA, 1992, 6.15[b]). It is difficult to imagine that knowing a study involves deception would not affect a person's desire to participate. The present wording gives researchers much greater latitude in limiting information provided to participants, thereby facilitating the use of deception.

One suggested method for dealing with the ethically distasteful, but scientifically important, practice of deceiving research participants is to have members of the proposed participant population evaluate the acceptability of research designs involving deception (Fisher & Fyrberg, 1994). Interestingly, potential participants are not uniformly opposed to deceptive research. They recognize its potential value to society and feel that the potential benefits of such research can outweigh the costs to participants (Fisher & Fyrberg, 1994).

Researchers are obligated to fully disclose to participants the true nature and purpose of the study and the reason deception was used as soon as possible following participation.[3] Effective and timely debriefing is extremely important to eliminating any negative effects the deception may have had on participants and to providing the educational benefits associated with debriefing. For example, false self-perceptions created by an experimental condition tend to persist; explicit discussion during debriefing might be needed to draw participants' attention to this issue (Stanley & Guido, 1996).

The use of deception in research with children is particularly problematic (R. A. Thompson, 1992). Children are more easily deceived because they trust adults; therefore, deceptive research has considerable potential for harm. Debriefing procedures used to resolve issues of deception following a study are also potentially harmful to children. Instead of benefiting children, the debriefing procedure might actually increase their confusion about their experiences in the study (R. A. Thompson, 1992). Moreover, if they do understand the nature of the deception, their trust in adult authority may be shaken, which could also be an upsetting and harmful experience for them (Macklin, 1992).

CASE EXAMPLE 12.9

A counseling researcher conducts a correlational study of the relation between locus of control and sociability. Unfortunately for the researcher, the only room available for conducting the study is a research room with an entire wall of one-way mirrors and microphones hanging from the ceiling. Several participants ask whether they are being observed and recorded. The researcher assures them that they are not and that he would have had to obtain their written consent to monitor their behavior in that manner. One participant responds that the researcher is probably lying to them because psychology research always involves "some kind of trick." The participants remain very suspicious, looking at the mirrored wall repeatedly. When the papers have been collected, another participant asks, "Now will you tell us what was really going on?"

CONFIDENTIALITY

Research participation is only truly anonymous when participants' identity is concealed from the researcher so that there is no practical way to determine which participant provided a particular set of data. Even if participants' names are not on the data sheets, their data are not necessarily anonymous; demographic data they provided could be used to identify them. For example, if most participants are of traditional college age in a university sample, a 44-year-old, divorced woman's data might easily be connected with her. Likewise, if the researcher gives each participant a number to avoid having them put their names on questionnaires, but keeps a list of the name-number combinations in case any data sets are incomplete, the data are not anonymous (at least until the list is destroyed). Whenever research data are not anonymous, researchers have an ethical obligation to conceal the identity of the participants by keeping any identifying data confidential (ACA, 2005, G.2.e; APA, 2002, 4.01). Researchers conducting studies involving the collection of individually identifiable health information from agencies or health care providers covered by HIPAA privacy regulations may be obligated to abide by the HIPAA standards that address security and confidentiality issues in the creation, storage, and disclosure of PHI (Privacy Rule, 2003, §§ 164.501, 164.508, 164.512[i]).[4]

During the data collection process, researchers are responsible for enacting privacy and security measures sufficient to ensure confidentiality. When conducting interview research, researchers must make sure that participants' voices cannot be heard by people passing by the room or by those in adjacent or adjoining rooms. Video and audio recordings of interviews should either be destroyed after being evaluated or stored in *very* secure locations because these records are an enormous threat to participants' confidentiality. Confidential research records should be stored in a secure setting with controlled access (e.g., a locked filing cabinet in a locked office). When sharing data with other researchers or reporting the results of a study in books, articles, or presentations, individual participants should not be identifiable (ACA, 2005, G.4.d; APA, 2002, 4.07, 8.14[a]). In general, only group results are presented. If the shared or presented data do reveal the identities of individual participants, the researcher must first obtain the participants' consent to use the data (ACA, 2005, G.4.d; APA, 2002, 4.07).

Research participants are sometimes asked to report illegal behaviors (e.g., drug use, corporal punishment of children) or other information that could potentially harm their reputation with their employer, alter insurance companies' willingness to insure them, and so on.

Participants are understandably reluctant to report these negative behaviors because research data are not necessarily protected from subpoena in legal proceedings. Researchers can protect participants by applying to the National Institutes of Health (NIH) for a "Certificate of Confidentiality" that will preserve the privacy of research data (Hoagwood, 1994). Under the statutory authority of section 301(d) of the Public Health Service Act (42 U.S.C. § 241[d]), the certificate protects researchers from being compelled to release confidential information regarding research participants. Many IRBs require researchers to obtain certificates as a condition for approving "high-risk" research concerning substance abuse or other legally sensitive issues (e.g., antisocial behavior).[5]

In rural and small-town settings, protecting participants' privacy can be particularly difficult. For example, recruitment procedures for intervention research (e.g., a study assessing the effect of an experimental treatment for ADHD) might make members of a community aware that a particular child has been diagnosed with the disorder (Fisher et al., 2002). Researchers need to implement additional precautions to minimize the risk that people not affiliated with the study will learn the identity of participants.

Limits of Confidentiality in Research

There are limitations on the confidentiality of information provided by research participants, just as for therapy clients, arising primarily from researchers' ethical obligation to protect the welfare of research participants (Bersoff & Bersoff, 1999). Researchers are obligated to explain these limitations (e.g., expression of suicidal intentions) to participants during the informed consent process (ACA, 2005, G.2.e; APA, 2002, 8.02[a]). Parents and children should be made aware of researchers' ethical and legal obligation to report suspicions of child abuse and neglect arising in research contexts (Kalichman, 1999), though some professionals have questioned the applicability of child abuse reporting laws to research contexts (e.g., Steinberg, Pynoos, Goenjian, Sossanabadi, & Sherr, 1999). It is unclear how the existence of a Certificate of Confidentiality would affect a researcher's obligation to report suspected child abuse to the proper authorities (Steinberg et al., 1999). Also, in research with children, the children and their parents should be told whether the parents will be informed of data indicating their child's involvement in suicidal activity, substance abuse, or other (specified) risky behaviors.

Multicultural populations are more likely to be recruited in studies of maladaptive developmental processes than in research concerning normative development (Scott-Jones, 1994). This phenomenon "may result in under- or overidentification of problem behaviors that require reporting" in multicultural research samples (Fisher et al., 2002, p. 1033). Researchers incur the obligation to develop culturally valid means of assessing clinical levels of psychopathology in children and criteria for assessing potential abuse in multicultural families. In this way, researchers can comply with mandatory reporting laws without unreasonably stigmatizing culturally acceptable family practices as "abuse."

Research involving the observation or interviewing of families presents a number of issues concerning confidentiality. The researchers cannot necessarily know in advance what might arise in the interactions among family members. Statements or behavior indicating child abuse or suicidal potential can place researchers in a situation in which they are legally and ethically obligated to violate a participant's confidentiality and report their concerns to parents or legal authorities (Bussell, 1994; Scott-Jones, 1994). This limitation on the confidentiality of the interview or observational data must be explained to participants beforehand.

Also, if a study involves the possibility of clinical referrals based on participants' responses, that should be stated in the consent form. An alternative procedure is to inform participants in the consent form of the importance of pursuing treatment if they experience symptoms like those described in the protocol and to provide all participants with information sheets regarding treatment referrals.

CASE EXAMPLE 12.10

A psychology researcher is conducting research with families. In her interview with a 12-year-old male family member, he discusses his use of alcohol and marijuana, both of which are illegal activities. Although his drug use has not created any dangerous consequences for his life yet, the researcher wonders whether she has an ethical or legal duty to inform his parents. After all, he could be injured while intoxicated or go on to experiment with other drugs.

Can There Be a "Duty to Warn" in a Research Context?

Although the existence of a clinical researcher's legal duty to warn has never been tested in court, it is certainly possible that mental health researchers could be viewed by the courts as having a legal duty to research participants similar to therapists' duty to prevent clients from harming themselves or someone else (Appelbaum & Rosenbaum, 1989). When conducting behavioral studies, researchers need to consider what their ethical responsibilities would be if a participant reported very severe depressive symptoms or significant suicidal potential (Stanton, Burker, & Kershaw, 1991).

A major consideration regarding the possible existence of a legal duty to warn in behavioral research is that a clinical researcher may not obtain sufficiently detailed information to make the research context analogous to a clinical intervention. For example, if a participant reports a very high level of anger on a questionnaire, a clinical researcher is not in a position to judge whether the individual represents a serious risk for violence. Research designs that employ participant interviews, in which researchers can probe further to evaluate the seriousness of participants' potential for violence toward themselves or particular individuals in their life, are likely to be considered much more similar to a therapist-client context (Appelbaum & Rosenbaum, 1989). Of course, most behavioral researchers are not clinicians, further complicating the issue. For instance, a cognitive researcher, as a non-clinician, can be viewed as lacking the training to form the type of "special relationship" that exists between a clinician and a client; therefore, the cognitive researcher is not competent to make a meaningful and valid professional judgment regarding a participant's dangerousness (Appelbaum & Rosenbaum, 1989).

Whether or not a legal duty to warn can be established for researchers, clearly it is important for both clinical and non-clinical researchers to address the potential clinical implications of their data collection procedures proactively, while the study is being designed. Researchers should be certain not to guarantee unconditional confidentiality during the informed consent process if there is any foreseeable circumstance in which they might find it necessary to violate that promise. If a study does involve the potential for intervention by the researchers or others, the consent forms for the study must state this possibility in the section on the limits of confidentiality (ACA, 2005, G.2.a.7; APA, 2002, Principle A, 8.02[a]).

Non-clinicians should seriously consider consulting with a clinical colleague to obtain input about the sorts of clinically significant responses that their research protocol might evoke and how to respond to participants' clinically provocative statements. It would also be prudent for non-clinicians conducting family interview research or research about suicidal behavior, anger, or other clinical topics to have a clinician on their research team. The clinician can competently evaluate videotape or audio recordings of interviews, as well as questionnaire responses, to assess the presence of clinical risk factors (Fisher & Rosendahl, 1990). The clinician can also follow up with at-risk participants during debriefing, provide appropriate referrals, and help participants resolve emotional reactions evoked by the study (Bussell, 1994).

CASE EXAMPLE 12.11

A counseling researcher undertakes a survey research project concerning anger. The consent form signed by participants guarantees unconditionally the confidentiality of their data. She has participants rate scenarios depicting different responses to anger-provoking stimuli in terms of the "appropriateness" of each response as a method of coping with anger. She then completes a structured interview with individual participants regarding their own methods of dealing with anger.

She interviews one participant who reports homicidal fantasies about his ex-wife, who was recently granted custody of their two young children following a hotly contested custody battle. The researcher completes the structured interview protocol but feels uncomfortable later about the seriousness of the threat this man might pose to his ex-wife and family. She knows the participant's name but is unsure about what action, if any, she should take.

ETHICAL ISSUES CONCERNING THE USE OF STUDENT SUBJECT POOLS

Many universities require students taking freshman-level psychology courses to participate in one or more research studies during the semester. Some programs give students extra credit points for fulfilling this course requirement; others do not. Sieber and Saks (1989) reported that 74% of psychology departments with graduate programs had subject pools; Landrum and Chastain (1999) found that 32.7% of undergraduate psychology departments had them. A major ethical issue regarding student subject pools is whether research participation for these students is truly voluntary (ACA, 2005, G.2.c). To provide students with a voluntary choice regarding research participation, the "Ethical Principles" requires that subject pool students be given "equitable alternative activities" for fulfilling their research requirement or earning extra credit (APA, 2002, 8.04[b]). Alternatives might include reading and summarizing a research article, designing a study to investigate a phenomenon, or attending a public lecture on campus. The major question about such alternatives is whether they are really equivalent to participation in a research study in terms of their educational value and the time and effort they require.

A second ethical issue is that some freshman students have not yet reached their 18th birthday. Because students younger than 18 cannot legally provide consent to participate in research, consent must be provided by their parents. Therefore, some provision must be made to obtain parental consent prior to including minors as participants in a study. Alternatively, students could be required to attest to the fact that they are 18 or older on the informed consent document they sign. If that procedure identifies students younger than 18, parental consent can be sought or the students can be directed to the alternatives to research participation.

The justification mentioned most often for having a departmental subject pool is that research participation is educational for the students. Students are afforded firsthand experience of how behavioral research is conducted, providing a valuable experiential supplement to the information concerning research methods they learn in class and from their reading. The quality of this educational component depends largely on researchers' efforts to make educational information, including handouts, available to participants and to provide thorough debriefing explanations (Nimmer & Handelsman, 1992; Sieber, 1999; Waite & Bowman, 1999). Just as IRBs protect the best interests of research participants, academic departments incur an obligation when they create a subject pool to promote the interests of these participants. Departments using a subject pool should appoint a faculty member or graduate assistant as subject pool coordinator to oversee the ethical treatment of subject pool participants, deal with participant complaints, and ensure that the educational goals of the subject pool are being addressed effectively.

The other, arguably more salient, justifications for the use of subject pools are the utilitarian considerations that faculty and students conducting research need participants, but students do not volunteer in sufficient numbers to satisfy this need. Furthermore, students who do volunteer are arguably not representative of the institution's general student population. Thus, in the interest of science (and to provide students with firsthand experience in behavioral research), students are coerced, at least to some extent, to participate. It must always be made clear to subject pool students that they have the same freedom as any other research participant to withdraw from participation without penalty while still receiving credit for attending the research session (ACA, 2005, G.2.c; APA, 2002, 8.04[a]). Fortunately for researchers, students very rarely elect this option.

A problem for researchers using student participants is the high rate of "no-shows" (i.e., students who sign up to participate but do not appear at the appointed time). Some faculty require additional (penalty) hours of research participation when students are reported as no-shows. Faculty members should remember that failure to appear is not necessarily an indication of laziness. Research participation is not an element of a student's usual routine; therefore, it is easily forgotten. (Faculty members certainly have their share of difficulty remembering appointments.) Penalizing no-shows again highlights the tension between the ethical expectation of voluntary research participation and participation as a course requirement.

ETHICS AND THE SCIENTIFIC MERIT OF RESEARCH

Researchers using human participants incur ethical obligations based simply on the fact that they are using participants' time (Rosenthal, 1994). Wasting participants' time on a meaningless research study demonstrates a lack of respect for participants as persons (ACA, 2005, G.1.a; APA, 2002, Principles B, E). Therefore, among researchers' most basic ethical obligations in designing a study is to make certain, by reviewing the relevant literature and consulting with colleagues, that the project has the potential to make a significant contribution to their field or to the participants. Of course, researchers can never know in advance what the outcome of their study will be.[6] Nevertheless, IRBs will typically ask researchers to provide information regarding the potential contributions of a proposed study (ACA, 2005, G.1.a; APA, 2002, 8.01). IRBs can reject a proposal on ethical grounds if they believe the study is not of sufficient potential value to justify the demands being placed on participants.

Ethical Issues in Selecting Research Samples

A study's value also depends on the representativeness and diversity of its participants (APA, 2003). For example, research on the effectiveness of cognitive-behavioral therapy in the treatment of depression is less valuable if the sample consists exclusively of adult white males. NIH has also issued regulations directing that women and minorities be adequately represented in any federally funded research if the results of the studies could potentially benefit, or have implications for, these diverse groups (NIH Guidelines, 1994). Diverse groups should be included in research samples unless there is a compelling justification for not doing so (ACA, 2005, G.1.g). The federal government has also issued preliminary guidance concerning the "Collection of Race and Ethnicity Data in Clinical Trials" that proposes guidelines to improve the standardization of data describing multicultural research samples (available at http://www.fda.gov/cder/guidance/index.htm).

ETHICAL ISSUES IN DATA COLLECTION AND ANALYSIS

The principal researcher on a project has an ethical responsibility to make certain that data collection procedures are conducted competently and professionally, whether the researcher collects the data personally or has colleagues, students, or other supervisees conduct the sessions (ACA, 2005, G.1.e; APA, 2002, 2.05). The researcher is also responsible for ensuring that protocols are scored correctly and that computer entry of data is accurate (Rosenthal, 1994). Fabricating data that were never collected and altering data are clearly the two most serious types of unethical behavior associated with data collection and analysis (ACA, 2005, G.4.a; APA, 2002, 8.10[a]). In addition, when researchers publish or present the results of a study, they are obligated to report nonsignificant findings and any results that disconfirm their hypotheses, along with significant results consistent with their hypotheses (ACA, 2005, G.4.b).

The decision to drop participants from a data set for any reason or to handle statistical outliers in a special way also has ethical implications. Whenever the collected data are manipulated in these ways, the researcher incurs an ethical duty to report how the data were handled and to provide the results that would have been obtained if the original data set had been left intact (Rosenthal, 1994).

Analyzing and reanalyzing data, which has been called "cooking the data," is a practice that is considered inappropriate by many psychometricians. However, Rosenthal (1994) regards such activities as making full use of the data that researchers and participants invested so much energy in creating. Of course, statistical techniques to adjust probability values should be employed when the same data are analyzed in a number of different ways, so the likelihood of obtaining statistically significant results is not inflated.

If errors pertaining to the analysis or reporting of results are discovered after a study has been published, the professional should endeavor to correct the error (ACA, 2005, G.4.c; APA, 2002, 8.10[b]). In such a circumstance, contacting the publisher to make arrangements for a printed correction or retraction statement is an appropriate course of action.

CASE EXAMPLE 12.12

A counseling psychology researcher is interested in studying the effect of different counseling styles on clients' perception of the therapist in an initial meeting. Each "client" (actually, college student) is interviewed by two therapists, in counterbalanced order. The researcher hypothesizes that a person-centered counseling style will be perceived more positively than a more directive, confrontational approach. He collects pilot data and finds that the directive style was rated more positively. The researcher wonders whether a difference in the attractiveness of the two therapists, rather than their counseling style, would account for the results of the pilot study.

He conducts another study in which only one therapist is used. She employs a person-centered approach with half of the participants and a directive approach with the other half. Participants are assigned randomly to the two conditions. The results of the second study are consistent with the researcher's hypothesis. The researcher concludes that the pilot data were invalid due to the confounding variable of therapist attractiveness. When he publishes the study, he reports only the methodology and results of the second study because he believes he should not publish invalid data.

ETHICAL ISSUES IN PUBLISHING RESEARCH RESULTS

Assigning Authorship Credit

Many researchers collaborate on projects with colleagues and students. When presenting or publishing research articles or books, it is necessary to determine which contributors to a project merit listing as authors (ACA, 2005, G.5.d; APA, 2002, 8.12[a], 8.12[b]). Authorship entails more than just assisting with data collection or making useful editorial contributions in the preparation of a research paper (Fine & Kurdek, 1993). The authors of a project are "those who have made substantial scientific contributions to a study," as well as those who have written the report of the research (APA, 2001, p. 6). Each person listed as an author should provide final approval of the manuscript before it is submitted for publication.

The order in which authors are listed on a project is intended to indicate "the relative scientific or professional contributions of the individuals involved, regardless of their relative status" (APA, 2002, 8.12[b]). In other words, senior researchers will not be listed first if their contributions to conceptualizing the study, collecting and interpreting the data, and writing up the report are not as substantial as those of other members of the research team (B. Thompson, 1994). Similarly, the faculty mentor of a student's dissertation study will generally not be the first author of an article based on the research because students should receive authorship credit commensurate with their contribution to a project (ACA, 2005, G.5.f; APA, 2002, 8.12[c]). However, if students complete their master's thesis requirement by taking primary responsibility for one study that is part of a four-study project conceptualized and developed by a faculty member, they are not ethically entitled to claim first authorship for the project merely because one part of it was their thesis (Shadish, 1994). Misunderstandings can be avoided by discussing the issue of authorship early on. Senior members of the research team bear primary responsibility for attending to these matters because they should be more familiar with the issues involved than students or first-time researchers (APA, 2002, 8.12[c]).

CASE EXAMPLE 12.13

A counseling professor and four graduate students conduct a research study. The study is designed by the professor, who develops the materials and procedures. The students conduct the data collection sessions and input the data on the professor's computer. The professor conducts the data analysis and writes an article summarizing the results of the project for journal publication. They agree that she will be listed as first author and that the students will be listed in alphabetical order as second through fifth authors because their contributions to the project were virtually identical.

Plagiarism

When information obtained from a published or unpublished source is used in a publication or presentation, professionals are ethically obligated to cite the source of the information or idea (ACA, 2005, G.5.a; APA, 2002, 8.11). Failure to do so constitutes *plagiarism,* which is the act of stealing another person's idea and presenting it as one's own. When the exact words of a source are presented, quotation marks are used and a citation, including the page number on which the quoted material appeared in the original source, is provided (APA, 2001).

Media Presentations of Research Findings

When professionals' research findings are presented on television or in a newspaper article, they cannot necessarily prevent the commentator or journalist from misrepresenting or misinterpreting the research results. Nevertheless, mental health professionals have an ethical obligation to try to minimize the probability of such mistakes and, if possible, to correct mistaken information presented to the public (ACA, 2005, C.6.c; APA, 2002, 1.01). Professional outlets (e.g., journals, books, organizational newsletters) are generally best for reporting research. Professionals who seek the glamour of mass media exposure face the risk of having their work misrepresented to the public, which could embarrass their profession.

Submitting Manuscripts for Journal Publication

Before submitting articles to academic journals, researchers should review the journal's "Instructions to Authors" section. These instructions usually specify the format and style to be used, where to submit the manuscript, and how to contact the editor. When reporting the results of research involving human participants, researchers should let the journal editor know that they obtained IRB approval for the informed consent procedure used in the study. Also, researchers should not submit data for publication to a journal if they have already published the data elsewhere because an author cannot give the copyright to more than one publisher (ACA, 2005, G.5.g; APA, 2002, 8.13). Neither should researchers submit a report of the same study to more than one journal at a time, hoping that at least one of the journals will accept the article (ACA, 2005, G.5.g; APA, 2001). If an article is rejected by a journal, the author is then free to pursue another outlet.

Reviewing Manuscripts Submitted for Publication

Most professional journals are peer reviewed. Manuscripts of books submitted to publishers are also generally sent to fellow professionals for review. Obviously, reviewers incur an ethical obligation to provide an unbiased, scholarly opinion regarding the quality of the manuscript. Recently, questions have been raised about the extent to which cultural bias among editors and reviewers for American psychology journals has limited the dissemination of cross-cultural and multicultural research (Pedersen, 2003). In addition to being fair, reviewers are also obligated to treat the material they review, and their judgment of its quality, confidentially; they also respect the authors' proprietary rights to the ideas and materials contained in the manuscript (ACA, 2005, G.5.h; APA, 2002, 8.15).

Another ethical issue in reviewing manuscripts concerns what Sternberg (2002) has referred to as "civility" in reviewing. Some reviewers seemingly go out of their way to be not only critical but also demeaning in their reviews. Sternberg (2002) refers to these as "savage reviews" (p. 3). Reviewers need to bear in mind that the duty to respect people's rights and dignity (APA, 2002, Principle E) also applies to their treatment of fellow professionals. The Kantian (1785/1964a) admonition to treat others only in ways that we would wish to be treated ourselves speaks to the unethical nature of hyperbolically negative reviews.

ETHICAL ISSUES IN CONDUCTING RESEARCH ON THE INTERNET

Researchers are often able to access larger and more specialized samples of participants by collecting data over the Internet. For example, a substantial sample of people with eating disorders might be recruited simply by contacting an Internet-based support group on the subject. Researchers are also becoming increasingly interested in studying Internet behavior itself (e.g., patterns of Internet use). However, both types of Internet research introduce a host of methodological and ethical concerns for researchers and IRBs. The external validity (i.e., generalizability) of Internet research is a concern because Internet users are not yet representative of the United States population; ethnic minority groups and people of lower socioeconomic status are especially underrepresented (Mathy et al., 2003). However, studies indicate that block sampling techniques can be used to ensure the representativeness of Internet research samples (Mathy et al., 2003).

Obtaining informed consent is a tricky issue since, at present, it is not generally feasible to get a signed consent form over the Internet. For studies concerning nonsensitive topics (e.g., a survey of television viewing habits), informed consent can be obtained using a "portal." Participants read a consent document screen, click their mouse on a button to indicate their consent, and gain access to the survey. Another cost-effective way to obtain informed consent is by having participants reply to a consent form sent to them via e-mail. For sensitive research topics (e.g., a survey of substance abuse behavior), researchers can present a consent form that participants can print out, sign, and mail to the researcher. (Alternatively, participants could request a consent form and postage-paid return envelope via e-mail, so they will not incur any expense.) When researchers receive a signed consent form, they can provide participants with a password that will enable them to access the survey questions.

A second important aspect of informed consent requires that participants understand the information conveyed about the study, but how is participant understanding to be assessed? Also, how can researchers be certain that participants are capable of providing consent (e.g., that adult participants are mentally competent)? What if a child completes a survey while posing as an adult? For example, a researcher might believe that he has received data for his sexual behavior study from a 30-year-old woman when the survey was actually completed by her nine-year-old son. Of course, participants can (and do) misidentify themselves in providing demographic data on paper-and-pencil forms and in telephone surveys as well (Mathy et al., 2003).[7]

Internet research not only gives researchers access to participants living near their university; they can potentially reach people throughout the world. However, it is extremely difficult to ensure that international participants can understand informed consent information and that the data they provide reflect a valid contribution to the study. Also, the risks to international participants resulting from research participation may be significantly greater, due to privacy and security issues associated with their sociopolitical situation.

Special issues also arise in the use of deception in Internet research. Although it would be easier to deceive online participants about relevant aspects of a research project, the use of deception in online research is more difficult to justify. How would researchers handle the required debriefing? What if participants were upset about having been misled?

Confidentiality is another very tricky topic in Internet research, just as it is for e-therapy. It is impossible to absolutely guarantee the confidentiality of information transmitted over the Internet (Anderson & Kanuka, 2003). Breaches of confidentiality can occur inadvertently (e.g., a virus affecting the researcher's computer) or through the deliberate acts of "hackers." The principle of nonmaleficence requires researchers to inform potential participants of these risks and to take reasonable steps to reduce the likelihood that breaches of privacy will occur, such as ensuring that participants are using computers and Internet connections "with physical safeguards and password protection locks to prevent unauthorized disclosure" of confidential information via the Internet (Mathy et al., 2003, p. 81). Participants should also be given instructions regarding the procedures to remove cookies, temporary files, and history files that could reveal their participation in the study to others using their computer (Mathy et al., 2003). For clinical research, HIPAA regulations would again be applicable to the duty to preserve the privacy of PHI collected or transmitted electronically. Participants' health information should be encrypted and stored in password-protected files on computers that are themselves password-protected (Mathy et al., 2003).

The ethical principle of competence takes on an additional dimension when researchers wish to conduct studies using the Internet. Researchers often do not possess cutting-edge knowledge of Internet technology. Clinicians and researchers "who are unable or unwilling to study computer science or computer systems for at least a semester prior to conducting Internet-mediated research (or practicing online) place their clinical participants (or clients) at considerable risk" (Mathy et al., 2003, p. 84). Consultation with people possessing this expertise will also help researchers to avoid many potential ethical pitfalls. As use of the Internet for research purposes increases, Internet researchers and IRB members will both need to receive training in the nuances of Internet technology, so researchers can provide technical information regarding security procedures to IRBs, and IRB members, in turn, can ask pertinent questions and provide competent consultation and recommendations.

Finally, issues regarding the extent to which Internet activity constitutes behavior in a public setting (e.g., naturalistic observation of chat room interactions), as opposed to private communication that should not be observed without the informed consent of the individuals involved, remain to be resolved (Anderson & Kanuka, 2003).

CASE EXAMPLE 12.14

A clinical psychologist submits an IRB proposal to conduct a study monitoring the frequency with which counselors and psychologists visit sexually explicit Web sites. He plans to send an e-mail message describing an online survey of Internet behavior to the members of ACA and APA. Participants will complete the online survey about the types of Web sites they visit most frequently and submit their data without indicating their name. When they submit their data, the researcher's server will deposit a "cookie" on the participant's computer that will track the participant's online behavior for the next year. The researcher asserts that he will not record the identity of the participants, so there is no risk of their being harmed by the deception. He argues that the deception is necessary because participants would alter the sites they visit if they were informed that their behavior was being monitored. Finally, he asserts that it is very important that we learn more about the nature of professional people's Internet behavior.

ETHICAL ISSUES IN CONDUCTING ANIMAL RESEARCH

Throughout the twentieth century, animal researchers and government agencies (e.g., NIH) have created and supported regulations concerning the humane treatment of animals in research. During the 1960s, the Pet Protection Act, subsequently known as the Animal Welfare Act (AWA) of 1966 (Pub. L. No. 89-544), was enacted by Congress to address the use of animals in research. The AWA gave the United States Department of Agriculture (USDA) responsibility for enforcement of the new law.

Institutions conducting behavioral and biomedical research involving animals are required to establish an Institutional Animal Care and Use Committee (IACUC), in accordance with guidelines published by the Applied Research Ethics National Association (ARENA) and the Office of Laboratory Animal Welfare (OLAW), to review and approve such research (ARENA & OLAW, 2002). The IACUC also inspects all animal facilities at its institution twice each year to make certain USDA regulations are being observed.

The use of animals in biomedical and behavioral research has become extremely controversial (Gluck & Kubacki, 1991; Plous, 1996a). Critics of animal research argue that it is unethical to cause animals pain and suffering unnecessarily. Supporters of animal research offer primarily utilitarian justifications: Animal research furthers our understanding of human behavior; assists in developing solutions to medical problems affecting human beings; and, in some instances, actually promotes the survival of the animal species involved. Proponents of the value of well-designed biomedical animal studies have also countered the argument about the cost of such studies to animals with a Kantian argument concerning the costs to people with serious illnesses of *not* conducting the studies (Kaplan, 1988). Nevertheless, psychologists' support for animal research has declined over time, and the positions of opponents and proponents of animal research have become increasingly polarized (Gluck & Kubacki, 1991).

Psychology students are somewhat ambivalent about animal research. Most oppose animal research involving pain or death and do not think psychology majors should be required to take an animal laboratory course (Plous, 1996b). One reason for their opposition to animal learning courses is that the animals are typically killed at the end of the course. On the other hand, students are not opposed in general to the use of animals in research or teaching. They believe that observational studies of animal learning and behavior are appropriate (Plous, 1996b).

Researchers conducting animal studies incur ethical and professional duties to treat animals humanely and to comply with relevant laws and government regulations (APA, 2002, 8.09). Ultimate responsibility for any problem or mistreatment that occurs in the lab rests with these researchers. Students and other personnel working in an animal lab must be adequately trained in research methods and in the care and handling of the species being studied (APA, 2002, 8.09[c]). Supervising researchers are obligated to monitor the behavior of their students and assistants to make certain that the animals are not harmed (APA, 2002, 8.09[b]).

Research procedures that involve pain or suffering are only permitted when no alternative methodology is available that will produce less suffering and when "the goal is justified by its prospective scientific, educational, or applied value" (APA, 2002, 8.09[e]). An institution's IACUC is responsible for evaluating the adequacy of researchers' justification for inflicting pain or suffering on animals. When the animals must be killed, the "Ethical Principles" stipulates that the method used should be quick and minimize pain (APA, 2002, 8.09[g]).

CASE EXAMPLE 12.15

Undergraduate students taking a course in experimental psychology are each assigned a specially bred white laboratory rat that they train in various conditioning tasks over the course of the semester. The students ask the laboratory instructor what the department does with the rats after the semester. Several are interested in adopting their rats as pets. The instructor informs the class that APA policy requires that the rats be killed because there would be no one to care for them while the university is closed between semesters and the animals would be totally helpless in any environment outside the lab. On the final day of the semester, a student takes his rat home. When the instructor discovers that the rat is missing, she contacts the student and threatens to fail him in the course unless he returns the rat. The student does return it, and the rat is "sacrificed" in accordance with APA guidelines.

PRACTICE CASE INVOLVING THE MODEL OF ETHICAL DECISION MAKING

In 1998, *Psychological Bulletin,* an APA journal, published a meta-analytic article concerning the long-term effects of childhood sexual abuse (CSA; Rind, Tromovitch, & Bauserman, 1998). The article analyzed data from a number of CSA studies and concluded that "CSA does not cause intense harm on a pervasive basis regardless of gender in the college population" (Rind et al., 1998, p. 46). The article went on to explain that definitional and methodological issues, such as lumping together both coercive and voluntary sexual contacts involving minors, "produce poor predictive validity" (Rind et al., 1998, p. 46).

The article's publication generated considerable controversy when it was misleadingly characterized as an endorsement of pedophilia (Ruark, 2001). People were extremely disturbed by the suggestion that sexual abuse could produce anything but disastrous consequences for every victimized child. Pedophiles, they believed, would focus on such a report to justify their immoral and illegal behavior. Moreover, they felt that psychological science had harmed children by presenting this information. As the controversy grew, APA yielded to popular and congressional pressure by issuing an apology for publishing the article (Ruark, 2001).

The apology generated additional controversy from researchers who attacked APA's tendency to mix science and politics in its treatment of issues. They argued that science should not have a political or social agenda. Empirical research must be guided by the data and present a balanced, objective interpretation of it, even when such a viewpoint is "politically incorrect."

Did APA behave appropriately in issuing an apology in this case?

SUMMARY

Research is an important aspect of many mental health professionals' work. Because personal values influence professionals' theoretical orientation and research interests, they must guard against conducting studies or presenting findings that are biased toward their subjective viewpoint. To increase multicultural awareness and understanding, researchers should use diverse participant groups whenever appropriate. Another aspect of multicultural research involves reexamining the traditional goal of finding the one right answer to a research question; instead, researchers might endeavor to describe the varied subjective perspectives characterizing different groups of participants.

The role of IRBs is to review their organization's proposed research studies to ensure that participants will not be harmed and that the studies are of sufficient quality to justify the use of participants' time and effort. Evaluating the relative importance of the potential risks and benefits associated with a study is one of the most difficult tasks for IRBs and researchers. IRBs also review informed consent procedures. The consent form provided to participants must be easily understood and explain the study in such a way that they can make an informed decision about their participation. For example, researchers are obligated to inform participants about any potential risks associated with the study and any limitations on the confidentiality of their data (e.g., mandatory reporting of child abuse). Additional informed consent considerations arise with special participant populations, such as legally incompetent individuals and children.

After participating in a study, participants should be debriefed as soon as possible. If information has been withheld or deception has been used for the sake of the study's validity, then full disclosure must be made during debriefing. Debriefing should also be educational for participants, particularly when the research sample is drawn from a student subject pool.

The Internet presents exciting new opportunities for researchers, but it also presents significant challenges to the ethical duties of informed consent and confidentiality. Researchers and IRBs will need to master this new technology to ensure that ethical standards for the protection of human participants are not compromised.

The use of animals in research has become increasingly controversial in recent years. IACUCs oversee the ethical and legal standards governing animal research. In any animal research laboratory, one or more supervising researchers are designated as having ultimate responsibility for the care and treatment of animals by all lab personnel. Today, animal research plays a more important role in biomedical research than in traditional behavioral studies.

NOTES

1. When international participants are involved in a treatment study (e.g., of the effectiveness of a new therapy for depression), researchers incur an ethical obligation to make the treatment available to people in those countries if its effectiveness is proven by the study.

2. There has been controversy concerning the age at which children ought to be allowed to provide self-consent for research participation. Shields and Johnson (1992) reported that children have cognitive capacities equal to those of adults for making consent decisions. It should be noted, however, that although the cognitive capacity to make competent decisions may exist in adolescents, experience in actually making decisions, which is a vital part of competent decision making, is usually lacking (Croxton, Churchill, & Fellin, 1988; Petersen & Leffert, 1995). In addition, even 14- or 15-year-olds may not possess the social competence to be able to act autonomously and give *voluntary* consent because of the influence the researcher, parent, or other authority figure might have over them (Scherer & Reppucci, 1988). Children are much more vulnerable to coercion than adults, though this changes as children reach adolescence (R. A. Thompson, 1992). Levine (1995a) suggested that adolescents should be permitted to provide self-consent for anonymous survey research and other studies involving no risk to participants.

3. Holmes (1976) referred to this debriefing process as "dehoaxing." He pointed out that when a researcher tells participants the truth about a study, they often do not believe it. They assume that the researcher, who lied before, is probably doing so again as part of the study.

4. Researchers obtaining health care information from HIPAA-covered entities (e.g., health insurers, health care providers) through collaborative arrangements would likely be affected by HIPAA, as would researchers working for covered entities. Researchers should consult the decision guidelines presented by the Department of Health and Human Services, Office for Civil Rights, titled "Am I a Covered Entity?" (available at http://www.hhs.gov/ocr/hipaa/).

5. On the other hand, Certificates of Confidentiality do not prevent researchers from *voluntarily* disclosing information about participants (e.g., evidence of child abuse). Therefore, researchers need to consider carefully any limitations they may wish to place on participants' confidentiality and tell participants of these limitations during the informed consent process.

6. If they could know the outcome in advance, the study would definitely be a waste of the participants' time and effort because the outcome would already be an established fact.

7. The flipside of the issue of informed consent in research conducted on the Internet involves the possibility that the *researchers* are not who they pretend to be. There is little protection for participants against unscrupulous researchers.

Chapter 13

Mental Health Professions and the Law

As discussed in Chapter 1, many of the professional activities of psychologists and counselors are guided by legal statutes as well as ethical guidelines. Some legal duties are mandated under federal laws, but the majority of statutes governing the treatment of clients with emotional disturbance or Mental Retardation are established by individual states. Although there is considerable agreement, the laws of individual states can vary, so it is extremely important for professionals to become familiar with the laws governing mental health practice in their state.

Mental health professionals interact with the legal system when they are involved in the involuntary commitment of a client to a psychiatric hospital (e.g., for suicide prevention). The issues of voluntary and involuntary treatment, and the ethical arguments for and against the use of coercive methods to prevent suicide, will be discussed in this chapter. Mental health professionals also function in a variety of roles within the legal system. These areas of professional specialization are referred to collectively as *forensic psychology*. Forensic psychologists are involved in matters pertaining to both criminal law and civil law, which involves noncriminal legal issues. In criminal matters, forensic experts might assist in determining a defendant's competence to stand trial or mental state at the time of the crime. In civil matters, they might offer expert testimony regarding a person's need for involuntary hospitalization based on an assessment of the individual's mental status and potential for violence. Forensic experts also frequently conduct child custody and child protective evaluations. Finally, situations in which legal and ethical considerations appear to conflict will be discussed as yet another context in which the ethical reasoning skills of professionals are tested.

LEGAL ISSUES IN HOSPITAL ADMISSION FOR PSYCHIATRIC TREATMENT

Competence

Most inpatient clients are admitted voluntarily, a process which assumes that clients are competent to choose to pursue treatment. Legally, the concept of personal competence centers on people's ability to make rational, deliberative decisions based on an accurate understanding of their circumstances. Thus, when the issue of individuals' competence is raised, the question to be decided is whether they understand what is going on and have the rational capacity to make deliberative choices based on their personal values.

Voluntary Treatment

The U.S. Supreme Court ruled that an incompetent individual cannot provide the informed consent necessary for voluntary hospitalization (*Zinermon v. Burch,* 1990) because clients must be competent to make an autonomous choice to pursue treatment. Autonomous choice entails, first, the absence of coercion (Carroll, 1991). In other words, clients are not being pressured to enter treatment with the threat of negative consequences (e.g., going to jail) for not pursuing treatment. Second, clients must be capable of understanding their situation and options and of making a rational, deliberative decision consistent with their values and beliefs. For example, if a client seeks admission to the hospital because it is the only safe haven that will permit her to escape the visitors from Mars who wish to extract her cerebrospinal fluid, it is unlikely that her decision would be deemed autonomous.

Clearly, there are degrees of autonomous functioning. Some clients request admission to a psychiatric facility based on their deliberative judgment that they need assistance with their emotional or substance abuse problems. These individuals demonstrate a high degree of autonomy. In many cases, clients' families or outpatient therapists will urge them to enter the hospital, with the assurance that they will be free to leave if they no longer wish to continue treatment. In deciding to take this advice, individuals still may be acting autonomously (i.e., consistent with their personal values and perceptions of the situation), though it could be argued that they demonstrate less autonomy than a person making an independent decision to pursue treatment (Wrightsman, Nietzel, & Fortune, 1998). In other cases, clients' families will threaten them with involuntary hospitalization if they refuse to accept voluntary admission to the hospital (Solomon, 1996). Mental health professionals making admissions evaluations at psychiatric hospitals sometimes present clients with the same limited menu of options. These clients have very little choice in "choosing" voluntary admission (Carroll, 1991).

Once admitted, even voluntary inpatient clients can face legal obstacles in attempting to leave the hospital if the mental health professionals responsible for their treatment do not believe they are ready for discharge. Essentially, clients deemed mentally ill and either potentially dangerous or incapable of attending to their basic physical needs can be held while civil commitment procedures are initiated, even though they have made a written request to be discharged. In most states, clients can be held up to three days after requesting discharge, even if commitment is not being sought, while the professionals responsible for their treatment determine whether their psychiatric condition requires additional hospitalization. Voluntary inpatient clients generally cannot be committed unless they demand to be discharged, leave the facility without medical permission, or refuse to consent to needed treatment.

CASE EXAMPLE 13.1

A counselor working in a psychiatric hospital has a client who requests discharge from an alcoholism treatment unit. The client has a history of depression and has made suicide attempts in the past. The counselor is concerned that the client will start drinking again if she is discharged. He urges the client to stay in the program, but to no avail. Finally, he tells her he believes that if she leaves the hospital, she will drink, become depressed, and attempt suicide. Therefore, if she demands to be discharged, commitment proceedings will be initiated on the basis that she poses a danger to herself. She agrees to stay voluntarily.

INVOLUNTARY HOSPITALIZATION: THE PSYCHIATRIC COMMITMENT PROCESS

Being deemed mentally ill is not sufficient grounds for hospitalizing people against their will. The vague and problematic nature of the concept of mental illness, discussed in Chapter 8, certainly raises questions about the appropriateness of using it as the sole criterion for depriving individuals of their civil liberties (Szasz, 1974). Although the legal requirements for commitment vary by state, usually people who are committed must (a) suffer from mental illness, (b) be dangerous to themselves or others or incapable of tending adequately to their basic physical needs, and (c) need inpatient hospitalization for treatment or care (Wrightsman et al., 1998).

The key element justifying most instances of involuntary commitment is individuals' inability to take care of their own basic needs (Turkheimer & Parry, 1992). Most courts do not require that people pose an "imminent" danger to themselves or others in order to commit them (Litwack & Schlesinger, 1999). In all cases, the ethical basis of involuntary hospitalization is concern for the welfare of clients and others potentially affected by their behavior. In other words, to be committed, clients must be judged to be incompetent as a function of mental illness in a way that threatens serious harm to themselves or others (Cohen & Cohen, 1999). Involuntary hospitalization is the most extreme expression of parentalism in mental health practice; mental health professionals actually decide to suspend clients' civil liberties "for their own good."

There are three types of legal psychiatric commitment. The most common type is *emergency commitment,* which occurs when clients are admitted involuntarily to a psychiatric hospital on an emergency basis, usually on the assertion that they are dangerous to themselves or others (Wrightsman et al., 1998). Emergency commitment does not require a court order and can be initiated by a law enforcement officer or mental health professional. The client is examined by a physician or mental health professional prior to emergency admission and committed on the basis of the professional's judgment. In most states, a commitment of this type has a maximum duration of 48 to 72 hours (Wrightsman et al., 1998). A preliminary hearing before a judge is needed to detain a person any longer.

CASE EXAMPLE 13.2

A patient being treated for a heart condition in a medical hospital is informed by his cardiologist that his condition cannot be treated effectively with medication, as the doctor had hoped. Rather, the patient will need to undergo an angioplasty procedure to reopen a clogged coronary artery. The patient is angered by this news because the cardiologist had previously assured him that medication would likely be sufficient. He refuses to consent to the angioplasty and demands to be discharged from the hospital. The cardiologist explains that he would be at extremely high risk for a life-threatening heart attack without the angioplasty procedure. The patient still demands immediate discharge.

The cardiologist consults a clinical psychologist on the hospital staff. After interviewing the patient, the psychologist informs the cardiologist that although the patient is clearly making an irrational decision, he is neither psychotic nor clinically depressed. The cardiologist tells her that the patient will likely have a heart attack and die without the procedure. The psychologist responds that people have the right to make bad judgments and that she cannot force the patient to remain in the hospital or undergo the procedure. The patient is discharged, against medical advice, later that day.

The other two types of involuntary commitment require a court order. *Involuntary hospitalization* in an inpatient facility involves an examination by a psychiatrist or other legally qualified mental health professional, followed by a court hearing concerning the results of the examination. If supposedly mentally ill clients do not have an attorney, one is appointed to represent their interests at the hearing. The hearing is generally before a judge, though in some states, the person for whom commitment is sought can elect to have a jury hear the case. Witnesses present evidence at the hearing and are cross-examined (Wrightsman et al., 1998). If the outcome of the hearing is that the person should be committed to a state facility, the commitment is generally not open-ended. If the person still meets the legal criteria for involuntary confinement after the initial period has elapsed, the commitment will need to be extended at another court hearing.

Outpatient commitment mandates that the person must attend treatment sessions at an outpatient facility (Wrightsman et al., 1998). It was developed to address the right of psychiatric clients, even involuntary ones, to be treated in the least restrictive setting appropriate to their treatment needs. These clients require treatment but do not need the protection of an inpatient setting (Hiday, 1996).

Consumer advocacy groups have questioned the ethical appropriateness of outpatient commitment on the grounds that these clients are not dangerous to themselves or others (or they would require inpatient hospitalization) and therefore should not be coerced to participate in treatment (Draine, 1997). Nevertheless, various forms of outpatient commitment have become increasingly popular as a means to prevent decompensation in outpatient clients and to increase the probability that conditionally discharged inpatient clients will pursue treatment in the community (Draine, 1997). The limited research that has been conducted on the effectiveness of outpatient commitment, summarized by Hiday (1996), indicates that the procedure is generally effective in improving clients' adjustment and reducing the likelihood of hospitalization, although more research is urgently needed (Draine, 1997).

CASE EXAMPLE 13.3

An adult heroin addict is arrested for drug dealing. The court grants her probation, provided she goes directly into an inpatient drug treatment facility and completes a three-month drug rehabilitation program successfully. Otherwise, she will be sent to prison. The individual enters a drug treatment program, but she makes little effort. She follows all the rules but is not really invested in understanding her problems and changing her life. A clinical psychologist accuses her of "jailing" (i.e., just passing time in the program without participating actively); he threatens to discharge her unless she shows greater urgency about changing her life. A week later, in spite of not having broken any program rules, the client is discharged, resulting in her being sentenced to prison.

THE RIGHTS OF PSYCHIATRIC INPATIENT CLIENTS

A *right* is defined as a legitimate claim to something. When people have legal rights, everyone else has a *duty* not to interfere with their exercise of those rights. Inpatient clients, whether voluntary or committed, have a number of civil and political rights, enumerated in court decisions and state statutes, that psychiatric facilities must provide (Slovenko, 1999). This "patient's bill of rights" includes the right to live in a safe environment, receive adequate food and shelter, have visitors, and participate in developing an individualized treatment plan. Several additional rights of clients are discussed below.

Right to Treatment

When people are committed for psychiatric treatment, the right to treatment follows naturally as part of the state's obligation for having deprived them of their liberty. Adults and children cannot be committed to a psychiatric facility simply to get them "off the streets"; they must receive treatment intended to improve their condition. The right to treatment was established in a 1971 court decision (*Wyatt v. Stickney,* 1971/1972).

Right to Refuse Treatment

When clients are committed involuntarily, the mental health professionals working with them are ethically obligated to provide treatment, but committed clients do not relinquish the right to refuse treatment. In other words, committed clients, like voluntary clients, can waive their right to treatment. However, mental health professionals responsible for their treatment might question whether they are competent to make this decision. They can deny clients the right to refuse treatment if they are deemed incompetent to make such a judgment and if their refusal is likely to result in harm to themselves or others (Wrightsman et al., 1998).

The crucial issue is *why* they are refusing to comply with the treatment plan, as well as the behavioral consequences of their refusal. For example, a client suffering from Schizophrenia, Paranoid Type is committed to a state hospital. He refuses to take the antipsychotic medication prescribed. When asked why he refuses, he tells his psychiatrist that the pills are poison and will kill him instantly. He has been assaultive toward the treatment staff on a number of occasions, believing that the food, toothpaste, and water on the ward are also being used to poison him. If a client's reason for refusing treatment is clearly irrational, a psychiatrist can argue that he is delusional and is not capable at present of understanding his situation rationally or perceiving circumstances accurately. Furthermore, his assaultiveness in his unmedicated delusional state makes it dangerous *not* to medicate him. On that basis, the psychiatrist can deem him incompetent to make such a decision and coerce him to take his medication. The burden of proof in this matter is always on those wanting to use coercion. Medicating people involuntarily is a very serious violation of their right to bodily privacy, which is protected by the First, Eighth, and Fourteenth Amendments to the United States Constitution.

Right to Least Restrictive Treatment

All clients, including involuntary ones, are entitled to treatment by the least intrusive or restrictive means possible. The "least restrictive appropriate setting for treatment" refers to the available treatment setting that provides clients with the greatest likelihood of improvement or cure and restricts their physical and social liberties no more than is necessary for effective treatment and for adequate protection against any dangers they might pose to themselves or others (*Dixon v. Weinberger,* 1975).

CASE EXAMPLE 13.4

A client suffering from Schizophrenia, Undifferentiated Type has been treated in an inpatient facility for the past three months. His condition is now stable, and he does not need to be in the hospital. However, he does not have a place to live, and there are no placements available in halfway houses or other community care facilities. The hospital administration insists that he be discharged because it is illegal to keep him in the restrictive hospital environment when he does not require that level of supervision. The counselor on the treatment team discharges him; she and the client plan that he will seek temporary housing at a nearby YMCA. Within days, he violates a YMCA rule and is told to leave. He becomes homeless.

ETHICAL CONSIDERATIONS IN SUICIDE PREVENTION

One of the most common reasons for considering hospitalizing clients involuntarily is to prevent them from committing suicide. The ethical codes of the mental health professions state that it is appropriate for professionals to violate their clients' confidentiality by inform-ing the police or medical personnel if they believe clients represent a danger to themselves (ACA, 2005, B.2.a; APA, 2002, 4.05[b]). However, suicide prevention is a matter of consid-erable ethical complexity because mental health professionals also profess a deep respect for the autonomy of each client. Clinicians believe that clients know what is best for them and should be afforded the respect of making their own decisions about how to conduct their lives (ACA, 2005, A.1.a; APA, 2002, Principle E). Professionals avoid imposing their values on clients out of this same respect for clients' personhood (ACA, 2005, A.4.b; APA, 2002, Principle E).

Nevertheless, clinicians engage in coercive, parentalistic suicide prevention procedures based on their duty to protect the welfare of their clients; interestingly, this duty is also grounded in their regard for clients as persons (Fairbairn, 1995). The ethical duty of non-maleficence is another important consideration in deciding whether to intervene to prevent clients from committing suicide. Clinicians do not want to cause harm to clients, yet they are divided regarding which course of action produces the most harm: preventing suicide and abridging clients' autonomy and right to self-determination, or allowing them to make their own choice and possibly lose their life as a result. Legitimate ethical duties conflict in the case of suicidal clients, creating an ethical dilemma for the clinician.

Why Do People Commit Suicide?

The traditional view of suicide among mental health professionals was that suicide is always an irrational act, resulting from depression, hopelessness, intense emotional pain, or psychosis (Shneidman, 1992). It is certainly true that individuals suffering from depressive disorders and the schizophrenias are at significantly elevated risk for suicide (Isometsa et al., 1994; Reid, 1998). However, some suicidologists have argued that although suicide is frequently an irrational act, it can also be a rational, autonomous act. To act autonomously, however, people must have "the capacity to make considered choices" and act on the basis of personal goals (Fairbairn, 1995, p. 164). Battin (1999) has added that rational people must also be capable of making a realistic appraisal of the world and their situation (i.e., not be delusional or seriously misinformed), have adequate information about present and likely future circumstances in their life, and be acting to avoid harm to themselves or others. People who are extremely depressed might not be considered rational because they are incapable of perceiving the possibility that their life circumstances could improve considerably.

Cases cited in support of the idea of rational suicide frequently involve the decisions of terminally ill people to end their lives in a painless manner or to be withdrawn from life-sustaining medical treatment (e.g., kidney dialysis). For example, in 1994, voters approved the Oregon Death With Dignity Act that makes it legal for a primary care physician to prescribe a medication for a competent, terminally ill person that will end the person's life (Ganzini, Fenn, Lee, Heintz, & Bloom, 1996). Hospice nurses in Oregon reported that terminally ill patients who chose to refuse food and fluids in order to hasten death generally did not exhibit symptoms of depression; rather, they chose to end their lives for seemingly sound reasons, like the desire to control the timing and nature of their impending death (Colburn, 2001; Ganzini et al., 2003). In 2001, the Netherlands became the first country to legalize assisted suicide for "terminally ill individuals enduring 'lasting and unbearable suffering'" (Cohen, 2001, p. A6).

Thomas Szasz (1999) has argued that euthanasia is actually suicide, so mental health professionals must decide where they stand on the fundamental issue of a person's right to commit suicide before they can determine the ethical acceptability of passive and active euthanasia. If the removal of life support (passive euthanasia) or the administration of a lethal drug (active euthanasia) is initiated by a patient, these acts are intended to cause the patient's death.[1] Thus, they are cases of suicide, though in cases of passive euthanasia, the cause of death is often reported to be the disease the person was dying from. Szasz (1999) points out that if a patient refused to continue life-sustaining dialysis but was shot on the way home, it would be a case of murder, not death from kidney disease.

Critics of the notion of "rational suicide" have asserted that people can never choose death rationally because they cannot have adequate knowledge of what they are choosing. No one knows what death is like; there is something "uncanny" about it (Devine, 1990).

The Ethical Argument for Suicide Prevention

The justification for coercive intervention to prevent suicide (e.g., involuntary hospitalization of the individual) is concern for clients' welfare, consistent with the ethical principle of nonmaleficence. According to active suicide prevention proponents, people who are depressed, intoxicated, psychotic, or in intense physical pain might perceive suicide as a rational solution to the problems in their life, but their belief is clearly irrational. They generally change their mind with the passage of time or after receiving mental health treatment (Goldblatt, 1999). Even terminally ill individuals are more likely to accept the continued use of life-prolonging medical treatment following successful treatment for depression (Farrenkopf & Bryan, 1999). Concern for the welfare of the survivors of the suicide (e.g., a client's family) is also an important consideration in preventing suicide.

Although the use of coercion, which involves controlling or exercising power over another person, does not appear to be consistent with respect for a client's autonomy, those favoring coercive suicide prevention argue that suicide is an irrational act, and irrational acts are never truly autonomous. For example, Kant argued that "to use the power of a free will for its own destruction is self-contradictory" (Kant, 1924/1963, p. 148). It makes no logical sense to exercise freedom by killing it.[2] Thus, according to Kant, in preventing clients from committing suicide, clinicians are not abridging their autonomy. Rather, they are working toward restoring clients' ability to engage in free, truly autonomous decision making by providing treatment for their psychiatric and emotional problems.

The metaethical justification for coercive suicide prevention is that our most fundamental duty toward persons is to preserve their lives. After all, if an individual is dead, other ethical duties, like respect for the individual's personhood and autonomy, cease to be of any practical importance. Thus, all of our specific duties toward individuals, including respect for their right to exercise self-determination, entail the duty to preserve human life.

Proponents of active suicide prevention argue that coercive interventions *following* a suicide attempt are also done out of respect for the person's autonomy. Providing medical treatment to save people's lives after a suicide attempt is no different from providing medical care when finding people unconscious; one assumes they did not intend to harm themselves (Fairbairn, 1995).

A final argument in support of active suicide prevention is that clinicians can be viewed as ethically and legally negligent for having failed to prevent a client's death (Shergill & Szmukler, 1998).

The Ethical Argument Against Suicide Prevention

One extreme position in this debate is that "coercive psychiatric suicide prevention" (i.e., hospitalizing a client involuntarily) is never appropriate (Szasz, 1999, p. 19). Active suicide prevention strips clients of their status as autonomous moral agents in the name of protecting their life. Suicidal individuals are deprived of their civil liberties, which is radically inconsistent with the values of a mental health professional (Szasz, 1986). People have a right to direct their own lives in the manner they choose, including making the autonomous decision to end it. The invocation of the concept of mental illness to explain suicidal behavior makes suicidal individuals less than people. In reality, there are many motivations to commit suicide, just as there are many motivations to join the army in wartime or to smoke cigarettes, both of which can be viewed as potentially suicidal acts.

Suicide prevention also involves the imposition of clinicians' values on suicidal individuals, specifically, the arbitrary value that suicidal acts are always "wrong" or "crazy." Clinicians cannot legitimately claim to respect clients' autonomy if they are only willing to do so when clients' free choices are consistent with the clinicians' values. Clinicians are supposed to respect autonomy unconditionally. Psychiatrists supportive of the Oregon Death With Dignity Act placed greater emphasis on a patient's right to self-determination, whereas opponents weighted the duty to protect and preserve life more strongly (Ganzini et al., 1996). Historically, prior to 1800, taking one's own life was regarded as a sin or crime, for which the actor bore responsibility (Szasz, 1986). Since that time, the supposed role of mental illness in suicide has resulted in the view that suicide is an insane act and that mental health professionals must protect suicidal individuals from their own irrational impulses.

Another ethical problem associated with coercive psychiatric suicide prevention is the ability of clinicians to accurately predict suicidal behavior. While most people experience suicidal thoughts and even discuss the possibility of committing suicide at one or more points in their lives, suicide is actually a low base rate behavior, which means that the vast majority of individuals judged to be at risk for suicide will not actually attempt it (Joiner, Walker, Rudd, & Jobes, 1999; Murphy, 1988; Shergill & Szmukler, 1998). Those opposed to coercive suicide prevention argue that a clinician's inability to accurately predict suicidal behavior further diminishes the legitimacy of depriving individuals of their civil liberties based on the belief that they are at elevated risk for suicide.

Although proponents of suicide prevention frequently cite the principle of nonmaleficence in support of their position, critics argue that "the utter infantilization and dehumanization of the suicidal person" does enormous harm (Szasz, 1999, p. 55). Clinicians "define suicide as an illness and thus deny that it is an act; or they acknowledge that it is an act but deny that it is 'rational' or 'truly voluntary,' annulling the moral significance of their acknowledgment" (Szasz, 1999, p. 128). Szasz's point is that coercive psychiatric suicide prevention subverts the sense of autonomy and personal responsibility that clinicians supposedly seek to foster in clients.

The metaethical justification cited by opponents of coercive suicide prevention is, oddly enough, the same as that presented by those who favor suicide prevention: respect for the personhood of suicidal individuals. The opponents of coercive suicide prevention argue that there is a metaethical contradiction inherent in the idea of using coercion against suicidal individuals in order to preserve their personhood because you cannot preserve their personhood by stripping them of it. Denying people their civil rights and interfering with their exercise of self-determination is, in fact, grossly *disrespectful* of the personhood that coercive suicide prevention supposedly seeks to preserve. Coercive suicide prevention also disrespects the personhood of suicidal individuals by denying their responsibility for controlling their suicidal impulses. Instead, mental health professionals assume responsibility for controlling these individuals' behavior. Does this pattern of "therapeutic" interaction not encourage dependency, which clinicians are ethically bound to avoid creating in clients (ACA, 2005, A. Introduction; APA, 2002, Principle E)? The manipulative display of suicidal behavior by some clients to "test" the extent of the therapist's concern suggests that clients perceive their therapist as responsible for preventing them from killing themselves.

Szasz (1999) points out that the considerable ethical costs of engaging in this infantilizing and dehumanizing practice are not even justified by the effectiveness of suicide prevention. Coercive psychiatric suicide prevention does not prevent suicide; the suicide rate has not decreased as a result of using these procedures (Szasz, 1999). In fact, some clients might act on a suicide threat out of fear of being put away in a mental hospital. Suicide has occurred throughout human history, since people discovered that they could cause their own death. Unfortunately, it will continue to occur, no matter what steps mental health professionals take to prevent it. The possibility of unwise, self-destructive choices is the price a society pays for truly valuing the freedom and autonomy of its people (Szasz, 1999).

Methods of Suicide Prevention

The least coercive intervention with suicidal clients is to discuss the matter, which usually involves attempts to persuade them that suicide is not the answer. Discussing clients' suicidal ideation affords them the opportunity to explore the issue. Opponents of coercive suicide prevention are comfortable with this type of intervention. "Those who desire to prevent a particular person from committing suicide must be content with their power, such as it might be, to persuade him to change his mind" (Szasz, 1999, p. 110). In many cases, intervening noncoercively will eliminate clients' serious intent to kill themselves (Fairbairn, 1995). Those who intervene with more coercive suicide prevention methods (e.g., confiscating clients' weapons, hospitalizing them involuntarily) actively prevent an attempt or undo the effects of the attempt after the fact, without clients' consent, with the justification that the clients are not acting autonomously, or at least not fully so, in deciding to commit suicide (Fairbairn, 1995).

Legal Aspects of Suicide Prevention

Legal authorities' acceptance of the expert judgments of psychiatrists and other mental health professionals as sufficient grounds for committing people involuntarily to a psychiatric hospital has opened up the possibility of malpractice litigation against clinicians for failing to accurately recognize and predict suicidal potential when clients under their care commit suicide (Szasz, 1986). Fairbairn (1995) suggests that many cases of involuntary hospitalization of potentially suicidal clients represent the self-interested parentalism of mental health professionals more concerned about the legal, financial, and professional consequences for themselves of having clients commit suicide than about the consequences for the people being hospitalized against their will. Many clinicians might believe that, in theory, respect for personal autonomy does entail that people have a right to kill themselves, but, regardless, they will never risk allowing their clients to exercise an autonomous choice of that type (Ganzini et al., 1996). In other words, people are free to decide to commit suicide, but not on the clinician's watch.

Fairbairn (1995) argues that clinicians have the right to prevent clients from exercising their autonomy and committing suicide because this autonomous act threatens to harm the clinician, legally as well as personally. However, this justification is not valid for mental health professionals because of their ethical duty to always give the best interests of their clients priority over their own. Clinicians need other types of justification that are rationally defensible (e.g., the welfare of the client) in order to ethically engage in coercive suicide prevention.

A final consideration that again highlights the ethical dilemma involved in coercive suicide prevention is that when a clinician violates clients' confidentiality by informing medical or legal authorities about clients' suicidal potential, clients can bring a civil malpractice suit against the clinician, claiming that the breach of confidentiality was unjustified. A jury would determine whether the clinician acted appropriately.

CASE EXAMPLE 13.5

A clinical psychologist receives a call from a neighbor who is concerned about her 16-year-old daughter. Her daughter has seemed depressed recently and, at dinner the previous night, asked whether there was any history of suicide in their family. The mother asks the psychologist to talk with her daughter to determine whether she is seriously contemplating suicide. The psychologist explains that he is headed out of town on vacation with his family, but he will stop by to talk with the daughter before leaving town.

The psychologist, who knows the daughter well, talks with her for 15 minutes. She is somewhat embarrassed. She says that she recently broke up with her boyfriend and has been wondering whether life is worth living. She becomes very tearful during their discussion. She tells him that if she did attempt suicide, she would do it by taking an overdose of pills, but she denies that she is going to try to kill herself. The psychologist asks her to promise not to harm herself and to go and talk to a colleague of his. She promises and thanks him for his concern.

The psychologist tells her parents they should make an appointment with his colleague, keep an eye on their daughter for any change in her condition, and remove any pills from their medicine cabinet. They thank him and offer to pay him for his time. He refuses politely, saying "What are friends for?" Two days later, the daughter kills herself by taking pills she had hidden in her room a week earlier. Her parents sue the psychologist for malpractice, claiming that he failed to accurately assess their daughter's suicidal potential.

FORENSIC PRACTICE IN THE MENTAL HEALTH PROFESSIONS

The role of mental health professionals in the legal system has expanded steadily since the mid-1800s. However, until fairly recently, expert testimony on such matters as competency, insanity, and civil commitment was nearly exclusively the province of psychiatrists. It was only during the 1960s that clinical psychologists began to be recognized as forensic "experts." During the 1970s, specialized graduate training in forensic psychology was introduced (Bartol & Bartol, 1999). Since that time, it has become an important, popular, and lucrative area of practice for mental health professionals (Hagen, 1997).

Professionals acting as forensic experts can provide testimony concerning a wide range of civil and criminal matters. Of course, they are ethically obligated to present only truthful testimony, including the limitations of their knowledge and conclusions (ACA, 2005, E.13.a; APA, 2002, 9.01[b]). But, what qualifies someone as an "expert" in forensic matters? The standards for the admissibility of expert testimony underwent significant revision during the 1990s (Brogdon, Adams, & Bahri, 2004). For many years, the Frye test, which stipulated that evidence presented by scientific experts was admissible only if it was based on data and theories "established to have gained general acceptance in the particular field in which it belongs," was the recognized benchmark (*Frye v. United States,* 1923). However, in 1993, the U.S. Supreme Court established a new standard concerning expert testimony in *Daubert v. Merrell Dow Pharmaceuticals.* In *Daubert,* the Court held that trial judges had a responsibility to ensure the relevance and reliability of scientific evidence by evaluating experts' testimony in relation to each of the following four factors: (a) whether the technique or theory (e.g., an actuarial model for evaluating potential for violence) can be or has been subjected to scientific test (i.e., is the theory *falsifiable?*); (b) whether the theory has been subjected to peer review or been published in the discipline; (c) whether an error rate associated with the theory has been established (e.g., a false positive rate for diagnosis of psychosis based on a test cut-off score); and (d) as in the Frye test, whether the theory is generally accepted within the relevant scientific discipline (Brogdon et al., 2004). The Supreme Court has since declared that the *Daubert* standard applies to all expert testimony (*Kumho Tire Company, Ltd. v. Carmichael,* 1999), which would include clinical judgments of mental health professionals when functioning as forensic expert witnesses. Thus, forensic experts have a "special responsibility for fairness and accuracy in their public statements" (Committee on Ethical Guidelines for Forensic Psychologists, 1991, VII.B).

The different aspects of forensic psychology are best conceptualized today as unique specialty areas of professional practice. Practicing in an area of forensic psychology (e.g., conducting child custody evaluations) should be preceded by the development of appropriate expertise through specialized training and supervised experience, along the lines adopted by APA for psychologists wishing to change their specialty area (Conger, 1976). In addition, the American Academy of Forensic Psychology and Division 41 of APA have published "Specialty Guidelines for Forensic Psychologists" that address professional and ethical issues affecting forensic specialists, including competence (Committee on Ethical Guidelines for Forensic Psychologists, 1991). Nevertheless, forensic psychology has become a very controversial area of mental health practice because of "experts" who will offer under oath whatever testimony a lawyer requests in exchange for a substantial fee (Pope et al., 2000).

Special Considerations in Forensic Assessment

In conducting assessments for legal proceedings (e.g., insanity evaluations, child custody evaluations), it is especially important for clinicians to clarify their role with all parties involved in the assessment (ACA, 2005, E.13.b; APA, 2002, 3.05[c]). Clients being assessed need to understand that the clinician is not their therapist but has been retained to conduct an evaluation in connection with legal proceedings. Also, clinicians should explain who hired them to conduct the assessment (e.g., the court, defense attorney, prosecutor's office), the purpose of the assessment (e.g., a determination of competence to stand trial), and what the results will be used for (e.g., report provided to the court). It is extremely important that clients understand the limits placed on the confidentiality of information they reveal during the assessment. In general, all information obtained from clients can be included in the assessment report.

Forensic clinicians should never assume that the judge or lawyers in a case have fully informed the client; clinicians should always disclose all relevant information to the client themselves prior to conducting the assessment. (The term *disclosure* is more generally applicable to forensic assessment than "informed consent" because there are circumstances under which clients cannot legally refuse to be evaluated. If clients refuse to participate, the assessment will be conducted from the available records.) In competency determinations, where there is likely reason to question clients' ability to provide autonomous informed consent, the client's legal counsel should also be a party to the informed consent discussion. Although forensic assessment generally involves a significant element of coercion, the clinician must inform clients that they have the right to refuse to participate. However, they should understand clearly, in consultation with their attorney, the consequences of such a refusal (e.g., potentially stricter sentence).

Countertransferential issues that can affect the objectivity of clinicians' judgment might be quite likely to arise in forensic contexts. Specifically, certain types of criminal charges (e.g., sexual assaults against children) or defendants (e.g., attractive, friendly) might evoke positive or negative countertransferential biases in the clinician. Clinicians need to be aware that their subjective value biases are potentially as important in this context as in conducting therapy.

CASE EXAMPLE 13.6

At the request of the district attorney's office, a forensic counselor is conducting an evaluation of a defendant charged with killing two children. She explains to the client what her role in the case is. She informs him that anything he tells her during the evaluation will not remain confidential and can be used in her evaluation report and testimony at the trial. He indicates his understanding and signs an informed consent document.

She begins the evaluation with intelligence testing. During the testing, the client says, "You're a head doctor, right?" She replies that she is a forensic diagnostician. He then says, "Why did I kill them?" She reminds him that she is not his therapist and of the limits on the confidentiality of their discussion. She then completes the intelligence testing and finds that he is mildly mentally retarded. She is no longer confident that he understood the informed consent procedure and is unsure how she should treat his admission of guilt.

Evaluating a Defendant's Competency to Stand Trial

Competency determinations permit a criminal trial to be postponed if defendants are considered unable (as opposed to just being unwilling) to do the following as a result of mental or physical illness or disability: (a) understand the charges brought against them and the potential consequences of those charges; (b) consult rationally with their lawyer, disclose information, and participate in legal decisions; (c) understand the adversarial nature of the legal proceedings; (d) behave appropriately in court; and (e) testify in their own defense (Conroy, 2003; Roesch, Zapf, Golding, & Skeem, 1999). People are presumed to be competent; therefore, incompetency must be proven by a preponderance of the evidence.

The issue of a defendant's competency can be raised before or during the criminal trial (Roesch et al., 1999). Competency determinations are conducted separately from criminal proceedings. If the question of a defendant's competency is raised, the judge orders an evaluation of the defendant by a psychiatrist or psychologist with expertise in forensic assessment. The evaluation can be conducted in a psychiatric hospital, outpatient mental health center, or jail, as ordered by the judge (Roesch et al., 1999). Forensic evaluators present an evaluation report to the court, offering their opinion as to whether the defendant's current mental status meets the criteria for competency. Competency is a legal issue, decided by a judge or jury, but most judges simply accept the evaluator's opinion, rather than conducting a formal competency hearing (Roesch et al., 1999). If evaluators conclude that a defendant is incompetent at present, they are generally required to address the issue of whether the defendant is likely to attain competence in the foreseeable future. Evaluators must then submit a separate report regarding the mental illness or disability responsible for the defendant's incompetency. The report should contain recommendations regarding appropriate treatment and the advisability of commitment.

In most jurisdictions, there are three possible outcomes in a competency determination. If defendants are deemed competent to stand trial, the trial will proceed. Second, If defendants are found to be incompetent, but likely to regain competence in the future, they will generally be committed to a psychiatric facility for a specified period to attain competency. The length of commitment varies by state statute (Roesch et al., 1999). Third, if defendants are judged incompetent and unlikely to become competent in the future, the charges are dismissed. In the final scenario, civil commitment proceedings are commenced if the defendant is believed to be mentally ill or mentally retarded and in need of hospitalization. If hospitalization is not warranted, the defendant will be discharged.

CASE EXAMPLE 13.7

The U.S. Supreme Court has ruled that it is unconstitutional to execute offenders who qualify for a diagnosis of Mental Retardation. A forensic counselor conducts an assessment of a woman convicted of murder and sentenced to death. The counselor, who opposes the death penalty on ethical grounds, explains the potential significance of the testing to the offender and explains the types of life skills deficits associated with mental retardation (e.g., problems with self-care and communication capabilities) in addition to poor performance on cognitive skills tests. Following the testing, the counselor has reason to question the validity of the offender's performance because she did not make a concerted effort to perform well on the tests. Nevertheless, he decides that these misgivings are too vague and subjective to include in his report, particularly considering the dire consequences (i.e., imposition of the death penalty) that could arise if authorities placed too much importance on his impression of the offender's level of effort.

Insanity as a Legal Defense

In most states, defendants plead "Not Guilty by Reason of Insanity" (NGRI) to claim that they were insane at the time they committed a crime. An insanity plea entails that defendants admit they committed the crime. In 1982, at the time John Hinkley attempted to assassinate President Reagan, federal courts and most state courts required that the prosecution prove beyond a reasonable doubt that the defendant was *not* insane. Following the Hinkley trial, the burden of proof changed in the federal courts and nearly all state courts; now, the defense must establish, "by clear and convincing evidence or a preponderance of the evidence," that defendants *were* insane at the time they committed the act, a much more difficult task (Borum & Fulero, 1999, p. 381).

The issue of insanity must be raised before the trial begins, as the defendant's plea in response to the charge; the insanity plea cannot be addressed unless the defendant is regarded as competent to stand trial (Conroy, 2003). After an insanity plea is entered, the defendant is required to undergo an evaluation by one or more forensic clinicians (psychiatrists or clinical psychologists). Both sides in the case (i.e., defense and prosecution) have the right to appoint experts to examine the defendant and to call these clinicians as expert witnesses in the trial (Wrightsman et al., 1998). The clinicians conducting the evaluation will report their findings on whether the defendant was mentally ill at the time the crime was committed. If the court finds defendants NGRI, they are committed to a psychiatric facility for evaluation of their need for treatment based on their current level of dangerousness. Jurors are not generally informed of the commitment process that follows an NGRI verdict (Golding, Skeem, Roesch, & Zapf, 1999).

In some states, those acquitted by reason of insanity spend less time in psychiatric hospitals, on the average, than people convicted of the same crimes spend in prison; in other states, they are confined for a longer period than people convicted of the same crimes (Borum & Fulero, 1999; Wrightsman et al., 1998). The NGRI defense is used in less than 1% of felony indictments and results in acquittal in approximately 15–25% of those cases (Borum & Fulero, 1999). It is used in less than 2% of capital (i.e., murder) cases in the United States (Steadman et al., 1993); only 14.3% of insanity pleas in one survey involved defendants charged with murder (Borum & Fulero, 1999). The rate of insanity acquittals showed a modest decline in the late 1980s and early to mid-1990s, following the furor over John Hinkley's insanity acquittal in 1982 (Cirincione & Jacobs, 1999). Contrary to popular belief, faking insanity has not generally been a successful method of avoiding punishment for clever defendants with slick lawyers (Lymburner & Roesch, 1999). However, defense claims of diminished capacity (resulting in diminished responsibility) as a consequence of mental retardation, temporary insanity, or intoxication at the time of the criminal act have increased in frequency over the years (Hagen, 1997).

Five rules or standards have been used by courts to establish whether defendants are insane. The first is the M'Naughten Rule, which dates back to 1843. Daniel M'Naughten had attempted to assassinate the Prime Minister of England, but had instead killed the Prime Minister's secretary. His legal defense was that he was delusional and did not know right from wrong (Wrightsman et al., 1998). The M'Naughten criterion states that defendants are legally insane if a defect of reason, resulting from a mental disease, prevented defendants from knowing the nature and quality of the acts they performed, or, if they knew they were performing the act, from understanding that the act was wrong (Steadman et al., 1993). Basically, psychotic disorders are the only potentially excusing conditions under the M'Naughten Rule. This rule was the criterion used by courts in most states until the 1960s (Steadman et al., 1993).

The Irresistible Impulse Rule was established in 1887. This precedent states that defendants are not legally responsible for their crime if, even though they knew that what they were doing was wrong, they could not stop themselves from performing the act because they were compelled beyond their will to commit the act (Wrightsman et al., 1998).

In 1954, the insanity defense was broadened further by a decision that established the Durham Rule (*Durham v. United States,* 1954). The rule, currently used only in New Hampshire, states that defendants are not criminally responsible if the unlawful act was the product of mental disease or defect. Under this rule, insanity could also be claimed based on the presence of a dissociative disorder or personality disorder (Wrightsman et al., 1998).

The American Law Institute (ALI) standard, developed in 1962, states that defendants are not responsible for their criminal acts if at the time of the acts, owing to mental disease or defect, they lacked the capacity to appreciate the criminal character of the act or to conform their behavior to the law. The ALI standard combines aspects of the M'Naughten and Irresistible Impulse Rules.

The Insanity Defense Reform Act (IDRA) was passed by the United States Congress in 1984 (Pub. L. No. 98-473) as the standard for insanity pleas in all federal courts. It is quite close to the standard set in the M'Naughten Rule. The defense must prove by clear and convincing evidence that defendants were suffering from a severe mental disorder that made them unable to appreciate the nature and quality of the act they were performing or that the act was wrong. Congress enacted the law in response to complaints that insanity pleas were too frequently successful and the public outcry when John Hinkley was found NGRI after he attempted to assassinate President Reagan (Steadman et al., 1993). At present, the vast majority of state courts use versions of the M'Naughten Rule or the ALI standard (Borum & Fulero, 1999; Golding et al., 1999). Three states (Idaho, Montana, and Utah) have no provision for an insanity defense.

Another reform of the insanity defense was the "Guilty, But Mentally Ill" (GBMI) verdict, which was first enacted in Michigan in 1975 (Steadman et al., 1993). At least a dozen other states have adopted similar provisions since that time (Borum & Fulero, 1999). This verdict does not eliminate the insanity defense, but it offers an additional alternative in arriving at a verdict for mentally ill defendants. When the GBMI verdict is applied, defendants receive the same sentence as others convicted of the crime, with the addition of requirements for mental health treatment during incarceration. Although initially popular, "the GBMI verdict has been severely criticized on both legal and conceptual grounds" (Borum & Fulero, 1999, p. 382).

The key ethical issue involved in the insanity defense is the ability of mental health professionals to determine a person's past mental state. Although this judgment can be extremely difficult to make, particularly in cases of temporary insanity, many forensic clinicians are very willing to offer opinions on cases that require this sort of "retrospective diagnostic clairvoyance" (Hagen, 1997, p. 123). Expert testimony is frequently presented on both sides of the issue, which is not surprising but makes it quite clear that a final, objective, scientific determination on the matter is not possible at present (Weiner, 1999). For example, a central issue in NGRI determinations is delusionality because the insanity defense relieves a mentally disordered individual of legal responsibility if she "acts upon a pathological, uncontrollable belief system that distorts her sense of reality, thereby impairing her capacity for rational choice" (Golding et al., 1999, p. 390). In contested cases, experts frequently disagree regarding the presence of delusions, as opposed to zealously held beliefs.

It is important to remember that forensic expert witnesses do not actually decide the issue of insanity, though verdicts are generally influenced by their expert clinical evaluations (Lymburner & Roesch, 1999). Expert witnesses simply present assessment information that the court interprets to decide the legal issue of insanity.

Prediction of Dangerousness

Contrary to the insanity defense evaluation process, predicting violent or suicidal behavior requires mental health professionals to make a judgment about people's *future* behavior based on current mental status and assessment data as well as information about their past behavior (Weiner, 1999). Predicting future dangerousness is also a formidable undertaking. Nevertheless, researchers in the area of risk assessment argue that actuarial prediction of risk for violence has improved considerably in recent years due to progress in identifying and validating risk factors for violence (Litwack & Schlesinger, 1999).

Many forensic clinicians use actuarial data from personality tests and interview assessments to determine a person's potential for violence. As discussed in Chapter 8, actuarial prediction can be a powerful tool for making clinical predictions and judgments, particularly for low base rate behaviors like violence (Arango, Calcedo Barba, Gonzalez-Salvador, & Calcedo Ordonez, 1999; Eccleston & Ward, 2004), provided that the model is sound and the individual being assessed is a member of a class of people (e.g., persons experiencing delusional thinking) for whom actuarial data have been compiled (Garb, 1998; Janus & Meehl, 1997; Shergill & Szmukler, 1998). Sound actuarial models can provide an objective standard that can be applied fairly and consistently by the courts (Janus & Meehl, 1997; Pope et al., 2000). Indeed, actuarial methods have proven more effective than clinical judgments in predicting violence in psychiatric populations (Arango et al., 1999; Eccleston & Ward, 2004).

Compelling evidence indicates that individuals currently experiencing psychotic symptoms involving a sense of being threatened and having their life controlled by external forces are at increased risk to commit violent acts against themselves or others, particularly when statements of violent intentions have been associated with the psychosis (Link & Steuve, 1994; Litwack & Schlesinger, 1999; Monahan, 1992). A history of repeated violence, particularly a recent history, and the likelihood that the individual will confront circumstances similar to ones that resulted in violent behavior in the past are also potent risk factors for violence (Arango et al., 1999; Litwack & Schlesinger, 1999; Megargee, 1993).

Critics have argued that most people in our society associate these predictors with an individual's potential for violence, so their use does not demonstrate any special capacity peculiar to mental health professionals (Hagen, 1997). An obvious limitation of such predictions is that situational factors, such as the behavior of the victim, play an extremely important part in violent acts (Megargee, 1995). In general, clinicians tend to focus too much on the individual's psychiatric condition in predicting violence, while underemphasizing the importance of interpersonal contexts and social variables, such as employment (Mulvey & Lidz, 1998). In fact, the vast majority of people suffering from mental disorders are not violent; alcoholism and drug abuse are much more potent predictors of violent behavior (Monahan, 1992).[3]

CASE EXAMPLE 13.8

A voluntary client suffering from Delusional Disorder, Persecutory Type requests discharge from a psychiatric hospital. When evaluated by a clinical psychologist, the client's condition is stable, though he still shows evidence of delusional beliefs that others intend to harm him. The client has a history of violence against people, but those incidents occurred when he was not taking his medication. He says that he intends to stay on his medication now so that he will not have to return to the hospital. The psychologist does not believe the client meets the legal standard for psychiatric commitment, so she recommends that he be discharged.

Five days later, having stopped taking his medication, he is questioned by a police officer who notices him running down a residential street, stopping to hide behind each tree. He gets into an altercation with the officer, manages to get the officer's gun, and kills him. The police officer's family sues the hospital and the psychologist for malpractice for discharging an individual who represented a significant risk for violence.

The degree of difficulty in predicting future violence becomes apparent whenever recently discharged psychiatric clients do commit violent acts: The clinicians responsible for their release assert that they are not legally or morally responsible for the client's actions because they had no way of knowing that the person would get into that situation or respond in that manner. However, legal responsibility for the violent acts of clients is something that mental health professionals have brought on themselves by asserting to judges and juries that they are indeed capable of predicting violence.

None of this is to say that clinicians cannot develop the competence to predict violence better than the average person. To generate their predictions, clinicians can use the following types of information: a skilled clinical assessment; the most effective actuarial prediction models, including base rate information for violence in the population to which the individual belongs; knowledge of recidivism rates for violent behavior, the circumstances of the individual's previous violent behavior and their similarity to circumstances the person is likely to face in the short-term future; the individual's capacity for empathy; current mental status; response to past treatment; and the evidence supporting the validity of each of these variables (ACA, 2005, E.5.a; APA, 2002, 9.01[a]; Litwack & Schlesinger, 1999; Weiner, 1999).[4] However, it is clearly inappropriate for a clinician to testify as a forensic "expert" in matters of violence without having developed a specialized competence in this area (ACA, 2005,

E.13.a; APA, 2002, 2.04). Mental health professionals are always ethically concerned with the welfare of others; they respect people's rights and dignity, and they recognize the limits of their professional competence. Before assuming the role of expert witness, clinicians should give careful consideration to these ethical duties and to their degree of certainty regarding any conclusions they intend to present under oath (ACA, 2005, E.13.a; APA, 2002, 9.01).

Child Custody Evaluations

Each year, more than one million families in the U.S. experience divorce (Bailey, 1998). Domestic courts generally become involved in determining child custody when the involved parties cannot resolve informally the amount and type of contact each parent (or other party seeking custody) will have with a child and the extent to which each will have decision-making authority for the child. The criteria taken into account in custody determinations are the following: the age and gender of the child; the child's preferences regarding a custodian; the quality of the child's interaction with each person seeking custody, as well as with any siblings or others (e.g., stepparents, stepsiblings) residing in the households; and the emotional and physical health of everyone relevant to the decision (Hess & Brinson, 1999). These cases are another setting in which mental health professionals conduct evaluations and offer expert testimony involving predictions about future behavior and events. APA has published guidelines for professionals involved in child custody evaluations (APA, 1994). In spite of the guidance provided, the questions involved in child custody determinations are sometimes extremely difficult for experts to address effectively based on the data available to them (Weiner, 1999).

Child custody evaluators conduct assessments designed to assess the parenting capacities of one or both parents, based on interview, testing, and observational data. The evaluation also assesses the personality functioning, developmental needs, and preferences of each child involved. Others living in the custodial households, including stepparents, stepsiblings, half siblings, and grandparents, are generally included in the examination of the home environment (Weiner, 1999). Clearly, the expertise of mental health professionals who are trained to make these evaluations can make a very positive contribution to the custody determination process "by providing competent, impartial information" (APA, 1994, p. 677).

As in other areas of forensic assessment, evaluators must be careful to obtain the informed consent of the individuals being evaluated, including the parent or guardian of any children being evaluated. The purpose of the evaluation and how the results will be used must be explained thoroughly. Parents should be informed at the outset of the process of the significant limitations placed on their confidentiality; everything they discuss with the evaluator can be included in the report (ACA, 2005, E.13.b; APA, 2002, 3.05[a], 9.03[a]). Also, child custody evaluators should not have a prior relationship with the child or parents, unless the court has ordered them to conduct the evaluation. Forensic evaluators should not present evaluative comments regarding any party to the case that they have not evaluated themselves (Knapp & VandeCreek, 2001).

Child custody decisions involve extremely weighty issues and difficult predictions. It is interesting that the guidelines mention that complaints have arisen about "the misuse of psychologists' influence" in such cases (APA, 1994, p. 677). For example, Bailey (1998) argues that unvalidated, biased viewpoints expressed by mental health professionals concerning paternal custody contributed to custody being awarded to fathers in only 10% of cases in 1990. Like assessments of dangerousness, predictions regarding parenting capabilities are extremely difficult to make unless the parent is exceptionally and obviously unfit. A clinician might note particular personality attributes in an assessment, such as "unresolved anger," but it would be extraordinarily speculative to testify as to how those attributes will affect the client's ability to function as a father. It would be far better to avoid presenting an opinion to the court regarding the relative merits of parents in the absence of considerable behavioral evidence. Clinicians should never be hesitant to admit when they simply do not have any valid data that will enable them to make a definite prediction (ACA, 2005, E.13.a; APA, 2002, 9.01[b], 9.02[b]). After all, the best long-term adjustment of children of divorce is related to their frequent contact with both parents, provided the parents do not experience ongoing personal conflict (Hess & Brinson, 1999).

CASE EXAMPLE 13.9

A forensic psychologist is hired to conduct a child custody evaluation by the attorney representing the child's father. The psychologist contacts the child's mother, but she declines to participate. During his evaluation of the child, the psychologist learns that the mother is a very strict, possibly abusive disciplinarian. In his report, he mentions his concerns about the mother's disciplinary practices because of his concern about the potential for abuse in the situation.

This area of professional practice requires competence concerning issues well beyond the range of normal clinical assessment (APA, 1994). Professionals competent to conduct custody evaluations using the MMPI-2, for example, should not only be familiar with the literature regarding the interpretation of MMPI-2 profiles, but of the differences they should expect between the profiles of individuals from the normative sample and those undergoing custody evaluations, two entirely different populations (Pope et al., 2000). Professionals are obligated to inform attorneys who contact them of the limits of their competence and make appropriate referrals to more qualified or experienced colleagues as needed (Pope et al., 2000).

As in other legal applications of mental health expertise, many clinicians are drawn to perform child custody evaluations because of the lucrative reimbursement available. Most evaluators are hired by one "side" in a case, and when clients and lawyers pay for an expensive evaluation, they expect the results to support their side. Failing to make a case for that parent (and, if possible, against the other parent) can have direct implications for the clinician's future business in conducting custody evaluations. Nevertheless, professional guidelines clearly require that "the psychologist should be impartial regardless of whether he or she is retained by the court or by a party to the proceedings" (APA, 1994, p. 678). Psychologists experienced in custody evaluations prefer to be appointed by the court or to be retained jointly by both attorneys in the case (Hess & Brinson, 1999).

The professional guidelines state that the parents' values that are relevant to parenting are an important aspect of the evaluation, which introduces considerable potential for the value biases of evaluators to influence the process (APA, 1994). An extremely difficult, yet important duty for evaluators is to avoid favoring parents whose approach to childrearing resembles their own (ACA, 2005, A.4.b; APA, 2002, Principle E). The potential for value biases increases when there are few objective determinants to guide clinicians' judgment. For example, if evaluators believe strongly in supporting the rights and autonomy of women within a male-dominated legal system, their value orientation could bias their perceptions of the relative desirability of granting custody to the mother, as opposed to the father (Keller, 1999).

The issue of physical, emotional, and sexual abuse of children is often raised in child custody cases, with or without justification (Hagen, 1997). Clinicians must be extraordinarily careful not to go beyond well-validated sources of behavioral data or unambiguous self-report information in offering professional judgments regarding these issues. For example, the interpretation of children's play with toys as data relevant to the issue of child abuse requires extensive validation in controlled behavioral studies, rather than clinical lore. Ethical mental health professionals should not make statements about "classic signs" of abuse, or of anything else, in the absence of objective, empirical evidence to support them (Hagen, 1997). The guidelines state that even evaluators competent to perform child custody evaluations may not be competent "to address these complex issues" of abuse (APA, 1994, p. 678).

A final matter pertaining to mental health professionals' role in child custody evaluations is that these evaluations tend to be quite expensive for parents. As a result, the process of obtaining expert testimony based on these evaluations to support parental fitness is inherently discriminatory against one parent (e.g., nonworking mother) if the parent has inadequate financial resources to obtain a competent evaluator. To avoid the unethical practice of discriminating against people based on their socioeconomic status (ACA, 2005, C.5; APA, 2002, 3.01), professionals can suggest to the attorney who contacts them about conducting an evaluation that both parents should receive competent evaluations.

Child Protection Evaluations

In cases of alleged abuse or neglect of a child, forensic experts in the area of child protection are frequently called upon to conduct evaluations of parents and children on behalf of the court, child welfare authorities, or some other interested party (e.g., parents) to determine whether children should be removed from their parents' home for their own protection. APA has published a set of specialty guidelines for clinicians conducting this type of forensic evaluation (APA Committee on Professional Practice and Standards, 1998). The guidelines emphasize that the best interest and well-being of the child are the most important considerations in these situations. Above all else, children must be protected from harm (i.e., abuse and neglect).

Like child custody evaluation, conducting child protection evaluations requires the specialized competence to provide complex judgments about the *future* behavior of parents (i.e., whether parents are likely to abuse their child) and make difficult predictions regarding the future impact of events on children (e.g., whether children will suffer emotional harm as a consequence of being separated from their parents). Child custody evaluators' areas of professional expertise should include the following: forensic practice, child and family development and psychopathology, types of child abuse, and the effect on children of being separated from their biological family (APA Committee on Professional Practice and Standards, 1998). Any expert opinion presented by an evaluator in a report or as an expert witness should be based on scientific knowledge that is valid for the population represented by the parents (e.g., African American) and children (e.g., adolescent) involved in the case.

Evaluators must also be aware of their biases for and against different types of people (e.g., based on gender, age, race, ethnicity, sexual orientation, socioeconomic status) in order to avoid discriminating against parents from diverse groups. If evaluators recognize that they cannot be objective in a case, they should not conduct the evaluation (APA Committee on Professional Practice and Standards, 1998). Professionals should also avoid compromising the welfare of a child by taking on multiple roles in child custody and child protection cases, such as functioning as both therapist and evaluator (Knapp & VandeCreek, 2001).

CASE EXAMPLE 13.10

Shortly after a counselor begins treating a child for depression, the child's father (who no longer lives with the child and her mother) is reported by the family's pediatrician for suspected physical abuse of the child. The child's mother asks the counselor to conduct an evaluation of the child to determine whether abuse has occurred and to make recommendations regarding the advisability of terminating the father's visitation rights. The counselor declines, telling the mother that her involvement as the child's therapist would make it inappropriate for her to conduct the independent evaluation. For one thing, if she becomes involved in the legal process, she feels it could compromise the confidentiality of the therapy relationship. The mother pleads with her, saying, "But she trusts you! She won't open up to anyone else." The counselor refuses, believing it would be unethical for her to conduct the evaluation.

General Ethical Concerns About Functioning as an Expert Witness

Sales and Simon (1993) stated that "a dramatic improvement in the quality of expert testimony could occur if experts reflected on their ethical obligations prior to becoming expert witnesses" (p. 244). They make an excellent point. Providing expert testimony, particularly in complex clinical matters (e.g., the assessment of an individual's potential for violence), is an extremely difficult task and one that has enormous implications for the lives of the people involved. Professionals should recognize the considerable ethical obligations they incur when they agree to present themselves as an expert witness in a legal proceeding.

To ethically claim competence to provide expert testimony in a case, professionals should be familiar with the scientific knowledge base for the testimony they will offer and possess an excellent knowledge of the laws and procedures relevant to their role as a forensic expert (ACA, 2005, E.13.a; APA, 2002, 2.01[f]). They should also understand the legal theories relevant to the testimony they will offer, so their testimony will be pertinent. In addition, before taking on a case, professionals have an ethical duty to make certain that they will have adequate time to prepare their testimony.

To support their case, many lawyers will try to influence the interpretation of a forensic evaluator's findings or how the findings will be presented in court. Forensic professionals must be very careful to insist upon reporting their findings honestly and candidly in their testimony (ACA, 2005, C.6.b; APA, 2002, Principle C, 5.01[a]). The objectivity and sense of social responsibility of forensic experts is what distinguishes them from "hired guns," whose job it is to support the case of the lawyer who retained them (APA, 2002, Principle C; Hess, 1999a, 1999b). The biased, unethical testimony of professionals selling their services as hired guns has compromised the integrity of the mental health professions (Sales & Simon, 1993). Due to the conflict of interest involved, forensic professionals cannot work on a contingent fee basis, as many lawyers do. In other words, professionals' fees cannot depend on their "side" winning the case (Committee on Ethical Guidelines for Forensic Psychologists, 1991, IV.B; Knapp & VandeCreek, 2001).

Forensic experts should be retained by the court or by an attorney in the case. If they are hired by a party in the case, the client could claim legal privilege in an attempt to prevent them from disclosing information in their testimony (Knapp & VandeCreek, 2001). As in all of the professional activities of clinicians, a primary obligation of a clinical professional consulting with defense attorneys or providing expert testimony for the defense is to protect the welfare of the defendant. In a recent New York case, a man with a long history of violence and hospitalizations for schizophrenia pleaded NGRI after murdering a woman by throwing her in front of a subway train (Barnes, 2000). His first trial ended in a hung jury. The defense team then decided to take him off his antipsychotic medication prior to his testimony at his second trial, so the jury could get a clearer picture of his mental state at the time of the crime (when he had also stopped taking his medication). The legal strategy did not work because the defendant struck a social worker and the judge ordered that he had to be offered his medication on a daily basis (Barnes, 2000). The defendant resumed taking his medication when it was offered and did not testify at the trial. A mental health professional involved in the defense of this individual would have an ethical obligation to object to the defense team's attempt to deliberately withhold treatment from the defendant without his consent.

Juries and judges place great importance on the testimony of forensic experts, so professionals must guard against the tendency to overstate their degree of certainty regarding an interpretation of assessment data in their testimony (Faust & Ziskin, 1988). They should always use a graded system of levels of confidence in presenting assessment interpretations, ranging from certain, based on the well-developed literature supporting an interpretation, to no expert opinion on an issue (Hess, 1999b). This point is important because when people think of themselves as experts, they may tend to overestimate their legitimate statistical confidence in a judgment (Garb, 1998). Similarly, forensic experts should not present a theory regarding behavior as fact; they should also point out whether any alternative theories have been developed in the profession that would lead to different conclusions (Sales & Simon, 1993).

CASE EXAMPLE 13.11

A forensic counselor has an excellent reputation among defense attorneys for presenting credible evidence that a jury will find compelling. He has been criticized by fellow forensic experts and prosecutors as a "hired gun" who will say anything under oath to assist the defense in exchange for a large fee. The counselor feels that there are at least two sides to every case. He enjoys the intellectual challenge of examining different perspectives on a case until he finds the one that meets the two conditions of presenting the defendant in a positive light and being as consistent as possible with the evidence in the case, including the evidence obtained in his evaluation of the client. He believes that criminal proceedings are adversarial and that his job is to present as strong a scientific case as possible for his side.

Finally, the objectivity required of forensic professionals entails that they avoid subjective judgments regarding the merit of a client's legal case based on their personal values and simply present information consistent with their scientific knowledge. Dr. Elizabeth Loftus, an experimental psychologist, has been a strong advocate of the need for a standard of unbiased professionalism in the forensic treatment of memory issues, grounded in objective experimental evidence (e.g., Loftus & Ketcham, 1994). Dr. Loftus was perceived by many as having violated her own standard when she refused to testify about her research findings in the trial of an accused Nazi, John Demjanjuk (Loftus & Ketcham, 1991). Scientists cannot ethically pick and choose the cases and causes entitled to the benefit of their objective data, based on their personal biases. This is a lesson that forensic psychology needs to learn from the American Civil Liberties Union. Everyone has an equal right to protection under the law, not just those whose situations you are in sympathy with. Dr. Loftus expressed discomfort about possibly advocating on behalf of a guilty individual if she had taken the witness stand (Loftus, 1987). Of course, a forensic psychologist's job is not to determine guilt or innocence but merely to present relevant findings.

WHAT IF ETHICS AND THE LAW CONFLICT?

As discussed in Chapter 1, ethics and law are not the same thing, but both involve important duties for mental health professionals. Professionals have an ethical obligation to obey the laws and regulations relevant to their profession (APA, 2002, 1.02), just as they have a duty to behave in accordance with their professional ethical code (ACA, 2005, C.1; APA, 2002, Introduction). However, in some instances, legal and ethical duties can conflict. This type of scenario presents mental health professionals with a different sort of ethical dilemma.

When a legal requirement conflicts with a professional ethical duty, mental health professionals must make the relevant parties aware of their commitment to the ethical code of their profession and endeavor to resolve the conflict (ACA, 2005, H.1.b; APA, 2002, 1.02). When professionals are served with a subpoena (i.e., a court document that requires the named individual to appear at a hearing, or at another location, to provide a deposition, courtroom testimony, or turn over records [Anderson, 1996]), they must consider both their legal duty to obey the court *and* their ethical duty to protect the confidential communications of their clients. In determining how to respond to the subpoena, they should first review the statutes concerning legal privilege for the state in which they practice. Suppose they discover that, in their state, there is no therapist-client privilege in criminal proceedings. (Actually, this would be true of most states.) Second, they should find out whether their clients want the information disclosed. If they do, professionals should obtain clients' consent to release the information and comply with the subpoena. If clients do not want the information released, or if professionals believe that releasing the information is not in their client's best interest, they should obtain the client's permission to contact the client's attorney. They would inform the attorney that providing the court with the information sought in the subpoena will place them in violation of the ethical code of their profession (ACA, 2005, B.2.c; APA, 2002, 1.02) and is against their client's wishes. They would then ask the attorney to file a motion to block the subpoena (ACA, 2005, B.2.c; Anderson, 1996; Arthur & Swanson, 1993). Therapists should also seek legal advice themselves and keep very careful records of their entire decision-making process (Anderson, 1996; Arthur & Swanson, 1993). If the subpoena is not withdrawn, they would have to decide whether to comply with the court order or risk being charged with contempt. Although mental health professionals are expected to advocate for their client's right to privacy with legal authorities, professional ethical codes do not require that they subject themselves to arrest by resisting a legal order (ACA, 2005, B.2; APA, 2002, 4.05[b]). If therapists do decide to provide the required records or testimony, they should still minimize the intrusion into their client's privacy by providing only information directly required by the court (ACA, 2005, B.2.d; APA, 2002, 4.04[a]).

For example, in 2003, the Women's Resource Center in Lawrence, Massachusetts, was ordered to provide counseling records for a 16-year-old client to the defense lawyers of the man she accused of raping her (Liptak, 2003a). The center refused to comply with the court order, arguing that the records were confidential and not directly germane to the criminal trial.

In this particular case, the Women's Resource Center was found to be in contempt of court for violating the order and assessed a $500-per-day fine until it complied (Liptak, 2003a).

One final note is that mental health professionals have an ethical obligation to work, individually and through their professional organizations, to change laws that are unjust and harmful to the people they serve.

CASE EXAMPLE 13.12

APA canceled its plans to hold its 1997 annual convention in New Orleans, Louisiana, after the state of Louisiana passed what the leadership of APA considered an unreasonably restrictive abortion law. APA acknowledged publicly that this law was the reason for canceling the convention plans, arguing that the decision was consistent with the ethical duty of psychologists to "work toward changing existing regulations that are not beneficial to the public interest" (APA, 1990, Principle 3[d]).

PRACTICE CASE INVOLVING THE MODEL OF ETHICAL DECISION MAKING

In 1979, Charles Singleton killed a grocery store clerk in Arkansas. He was convicted of murder and sentenced to be executed. Concerns about Mr. Singleton's mental health developed in 1987 when he reported that "his prison cell was possessed by demons and that a prison doctor had implanted a device in his ear" (Liptak, 2003b, p. A27). After a number of medical evaluations concluded he was psychotic, Mr. Singleton's lawyers argued that he was mentally incompetent and should not be executed. (In 1986, the United States Supreme Court had ruled the execution of an insane individual unconstitutional on the basis of the Eighth Amendment prohibition against cruel and unusual punishment.) He had been treated with antipsychotic medications over the years, and the medication did reduce his psychotic symptomatology. Sometimes, he took medication voluntarily; at other times, he was medicated against his will, with the justification that "he posed a danger to himself and to others" (Liptak, 2003b, p. A27).

In February, 2003, a federal appeals court ruled that Mr. Singleton could be medicated involuntarily to treat his psychosis and reduce his dangerousness to himself and others, even though a major implication of this treatment was that he would be regarded as legally sane and eligible for execution. The Supreme Court has ruled in the past that a convict can be medicated against his will in some circumstances, such as when his behavior puts correctional officers at risk when dealing with the prisoner or the prisoner represents a suicide risk. However, the issue of providing involuntary antipsychotic medication in order to make a prisoner eligible for execution has not been addressed by the Supreme Court.

Is it ethically appropriate for mental health professionals to provide involuntary treatment to Mr. Singleton under these circumstances?

SUMMARY

This chapter addressed the areas in which the mental health professions interface with the legal system. Each state has statutes concerning the rights of hospitalized psychiatric clients, hospital discharge procedures, and the involuntary commitment process. Clients can be hospitalized involuntarily on a temporary, emergency basis. Longer-term commitment requires a judge's order, as does commitment to mandated outpatient treatment. The process of suicide prevention, which often involves hospitalizing clients involuntarily, has proven very controversial because of its inconsistency with mental health professionals' respect for the autonomy of clients. The opposing schools of thought on this issue were presented in detail.

Mental health professionals who specialize in forensic psychology conduct evaluations in connection with civil or criminal legal proceedings. These professionals might evaluate the competency of criminal defendants to stand trial, including those who enter a plea of NGRI. They also might be retained to provide expert testimony in their specialty area (e.g., long-term effects of abuse, accuracy of eyewitness testimony). Forensic clinicians also conduct child protection and child custody evaluations. Expert witnesses should only offer an opinion in a court proceeding when they have valid data to support their statements. In addition, they should explain their role in the evaluation process to those involved (e.g., clients and attorneys).

Mental health professionals occasionally become involved in legal proceedings unintentionally when their client records are subpoenaed. If their client does not want the information presented, they should claim privilege on the client's behalf and attempt to have the subpoena withdrawn.

NOTES

1. Removing irreversibly comatose patients from life support is obviously not relevant to the issue of suicide because they are not capable of making a choice. Arguably, such situations are also not potentially cases of murder because their lives have already really ended. Medical technology can keep people's bodies alive when they are no longer capable of performing any of the functions we associate with living (e.g., interacting, thinking, or feeling). These capacities of living persons are what make the preservation of life so important to humankind. Since these capacities are no longer present, and there is no hope that they will be regained in the future, the person is really already dead (Jamison, 1999).

2. On the other hand, suicide as self-sacrifice, which is intended to preserve the lives of others, may be permissible for Kant.

3. Individuals who combine these two predictors (i.e., have a major psychiatric diagnosis *and* abuse substances) are at particularly elevated risk for violent crime (Eccleston & Ward, 2004).

4. Professionals interested in learning more about assessment methods useful in the prediction of violence can consult the following sources: *Handbook of Forensic Psychology,* edited by W. O'Donohue and E. Levensky, published by Elsevier (2004); and *The Handbook of Forensic Psychology,* edited by A. K. Hess and I. B. Weiner, published by Wiley (1999).

Chapter 14

State Boards, Ethics Committees, and Ethics Complaints

WHEN PROFESSIONALS IDENTIFY UNETHICAL CONDUCT

Informal Resolution

Professionals are collegial, which means that they regard each other as equals and as colleagues. Thus, mental health professionals expect their colleagues to behave as ethical professionals (ACA, 2005, H.2.a; APA, 2002, 1.04). In the spirit of collegiality, if mental health professionals believe that another professional may be violating an ethical principle or standard, their first step should be to informally discuss their concern with the professional involved (ACA, 2005, H.2.b; APA, 2002, 1.04). For example, suppose a psychologist had observed her colleague drinking from a flask in the restroom between therapy sessions and became concerned that her colleague's drinking might be interfering with his competence as a therapist. It would be the psychologist's ethical duty to bring the issue to the colleague's attention. Many ethical violations can be avoided or resolved by an informal discussion in which one professional approaches another in a nonjudgmental manner as a concerned colleague interested in protecting colleagues from placing themselves in professional jeopardy and from potentially harming the people they serve (APA, 2002, 3.04).

At the same time, the psychologist should make it clear that the interests of her colleague's clients and those of the profession will not allow her to ignore a continuation of the behavior. Members of a profession have a duty to uphold the ethical standards of the profession; they are the first line of defense against ethical violations that can cause harm and erode public confidence in the profession. If the psychologist were convinced that she had addressed the issue effectively, she need not take any further action, other than to monitor the situation.

On the other hand, suppose one of the psychologist's clients told her she had observed the other professional's unethical behavior. If the psychologist believed that her colleague would know that the client was the source of the information, the psychologist would have a duty to preserve the client's confidentiality and would not be able to discuss that specific incident with her colleague (ACA, 2005, H.2.b; APA, 2002, 1.04). Suspected ethical violations by a fellow professional do not constitute sufficient grounds to violate anyone's right to confidentiality. The psychologist could look for other evidence of a drinking problem that she could discuss with the colleague. She could also ask the client's permission to discuss her report with the colleague; however, in general, it is not desirable to ask clients to waive their right to confidentiality unless the ethical violation is of an extremely serious nature because clients might feel pressured to agree to the waiver, even if they feel very uncomfortable about doing so.

If professionals' efforts to resolve a colleague's apparent ethical violation informally are not successful, or if the unethical behavior is so severe that it does not lend itself to an informal resolution (e.g., a faculty member was involved in an inappropriate sexual relationship with a student that contributed to the student's suicide attempt), professionals should report the matter to their colleague's state licensing board and to the ethics committee of the colleague's state or national professional organization (ACA, 2005, H.2.c; APA, 2002, 1.05).

In all of these matters, protecting the confidentiality of people reporting possible violations is a major concern. Recipients of professional services (e.g., clients, supervisees, students) who tell a professional about an ethical violation should be encouraged to proceed with a formal complaint. The procedure for filing a complaint should be explained to them, as well as the protections provided to prevent retaliation against them for making a legitimate complaint. Ultimately, though, a state board or an ethics committee must be able to identify and interview a complainant in order to investigate and, if necessary, adjudicate a complaint.

CASE EXAMPLE 14.1

A psychology professor receives a faculty research award. In a newspaper article describing his achievement, he is credited with having authored two books. A departmental colleague reading the article knows that the only two "books" the professor was involved with were his contribution of a chapter to an edited volume (he was not one of the book's editors) and his authorship of a study guide for an online course.

Although she considers the professor's characterization of these achievements to be unethical, she decides not to pursue the matter with him because he might be technically accurate about having been involved in the publication of two "books." Besides, the university's media people might have misrepresented his record to the newspaper.

Dealing With More Serious Unethical Behavior

Serious ethical violations that involve the potential for harm to clients (e.g., a sexual relationship with a client) should not be resolved informally between colleagues. Rather, such violations should be reported to the appropriate ethics committee or state board to make certain that the victim of the abuse receives adequate assistance in resolving the emotional harm produced by the situation and that professionals receive the supervision and rehabilitation needed before being permitted to practice again (ACA, 2005, H.2.c; APA, 2002, 1.05). Professionals' failure to report such serious violations is itself unethical. This type of behavior threatens the trust that the public bestows on mental health professionals because it suggests that professionals are simply covering up for one another (Quadrio, 1994).

In academic settings, a problem sometimes develops in which the people with firsthand knowledge of the ethical violation (e.g., students who were demeaned repeatedly by a faculty member for disagreeing effectively with the professor during class discussions) might be unwilling to file a complaint because they will need to take additional classes from the professor. They might believe they can avoid the problem in the future by never disagreeing with the faculty member, but they might tell another faculty member about the situation in confidence. In such a circumstance, the professional who learns of a colleague's unethical behavior could be guilty of violating the students' confidentiality by filing a complaint on the students' behalf. The professional must try to resolve the confidentiality issue with the students (e.g., by encouraging them to report the unethical instructor's actions to prevent future harm to other students), but if it cannot be resolved, the professional still must not file the complaint (ACA, 2005, H.2.c; APA, 2002, 1.05). The students' wish for the matter to remain confidential has to be given priority.

STATE BOARDS OF PSYCHOLOGY AND COUNSELING

State governments regulate the practice of professions when such regulation is considered to be in the public interest. State boards for psychology and counseling serve as gatekeepers for professions: They assess the academic qualifications of applicants for licensure and administer licensing examinations. They also screen applicants for past or current records of felony convictions, ethics complaints, ethics investigations, judgments affecting their license status, and malpractice lawsuits to make certain that individuals of questionable moral character are not permitted to be licensed as professionals in their state. The state board monitors its licensees' compliance with the ethical code of the profession and state board rules (e.g., annual requirement for continuing education hours). Also, once a professional is licensed in a jurisdiction, the state board is the government agency that will receive, investigate, and adjudicate any ethics complaints brought against the professional. Board members are political appointees; generally, the governor of the state is responsible for selecting them. Most state boards have three types of members: doctoral-level, licensed members of the profession; master's-level, licensed professionals; and public members who are not associated with the profession. As a consequence of being licensed, professionals place themselves under the authority of their state board.

State Board Procedures for Investigating Ethics Complaints

When a client, student, supervisee, fellow professional, or other recipient of professional services files a complaint against a mental health professional, the state board of the profession will initiate an investigation. A complaint may also be referred to the board by the ethics committee of a state or national professional organization. Anonymous complaints are not accepted by state boards. Furthermore, if professionals are convicted of a felony or violation of a law involving moral turpitude, the board will pursue action against them.

Although the procedures used by state boards to investigate ethics complaints vary, complaints are generally prioritized based on the risk of harm to the public represented by the alleged violation (e.g., a client's allegation of therapist sexual abuse would be addressed before a dispute over fees). The board's first step is contacting the complainant to obtain sufficient information to evaluate whether the complaint falls within the jurisdiction of the board. If it does, the professional is then asked to provide a written response to the complaint. This preliminary investigation will result in either a recommendation to dismiss the complaint or, if probable cause exists that a board rule has been violated, referral to a disciplinary panel of the board.

The board's disciplinary panel will conduct any further investigation needed before recommending dismissal of the complaint or sanctions against a professional. The investigation might include an informal hearing to resolve the investigation. Of course, professionals always have the right to contest a complaint more formally and request an adjudicative hearing.

CASE EXAMPLE 14.2

A university student tells the instructor of her counseling methods course that she was sexually abused by her counselor during the previous year. The instructor encourages her to file a formal complaint with the state board, but she asks him to file the complaint, saying she is too uncomfortable about confronting her counselor publicly.

State Board Sanctions for Unethical Conduct

When an ethical complaint is supported adequately by the facts obtained by the state board, the board can impose sanctions, including the following actions: temporary suspension of professional license, license revocation, probation, reprimand (sometimes referred to as a "letter of instruction"), and monetary fine. Any sanction other than revocation of a license can, and usually will, involve rehabilitation in the form of additional continuing education requirements, completion of a professional ethics course, reexamination for licensure, supervision of practice for a period of time, limitations on services the professionals can provide or on classes of clients they can work with, or restrictions on their ability to supervise others.

A finding of guilt has serious implications for professionals' careers. The professionals' national organization (e.g., ACA, APA) is notified and may initiate an ethics investigation. License applications and employment applications (e.g., to work for an MCO) always require that applicants indicate whether any action has been taken against them by a state licensing board. Because employers could be held liable for malpractice by their employees, they are very unlikely to hire a professional with a history of ethics violations. In addition, professionals might have difficulty obtaining malpractice insurance; if an insurer agrees to provide coverage, they will probably have to pay much higher than normal premiums.

Professionals facing serious ethics charges will sometimes choose to resign their license to avoid formal adjudication of a complaint. However, a record of the circumstances of the resignation, like that of sanctions imposed, will follow them if they ever attempt to apply for licensure elsewhere.

CASE EXAMPLE 14.3

A man diagnosed as suffering from Dissociative Identity Disorder initiates treatment with a counselor. During the treatment, a number of alternative personalities ("alters") emerge. It becomes clear to the clinician that these alters are related to episodes of severe physical and sexual abuse that occurred during the client's childhood. She decides to confront these childhood traumas with her client. His condition worsens, and his family files an ethics complaint with the counselor's state board, asserting that the treatment resulted in her client developing Posttraumatic Stress Disorder.

PROFESSIONAL ORGANIZATIONS' ETHICS COMMITTEES

Professional organizations (e.g., APA, ACA) have standing ethics committees that formulate the ethical code of the profession and receive, investigate, and adjudicate complaints of unethical conduct against their members (ACA Ethics Committee, 1997b; APA Ethics Committee, 2002). The ethics committee can also require members to "show cause" why they should not be expelled from membership if a judgment (e.g., license revocation, expulsion from membership, felony conviction) involving a serious ethical infraction has been made against them by a state licensing board, state professional association, or criminal court (APA Ethics Committee, 2002). Finally, the ethics committee also addresses the ethical acceptability of applicants for membership in the organization if the applicants have reported prior or current ethics complaints, investigations, or lawsuits on their membership application (Flescher, 1991).

Ethics Committee Procedures for Investigating Ethical Violations

An ethics committee responds to complaints of professional misconduct filed with them by members of the association or by the general public (ACA Ethics Committee, 1997b; APA Ethics Committee, 2002).[1] Again, complaints cannot be filed anonymously. When the complaint falls within the jurisdiction of the committee (i.e., involves a complaint against a member of the organization), the committee will first determine whether there is sufficient cause for action on the complaint (ACA Ethics Committee, 1997b; APA Ethics Committee, 2002). This determination may require requesting additional information from the complainant. The matter will be closed if the information provided does not constitute sufficient grounds for the committee to investigate (ACA Ethics Committee, 1997b; APA Ethics Committee, 2002).

If, on the other hand, the alleged behavior of the professional constitutes a violation of the ethical code, professionals will be notified of the complaint (ACA Ethics Committee, 1997b; APA Ethics Committee, 2002). They then have 30 days to respond. Professionals are free to consult legal counsel, but must respond to the complaint themselves. If, at the conclusion of this process, cause for action is believed to exist, a formal investigation will be initiated. A letter delineating the charges will be sent to the professional (APA Ethics Committee, 2002). The ethics committee may request professionals to appear before them to provide pertinent information. At the conclusion of the investigation, the ethics committee will make a decision and inform the professional and the complainant of the outcome (ACA Ethics Committee, 1997b; APA Ethics Committee, 2002).

Most Common Types of Ethics Complaints

In 2003, the APA Ethics Committee received a total of 61 ethics complaints, representing a rate of less than 1 complaint for every 1,000 APA members (APA Ethics Committee, 2004).

The most frequent categories of complaint were sexual misconduct with adults and insurance and fee problems, each of which was involved in 32% of the complaints filed. Nonsexual dual relationships were a factor in 16% of complaints, followed by child custody evaluation (4%), test misuse (4%), and hospitalization (4%) complaints (APA Ethics Committee, 2004).[2]

Sanctions for Unethical Conduct

The ethics committees of professional organizations may dismiss the charges for a violation if it is trivial or has already been corrected, although the ethics committee may still send the professional an educative letter concerning the violation. In 2003, APA dismissed 8% of cases arising from ethics complaints (APA Ethics Committee, 2004). For violations not likely to cause harm or seriously damage the profession, the ethics committee can decide to reprimand the professional (APA Ethics Committee, 2002). When a violation is likely to cause harm to another person, but not significant harm, the ethics committee might recommend that the professional be censured or placed on probation by the organization (ACA Ethics Committee, 1997b; APA Ethics Committee, 2002). In 2003, APA recommended reprimand or censure in 58% of cases (APA Ethics Committee, 2004). The ACA Ethics Committee (1997b) has the additional option of suspending a counselor from membership in the organization, generally with remedial requirements that must be completed during the suspension.

The most severe action that a professional organization can take against members who have committed a serious ethical violation is to recommend to its board of directors that they be expelled from the organization or allowed to resign under stipulated conditions (ACA Ethics Committee, 1997b; APA Ethics Committee, 2002).[3] In 2003, 33% of ethics cases investigated by the APA Ethics Committee resulted in recommendations for loss of APA membership (APA Ethics Committee, 2004). In taking this action, the ethics committee can also inform the offender's state board of the complaint and the committee's action (APA Ethics Committee, 2002). The state board may then investigate and take action against the professional's license.

The professional can accept the decision of the ethics committee or request a formal hearing on the charges before a three-member hearing committee, which must include at least two members of the organization (APA Ethics Committee, 2002). The hearing committee will call witnesses, if needed, and then decide whether to accept the recommendation of the ethics committee, alter the sanctions, or dismiss the charges (APA Ethics Committee, 2002).

DEALING APPROPRIATELY WITH A STATE BOARD OR ETHICS COMMITTEE INQUIRY

Mental health professionals have an obligation to cooperate fully with an ethics investigation undertaken by their state board or any duly authorized ethics committee (ACA, 2005, H.3; APA, 2002, 1.06). Although all professionals hope they will never be contacted regarding an ethics inquiry, it is important to know how to handle such an inquiry in an appropriate, professional manner. First, before launching into a defense of their behavior, professionals should make certain that they do not exacerbate the situation by violating the confidentiality of a complainant or anyone else. If professionals receive a phone call from a member of an ethics committee, it would be inappropriate for them to even acknowledge that they know or have treated a client until they receive a written waiver, signed by the complainant, permitting them to disclose information to the committee. Professionals should inform the caller that they would be glad to cooperate in any way they can as soon as they have received the required permission form allowing them to discuss the matter with the committee.

Second, when the nature of the complaint and the formal documentation have been provided, professionals should definitely consult an attorney who is competent and experienced in handling such matters to, at a minimum, review the response they have prepared to the board's inquiry. Professionals who believe they are blameless in the situation should not assume that they do not need expert guidance in preparing their response to the complaint. The investigation and adjudication of ethics complaints are legal matters; attorneys have a great deal more expertise in handling them than most mental health professionals. Finally, professionals should provide relevant documentation to their attorney and, as instructed, to the state board or ethics committee. They certainly should not attempt to create, alter, or destroy records to support their case. If documentation concerning the matter does not exist, simply report that fact.

CASE EXAMPLE 14.4

A psychologist receives a phone call from a person who says she is from his state board. The caller names one of the psychologist's clients and says that the client has filed a complaint against him regarding inappropriate fee charges. The caller goes on to say that she has obtained the permission of the client to discuss the matter with him and that she wants to hear his version of the events in question. He responds by pointing out that the client has received a diagnosis of Borderline Personality Disorder and that she is frequently very manipulative.

The caller then says, "So, you think I'm manipulative? Well, just wait until I play the recording of this conversation for the state board. You've violated my confidentiality, as well as displaying your total contempt for me. You're finished as a therapist, Charlie!"

LEGAL COMPLAINTS AGAINST MENTAL HEALTH PROFESSIONALS

Most legal proceedings brought against the professional conduct of mental health professionals are civil actions (e.g., malpractice suits). However, some circumstances can result in criminal charges against a professional, such as Medicaid or insurance fraud. Also, in some states, sexual relations with a client can result in a felony sexual misconduct charge. These legal proceedings are conducted independently of any ethics committee or state board investigation of professional ethics violations, although it is possible that the records of an ethics investigation could be subpoenaed as part of a civil or criminal case.

As stated earlier, conviction of a felony or a crime involving moral turpitude can also be grounds for sanctions against a professional by a state board or ethics committee. Even if the crime (e.g., bank robbery) has no apparent relation to the individual's professional conduct, the dishonesty and disregard for the law involved in such an act will likely constitute grounds for revocation of the individual's license and expulsion from a professional organization.

AVOIDING DIFFICULTIES BY FUNCTIONING AS AN ETHICAL PROFESSIONAL

Throughout this book, ethical mental health professionals have been shown to combine virtue with knowledge. Ethical professionals want to serve humankind in a positive manner through their teaching, research, and applied work. They respect those they serve as persons and do not exploit them. They feel a responsibility to each individual affected by their work, to their profession, and to society as a whole to provide only the highest quality professional services possible. These virtuous motivations are fundamental to ethical professional practice.

However, behaving ethically as mental health professionals also requires knowledge. Ethical professionals must be familiar with both the ethical code of their profession and the metaethical origins of their professional ethical duties in order to be capable of rationally resolving situations involving apparent conflicts between ethical duties. They must strive to develop competence in ethical reasoning, so they will recognize when a situation involves ethical complexity and can devise a rational, ethically appropriate course of action that gives each relevant ethical consideration the respect it merits. Functioning as an ethical professional is difficult; the "Ethical Principles" states that ethical professionalism requires "a personal commitment and a lifelong effort to act ethically" (APA, 2002, Preamble). Nevertheless, ethical competence is certainly achievable. The model of ethical decision making presented in Chapter 5 will assist professionals in pursuing this goal.

To prevent the occurrence of unethical behavior, ethical professionals always endeavor to address foreseeable ethical issues proactively, at the outset of a professional relationship (Smith, 2003b). They scrupulously avoid engaging in any professional activity outside the range of their competence. Also, they have a sound working knowledge of their professional ethical code. They also know that in many situations an ethical course of action may be prescribed by state board rules; relevant federal, state, and local statutes; or the organizational or institutional policies of their employer.

Ethical professionals are always sensitive to their duty to obtain the informed consent of clients, research participants, and students. They reflect carefully on the informed consent procedure they intend to use to make certain it will be understood by the people they will be working with. They also ensure that they identify and explain any potential risks arising from clients' agreement to interact with them professionally (e.g., the limits of confidentiality). They consider the possibility that some or all of the people with whom they work may not be competent to provide consent and take appropriate steps to avoid exploiting such individuals.

They offer professional services only within their areas of competence, and they openly acknowledge the limitations of their expertise. Ethical professionals work at maintaining a high level of competence and professionalism by pursuing continuing education opportunities. When offering an expert opinion or conducting assessments in forensic settings, ethical professionals are careful to base all their statements on the available data. They make sure that their assessment techniques are appropriate for the issue and the population they are assessing.

Ethical professionals understand the importance of keeping careful, confidential records of their professional activities. They keep records regarding all contacts with clients (e.g., telephone conversations, e-mail exchanges, cancelled sessions, counseling sessions) and contacts concerning clients (e.g., supervision sessions, consultations), with sufficient detail "for continuity in the event that another psychologist takes over delivery of services" (APA Committee on Professional Practice and Standards, 1993, p. 985). Professionals recognize that thorough documentation of their activities can be extremely helpful in resolving complex ethical situations and are a tremendous asset if any aspect of their professional activity is reviewed by an ethics panel. Conscientiously kept records provide reviewers and investigators with information regarding a professional's behavior, attitudes, and professionalism at the time a situation occurred. Although their records are thorough, they do not include irrelevant or outdated information, particularly when the information could harm the client if disclosed (e.g., outdated assessment results; APA Committee on Professional Practice and Standards, 1993). Furthermore, they do not alter records after recording them. They may always elect to append additional material to a record, indicating the date on which the subsequent material was added. In recording personal information about people they serve, professionals are always sensitive to the fact that their records could be reviewed in a legal context (APA Committee on Professional Practice and Standards, 1993). Ethical professionals maintain clear, accurate financial records for all of their professional activities. They discuss fees and billing procedures thoroughly with consumers at the outset of their professional relationship.

Ethical professionals are always aware of the confidential nature of many of their professional activities. They deeply respect the individual's right to privacy and develop positive habits regarding the protection of privacy. When it is unclear whether a communication (e.g., with a student or research participant) qualifies as confidential, they err on the side of caution by not disclosing the information to anyone. An ethical professional is not a gossip.

Whenever ethical professionals are uncertain about the correct ethical response to a particular situation or about the ethicality of a proposed course of action, they realize that an excellent way to avoid ethical missteps is to consult more experienced colleagues, members of the ethics committee of their professional organization (ACA Ethics Committee, 1997a), a competent legal authority, or other resources appropriate to the context.[4] Consultation takes time and is often overlooked because of the time pressure professionals are under in an ethically complex situation to make a decision and *do something,* but ethical professionals always remember that when it comes to sound ethical decision making, haste makes mistakes. They prevent ethical problems from developing by avoiding impulsive action; they take the time needed to reflect on situations outside the range of their everyday professional experience. They do not allow themselves to be pressured into acting without careful forethought.

CASE EXAMPLE 14.5

A clinical psychologist in private practice finishes her last session of the day. She and the client engage in a bit of small talk, and he says he will walk out to the parking lot with her. The statement catches her off guard, but she wants to leave and sees no harm in leaving with him, so she agrees and gathers her belongings. When they get out to the parking lot, they stand by her car and the client asks her about her plans for the weekend. She is a bit uncomfortable with this inquiry about her personal life, but she decides she would appear defensive if she evaded the question, so she says that she'll probably stay at home and catch up on some reading. He touches her arm and suggests that since he has no plans either, maybe they could get together for lunch on Saturday. At this point, she is totally flustered. She does not feel it would be appropriate to get into a discussion of professional boundaries in the parking lot, so she just says that she thinks she will be busy on Saturday and quickly jumps into her car. He says, "Well, I'll give you a call."

She wonders how things got so out of hand so quickly after a very productive session. She also wonders what her client is thinking about the whole conversation and how she should respond if he does call.

Finally, self-awareness is a key aspect of professionalism. Ethical professionals must understand the multicultural subtleties of relationships in order to be sensitive to the ethical dimension present in every aspect of their work (APA, 2003). As discussed throughout this book, they need to be aware of their personal values, so they can identify situations in which their values might affect their perception of and behavior toward those they serve professionally.[5] Self-awareness is also the key to preventing personal problems from impairing professional performance. Ethical professionals recognize that unresolved personal issues can gradually subvert their professional competence and grease the slide into the abyss of burnout or an unethical dual relationship.

Professionals are sensitive to the many warning signs of personal impairment or the early stages of burnout. For example, they might recognize that they no longer look forward to going to work, are not concentrating as well at work, are looking forward more than they reasonably should to seeing particular clients each week, are missing supervision sessions with their employees with increasing frequency, or that their after-work drinking has increased. Each of these scenarios, along with countless others described throughout this book, should be clear indicators to ethical professionals that they are not operating at their normal level of professionalism. Mental health professionals should not assume they are invulnerable to impairment; they need to be able to recognize when they are overextended in their personal and professional life and need to reduce their burden. Resolving personal problems may involve seeking professional help (a very difficult admission for many clinicians, although they think everyone else would benefit from talking to a professional), or perhaps just cutting back on their caseload or taking a vacation. The point is that ethical professionals recognize that taking care of themselves and their own problems are *professional* duties; they cannot function competently as professionals if they fail to attend to the important issues in their personal lives. Remember, competent professionals are aware of both their strengths *and* limitations.

PRACTICE CASE INVOLVING THE MODEL OF ETHICAL DECISION MAKING

A 22-year-old, African American female client consults a counselor for complaints of depression and low self-esteem. During the intake interview, she reveals that she had been in treatment with another counselor in a nearby town for the previous three years. However, when the counselor asks for her permission to contact her previous counselor, she refuses. After some further probing by the counselor, she reveals that she had been involved in a sexual relationship with her former counselor for most of the time she saw him professionally. The counselor had ended the sexual relationship recently, and she had then stopped seeing him for counseling. She suspected that he had become sexually involved with another of his clients because she had seen him at a restaurant with a young woman she had seen and talked to once in his waiting room.

The counselor expresses her dismay about how the client was exploited by her previous counselor and encourages her to file a formal complaint with the state board, so disciplinary action can be taken against him. The client refuses. She says that her husband does not know about the affair, and she does not want him to find out. She also says that she is in love with the counselor and still hopes to reconcile with him. She says that even if they do not get back together, she would never do anything to hurt her former counselor because she had wanted the relationship as much as he did. She again expresses an interest in working with the new counselor on her feelings of depression and her low self-esteem. However, she makes it quite clear that she wants the situation with her former counselor to be kept confidential.

What should the counselor do?

SUMMARY

If a mental health professional is aware of a colleague's unethical behavior, the professional is obligated to try to resolve the issue informally with the colleague. If this attempt fails or the misconduct is too serious for informal resolution, the professional should report the behavior to the applicable state board or professional organization. If a student, supervisee, therapy client, or other person served by a mental health professional indicates knowledge of professional misconduct, this person should be encouraged to file a complaint.

Both state boards for counseling and psychology and national professional organizations (e.g., ACA, APA) are responsible for handling ethics complaints against professionals. If they determine that sufficient cause exists to pursue an investigation, professionals are obligated to cooperate fully. The procedure for handling a complaint was described in this chapter. State board sanctions for misconduct include suspension or revocation of the professional's license to practice, mandatory training, or monetary fine, whereas ethics committees can force a professional to resign from the professional organization.

Ethical professionals are motivated to uphold the standards of their profession by functioning in a competent manner. They value those they serve and show respect for persons' autonomy and right to privacy. Furthermore, ethical professionals strive to attain the knowledge that will allow them to reason ethically. They are familiar with their profession's code of ethics as well as pertinent federal, state, and local laws and regulations. Professionals who are sensitive to their personal values and to the warning signs of impairment will be able to prevent many ethical problems from developing. Finally, ethical professionals do not make decisions without deliberating about them sufficiently. They think through the relevant considerations carefully, gathering information as needed, and use their ethical reasoning skills to resolve ethical dilemmas effectively.

NOTES

1. The procedures described in this section are those adopted by the APA Ethics Committee (2002). The policies of the ACA Ethics Committee (1997b) are very similar and address the same issues.

2. These categories and percentages of ethical violations are roughly comparable to those received by state boards, although a large proportion of the disciplinary actions taken by state boards in recent years concern failure of licensees to meet continuing education requirements. APA does not impose its own continuing education requirement on its members.

3. APA rules prevent a member from resigning during an ethics investigation to ensure that the APA Ethics Committee will retain jurisdiction over the complaint until it has been resolved. However, in

2001, APA created an adjudication option of "stipulated resignation" that, in some circumstances, permits members to resign rather than be expelled from the organization after signing an affidavit acknowledging the validity of an ethics committee judgment against them.

4. Professionals and students can contact the American Psychological Association (APA) via their Web site (http://www.apa.org). The Web address for the American Counseling Association (ACA) is http://www.counseling.org. Both sites provide extensive information regarding ethical issues, including contact information for the organization's ethics committee.

5. A self-study program, like the one described in Chapter 11 (Vachon & Agresti, 1992), can assist professionals in this process.

References

AAAPP declares its own "war on drugs." (1995, March). *The Scientist Practitioner, 4*(3), 2–5.

Academy of Management. (2003). *Code of ethical conduct.* Retrieved June 16, 2004, from http://myaom.pace.edu/octane8admin/websites/ProfessionalDevelopment/default.asp?id=126

Acker, G. M. (1999). The impact of clients' mental illness on social workers' job satisfaction and burnout. *Health and Social Work, 24,* 112–119.

Adair, J. G., Dushenko, T. W., & Lindsay, R. C. L. (1985). Ethical regulations and their impact on research practice. *American Psychologist, 40,* 59–72.

Aiken, L. S., West, S. G., Sechrest, L., Reno, R. R., Roediger, H. L., III, Scarr, S., et al. (1990). Graduate training in statistics, methodology, and measurement in psychology: A survey of PhD programs in North America. *American Psychologist, 45,* 721–734.

Allard, G., Butler, J., Faust, D., & Shea, M. T. (1995). Errors in hand scoring objective personality tests: The case of the Personality Diagnostic Questionnaire—Revised (PDQ-R). *Professional Psychology: Research and Practice, 26,* 304–308.

Allen, M., D'Alessio, D., Emmers, T. M., & Gebhardt, L. (1996). The role of educational briefings in mitigating effects of experimental exposure to violent sexually explicit material: A meta-analysis. *Journal of Sex Research, 33,* 135–141.

Ambrose, P. A., Jr. (1997). Challenges for mental health service providers: The perspective of managed care organizations. In J. N. Butcher (Ed.), *Personality assessment in managed health care: Using the MMPI-2 in treatment planning* (pp. 61–72). New York: Oxford University Press.

American Association for Marriage and Family Therapy. (1991). *AAMFT code of ethics.* Washington, DC: Author.

American Counseling Association. (1995). *Code of ethics and standards of practice.* Alexandria, VA: Author.

American Counseling Association. (1999). *Ethical standards for Internet online counseling.* Alexandria, VA: Author.

American Counseling Association (in cooperation with the Association for Assessment in Counseling). (2003). *Responsibilities of users of standardized tests* (3rd ed.). Alexandria, VA: Author.

American Counseling Association. (2005). *Code of ethics.* Alexandria, VA: Author.

American Counseling Association Ethics Committee. (1997a). *Policies and procedures for responding to members' requests for interpretations of the ethical standards.* Alexandria, VA: American Counseling Association.

American Counseling Association Ethics Committee. (1997b). *Policies and procedures for processing complaints of ethical violations.* Alexandria, VA: American Counseling Association.

American Educational Research Association, American Psychological Association, & National Council on Measurement in Education. (1999). *Standards for educational and psychological testing.* Washington, DC: American Educational Research Association.

American Psychiatric Association. (2000). *Diagnostic and statistical manual of mental disorders (DSM-IV-TR)* (4th ed., Text Revision). Washington, DC: Author.

American Psychiatric Association. (2003). *The principles of medical ethics, with annotations especially applicable to psychiatry.* Washington, DC: Author.

American Psychological Association. (1952). Discussion on ethics. *American Psychologist, 7,* 425–455.

American Psychological Association. (1953). *Ethical standards of psychologists.* Washington, DC: Author.

American Psychological Association. (1958). Standards of ethical behavior for psychologists. *American Psychologist, 13,* 268–271.

American Psychological Association. (1963). Ethical standards of psychologists. *American Psychologist, 18,* 56–60.

American Psychological Association. (1968). Ethical standards of psychologists. *American Psychologist, 23,* 357–361.

American Psychological Association. (1979). *Ethical standards of psychologists.* Washington, DC: Author.

American Psychological Association. (1981a). Ethical principles of psychologists. *American Psychologist, 36,* 633–638.

American Psychological Association. (1981b). Specialty guidelines for the delivery of services by clinical psychologists, counseling psychologists, industrial/organizational psychologists, and school psychologists. *American Psychologist, 36,* 639–681.

American Psychological Association. (1987). General guidelines for providers of psychological services. *American Psychologist, 42,* 712–723.

American Psychological Association. (1990). Ethical principles of psychologists (Amended June 2, 1989). *American Psychologist, 45,* 390–395.

American Psychological Association. (1992). Ethical principles of psychologists and code of conduct. *American Psychologist, 47,* 1597–1611.

American Psychological Association. (1993). Guidelines for providers of psychological services to ethnic, linguistic, and culturally diverse populations. *American Psychologist, 48,* 45–48.

American Psychological Association. (1994). Guidelines for child custody evaluations in divorce proceedings. *American Psychologist, 49,* 677–680.

American Psychological Association. (2001). *Publication manual of the American Psychological Association* (5th ed.). Washington, DC: Author.

American Psychological Association. (2002). Ethical principles of psychologists and code of conduct. *American Psychologist, 57,* 1060–1073.

American Psychological Association. (2003). Guidelines on multicultural education, training, research, practice, and organizational change for psychologists. *American Psychologist, 58,* 377–402.

American Psychological Association, Committee for the Protection of Human Participants in Research. (1982). *Ethical principles in the conduct of research with human participants.* Washington, DC: Author.

American Psychological Association, Committee on Animal Research and Ethics. (1993). *Guidelines for ethical conduct in the care and use of animals.* Washington, DC: Author.

American Psychological Association, Committee on Ethical Standards of Psychologists. (1958). Standards of ethical behavior for psychologists: Report of the committee on ethical standards of psychologists. *American Psychologist, 13,* 266–267.

American Psychological Association, Committee on Professional Practice and Standards. (1993). Record keeping guidelines. *American Psychologist, 48,* 984–986.

American Psychological Association, Committee on Professional Practice and Standards. (1998). *Guidelines for psychological evaluations in child protection matters.* Washington, DC: Author.

American Psychological Association, Committee on Subdoctoral Education, Education and Training Board. (1955). The training of technical workers in psychology at the subdoctoral level. *American Psychologist, 10,* 541–545.

American Psychological Association Ethics Committee. (1997). APA statement concerning services by telephone, teleconferencing, and Internet. Retrieved January 30, 2004, from http://www.apa.org/ethics/stmnt01.html

American Psychological Association Ethics Committee. (2002). Rules and procedures. *American Psychologist, 57,* 626–645.

American Psychological Association Ethics Committee. (2004). Report of the ethics committee, 2003. *American Psychologist, 59,* 434–441.

American Psychological Association, Research Office. (2000). *2000 APA directory survey.* Retrieved December 2, 2004, from http://research.apa.org/2000membershipt4.pdf

Americans With Disabilities Act of 1990, 42 U.S.C.A. § 1201 *et seq.* (West 1993).

Anderson, B. S. (1996). *The counselor and the law* (4th ed.). Alexandria, VA: American Counseling Association.

Anderson, T., & Kanuka, H. (2003). *E-research: Methods, strategies, and issues.* Boston: Allyn & Bacon.

Animal Welfare Act of 1966, 7 U.S.C. § 2131 *et seq.* (West 1994).

Appelbaum, P. S., & Rosenbaum, A. (1989). Tarasoff and the researcher: Does the duty to protect apply in the research setting? *American Psychologist, 44,* 885–894.

Applied Research Ethics National Association, & Office of Laboratory Animal Welfare. (2002). *Institutional animal care and use committee guidebook* (2nd ed.). Bethesda, MD: National Institutes of Health.

Arango, C., Calcedo Barba, A., Gonzalez-Salvador, T., & Calcedo Ordonez, A. (1999). Violence in inpatients with schizophrenia: A prospective study. *Schizophrenia Bulletin, 25,* 493–503.

Areen, J. (1992). Legal constraints on social research with children. In B. Stanley & J. E. Sieber (Eds.), *Social research on children and adolescents: Ethical issues* (pp. 7–28). Newbury Park, CA: Sage.

Aristotle. (1947). Nicomachean ethics (W. D. Ross, Trans.). In R. McKeon (Ed.), *Introduction to Aristotle* (pp. 300–543). New York: Modern Library.

Arizmendi, T. G., Beutler, L. E., Shanfield, S. B., Crago, M., & Hagaman, R. (1985). Client-therapist value similarity and psychotherapy outcome: A microscopic analysis. *Psychotherapy: Theory, Research, and Practice, 22,* 16–21.

Aronow, H. A. (1993, May). Sex between HIV+ partners: What are the options? *Being Alive, 3,* 13.

Arthur, G. L., Jr., & Swanson, C. D. (1993). *The ACA legal series: Vol. 6. Confidentiality and privileged communication* (T. P. Remley, Jr., Series Ed.). Alexandria, VA: American Counseling Association.

Association for Counselor Education. (1990). Standards for counseling supervisors. *Journal of Counseling and Development, 69,* 30–32.

Ax, R. K., Forbes, M. R., & Thompson, D. D. (1997). Prescription privileges for psychologists: A survey of predoctoral interns and directors of training. *Professional Psychology: Research and Practice, 28,* 509–514.

Bailey, G. R., Jr. (1998). Ethical and professional considerations in child custody evaluations. *Journal of Psychological Practice, 4,* 1–19.

Barak, A. (1999). Psychological applications on the Internet: A discipline on the threshold of a new millennium. *Applied and Preventive Psychology, 8,* 231–245.

Barlow, D. H., Gorman, J. M., Shear, M. K., & Woods, S. W. (2000). Cognitive-behavioral therapy, imipramine, or their combination for panic disorder: A randomized controlled trial. *Journal of the American Medical Association, 283,* 2529–2536.

Barnes, J. E. (2000, March 23). Insanity defense fails for man who threw woman onto track. *The New York Times,* pp. A1, A29.

Bartol, C. R., & Bartol, A. M. (1999). History of forensic psychology. In A. K. Hess & I. B. Weiner (Eds.), *The handbook of forensic psychology* (2nd ed., pp. 3–23). New York: Wiley.

Battin, M. P. (1999). Can suicide be rational? Yes, sometimes. In J. L. Werth, Jr. (Ed.), *Contemporary perspectives on rational suicide* (pp. 13–21). Philadelphia: Brunner/Mazel.

Baumrind, D. (1990). Doing good well. In I. E. Sigel (Series Ed.), C. B. Fisher, & W. W. Tryon (Vol. Eds.), *Annual advances in applied developmental psychology: Vol. 4. Ethics in applied developmental psychology: Emerging issues in an emerging field* (pp. 17–28). Norwood, NJ: Ablex.

Beauchamp, T. L., & Childress, J. F. (1979). *Principles of biomedical ethics.* Oxford: Oxford University Press.

Beck, A. T., Steer, R. A., & Brown, G. K. (1996). *BDI-II manual.* San Antonio, TX: The Psychological Corporation.

Beecher, H. K. (1970). *Research and the individual: Human studies.* Boston: Little, Brown.

Belar, C. D. (1997). Psychological assessment in capitated care: Challenges and opportunities. In J. N. Butcher (Ed.), *Personality assessment in managed health care: Using the MMPI-2 in treatment planning* (pp. 73–80). New York: Oxford University Press.

Bell, D. (1999). Ethical issues in the prevention of suicide in prison. *Australian and New Zealand Journal of Psychiatry, 33,* 723–728.

The Belmont Report: Ethical Principles and Guidelines for the Protection of Human Subjects of Research, 44 Fed. Reg. 23192 (1979).

Bentham, J. (1948). An introduction to the principles of morals and legislation. In W. Harrison (Ed.), *A fragment on government and an introduction to the principles of morals and legislation* (pp. 113–435). Oxford: Basil Blackwell. (Original work published 1789)

Bergin, A. E. (1980). Psychotherapy and religious values. *Journal of Consulting and Clinical Psychology, 48,* 95–105.

Bergin, A. E. (1991). Values and religious issues in psychotherapy and mental health. *American Psychologist, 46,* 394–403.

Bergin, A. E., Payne, I. R., & Richards, P. S. (1996). Values in psychotherapy. In E. P. Shafranske (Ed.), *Religion and the clinical practice of psychology* (pp. 297–325). Washington, DC: American Psychological Association.

Bersoff, D. M. (2003a). Ethics codes and how they are enforced. In D. M. Bersoff (Ed.), *Ethical conflicts in psychology* (3rd ed., pp. 1–2). Washington, DC: American Psychological Association.

Bersoff, D. M. (2003b). HIPAA: Federal regulations of healthcare records. In D. M. Bersoff (Ed.), *Ethical conflicts in psychology* (3rd ed., pp. 526–528). Washington, DC: American Psychological Association.

Bersoff, D. M., & Bersoff, D. N. (1999). Ethical perspectives in clinical research. In P. C. Kendall, J. N. Butcher, & G. N. Holmbeck (Eds.), *Handbook of research methods in clinical psychology* (2nd ed., pp. 31–53). New York: Wiley.

Beutler, L. E., Pollack, S., & Jobe, A. (1978). "Acceptance," values, and therapeutic change. *Journal of Consulting and Clinical Psychology, 46,* 198–199.

Blanck, P. D., Bellack, A. S., Rosnow, R. L., Rotheram-Borus, M. J., & Schooler, N. R. (1992). Scientific rewards and conflicts of ethical choices in human subjects research. *American Psychologist, 47,* 959–965.

Blevins-Knabe, B. (1992). The ethics of dual relationships in higher education. *Ethics and Behavior, 2,* 151–163.

Bloom, J. W. (1998). The ethical practice of WebCounseling. *British Journal of Guidance and Counselling, 26,* 53–59.

Bodenheimer, T. (1997). The Oregon health plan: Lessons for the nation. *New England Journal of Medicine, 337,* 720–723.

Bonanno, G. A., Znoj, H., Siddique, H. I., & Horowitz, M. J. (1999). Verbal-autonomic dissociation and adaptation to midlife conjugal loss: A follow-up at 25 months. *Cognitive Therapy and Research, 23,* 605–624.

Boothby, J. L., & Clements, C. B. (2000). A national survey of correctional psychologists. *Criminal Justice and Behavior, 27,* 716–732.

Borum, R., & Fulero, S. M. (1999). Empirical research on the insanity defense and attempted reforms: Evidence toward informed policy. *Law and Human Behavior, 23,* 375–394.

Brandt, R. B. (1959). *Ethical theory: The problems of normative and critical ethics.* Englewood Cliffs, NJ: Prentice-Hall.

Bridwell, A. M., & Ford, G. G. (1996). Interpersonal variables affecting attributions of defensiveness. *Current Psychology, 15,* 137–146.

Briere, J. N., & Elliott, D. M. (1994). Immediate and long-term impacts of child sexual abuse. *The Future of Children, 4,* 54–69.

Brill, C. K. (2001). Looking at the social work profession through the eye of the NASW Code of Ethics. *Research on Social Work Practice, 11,* 223–234.

Brogdon, M. G., Sr., Adams, J. H., & Bahri, R. (2004). Psychology and the law. In W. T. O'Donohue & E. R. Levensky (Eds.), *Handbook of forensic psychology: Resource for mental health and legal professionals* (pp. 3–26). San Diego, CA: Elsevier.

Brown, F. (1982). The ethics of psychodiagnostic assessment. In M. Rosenbaum (Ed.), *Ethics and values in psychotherapy* (pp. 96–106). New York: Free Press.

Brown, J., Cohen, P., Johnson, J. G., & Smailes, E. M. (1999). Childhood abuse and neglect: Specificity and effects on adolescent and young adult depression and suicidality. *Journal of the American Academy of Child and Adolescent Psychiatry, 38,* 1490–1496.

Brunswig, K. A., & Parham, R. W. (2004). Psychology in a secure setting. In W. T. O'Donohue & E. R. Levensky (Eds.), *Handbook of forensic psychology: Resource for mental health and legal professionals* (pp. 851–871). San Diego, CA: Elsevier.

Bryan, L. A. (2001). Neither mask nor mirror: One therapist's journey to ethically integrate feminist family therapy and multiculturalism. *Journal of Feminist Family Therapy, 12,* 105–121.

Buchanan, T. (2002). Online assessment: Desirable or dangerous? *Professional Psychology: Research and Practice, 33,* 148–154.

Bussell, D. A. (1994). Ethical issues in observational family research. *Family Process, 33,* 361–376.

Butcher, J. N. (1997a). Assessment and treatment in the era of managed care. In J. N. Butcher (Ed.), *Personality assessment in managed health care: Using the MMPI-2 in treatment planning* (pp. 3–12). New York: Oxford University Press.

Butcher, J. N. (1997b). Use of computer-based personality test reports in treatment planning. In J. N. Butcher (Ed.), *Personality assessment in managed health care: Using the MMPI-2 in treatment planning* (pp. 153–172). New York: Oxford University Press.

Butcher, J. N., Graham, J. R., Ben-Porath, Y. S., Tellegen, A., Dahlstrom, W. G., & Kaemmer, B. (2001). *MMPI-2 (Minnesota Multiphasic Personality Inventory-2): Manual for administration, scoring, and interpretation* (Rev. ed.). Minneapolis: University of Minnesota Press.

Butler, J. (1950). *Five sermons preached at the Rolls Chapel and a dissertation upon the nature of virtue.* Indianapolis, IN: Bobbs-Merrill. (Original work published 1726)

Butterfield, F. (2003, October 22). Study finds hundreds of thousands of inmates mentally ill. *The New York Times,* p. A16.

Camara, W. J., & Schneider, D. L. (1994). Integrity tests: Facts and unresolved issues. *American Psychologist, 49,* 112–119.

Carroll, J. S. (1991). Consent to mental health treatment: A theoretical analysis of coercion, freedom, and control. *Behavioral Sciences and the Law, 9,* 129–142.

Carson, R. C. (1990). Assessment: What role the assessor? *Journal of Personality Assessment, 54,* 435–445.

Carson, R. C., Butcher, J. N., & Mineka, S. (2000). *Abnormal psychology and modern life* (11th ed.). Boston: Allyn & Bacon.

Catalano, S. (1997). The challenges of clinical practice in small or rural communities: Case studies in managing dual relationships in and outside of therapy. *Journal of Contemporary Psychotherapy, 27,* 23–35.

Center, C., Davis, M., Detre, T., Ford, D. E., Hansbrough, W., Hendin, H., et al. (2003). Confronting depression and suicide in physicians: A consensus statement. *Journal of the American Medical Association, 289,* 3161–3166.

Chafetz, M. D., & Buelow, G. (1994). A training model for psychologists with prescription privileges: Clinical pharmacopsychologists. *Professional Psychology: Research and Practice, 25,* 149–153.

Chenneville, T. (2000). HIV, confidentiality, and duty to protect: A decision-making model. *Professional Psychology: Research and Practice, 31,* 661–670.

Cirincione, C., & Jacobs, C. (1999). Identifying insanity acquittals: Is it any easier? *Law and Human Behavior, 23,* 487–497.

Clarkin, J. F., & Levy, K. N. (2004). The influence of client variables on psychotherapy. In M. J. Lambert (Ed.), *Bergin and Garfield's handbook of psychotherapy and behavior change* (5th ed., pp. 194–226). New York: Wiley.

Cohen, E. D., & Cohen, G. S. (1999). *The virtuous therapist: Ethical practice of counseling & psychotherapy.* Belmont, CA: Wadsworth.

Cohen, R. (2001, April 12). Horror expressed in Germany over Dutch euthanasia. *The New York Times,* p. A6.

Colburn, D. (2001, March 11). Assisted suicide law gave a dying woman in Oregon the freedom to determine . . . 'It's time.' *Staten Island Sunday Advance,* p. A12.

Committee on Ethical Guidelines for Forensic Psychologists. (1991). Specialty guidelines for forensic psychologists. *Law and Human Behavior, 15,* 655–665.

Conger, J. J. (1976). Proceedings of the American Psychological Association, Incorporated, for the year 1975: Minutes of the annual meeting of the Council of Representatives, August 29 and September 2, 1975, Chicago, Illinois, and January 23–25, 1976, Washington, DC. *American Psychologist, 31,* 406–434.

Conroy, M. A. (2003, Fall). Evaluating competence to stand trial: The rules have changed. *Texas Psychologist, 54*(3), 26–27.

Cook-Deegan, R. M. (2000). Protecting the vulnerable in brain research. *Cerebrum: The Dana Forum on Brain Science, 2*(2), 73–91.

Cottone, R. R., Mannis, J., & Lewis, T. (1996). Uncovering secret extramarital affairs in marriage counseling. *The Family Journal, 4,* 109–115.

Cottone, R. R., & Tarvydas, V. M. (2003). *Ethical and professional issues in counseling* (2nd ed.). Upper Saddle River, NJ: Merrill Prentice Hall.

Croxton, T. A., Churchill, S. R., & Fellin, P. (1988). Counseling minors without parental consent. *Child Welfare, 67,* 3–14.

Cutler, D. L., McFarland, B. H., & Winthrop, K. (1998). Mental health in the Oregon health plan: Fragmentation or integration? *Administration and Policy in Mental Health, 25,* 361–386.

Daubert v. Merrell Dow Pharmaceuticals, Inc., 113 S. Ct. 2786, 509 U.S. 579 (1993).

DeAngelis, T. (1993, March). Practitioner advertising affected by FTC order. *APA Monitor,* p. 7.

Delano, S. J., & Zucker, J. L. (1994). Protecting mental health research subjects without prohibiting progress. *Hospital and Community Psychology, 45,* 601–603.

deMayo, R. A. (2002). Academic interests and experiences of doctoral students in clinical psychology: Implications for prescription privilege training. *Professional Psychology: Research and Practice, 33,* 499–501.

Devine, P. E. (1990). On choosing death. In J. Donnelly (Ed.), *Suicide: Right or wrong?* (pp. 201–205). Buffalo, NY: Prometheus Books.

Dewey, J. (1930). *Human nature and conduct.* New York: Modern Library.

Dixon v. Weinberger, 405 F. Supp. 974 (D.C. 1975).

Downey, R. G., Sinnett, E. R., & Seeberger, W. (1998). The changing face of MMPI practice. *Psychological Reports, 83,* 1267–1272.

Downs, A. M., & De Vincenzi, I. (1996). Probability of heterosexual transmission of HIV: Relationship to the number of unprotected sexual contacts. *Journal of Acquired Immune Deficiency Syndromes and Human Retrovirology, 11,* 388–395.

Draine, J. (1997). Conceptualizing services research on outpatient commitment. *Journal of Mental Health Administration, 24,* 306–315.

Dubin, S. S. (1972). Obsolescence or lifelong education: A choice for the professional. *American Psychologist, 27,* 486–496.

Durham v. United States, 214 F.2d 862 (1954).

Eccleston, L., & Ward, T. (2004). Assessment of dangerousness and criminal responsibility. In W. T. O'Donohue & E. R. Levensky (Eds.), *Handbook of forensic psychology: Resource for mental health and legal professionals* (pp. 85–101). San Diego, CA: Elsevier.

Epley, N., & Huff, C. (1998). Suspicion, affective response, and educational benefit as a result of deception in psychology research. *Personality and Social Psychology Bulletin, 24,* 759–768.

Ethics Committee statement on military and confidentiality. (1993, September). *APA Monitor,* p. 51.

Exner, J. E., Jr. (1993). *The Rorschach: A comprehensive system. Vol. 1. Basic Foundations* (3rd ed.). New York: Wiley.

Eysenck, H. J. (1952). The effects of psychotherapy: An evaluation. *Journal of Consulting Psychology, 16,* 319–324.

Fairbairn, G. J. (1995). *Contemplating suicide: The language and ethics of self harm.* London, UK: Routledge.

Family Educational Rights and Privacy Act, 20 U.S.C. § 1232g (1974).

Farrenkopf, T., & Bryan, J. (1999). Psychological consultation under Oregon's 1994 Death With Dignity Act: Ethics and procedures. *Professional Psychology: Research and Practice, 30,* 245–249.

Faust, D., & Ziskin, J. (1988, July 1). The expert witness in psychology and psychiatry. *Science, 241,* 31–35.

Fellows, L. K. (1998). Competency and consent in dementia. *Journal of the American Geriatrics Society, 46,* 922–926.

Findholt, N., & Robrecht, L. C. (2002). Legal and ethical considerations in research with sexually active adolescents: The requirement to report statutory rape. *Perspectives on Sexual and Reproductive Health, 34,* 259–264.

Fine, M. A., & Kurdek, L. A. (1993). Reflections on determining authorship credit and authorship order on faculty-student collaborations. *American Psychologist, 48,* 1141–1147.

Fischer, L., & Sorenson, G. P. (1996). *School law for counselors, psychologists, and social workers* (3rd ed.). White Plains, NY: Longman.

Fisher, C. B. (2003). *Decoding the ethics code: A practical guide for psychologists.* Thousand Oaks, CA: Sage.

Fisher, C. B., & Fried, A. L. (2003). Internet-mediated psychological services and the American Psychological Association ethics code. *Psychotherapy: Theory, Research, Practice, Training, 40,* 103–111.

Fisher, C. B., & Fyrberg, D. (1994). Participant partners: College students weigh the costs and benefits of deceptive research. *American Psychologist, 49,* 417–427.

Fisher, C. B., Hoagwood, K., Boyce, C., Duster, T., Frank, D. A., Grisso, T., et al. (2002). Research ethics for mental health science involving ethnic minority children and youths. *American Psychologist, 57,* 1024–1040.

Fisher, C. B., & Rosendahl, S. A. (1990). Psychological risks and remedies of research participation. In I. E. Sigel (Series Ed.), C. B. Fisher & W. W. Tryon (Vol. Eds.), *Annual advances in applied developmental psychology: Vol. 4. Ethics in applied developmental psychology: Emerging issues in an emerging field* (pp. 43–59). Norwood, NJ: Ablex.

Flescher, I. (1991). Ethical implications in screening for ethics violations *Ethics and Behavior, 1,* 259–271.

Fletcher, J. (1966). *Situation ethics: The new morality.* Philadelphia: Westminster Press.

Ford, G. G. (1996). An existential model for promoting life change: Confronting the disease concept. *Journal of Substance Abuse Treatment, 13,* 151–158.

Ford, G. G. (2001). *Ethical reasoning in the mental health professions.* Boca Raton, FL: CRC Press.

Frankl, V. E. (1963). *Man's search for meaning.* New York: Washington Square Press.

Freud, S. (1961). The ego and the id. In J. Strachey (Ed. and Trans.), *The standard edition of the complete psychological works of Sigmund Freud* (Vol. 19, pp. 3–66). London: Hogarth Press. (Original work published 1923)

Frye v. United States, 54 App. D.C. 46, 47, 293 F. 1013, 1014 (1923).

Gabbard, G. O. (1994). Reconsidering the American Psychological Association's policy on sex with former patients: Is it justifiable? *Professional Psychology: Research and Practice, 25,* 329–335.

Galassi, J. P. (1991). Issues in clinical-analogue research versus issues in research compliance. *Psychological Reports, 69,* 82.

Ganzini, L., Fenn, D. S., Lee, M. A., Heintz, R. T., & Bloom, J. D. (1996). Attitudes of Oregon psychiatrists toward physician-assisted suicide. *American Journal of Psychiatry, 153,* 1469–1475.

Ganzini, L., Goy, E. R., Miller, L. L., Harvath, T. A., Jackson, A., & Delorit, M. A. (2003). Nurses' experience with hospice patients who refuse food and fluids to hasten death. *New England Journal of Medicine, 349,* 359–365.

Garb, H. N. (1998). *Studying the clinician: Judgment research and psychological assessment.* Washington, DC: American Psychological Association.

Geisinger, K. F. (1994). Cross-cultural normative assessment: Translation and adaptation issues influencing the normative interpretation of assessment instruments. *Psychological Assessment, 6,* 304–312.

Geisinger, K. F. (1998). Psychometric issues in test interpretation. In J. Sandoval, C. L. Frisby, K. F. Geisinger, J. D. Scheuneman, & J. R. Grenier (Eds.), *Test interpretation and diversity: Achieving equity in assessment* (pp. 17–30). Washington, DC: American Psychological Association.

Geisinger, K. F., Boodoo, G., & Noble, J. P. (2002). The psychometrics of testing individuals with disabilities. In R. B. Ekstrom & D. K. Smith (Eds.), *Assessing individuals with disabilities* (pp. 33–42). Washington, DC: American Psychological Association.

Geisinger, K. F., & Carlson, J. F. (1998). Training psychologists to assess members of a diverse society. In J. Sandoval, C. L. Frisby, K. F. Geisinger, J. D. Scheuneman, & J. R. Grenier (Eds.), *Test interpretation and diversity: Achieving equity in assessment* (pp. 375–386). Washington, DC: American Psychological Association.

Gergen, K. J. (1990). Therapeutic professions and the diffusion of deficit. *Journal of Mind and Behavior, 11,* 353–367.

Ginzburg, K., Solomon, Z., & Bleich, A. (2002). Repressive coping style, acute stress disorder, and posttraumatic stress disorder after myocardial infarction. *Psychosomatic Medicine, 64,* 748–757.

Gist, R., & Lubin, B. (Eds.). (1999). *Response to disaster: Psychosocial, community, and ecological approaches.* Philadelphia: Brunner.

Glancy, G. D., Regehr, C., & Bryant, A. G. (1998). Confidentiality in crisis: Part II—Confidentiality of treatment records. *Canadian Journal of Psychiatry, 43,* 1006–1011.

Glass, T. A. (1998). Ethical issues in group therapy. In R. M. Anderson, Jr., T. L. Needels, & H. V. Hall (Eds.), *Avoiding ethical misconduct in psychology specialty areas* (pp. 95–126). Springfield, IL: Charles C Thomas.

Gluck, J. P., & Kubacki, S. R. (1991). Animals in biomedical research: The undermining effect of the rhetoric of the besieged. *Ethics and Behavior, 1,* 157–173.

Glueckhauf, R. L., Pickett, T. C., Ketterson, T. U., Loomis, J. S., & Rozensky, R. H. (2003). Preparation for the delivery of telehealth services: A self-study framework for expansion of practice. *Professional Psychology: Research and Practice, 34,* 159–163.

Golann, S. E. (1970). Ethical standards for psychology: Development and revision, 1938–1968. *Annals of the New York Academy of Sciences, 169,* 398–405.

Goldblatt, M. J. (1999). Rational suicide: A psychiatrist against. In J. L. Werth, Jr. (Ed.), *Contemporary perspectives on rational suicide* (pp. 114–120). Philadelphia: Brunner/Mazel.

Golding, S. L., Skeem, J. L., Roesch, R., & Zapf, P. A. (1999). The assessment of criminal responsibility: Current controversies. In A. K. Hess & I. B. Weiner (Eds.), *The handbook of forensic psychology* (2nd ed., pp. 379–408). New York: Wiley.

Goode, E. (2002, March 26). Psychologists get prescription pads and furor erupts. *The New York Times,* pp. F1, F4.

Gottesman, I. I., & Prescott, C. A. (1989). Abuses of the MacAndrew MMPI Alcoholism Scale: A critical review. *Clinical Psychology Review, 9,* 223–242.

Grant, B. F. (1997). Prevalence and correlates of alcohol use and DSM-IV alcohol dependence in the United States: Results of the National Longitudinal Alcohol Epidemiologic Survey. *Journal of Studies on Alcohol, 58,* 464–473.

Grimm, D. W. (1994). Therapist spiritual and religious values in psychotherapy. *Counseling and Values, 38,* 154–164.

Grisso, T. (1992). Minors' assent to behavioral research without parental consent. In B. Stanley & J. E. Sieber (Eds.), *Social research on children and adolescents: Ethical issues* (pp. 109–127). Newbury Park, CA: Sage.

Grisso, T. (1996). Voluntary consent to research participation in the institutional context. In B. H. Stanley, J. E. Sieber, & G. B. Melton (Eds.), *Research ethics: A psychological approach* (pp. 203–224). Lincoln: University of Nebraska Press.

Gustafson, K. E., & McNamara, J. R. (1987). Confidentiality with minor clients: Issues and guidelines for therapists. *Professional Psychology: Research and Practice, 18,* 503–508.

Gustafson, K. E., McNamara, J. R., & Jensen, J. A. (1994). Parents' informed consent decisions regarding psychotherapy for their children: Consideration of therapeutic risks and benefits. *Professional Psychology: Research and Practice, 25,* 16–22.

Guthrie, R. V. (1998). *Even the rat was white: A historical view of psychology* (2nd ed.). Boston: Allyn & Bacon.

Haas, L. J., Malouf, J. L., & Mayerson, N. H. (1986). Ethical dilemmas in psychological practice: Results of a national survey. *Professional Psychology: Research and Practice, 17,* 316–321.

Hagen, M. A. (1997). *Whores of the court: The fraud of psychiatric testimony and the rape of American justice.* New York: HarperCollins.

Hall, C. C. I. (1997). Cultural malpractice: The growing obsolescence of psychology with the changing U.S. population. *American Psychologist, 52,* 642–651.

Hammond, O. W. (1998). Ethical considerations in program evaluation. In R. M. Anderson, Jr., T. L. Needels, & H. V. Hall (Eds.), *Avoiding ethical misconduct in psychology specialty areas* (pp. 142–153). Springfield, IL: Charles C. Thomas.

Hargrove, D. S. (1991). Training Ph.D. psychologists for rural service: A report from Nebraska. *Community Mental Health Journal, 27,* 293–298.

Hayes, S. C., & Chang, G. (2002). Invasion of the body snatchers: Prescription privileges, professional schools, and the drive to create a new behavioral health profession. *Clinical Psychology: Science and Practice, 9,* 264–269.

Health Insurance Portability and Accountability Act of 1996, Pub. L. No. 104–191, 110 Stat. 1936 (1997).

Heiby, E. M. (2002). Concluding remarks on the debate about prescription privileges for psychologists. *Journal of Clinical Psychology, 58,* 709–722.

Heinlen, K. T., Welfel, E. R., Richmond, E. N., & O'Donnell, M. S. (2003). The nature, scope, and ethics of psychologists' e-therapy Web sites: What consumers find when surfing the Web. *Psychotherapy: Theory, Research, Practice, Training, 40,* 112–124.

Heinlen, K. T., Welfel, E. R., Richmond, E. N., & Rak, C. F. (2003). The scope of WebCounseling: A survey of services and compliance with NBCC S*tandards for the Ethical Practice of WebCounseling. Journal of Counseling and Development, 81,* 61–69.

Helms, J. E. (2003). A pragmatic view of social justice. *The Counseling Psychologist, 31,* 305–313.

Helms, J. E., Malone, L. S., Henze, K., Satiani, A., Perry, J., & Warren, A. (2003). First annual diversity challenge: "How to survive teaching courses on race and culture." *Journal of Multicultural Assessment and Development, 31,* 3–11.

Hess, A. K. (1999a). Serving as an expert witness. In A. K. Hess & I. B. Weiner (Eds.), *The handbook of forensic psychology* (2nd ed., pp. 521–555). New York: Wiley.

Hess, A. K. (1999b). Practicing principled forensic psychology: Legal, ethical, and moral considerations. In A. K. Hess & I. B. Weiner (Eds.), *The handbook of forensic psychology* (2nd ed., pp. 673–699). New York: Wiley.

Hess, K. D., & Brinson, P. (1999). Mediating domestic law issues. In A. K. Hess & I. B. Weiner (Eds.), *The handbook of forensic psychology* (2nd ed., pp. 63–103). New York: Wiley.

Hiday, V. A. (1996). Outpatient commitment: Official coercion in the community. In D. L. Dennis & J. Monahan (Eds.), *Coercion and aggressive community treatment: A new frontier in mental health law* (pp. 29–47). New York: Plenum.

Hines, A. H., Ader, D. N., Chang, A. S., & Rundell, J. R. (1998). Dual agency, dual relationships, boundary crossings, and associated boundary violations: A survey of military and civilian psychiatrists. *Military Medicine, 163,* 826–833.

Hoagwood, K. (1994). The certificate of confidentiality at the National Institute of Mental Health: Discretionary considerations in its applicability in research on child and adolescent mental disorders. *Ethics and Behavior, 4,* 123–131.

Hochhauser, M. (1999). Informed consent and patient's rights documents: A right, a rite, or a rewrite? *Ethics and Behavior, 9,* 1–20.

Hoffman, R. M. (1995). Sexual dual relationships in counseling: Confronting the issues. *Counseling and Values, 40,* 15–23.

Holmes, D. S. (1976). Debriefing after psychological experiments. *American Psychologist, 31,* 858–875.

Holroyd, J. C., & Brodsky, A. M. (1977). Psychologists' attitudes and practices regarding erotic and nonerotic physical contact with patients. *American Psychologist, 32,* 843–849.

Houghkirk, E. (1977). Everything you have always wanted your clients to know but have been afraid to tell them. *Journal of Marriage and Family Counseling, 3,* 27–33.

Howard, K. I., Kopta, S. M., Krause, M. S., & Orlinsky, D. E. (1986). The dose-effect relationship in psychotherapy. *American Psychologist, 41,* 159–164.

Hunsley, J., & Bailey, J. M. (1999). The clinical utility of the Rorschach: Unfulfilled promises and an uncertain future. *Psychological Assessment, 11,* 266–277.

Insanity Defense Reform Act of 1984, 18 U.S.C.S. § 17 (West 1998).

International Society for Mental Health Online. (2000). *Suggested principles for the online provision of mental health services.* Retrieved January 29, 2004, from http://ismho.org/suggestions.html

International Society for Mental Health Online. (2002). *Assessing a person's suitability for online therapy.* Retrieved November 11, 2003, from http://www.ismho.org/casestudy/ccsgas.htm

Isometsa, E. T., Henriksson, M. M., Aro, H. M., Heikkinen, M. E., Kuoppasalmi, K. I., & Lonnqvist, J. K. (1994). Suicide in major depression. *American Journal of Psychiatry, 151,* 530–536.

Jaffee v. Redmond, 518 U.S. 1 (1996).

Jamison, S. (1999). Psychology and rational suicide: The special case of assisted dying. In J. L. Werth, Jr. (Ed.), *Contemporary perspectives on rational suicide* (pp. 128–134). Philadelphia: Brunner/Mazel.

Janus, E. S., & Meehl, P. E. (1997). Assessing the legal standard for predictions of dangerousness in sex offender commitment proceedings. *Psychology, Public Policy, and Law, 3,* 33–64.

Jellinek, M., & Parmelee, D. (1977). Is there a role for medical ethics in postgraduate psychiatry courses? *American Journal of Psychiatry, 134,* 1438–1439.

Joiner, T. E., Jr., Walker, R. L., Rudd, M. D., & Jobes, D. A. (1999). Scientizing and routinizing the assessment of suicidality in outpatient practice. *Professional Psychology: Research and Practice, 5,* 447–453.

Kalichman, S. C. (1999). *Mandated reporting of suspected child abuse: Ethics, law, and policy* (2nd ed.). Washington, DC: American Psychological Association.

Kant, I. (1909). On a supposed right to tell lies from benevolent motives. In T. K. Abbott (Trans.), *Kant's critique of practical reason and other works on the theory of ethics* (pp. 361–365). London: Longmans, Green, & Co. (Original work published 1797)

Kant, I. (1956). *Critique of practical reason* (L. W. Beck, Trans.). New York: Bobbs-Merrill. (Original work published 1788)

Kant, I. (1963). *Lectures on ethics* (L. Infield, Trans.). New York: Harper & Row. (Original work published 1924)

Kant, I. (1964a). *Groundwork of the metaphysic of morals* (H. J. Patton, Trans.). New York: Harper & Row. (Original work published 1785)

Kant, I. (1964b). *The metaphysical principles of virtue* (J. Ellington, Trans.). New York: Bobbs-Merrill. (Original work published 1797)

Kaplan, J. (1988). The use of animals in research. *Science, 242,* 839–840.

Kazdin, A. E. (2004). Psychotherapy for children and adolescents. In M. J. Lambert (Ed.), *Bergin and Garfield's handbook of psychotherapy and behavior change* (5th ed., pp. 543–589). New York: Wiley.

Keller, S. A. (1999). Split loyalties: The conflicting demands of individual treatment goals and parental responsibility. *Women and Therapy, 22,* 117–131.

Kelly, T. A., & Strupp, H. H. (1992). Patient and therapist values in psychotherapy: Perceived changes, assimilation, similarity, and outcome. *Journal of Consulting and Clinical Psychology, 60,* 34–40.

Kendall, P. C. (1998). Empirically supported psychological therapies. *Journal of Consulting and Clinical Psychology, 66,* 3–6.

Keppel, G., Saufley, W. H., Jr., & Tokunaga, H. (1992). *Introduction to design and analysis* (2nd ed.). New York: W. H. Freeman.

Kitchener, K. S. (1984). Intuition, critical evaluation, and ethical principles: The foundation for ethical decisions in counseling psychology. *The Counseling Psychologist, 12*(3), 43–55.

Kitchener, K. S. (2000). *Foundations of ethical practice, research, and teaching in psychology.* Mahwah, NJ: Lawrence Erlbaum.

Kitchener, R. F. (1980). Ethical relativism and behavior therapy. *Journal of Consulting and Clinical Psychology, 48,* 1–7.

Kitchener, R. F. (1991). The ethical foundations of behavior therapy. *Ethics and Behavior, 1,* 221–238.

Klein, K., & Cheuvront, B. (1990). The subject-experimenter contract: A reexamination of subject pool contamination. *Teaching of Psychology, 17,* 166–169.

Knapp, S., & VandeCreek, L. (2001). Ethical issues in personality assessment in forensic psychology. *Journal of Personality Assessment, 77,* 242–254.

Koocher, G. P., & Keith-Spiegel, P. (1998). *Ethics in psychology: Professional standards and cases* (2nd ed.). New York: Oxford University Press.

Korn, J. H., Huelsman, T. J., Reed, C. K. S., & Aiello, M. (1992). Perceived ethicality of guided imagery in rape research. *Ethics and Behavior, 2,* 1–14.

Kumho Tire Company, Ltd. v. Carmichael, 119 S. Ct. 1167, 1176, 526 U.S. 137 (1999).

Lambert, M. J., & Ogles, B. M. (2004). The efficacy and effectiveness of psychotherapy. In M. J. Lambert (Ed.), *Bergin and Garfield's handbook of psychotherapy and behavior change* (5th ed., pp. 139–193). New York: Wiley.

Landrum, R. E., & Chastain, G. (1999). Subject pool policies in undergraduate-only departments: Results from a nationwide survey. In G. Chastain & R. E. Landrum (Eds.), *Protecting human subjects: Departmental subject pools and institutional review boards* (pp. 25–42). Washington, DC: American Psychological Association.

Laosa, L. M. (1990). Population generalizability, cultural sensitivity, and ethical dilemmas. In I. E. Sigel (Series Ed.), C. B. Fisher & W. W. Tryon (Vol. Eds.), *Annual advances in applied developmental psychology: Vol. 4. Ethics in applied developmental psychology: Emerging issues in an emerging field* (pp. 227–251). Norwood, NJ: Ablex.

Lazarus, A. A. (1995). Multimodal therapy. In R. J. Corsini & D. Wedding (Eds.), *Current psychotherapies* (5th ed., pp. 322–355). Itasca, IL: F. E. Peacock.

Lefley, H. P. (2002). Ethical issues in mental health services for culturally diverse communities. In P. Backlar & D. L. Cutler (Eds.), *Ethics in community mental health care: Commonplace concerns* (pp. 3–22). New York: Plenum.

Levine, R. J. (1995a). Adolescents as research subjects without permission of their parents or guardians: Ethical considerations. *Journal of Adolescent Health, 17,* 287–297.

Levine, R. J. (1995b). Children as research subjects: Ethical and legal considerations. *Child and Adolescent Psychiatric Clinics of North America, 4,* 853–868.

Lilienfeld, S. O., & Marino, L. (1995). Mental disorder as a Roschian concept: A critique of Wakefield's "harmful dysfunction" analysis. *Journal of Abnormal Psychology, 104,* 411–420.

Link, B. G. (1987). Understanding labeling effects in the area of mental disorders: An assessment of the effects of expectations of rejection. *American Sociological Review, 52,* 96–112.

Link, B. G., Cullen, F. T., Frank, J., & Wozniak, J. F. (1987). The social rejection of former mental patients: Understanding why labels matter. *American Journal of Sociology, 92,* 1461–1500.

Link, B. G., & Steuve, A. (1994). Psychotic symptoms and the violent/illegal behavior of mental patients compared to community controls. In J. Monahan & H. J. Steadman (Eds.), *Violence and mental disorder: Developments in risk assessment* (pp. 137–159). Chicago: University of Chicago Press.

Liptak, A. (2003a, January 26). Privacy of rape accusers clashes with trial rights. *The New York Times,* p. A16.

Liptak, A. (2003b, February 11). State can make inmate sane enough to execute, court rules. *The New York Times,* pp. A1, A27.

Litwack, T. R., & Schlesinger, L. B. (1999). Dangerousness risk assessments: Research, legal, and clinical considerations. In A. K. Hess & I. B. Weiner (Eds.), *The handbook of forensic psychology* (2nd ed., pp. 171–217). New York: Wiley.

Loftus, E. (1987, June 29). Trials of an expert witness. *Newsweek, 109,* pp. 10–11.

Loftus, E., & Ketcham, K. (1991). *Witness for the defense: The accused, the eyewitness, and the expert who puts memory on trial.* New York: St. Martin's Press.

Loftus, E., & Ketcham, K. (1994). *The myth of repressed memory.* New York: St. Martin's Press.

Luepker, E. T. (1999). Effects of practitioners' sexual misconduct: A follow-up study. *Journal of the American Academy of Psychiatry and the Law, 27,* 51–63.

Luster, T., & Small, S. A. (1997). Sexual abuse history and problems in adolescence: Exploring the effects of moderating variables. *Journal of Marriage and the Family, 59,* 131–142.

Lydon, C. (1972, July 26). Eagleton tells of shock therapy on two occasions. *The New York Times,* pp. A1, A20.

Lymburner, J. A., & Roesch, R. (1999). The insanity defense: Five years of research. *International Journal of Law and Psychiatry, 22,* 213–240.

MacAndrew, C. (1965). The differentiation of male alcoholic outpatients from nonalcoholic psychiatric outpatients by means of the MMPI. *Quarterly Journal of Studies on Alcohol, 26,* 238–246.

Maccoby, E. E. (1990). Gender and relationships: A developmental account. *American Psychologist, 45,* 513–520.

MacKay, E., & O'Neill, P. (1992). What creates the dilemma in ethical dilemmas? Examples from psychological practice. *Ethics and Behavior, 2,* 227–244.

Macklin, R. (1992). Autonomy, beneficence, and child development. In B. Stanley & J. E. Sieber (Eds.), *Social research on children and adolescents: Ethical issues* (pp. 88–105). Newbury Park, CA: Sage.

Manhal-Baugus, M. (2001). E-therapy: Practical, ethical, and legal issues. *CyberPsychology & Behavior, 4,* 551–563.

Mann, T. (1994). Informed consent for psychological research: Do subjects comprehend consent forms and understand their legal rights? *Psychological Science, 5,* 140–143.

Margolin, G. (1998). Ethical issues in marital therapy. In R. M. Anderson, Jr., T. L. Needels, & H. V. Hall (Eds.), *Avoiding ethical misconduct in psychology specialty areas* (pp. 78–94). Springfield, IL: Charles C Thomas.

Marino, I. R., & Cirillo, C. (2004). Clinical trials or exploitation? *Science, 306,* 54–55.

Martin, S. (1999, July/August). Revision of ethics code calls for stronger former client sex rule. *APA Monitor,* p. 44.

Masi, D., & Freedman, M. (2001). The use of telephone and on line technology in assessment, counseling, and therapy. *Employee Assistance Quarterly, 16*(3), 49–63.

Mathy, R. M., Kerr, D. L., & Haydin, B. M. (2003). Methodological rigor and ethical considerations in Internet-mediated research. *Psychotherapy: Theory, Research, Practice, Training, 40,* 77–85.

Mattison, D., Jayaratne, S., & Croxton, T. (2002). Client or former client? Implications of ex-client definition on social work practice. *Social Work, 47,* 55–64.

McCarthy, W. C., & Frieze, I. H. (1999). Negative aspects of therapy: Client perceptions of therapists' social influence, burnout, and quality of care. *Journal of Social Issues, 55,* 33–50.

McCarty, D., & Clancy, C. (2002). Telehealth: Implications for social work practice. *Social Work, 47,* 153–161.

McFall, R. M. (2002). Training for prescriptions vs. prescriptions for training: Where are we now? Where should we be? How do we get there? *Journal of Clinical Psychology, 58,* 659–676.

McMahon, M. (1997). Criminalising professional misconduct: Legislative regulation of psychotherapist-patient sex. *Psychiatry, Psychology and Law, 4,* 177–193.

McMinn, M. R., Buchanan, T., Ellens, B. M., & Ryan, M. K. (1999). Technology, professional practice, and ethics: Survey findings and implications. *Professional Psychology: Research and Practice, 30,* 165–172.

McMinn, M. R., Ellens, B. M., & Soref, E. (1999). Ethical perspectives and practice behaviors involving computer-based test interpretation. *Assessment, 6,* 71–77.

McMurtrie, B. (2001, December 14). Psychology association kills anti-bias proposal. *Chronicle of Higher Education,* p. A29.

McShane, R. H., & Rowe, D. (1994). Access to psychiatric records: Bane or boon? *Journal of Mental Health, 3,* 301–309.

Meehl, P. E., & Rosen, A. (1955). Antecedent probability and the efficacy of psychometric signs, patterns, or cutting scores. *Psychological Bulletin, 52,* 194–216.

Megargee, E. I. (1993). Aggression and violence. In P. B. Sutker & H. E. Adams (Eds.), *Comprehensive handbook of psychopathology* (2nd ed., pp. 617–644). New York: Plenum.

Megargee, E. I. (1995). Assessing and understanding aggressive and violent patients. In J. N. Butcher (Ed.), *Clinical personality assessment: Practical considerations* (pp. 395–409). New York: Oxford University Press.

Michaels, T. F., & Oetting, E. R. (1979). The informed consent dilemma: An empirical approach. *Journal of Social Psychology, 109,* 223–230.

Milan, M. A., Chin, C. E., & Nguyen, Q. X. (1999). Practicing psychology in correctional settings: Assessment, treatment, and substance abuse programs. In A. K. Hess & I. B. Weiner (Eds.), *The handbook of forensic psychology* (2nd ed., pp. 580–602). New York: Wiley.

Miles, S. H. (2004). *The Hippocratic oath and the ethics of medicine.* New York: Oxford University Press.

Milgram, S. (1963). Behavioral study of obedience. *Journal of Abnormal and Social Psychology, 67,* 371–378.

Mill, J. S. (1910). Utilitarianism. In *Utilitarianism, on liberty, and representative government* (pp. 1–60). London: J. M. Dent & Sons. (Original work published 1863)

Miller, L. (1998). Our own medicine: Traumatized psychotherapists and the stresses of doing therapy. *Psychotherapy, 35,* 137–146.

Mills, L. B., & Huebner, E. S. (1998). A prospective study of personality characteristics, occupational stressors, and burnout among school psychology practitioners. *Journal of School Psychology, 36,* 103–120.

Mobley, M. J. (1999). Psychotherapy with criminal offenders. In A. K. Hess & I. B. Weiner (Eds.), *The handbook of forensic psychology* (2nd ed., pp. 603–639). New York: Wiley.

Monahan, J. (1992). Mental disorder and violent behavior: Perceptions and evidence. *American Psychologist, 47,* 511–521.

Moore, G. E. (1962). *Principia ethica.* London: Cambridge University Press.

Moreland, K. L. (1987). Computer-based test interpretations: Advice to the consumer. *Applied Psychology: An International Review, 36,* 385–399.

Mueller, J. H., & Furedy, J. J. (2001, September). Reviewing for risk: What's the evidence that it works? *APS Observer,* pp. 1, 26–28.

Muller, R. T., & Diamond, T. (1999). Father and mother physical abuse and child aggressive behaviour in two generations. *Canadian Journal of Behavioural Science, 31,* 221–228.

Mulvey, E. P., & Lidz, C. W. (1998). Clinical prediction of violence as a conditional judgment. *Social Psychiatry and Psychiatric Epidemiology, 33*(Suppl. 1), S107–S113.

Murphy, D. A., O'Keefe, Z. H., & Kaufman, A. H. (1999). Improving comprehension and recall of information for an HIV vaccine trial among women at risk for HIV: Reading level simplification and inclusion of pictures to illustrate key concepts. *AIDS Education and Prevention, 11,* 389–399.

Murphy, G. E. (1988). The prediction of suicide. In S. Lesse (Ed.), *What we know about suicidal behavior and how to treat it* (pp. 47–58). Northvale, NJ: Jason Aronson.

Murphy, K. R., & Davidshofer, C. O. (1994). *Psychological testing: Principles and applications* (3rd ed.). Englewood Cliffs, NJ: Prentice Hall.

National Association of Social Workers. (1982). *NASW standards for continuing professional education.* Washington, DC: Author.

National Association of Social Workers. (1989). *NASW standards for the practice of clinical social work.* Washington, DC: Author.

National Association of Social Workers. (1999). *Code of ethics of the National Association of Social Workers.* Washington, DC: Author.

National Board for Certified Counselors. (2001). *The practice of Internet counseling.* Greensboro, NC: Author.

National Commission for the Protection of Human Subjects of Biomedical and Behavioral Research (NCPHS). (1977). *Research involving children: Report and recommendations* (DHEW Publication No. [OS] 77-0004). Washington, DC: U.S. Government Printing Office.

National Institutes of Health. (1998, March 6). NIH policy and guidelines on the inclusion of children as participants in research involving human subjects. *NIH Guide for Grants and Contracts.* Retrieved June 19, 2004, from http://grants1.nih.gov/grants/guide/noticefiles/not98024.html

National Institutes of Health Guidelines on the Inclusion of Women and Minorities as Subjects in Clinical Research, 59 Fed. Reg. 11146-11151 (1994).

National Research Act of 1974, 42 U.S.C. § 241 *et seq.* (West 1994).

National Science Foundation. (2004). *Science and engineering degrees: 1966–2001.* Retrieved June 8, 2005, from http://www.nsf.gov/statistics/nsf04311

Naughton, J. M. (1972, August 1). Successor sought: O'Brien and Muskie in running—Dakotan to address nation. *The New York Times,* pp. A1, A24.

Newman, R., Phelps, R., Sammons, M. T., Dunivin, D. L., & Cullen, E. A. (2000). Evaluation of the psychopharmacology demonstration project: A retrospective analysis. *Professional Psychology: Research and Practice, 31,* 598–603.

Nimmer, J. G., & Handelsman, M. M. (1992). Effects of subject pool policy on student attitudes toward psychology and psychological research. *Teaching of Psychology, 19,* 141–144.

Norcross, J. C. (2001). Purposes, processes, and products of the task force on empirically supported therapy relationships. *Psychotherapy: Theory, Research, Practice, Training, 38,* 345–356.

Norcross, J. C. (Ed.). (2002). *Psychotherapy relationships that work: Therapist contributions and responsiveness to patients.* New York: Oxford University Press.

Ogloff, J. R. P., & Otto, R. K. (1991). Are research participants truly informed? Readability of informed consent forms used in research. *Ethics and Behavior, 1,* 239–252.

Oliansky, A. (1991). A confederate's perspective on deception. *Ethics and Behavior, 1,* 253–258.

Olson, M. M., Russell, C. S., & White, M. B. (2001). Technological implications for clinical supervision and practice. *The Clinical Supervisor, 20,* 201–215.

Ondrusek, N., Abramovitch, R., Pencharz, P., & Koren, G. (1998). Empirical examination of the ability of children to consent to clinical research. *Journal of Medical Ethics, 24,* 158–165.

Oravec, J. A. (2000). Online counseling and the Internet: Perspectives for mental health care supervision and education. *Journal of Mental Health, 9,* 121–135.

Ortmann, A., & Hertwig, R. (1997). Is deception acceptable? *American Psychologist, 52,* 746–747.

Parrott, J., Strathdee, G., & Brown, P. (1988). Patient access to psychiatric records: The patient's view. *Journal of the Royal Society of Medicine, 81,* 520–522.

Pearson, B., & Piazza, N. (1997). Classification of dual relationships in the helping professions. *Counselor Education and Supervision, 37,* 89–99.

Pedersen, P. B. (1997). The cultural context of the American Counseling Association Code of Ethics. *Journal of Counseling & Development, 76,* 23–28.

Pedersen, P. B. (2001). Multiculturalism and the paradigm shift in counselling: Controversies and alternative futures. *Canadian Journal of Counselling, 35,* 15–25.

Pedersen, P. B. (2003). Culturally biased assumptions in counseling psychology. *The Counseling Psychologist, 31,* 396–403.

Peele, S. (1990). Behavior in a vacuum: Social-psychological theories of addiction that deny the social and psychological meanings of behavior. *Journal of Mind and Behavior, 11,* 513–529.

Petersen, A. C., & Leffert, N. (1995). Developmental issues influencing guidelines for adolescent health research: A review. *Journal of Adolescent Health, 17,* 298–305.

Pettifor, J. L. (2001). Are professional codes of ethics relevant for multicultural counselling? *Canadian Journal of Counselling, 35,* 26–35.

Piller, C. (2001, November 7). Web mishap: Kids' psychological files posted. *Los Angeles Times,* pp. A1, A22.

Pittenger, D. J. (2002). Deception in research: Distinctions and solutions from the perspective of utilitarianism. *Ethics and Behavior, 12,* 117–142.

Plaut, S. M. (1997). Boundary violations in professional-client relationships: Overview and guidelines for prevention. *Sexual and Marital Therapy, 12,* 77–94.

Plous, S. (1996a). Attitudes toward the use of animals in psychological research and education: Results from a national survey of psychologists. *American Psychologist, 51,* 1167–1180.

Plous, S. (1996b). Attitudes toward the use of animals in psychological research and education: Results from a national survey of psychology majors. *Psychological Science, 7,* 352–358.

Pollack, D. A., McFarland, B. H., George, R. A., & Angell, R. H. (1994). Prioritization of mental health services in Oregon. *The Milbank Quarterly, 72,* 515–553.

Pope, K. S. (1989). Therapist-patient sex syndrome: A guide for attorneys and subsequent therapists to assessing damage. In G. Gabbard (Ed.), *Sexual exploitation in professional relationships* (pp. 39–55). Washington, DC: American Psychiatric Press.

Pope, K. S. (1991). Dual relationships in psychotherapy. *Ethics and Behavior, 1,* 21–34.

Pope, K. S., & Bouhoutsos, J. C. (1986). *Sexual intimacy between therapists and patients.* New York: Praeger.

Pope, K. S., Butcher, J. N., & Seelen, J. (2000). *The MMPI, MMPI-2, & MMPI-A in court: A practical guide for expert witnesses and attorneys* (2nd ed.). Washington, DC: American Psychological Association.

Popper, K. R. (1965). *Conjectures and refutations: The growth of scientific knowledge* (2nd ed.). New York: Basic Books.

Porter, J. (1996). Regulatory considerations in research involving children and adolescents with mental disorders. In K. Hoagwood, P. S. Jensen, & C. B. Fisher (Eds.), *Ethical issues in mental health research with children and adolescents* (pp. 15–28). Mahwah, NJ: Lawrence Erlbaum.

Powell, M. P., & Vacha-Haase, T. (1994). Issues related to research with children: What counseling psychologists need to know. *The Counseling Psychologist, 22,* 444–453.

Prediger, D. J. (1994). Multicultural assessment standards: A compilation for counselors. *Measurement and Evaluation in Counseling and Development, 27,* 68–73.

Privacy Rule, 45 C.F.R. § 160 & 164 (2003).

Prochaska, J. O., & Norcross, J. C. (1999). *Systems of psychotherapy: A transtheoretical analysis* (4th ed.). Pacific Grove, CA: Brooks/Cole.

Protection of Human Subjects, 45 C.F.R. 46 (2001).

Quadrio, C. (1994). Sexual abuse involving therapists, clergy and judiciary: Closed ranks, collusions and conspiracies of silence. *Psychiatry, Psychology and Law, 1,* 189–198.

Quinn, T. C., Glasser, D., Cannon, R. O., Matuszak, D. L., Dunning, R. W., Kline, R. L., et al. (1988). Human immunodeficiency virus infection among patients attending clinics for sexually transmitted diseases. *New England Journal of Medicine, 318,* 197–203.

Ragusea, A. S., & VandeCreek, L. (2003). Suggestions for the ethical practice of online psychotherapy. *Psychotherapy: Theory, Research, Practice, Training, 40,* 94–102.

Raskin, N. J., & Rogers, C. R. (1995). Person-centered therapy. In R. J. Corsini & D. Wedding (Eds.), *Current psychotherapies* (5th ed., pp. 128–161). Itasca, IL: F. E. Peacock.

Rawls, J. (1971). *A theory of justice.* Cambridge, MA: Harvard University Press.

Reid, S. (1998). Suicide in schizophrenia: A review of the literature. *Journal of Mental Health, 7,* 345–353.

Remley, T. P., Jr., Herlihy, B., & Herlihy, S. B. (1997). The U.S. Supreme Court decision in Jaffee v. Redmond: Implications for counselors. *Journal of Counseling and Development, 75,* 213–218.

Richards, P. S., & Davison, M. L. (1989). The effects of theistic and atheistic counselor values on client trust: A multidimensional scaling analysis. *Counseling and Values, 33,* 109–120.

Rind, B., Tromovitch, P., & Bauserman, R. (1998). A meta-analytic examination of assumed properties of child sexual abuse using college samples. *Psychological Bulletin, 124,* 22–53.

Roback, H. B., Moore, R. F., Bloch, F. S., & Shelton, M. (1996). Confidentiality in group psychotherapy: Empirical findings and the law. *International Journal of Group Psychotherapy, 46,* 117–135.

Robiner, W. N., Arbisi, P. A., & Edwall, G. E. (1994). The basis for the doctoral degree for psychology licensure. *Clinical Psychology Review, 14,* 227–254.

Robinson, P., & Serfaty, M. (2003). Computers, e-mail, and therapy in eating disorders. *European Eating Disorders Review, 11,* 210–221.

Roesch, R., Zapf, P. A., Golding, S. L., & Skeem, J. L. (1999). Defining and assessing competency to stand trial. In A. K. Hess & I. B. Weiner (Eds.), *The handbook of forensic psychology* (2nd ed., pp. 327–349). New York: Wiley.

Rogers, C. R. (1961). *On becoming a person.* Boston: Houghton Mifflin.

Rogers, C. R., & Skinner, B. F. (1956). Some issues concerning the control of human behavior. *Science, 124,* 1057–1066.

Rosenbaum, M. (1982). Ethical problems of group psychotherapy. In M. Rosenbaum (Ed.), *Ethics and values in psychotherapy* (pp. 237–257). New York: Free Press.

Rosenthal, R. (1994). Science and ethics in conducting, analyzing, and reporting psychological research. *Psychological Science, 5,* 127–134.

Rosovsky, H., & Hartley, M. (2002). *Evaluation and the academy: Are we doing the right thing?* Cambridge, MA: American Academy of Arts and Sciences.

Roth, L. H., Wolford, J., & Meisel, A. (1980). Patient access to records: Tonic or toxin? *American Journal of Psychiatry, 137,* 592–596.

Rovi, S., Chen, P. H., & Johnson, M. S. (2004). The economic burden of hospitalizations associated with child abuse and neglect. *American Journal of Public Health, 94,* 586–590.

Ruark, J. K. (2001, June 1). American Psychological Association journal accused of bowing to political pressure. *The Chronicle of Higher Education,* p. A14.

Russell, B. (1945). *A history of Western philosophy.* New York: Simon and Schuster.

Sales, B. D., & Simon, L. (1993). Institutional constraints on the ethics of expert testimony. *Ethics and Behavior, 3,* 231–249.

Sampson, J. P., Jr., Kolodinsky, R. W., & Greeno, B. P. (1997). Counseling on the information highway: Future possibilities and potential problems. *Journal of Counseling and Development, 75,* 203–212.

Sampson, J. P., Jr., Purgar, M. P., & Shy, J. D. (2003). Computer-based test interpretation in career assessment: Ethical and professional issues. *Journal of Career Assessment, 11,* 22–39.

Sanderson, W. C. (2003). Why empirically supported psychological treatments are important. *Behavior Modification, 27,* 290–299.

Sandoval, J. (1998). Critical thinking in test interpretation. In J. Sandoval, C. L. Frisby, K. F. Geisinger, J. D. Scheuneman, & J. R. Grenier (Eds.), *Test interpretation and diversity: Achieving equity in assessment* (pp. 31–49). Washington, DC: American Psychological Association.

Sarbin, T. R. (1990). Toward the obsolescence of the schizophrenia hypothesis. *Journal of Mind and Behavior, 11,* 259–283.

Sarbin, T. R. (1997). On the futility of psychiatric diagnostic manuals (DSMs) and the return of personal agency. *Applied and Preventive Psychology, 6,* 233–243.

Scherer, D. G., & Reppucci, N. D. (1988). Adolescents' capacities to provide voluntary informed consent: The effects of parental influence and medical dilemmas. *Law and Human Behavior, 12,* 123–141.

Schwehn, J., & Schau, C. G. (1990). Psychotherapy as a process of value stabilization. *Counseling and Values, 35,* 24–30.

Scott-Jones, D. (1994). Ethical issues in reporting and referring in research with low-income minority children. *Ethics and Behavior, 4,* 97–108.

Sechrest, L., & Coan, J. A. (2002). Preparing psychologists to prescribe. *Journal of Clinical Psychology, 58,* 649–658.

Shadish, W. R. (1994). APA ethics and student authorship on master's theses. *American Psychologist, 49,* 1096.

Sharkey, J. (1997, September 28). You're not bad, you're sick. It's in the book. *The New York Times,* pp. 1, 5.

Shergill, S. S., & Szmukler, G. (1998). How predictable is violence and suicide in community psychiatric practice? *Journal of Mental Health, 7,* 393–401.

Shields, J. M., & Johnson, A. (1992). Collision between law and ethics: Consent for treatment with adolescents. *Bulletin of the American Academy of Psychiatry and Law, 20,* 309–323.

Shneidman, E. S. (1992). Rational suicide and psychiatric disorders. *New England Journal of Medicine, 326,* 889–890.

Sidman, M. (1999). Coercion in educational settings. *Behaviour Change, 16,* 79–88.

Sieber, J. E. (1999). What makes a subject pool (un)ethical? In G. Chastain & R. E. Landrum (Eds.), *Protecting human subjects: Departmental subject pools and institutional review boards* (pp. 43–64). Washington, DC: American Psychological Association.

Sieber, J. E., & Saks, M. J. (1989). A census of subject pool characteristics and policies. *American Psychologist, 44,* 1053–1061.

Singh, S. N., Mishra, S., & Kim, D. (1998). Research-related burnout among faculty in higher education. *Psychological Reports, 83,* 463–473.

Sireci, S. G., & Geisinger, K. F. (1998). Equity issues in employment testing. In J. Sandoval, C. L. Frisby, K. F. Geisinger, J. D. Scheuneman, & J. R. Grenier (Eds.), *Test interpretation and diversity: Achieving equity in assessment* (pp. 105–140). Washington, DC: American Psychological Association.

Skorupa, J., & Agresti, A. A. (1993). Ethical beliefs about burnout and continued professional practice. *Professional Psychology: Research and Practice, 24,* 281–285.

Slater, L. (2003, January 26). Full disclosure. *The New York Times,* Section 6, pp. 11–12.

Slovenko, R. (1999). Civil competency. In A. K. Hess & I. B. Weiner (Eds.), *The handbook of forensic psychology* (2nd ed., pp. 151–167). New York: Wiley.

Smart, J. J. C., & Williams, B. (1973). *Utilitarianism: For and against.* London: Cambridge University Press.

Smart, R. N. (1958). Negative utilitarianism. *Mind, 67,* 542–543.

Smith, D. (2003a, January). 10 ways practitioners can avoid frequent ethical pitfalls. *Monitor on Psychology,* pp. 50–55.

Smith, D. (2003b, January). In an ethical bind? *Monitor on Psychology,* p. 61.

Smith, J. A., Harre, R., & Van Langenhove, L. (1995). *Rethinking psychology.* London, UK: Sage.

Smith, S. D., & Reynolds, C. (2002). Cyber-psychotherapy. *Annals of the American Psychotherapy Association, 5*(2), 20–22.

Smith, T. S., McGuire, J., Abbott, D., & Blau, B. (1991). Clinical ethical decision making: An investigation of the rationales used to justify doing less than one believes one should. *Professional Psychology: Research and Practice, 22,* 235–239.

Smyer, M. A., Balster, R. L., Egli, D., Johnson, D. L., Kilbey, M. M., Leith, N. J., et al. (1993). Summary of the report of the ad hoc task force on psychopharmacology of the American Psychological Association. *Professional Psychology: Research and Practice, 24,* 394–403.

Society for Industrial and Organizational Psychology, Inc. (1987). *Principles for the validation and use of personnel selection procedures* (3rd ed.). College Park, MD: Author.

Society for Industrial and Organizational Psychology, Inc. (1994). *Guidelines for education and training at the master's level in industrial-organizational psychology.* Arlington Heights, IL: Author.

Society for Industrial and Organizational Psychology, Inc. (1999). *Guidelines for education and training at the doctoral level in industrial-organizational psychology.* Bowling Green, OH: Author.

Solomon, P. (1996). Research on the coercion of persons with severe mental illness. In D. L. Dennis & J. Monahan (Eds.), *Coercion and aggressive community treatment: A new frontier in mental health law* (pp. 129–145). New York: Plenum.

Somer, E., & Saadon, M. (1999). Therapist-client sex: Clients' retrospective reports. *Professional Psychology: Research and Practice, 30,* 504–509.

Stanley, B. H., & Guido, J. R. (1996). Informed consent: Psychological and empirical issues. In B. H. Stanley, J. E. Sieber, & G. B. Melton (Eds.), *Research ethics: A psychological approach* (pp. 105–128). Lincoln: University of Nebraska Press.

Stanton, A. L., Burker, E. J., & Kershaw, D. (1991). Effects of researcher follow-up of distressed subjects: Tradeoff between validity and ethical responsibility. *Ethics and Behavior, 1,* 105–112.

Steadman, H. J., McGreevy, M. A., Morissey, J. P., Callahan, L. A., Robbins, P. C., & Cirincione, C. (1993). *Before and after Hinckley: Evaluating insanity defense reform.* New York: Guilford.

Stein, E. J., Furedy, R. L., Simonton, M. J., & Neuffer, C. H. (1979). Patient access to medical records on a psychiatric inpatient unit. *American Journal of Psychiatry, 136,* 327–329.

Steinberg, A. M., Pynoos, R. S., Goenjian, A. K., Sossanabadi, H., & Sherr, L. (1999). Are researchers bound by child abuse reporting laws? *Child Abuse and Neglect, 23,* 771–777.

Sternberg, R. J. (2002, January). On civility in reviewing. *APS Observer,* pp. 3, 34.

Stevens, J., Yock, T., & Perlman, B. (1979). Comparing master's clinical training with professional responsibilities in community mental health centers. *Professional Psychology: Research and Practice, 10,* 20–27.

Strom-Gottfried, K. (1999). Professional boundaries: An analysis of violations by social workers. *Families in Society, 80,* 439–449.

Sue, D. W., Carter, R. T., Casas, J. M., Fouad, N. A., Ivey, A. E., Jensen, M., et al. (1998). *Multicultural counseling competencies: Individual and organizational development.* Thousand Oaks, CA: Sage.

Summers, C. (1992). Militarism, human welfare, and the APA Ethical Principles of Psychologists. *Ethics and Behavior, 2,* 287–310.

Swenson, C. C., & Hanson, R. F. (1998). Sexual abuse of children: Assessment, research, and treatment. In J. R. Lutzker (Ed.), *Handbook of child abuse research and treatment* (pp. 475–499). New York: Plenum.

Szasz, T. (1974). *The myth of mental illness: Foundations of a theory of personal conduct* (Rev. ed.). New York: HarperCollins.

Szasz, T. (1986). The case against suicide prevention. *American Psychologist, 41,* 806–812.

Szasz, T. (1999). *Fatal freedom: The ethics and politics of suicide.* Westport, CT: Praeger.

Tallent, N. (1987). Computer-generated psychological reports: A look at the modern psychometric machine. *Journal of Personality Assessment, 51,* 95–108.

Tarasoff v. Board of Regents of the University of California, 13 Cal. 3d 177, 529 P. 2d 533 (1974), *vacated,* 17 Cal. 3d 425, 551 P. 2d 334 (1976).

Taylor, C. B., & Luce, K. H. (2003). Computer- and Internet-based psychotherapy interventions. *Current Directions in Psychological Science, 12,* 18–22.

Texas Family Code, Title 2(A) § 32.004 (West 2000).

Thapar v. Zezulka, 994 S.W.2d 635 (1999).

Thompson, B. (1994). The big picture(s) in deciding authorship order. *American Psychologist, 49,* 1095–1096.

Thompson, R. A. (1992). Developmental changes in research risk and benefit. In B. Stanley & J. E. Sieber (Eds.), *Social research on children and adolescents: Ethical issues* (pp. 31–64). Newbury Park, CA: Sage.

Thoreson, R. W., Shaughnessy, P., & Frazier, P. A. (1995). Sexual contact during and after professional relationships: Practices and attitudes of female counselors. *Journal of Counseling and Development, 74,* 84–89.

Thoreson, R. W., Shaughnessy, P., Heppner, P. P., & Cook, S. W. (1993). Sexual contact during and after the professional relationship: Attitudes and practices of male counselors. *Journal of Counseling and Development, 71,* 429–434.

Thorndike, E. L. (1911). *Animal intelligence.* New York: Macmillan.

Thorndike, E. L. (1940). *Human nature and the social order.* New York: Macmillan.

Tillman, J. G. (1998). Psychodynamic psychotherapy, religious beliefs, and self-disclosure. *American Journal of Psychotherapy, 52,* 273–286.

Treppa, J. A. (1998). A practitioner's guide to ethical decision-making. In R. M. Anderson, Jr., T. L. Needels, & H. V. Hall (Eds.), *Avoiding ethical misconduct in psychology specialty areas* (pp. 26–41). Springfield, IL: Charles C Thomas.

Tsemberis, S., Miller, A. C., & Gartner, D. (1996). Expert judgments of computer-based and clinician-written reports. *Computers in Human Behavior, 12,* 167–175.

Tseng, H. M., Macleod, H. A., & Wright, P. (1997). Computer anxiety and measurement of mood change. *Computers in Human Behavior, 13,* 305–316.

Tseng, H. M., Tiplady, B., Macleod, H. A., & Wright, P. (1998). Computer anxiety: A comparison of pen-based personal digital assistants, conventional computer and paper assessment of mood and performance. *British Journal of Psychology, 89,* 599–610.

Tucker, G. J. (1998). Putting *DSM-IV* in perspective. *American Journal of Psychiatry, 155,* 159–161.

Turkheimer, E., & Parry, C. D. H. (1992). Why the gap? Practice and policy in civil commitment hearings *American Psychologist, 47,* 646–655.

Tymchuk, A. J. (1981). Ethical decision making and psychological treatment. *Journal of Psychiatric Treatment and Evaluation, 3,* 507–513.

Tymchuk, A. J. (1986). Guidelines for ethical decision making. *Canadian Psychology, 27,* 36–43.

Tymchuk, A. J., & Ouslander, J. G. (1990). Optimizing the informed consent process with elderly people. *Educational Gerontology, 16,* 245–257.

Uniform Guidelines on Employee Selection Procedures, 43 Fed. Reg. 38290 (1978).

Vachon, D. O., & Agresti, A. A. (1992). A training proposal to help mental health professionals clarify and manage implicit values in the counseling process. *Professional Psychology: Research and Practice, 6,* 509–514.

VandeCreek, L., & Knapp, S. (1993). *Tarasoff and beyond: Legal and clinical considerations in the treatment of life-endangering patients* (Rev. ed.). Sarasota, FL: Professional Resource Press.

Velasquez, R. J., & Callahan, W. J. (1992). Psychological testing of Hispanic Americans in clinical settings: Overview and issues. In K. F. Geisinger (Ed.), *Psychological testing of Hispanics* (pp. 253–265). Washington, DC: American Psychological Association.

Vodanovich, S. J., & Piotrowski, C. (2001). Internet-based instruction: A national survey of psychology faculty. *Journal of Instructional Psychology, 28,* 253–255.

Vredenburgh, L. D., Carlozzi, A. F., & Stein, L. B. (1999). Burnout in counseling psychologists: Type of practice setting and pertinent demographics. *Counselling Psychology Quarterly, 12,* 293–302.

Waite, B. M., & Bowman, L. L. (1999). Research participation among general psychology students at a metropolitan comprehensive public university. In G. Chastain & R. E. Landrum (Eds.), *Protecting human subjects: Departmental subject pools and institutional review boards* (pp. 69–85). Washington, DC: American Psychological Association.

Wallace, J. D. (1988). *Moral relevance and moral conflict.* Ithaca, NY: Cornell University Press.

Walters, G. D., White, T. W., & Greene, R. L. (1988). Use of the MMPI to identify malingering and exaggeration of psychiatric symptomatology in male prison inmates. *Journal of Consulting and Clinical Psychology, 56,* 111–117.

Watson, J. C., Tenenbaum, G., Lidor, R., & Alfermann, D. (2001). ISSP position stand on the use of the Internet in sport psychology. *International Journal of Sport Psychology, 32,* 207–222.

Weiner, I. B. (1999). Writing forensic reports. In A. K. Hess & I. B. Weiner (Eds.), *The handbook of forensic psychology* (2nd ed., pp. 501–520). New York: Wiley.

Welfel, E. R. (2003, May-June). E-therapy: A question of ethics: A review of the professional issues involved in this controversial medium. *Behavioral Health Management, 23*(3), 17–19.

West, P. L., Mustaine, B. L., & Wyrick, B. (1999). State regulations and the ACA Code of Ethics and Standards of Practice: Oil and water for the substance abuse counselor. *Journal of Addictions and Offender Counseling, 20,* 35–46.

Westen, D., & Morrison, K. (2001). A multidimensional meta-analysis of treatments for depression, panic, and generalized anxiety disorder: An empirical examination of the status of empirically supported therapies. *Journal of Consulting and Clinical Psychology, 69,* 875–899.

Whitecotton, S. M., Sanders, D. E., & Norris, K. B. (1998). Improving predictive accuracy with a combination of human intuition and mechanical decision aids. *Organizational Behavior and Human Decision Processes, 76,* 325–348.

Williams, M. H. (1992). Exploitation and inference: Mapping the damage from therapist-patient sexual involvement. *American Psychologist, 47,* 412–421.

Wrightsman, L. S., Nietzel, M. T., & Fortune, W. H. (1998). *Psychology and the legal system* (4th ed.). Pacific Grove, CA: Brooks/Cole.

Wyatt v. Stickney, 325 F. Supp. 781 (M.D. Ala. 1971) and 344 F. Supp. 373 (M.D. Ala. 1972).

Yanagida, E. H. (1998). Ethical dilemmas in the clinical practice of child psychology. In R. M. Anderson, Jr., T. L. Needels, & H. V. Hall (Eds.), *Avoiding ethical misconduct in psychology specialty areas* (pp. 47–77). Springfield, IL: Charles C Thomas.

Yoshino, A., Shigemura, J., Kobayashi, Y., Nomura, S., Shishikura, K., Den, R., et al. (2001). Telepsychiatry: Assessment of televideo psychiatric interview reliability with present- and next-generation Internet infrastructures. *Acta Psychiatrica Scandinavica, 104,* 223–226.

Young, D. R., Hooker, D. T., & Freeberg, F. E. (1990). Informed consent documents: Increasing comprehension by reducing reading level. *IRB: A Review of Human Subjects Research, 12*(3), 1–5.

Zeiger, M., & Lewis, J. E. (1998). The spiritually responsible therapist: Religious material in the psychotherapeutic setting. *Psychotherapy, 35,* 415–424.

Zinermon v. Burch, 494 U.S. 113 (1990).

Appendix A

"Ethical Principles of Psychologists and Code of Conduct"

2002

CONTENTS

INTRODUCTION AND APPLICABILITY

PREAMBLE

GENERAL PRINCIPLES

ETHICAL STANDARDS

INTRODUCTION AND APPLICABILITY

The American Psychological Association's (APA's) Ethical Principles of Psychologists and Code of Conduct (hereinafter referred to as the Ethics Code) consists of an Introduction, a Preamble, five General Principles (A–E), and specific Ethical Standards. The Introduction discusses the intent, organization, procedural considerations, and scope of application of the Ethics Code. The Preamble and General Principles are aspirational goals to guide psychologists toward the highest ideals of psychology. Although the Preamble and General Principles are not themselves enforceable rules, they should be considered by psychologists in arriving at an ethical course of action. The Ethical Standards set forth enforceable rules for conduct as psychologists. Most of the Ethical Standards are written broadly, in order to apply to psychologists in varied roles, although the application of an Ethical Standard may vary depending on the context. The Ethical Standards are not exhaustive. The fact that a given conduct is not specifically addressed by an Ethical Standard does not mean that it is necessarily either ethical or unethical.

This Ethics Code applies only to psychologists' activities that are part of their scientific, educational, or professional roles as psychologists. Areas covered include but are not limited to the clinical, counseling, and school practice of psychology; research; teaching; supervision of trainees; public service; policy development; social intervention; development of assessment instruments; conducting assessments; educational counseling; organizational consulting; forensic activities; program design and evaluation; and administration. This Ethics Code applies to these activities across a variety of contexts, such as in person, postal, telephone, internet, and other electronic transmissions. These activities shall be distinguished from the purely private conduct of psychologists, which is not within the purview of the Ethics Code.

Membership in the APA commits members and student affiliates to comply with the standards of the APA Ethics Code and to the rules and procedures used to enforce them. Lack of awareness or misunderstanding of an Ethical Standard is not itself a defense to a charge of unethical conduct.

The procedures for filing, investigating, and resolving complaints of unethical conduct are described in the current Rules and Procedures of the APA Ethics Committee. APA may impose sanctions on its members for violations of the standards of the Ethics Code, including termination of APA membership, and may notify other bodies and individuals of its actions. Actions that violate the standards of the Ethics Code may also lead to the imposition of sanctions on psychologists or students whether or not they are APA members by bodies other than APA, including state psychological associations, other professional groups, psychology boards, other state or federal agencies, and payors for health services. In addition, APA may take action against a member after his or her conviction of a felony, expulsion or suspension from an affiliated state psychological association, or suspension or loss of licensure. When the sanction to be imposed by APA is less than expulsion, the 2001 Rules and Procedures do not guarantee an opportunity for an in-person hearing, but generally provide that complaints will be resolved only on the basis of a submitted record.

The Ethics Code is intended to provide guidance for psychologists and standards of professional conduct that can be applied by the APA and by other bodies that choose to adopt them. The Ethics Code is not intended to be a basis of civil liability. Whether a psychologist has violated the Ethics Code standards does not by itself determine whether the psychologist is legally liable in a court action, whether a contract is enforceable, or whether other legal consequences occur.

The modifiers used in some of the standards of this Ethics Code (e.g., *reasonably, appropriate, potentially*) are included in the standards when they would (1) allow professional judgment on the part of psychologists, (2) eliminate injustice or inequality that would occur without the modifier, (3) ensure applicability across the broad range of activities conducted by psychologists, or (4) guard against a set of rigid rules that might be quickly outdated. As used in this Ethics Code, the term *reasonable* means the prevailing professional judgment of psychologists engaged in similar activities in similar circumstances, given the knowledge the psychologist had or should have had at the time.

In the process of making decisions regarding their professional behavior, psychologists must consider this Ethics Code in addition to applicable laws and psychology board regulations. In applying the Ethics Code to their professional work, psychologists may consider other materials and guidelines that have been adopted or endorsed by scientific and professional psychological organizations and the dictates of their own conscience, as well as consult with others within the field. If this Ethics Code establishes a higher standard of conduct than is required by law, psychologists must meet the higher ethical standard. If psychologists' ethical responsibilities conflict with law, regulations, or other governing legal authority, psychologists make known their commitment to this Ethics Code and take steps to resolve the conflict in a responsible manner. If the conflict is unresolvable via such means, psychologists may adhere to the requirements of the law, regulations, or other governing authority in keeping with basic principles of human rights.

PREAMBLE

Psychologists are committed to increasing scientific and professional knowledge of behavior and people's understanding of themselves and others and to the use of such knowledge to improve the condition of individuals, organizations, and society. Psychologists respect and protect civil and human rights and the central importance of freedom of inquiry and expression in research, teaching, and publication. They strive to help the public in developing informed judgments and choices concerning human behavior. In doing so, they perform many roles, such as researcher, educator, diagnostician, therapist, supervisor, consultant, administrator, social interventionist, and expert witness. This Ethics Code provides a common set of principles and standards upon which psychologists build their professional and scientific work.

This Ethics Code is intended to provide specific standards to cover most situations encountered by psychologists. It has as its goals the welfare and protection of the individuals and groups with whom psychologists work and the education of members, students, and the public regarding ethical standards of the discipline.

The development of a dynamic set of ethical standards for psychologists' work-related conduct requires a personal commitment and lifelong effort to act ethically; to encourage ethical behavior by students, supervisees, employees, and colleagues; and to consult with others concerning ethical problems.

GENERAL PRINCIPLES

This section consists of General Principles. General Principles, as opposed to Ethical Standards, are aspirational in nature. Their intent is to guide and inspire psychologists toward the very highest ethical ideals of the profession. General Principles, in contrast to Ethical Standards, do not represent obligations and should not form the basis for imposing sanctions. Relying upon General Principles for either of these reasons distorts both their meaning and purpose.

Principle A: Beneficence and Nonmaleficence

Psychologists strive to benefit those with whom they work and take care to do no harm. In their professional actions, psychologists seek to safeguard the welfare and rights of those with whom they interact professionally and other affected persons, and the welfare of animal subjects of research. When conflicts occur among psychologists' obligations or concerns, they attempt to resolve these conflicts in a responsible fashion that avoids or minimizes harm. Because psychologists' scientific and professional judgments and actions may affect the lives of others, they are alert to and guard against personal, financial, social, organizational, or political factors that might lead to misuse of their influence. Psychologists strive to be aware of the possible effect of their own physical and mental health on their ability to help those with whom they work.

Principle B: Fidelity and Responsibility

Psychologists establish relationships of trust with those with whom they work. They are aware of their professional and scientific responsibilities to society and to the specific communities in which they work. Psychologists uphold professional standards of conduct, clarify their professional roles and obligations, accept appropriate responsibility for their behavior, and seek to manage conflicts of interest that could lead to exploitation or harm. Psychologists consult with, refer to, or cooperate with other professionals and institutions to the extent needed to serve the best interests of those with whom they work. They are concerned about the ethical compliance of their colleagues' scientific and professional conduct. Psychologists strive to contribute a portion of their professional time for little or no compensation or personal advantage.

Principle C: Integrity

Psychologists seek to promote accuracy, honesty, and truthfulness in the science, teaching, and practice of psychology. In these activities psychologists do not steal, cheat, or engage in fraud, subterfuge, or intentional misrepresentation of fact. Psychologists strive to keep their promises and to avoid unwise or unclear commitments. In situations in which deception may be ethically justifiable to maximize benefits and minimize harm, psychologists have a serious obligation to consider the need for, the possible consequences of, and their responsibility to correct any resulting mistrust or other harmful effects that arise from the use of such techniques.

Principle D: Justice

Psychologists recognize that fairness and justice entitle all persons to access to and benefit from the contributions of psychology and to equal quality in the processes, procedures, and services being conducted by psychologists. Psychologists exercise reasonable judgment and take precautions to ensure that their potential biases, the boundaries of their competence, and the limitations of their expertise do not lead to or condone unjust practices.

Principle E: Respect for People's Rights and Dignity

Psychologists respect the dignity and worth of all people, and the rights of individuals to privacy, confidentiality, and self-determination. Psychologists are aware that special safeguards may be necessary to protect the rights and welfare of persons or communities whose vulnerabilities impair autonomous decision making. Psychologists are aware of and respect cultural, individual, and role differences, including those based on age, gender, gender identity, race, ethnicity, culture, national origin, religion, sexual orientation, disability, language, and socioeconomic status and consider these factors when working with members of such groups. Psychologists try to eliminate the effect on their work of biases based on those factors, and they do not knowingly participate in or condone activities of others based upon such prejudices.

ETHICAL STANDARDS

1. Resolving Ethical Issues

1.01 Misuse of Psychologists' Work

If psychologists learn of misuse or misrepresentation of their work, they take reasonable steps to correct or minimize the misuse or misrepresentation.

1.02 Conflicts Between Ethics and Law, Regulations, or Other Governing Legal Authority

If psychologists' ethical responsibilities conflict with law, regulations, or other governing legal authority, psychologists make known their commitment to the Ethics Code and take steps to resolve the conflict. If the conflict is unresolvable via such means, psychologists may adhere to the requirements of the law, regulations, or other governing legal authority.

1.03 Conflicts Between Ethics and Organizational Demands

If the demands of an organization with which psychologists are affiliated or for whom they are working conflict with this Ethics Code, psychologists clarify the nature of the conflict, make known their commitment to the Ethics Code, and to the extent feasible, resolve the conflict in a way that permits adherence to the Ethics Code.

1.04 Informal Resolution of Ethical Violations

When psychologists believe that there may have been an ethical violation by another psychologist, they attempt to resolve the issue by bringing it to the attention of that individual, if an informal resolution appears appropriate and the intervention does not violate any confidentiality rights that may be involved. (See also Standards 1.02, Conflicts Between Ethics and Law, Regulations, or Other Governing Legal Authority, and 1.03, Conflicts Between Ethics and Organizational Demands.)

1.05 Reporting Ethical Violations

If an apparent ethical violation has substantially harmed or is likely to substantially harm a person or organization and is not appropriate for informal resolution under Standard 1.04, Informal Resolution of Ethical Violations, or is not resolved properly in that fashion, psychologists take further action appropriate to the situation. Such action might include referral to state or national committees on professional ethics, to state licensing boards, or to the appropriate institutional authorities. This standard does not apply when an intervention would violate confidentiality rights or when psychologists have been retained to review the work of another psychologist whose professional conduct is in question. (See also Standard 1.02, Conflicts Between Ethics and Law, Regulations, or Other Governing Legal Authority.)

1.06 Cooperating With Ethics Committees

Psychologists cooperate in ethics investigations, proceedings, and resulting requirements of the APA or any affiliated state psychological association to which they belong. In doing so, they address any confidentiality issues. Failure to cooperate is itself an ethics violation. However, making a request for deferment of adjudication of an ethics complaint pending the outcome of litigation does not alone constitute noncooperation.

1.07 Improper Complaints

Psychologists do not file or encourage the filing of ethics complaints that are made with reckless disregard for or willful ignorance of facts that would disprove the allegation.

1.08 Unfair Discrimination Against Complainants and Respondents

Psychologists do not deny persons employment, advancement, admissions to academic or other programs, tenure, or promotion, based solely upon their having made or their being the subject of an ethics complaint. This does not preclude taking action based upon the outcome of such proceedings or considering other appropriate information.

2. Competence

2.01 Boundaries of Competence

(a) Psychologists provide services, teach, and conduct research with populations and in areas only within the boundaries of their competence, based on their education, training, supervised experience, consultation, study, or professional experience.

(b) Where scientific or professional knowledge in the discipline of psychology establishes that an understanding of factors associated with age, gender, gender identity, race, ethnicity, culture, national origin, religion, sexual orientation, disability, language, or socioeconomic status is essential for effective implementation of their services or research, psychologists have or obtain the training, experience, consultation, or supervision necessary to ensure the competence of their services, or they make appropriate referrals, except as provided in Standard 2.02, Providing Services in Emergencies.

(c) Psychologists planning to provide services, teach, or conduct research involving populations, areas, techniques, or technologies new to them undertake relevant education, training, supervised experience, consultation, or study.

(d) When psychologists are asked to provide services to individuals for whom appropriate mental health services are not available and for which psychologists have not obtained the competence necessary, psychologists with closely related prior training or experience may provide such services in order to ensure that services are not denied if they make a reasonable effort to obtain the competence required by using relevant research, training, consultation, or study.

(e) In those emerging areas in which generally recognized standards for preparatory training do not yet exist, psychologists nevertheless take reasonable steps to ensure the competence of their work and to protect clients/patients, students, supervisees, research participants, organizational clients, and others from harm.

(f) When assuming forensic roles, psychologists are or become reasonably familiar with the judicial or administrative rules governing their roles.

2.02 Providing Services in Emergencies

In emergencies, when psychologists provide services to individuals for whom other mental health services are not available and for which psychologists have not obtained the necessary training, psychologists may provide such services in order to ensure that services are not denied. The services are discontinued as soon as the emergency has ended or appropriate services are available.

2.03 Maintaining Competence

Psychologists undertake ongoing efforts to develop and maintain their competence.

2.04 Bases for Scientific and Professional Judgments

Psychologists' work is based upon established scientific and professional knowledge of the discipline. (See also Standards 2.01e, Boundaries of Competence, and 10.01b, Informed Consent to Therapy.)

2.05 Delegation of Work to Others

Psychologists who delegate work to employees, supervisees, or research or teaching assistants or who use the services of others, such as interpreters, take reasonable steps to (1) avoid delegating such work to persons who have a multiple relationship with those being served that would likely lead to exploitation or loss of objectivity; (2) authorize only those responsibilities that such persons can be expected to perform competently on the basis of their education, training, or experience, either independently or with the level of supervision being provided; and (3) see that such persons perform these services competently. (See also Standards 2.02, Providing Services in Emergencies; 3.05, Multiple Relationships; 4.01, Maintaining Confidentiality; 9.01, Bases for Assessments; 9.02, Use of Assessments; 9.03, Informed Consent in Assessments; and 9.07, Assessment by Unqualified Persons.)

2.06 Personal Problems and Conflicts

(a) Psychologists refrain from initiating an activity when they know or should know that there is a substantial likelihood that their personal problems will prevent them from performing their work-related activities in a competent manner.

(b) When psychologists become aware of personal problems that may interfere with their performing work-related duties adequately, they take appropriate measures, such as obtaining professional consultation or assistance, and determine whether they should limit, suspend, or terminate their work-related duties. (See also Standard 10.10, Terminating Therapy.)

3. Human Relations

3.01 Unfair Discrimination

In their work-related activities, psychologists do not engage in unfair discrimination based on age, gender, gender identity, race, ethnicity, culture, national origin, religion, sexual orientation, disability, socioeconomic status, or any basis proscribed by law.

3.02 Sexual Harassment

Psychologists do not engage in sexual harassment. Sexual harassment is sexual solicitation, physical advances, or verbal or nonverbal conduct that is sexual in nature, that occurs in connection with the psychologist's activities or roles as a psychologist, and that either (1) is unwelcome, is offensive, or creates a hostile workplace or educational environment, and the psychologist knows or is told this or (2) is sufficiently severe or intense to be abusive to a reasonable person in the context. Sexual harassment can consist of a single intense or severe act or of multiple persistent or pervasive acts. (See also Standard 1.08, Unfair Discrimination Against Complainants and Respondents.)

3.03 Other Harassment

Psychologists do not knowingly engage in behavior that is harassing or demeaning to persons with whom they interact in their work based on factors such as those persons' age, gender, gender identity, race, ethnicity, culture, national origin, religion, sexual orientation, disability, language, or socioeconomic status.

3.04 Avoiding Harm

Psychologists take reasonable steps to avoid harming their clients/patients, students, supervisees, research participants, organizational clients, and others with whom they work, and to minimize harm where it is foreseeable and unavoidable.

3.05 Multiple Relationships

(a) A multiple relationship occurs when a psychologist is in a professional role with a person and (1) at the same time is in another role with the same person, (2) at the same time is in a relationship with a person closely associated with or related to the person with whom the psychologist has the professional relationship, or (3) promises to enter into another relationship in the future with the person or a person closely associated with or related to the person.

A psychologist refrains from entering into a multiple relationship if the multiple relationship could reasonably be expected to impair the psychologist's objectivity, competence, or effectiveness in performing his or her functions as a psychologist, or otherwise risks exploitation or harm to the person with whom the professional relationship exists.

Multiple relationships that would not reasonably be expected to cause impairment or risk exploitation or harm are not unethical.

(b) If a psychologist finds that, due to unforeseen factors, a potentially harmful multiple relationship has arisen, the psychologist takes reasonable steps to resolve it with due regard for the best interests of the affected person and maximal compliance with the Ethics Code.

(c) When psychologists are required by law, institutional policy, or extraordinary circumstances to serve in more than one role in judicial or administrative proceedings, at the outset they clarify role expectations and the extent of confidentiality and thereafter as changes occur. (See also Standards 3.04, Avoiding Harm, and 3.07, Third-Party Requests for Services.)

3.06 Conflict of Interest

Psychologists refrain from taking on a professional role when personal, scientific, professional, legal, financial, or other interests or relationships could reasonably be expected to (1) impair their objectivity, competence, or effectiveness in performing their functions as psychologists or (2) expose the person or organization with whom the professional relationship exists to harm or exploitation.

3.07 Third-Party Requests for Services

When psychologists agree to provide services to a person or entity at the request of a third party, psychologists attempt to clarify at the outset of the service the nature of the relationship with all individuals or organizations involved. This clarification includes the role of the psychologist (e.g., therapist, consultant, diagnostician, or expert witness), an identification of who is the client, the probable uses of the services provided or the information obtained, and the fact that there may be limits to confidentiality. (See also Standards 3.05, Multiple Relationships, and 4.02, Discussing the Limits of Confidentiality.)

3.08 Exploitative Relationships

Psychologists do not exploit persons over whom they have supervisory, evaluative, or other authority such as clients/patients, students, supervisees, research participants, and employees. (See also Standards 3.05, Multiple Relationships; 6.04, Fees and Financial Arrangements; 6.05, Barter With Clients/Patients; 7.07, Sexual Relationships With Students and Supervisees; 10.05, Sexual Intimacies With Current Therapy Clients/Patients; 10.06, Sexual Intimacies With Relatives or Significant Others of Current Therapy Clients/Patients; 10.07, Therapy With Former Sexual Partners; and 10.08, Sexual Intimacies With Former Therapy Clients/Patients.)

3.09 Cooperation With Other Professionals

When indicated and professionally appropriate, psychologists cooperate with other professionals in order to serve their clients/patients effectively and appropriately. (See also Standard 4.05, Disclosures.)

3.10 Informed Consent

(a) When psychologists conduct research or provide assessment, therapy, counseling, or consulting services in person or via electronic transmission or other forms of communication, they obtain the informed consent of the individual or individuals using language that is reasonably understandable to that person or persons except when conducting such activities without consent is mandated by law or governmental regulation or as otherwise provided in this Ethics Code. (See also Standards 8.02, Informed Consent to Research; 9.03, Informed Consent in Assessments; and 10.01, Informed Consent to Therapy.)

(b) For persons who are legally incapable of giving informed consent, psychologists nevertheless (1) provide an appropriate explanation, (2) seek the individual's assent, (3) consider such persons' preferences and best interests, and (4) obtain appropriate permission from a legally authorized person, if such substitute consent is permitted or required by law. When consent by a legally authorized person is not permitted or required by law, psychologists take reasonable steps to protect the individual's rights and welfare.

(c) When psychological services are court ordered or otherwise mandated, psychologists inform the individual of the nature of the anticipated services, including whether the services are court ordered or mandated and any limits of confidentiality, before proceeding.

(d) Psychologists appropriately document written or oral consent, permission, and assent. (See also Standards 8.02, Informed Consent to Research; 9.03, Informed Consent in Assessments; and 10.01, Informed Consent to Therapy.)

3.11 Psychological Services Delivered To or Through Organizations

(a) Psychologists delivering services to or through organizations provide information beforehand to clients and when appropriate those directly affected by the services about (1) the nature and objectives of the services, (2) the intended recipients, (3) which of the individuals are clients, (4) the relationship the psychologist will have with each person and the organization, (5) the probable uses of services provided and information obtained, (6) who will have access to the information, and (7) limits of confidentiality. As soon as feasible, they provide information about the results and conclusions of such services to appropriate persons.

(b) If psychologists will be precluded by law or by organizational roles from providing such information to particular individuals or groups, they so inform those individuals or groups at the outset of the service.

3.12 Interruption of Psychological Services

Unless otherwise covered by contract, psychologists make reasonable efforts to plan for facilitating services in the event that psychological services are interrupted by factors such as the psychologist's illness, death, unavailability, relocation, or retirement or by the client's/ patient's relocation or financial limitations. (See also Standard 6.02c, Maintenance, Dissemination, and Disposal of Confidential Records of Professional and Scientific Work.)

4. Privacy And Confidentiality

4.01 Maintaining Confidentiality

Psychologists have a primary obligation and take reasonable precautions to protect confidential information obtained through or stored in any medium, recognizing that the extent and limits of confidentiality may be regulated by law or established by institutional rules or professional or scientific relationship. (See also Standard 2.05, Delegation of Work to Others.)

4.02 Discussing the Limits of Confidentiality

(a) Psychologists discuss with persons (including, to the extent feasible, persons who are legally incapable of giving informed consent and their legal representatives) and organizations with whom they establish a scientific or professional relationship (1) the relevant limits of confidentiality and (2) the foreseeable uses of the information generated through their psychological activities. (See also Standard 3.10, Informed Consent.)

(b) Unless it is not feasible or is contraindicated, the discussion of confidentiality occurs at the outset of the relationship and thereafter as new circumstances may warrant.

(c) Psychologists who offer services, products, or information via electronic transmission inform clients/patients of the risks to privacy and limits of confidentiality.

4.03 Recording

Before recording the voices or images of individuals to whom they provide services, psychologists obtain permission from all such persons or their legal representatives. (See also Standards 8.03, Informed Consent for Recording Voices and Images in Research; 8.05, Dispensing With Informed Consent for Research; and 8.07, Deception in Research.)

4.04 Minimizing Intrusions on Privacy

(a) Psychologists include in written and oral reports and consultations, only information germane to the purpose for which the communication is made.

(b) Psychologists discuss confidential information obtained in their work only for appropriate scientific or professional purposes and only with persons clearly concerned with such matters.

4.05 Disclosures

(a) Psychologists may disclose confidential information with the appropriate consent of the organizational client, the individual client/patient, or another legally authorized person on behalf of the client/patient unless prohibited by law.

(b) Psychologists disclose confidential information without the consent of the individual only as mandated by law, or where permitted by law for a valid purpose such as to (1) provide needed professional services; (2) obtain appropriate professional consultations; (3) protect the client/patient, psychologist, or others from harm; or (4) obtain payment for services from a client/patient, in which instance disclosure is limited to the minimum that is necessary to achieve the purpose. (See also Standard 6.04e, Fees and Financial Arrangements.)

4.06 Consultations

When consulting with colleagues, (1) psychologists do not disclose confidential information that reasonably could lead to the identification of a client/patient, research participant, or other person or organization with whom they have a confidential relationship unless they have obtained the prior consent of the person or organization or the disclosure cannot be avoided, and (2) they disclose information only to the extent necessary to achieve the purposes of the consultation. (See also Standard 4.01, Maintaining Confidentiality.)

4.07 Use of Confidential Information for Didactic or Other Purposes

Psychologists do not disclose in their writings, lectures, or other public media, confidential, personally identifiable information concerning their clients/patients, students, research participants, organizational clients, or other recipients of their services that they obtained during the course of their work, unless (1) they take reasonable steps to disguise the person or organization, (2) the person or organization has consented in writing, or (3) there is legal authorization for doing so.

5. Advertising and Other Public Statements

5.01 Avoidance of False or Deceptive Statements

(a) Public statements include but are not limited to paid or unpaid advertising, product endorsements, grant applications, licensing applications, other credentialing applications, brochures, printed matter, directory listings, personal resumes or curricula vitae, or comments for use in media such as print or electronic transmission, statements in legal proceedings, lectures and public oral presentations, and published materials. Psychologists do not knowingly make public statements that are false, deceptive, or fraudulent concerning their research, practice, or other work activities or those of persons or organizations with which they are affiliated.

(b) Psychologists do not make false, deceptive, or fraudulent statements concerning (1) their training, experience, or competence; (2) their academic degrees; (3) their credentials; (4) their institutional or association affiliations; (5) their services; (6) the scientific or clinical basis for, or results or degree of success of, their services; (7) their fees; or (8) their publications or research findings.

(c) Psychologists claim degrees as credentials for their health services only if those degrees (1) were earned from a regionally accredited educational institution or (2) were the basis for psychology licensure by the state in which they practice.

5.02 Statements by Others

(a) Psychologists who engage others to create or place public statements that promote their professional practice, products, or activities retain professional responsibility for such statements.

(b) Psychologists do not compensate employees of press, radio, television, or other communication media in return for publicity in a news item. (See also Standard 1.01, Misuse of Psychologists' Work.)

(c) A paid advertisement relating to psychologists' activities must be identified or clearly recognizable as such.

5.03 Descriptions of Workshops and
Non-Degree-Granting Educational Programs

To the degree to which they exercise control, psychologists responsible for announcements, catalogs, brochures, or advertisements describing workshops, seminars, or other non-degree-granting educational programs ensure that they accurately describe the audience for which the program is intended, the educational objectives, the presenters, and the fees involved.

5.04 Media Presentations

When psychologists provide public advice or comment via print, internet, or other electronic transmission, they take precautions to ensure that statements (1) are based on their professional knowledge, training, or experience in accord with appropriate psychological literature and practice; (2) are otherwise consistent with this Ethics Code; and (3) do not indicate that a professional relationship has been established with the recipient. (See also Standard 2.04, Bases for Scientific and Professional Judgments.)

5.05 Testimonials

Psychologists do not solicit testimonials from current therapy clients/patients or other persons who because of their particular circumstances are vulnerable to undue influence.

5.06 In-Person Solicitation

Psychologists do not engage, directly or through agents, in uninvited in-person solicitation of business from actual or potential therapy clients/patients or other persons who because of their particular circumstances are vulnerable to undue influence. However, this prohibition does not preclude (1) attempting to implement appropriate collateral contacts for the purpose of benefiting an already engaged therapy client/patient or (2) providing disaster or community outreach services.

6. Record Keeping and Fees

6.01 Documentation of Professional and
Scientific Work and Maintenance of Records

Psychologists create, and to the extent the records are under their control, maintain, disseminate, store, retain, and dispose of records and data relating to their professional and scientific work in order to (1) facilitate provision of services later by them or by other professionals, (2) allow for replication of research design and analyses, (3) meet institutional requirements, (4) ensure accuracy of billing and payments, and (5) ensure compliance with law. (See also Standard 4.01, Maintaining Confidentiality.)

6.02 Maintenance, Dissemination, and Disposal of
Confidential Records of Professional and Scientific Work

(a) Psychologists maintain confidentiality in creating, storing, accessing, transferring, and disposing of records under their control, whether these are written, automated, or in any other medium. (See also Standards 4.01, Maintaining Confidentiality, and 6.01, Documentation of Professional and Scientific Work and Maintenance of Records.)

(b) If confidential information concerning recipients of psychological services is entered into databases or systems of records available to persons whose access has not been consented to by the recipient, psychologists use coding or other techniques to avoid the inclusion of personal identifiers.

(c) Psychologists make plans in advance to facilitate the appropriate transfer and to protect the confidentiality of records and data in the event of psychologists' withdrawal from positions or practice. (See also Standards 3.12, Interruption of Psychological Services, and 10.09, Interruption of Therapy.)

6.03 Withholding Records for Nonpayment

Psychologists may not withhold records under their control that are requested and needed for a client's/patient's emergency treatment solely because payment has not been received.

6.04 Fees and Financial Arrangements

(a) As early as is feasible in a professional or scientific relationship, psychologists and recipients of psychological services reach an agreement specifying compensation and billing arrangements.

(b) Psychologists' fee practices are consistent with law.

(c) Psychologists do not misrepresent their fees.

(d) If limitations to services can be anticipated because of limitations in financing, this is discussed with the recipient of services as early as is feasible. (See also Standards 10.09, Interruption of Therapy, and 10.10, Terminating Therapy.)

(e) If the recipient of services does not pay for services as agreed, and if psychologists intend to use collection agencies or legal measures to collect the fees, psychologists first inform the person that such measures will be taken and provide that person an opportunity to make prompt payment. (See also Standards 4.05, Disclosures; 6.03, Withholding Records for Nonpayment; and 10.01, Informed Consent to Therapy.)

6.05 Barter With Clients/Patients

Barter is the acceptance of goods, services, or other nonmonetary remuneration from clients/patients in return for psychological services. Psychologists may barter only if (1) it is not clinically contraindicated, and (2) the resulting arrangement is not exploitative. (See also Standards 3.05, Multiple Relationships, and 6.04, Fees and Financial Arrangements.)

6.06 Accuracy in Reports to Payors and Funding Sources

In their reports to payors for services or sources of research funding, psychologists take reasonable steps to ensure the accurate reporting of the nature of the service provided or research conducted, the fees, charges, or payments, and where applicable, the identity of the provider, the findings, and the diagnosis. (See also Standards 4.01, Maintaining Confidentiality; 4.04, Minimizing Intrusions on Privacy; and 4.05, Disclosures.)

6.07 Referrals and Fees

When psychologists pay, receive payment from, or divide fees with another professional, other than in an employer-employee relationship, the payment to each is based on the services provided (clinical, consultative, administrative, or other) and is not based on the referral itself. (See also Standard 3.09, Cooperation With Other Professionals.)

7. Education and Training

7.01 Design of Education and Training Programs

Psychologists responsible for education and training programs take reasonable steps to ensure that the programs are designed to provide the appropriate knowledge and proper experiences, and to meet the requirements for licensure, certification, or other goals for which claims are made by the program. (See also Standard 5.03, Descriptions of Workshops and Non-Degree-Granting Educational Programs.)

7.02 Descriptions of Education and Training Programs

Psychologists responsible for education and training programs take reasonable steps to ensure that there is a current and accurate description of the program content (including participation in required course- or program-related counseling, psychotherapy, experiential groups, consulting projects, or community service), training goals and objectives, stipends and benefits, and requirements that must be met for satisfactory completion of the program. This information must be made readily available to all interested parties.

7.03 Accuracy in Teaching

(a) Psychologists take reasonable steps to ensure that course syllabi are accurate regarding the subject matter to be covered, bases for evaluating progress, and the nature of course experiences. This standard does not preclude an instructor from modifying course content or requirements when the instructor considers it pedagogically necessary or desirable, so long as students are made aware of these modifications in a manner that enables them to fulfill course requirements. (See also Standard 5.01, Avoidance of False or Deceptive Statements.)

(b) When engaged in teaching or training, psychologists present psychological information accurately. (See also Standard 2.03, Maintaining Competence.)

7.04 Student Disclosure of Personal Information

Psychologists do not require students or supervisees to disclose personal information in course- or program-related activities, either orally or in writing, regarding sexual history, history of abuse and neglect, psychological treatment, and relationships with parents, peers, and spouses or significant others except if (1) the program or training facility has clearly identified this requirement in its admissions and program materials or (2) the information is necessary to evaluate or obtain assistance for students whose personal problems could reasonably be judged to be preventing them from performing their training- or professionally related activities in a competent manner or posing a threat to the students or others.

7.05 Mandatory Individual or Group Therapy

(a) When individual or group therapy is a program or course requirement, psychologists responsible for that program allow students in undergraduate and graduate programs the option of selecting such therapy from practitioners unaffiliated with the program. (See also Standard 7.02, Descriptions of Education and Training Programs.)

(b) Faculty who are or are likely to be responsible for evaluating students' academic performance do not themselves provide that therapy. (See also Standard 3.05, Multiple Relationships.)

7.06 Assessing Student and Supervisee Performance

(a) In academic and supervisory relationships, psychologists establish a timely and specific process for providing feedback to students and supervisees. Information regarding the process is provided to the student at the beginning of supervision.

(b) Psychologists evaluate students and supervisees on the basis of their actual performance on relevant and established program requirements.

7.07 Sexual Relationships With Students and Supervisees

Psychologists do not engage in sexual relationships with students or supervisees who are in their department, agency, or training center or over whom psychologists have or are likely to have evaluative authority. (See also Standard 3.05, Multiple Relationships.)

8. Research and Publication

8.01 Institutional Approval

When institutional approval is required, psychologists provide accurate information about their research proposals and obtain approval prior to conducting the research. They conduct the research in accordance with the approved research protocol.

8.02 Informed Consent to Research

(a) When obtaining informed consent as required in Standard 3.10, Informed Consent, psychologists inform participants about (1) the purpose of the research, expected duration, and procedures; (2) their right to decline to participate and to withdraw from the research once participation has begun; (3) the foreseeable consequences of declining or withdrawing; (4) reasonably foreseeable factors that may be expected to influence their willingness to participate such as potential risks, discomfort, or adverse effects; (5) any prospective research benefits; (6) limits of confidentiality; (7) incentives for participation; and (8) whom to contact for questions about the research and research participants' rights. They provide opportunity for the prospective participants to ask questions and receive answers. (See also Standards 8.03, Informed Consent for Recording Voices and Images in Research; 8.05, Dispensing With Informed Consent for Research; and 8.07, Deception in Research.)

(b) Psychologists conducting intervention research involving the use of experimental treatments clarify to participants at the outset of the research (1) the experimental nature of the treatment; (2) the services that will or will not be available to the control group(s) if appropriate; (3) the means by which assignment to treatment and control groups will be made; (4) available treatment alternatives if an individual does not wish to participate in the research or wishes to withdraw once a study has begun; and (5) compensation for or monetary costs of participating including, if appropriate, whether reimbursement from the participant or a third-party payor will be sought. (See also Standard 8.02a, Informed Consent to Research.)

8.03 Informed Consent for Recording Voices and Images in Research

Psychologists obtain informed consent from research participants prior to recording their voices or images for data collection unless (1) the research consists solely of naturalistic observations in public places, and it is not anticipated that the recording will be used in a manner that could cause personal identification or harm, or (2) the research design includes deception, and consent for the use of the recording is obtained during debriefing. (See also Standard 8.07, Deception in Research.)

8.04 Client/Patient, Student, and Subordinate Research Participants

(a) When psychologists conduct research with clients/patients, students, or subordinates as participants, psychologists take steps to protect the prospective participants from adverse consequences of declining or withdrawing from participation.

(b) When research participation is a course requirement or an opportunity for extra credit, the prospective participant is given the choice of equitable alternative activities.

8.05 Dispensing With Informed Consent for Research

Psychologists may dispense with informed consent only (1) where research would not reasonably be assumed to create distress or harm and involves (a) the study of normal educational practices, curricula, or classroom management methods conducted in educational settings; (b) only anonymous questionnaires, naturalistic observations, or archival research for which disclosure of responses would not place participants at risk of criminal or civil liability or damage their financial standing, employability, or reputation, and confidentiality is protected; or (c) the study of factors related to job or organization effectiveness conducted in organizational settings for which there is no risk to participants' employability, and confidentiality is protected or (2) where otherwise permitted by law or federal or institutional regulations.

8.06 Offering Inducements for Research Participation

(a) Psychologists make reasonable efforts to avoid offering excessive or inappropriate financial or other inducements for research participation when such inducements are likely to coerce participation.

(b) When offering professional services as an inducement for research participation, psychologists clarify the nature of the services, as well as the risks, obligations, and limitations. (See also Standard 6.05, Barter With Clients/Patients.)

8.07 Deception in Research

(a) Psychologists do not conduct a study involving deception unless they have determined that the use of deceptive techniques is justified by the study's significant prospective scientific, educational, or applied value and that effective nondeceptive alternative procedures are not feasible.

(b) Psychologists do not deceive prospective participants about research that is reasonably expected to cause physical pain or severe emotional distress.

(c) Psychologists explain any deception that is an integral feature of the design and conduct of an experiment to participants as early as is feasible, preferably at the conclusion of their participation, but no later than at the conclusion of the data collection, and permit participants to withdraw their data. (See also Standard 8.08, Debriefing.)

8.08 Debriefing

(a) Psychologists provide a prompt opportunity for participants to obtain appropriate information about the nature, results, and conclusions of the research, and they take reasonable steps to correct any misconceptions that participants may have of which the psychologists are aware.

(b) If scientific or humane values justify delaying or withholding this information, psychologists take reasonable measures to reduce the risk of harm.

(c) When psychologists become aware that research procedures have harmed a participant, they take reasonable steps to minimize the harm.

8.09 Humane Care and Use of Animals in Research

(a) Psychologists acquire, care for, use, and dispose of animals in compliance with current federal, state, and local laws and regulations, and with professional standards.

(b) Psychologists trained in research methods and experienced in the care of laboratory animals supervise all procedures involving animals and are responsible for ensuring appropriate consideration of their comfort, health, and humane treatment.

(c) Psychologists ensure that all individuals under their supervision who are using animals have received instruction in research methods and in the care, maintenance, and handling of the species being used, to the extent appropriate to their role. (See also Standard 2.05, Delegation of Work to Others.)

(d) Psychologists make reasonable efforts to minimize the discomfort, infection, illness, and pain of animal subjects.

(e) Psychologists use a procedure subjecting animals to pain, stress, or privation only when an alternative procedure is unavailable and the goal is justified by its prospective scientific, educational, or applied value.

(f) Psychologists perform surgical procedures under appropriate anesthesia and follow techniques to avoid infection and minimize pain during and after surgery.

(g) When it is appropriate that an animal's life be terminated, psychologists proceed rapidly, with an effort to minimize pain and in accordance with accepted procedures.

8.10 Reporting Research Results

(a) Psychologists do not fabricate data. (See also Standard 5.01a, Avoidance of False or Deceptive Statements.)

(b) If psychologists discover significant errors in their published data, they take reasonable steps to correct such errors in a correction, retraction, erratum, or other appropriate publication means.

8.11 Plagiarism

Psychologists do not present portions of another's work or data as their own, even if the other work or data source is cited occasionally.

8.12 Publication Credit

(a) Psychologists take responsibility and credit, including authorship credit, only for work they have actually performed or to which they have substantially contributed. (See also Standard 8.12b, Publication Credit.)

(b) Principal authorship and other publication credits accurately reflect the relative scientific or professional contributions of the individuals involved, regardless of their relative status. Mere possession of an institutional position, such as department chair, does not justify authorship credit. Minor contributions to the research or to the writing for publications are acknowledged appropriately, such as in footnotes or in an introductory statement.

(c) Except under exceptional circumstances, a student is listed as principal author on any multiple-authored article that is substantially based on the student's doctoral dissertation. Faculty advisors discuss publication credit with students as early as feasible and throughout the research and publication process as appropriate. (See also Standard 8.12b, Publication Credit.)

8.13 Duplicate Publication of Data

Psychologists do not publish, as original data, data that have been previously published. This does not preclude republishing data when they are accompanied by proper acknowledgment.

8.14 Sharing Research Data for Verification

(a) After research results are published, psychologists do not withhold the data on which their conclusions are based from other competent professionals who seek to verify the substantive claims through reanalysis and who intend to use such data only for that purpose, provided that the confidentiality of the participants can be protected and unless legal rights concerning proprietary data preclude their release. This does not preclude psychologists from requiring that such individuals or groups be responsible for costs associated with the provision of such information.

(b) Psychologists who request data from other psychologists to verify the substantive claims through reanalysis may use shared data only for the declared purpose. Requesting psychologists obtain prior written agreement for all other uses of the data.

8.15 Reviewers

Psychologists who review material submitted for presentation, publication, grant, or research proposal review respect the confidentiality of and the proprietary rights in such information of those who submitted it.

9. Assessment

9.01 Bases for Assessments

(a) Psychologists base the opinions contained in their recommendations, reports, and diagnostic or evaluative statements, including forensic testimony, on information and techniques sufficient to substantiate their findings. (See also Standard 2.04, Bases for Scientific and Professional Judgments.)

(b) Except as noted in 9.01c, psychologists provide opinions of the psychological characteristics of individuals only after they have conducted an examination of the individuals adequate to support their statements or conclusions. When, despite reasonable efforts, such an examination is not practical, psychologists document the efforts they made and the result of those efforts, clarify the probable impact of their limited information on the reliability and validity of their opinions, and appropriately limit the nature and extent of their conclusions or recommendations. (See also Standards 2.01, Boundaries of Competence, and 9.06, Interpreting Assessment Results.)

(c) When psychologists conduct a record review or provide consultation or supervision and an individual examination is not warranted or necessary for the opinion, psychologists explain this and the sources of information on which they based their conclusions and recommendations.

9.02 Use of Assessments

(a) Psychologists administer, adapt, score, interpret, or use assessment techniques, interviews, tests, or instruments in a manner and for purposes that are appropriate in light of the research on or evidence of the usefulness and proper application of the techniques.

(b) Psychologists use assessment instruments whose validity and reliability have been established for use with members of the population tested. When such validity or reliability has not been established, psychologists describe the strengths and limitations of test results and interpretation.

(c) Psychologists use assessment methods that are appropriate to an individual's language preference and competence, unless the use of an alternative language is relevant to the assessment issues.

9.03 Informed Consent in Assessments

(a) Psychologists obtain informed consent for assessments, evaluations, or diagnostic services, as described in Standard 3.10, Informed Consent, except when (1) testing is mandated by law or governmental regulations; (2) informed consent is implied because testing is conducted as a routine educational, institutional, or organizational activity (e.g., when participants voluntarily agree to assessment when applying for a job); or (3) one purpose of the testing is to evaluate decisional capacity. Informed consent includes an explanation of the nature and purpose of the assessment, fees, involvement of third parties, and limits of confidentiality and sufficient opportunity for the client/patient to ask questions and receive answers.

(b) Psychologists inform persons with questionable capacity to consent or for whom testing is mandated by law or governmental regulations about the nature and purpose of the proposed assessment services, using language that is reasonably understandable to the person being assessed.

(c) Psychologists using the services of an interpreter obtain informed consent from the client/patient to use that interpreter, ensure that confidentiality of test results and test security are maintained, and include in their recommendations, reports, and diagnostic or evaluative statements, including forensic testimony, discussion of any limitations on the data obtained. (See also Standards 2.05, Delegation of Work to Others; 4.01, Maintaining Confidentiality; 9.01, Bases for Assessments; 9.06, Interpreting Assessment Results; and 9.07, Assessment by Unqualified Persons.)

9.04 Release of Test Data

(a) The term *test data* refers to raw and scaled scores, client/patient responses to test questions or stimuli, and psychologists' notes and recordings concerning client/patient statements and behavior during an examination. Those portions of test materials that include client/patient responses are included in the definition of *test data*. Pursuant to a client/patient release, psychologists provide test data to the client/patient or other persons identified in the release. Psychologists may refrain from releasing test data to protect a client/patient or others from substantial harm or misuse or misrepresentation of the data or the test, recognizing that in many instances release of confidential information under these circumstances is regulated by law. (See also Standard 9.11, Maintaining Test Security.)

(b) In the absence of a client/patient release, psychologists provide test data only as required by law or court order.

9.05 Test Construction

Psychologists who develop tests and other assessment techniques use appropriate psychometric procedures and current scientific or professional knowledge for test design, standardization, validation, reduction or elimination of bias, and recommendations for use.

9.06 Interpreting Assessment Results

When interpreting assessment results, including automated interpretations, psychologists take into account the purpose of the assessment as well as the various test factors, test-taking abilities, and other characteristics of the person being assessed, such as situational, personal, linguistic, and cultural differences, that might affect psychologists' judgments or reduce the accuracy of their interpretations. They indicate any significant limitations of their interpretations. (See also Standards 2.01b and c, Boundaries of Competence, and 3.01, Unfair Discrimination.)

9.07 Assessment by Unqualified Persons

Psychologists do not promote the use of psychological assessment techniques by unqualified persons, except when such use is conducted for training purposes with appropriate supervision. (See also Standard 2.05, Delegation of Work to Others.)

9.08 Obsolete Tests and Outdated Test Results

(a) Psychologists do not base their assessment or intervention decisions or recommendations on data or test results that are outdated for the current purpose.

(b) Psychologists do not base such decisions or recommendations on tests and measures that are obsolete and not useful for the current purpose.

9.09 Test Scoring and Interpretation Services

(a) Psychologists who offer assessment or scoring services to other professionals accurately describe the purpose, norms, validity, reliability, and applications of the procedures and any special qualifications applicable to their use.

(b) Psychologists select scoring and interpretation services (including automated services) on the basis of evidence of the validity of the program and procedures as well as on other appropriate considerations. (See also Standard 2.01b and c, Boundaries of Competence.)

(c) Psychologists retain responsibility for the appropriate application, interpretation, and use of assessment instruments, whether they score and interpret such tests themselves or use automated or other services.

9.10 Explaining Assessment Results

Regardless of whether the scoring and interpretation are done by psychologists, by employees or assistants, or by automated or other outside services, psychologists take reasonable steps to ensure that explanations of results are given to the individual or designated representative unless the nature of the relationship precludes provision of an explanation of results (such as in some organizational consulting, preemployment or security screenings, and forensic evaluations), and this fact has been clearly explained to the person being assessed in advance.

9.11. Maintaining Test Security

The term *test materials* refers to manuals, instruments, protocols, and test questions or stimuli and does not include *test data* as defined in Standard 9.04, Release of Test Data. Psychologists make reasonable efforts to maintain the integrity and security of test materials and other assessment techniques consistent with law and contractual obligations, and in a manner that permits adherence to this Ethics Code.

10. Therapy

10.01 Informed Consent to Therapy

(a) When obtaining informed consent to therapy as required in Standard 3.10, Informed Consent, psychologists inform clients/patients as early as is feasible in the therapeutic relationship about the nature and anticipated course of therapy, fees, involvement of third parties, and limits of confidentiality and provide sufficient opportunity for the client/patient to ask questions and receive answers. (See also Standards 4.02, Discussing the Limits of Confidentiality, and 6.04, Fees and Financial Arrangements.)

(b) When obtaining informed consent for treatment for which generally recognized techniques and procedures have not been established, psychologists inform their clients/patients of the developing nature of the treatment, the potential risks involved, alternative treatments that may be available, and the voluntary nature of their participation. (See also Standards 2.01e, Boundaries of Competence, and 3.10, Informed Consent.)

(c) When the therapist is a trainee and the legal responsibility for the treatment provided resides with the supervisor, the client/patient, as part of the informed consent procedure, is informed that the therapist is in training and is being supervised and is given the name of the supervisor.

10.02 Therapy Involving Couples or Families

(a) When psychologists agree to provide services to several persons who have a relationship (such as spouses, significant others, or parents and children), they take reasonable steps to clarify at the outset (1) which of the individuals are clients/patients and (2) the relationship the psychologist will have with each person. This clarification includes the psychologist's role and the probable uses of the services provided or the information obtained. (See also Standard 4.02, Discussing the Limits of Confidentiality.)

(b) If it becomes apparent that psychologists may be called on to perform potentially conflicting roles (such as family therapist and then witness for one party in divorce proceedings), psychologists take reasonable steps to clarify and modify, or withdraw from, roles appropriately. (See also Standard 3.05c, Multiple Relationships.)

10.03 Group Therapy

When psychologists provide services to several persons in a group setting, they describe at the outset the roles and responsibilities of all parties and the limits of confidentiality.

10.04 Providing Therapy to Those Served by Others

In deciding whether to offer or provide services to those already receiving mental health services elsewhere, psychologists carefully consider the treatment issues and the potential client's/patient's welfare. Psychologists discuss these issues with the client/patient or another legally authorized person on behalf of the client/patient in order to minimize the risk of confusion and conflict, consult with the other service providers when appropriate, and proceed with caution and sensitivity to the therapeutic issues.

10.05 Sexual Intimacies With Current Therapy Clients/Patients

Psychologists do not engage in sexual intimacies with current therapy clients/patients.

10.06 Sexual Intimacies With Relatives or Significant Others of Current Therapy Clients/Patients

Psychologists do not engage in sexual intimacies with individuals they know to be close relatives, guardians, or significant others of current clients/patients. Psychologists do not terminate therapy to circumvent this standard.

10.07 Therapy With Former Sexual Partners

Psychologists do not accept as therapy clients/patients persons with whom they have engaged in sexual intimacies.

10.08 Sexual Intimacies With Former Therapy Clients/Patients

(a) Psychologists do not engage in sexual intimacies with former clients/patients for at least two years after cessation or termination of therapy.

(b) Psychologists do not engage in sexual intimacies with former clients/patients even after a two-year interval except in the most unusual circumstances. Psychologists who engage in such activity after the two years following cessation or termination of therapy and of having no sexual contact with the former client/patient bear the burden of demonstrating that there has been no exploitation, in light of all relevant factors, including (1) the amount of time that has passed since therapy terminated; (2) the nature, duration, and intensity of the therapy; (3) the circumstances of termination; (4) the client's/patient's personal history; (5) the client's/patient's current mental status; (6) the likelihood of adverse impact on the client/patient; and (7) any statements or actions made by the therapist during the course of therapy suggesting or inviting the possibility of a posttermination sexual or romantic relationship with the client/patient. (See also Standard 3.05, Multiple Relationships.)

10.09 Interruption of Therapy

When entering into employment or contractual relationships, psychologists make reasonable efforts to provide for orderly and appropriate resolution of responsibility for client/patient care in the event that the employment or contractual relationship ends, with paramount consideration given to the welfare of the client/patient. (See also Standard 3.12, Interruption of Psychological Services.)

10.10 Terminating Therapy

(a) Psychologists terminate therapy when it becomes reasonably clear that the client/ patient no longer needs the service, is not likely to benefit, or is being harmed by continued service.

(b) Psychologists may terminate therapy when threatened or otherwise endangered by the client/patient or another person with whom the client/patient has a relationship.

(c) Except where precluded by the actions of clients/patients or third-party payors, prior to termination psychologists provide pretermination counseling and suggest alternative service providers as appropriate.

History and Effective Date Footnote

This version of the APA Ethics Code was adopted by the American Psychological Association's Council of Representatives during its meeting, August 21, 2002, and is effective beginning June 1, 2003. Inquiries concerning the substance or interpretation of the APA Ethics Code should be addressed to the Director, Office of Ethics, American Psychological Association, 750 First Street, NE, Washington, DC 20002–4242. The Ethics Code and information regarding the Code can be found on the APA web site, http://www.apa.org/ethics. The standards in this Ethics Code will be used to adjudicate complaints brought concerning alleged conduct occurring on or after the effective date. Complaints regarding conduct occurring prior to the effective date will be adjudicated on the basis of the version of the Ethics Code that was in effect at the time the conduct occurred.

The APA has previously published its Ethics Code as follows:

American Psychological Association. (1953). *Ethical standards of psychologists*. Washington, DC: Author.

American Psychological Association. (1959). Ethical standards of psychologists. *American Psychologist, 14*, 279–282.

American Psychological Association. (1963). Ethical standards of psychologists. *American Psychologist, 18*, 56–60.

American Psychological Association. (1968). Ethical standards of psychologists. *American Psychologist, 23,* 357–361.

American Psychological Association. (1977, March). Ethical standards of psychologists. *APA Monitor,* 22–23.

American Psychological Association. (1979). *Ethical standards of psychologists.* Washington, DC: Author.

American Psychological Association. (1981). Ethical principles of psychologists. *American Psychologist, 36,* 633–638.

American Psychological Association. (1990). Ethical principles of psychologists (Amended June 2, 1989). *American Psychologist, 45,* 390–395.

American Psychological Association. (1992). Ethical principles of psychologists and code of conduct. *American Psychologist, 47,* 1597–1611.

Request copies of the APA's Ethical Principles of Psychologists and Code of Conduct from the APA Order Department, 750 First Street, NE, Washington, DC 20002–4242, or phone (202) 336–5510.

Appendix B

ACA *Code of Ethics*

As approved by the ACA Governing Council

2005

MISSION

The mission of the American Counseling Association is to enhance the quality of life in society by promoting the development of professional counselors, advancing the counseling profession, and using the profession and practice of counseling to promote respect for human dignity and diversity.

CONTENTS

ACA CODE OF ETHICS PREAMBLE

The American Counseling Association is an educational, scientific, and professional organization whose members work in a variety of settings and serve in multiple capacities. ACA members are dedicated to the enhancement of human development throughout the life span. Association members recognize diversity and embrace a cross-cultural approach in support of the worth, dignity, potential, and uniqueness of people within their social and cultural contexts.

Professional values are an important way of living out an ethical commitment. Values inform principles. Inherently held values that guide our behaviors or exceed prescribed behaviors are deeply ingrained in the counselor and developed out of personal dedication, rather than the mandatory requirement of an external organization.

ACA CODE OF ETHICS PURPOSE

The *ACA Code of Ethics* serves five main purposes:

1. The *Code* enables the association to clarify to current and future members, and to those served by members, the nature of the ethical responsibilities held in common by its members.

2. The *Code* helps support the mission of the association.

3. The *Code* establishes principles that define ethical behavior and best practices of association members.

4. The *Code* serves as an ethical guide designed to assist members in constructing a professional course of action that best serves those utilizing counseling services and best promotes the values of the counseling profession.

5. The *Code* serves as the basis for processing of ethical complaints and inquiries initiated against members of the association.

The *ACA Code of Ethics* contains eight main sections that address the following areas:

Section A: The Counseling Relationship

Section B: Confidentiality, Privileged Communication, and Privacy

Section C: Professional Responsibility

Section D: Relationships With Other Professionals

Section E: Evaluation, Assessment, and Interpretation

Section F: Supervision, Training, and Teaching

Section G: Research and Publication

Section H: Resolving Ethical Issues

Each section of the *ACA Code of Ethics* begins with an Introduction. The introductions to each section discuss what counselors should aspire to with regard to ethical behavior and responsibility. The Introduction helps set the tone for that particular section and provides a starting point that invites reflection on the ethical mandates contained in each part of the *ACA Code of Ethics.*

When counselors are faced with ethical dilemmas that are difficult to resolve, they are expected to engage in a carefully considered ethical decision-making process. Reasonable differences of opinion can and do exist among counselors with respect to the ways in which values, ethical principles, and ethical standards would be applied when they conflict. While there is no specific ethical decision-making model that is most effective, counselors are expected to be familiar with a credible model of decision making that can bear public scrutiny and its application.

Through a chosen ethical decision-making process and evaluation of the context of the situation, counselors are empowered to make decisions that help expand the capacity of people to grow and develop.

A brief glossary is given to provide readers with a concise description of some of the terms used in the *ACA Code of Ethics*.

Section A

The Counseling Relationship

Introduction

Counselors encourage client growth and development in ways that foster the interest and welfare of clients and promote formation of healthy relationships. Counselors actively attempt to understand the diverse cultural backgrounds of the clients they serve. Counselors also explore their own cultural identities and how these affect their values and beliefs about the counseling process.

Counselors are encouraged to contribute to society by devoting a portion of their professional activity to services for which there is little or no financial return (pro bono publico).

A.1. Welfare of Those Served by Counselors

A.1.a. Primary Responsibility   The primary responsibility of counselors is to respect the dignity and to promote the welfare of clients.

A.1.b. Records   Counselors maintain records necessary for rendering professional services to their clients and as required by laws, regulations, or agency or institution procedures. Counselors include sufficient and timely documentation in their client records to facilitate the delivery and continuity of needed services. Counselors take reasonable steps to ensure that documentation in records accurately reflects client progress and services provided. If errors are made in client records, counselors take steps to properly note the correction of such errors according to agency or institutional policies. *(See A.12.g.7., B.6., B.6.g., G.2.j.)*

A.1.c. Counseling Plans   Counselors and their clients work jointly in devising integrated counseling plans that offer reasonable promise of success and are consistent with abilities and circumstances of clients. Counselors and clients regularly review counseling plans to assess their continued viability and effectiveness, respecting the freedom of choice of clients. *(See A.2.a., A.2.d., A.12.g.)*

A.1.d. Support Network Involvement   Counselors recognize that support networks hold various meanings in the lives of clients and consider enlisting the support, understanding, and involvement of others (e.g., religious/spiritual/community leaders, family members, friends) as positive resources, when appropriate, with client consent.

A.1.e. Employment Needs   Counselors work with their clients considering employment in jobs that are consistent with the overall abilities, vocational limitations, physical restrictions, general temperament, interest and aptitude patterns, social skills, education, general qualifications, and other relevant characteristics and needs of clients. When appropriate, counselors appropriately trained in career development will assist in the placement of clients in positions that are consistent with the interest, culture, and the welfare of clients, employers, and/or the public.

A.2. Informed Consent in the Counseling Relationship
(See A.12.g., B.5., B.6.b., E.3., E.13.b., F.1.c., G.2.a.)

A.2.a. Informed Consent   Clients have the freedom to choose whether to enter into or remain in a counseling relationship and need adequate information about the counseling process and the counselor. Counselors have an obligation to review in writing and verbally with clients the rights and responsibilities of both the counselor and the client. Informed consent is an ongoing part of the counseling process, and counselors appropriately document discussions of informed consent throughout the counseling relationship.

A.2.b. Types of Information Needed   Counselors explicitly explain to clients the nature of all services provided. They inform clients about issues such as, but not limited to, the following: the purposes, goals, techniques, procedures, limitations, potential risks, and benefits of services; the counselor's qualifications, credentials, and relevant experience; continuation of services upon the incapacitation or death of a counselor; and other pertinent information. Counselors take steps to ensure that clients understand the implications of diagnosis, the intended use of tests and reports, fees, and billing arrangements. Clients have the right to confidentiality and to be provided with an explanation of its limitations (including how supervisors and/or treatment team professionals are involved); to obtain clear information about their records; to participate in the ongoing counseling plans; and to refuse any services or modality change and to be advised of the consequences of such refusal.

A.2.c. Developmental and Cultural Sensitivity   Counselors communicate information in ways that are both developmentally and culturally appropriate. Counselors use clear and understandable language when discussing issues related to informed consent. When clients have difficulty understanding the language used by counselors, they provide necessary services (e.g., arranging for a qualified interpreter or translator) to ensure comprehension by clients. In collaboration with clients, counselors consider cultural implications of informed consent procedures and, where possible, counselors adjust their practices accordingly.

A.2.d. Inability to Give Consent   When counseling minors or persons unable to give voluntary consent, counselors seek the assent of clients to services, and include them in decision making as appropriate. Counselors recognize the need to balance the ethical rights of clients to make choices, their capacity to give consent or assent to receive services, and parental or familial legal rights and responsibilities to protect these clients and make decisions on their behalf.

A.3. Clients Served by Others

When counselors learn that their clients are in a professional relationship with another mental health professional, they request release from clients to inform the other professionals and strive to establish positive and collaborative professional relationships.

A.4. Avoiding Harm and Imposing Values

A.4.a. Avoiding Harm   Counselors act to avoid harming their clients, trainees, and research participants and to minimize or to remedy unavoidable or unanticipated harm.

A.4.b. Personal Values   Counselors are aware of their own values, attitudes, beliefs, and behaviors and avoid imposing values that are inconsistent with counseling goals. Counselors respect the diversity of clients, trainees, and research participants.

A.5. Roles and Relationships With Clients *(See F.3., F.10., G.3.)*

A.5.a. Current Clients   Sexual or romantic counselor–client interactions or relationships with current clients, their romantic partners, or their family members are prohibited.

A.5.b. Former Clients   Sexual or romantic counselor–client interactions or relationships with former clients, their romantic partners, or their family members are prohibited for a period of 5 years following the last professional contact. Counselors, before engaging in sexual or romantic interactions or relationships with clients, their romantic partners, or client family members after 5 years following the last professional contact, demonstrate forethought and document (in written form) whether the interactions or relationship can be viewed as exploitive in some way and/or whether there is still potential to harm the former client; in cases of potential exploitation and/or harm, the counselor avoids entering such an interaction or relationship.

A.5.c. Nonprofessional Interactions or Relationships (Other Than Sexual or Romantic Interactions or Relationships)   Counselor–client nonprofessional relationships with clients, former clients, their romantic partners, or their family members should be avoided, except when the interaction is potentially beneficial to the client. *(See A.5.d.)*

A.5.d. Potentially Beneficial Interactions   When a counselor–client nonprofessional interaction with a client or former client may be potentially beneficial to the client or former client, the counselor must document in case records, prior to the interaction (when feasible), the rationale for such an interaction, the potential benefit, and anticipated consequences for the client or former client and other individuals significantly involved with the client or former client. Such interactions should be initiated with appropriate client consent. Where unintentional harm occurs to the client or former client, or to an individual significantly involved with the client or former client, due to the nonprofessional interaction, the counselor must show evidence of an attempt to remedy such harm. Examples of potentially beneficial interactions include, but are not limited to, attending a formal ceremony (e.g., a wedding/commitment ceremony or graduation); purchasing a service or product provided by a client or former client (excepting unrestricted bartering); hospital visits to an ill family member; mutual membership in a professional association, organization, or community. *(See A.5.c.)*

A.5.e. Role Changes in the Professional Relationship   When a counselor changes a role from the original or most recent contracted relationship, he or she obtains informed consent from the client and explains the right of the client to refuse services related to the change. Examples of role changes include

1. changing from individual to relationship or family counseling, or vice versa;
2. changing from a nonforensic evaluative role to a therapeutic role, or vice versa;

3. changing from a counselor to a researcher role (i.e., enlisting clients as research participants), or vice versa; and

4. changing from a counselor to a mediator role, or vice versa.

Clients must be fully informed of any anticipated consequences (e.g., financial, legal, personal, or therapeutic) of counselor role changes.

A.6. Roles and Relationships at Individual, Group, Institutional, and Societal Levels

A.6.a. Advocacy   When appropriate, counselors advocate at individual, group, institutional, and societal levels to examine potential barriers and obstacles that inhibit access and/or the growth and development of clients.

A.6.b. Confidentiality and Advocacy   Counselors obtain client consent prior to engaging in advocacy efforts on behalf of an identifiable client to improve the provision of services and to work toward removal of systemic barriers or obstacles that inhibit client access, growth, and development.

A.7. Multiple Clients

When a counselor agrees to provide counseling services to two or more persons who have a relationship, the counselor clarifies at the outset which person or persons are clients and the nature of the relationships the counselor will have with each involved person. If it becomes apparent that the counselor may be called upon to perform potentially conflicting roles, the counselor will clarify, adjust, or withdraw from roles appropriately. *(See A.8.a., B.4.)*

A.8. Group Work *(See B.4.a.)*

A.8.a. Screening   Counselors screen prospective group counseling/therapy participants. To the extent possible, counselors select members whose needs and goals are compatible with goals of the group, who will not impede the group process, and whose well-being will not be jeopardized by the group experience.

A.8.b. Protecting Clients   In a group setting, counselors take reasonable precautions to protect clients from physical, emotional, or psychological trauma.

A.9. End-of-Life Care for Terminally Ill Clients

A.9.a. Quality of Care   Counselors strive to take measures that enable clients

1. to obtain high quality end-of-life care for their physical, emotional, social, and spiritual needs;

2. to exercise the highest degree of self-determination possible;

3. to be given every opportunity possible to engage in informed decision making regarding their end-of-life care; and

4. to receive complete and adequate assessment regarding their ability to make competent, rational decisions on their own behalf from a mental health professional who is experienced in end-of-life care practice.

A.9.b. Counselor Competence, Choice, and Referral Recognizing the personal, moral, and competence issues related to end-of-life decisions, counselors may choose to work or not work with terminally ill clients who wish to explore their end-of-life options. Counselors provide appropriate referral information to ensure that clients receive the necessary help.

A.9.c. Confidentiality Counselors who provide services to terminally ill individuals who are considering hastening their own deaths have the option of breaking or not breaking confidentiality, depending on applicable laws and the specific circumstances of the situation and after seeking consultation or supervision from appropriate professional and legal parties. *(See B.5.c.,B.7.c.)*

A.10. Fees and Bartering

A.10.a. Accepting Fees From Agency Clients Counselors refuse a private fee or other remuneration for rendering services to persons who are entitled to such services through the counselor's employing agency or institution. The policies of a particular agency may make explicit provisions for agency clients to receive counseling services from members of its staff in private practice. In such instances, the clients must be informed of other options open to them should they seek private counseling services.

A.10.b. Establishing Fees In establishing fees for professional counseling services, counselors consider the financial status of clients and locality. In the event that the established fee structure is inappropriate for a client, counselors assist clients in attempting to find comparable services of acceptable cost.

A.10.c. Nonpayment of Fees If counselors intend to use collection agencies or take legal measures to collect fees from clients who do not pay for services as agreed upon, they first inform clients of intended actions and offer clients the opportunity to make payment.

A.10.d. Bartering Counselors may barter only if the relationship is not exploitive or harmful and does not place the counselor in an unfair advantage, if the client requests it, and if such arrangements are an accepted practice among professionals in the community. Counselors consider the cultural implications of bartering and discuss relevant concerns with clients and document such agreements in a clear written contract.

A.10.e. Receiving Gifts Counselors understand the challenges of accepting gifts from clients and recognize that in some cultures, small gifts are a token of respect and showing gratitude. When determining whether or not to accept a gift from clients, counselors take into account the therapeutic relationship, the monetary value of the gift, a client's motivation for giving the gift, and the counselor's motivation for wanting or declining the gift.

A.11. Termination and Referral

A.11.a. Abandonment Prohibited Counselors do not abandon or neglect clients in counseling. Counselors assist in making appropriate arrangements for the continuation of treatment, when necessary, during interruptions such as vacations, illness, and following termination.

A.11.b. Inability to Assist Clients If counselors determine an inability to be of professional assistance to clients, they avoid entering or continuing counseling relationships. Counselors are knowledgeable about culturally and clinically appropriate referral resources and suggest these alternatives. If clients decline the suggested referrals, counselors should discontinue the relationship.

A.11.c. Appropriate Termination   Counselors terminate a counseling relationship when it becomes reasonably apparent that the client no longer needs assistance, is not likely to benefit, or is being harmed by continued counseling. Counselors may terminate counseling when in jeopardy of harm by the client, or another person with whom the client has a relationship, or when clients do not pay fees as agreed upon. Counselors provide pretermination counseling and recommend other service providers when necessary.

A.11.d. Appropriate Transfer of Services   When counselors transfer or refer clients to other practitioners, they ensure that appropriate clinical and administrative processes are completed and open communication is maintained with both clients and practitioners.

A.12. Technology Applications

A.12.a. Benefits and Limitations   Counselors inform clients of the benefits and limitations of using information technology applications in the counseling process and in business/ billing procedures. Such technologies include but are not limited to computer hardware and software, telephones, the World Wide Web, the Internet, online assessment instruments and other communication devices.

A.12.b. Technology-Assisted Services   When providing technology-assisted distance counseling services, counselors determine that clients are intellectually, emotionally, and physically capable of using the application and that the application is appropriate for the needs of clients.

A.12.c. Inappropriate Services   When technology-assisted distance counseling services are deemed inappropriate by the counselor or client, counselors consider delivering services face to face.

A.12.d. Access   Counselors provide reasonable access to computer applications when providing technology-assisted distance counseling services.

A.12.e. Laws and Statutes   Counselors ensure that the use of technology does not violate the laws of any local, state, national, or international entity and observe all relevant statutes.

A.12.f. Assistance   Counselors seek business, legal, and technical assistance when using technology applications, particularly when the use of such applications crosses state or national boundaries.

A.12.g. Technology and Informed Consent   As part of the process of establishing informed consent, counselors do the following:

1. Address issues related to the difficulty of maintaining the confidentiality of electronically transmitted communications.

2. Inform clients of all colleagues, supervisors, and employees, such as Informational Technology (IT) administrators, who might have authorized or unauthorized access to electronic transmissions.

3. Urge clients to be aware of all authorized or unauthorized users including family members and fellow employees who have access to any technology clients may use in the counseling process.

4. Inform clients of pertinent legal rights and limitations governing the practice of a profession over state lines or international boundaries.

5. Use encrypted Web sites and e-mail communications to help ensure confidentiality when possible.

6. When the use of encryption is not possible, counselors notify clients of this fact and limit electronic transmissions to general communications that are not client specific.

7. Inform clients if and for how long archival storage of transaction records are maintained.

8. Discuss the possibility of technology failure and alternate methods of service delivery.

9. Inform clients of emergency procedures, such as calling 911 or a local crisis hotline, when the counselor is not available.

10. Discuss time zone differences, local customs, and cultural or language differences that might impact service delivery.

11. Inform clients when technologyassisted distance counseling services are not covered by insurance. *(See A.2.)*

A.12.h. Sites on the World Wide Web   Counselors maintaining sites on the World Wide Web (the Internet) do the following:

1. Regularly check that electronic links are working and professionally appropriate.

2. Establish ways clients can contact the counselor in case of technology failure.

3. Provide electronic links to relevant state licensure and professional certification boards to protect consumer rights and facilitate addressing ethical concerns.

4. Establish a method for verifying client identity.

5. Obtain the written consent of the legal guardian or other authorized legal representative prior to rendering services in the event the client is a minor child, an adult who is legally incompetent, or an adult incapable of giving informed consent.

6. Strive to provide a site that is accessible to persons with disabilities.

7. Strive to provide translation capabilities for clients who have a different primary language while also addressing the imperfect nature of such translations.

8. Assist clients in determining the validity and reliability of information found on the World Wide Web and other technology applications.

Section B

Confidentiality, Privileged Communication, and Privacy

Introduction

Counselors recognize that trust is a cornerstone of the counseling relationship. Counselors aspire to earn the trust of clients by creating an ongoing partnership, establishing and upholding appropriate boundaries, and maintaining confidentiality. Counselors communicate the parameters of confidentiality in a culturally competent manner.

B.1. Respecting Client Rights

B.1.a. Multicultural/Diversity Considerations Counselors maintain awareness and sensitivity regarding cultural meanings of confidentiality and privacy. Counselors respect differing views toward disclosure of information. Counselors hold ongoing discussions with clients as to how, when, and with whom information is to be shared.

B.1.b. Respect for Privacy Counselors respect client rights to privacy. Counselors solicit private information from clients only when it is beneficial to the counseling process.

B.1.c. Respect for Confidentiality Counselors do not share confidential information without client consent or without sound legal or ethical justification.

B.1.d. Explanation of Limitations At initiation and throughout the counseling process, counselors inform clients of the limitations of confidentiality and seek to identify foreseeable situations in which confidentiality must be breached. *(See A.2.b.)*

B.2. Exceptions

B.2.a. Danger and Legal Requirements The general requirement that counselors keep information confidential does not apply when disclosure is required to protect clients or identified others from serious and foreseeable harm or when legal requirements demand that confidential information must be revealed. Counselors consult with other professionals when in doubt as to the validity of an exception. Additional considerations apply when addressing end-of-life issues. *(See A.9.c.)*

B.2.b. Contagious, Life-Threatening Diseases When clients disclose that they have a disease commonly known to be both communicable and life threatening, counselors may be justified in disclosing information to identifiable third parties, if they are known to be at demonstrable and high risk of contracting the disease. Prior to making a disclosure, counselors confirm that there is such a diagnosis and assess the intent of clients to inform the third parties about their disease or to engage in any behaviors that may be harmful to an identifiable third party.

B.2.c. Court-Ordered Disclosure   When subpoenaed to release confidential or privileged information without a client's permission, counselors obtain written, informed consent from the client or take steps to prohibit the disclosure or have it limited as narrowly as possible due to potential harm to the client or counseling relationship.

B.2.d. Minimal Disclosure   To the extent possible, clients are informed before confidential information is disclosed and are involved in the disclosure decision-making process. When circumstances require the disclosure of confidential information, only essential information is revealed.

B.3. Information Shared With Others

B.3.a. Subordinates   Counselors make every effort to ensure that privacy and confidentiality of clients are maintained by subordinates, including employees, supervisees, students, clerical assistants, and volunteers. *(See F.1.c.)*

B.3.b. Treatment Teams   When client treatment involves a continued review or participation by a treatment team, the client will be informed of the team's existence and composition, information being shared, and the purposes of sharing such information.

B.3.c. Confidential Settings   Counselors discuss confidential information only in settings in which they can reasonably ensure client privacy.

B.3.d. Third-Party Payers   Counselors disclose information to third-party payers only when clients have authorized such disclosure.

B.3.e. Transmitting Confidential Information   Counselors take precautions to ensure the confidentiality of information transmitted through the use of computers, electronic mail, facsimile machines, telephones, voicemail, answering machines, and other electronic or computer technology. *(See A.12.g.)*

B.3.f. Deceased Clients   Counselors protect the confidentiality of deceased clients, consistent with legal requirements and agency or setting policies.

B.4. Groups and Families

B.4.a. Group Work   In group work, counselors clearly explain the importance and parameters of confidentiality for the specific group being entered.

B.4.b. Couples and Family Counseling   In couples and family counseling, counselors clearly define who is considered "the client" and discuss expectations and limitations of confidentiality. Counselors seek agreement and document in writing such agreement among all involved parties having capacity to give consent concerning each individual's right to confidentiality and any obligation to preserve the confidentiality of information known.

B.5. Clients Lacking Capacity to Give Informed Consent

B.5.a. Responsibility to Clients When counseling minor clients or adult clients who lack the capacity to give voluntary, informed consent, counselors protect the confidentiality of information received in the counseling relationship as specified by federal and state laws, written policies, and applicable ethical standards.

B.5.b. Responsibility to Parents and Legal Guardians Counselors inform parents and legal guardians about the role of counselors and the confidential nature of the counseling relationship. Counselors are sensitive to the cultural diversity of families and respect the inherent rights and responsibilities of parents/guardians over the welfare of their children/charges according to law. Counselors work to establish, as appropriate, collaborative relationships with parents/guardians to best serve clients.

B.5.c. Release of Confidential Information When counseling minor clients or adult clients who lack the capacity to give voluntary consent to release confidential information, counselors seek permission from an appropriate third party to disclose information. In such instances, counselors inform clients consistent with their level of understanding and take culturally appropriate measures to safeguard client confidentiality.

B.6. Records

B.6.a. Confidentiality of Records Counselors ensure that records are kept in a secure location and that only authorized persons have access to records.

B.6.b. Permission to Record Counselors obtain permission from clients prior to recording sessions through electronic or other means.

B.6.c. Permission to Observe Counselors obtain permission from clients prior to observing counseling sessions, reviewing session transcripts, or viewing recordings of sessions with supervisors, faculty, peers, or others within the training environment.

B.6.d. Client Access Counselors provide reasonable access to records and copies of records when requested by competent clients. Counselors limit the access of clients to their records, or portions of their records, only when there is compelling evidence that such access would cause harm to the client. Counselors document the request of clients and the rationale for withholding some or all of the record in the files of clients. In situations involving multiple clients, counselors provide individual clients with only those parts of records that related directly to them and do not include confidential information related to any other client.

B.6.e. Assistance With Records When clients request access to their records, counselors provide assistance and consultation in interpreting counseling records.

B.6.f. Disclosure or Transfer Unless exceptions to confidentiality exist, counselors obtain written permission from clients to disclose or transfer records to legitimate third parties. Steps are taken to ensure that receivers of counseling records are sensitive to their confidential nature. *(See A.3., E.4.)*

B.6.g. Storage and Disposal After Termination Counselors store records following termination of services to ensure reasonable future access, maintain records in accordance with state and federal statutes governing records, and dispose of client records and other sensitive materials in a manner that protects client confidentiality. When records are of an artistic nature, counselors obtain client (or guardian) consent with regards to handling of such records or documents. *(See A.1.b.)*

B.6.h. Reasonable Precautions   Counselors take reasonable precautions to protect client confidentiality in the event of the counselor's termination of practice, incapacity, or death. *(See C.2.h.)*

B.7. Research and Training

B.7.a. Institutional Approval   When institutional approval is required, counselors provide accurate information about their research proposals and obtain approval prior to conducting their research. They conduct research in accordance with the approved research protocol.

B.7.b. Adherence to Guidelines   Counselors are responsible for understanding and adhering to state, federal, agency, or institutional policies or applicable guidelines regarding confidentiality in their research practices.

B.7.c. Confidentiality of Information Obtained in Research   Violations of participant privacy and confidentiality are risks of participation in research involving human participants. Investigators maintain all research records in a secure manner. They explain to participants the risks of violations of privacy and confidentiality and disclose to participants any limits of confidentiality that reasonably can be expected. Regardless of the degree to which confidentiality will be maintained, investigators must disclose to participants any limits of confidentiality that reasonably can be expected. *(See G.2.e.)*

B.7.d. Disclosure of Research Information   Counselors do not disclose confidential information that reasonably could lead to the identification of a research participant unless they have obtained the prior consent of the person. Use of data derived from counseling relationships for purposes of training, research, or publication is confined to content that is disguised to ensure the anonymity of the individuals involved. *(See G.2.a., G.2.d.)*

B.7.e. Agreement for Identification   Identification of clients, students, or supervisees in a presentation or publication is permissible only when they have reviewed the material and agreed to its presentation or publication. *(See G.4.d.)*

B.8. Consultation

B.8.a. Agreements   When acting as consultants, counselors seek agreements among all parties involved concerning each individual's rights to confidentiality, the obligation of each individual to preserve confidential information, and the limits of confidentiality of information shared by others.

B.8.b. Respect for Privacy   Information obtained in a consulting relationship is discussed for professional purposes only with persons directly involved with the case. Written and oral reports present only data germane to the purposes of the consultation, and every effort is made to protect client identity and to avoid undue invasion of privacy.

B.8.c. Disclosure of Confidential Information   When consulting with colleagues, counselors do not disclose confidential information that reasonably could lead to the identification of a client or other person or organization with whom they have a confidential relationship unless they have obtained the prior consent of the person or organization or the disclosure cannot be avoided. They disclosure information only to the extent necessary to achieve the purpose of the consultation. *(See D.2.D)*

Section C

Professional Responsibility

Introduction

Counselors aspire to open, honest, and accurate communication in dealing with the public and other professionals. They practice in a nondiscriminatory manner within the boundaries of professional and personal competence and have a responsibility to abide by the *ACA Code of Ethics*. Counselors actively participate in local, state, and national associations that foster the development and improvement of counseling. Counselors advocate to promote change at the individual, group, institutional, and societal levels that improve the quality of life for individuals and groups and remove potential barriers to the provision or access of appropriate services being offered. Counselors have a responsibility to the public to engage in counseling practices that are based on rigorous research methodologies. In addition, counselors engage in self-care activities to maintain and promote their emotional, physical, mental, and spiritual well-being to best meet their professional responsibilities.

C.1. Knowledge of Standards

Counselors have a responsibility to read, understand, and follow the *ACA Code of Ethics* and adhere to applicable laws and regulations.

C.2. Professional Competence

C.2.a. Boundaries of Competence   Counselors practice only within the boundaries of their competence, based on their education, training, supervised experience, state and national professional credentials, and appropriate professional experience. Counselors gain knowledge, personal awareness, sensitivity, and skills pertinent to working with a diverse client population. *(See A.9.b., C.4.e., E.2., F.2., F.11.b.)*

C.2.b. New Specialty Areas of Practice   Counselors practice in specialty areas new to them only after appropriate education, training, and supervised experience. While developing skills in new specialty areas, counselors take steps to ensure the competence of their work and to protect others from possible harm. *(See F.6.f.)*

C.2.c. Qualified for Employment   Counselors accept employment only for positions for which they are qualified by education, training, supervised experience, state and national professional credentials, and appropriate professional experience. Counselors hire for professional counseling positions only individuals who are qualified and competent for those positions.

C.2.d. Monitor Effectiveness Counselors continually monitor their effectiveness as professionals and take steps to improve when necessary. Counselors in private practice take reasonable steps to seek peer supervision as needed to evaluate their efficacy as counselors.

C.2.e. Consultation on Ethical Obligations Counselors take reasonable steps to consult with other counselors or related professionals when they have questions regarding their ethical obligations or professional practice.

C.2.f. Continuing Education Counselors recognize the need for continuing education to acquire and maintain a reasonable level of awareness of current scientific and professional information in their fields of activity. They take steps to maintain competence in the skills they use, are open to new procedures, and keep current with the diverse populations and specific populations with whom they work.

C.2.g. Impairment Counselors are alert to the signs of impairment from their own physical, mental, or emotional problems and refrain from offering or providing professional services when such impairment is likely to harm a client or others. They seek assistance for problems that reach the level of professional impairment, and, if necessary, they limit, suspend, or terminate their professional responsibilities until such time it is determined that they may safely resume their work. Counselors assist colleagues or supervisors in recognizing their own professional impairment and provide consultation and assistance when warranted with colleagues or supervisors showing signs of impairment and intervene as appropriate to prevent imminent harm to clients. *(See A.11.b., F.8.b.)*

C.2.h. Counselor Incapacitation or Termination of Practice When counselors leave a practice, they follow a prepared plan for transfer of clients and files. Counselors prepare and disseminate to an identified colleague or "records custodian" a plan for the transfer of clients and files in the case of their incapacitation, death, or termination of practice.

C.3. Advertising and Soliciting Clients

C.3.a. Accurate Advertising When advertising or otherwise representing their services to the public, counselors identify their credentials in an accurate manner that is not false, misleading, deceptive, or fraudulent.

C.3.b. Testimonials Counselors who use testimonials do not solicit them from current clients nor former clients nor any other persons who may be vulnerable to undue influence.

C.3.c. Statements by Others Counselors make reasonable efforts to ensure that statements made by others about them or the profession of counseling are accurate.

C.3.d. Recruiting Through Employment Counselors do not use their places of employment or institutional affiliation to recruit or gain clients, supervisees, or consultees for their private practices.

C.3.e. Products and Training Advertisements Counselors who develop products related to their profession or conduct workshops or training events ensure that the advertisements concerning these products or events are accurate and disclose adequate information for consumers to make informed choices. *(See C.6.d.)*

C.3.f. Promoting to Those Served   Counselors do not use counseling, teaching, training, or supervisory relationships to promote their products or training events in a manner that is deceptive or would exert undue influence on individuals who may be vulnerable. However, counselor educators may adopt textbooks they have authored for instructional purposes.

C.4. Professional Qualifications

C.4.a. Accurate Representation   Counselors claim or imply only professional qualifications actually completed and correct any known misrepresentations of their qualifications by others. Counselors truthfully represent the qualifications of their professional colleagues. Counselors clearly distinguish between paid and volunteer work experience and accurately describe their continuing education and specialized training. *(See C.2.a.)*

C.4.b. Credentials   Counselors claim only licenses or certifications that are current and in good standing.

C.4.c. Educational Degrees   Counselors clearly differentiate between earned and honorary degrees.

C.4.d. Implying Doctoral-Level Competence   Counselors clearly state their highest earned degree in counseling or closely related field. Counselors do not imply doctoral-level competence when only possessing a master's degree in counseling or a related field by referring to themselves as "Dr." in a counseling context when their doctorate is not in counseling or related field.

C.4.e. Program Accreditation Status   Counselors clearly state the accreditation status of their degree programs at the time the degree was earned.

C.4.f. Professional Membership   Counselors clearly differentiate between current, active memberships and former memberships in associations. Members of the American Counseling Association must clearly differentiate between professional membership, which implies the possession of at least a master's degree in counseling, and regular membership, which is open to individuals whose interests and activities are consistent with those of ACA but are not qualified for professional membership.

C.5. Nondiscrimination

Counselors do not condone or engage in discrimination based on age, culture, disability, ethnicity, race, religion/ spirituality, gender, gender identity, sexual orientation, marital status/ partnership, language preference, socioeconomic status, or any basis proscribed by law. Counselors do not discriminate against clients, students, employees, supervisees, or research participants in a manner that has a negative impact on these persons.

C.6. Public Responsibility

C.6.a. Sexual Harassment   Counselors do not engage in or condone sexual harassment. Sexual harassment is defined as sexual solicitation, physical advances, or verbal or nonverbal conduct that is sexual in nature, that occurs in connection with professional activities or roles, and that either

1. is unwelcome, is offensive, or creates a hostile workplace or learning environment, and counselors know or are told this; or

2. is sufficiently severe or intense to be perceived as harassment to a reasonable person in the context in which the behavior occurred. Sexual harassment can consist of a single intense or severe act or multiple persistent or pervasive acts.

C.6.b. Reports to Third Parties   Counselors are accurate, honest, and objective in reporting their professional activities and judgments to appropriate third parties, including courts, health insurance companies, those who are the recipients of evaluation reports, and others. *(See B.3., E.4.)*

C.6.c. Media Presentations   When counselors provide advice or comment by means of public lectures, demonstrations, radio or television programs, prerecorded tapes, technology-based applications, printed articles, mailed material, or other media, they take reasonable precautions to ensure that

1. the statements are based on appropriate professional counseling literature and practice,

2. the statements are otherwise consistent with the *ACA Code of Ethics,* and

3. the recipients of the information are not encouraged to infer that a professional counseling relationship has been established.

C.6.d. Exploitation of Others   Counselors do not exploit others in their professional relationships. *(See C.3.e.)*

C.6.e. Scientific Bases for Treatment Modalities   Counselors use techniques/ procedures/modalities that are grounded in theory and/or have an empirical or scientific foundation. Counselors who do not must define the techniques/procedures as "unproven" or "developing" and explain the potential risks and ethical considerations of using such techniques/ procedures and take steps to protect clients from possible harm. *(See A.4.a., E.5.c., E.5.d.)*

C.7. Responsibility to Other Professionals

C.7.a. Personal Public Statements   When making personal statements in a public context, counselors clarify that they are speaking from their personal perspectives and that they are not speaking on behalf of all counselors or the profession.

Section D

Relationships With Other Professionals

Introduction

Professional counselors recognize that the quality of their interactions with colleagues can influence the quality of services provided to clients. They work to become knowledgeable about colleagues within and outside the field of counseling. Counselors develop positive working relationships and systems of communication with colleagues to enhance services to clients.

D.1. Relationships With Colleagues, Employers, and Employees

D.1.a. Different Approaches   Counselors are respectful of approaches to counseling services that differ from their own. Counselors are respectful of traditions and practices of other professional groups with which they work.

D.1.b. Forming Relationships   Counselors work to develop and strengthen interdisciplinary relations with colleagues from other disciplines to best serve clients.

D.1.c. Interdisciplinary Teamwork   Counselors who are members of interdisciplinary teams delivering multifaceted services to clients, keep the focus on how to best serve the clients. They participate in and contribute to decisions that affect the well-being of clients by drawing on the perspectives, values, and experiences of the counseling profession and those of colleagues from other disciplines. *(See A.1.a.)*

D.1.d. Confidentiality   When counselors are required by law, institutional policy, or extraordinary circumstances to serve in more than one role in judicial or administrative proceedings, they clarify role expectations and the parameters of confidentiality with their colleagues. *(See B.1.c., B.1.d., B.2.c., B.2.d., B.3.b.)*

D.1.e. Establishing Professional and Ethical Obligations   Counselors who are members of interdisciplinary teams clarify professional and ethical obligations of the team as a whole and of its individual members. When a team decision raises ethical concerns, counselors first attempt to resolve the concern within the team. If they cannot reach resolution among team members, counselors pursue other avenues to address their concerns consistent with client well-being.

D.1.f. Personnel Selection and Assignment   Counselors select competent staff and assign responsibilities compatible with their skills and experiences.

D.1.g. Employer Policies   The acceptance of employment in an agency or institution implies that counselors are in agreement with its general policies and principles. Counselors strive to reach agreement with employers as to acceptable standards of conduct that allow for changes in institutional policy conducive to the growth and development of clients.

D.1.h. Negative Conditions   Counselors alert their employers of inappropriate policies and practices. They attempt to effect changes in such policies or procedures through constructive action within the organization. When such policies are potentially disruptive or damaging to clients or may limit the effectiveness of services provided and change cannot be effected, counselors take appropriate further action. Such action may include referral to appropriate certification, accreditation, or state licensure organizations, or voluntary termination of employment.

D.1.i. Protection From Punitive Action   Counselors take care not to harass or dismiss an employee who has acted in a responsible and ethical manner to expose inappropriate employer policies or practices.

D.2. Consultation

D.2.a. Consultant Competency   Counselors take reasonable steps to ensure that they have the appropriate resources and competencies when providing consultation services. Counselors provide appropriate referral resources when requested or needed. *(See C.2.a.)*

D.2.b. Understanding Consultees   When providing consultation, counselors attempt to develop with their consultees a clear understanding of problem definition, goals for change, and predicted consequences of interventions selected.

D.2.c. Consultant Goals   The consulting relationship is one in which consultee adaptability and growth toward self-direction are consistently encouraged and cultivated.

D.2.d. Informed Consent in Consultation   When providing consultation, counselors have an obligation to review, in writing and verbally, the rights and responsibilities of both counselors and consultees. Counselors use clear and understandable language to inform all parties involved about the purpose of the services to be provided, relevant costs, potential risks and benefits, and the limits of confidentiality. Working in conjunction with the consultee, counselors attempt to develop a clear definition of the problem, goals for change, and predicted consequences of interventions that are culturally responsive and appropriate to the needs of consultees. *(See A.2.a., A.2.b.)*

Section E

Evaluation, Assessment, and Interpretation

Introduction

Counselors use assessment instruments as one component of the counseling process, taking into account the client personal and cultural context. Counselors promote the well-being of individual clients or groups of clients by developing and using appropriate educational, psychological, and career assessment instruments.

E.1. General

E.1.a. Assessment The primary purpose of educational, psychological, and career assessment is to provide measurements that are valid and reliable in either comparative or absolute terms. These include, but are not limited to, measurements of ability, personality, interest, intelligence, achievement, and performance. Counselors recognize the need to interpret the statements in this section as applying to both quantitative and qualitative assessments.

E.1.b. Client Welfare Counselors do not misuse assessment results and interpretations, and they take reasonable steps to prevent others from misusing the information these techniques provide. They respect the client's right to know the results, the interpretations made, and the bases for counselors' conclusions and recommendations.

E.2. Competence to Use and Interpret Assessment Instruments

E.2.a. Limits of Competence Counselors utilize only those testing and assessment services for which they have been trained and are competent. Counselors using technology assisted test interpretations are trained in the construct being measured and the specific instrument being used prior to using its technology based application. Counselors take reasonable measures to ensure the proper use of psychological and career assessment techniques by persons under their supervision. *(See A.12.)*

E.2.b. Appropriate Use Counselors are responsible for the appropriate application, scoring, interpretation, and use of assessment instruments relevant to the needs of the client, whether they score and interpret such assessments themselves or use technology or other services.

E.2.c. Decisions Based on Results Counselors responsible for decisions involving individuals or policies that are based on assessment results have a thorough understanding of educational, psychological, and career measurement, including validation criteria, assessment research, and guidelines for assessment development and use.

E.3. Informed Consent in Assessment

E.3.a. Explanation to Clients   Prior to assessment, counselors explain the nature and purposes of assessment and the specific use of results by potential recipients. The explanation will be given in the language of the client (or other legally authorized person on behalf of the client), unless an explicit exception has been agreed upon in advance. Counselors consider the client's personal or cultural context, the level of the client's understanding of the results, and the impact of the results on the client. *(See A.2., A.12.g., F.1.c.)*

E.3.b. Recipients of Results   Counselors consider the examinee's welfare, explicit understandings, and prior agreements in determining who receives the assessment results. Counselors include accurate and appropriate interpretations with any release of individual or group assessment results. *(See B.2.c., B.5.)*

E.4. Release of Data to Qualified Professionals

Counselors release assessment data in which the client is identified only with the consent of the client or the client's legal representative. Such data are released only to persons recognized by counselors as qualified to interpret the data. *(See B.1., B.3., B.6.b.)*

E.5. Diagnosis of Mental Disorders

E.5.a. Proper Diagnosis   Counselors take special care to provide proper diagnosis of mental disorders. Assessment techniques (including personal interview) used to determine client care (e.g., locus of treatment, type of treatment, or recommended follow-up) are carefully selected and appropriately used.

E.5.b. Cultural Sensitivity   Counselors recognize that culture affects the manner in which clients' problems are defined. Clients' socioeconomic and cultural experiences are considered when diagnosing mental disorders. *(See A.2.c.)*

E.5.c. Historical and Social Prejudices in the Diagnosis of Pathology   Counselors recognize historical and social prejudices in the misdiagnosis and pathologizing of certain individuals and groups and the role of mental health professionals in perpetuating these prejudices through diagnosis and treatment.

E.5.d. Refraining From Diagnosis   Counselors may refrain from making and/or reporting a diagnosis if they believe it would cause harm to the client or others.

E.6. Instrument Selection

E.6.a. Appropriateness of Instruments   Counselors carefully consider the validity, reliability, psychometric limitations, and appropriateness of instruments when selecting assessments.

E.6.b. Referral Information   If a client is referred to a third party for assessment, the counselor provides specific referral questions and sufficient objective data about the client to ensure that appropriate assessment instruments are utilized. *(See A.9.b., B.3.)*

E.6.c. Culturally Diverse Populations Counselors are cautious when selecting assessments for culturally diverse populations to avoid the use of instruments that lack appropriate psychometric properties for the client population. *(See A.2.c., E.5.b.)*

E.7. Conditions of Assessment Administration *(See A.12.b., A.12.d.)*

E.7.a. Administration Conditions Counselors administer assessments under the same conditions that were established in their standardization. When assessments are not administered under standard conditions, as may be necessary to accommodate clients with disabilities, or when unusual behavior or irregularities occur during the administration, those conditions are noted in interpretation, and the results may be designated as invalid or of questionable validity.

E.7.b. Technological Administration Counselors ensure that administration programs function properly and provide clients with accurate results when technological or other electronic methods are used for assessment administration.

E.7.c. Unsupervised Assessments Unless the assessment instrument is designed, intended, and validated for self-administration and/or scoring, counselors do not permit inadequately supervised use.

E.7.d. Disclosure of Favorable Conditions Prior to administration of assessments, conditions that produce most favorable assessment results are made known to the examinee.

E.8. Multicultural Issues/Diversity in Assessment

Counselors use with caution assessment techniques that were normed on populations other than that of the client. Counselors recognize the effects of age, color, culture, disability, ethnic group, gender, race, language preference, religion, spirituality, sexual orientation, and socio-economic status on test administration and interpretation, and place test results in proper perspective with other relevant factors. *(See A.2.c., E.5.b.)*

E.9. Scoring and Interpretation of Assessments

E.9.a. Reporting In reporting assessment results, counselors indicate reservations that exist regarding validity or reliability due to circumstances of the assessment or the inappropriateness of the norms for the person tested.

E.9.b. Research Instruments Counselors exercise caution when interpreting the results of research instruments not having sufficient technical data to support respondent results. The specific purposes for the use of such instruments are stated explicitly to the examinee.

E.9.c. Assessment Services Counselors who provide assessment scoring and interpretation services to support the assessment process confirm the validity of such interpretations. They accurately describe the purpose, norms, validity, reliability, and applications of the procedures and any special qualifications applicable to their use. The public offering of an automated test interpretations service is considered a professional-to-professional consultation. The formal responsibility of the consultant is to the consultee, but the ultimate and overriding responsibility is to the client. *(See D.2.)*

E.10. Assessment Security

Counselors maintain the integrity and security of tests and other assessment techniques consistent with legal and contractual obligations. Counselors do not appropriate, reproduce, or modify published assessments or parts thereof without acknowledgment and permission from the publisher.

E.11. Obsolete Assessments and Outdated Results

Counselors do not use data or results from assessments that are obsolete or outdated for the current purpose. Counselors make every effort to prevent the misuse of obsolete measures and assessment data by others.

E.12. Assessment Construction

Counselors use established scientific procedures, relevant standards, and current professional knowledge for assessment design in the development, publication, and utilization of educational and psychological assessment techniques.

E.13. Forensic Evaluation: Evaluation for Legal Proceedings

E.13.a. Primary Obligations   When providing forensic evaluations, the primary obligation of counselors is to produce objective findings that can be substantiated based on information and techniques appropriate to the evaluation, which may include examination of the individual and/or review of records. Counselors are entitled to form professional opinions based on their professional knowledge and expertise that can be supported by the data gathered in evaluations. Counselors will define the limits of their reports or testimony, especially when an examination of the individual has not been conducted.

E.13.b. Consent for Evaluation   Individuals being evaluated are informed in writing that the relationship is for the purposes of an evaluation and is not counseling in nature, and entities or individuals who will receive the evaluation report are identified. Written consent to be evaluated is obtained from those being evaluated unless a court orders evaluations to be conducted without the written consent of individuals being evaluated. When children or vulnerable adults are being evaluated, informed written consent is obtained from a parent or guardian.

E.13.c. Client Evaluation Prohibited   Counselors do not evaluate individuals for forensic purposes they currently counsel or individuals they have counseled in the past. Counselors do not accept as counseling clients individuals they are evaluating or individuals they have evaluated in the past for forensic purposes.

E.13.d. Avoid Potentially Harmful Relationships   Counselors who provide forensic evaluations avoid potentially harmful professional or personal relationships with family members, romantic partners, and close friends of individuals they are evaluating or have evaluated in the past.

Section F

Supervision, Training, and Teaching

Introduction

Counselors aspire to foster meaningful and respectful professional relationships and to maintain appropriate boundaries with supervisees and students. Counselors have theoretical and pedagogical foundations for their work and aim to be fair, accurate, and honest in their assessments of counselors-in-training.

F.1. Counselor Supervision and Client Welfare

F.1.a. Client Welfare A primary obligation of counseling supervisors is to monitor the services provided by other counselors or counselors-in-training. Counseling supervisors monitor client welfare and supervisee clinical performance and professional development. To fulfill these obligations, supervisors meet regularly with supervisees to review case notes, samples of clinical work, or live observations. Supervisees have a responsibility to understand and follow the *ACA Code of Ethics*.

F.1.b. Counselor Credentials Counseling supervisors work to ensure that clients are aware of the qualifications of the supervisees who render services to the clients. *(See A.2.b.)*

F.1.c. Informed Consent and Client Rights Supervisors make supervisees aware of client rights including the protection of client privacy and confidentiality in the counseling relationship. Supervisees provide clients with professional disclosure information and inform them of how the supervision process influences the limits of confidentiality. Supervisees make clients aware of who will have access to records of the counseling relationship and how these records will be used. *(See A.2.b., B.1.d.)*

F.2. Counselor Supervision Competence

F.2.a. Supervisor Preparation Prior to offering clinical supervision services, counselors are trained in supervision methods and techniques. Counselors who offer clinical supervision services regularly pursue continuing education activities including both counseling and supervision topics and skills. *(See C.2.a., C.2.f.)*

F.2.b. Multicultural Issues/Diversity in Supervision Counseling supervisors are aware of and address the role of multiculturalism/diversity in the supervisory relationship.

F.3. Supervisory Relationships

F.3.a. Relationship Boundaries With Supervisees   Counseling supervisors clearly define and maintain ethical professional, personal, and social relationships with their supervisees. Counseling supervisors avoid nonprofessional relationships with current supervisees. If supervisors must assume other professional roles (e.g., clinical and administrative supervisor, instructor) with supervisees, they work to minimize potential conflicts and explain to supervisees the expectations and responsibilities associated with each role. They do not engage in any form of nonprofessional interaction that may compromise the supervisory relationship.

F.3.b. Sexual Relationships   Sexual or romantic interactions or relationships with current supervisees are prohibited.

F.3.c. Sexual Harassment   Counseling supervisors do not condone or subject supervisees to sexual harassment. *(See C.6.a.)*

F.3.d. Close Relatives and Friends   Counseling supervisors avoid accepting close relatives, romantic partners, or friends as supervisees.

F.3.e. Potentially Beneficial Relationships   Counseling supervisors are aware of the power differential in their relationships with supervisees. If they believe nonprofessional relationships with a supervisee may be potentially beneficial to the supervisee, they take precautions similar to those taken by counselors when working with clients. Examples of potentially beneficial interactions or relationships include attending a formal ceremony; hospital visits; providing support during a stressful event; or mutual membership in a professional association, organization, or community. Counseling supervisors engage in open discussions with supervisees when they consider entering into relationships with them outside of their roles as clinical and/or administrative supervisors. Before engaging in nonprofessional relationships, supervisors discuss with supervisees and document the rationale for such interactions, potential benefits or drawbacks, and anticipated consequences for the supervisee. Supervisors clarify the specific nature and limitations of the additional role(s) they will have with the supervisee.

F.4. Supervisor Responsibilities

F.4.a. Informed Consent for Supervision   Supervisors are responsible for incorporating into their supervision the principles of informed consent and participation. Supervisors inform supervisees of the policies and procedures to which they are to adhere and the mechanisms for due process appeal of individual supervisory actions.

F.4.b. Emergencies and Absences   Supervisors establish and communicate to supervisees procedures for contacting them or, in their absence, alternative on-call supervisors to assist in handling crises.

F.4.c. Standards for Supervisees   Supervisors make their supervisees aware of professional and ethical standards and legal responsibilities. Supervisors of postdegree counselors encourage these counselors to adhere to professional standards of practice. *(See C.1.)*

F.4.d. Termination of the Supervisory Relationship   Supervisors or supervisees have the right to terminate the supervisory relationship with adequate notice. Reasons for withdrawal are provided to the other party. When cultural, clinical, or professional issues are crucial to the viability of the supervisory relationship, both parties make efforts to resolve differences.

When termination is warranted, supervisors make appropriate referrals to possible alternative supervisors.

F.5. Counseling Supervision Evaluation, Remediation, and Endorsement

F.5.a. Evaluation　Supervisors document and provide supervisees with ongoing performance appraisal and evaluation feedback and schedule periodic formal evaluative sessions throughout the supervisory relationship.

F.5.b. Limitations　Through ongoing evaluation and appraisal, supervisors are aware of the limitations of supervisees that might impede performance. Supervisors assist supervisees in securing remedial assistance when needed. They recommend dismissal from training programs, applied counseling settings, or state or voluntary professional credentialing processes when those supervisees are unable to provide competent professional services. Supervisors seek consultation and document their decisions to dismiss or refer supervisees for assistance. They ensure that supervisees are aware of options available to them to address such decisions. *(See C.2.g.)*

F.5.c. Counseling for Supervisees　If supervisees request counseling, supervisors provide them with acceptable referrals. Counselors do not provide counseling services to supervisees. Supervisors address interpersonal competencies in terms of the impact of these issues on clients, the supervisory relationship, and professional functioning. *(See F.3.a.)*

F.5.d. Endorsement　Supervisors endorse supervisees for certification, licensure, employment, or completion of an academic or training program only when they believe supervisees are qualified for the endorsement. Regardless of qualifications, supervisors do not endorse supervisees whom they believe to be impaired in any way that would interfere with the performance of the duties associated with the endorsement.

F.6. Responsibilities of Counselor Educators

F.6.a. Counselor Educators　Counselor educators who are responsible for developing, implementing, and supervising educational programs are skilled as teachers and practitioners. They are knowledgeable regarding the ethical, legal, and regulatory aspects of the profession, are skilled in applying that knowledge, and make students and supervisees aware of their responsibilities. Counselor educators conduct counselor education and training programs in an ethical manner and serve as role models for professional behavior. *(See C.1., C.2.a., C.2.c.)*

F.6.b. Infusing Multicultural Issues/Diversity　Counselor educators infuse material related to multicultluralism/diversity into all courses and workshops for the development of professional counselors.

F.6.c. Integration of Study and Practice　Counselor educators establish education and training programs that integrate academic study and supervised practice.

F.6.d. Teaching Ethics　Counselor educators make students and supervisees aware of the ethical responsibilities and standards of the profession and the ethical responsibilities of students to the profession. Counselor educators infuse ethical considerations throughout the curriculum. *(See C.1.)*

F.6.e. Peer Relationships　Counselor educators make every effort to ensure that the rights of peers are not compromised when students or supervisees lead counseling groups or provide clinical supervision. Counselor educators take steps to ensure that students and supervisees understand they have the same ethical obligations as counselor educators, trainers, and supervisors.

F.6.f. Innovative Theories and Techniques   When counselor educators teach counseling techniques/procedures that are innovative, without an empirical foundation, or without a well-grounded theoretical foundation, they define the counseling techniques/procedures as "unproven" or "developing" and explain to students the potential risks and ethical considerations of using such techniques/procedures.

F.6.g. Field Placements   Counselor educators develop clear policies within their training programs regarding field placement and other clinical experiences. Counselor educators provide clearly stated roles and responsibilities for the student or supervisee, the site supervisor, and the program supervisor. They confirm that site supervisors are qualified to provide supervision and inform site supervisors of their professional and ethical responsibilities in this role.

F.6.h. Professional Disclosure   Before initiating counseling services, counselors-in-training disclose their status as students and explain how this status affects the limits of confidentiality. Counselor educators ensure that the clients at field placements are aware of the services rendered and the qualifications of the students and supervisees rendering those services. Students and supervisees obtain client permission before they use any information concerning the counseling relationship in the training process. *(See A.2.b.)*

F.7. Student Welfare

F.7.a. Orientation   Counselor educators recognize that orientation is a developmental process that continues throughout the educational and clinical training of students. Counseling faculty provide prospective students with information about the counselor education program's expectations:

1. the type and level of skill and knowledge acquisition required for successful completion of the training;
2. program training goals, objectives, and mission, and subject matter to be covered;
3. bases for evaluation;
4. training components that encourage self-growth or self-disclosure as part of the training process;
5. the type of supervision settings and requirements of the sites for required clinical field experiences;
6. student and supervisee evaluation and dismissal policies and procedures; and
7. up-to-date employment prospects for graduates.

F.7.b. Self-Growth Experiences   Counselor education programs delineate requirements for self-disclosure or self-growth experiences in their admission and program materials. Counselor educators use professional judgment when designing training experiences they conduct that require student and supervisee selfgrowth or self-disclosure. Students and supervisees are made aware of the ramifications their self-disclosure may have when counselors whose primary role as teacher, trainer, or supervisor requires acting on ethical obligations to the profession. Evaluative components of experiential training experiences explicitly delineate predetermined academic standards that are separate and do not depend on the student's level of selfdisclosure. Counselor educators may require trainees to seek professional help to address any personal concerns that may be affecting their competency.

F.8. Student Responsibilities

F.8.a. Standards for Students   Counselors-in-training have a responsibility to understand and follow the *ACA Code of Ethics* and adhere to applicable laws, regulatory policies, and rules and policies governing professional staff behavior at the agency or placement setting. Students have the same obligation to clients as those required of professional counselors. *(See C.1., H.1.)*

F.8.b. Impairment   Counselors-in-training refrain from offering or providing counseling services when their physical, mental, or emotional problems are likely to harm a client or others. They are alert to the signs of impairment, seek assistance for problems, and notify their program supervisors when they are aware that they are unable to effectively provide services. In addition, they seek appropriate professional services for themselves to remediate the problems that are interfering with their ability to provide services to others. *(See A.1., C.2.d., C.2.g.)*

F.9. Evaluation and Remediation of Students

F.9.a. Evaluation   Counselors clearly state to students, prior to and throughout the training program, the levels of competency expected, appraisal methods, and timing of evaluations for both didactic and clinical competencies. Counselor educators provide students with ongoing performance appraisal and evaluation feedback throughout the training program.

F.9.b. Limitations   Counselor educators, throughout ongoing evaluation and appraisal, are aware of and address the inability of some students to achieve counseling competencies that might impede performance. Counselor educators

1. assist students in securing remedial assistance when needed,
2. seek professional consultation and document their decision to dismiss or refer students for assistance, and
3. ensure that students have recourse in a timely manner to address decisions to require them to seek assistance or to dismiss them and provide students with due process according to institutional policies and procedures. *(See C.2.g.)*

F.9.c. Counseling for Students   If students request counseling or if counseling services are required as part of a remediation process, counselor educators provide acceptable referrals.

F.10. Roles and Relationships Between Counselor Educators and Students

F.10.a. Sexual or Romantic Relationships   Sexual or romantic interactions or relationships with current students are prohibited.

F.10.b. Sexual Harassment   Counselor educators do not condone or subject students to sexual harassment. *(See C.6.a.)*

F.10.c. Relationships With Former Students   Counselor educators are aware of the power differential in the relationship between faculty and students. Faculty members foster open discussions with former students when considering engaging in a social, sexual, or other intimate relationship. Faculty members discuss with the former student how their former relationship may affect the change in relationship.

F.10.d. Nonprofessional Relationships Counselor educators avoid nonprofessional or ongoing professional relationships with students in which there is a risk of potential harm to the student or that may compromise the training experience or grades assigned. In addition, counselor educators do not accept any form of professional services, fees, commissions, reimbursement, or remuneration from a site for student or supervisee placement.

F.10.e. Counseling Services Counselor educators do not serve as counselors to current students unless this is a brief role associated with a training experience.

F.10.f. Potentially Beneficial Relationships Counselor educators are aware of the power differential in the relationship between faculty and students. If they believe a nonprofessional relationship with a student may be potentially beneficial to the student, they take precautions similar to those taken by counselors when working with clients. Examples of potentially beneficial interactions or relationships include, but are not limited to, attending a formal ceremony; hospital visits; providing support during a stressful event; or mutual membership in a professional association, organization, or community. Counselor educators engage in open discussions with students when they consider entering into relationships with students outside of their roles as teachers and supervisors. They discuss with students the rationale for such interactions, the potential benefits and drawbacks, and the anticipated consequences for the student. Educators clarify the specific nature and limitations of the additional role(s) they will have with the student prior to engaging in a nonprofessional relationship. Nonprofessional relationships with students should be time-limited and initiated with student consent.

F.11. Multicultural/Diversity Competence in Counselor Education and Training Programs

F.11.a. Faculty Diversity Counselor educators are committed to recruiting and retaining a diverse faculty.

F.11.b. Student Diversity Counselor educators actively attempt to recruit and retain a diverse student body. Counselor educators demonstrate commitment to multicultural/diversity competence by recognizing and valuing diverse cultures and types of abilities students bring to the training experience. Counselor educators provide appropriate accommodations that enhance and support diverse student well-being and academic performance.

F.11.c. Multicultural/Diversity Competence Counselor educators actively infuse multicultural/diversity competency in their training and supervision practices. They actively train students to gain awareness, knowledge, and skills in the competencies of multicultural practice. Counselor educators include case examples, role-plays, discussion questions, and other classroom activities that promote and represent various cultural perspectives.

Section G

Research and Publication

Introduction

Counselors who conduct research are encouraged to contribute to the knowledge base of the profession and promote a clearer understanding of the conditions that lead to a healthy and more just society. Counselors support efforts of researchers by participating fully and willingly whenever possible. Counselors minimize bias and respect diversity in designing and implementing research programs.

G.1. Research Responsibilities

G.1.a. Use of Human Research Participants   Counselors plan, design, conduct, and report research in a manner that is consistent with pertinent ethical principles, federal and state laws, host institutional regulations, and scientific standards governing research with human research participants.

G.1.b. Deviation From Standard Practice   Counselors seek consultation and observe stringent safeguards to protect the rights of research participants when a research problem suggests a deviation from standard or acceptable practices.

G.1.c. Independent Researchers   When independent researchers do not have access to an Institutional Review Board (IRB), they should consult with researchers who are familiar with IRB procedures to provide appropriate safeguards.

G.1.d. Precautions to Avoid Injury   Counselors who conduct research with human participants are responsible for the welfare of participants throughout the research process and should take reasonable precautions to avoid causing injurious psychological, emotional, physical, or social effects to participants.

G.1.e. Principal Researcher Responsibility   The ultimate responsibility for ethical research practice lies with the principal researcher. All others involved in the research activities share ethical obligations and responsibility for their own actions.

G.1.f. Minimal Interference   Counselors take reasonable precautions to avoid causing disruptions in the lives of research participants that could be caused by their involvement in research.

G.1.g. Multicultural/Diversity Considerations in Research   When appropriate to research goals, counselors are sensitive to incorporating research procedures that take into account cultural considerations. They seek consultation when appropriate.

G.2. Rights of Research Participants *(See A.2, A.7.)*

G.2.a. Informed Consent in Research   Individuals have the right to consent to become research participants. In seeking consent, counselors use language that

1. accurately explains the purpose and procedures to be followed,
2. identifies any procedures that are experimental or relatively untried,
3. describes any attendant discomforts and risks,
4. describes any benefits or changes in individuals or organizations that might be reasonably expected,
5. discloses appropriate alternative procedures that would be advantageous for participants,
6. offers to answer any inquiries concerning the procedures,
7. describes any limitations on confidentiality,
8. describes the format and potential target audiences for the dissemination of research findings, and
9. instructs participants that they are free to withdraw their consent and to discontinue participation in the project at any time without penalty.

G.2.b. Deception   Counselors do not conduct research involving deception unless alternative procedures are not feasible and the prospective value of the research justifies the deception. If such deception has the potential to cause physical or emotional harm to research participants, the research is not conducted, regardless of prospective value. When the methodological requirements of a study necessitate concealment or deception, the investigator explains the reasons for this action as soon as possible during the debriefing.

G.2.c. Student/Supervisee Participation   Researchers who involve students or supervisees in research make clear to them that the decision regarding whether or not to participate in research activities does not affect one's academic standing or supervisory relationship. Students or supervisees who choose not to participate in educational research are provided with an appropriate alternative to fulfill their academic or clinical requirements.

G.2.d. Client Participation   Counselors conducting research involving clients make clear in the informed consent process that clients are free to choose whether or not to participate in research activities. Counselors take necessary precautions to protect clients from adverse consequences of declining or withdrawing from participation.

G.2.e. Confidentiality of Information   Information obtained about research participants during the course of an investigation is confidential. When the possibility exists that others may obtain access to such information, ethical research practice requires that the possibility, together with the plans for protecting confidentiality, be explained to participants as a part of the procedure for obtaining informed consent.

G.2.f. Persons Not Capable of Giving Informed Consent   When a person is not capable of giving informed consent, counselors provide an appropriate explanation to, obtain agreement for participation from, and obtain the appropriate consent of a legally authorized person.

G.2.g. Commitments to Participants   Counselors take reasonable measures to honor all commitments to research participants. *(See A.2.c.)*

G.2.h. Explanations After Data Collection   After data are collected, counselors provide participants with full clarification of the nature of the study to remove any misconceptions participants might have regarding the research. Where scientific or human values justify delaying or withholding information, counselors take reasonable measures to avoid causing harm.

G.2.i. Informing Sponsors   Counselors inform sponsors, institutions, and publication channels regarding research procedures and outcomes. Counselors ensure that appropriate bodies and authorities are given pertinent information and acknowledgement.

G.2.j. Disposal of Research Documents and Records   Within a reasonable period of time following the completion of a research project or study, counselors take steps to destroy records or documents (audio, video, digital, and written) containing confidential data or information that identifies research participants. When records are of an artistic nature, researchers obtain participant consent with regard to handling of such records or documents. *(See B.4.a, B.4.g.)*

G.3. Relationships With Research Participants (When Research Involves Intensive or Extended Interactions)

G.3.a. Nonprofessional Relationships   Nonprofessional relationships with research participants should be avoided.

G.3.b. Relationships With Research Participants   Sexual or romantic counselor–research participant interactions or relationships with current research participants are prohibited.

G.3.c. Sexual Harassment and Research Participants   Researchers do not condone or subject research participants to sexual harassment.

G.3.d. Potentially Beneficial Interactions   When a nonprofessional interaction between the researcher and the research participant may be potentially beneficial, the researcher must document, prior to the interaction (when feasible), the rationale for such an interaction, the potential benefit, and anticipated consequences for the research participant. Such interactions should be initiated with appropriate consent of the research participant. Where unintentional harm occurs to the research participant due to the nonprofessional interaction, the researcher must show evidence of an attempt to remedy such harm.

G.4. Reporting Results

G.4.a. Accurate Results   Counselors plan, conduct, and report research accurately. They provide thorough discussions of the limitations of their data and alternative hypotheses. Counselors do not engage in misleading or fraudulent research, distort data, misrepresent data, or deliberately bias their results. They explicitly mention all variables and conditions known to the investigator that may have affected the outcome of a study or the interpretation of data. They describe the extent to which results are applicable for diverse populations.

G.4.b. Obligation to Report Unfavorable Results   Counselors report the results of any research of professional value. Results that reflect unfavorably on institutions, programs, services, prevailing opinions, or vested interests are not withheld.

G.4.c. Reporting Errors   If counselors discover significant errors in their published research, they take reasonable steps to correct such errors in a correction erratum, or through other appropriate publication means.

G.4.d. Identity of Participants   Counselors who supply data, aid in the research of another person, report research results, or make original data available take due care to disguise the identity of respective participants in the absence of specific authorization from the participants to do otherwise. In situations where participants self-identify their involvement in research studies, researchers take active steps to ensure that data is adapted/changed to protect the identity and welfare of all parties and that discussion of results does not cause harm to participants.

G.4.e. Replication Studies   Counselors are obligated to make available sufficient original research data to qualified professionals who may wish to replicate the study.

G.5. Publication

G.5.a. Recognizing Contributions   When conducting and reporting research, counselors are familiar with and give recognition to previous work on the topic, observe copyright laws, and give full credit to those to whom credit is due.

G.5.b. Plagiarism   Counselors do not plagiarize, that is, they do not present another person's work as their own work.

G.5.c. Review/Republication of Data or Ideas   Counselors fully acknowledge and make editorial reviewers aware of prior publication of ideas or data where such ideas or data are submitted for review or publication.

G.5.d. Contributors   Counselors give credit through joint authorship, acknowledgment, footnote statements, or other appropriate means to those who have contributed significantly to research or concept development in accordance with such contributions. The principal contributor is listed first and minor technical or professional contributions are acknowledged in notes or introductory statements.

G.5.e. Agreement of Contributors   Counselors who conduct joint research with colleagues or students/supervisees establish agreements in advance regarding allocation of tasks, publication credit, and types of acknowledgement that will be received.

G.5.f. Student Research   For articles that are substantially based on students course papers, projects, dissertations or theses, and on which students have been the primary contributors, they are listed as principal authors.

G.5.g. Duplicate Submission   Counselors submit manuscripts for consideration to only one journal at a time. Manuscripts that are published in whole or in substantial part in another journal or published work are not submitted for publication without acknowledgment and permission from the previous publication.

G.5.h. Professional Review   Counselors who review material submitted for publication, research, or other scholarly purposes respect the confidentiality and proprietary rights of those who submitted it. Counselors use care to make publication decisions based on valid and defensible standards. Counselors review article submissions in a timely manner and based on their scope and competency in research methodologies. Counselors who serve as reviewers at the request of editors or publishers make every effort to only review materials that are within their scope of competency and use care to avoid personal biases.

Section H

Resolving Ethical Issues

Introduction

Counselors behave in a legal, ethical, and moral manner in the conduct of their professional work. They are aware that client protection and trust in the profession depend on a high level of professional conduct. They hold other counselors to the same standards and are willing to take appropriate action to ensure that these standards are upheld.

Counselors strive to resolve ethical dilemmas with direct and open communication among all parties involved and seek consultation with colleagues and supervisors when necessary. Counselors incorporate ethical practice into their daily professional work. They engage in ongoing professional development regarding current topics in ethical and legal issues in counseling.

H.1. Standards and the Law *(See F.9.a.)*

H.1.a. Knowledge Counselors understand the *ACA Code of Ethics* and other applicable ethics codes from other professional organizations or from certification and licensure bodies of which they are members. Lack of knowledge or misunderstanding of an ethical responsibility is not a defense against a charge of unethical conduct.

H.1.b. Conflicts Between Ethics and Laws If ethical responsibilities conflict with law, regulations, or other governing legal authority, counselors make known their commitment to the *ACA Code of Ethics* and take steps to resolve the conflict. If the conflict cannot be resolved by such means, counselors may adhere to the requirements of law, regulations, or other governing legal authority.

H.2. Suspected Violations

H.2.a. Ethical Behavior Expected Counselors expect colleagues to adhere to the *ACA Code of Ethics*. When counselors possess knowledge that raises doubts as to whether another counselor is acting in an ethical manner, they take appropriate action. *(See H.2.b., H.2.c.)*

H.2.b. Informal Resolution When counselors have reason to believe that another counselor is violating or has violated an ethical standard, they attempt first to resolve the issue informally with the other counselor if feasible, provided such action does not violate confidentiality rights that may be involved.

H.2.c. Reporting Ethical Violations   If an apparent violation has substantially harmed, or is likely to substantially harm a person or organization and is not appropriate for informal resolution or is not resolved properly, counselors take further action appropriate to the situation. Such action might include referral to state or national committees on professional ethics, voluntary national certification bodies, state licensing boards, or to the appropriate institutional authorities. This standard does not apply when an intervention would violate confidentiality rights or when counselors have been retained to review the work of another counselor whose professional conduct is in question.

H.2.d. Consultation   When uncertain as to whether a particular situation or course of action may be in violation of the *ACA Code of Ethics,* counselors consult with other counselors who are knowledgeable about ethics and the *ACA Code of Ethics,* with colleagues, or with appropriate authorities

H.2.e. Organizational Conflicts   If the demands of an organization with which counselors are affiliated pose a conflict with the *ACA Code of Ethics,* counselors specify the nature of such conflicts and express to their supervisors or other responsible officials their commitment to the *ACA Code of Ethics.* When possible, counselors work toward change within the organization to allow full adherence to the *ACA Code of Ethics.* In doing so, they address any confidentiality issues.

H.2.f. Unwarranted Complaints   Counselors do not initiate, participate in, or encourage the filing of ethics complaints that are made with reckless disregard or willful ignorance of facts that would disprove the allegation.

H.2.g. Unfair Discrimination Against Complainants and Respondents   Counselors do not deny persons employment, advancement, admission to academic or other programs, tenure, or promotion based solely upon their having made or their being the subject of an ethics complaint. This does not preclude taking action based upon the outcome of such proceedings or considering other appropriate information.

H.3. Cooperation With Ethics Committees

Counselors assist in the process of enforcing the *ACA Code of Ethics.* Counselors cooperate with investigations, proceedings, and requirements of the ACA Ethics Committee or ethics committees of other duly constituted associations or boards having jurisdiction over those charged with a violation. Counselors are familiar with the *ACA Policy and Procedures for Processing Complains of Ethical Violations* and use it as a reference for assisting in the enforcement of the *ACA Code of Ethics.*

Glossary of Terms

Advocacy – promotion of the well-being of individuals and groups, and the counseling profession within systems and organizations. Advocacy seeks to remove barriers and obstacles that inhibit access, growth, and development.

Assent – to demonstrate agreement, when a person is otherwise not capable or competent to give formal consent (e.g., informed consent) to a counseling service or plan.

Client – an individual seeking or referred to the professional services of a counselor for help with problem resolution or decision making.

Counselor – a professional (or a student who is a counselorin-training) engaged in a counseling practice or other counseling-related services. Counselors fulfill many roles and responsibilities such as counselor educators, researchers, supervisors, practitioners, and consultants.

Counselor Educator – a professional counselor engaged primarily in developing, implementing, and supervising the educational preparation of counselors-in-training.

Counselor Supervisor – a professional counselor who engages in a formal relationship with a practicing counselor or counselor-in-training for the purpose of overseeing that individual's counseling work or clinical skill development.

Culture – membership in a socially constructed way of living, which incorporates collective values, beliefs, norms, boundaries, and lifestyles that are cocreated with others who share similar worldviews comprising biological, psychosocial, historical, psychological, and other factors.

Diversity – the similarities and differences that occur within and across cultures, and the intersection of cultural and social identities.

Documents – any written, digital, audio, visual, or artistic recording of the work within the counseling relationship between counselor and client.

Examinee – a recipient of any professional counseling service that includes educational, psychological, and career appraisal utilizing qualitative or quantitative techniques.

Forensic Evaluation – any formal assessment conducted for court or other legal proceedings.

Multicultural/Diversity Competence – a capacity whereby counselors possess cultural and diversity awareness and knowledge about self and others, and how this awareness and knowledge is applied effectively in practice with clients and client groups.

Multicultural/Diversity Counseling – counseling that recognizes diversity and embraces approaches that support the worth, dignity, potential, and uniqueness of individuals within their historical, cultural, economic, political, and psychosocial contexts.

Student – an individual engaged in formal educational preparation as a counselor-in-training.

Supervisee – a professional counselor or counselor-in-training whose counseling work or clinical skill development is being overseen in a formal supervisory relationship by a qualified trained professional.

Supervisor – counselors who are trained to oversee the professional clinical work of counselors and counselors-in-training.

Teaching – all activities engaged in as part of a formal educational program designed to lead to a graduate degree in counseling.

Training – the instruction and practice of skills related to the counseling profession. Training contributes to the ongoing proficiency of students and professional counselors.

Index

About the Author

Gary G. Ford, Ph.D., is a professor in the Department of Psychology at Stephen F. Austin State University. He teaches both undergraduate and graduate courses, such as professional ethics, theories of personality, personality assessment, history and systems of psychology, human consciousness, existential psychology, and psychopathology. He is also actively involved in providing practicum supervision in the clinical psychology graduate program. He has published in the areas of professional ethics, substance abuse, psychological defense, existential psychology, and sports psychology. He served on the editorial board of *Journal of Research in Personality* for six years.

Dr. Ford received his Ph.D. in clinical psychology from Fordham University, Bronx, New York, and his M.A. in philosophy from the University of Illinois at Urbana–Champaign. His interdisciplinary academic background in philosophy and psychology has provided him with a unique perspective on the complex task of developing an ethics book for mental health professionals that will enable them to reason effectively when confronted with the ethical conflicts that invariably arise in their professional practice. He has been a licensed clinical psychologist for nearly 20 years and has been affiliated with Veterans Administration Medical Centers and worked in private practice. He has served on IRBs and ethics committees in both hospitals and universities. He has administered psychology licensing examinations as an oral examiner for the Texas State Board of Examiners of Psychologists and conducted continuing education workshops in professional ethics.